Hurtig Publishers Ltd.
1302, Oxford Tower
10235 - 101 Street
Edmonton, Alberta
Canada T5J 3G1

Every attempt has been made to identify and credit sources for
photographs. The publisher would appreciate receiving
information as to any inaccuracies in the credits for
subsequent editions.

Canadian Cataloguing in Publication Data

Main entry under title:
The Junior Encyclopedia of Canada

Editor in Chief: James H. Marsh

ISBN 0-88830-334-3 (set) —ISBN 088830-335-1
(v. 1). —ISBN 0-88830-336-X (v. 2). —ISBN
0-88830-337-8 (v. 3). —ISBN 0-88830-338-6
(v. 4). —ISBN 0-88830-339-4 (v. 5).

1. Canada—Dictionaries and encyclopedias—
Juvenile literature   I. Marsh, James H.

FC23.J86 1990   j971'.003   C90-090120-9
F1006.J86 1990

Designed, typeset, and manufactured
in Canada

Cover photo by Roland Weber/Masterfile

ACKNOWLEDGEMENT

Hurtig Publishers gratefully acknowledges

the generous assistance of

The Department of Communications

and

The CRB Foundation,

without whose support

The Junior Encyclopedia of Canada

could not have been published

FOREWORD

This is the first work of its kind ever developed in Canada. After we published *The Canadian Encyclopedia* in 1985 we received many requests, from all across Canada, from parents, teachers, students and librarians, to produce an encyclopedia for young Canadians.

We decided at the outset that our new *Junior Encyclopedia* could not be simply a rewrite or condensation of the adult encyclopedia. We would have to start all over and begin a brand new, comprehensive work. We also decided that the new encyclopedia must be beautiful as well as useful. We wanted to produce a very attractive set of books that young Canadians would be drawn to, and find easy and interesting to use. The costs of such a project are enormous. From the time of its conception in 1986, to publication in 1990, *The Junior Encyclopedia of Canada* has become the largest, most expensive publishing project in the history of Canada.

We could not have begun work on such an ambitious undertaking without the enthusiasm and assistance of The Honourable Flora MacDonald and The Honourable Marcel Masse of the Department of Communications, and their supportive staff, especially Esther Rosenberg-Paritsky. Their early appreciation of the need for this work encouraged us to proceed when the difficulties and problems seemed insurmountable.

The financial assistance supplied by the Department of Communications was matched with a generous grant from The CRB Foundation of Montreal, in keeping with its interest in helping young Canadians to increase their understanding of their history, heritage, and culture. Charles and Andrea Bronfman and senior staff members Tom Axworthy and Ann Dadson, were of inestimable help. It is not possible to thank The CRB Foundation and the Department of Communications adequately. Suffice to say, without their faith and confidence, *The Junior Encyclopedia of Canada* would never have been published.

While scores of other Canadians, all across our country, have been indispensable to the successful publication of the encyclopedia, two deserve very special mention. James Marsh, our Editor in Chief, has been, once again, simply brilliant in the complex planning and successful completion of the massive editorial challenge. And, Barry Hicks, Vice-President of Hurtig Publishers, has been a tower of strength for the entire project, especially in the financial, production, and fullfillment areas.

Sheila Birmingham, Carol Woo, Debra MacGregor, Nancy Foulds, Gail Kudelik, Robyn Ross, and Kay Hurtig made very special contributions to the making of the encyclopedia, along with Bob Young (design), Rick Checkland (maps), and Kathy Garnsworthy (index).

Many, many others deserve special thanks. At the top of the list must come Special Advisor Dr Myer Horowitz, the Bank of Montreal and Ronalds Printing. Thanks are also due to Joyce Zemans and Peter Brown of the Canada Council; Mona Goldstein and Yves Blain of Wunderman Worldwide; and George Melnyk of the Alberta Foundation for the Literary Arts. Hurtig Publishers continues to enjoy a special relationship with the University of Alberta, which played an integral role in providing technical advice, computing, library resources, and the support of its academic staff. We were also fortunate in having the co-operation of so many schools and libraries in testing materials and compiling lists of questions that young readers ask about.

Finally, our staff at Hurtig Publishers have been superb. Their extra effort and consistent dedication have been truly wonderful. Thank you to Rhonda Bouchard, Sharon Burton, Tracy Yaeger, Kendra Brunt, Laurie Verstraete, Suzanne Harkin, Marie Triggs, Weylin Willis.

Mel Hurtig
Publisher
Edmonton, Jan 1990

PREFACE

The Junior Encyclopedia provides Canadian students with the information that they need to complete school assignments or to satisfy their curiosity about their country.

Many people think of Canada as a relatively young nation. Yet, the native people occupied this part of the world at least 12 000 years ago. Europeans settled here almost 400 years ago. The story of Canada is full of adventure, conflict, and accomplishment. It is a story of survival in a challenging environment; of forging a union of many cultures; and of following a separate destiny in North America while being drawn ever closer to our powerful American neighbour to the south. It is a story that is not told often enough, or thoroughly enough.

It is very difficult for a general encyclopedia, which seeks to cover the whole world, to provide a true indication of the complex nature of Canada. Most of these works are prepared outside Canada for a larger market in the United States or Europe. The Canadian aspects of topics such as dinosaurs, the senate, the environment, economics, growth of cities, architecture, native people, and many more important topics might rate only a few sentences in a general encyclopedia. The Junior Encyclopedia of Canada provides extensive information, from a Canadian point of view, on these and 4100 other subjects.

Together with some 3000 illustrations, the entries of the encyclopedia provide the most complete portrait of Canada that has ever been available to young Canadians.

The articles in The Junior Encyclopedia of Canada are written in simple language and are clearly organized to help students find facts quickly. The editors paid particular attention to topics that students are likely to encounter in school work, such as the provinces, prejudice and discrimination, federalism, ethnic groups, language, Parliament, and Canadian men and women in all areas of society. Entries on mammals, fish, birds, flowers, and similar articles are written with younger readers in mind. Some entries, such as culture and economics, are aimed at older students, who are most likely to consult them.

The entries were read by experts and checked by researchers to ensure that they are accurate. They were read by hundreds of students in class to make sure that they were understandable. Many entries were changed as a result of questions raised by students who read the entries, or as a result of lists of questions compiled by librarians across the country.

The Junior Encyclopedia of Canada is a tribute to the dedication of a skilled staff and the inspiration of Mel Hurtig. It is dedicated to young Canadians who will discover here the immense beauty, wealth, and opportunity that is Canada.

James H. Marsh
Editor in Chief
January 1990

STAFF

Publisher
Mel Hurtig

Editor in Chief
James H. Marsh

**Vice President,
Finance and Production**
Barry Hicks

Editorial Manager
Debra MacGregor

**Project Co-ordinator
Data Manager/Page Make-Up**
Sheila Birmingham

**Assistant to Editor in Chief
Illustrations Editor**
Carol Woo

Editor
Nancy Brown Foulds

**Consulting Editor
Contributing Editor**
Carlotta Lemieux

Contributing Editors
Daniel Francis
Sean McCutcheon
Rosemary Shipton

**Office Manager
Illustrations Assistant**
Robyn Ross

Senior Researcher
Gail E. Kudelik

Researchers
Muriel Draaisma
Stanley B. Gordon
Kathryn Chase Merrett
Roberta Staley
Kay Hurtig

Proofreaders
Vincent P. Ambrock
Tim Black
Carolyn King

Data Entry
Arlene Birmingham
Beverly Higgins

Translator
Penny Williams

Indexing
Kathy Garnsworthy

Hurtig Publishers
Tracy Yaeger
Rhonda Bouchard
Kendra Brunt
Suzanne Harkin
Marie Triggs
Laurie Verstraete
Weylin Willis

PRODUCTION

Typesetting/Computing
Printing Services,
University of Alberta
Len Young, Director
Earl Olsen
James MacLachlan
Claire Burke
Douglas J. Martin
Mabel Chan

Design
Roberge Hoffman Young
Graphic Design Inc.

Graphs
Omar Sanchez,
Penta Electronic Graphic Design
and Production

Cartography
Rick Checkland,
Ricarte Mapping

Printing
Ronalds Printing
Montreal, division of
Québecor Printing (Canada) Inc.

Binding
The Bryant Press Ltd

CONTRIBUTORS AND CONSULTANTS

Abella, Professor Irving
Department of History
Glendon College
York University

Adams, Peter
MPP
Trent University

Armstrong, Joe C.W.
Author, Historian/Toronto

Arsenault, Céline
Botaniste
Jardin botanique de Montréal

Artibise, Alan F.J.
School of Community and Regional
Planning
University of British Columbia

Asch, Professor Michael
Department of Anthropology
University of Alberta

Aubrey, Irene E.
Chief, Children's Literature Service
National Library of Canada/Ottawa

Backhouse, Professor Constance
Faculty of Law
University of Western Ontario

Baglole, Harry
Director, Institute of Island Studies
University of Prince Edward Island

Baker, Dr. Melvin
President's Office
Memorial University

Barclay, Professor Harold B.
Department of Anthropology
University of Alberta

Basinger, Professor James
Department of Geological Sciences
University of Saskatchewan

Bélanger, Professor Réal
Département d'histoire
Université Laval

Bennett, Susan
Research and Reference Librarian
Ontario Agricultural Museum/Milton

Bishop, Mary F.
Department of Health Care
and Epidemiology
University of British Columbia

Blackwell, John D.
Lecturer in History
St. Francis Xavier University

Bonisteel, Roy
Author-Broadcaster/Trenton

Booth, Professor David
Elementary Department
Faculty of Education
University of Toronto

Boothe, Professor Paul
Department of Economics
University of Alberta

Breen, Professor David
Department of History
University of British Columbia

Brown, D. Murray
Professor of Agrometeorology
Department of Land Resource Science
Ontario Agricultural College
University of Guelph

Burnet, Jean
Chairman, Board of Directors
Chief Executive Officer
Multicultural History Society
of Ontario/Toronto

Butts, Edward
Writer/Mississauga

Cameron, Christina
Director General
National Historic Parks and Sites
Environment Canada/Ottawa

Chambers, Professor E.J.
Faculty of Business
University of Alberta

Chambers, Professor Thomas F.
Canadore College/North Bay

Chandler, Dr. F.W.
Geological Survey of Canada/Ottawa

Charlesworth, Professor H.A.K.
Department of Geology
University of Alberta

Citizens Inquiry Bureau
Government of Ontario/Toronto

Clarke, J.Y.
President
Canadian Maritime Industries
Association/Ottawa

Coates, Professor Kenneth
Department of History
University of Victoria

Colombo, John Robert
Author and Editor/Toronto

Conolly, Professor L.W.
Associate Vice-President, Academic
University of Guelph

Cosper, Professor Ronald L.
Department of Sociology
St. Mary's University

Côté, Sylvain
Entomologist/St-Jean-sur-Richelieu

Cumming, Professor Bruce
Department of Biology
Fredericton Campus
University of New Brunswick

Currie, Philip J.
Head, Dinosaur Research Programme
Tyrrell Museum of
Palaeontology/Drumheller

Cyr, Professor André
Département de biologie
Faculté des sciences
Université de Sherbrooke

Dahl, Edward H.
Early Cartography Specialist
National Archives of Canada/Ottawa

Dahlby, Professor B.
Department of Economics
University of Alberta

Danks, Dr. Hugh
Biological Survey of Canada
Zoology Division
National Museum of Natural Sciences/
Ottawa

de Montigny, Valerie
Writer/Gatineau

DeFelice, Professor James
Department of Drama
University of Alberta

Denham, Professor Ross A.
Department of Accounting
Faculty of Business
University of Alberta

Denton, Peter H.
Writer/Ancaster

Dewhirst, John
Archaeo Tech Associates/Victoria

Dionne, Réne
Département des lettres françaises
Université d'Ottawa

Draper, Professor James A.
Professor of Adult Education
OISE/Toronto

Dufresne, Benoit
Assistant Program Director/
Music Director
CFMI/New Westminster

Durand, Lucette
Biologist/Montréal

Edwards, Professor Joyce
Faculty of Education
University of Alberta

Elliott, Ross
Curriculum Supervisor
Burin Integrated School
Board/Marystown

Ellis, Sarah
Writer/Vancouver

Fenton, M.B.
Consultant/Ottawa

Fisher, Professor Robin
Department of History
Simon Fraser University

Fizzard, Professor Garfield
Faculty of Education
Memorial University

Fredeen, Howard
Consultant/Lacombe

Friesen, Professor John W.
Faculty of Education
University of Calgary

Gall, Professor Gerald
Faculty of Law
University of Alberta

Gardner, David
Consultant/Toronto

Geist, Professor Valerius
Faculty of Environmental Design
University of Calgary

Gendreau, Dr. Paul
Director of Research
Centracare St John Inc./St John

Gibbons, Professor Kenneth
Department of Political Science
University of Winnipeg

Goa, David
Curator of Folk Life
Provincial Museum of
Alberta/Edmonton

Godard, Dr. Barbara
Department of English
York University

Gotlieb, Professor C.C.
Department of Computer Science
University of Toronto

Grey, Professor Julius
Faculty of Law
McGill University

Guidotti, Dr. Tee L.
Occupational Medicine
University of Alberta

Hanna, David B.
Department of Geography
Université du Québec à Montréal

Harris, Stephen J.
Directorate of History
Department of National
Defence/Ottawa

Henry, Jeanne
Consultant
University of Alberta

Hillmer, Norman
Senior Historian
Directorate of History
Department of National
Defence/Ottawa

Hogg, Professor Peter W.
Osgoode Hall Law School
York University

Holman, Harry
Provincial Archivist/Charlottetown

Hopkins, Joyce
Career Resource Centre
Hamilton Public Library/Hamilton

Humber, William
Chairman, Continuing Education
Seneca College/Toronto

Irwin, Neal A.
Managing Director
IBI Group/Toronto

Israel, Dr. W.
Department of Physics
University of Alberta

Jenkinson, Professor David
Department of Curriculum:
Humanities and Social Sciences
Faculty of Education
University of Manitoba

Jobe, Professor Ronald
Faculty of Education
University of British Columbia

Johnston, C. Fred
Associate Professor of Education
Queen's University

Jones, Professor A.R.C.
Faculty of Agriculture
McGill University

Jones, Professor Raymond E.
Department of English
University of Alberta

Jorgensen, Professor Erik
Arbor Consultants/Guelph

Juliebö, Professor Moira
Department of Elementary Education
University of Alberta

Kernaghan, Dr. K.
Department of Politics and
Administrative Studies
Brock University

Knight, Professor David B.
Department of Geography
Carleton University

Koller, Katherine
Writer/Edmonton

Lachance, Stephanie
Writer/Gentilly

Lacombe, Claire
Writer/Montréal

Lacoursière, Professor Estelle
Département de chimie-biologie
Université du Québec à Trois-Rivières

Leclair, Professor Raymond
Département de chimie-biologie
Université du Québec à Trois-Rivières

Leier, Margaret
Writer/Victoria

Lozowski, Professor E.P.
Department of Geography
University of Alberta

MacKay, Donald
Writer/Montréal

McDiarmid, Louise
Writer and Storyteller/Ottawa

McGhee, Robert
Archaeologist/Woodlawn

McKeracher, Peter
Durham College/Oshawa

McMordie, Professor Michael
Faculty of Environmental Design
University of Calgary

Mills, Professor David
Department of History
University of Alberta

Moore, Christopher
Writer/Toronto

Morissette, Professor Yves-Marie
Faculty of Law
McGill University

Morrison, Professor William
Centre for Northern Studies
Lakehead University

Moyles, Professor Gordon
Department of English
University of Alberta

Mulligan, Terry David
Writer/Vancouver

Nash, Knowlton
Broadcaster/Toronto

Nowak, Professor W.S.W.
Department of Geography
Memorial University

Nowlan, Michael O.
Acting Assistant Director
Program Development and
Implementation Branch
New Brunswick Department
of Education/Fredericton

Osborne, Professor Ken
Faculty of Education
University of Manitoba

Pattie, Donald
Biological Science, NAIT

Pederson, R. Cole
Writer/St. Albert

Peers, Laura
Consultant/Uxbridge

Percy, Professor John
Department of Astronomy
Erindale College
University of Toronto

Pitt, Robert D.
Department of English Language
and Literature
Memorial University

Priamo, Carol
Writer/Toronto

Price, Professor M.A.
Chairman, Department of Animal
Science
Faculty of Agriculture and Forestry
University of Alberta

Pringle, Alexander
Barrister and Solicitor/Edmonton

Purves, Becky J.
Assistant Registrar
Office of the Registrar
University of Alberta

Rasmussen, John
Writer/Edmonton

Reid, Susan
Executive Director
ACCIS-The Graduate Workforce
Professionals/Toronto

Ricard, Dr. Marcelle
Department of Psychology
Université de Montréal

Richards, Leslie
Writer/Victoria

Robinson, Paul
Writer/Dartmouth

Rocan, Claude
Writer/Ottawa

Rompkey, Professor Ronald G.
Department of English
Memorial University

Roseberry, Luc
Département d'océanographie
Université du Québec à Rimouski

Ross, J.S.
Professor Emeritus

Ross, Professor W.A.
Faculty of Environmental Design
University of Calgary

Rowe, Professor emeritus J.S.
Department of Crop Science
and Plant Ecology
University of Saskatchewan

Runnalls, O.J.C.
Professor Emeritus,
Nuclear Engineering and
Energy Studies, Toronto

Rutter, Professor N.W.
Department of Geology
University of Alberta

Ruzzier, Laura
Multiculturalism Sector
Secretary of State Department/Ottawa

Schwartz, Professor Bernard
Department of Elementary Education
University of Alberta

Skeoch, Alan
Agricultural Historian
Head of History
Parkdale Collegiate
Institute/Mississauga

Smith, Professor Larry
Department of Economics
University of Waterloo

Smith, Professor P.J.
Department of Geography
University of Alberta

Smith, T.B.
Barrister and Solicitor/Ottawa

Stanley, Laurie C.C.
Assistant Professor of History
St. Francis Xavier University

Stoskopf, Professor Neal C.
Department of Crop Science
Ontario Agricultural College
University of Guelph

Stott, Professor Jon C.
Department of English
University of Alberta

Therrien, Julie
Biologist
Environmental Education
Université du Québec à Trois-Rivières

Thomas, Audrey M.
Consultant/Victoria

Thompson, Professor Dixon
Faculty of Environmental Design
University of Calgary

Troper, Professor Harold
History
Ontario Institute for
Studies in Education/Toronto

Trott, Professor Elizabeth
Department of Philosophy
Victoria College
University of Toronto

Vachon, Auguste
Saint-Laurent Herald
Canadian Heraldic Authority/Ottawa

van Zyll de Jong, C.G.
Curator, Mammalogy Section
National Museum of Natural
Sciences/Ottawa

Veeman, Professor Michele
Department of Rural Economy
Faculty of Agriculture and Forestry
University of Alberta

Waite, Professor P.B.
Department of History
Dalhousie University

Wallis, Cliff
Cottonwood Consultants/Calgary

Wershler, Cleve
Sweetgrass Consultants/Calgary

White, Professor Graham
Department of Political Science
University of Toronto

Wilkinson, Professor Bruce W.
Department of Economics
University of Alberta

Winters, Kenneth
Writer/Orono

Wolfe, Professor Fred
Chairman, Department of Food Science
Faculty of Agriculture and Forestry
University of Alberta

Wolforth, Professor John
Faculty of Education
McGill University

Woodcock, George
Writer/Vancouver

Wright, Janet
Architectural Historian
National Historic Parks and Sites
Environment Canada/Ottawa

Yaffe, Dr. Mark
Associate Professor of Family Medicine
McGill University
St. Mary's Hospital Centre/Montréal

Yip-Choy, Jennifer
Director, Career and Placement
Services
University of Alberta

Young, Professor H. Clifton
Faculty of Business
University of Alberta

Zola, Professor Meguido
Faculty of Education
Simon Fraser University

SPECIAL ACKNOWLEDGEMENTS

Libraries

VANCOUVER

Janice Douglas
Co-ordinator of Children's and Young
Adult Services, Vancouver Public
Library

Liz Austrom
Co-ordinator of Curriculum Resources,
Vancouver Board of School Trustees

Ken Walters
Teacher-Librarian, Lord Strathcona
Elementary School

Wendy Shaw
Teacher-Librarian, Templeton
Secondary School

EDMONTON

Bob Bell
Supervisor, Children's Division,
Edmonton Public Library

MONTREAL

Joanne Stanbridge
Children's Librarian
Westmount Public Library

Eleanor London
Côte-St-Luc Public Library

Audrey Ballard
Library Consultant, Lakeshore School
Board, Beaconsfield

LONDON

Joan Devereux, Librarian, Evelyn
Harrison Public School

Marion Walls, Emily Carr
Elementary School

Alastair L. Neely, History Librarian,
London Public Libraries

TORONTO

Lynda Robbins, Branch Head,
Patricia Hall, Children's Librarian
Forest Hill Library,
Toronto Public Library

Gail Culligan
Nancy Chavner
Co-ordinator of Children's and Young
Adult Services
East York Public Library

Irma Lambourne, Librarian,
Glenview School

Iris Harvey,
King Edward Public School

Joan McGrath, Library Consultant,
Toronto Board of Education

HALIFAX

Hope Bridgewater, Children's and
Young Adult Services Co-ordinator,
Halifax City Regional Library

Bertha B. Currie
Mary Louise Mills
Supervisor of Library Services,
Halifax District School Board

Schools

Sheila Pritchard, Learning Resources
Consultant, Edmonton Public
School Board

F. Deane Jensen, Supervisor,
Curriculum, Edmonton Public
School Board

Doris Severyn, Baturyn Elementary
School, Edmonton, Alta

Diane Antoniuk, Irene Heffel,
Debbie Lamoriss, Linda Thompson,
Dan Knott Junior High School,
Edmonton, Alta

Myrna Andruko, Irene Hrechuk,
Kerry Langman, Elaine O'Hare,
Larry Soper,
Ottewell Junior High School,
Edmonton, Alta

Bob Niven, Dovercourt Elementary
School, Edmonton, Alta

Lise Dropko, Evansdale Elementary
School, Edmonton, Alta

Lois Voegtlin, Parkview
Elementary-Junior High School,
Edmonton, Alta

Sandra Sawchuck,
Westbrook Elementary School,
Edmonton, Alta

Myron Yates, Georgetown
Elementary School, Georgetown, P.E.I.

B.G. Malone, Ellenvale Junior High
School, Dartmouth, N.S.

Shirley Augustine, Emerson
Elementary School, Winnipeg, Man.

Nancy Jacobson, Sir John A. Macdonald
School, Thunder Bay, Ont.

Sharen McDonald, Hudson High
School, Hudson Heights, Quebec

Anne Jones, John Rennie High School,
Pointe Claire, Que.

Avrille Gosling, James Thomson
Elementary School, Powell River, B.C.

Evelyn Bennett, Newtown
Elementary School,
Mount Pearl, Nfld

Mary Mesheau, Assiniboine School,
Oromocto, N.B.

Nancy Porcina, Princess Margaret
School, Prince Albert, Sask.

HOW TO USE THE ENCYCLOPEDIA

Encyclopedia articles condense information into as few words as possible, concentrating on the most important features of a topic. Larger topics, such as botany, are broken down under many headings so that information can be found easily. Thus there are separate entries on individual plants, such as the rose or larkspur.

Article Titles Topics in *The Junior Encyclopedia* are arranged alphabetically, like words in a dictionary. They are listed in boldface under entry titles, and marked by a coloured square, for example, ■ **Aviation.**

The reader should first look for the topic in this alphabetical listing. Thus **Confederation** will be found in the Cs, between **Concordia University** and **Confederation of National Trade Unions.**

In many cases, a single entry will provide all the information you need. However, much more can be learned about every subject, both within the encyclopedia, and by following leads provided at the end of the articles.

Cross References guide the reader to other entries in the encyclopedia that treat different aspects of a topic. For example, the article on diabetes presents a brief summary of the disease and how a treatment was found in Canada. The list of entries under the heading ▷ RELATED ARTICLES leads to biographies of the scientists who discovered the treatment and to an article on the drug insulin.

See References In some cases, *see* references send the reader directly to another title. For example, the listing for Canadian Museum of Civilization sends the reader to the article **Museum.**

See references are also found after many brief entries. For example, the entry **Chippewyan** has a brief description of that native group and ends with the reference *See* **Native People: Eastern Woodlands,** which has a more detailed treatment.

Index If the topic is not listed among the entries, the reader should turn to the index in Volume 5. (Further information on how to use the index is found at the beginning of the index.)

Suggested Reading Many articles list one or more books under the heading ▷ SUGGESTED READING: These books are available in most libraries and contain more information on a topic. Most can be read by students ages 8 to 15.

Other Canadian reference books, such as the *National Atlas of Canada, The Canada Year Book*, and *The Canadian Encyclopedia*, contain further information. The many volumes of the Dictionary of Canadian Biography contain the most extensive information on Canadians who died before 1900. Many articles, for example, those on the towns and cities, contain addresses to which you can write and ask for information.

Independent Research As your research progresses, you will find that one source leads to another.

Many books include bibliographies (lists of books) which may lead in yet other directions.

Magazines are good sources of up-to-date information and photographs. Librarians often have books which "index" magazine articles or group them by subject. There is also a subject index to children's magazines, called *Children's Magazine Guide*.

There are many ways to use the resources in a library. The librarian can show you how to use the Subject Catalogue, which lists all the books it has on a subject. General subjects, such as genetics or medicine, are more difficult to research than specific subjects, such as Sir Frederick Banting.

Research requires patience and imagination. Research skills are a valuable asset, not only for school work, but for many jobs later in life.

RESEARCH AIDS

Most of the information in the encyclopedia is contained in the text of the entries. Some of the facts are summarized in separate fact boxes or tables, with facts for quick reference. All of the provinces and territories, for example, contain one of these fact sheets.

Maps are used to show locations of places, such as Charlottetown, P.E.I., or the distribution of features, such as Natural Regions. All the provinces and territories have full-page maps. Many maps also contain photographs.

Graphs help to show trends or comparisons, such as population growth or economic activity in the cities.

Time Lines accompany many articles to help place an event or person in time. For example, every biography of a prime minister has a time line showing who preceded and who followed him.

Artwork The hundreds of pieces of new artwork in the encyclopedia have been carefully researched by experts and drawn by talented artists. They contain a great deal of information that cannot be described in the text.

Sidebars Many entries in the encyclopedia have sidebars (located in the narrow half-column), with additional information of related interest. Often these are biographies of people dealt with in the main article, such as a boxer in the entry on boxing, or a fashion designer in the entry on design. The sidebars also contain definitions of difficult terms.

Statistics are one of the most changeable forms of information. Wherever possible, the entries give the most recent and reliable figures available. However, particular emphasis is placed on statistics that can be compared with other articles. Census figures are the most reliable available to us and can be used to compare a place such as London, Ont., to another, such as Regina, Saskatchewan. Canada held a census in 1981 and another in 1986. The encyclopedia contains figures from both of these.

Text Over 1 million words contain the important facts on each topic.

Main Sub-Head helps guide the reader to the part of the topic of most interest.

Photographs present an image of what is described in the text and add useful visual information.

Captions describe the photographs and artwork and give the source, in this case, the photographer Thomas Kitchin.

Minor Sub-Head gives further guidance to the reader in finding information.

Careers Over 100 careers, from accounting to zoology, are described in sidebars.

Mini-biographies of Canadians who made contributions in the areas described in articles in the text.

Running Heads help guide the reader to articles throughout the alphabet. On a right-hand page, the running head lists the last article on the page. On a left-hand page, it lists the first article.

Page Number Each volume begins on page one. References in the index list these page numbers and the volume in which the subject appears.

Addresses for More Information are listed at the end of many articles.

Related Articles lead the reader to other entries in the encyclopedia that contain information on a different aspect of the topic.

Suggested Reading lists books and magazines containing information on the topic.

Article Titles are listed alphabetically throughout the encyclopedia.

Definitions begin many articles. The origins of words are often given as an aid to understanding.

Sidebar Summaries provide quick reference, dates, definitions, and a great deal more.

Historical Background is provided for most topics, often with an accompanying "Time Line" in the margin.

bone whistle. On either side of the body were small piles of charcoal, where fires had been built at the bottom of the pit. Since it would have taken a band of hunters about a week to build a grave of this size, this adolescent must have been very special, or else very fearful, to the group who buried him.

Cliff at Head-Smashed-In Buffalo Jump. The native people stampeded the bison over this cliff to their death (photo by Thomas Kitchin).

Head-Smashed-In Buffalo Jump is one of hundreds of animal killing sites on the Canadian plains. It is in the Porcupine Hills in southern Alberta. The site consists of a cliff 10 metres high, with a large natural basin to the west, surrounded by hills and crisscrossed by streams. For over 5000 years (3500 BC to 1750 AD), groups of native people used the site to stampede large numbers of bison to their death. They built several rock cairns among the streams in the basin to make a network of drive lanes leading up to the cliff. Then they herded the bison into the lanes and drove them forward over the cliff. Many bison were killed outright in the fall, and those that were wounded were quickly killed off by hunters waiting below with clubs, arrows, and spears. Archaeologists

Bison Jump found at Head-Smashed-In Buffalo Jump. Archaeologists have uncovered bones and some 5000 arrow and spear points at the site (photo by Thomas Kitchin).

have excavated butchered bones and stone tools at the base of the cliff and have recovered over 5000 arrow and spear points. Some of the rock used to make the knives and arrowheads came from as far away as Wyoming and North Dakota, which shows the extent of trade among native groups. Because it is one of the oldest and best-preserved jump sites, Head-Smashed-In has been named both an Alberta Historical Resource Site and a United Nations World Heritage Site.

ARCHAEOLOGY IN CANADA
The history of archaeology in Canada can be divided into three main periods: early collectors, professional archaeologists, and compulsory legislation.

Early Collectors The first "archaeologists" in Canada were amateur collectors who enjoyed looking for relics or curiosities in old Indian cemeteries. Unfortunately, their hasty and unscientific methods probably destroyed more evidence of native culture than was found. Gradually, collections of artifacts were put together, which became the basis for many new museums in cities in central and eastern Canada after 1850. The most important collection was made by scientists employed by the Geological Survey of Canada. In 1911 their museum became the Victoria Memorial Museum in Ottawa, and today their archaeological collection is part of the Canadian Museum of Civilization.

Professional Archaeologists In 1925 the first anthropology department was established at the University of Toronto, with offices located in the Royal Ontario Museum. Gradually, other universities across Canada set up similar departments, where archaeology was taught as part of the anthropology program. It was not until 1964 that the University of Calgary organized the first separate archaeology department.

Archaeologists employed by both universities and the major museums excavated sites in many parts of Canada, though they were often hampered by lack of money. In 1961 the Canada Council began to fund archaeological research. The Quiet Revolution in Quebec in the 1960s and Centennial Year in 1967 also made the public much more aware of its heritage, including what archaeologists have found out about the past. As a result, there has been a tremendous expansion in the field. The Archaeological Survey of Canada was founded in 1971, and there

mids of varying size have been designed by Peter Hemingway to cover a series of buried concrete chambers which house plants from tropical, temperate, and arid zones.

Finally, some Post-Modern architects have turned back to the past. In his design for the Canadian Centre for Architecture (1989), in Montreal, architect Peter Rose showed a renewed interest in the Beaux-Arts. The Royal Architectural Institute of Canada, 328 Somerset Street, West, Ottawa, Ont., K2P 0J9, can be contacted for more information.

▷ RELATED ARTICLES: **Barns; Grain Elevators; Heritage Conservation; House; Parliament Buildings;** and biographies of **Raymond Affleck; Baillairgé Family; Douglas Cardinal; Arthur Erickson; John Lyle; Raymond Moriyama; John B. Parkin; Francis Rattenbury; Moshe Safdie; Ronald Thom; Eberhard Zeidler.** *See also* entries on individual buildings: **Canadian Museum of Civilization; Christ Church Cathedral; CN Tower; Kingston City Hall; Province House.**

▷ SUGGESTED READING: Ruth Cawker and William Bernstein, *Contemporary Canadian Architecture* (1988); Alan Gowans, *Building Canada* (1966); Ron MacGregor and others, *Canadian Art: Building a Heritage* (1987); Moshe Safdie, *Form and Purpose* (1982); Leon Whiteson, *Modern Canadian Architecture* (1983).

■ **Archives**
Archives are places where permanent

St Mary's Catholic Church, Red Deer, Alta. Architect Douglas Cardinal's moulded shapes are a sharp contrast to the rigid lines of the International style (photo by Roy Ooms/Take Stock Inc.).

Paris Opera House Canadian architects' fame and work are spreading to other countries. Canadian architect Carlos Ott designed the new Paris Opera House, one of the most important new buildings in Paris (courtesy NORR Partnership Ltd).

records are kept. The word *archives* also refers to the records themselves. Governments, institutions, corporations, clubs, and individuals all produce records of their everyday activities. Most of these records are thrown away almost immediately, but others have value as a history of the particular organization or person. It is these significant records that are collected in archives. The people who look after them are called *archivists.*

Many institutions keep their own archives, but the largest archives in Canada are maintained by the federal and provincial governments. Several cities also have archives, including Toronto, Vancouver, Edmonton, Calgary, and Ottawa.

The National Archives of Canada in Ottawa is the most important archives in Canada. It traces its roots back to 1872. From 1912 to 1987 it was called the Public Archives of Canada. It keeps records from all federal government departments, as well as maps, paintings, books, photographs, films, sound recordings, music scores, architectural drawings, medals, and other objects. It also collects letters and diaries from politicians, scientists, writers, and other individuals who are of national interest.

What Archives Do Archivists collect

The Junior Encyclopedia of Canada

A Mari usque ad Mare

A Mari usque ad Mare is Canada's motto (Latin for "From Sea to Sea"). Like the term "dominion," it comes from the Bible, Psalm 72, Verse 8: "He shall have dominion also from sea to sea...." The motto was adopted officially in 1921, when it was included in a new design for Canada's coat of arms. In French, the words are "D'un océan à l'autre."

Canada's Coat of Arms includes Canada's motto, A Mari usque ad Mare. It means "From Sea to Sea" (courtesy NAC/artist Karen E. Bailey).

Abalone

Abalone are also called ear shells or sea ears, because of the ear shape of the shell. They are a kind of mollusc. They live in marine environments, attached to rocks in shallow water, but some are found as deep as 375 metres. There are two species of abalone in Canada. The pinto abalone (*Haliotis kamtschatkana*) is found along the entire B.C. coast. The northern green abalone (*H. walallensis*) is found only in the waters at the southern edge of B.C.

The abalone uses its powerful foot to attach itself so firmly to a rock that a lever is needed to pry it loose. Its red-green shell has four to eight holes, through which the animal eliminates water and its own waste. Abalone feeds on algae. The soft muscular parts are choice gourmet food, grilled as steak or ground up in a bisque. The pearly iridescence of the inner shell has made it popular among Northwest Coast Indians, who use it for jewellery and inlays.

Abbotsford

Abbotsford, B.C., is on the south bank of the Fraser River, just east of Vancouver. The original village was named for Harry Abbott, an official with the Canadian Pacific Railway. It was originally one of several farming centres in the fertile Fraser Valley. More recently, several industries have located there. Many residents of Abbotsford commute the short distance to work in Vancouver. A famous air show brings thousands of visitors every year. The population in 1986 was 14 496. For information, contact the Municipal Clerk, 34194 Marshall Road, Abbotsford, B.C., V2S 5E4.

Abbott, Sir John Joseph Caldwell

Abbott was a graduate of McGill University, where he trained as a lawyer and later taught law. Meanwhile, he practised as a lawyer, as well as serving as an elected

Sir John Joseph Caldwell Abbott
3RD PRIME MINISTER OF CANADA

Born: March 12, 1821, at St Andrews East,
Lower Canada [Quebec]
Died: October 30, 1893, Montreal, Que.
Occupation: Lawyer
Political Party: Conservative
First Elected: 1857
Chosen Leader: 1891
Period as Prime Minister: June 16, 1891, to
November 24, 1892
Note: first Prime Minister born in Canada.
(PHOTO COURTESY NAC/PA33933)

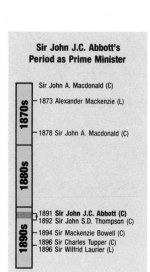

**Sir John J.C. Abbott's
Period as Prime Minister**

1870s	Sir John A. Macdonald (C)
	1873 Alexander Mackenzie (L)
	1878 Sir John A. Macdonald (C)
1880s	
1890s	1891 **Sir John J.C. Abbott (C)**
	1892 Sir John S.D. Thompson (C)
	1894 Sir Mackenzie Bowell (C)
	1896 Sir Charles Tupper (C)
	1896 Sir Wilfrid Laurier (L)

*Maude Abbott was one
of Canada's earliest
women doctors and a
world authority on heart
disease (courtesy
NAC/C-9479).*

politician both before and after Confederation. In 1887 he was appointed to the Senate.

In 1891, when John A. Macdonald died, Abbott became prime minister mainly because the Conservative Party could not agree on Macdonald's successor. The logical choice would have been Sir John Thompson, but he was a Roman Catholic. A sufficient number of Conservatives were not yet ready for a Catholic prime minister. So the choice fell on Abbott who himself said that he was chosen "because I am not particularly obnoxious to anyone." Abbott ruled from the Senate while Thompson spoke for him in the House of Commons. Abbott thus became the first Canadian-born prime minister. He retired owing to ill health after only a year and a half.

Abbott was thus an interim choice as prime minister. Macdonald considered him selfish. When someone remarked that Abbott had a disarming smile, Macdonald had replied, "Yes, a sweet smile — from the teeth outwards." But Abbott was really better than that. He and Thompson were determined to scrub the Conservative Party clean after recent scandals. Like a puppy, the party did not much like the process, but it emerged much the better for it.

▷ SUGGESTED READING: Chris Ondaatje, *The Prime Ministers of Canada* (1985).

■ Abbott, Maude Elizabeth Seymour

Doctor, medical researcher (*born in 1869 at St Andrews East, Que.; died in 1940 at Montreal, Que.*). Maude Abbott was one of Canada's earliest women doctors and a world authority on heart disease. She received her medical degree in 1894, when it was still very difficult for a woman to qualify as a doctor. Most universities did not accept women as medical students. She completed her training in Europe, where she studied under some of the foremost authorities of her day.

Despite her many qualifications and outstanding exam results, the most Abbott could do on her return to Montreal in 1897 was to open a small practice for women and children. All other opportunities were closed to her, because she was a woman. Finally, in 1898 she was appointed assistant curator at McGill Medical Museum, where she spent most of the rest of her life. Although she created order out of chaos at the museum and was the author of more than 100 publications, she never rose above the rank of assistant professor at McGill. Nevertheless, she was known around the world as an authority on heart disease. When she died, a leading heart specialist called her "a living force in the medicine of her generation."

▷ RELATED ARTICLE: **Doctors and Medicine**.

■ Abenaki

The Abenaki are an Algonquian-speaking group that once lived in present-day Maine and New England. They lived in villages along the major rivers in the seasons when the fish could be harvested. During other seasons they moved in family groups to the coast or to small camps farther inland. They used these camps as trapping bases during the fur trade. When the trade declined they found work in lumbering, canoe making, and basketry. They were devastated by European diseases in the 17th century. Many of the survivors moved to Quebec, where they are still known for their crafts and lively folklore. *See* **Native People: Eastern Woodlands.**

■ Aberdeen and Temair, Ishbel Maria Gordon, Marchioness of

Reformer, feminist (*born in 1857 at London, England; died in 1939 at Aberdeen, Scotland*). As wife of the governor general, Lady Aberdeen played a leading role in Canadian society, but it was different from that of most governor generals' wives. She was a dedicated reformer, determined to help those in need. In particular, she wanted to help women play a greater part in the life of the nation.

Lady Aberdeen was in Canada from 1893 to 1898 and is remembered especially for forming the National Council of Women (1893) and the Victorian Order of Nurses (1897). The Victorian Order of Nurses brought nursing care to the poor in their homes. The National Council championed causes that were of concern to women, including broader education for girls. With Lady Aberdeen as its president, the organization gained far more notice than it would otherwise have done. Lady Aberdeen's influence continued long after she left Canada. In 1909, for example, she chaired a meeting in Toronto of the International Council of Women that declared its support for women's right to vote.

▷ RELATED ARTICLES: **Woman Suffrage; Women's Organizations.**

▷ SUGGESTED READING: Doris French, *Ishbel and the Empire* (1988).

Lady Aberdeen was a dedicated reformer who was determined to help those in need. She founded the Victorian Order of Nurses (courtesy NAC/C-22760).

■ Aberdeen and Temair, John Campbell Gordon, 1st Marquess of

Governor general (*born in 1847 at Edinburgh, Scotland; died in 1934 at Tarland, Scotland*). Lord Aberdeen was governor general of Canada from 1893 to 1898. During these years, Canada had a series of Conservative governments, until 1896, when Wilfrid Laurier became prime minister. Aberdeen found it hard to get along with the Conservative leaders. He caused controversy in 1896 when he refused to approve a list of appointments put forward by PM Sir Charles Tupper.

In Britain, Aberdeen sat in the House of Lords as a Liberal, and he was a strong believer in Liberal policies. He was also a keen social reformer. On his family estate in Scotland, he had established hospitals, schools, and clubs to make life better for the poorer people, and he encouraged similar projects in Canada. Aberdeen returned to England before the expiry of his term, partly because he lost money investing in an orchard in Vernon, B.C. He later served as lord lieutenant of Ireland (1905-15).

■ Aberhart, William

Premier of Alberta (*born in 1878 at Hibbert Township, Perth County, Ont.; died in 1943 at Vancouver, B.C.*). As premier of Alberta from 1935 to 1943, William Aberhart was leader of the first Social Credit government in the world. He had earlier gained fame as a radio preacher, known throughout the prairies as "Bible Bill."

Teacher and Preacher Aberhart began his career as a school teacher and lay preacher in Brantford, Ontario. Moving to Calgary in 1910, he became principal of Crescent Heights High School in 1915. Meanwhile, he taught Bible classes and served as the unofficial minister of a Baptist church in Calgary. He began broadcasting Sunday afternoon services in 1925, and in 1927 he opened his own religious training school, the Calgary Prophetic Bible Institute. From there he broadcast his "Back to the Bible Hour" radio program, which attracted over 300 000 listeners.

Politician In the early 1930s, as the Great Depression caused increasing hardship, Aberhart began to preach about a new theory called Social Credit. He believed that Social Credit could solve the problems of the Depression. During the 1935 provincial elections, he announced that a Social Credit government would give each adult Albertan, every month, a

Lord Aberdeen was a strong believer in Liberal policies and found it hard to co-operate with Canada's Conservative leaders (artwork by Irma Council).

William Aberhart became well known to Albertans through his radio broadcast, "Back to the Bible Hour." He became premier in 1935, promising that his theory of Social Credit would bring Alberta out of the Great Depression (courtesy NAC/C-9448).

dividend worth $25 — called "funny money" by his critics. Albertans, who could not understand why there was "poverty in the midst of plenty," were attracted to Aberhart's ideas.

Although Aberhart himself did not run in the elections, he promoted Social Credit so successfully that the party won 56 of the 63 seats in the legislature.

Aberhart was promptly sworn in as premier. A by-election was then held so that he could be elected a member of the legislature.

Aberhart remained premier until his death, though he was unable to fulfil his promised reforms. They encroached on federal powers and were quickly disallowed by the federal government. Nevertheless, Albertans continued to vote for the Social Credit Party into the 1970s.

▷ RELATED ARTICLE: **Social Credit.**

▷ SUGGESTED READING: David R. Elliott, *Bible Bill: A Biography of William Aberhart* (1987).

■ Aboriginal Rights

Aboriginal rights are the rights of the native people of Canada. They are partly based on the fact that the native people used the land long before the arrival of European settlers. They are also based on the fact that the native people were organized in societies.

The Royal Proclamation of 1763 set aside a large area of land for the use of native people. Since then, rights have been guaranteed in treaties, international law, and court cases. Aboriginal rights are also guaranteed by the Constitution Act, 1982. However, native leaders and the federal and provincial governments do not agree about what these rights include. It is usually agreed that they refer to land and resources. Native groups claim that their rights also extend to their culture. Many also claim a right to govern themselves. The question of aboriginal rights is one of the most important in the lives of the native people in Canada today. They also present a major challenge to the governments of Canada.

▷ RELATED ARTICLES: **Indian Treaties; Land Claims; Royal Proclamation of 1763** and various entries under **Native People.**

■ Abortion

Abortion is the term which describes the ending of a pregnancy, especially when it is ended deliberately. Abortion is one of the most controversial issues in society today. Abortion was made illegal in Canada in the 19th century. Nevertheless, many women continued to seek abortions to end unwanted pregnancies. Some sought help from doctors or non-medical people. Others tried to perform the abortions themselves. As a result, many women were maimed or killed. During the 1960s, while restrictions on abortion were relaxed around the world, Canadian law still treated abortion as a crime. The maximum penalty for a conviction was life imprisonment.

The 1969 Amendment In 1969 Parliament amended the Criminal Code, permitting abortions under certain circumstances. The abortion had to take place at an approved hospital. Second, the abortion could only be performed if the hospital had established an abortion committee. These committees could approve an abortion if they decided that the continuation of the pregnancy would pose a danger to a woman's "life or health." Because the law was difficult to interpret, the amendment was considered unsatisfactory both by those who opposed abortion and by those who wanted abortion left to the choice of the individual. The new law did not, for example, define "life" or "health." Each committee made its own rules. One of the principles of law is that it must be applied equally to everyone.

This was not possible if each committee could interpret the rules differently. In some areas of the country, no committees were ever formed. Hence, a woman had to leave these areas to get an abortion.

Challenges to the New Law The uncertainty of the law confused and angered people on both sides of the issue. It has been challenged several times in the courts. Dr Henry Morgentaler, a Montreal doctor, set up abortion clinics in several Canadian cities. In 1973 the police charged him under the Criminal Code. A jury found him not guilty. In 1974 the Quebec Court of Appeal overturned the jury finding. In 1975 the Supreme Court of Canada upheld the Quebec Court's decision, and Morgentaler went to prison. Morgentaler was tried by jury twice more and acquitted each time. In 1988, as a result of another appeal by Morgentaler, the Supreme Court struck down the existing law, as unconstitutional under the new Charter of Rights.

After 1988 there was therefore no valid abortion law in Canada. The Supreme Court refused to rule on whether or not the fetus has rights. It handed the whole matter back to Parliament. In 1989 several men asked the courts to prevent individual women from having abortions. Courts in Alberta and Ontario refused. In Quebec, the request was granted, upheld by the Quebec Court of Appeal, and then struck down by the Supreme Court.

Continuing Controversy The issue of abortion is difficult to resolve because there is no agreement throughout society on some of the key points. For example, those who oppose abortion claim that a fetus is a human life, right from the time of conception. Hence, they call their position "Pro-Life." Those who defend abortion argue that a woman should control her own body and that the state has no right to force her to complete a pregnancy. Hence, this position is often called "Pro-Choice." The two sides have had a long and vociferous debate in the media. Supporters of each position have broken the law to express their point of view.

In 1989, the Conservative government proposed a new law, which would permit abortions only if a doctor judged that the woman's health was in danger. The proposal was criticized from both sides. It was unclear if the law would pass.

▷ Suggested Reading: Edward F. Dolan, *Matters of Life and Death* (1982); Sue Johanson, *Talk Sex* (1988); Helen Fogwell Porter, *January, February, June or July* (1988); Mary Razzell, *Snow Apples* (1984).

■ Acadia

Acadians are the French-speaking people of Atlantic Canada. You might meet them in the industrial town of Bathurst in New Brunswick, on a farm near Tignish on Prince Edward Island, around the fishing port of Cheticamp in Nova Scotia, or on the university campus in Moncton, N.B. The Acadians and their ancestors have lived around the Bay of Fundy and the Gulf of St Lawrence for more than 350 years. Today, Acadian communities are found in all the Maritime provinces and also in parts of Quebec.

The name Acadia is old. In 1524 explorer Giovanni da Verrazzano put the name "Arcadie" (which refers to a legendary place of beauty and peace) on his map of the east coast of North America. Gradually, the mapmakers moved the word northeast towards Atlantic Canada. The Micmac Indians used the word "cadie" or "chadie" for a safe, sheltered harbour. "Arcadie," perhaps mixed with "cadie," produced the name of Acadie or Acadia.

HISTORY

Exploration and Settlement Fur trader Pierre Du Gua de Monts brought the first European settlers to Acadia in 1604. The King of France had given him the privilege of being the only Frenchman allowed to trade for furs or build settlements anywhere in New France. The group of men led by de Monts spent their first winter in Acadia at Île Sainte-Croix. The next year they settled at Port-Royal, where they built the habitation. Between 1604 and 1607, Samuel de Champlain, who was one of de Monts' men, explored and mapped much of the southern Atlantic coast. In the first years, many of the men died of scurvy, but slowly they learned to live in the New World. To keep them happy, Champlain founded the Order of Good Cheer, and all the members competed to see who could prepare the best meals. In 1607, however, de Monts learned that the King of France intended to take away his special privileges, so he closed the settlement in Acadia. Port-Royal remained unoccupied until 1610, when a small group of colonists arrived, led by Jean de Biencourt.

After this, rival fur traders and colonizers — the Biencourts, the Denys, the La Tours, and others — fought over Acadia for many years. They built forts and trading posts on the Bay of Fundy, along the Atlantic coast, and in the Gulf of St Lawrence. They fought each other and the English to control the trade of Acadia.

Order of Good Cheer
Samuel de Champlain founded the Order of Good Cheer at Port-Royal in 1606.

The French had suffered a terrible winter at Sainte Croix Island. Many died of scurvy.

They moved the colony to Port-Royal and enjoyed a more pleasant winter.

In this happier time, Champlain established the Order to keep up spirits and pass the time. Members took turns hunting and leading a procession to the table.

In 1632, Isaac de Razilly brought over 300 settlers from France to settle at Port-Royal. Upon his death, Charles de Menou d'Aulnay gained control of the colony. In 1645 d'Aulnay, who commanded Port-Royal, attacked the fort of his rival Charles de La Tour on the Saint John River. La Tour was away and the fort surrendered. His wife, Françoise, was forced to watch as d'Aulnay hanged her men, and she died soon afterwards. Yet when d'Aulnay died five years later, La Tour married his widow and took over at Port-Royal.

By 1671 there were about 400 settlers in Acadia, mostly around Port-Royal. Most of these first Acadians were French, but some were Scots or Basque. They fished, trapped, and traded with their Micmac neighbours, and some married Micmacs. Others started farms around Port-Royal, and a small, settled community began to develop.

The Wars for Acadia Acadia lay in a boundary zone, fought over by British and French, and it was never left in peace for long. The English colonies of New England were closer to Acadia than to any other French settlements. In peacetime the English came to trade, and in war they came to conquer. In 1613 English colonists from Virginia led by Samuel Argall burned Port-Royal. The British attacked again in 1629. They captured Port-Royal in 1654 and controlled Acadia until France regained it in 1670. The English attacked again in 1690, 1704, and in 1707. With so much fighting and so many changes of command, the Acadians became a people without strong ties to either side.

In 1710 the British captured Port-Royal yet again, and in 1713 the Treaty of Utrecht gave Acadia permanently to Britain. Port-Royal was renamed Annapolis Royal, and a British commander with a small garrison of soldiers replaced the French governor and his garrison. However, most of the Acadians stayed on under British rule.

The Acadian People Despite the wars, the tiny colony of Acadia kept growing. The 400 people of 1671 became 1400 by 1701. By the 1750s, there would be 13 000 Acadians. As their numbers grew, the Acadians began to move out from Port-Royal to settle at Beaubassin, Grand Pré, and other places around the Bay of Fundy. They were a healthy people. They had big families, and as they married it began to seem that all Acadians were related.

The Acadian people were mostly farmers. To hold back the huge tides of the Bay of Fundy, they built dykes on the marshlands around Port-Royal. As rainwater and melting snow drained the salt out of

Major Acadian Settlements to 1713

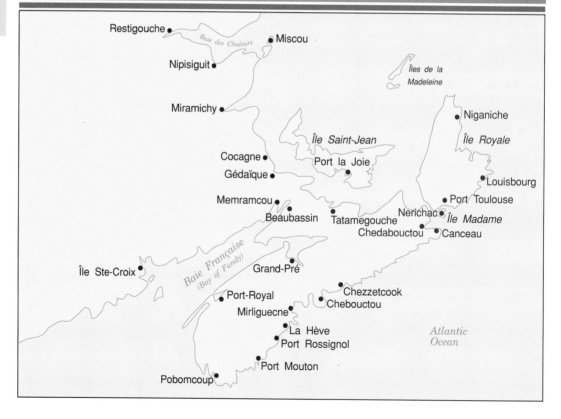

the newly dyked land, rich farm fields became available. The settlers raised crops and animals, and they planted fruit trees. They built mills to grind their grain and to cut lumber for their homes, barns, boats, and furniture. They ate what they needed from their produce and traded the remainder for tools, molasses, fabrics, and other things they could not easily make themselves.

They were becoming an independent and self-reliant community even before the British took control. Until 1713, they had French governors and seigneurs (the heirs of d'Aulnay and the La Tours), but these rulers tended to be driven away whenever the British attacked, and the Acadians learned to live without them. The government in France was too far off to have much influence. New Englanders were officially the enemy, but New England was the closest place with which Acadians could trade. They began to refer to the New Englanders as "our friends the enemy." The Acadians were a people caught between two empires, yet were part of neither.

The Deportation In the years immediately following 1713, hardly any British settlers arrived in Acadia, so the new British governors had to get along with the people who were already there. The Acadians agreed to obey the new rulers, but they refused to promise to fight against France. The British governors had to accept this, and they called the Acadians "the French neutrals." For the Acadians, little in their lives changed because of British rule. Despite living under foreigners, they prospered.

This began to change after 1749. France still hoped to regain Acadia and had tried to capture Annapolis Royal in 1744. Then, in 1749, the British founded Halifax and brought the first large group of English-speaking settlers to Nova Scotia. This gave the British governors more power to deal with their French subjects. When fighting between Britain and France began again in 1755, the British tried to force the Acadians to take the same oath of allegiance that other British subjects took. The Acadians continued to argue that they should be neutral. But they were French-speaking, and the British were not sure they could be trusted, so the British decided to get rid of them.

That summer and fall of 1755, British troops rounded up over 7000 Acadians. In every Acadian community around the Bay of Fundy, the soldiers burned Acadian homes and herded Acadian prisoners onto ships, which carried them off to the American colonies, from Massachusetts south to Georgia. The big Acadian fam-

Oath of Allegiance

England demanded an oath of loyalty from all its conquered subjects.

The Acadians would agree only to be neutral. They would not take up arms against France or England.

In 1730 Governor Philipps agreed to this compromise.

In 1755 the English used the oath to settle the Acadian problem once and for all.

They used the Acadians' refusal to swear the oath of loyalty as an excuse to deport them.

French Ancestry in Modern Acadia

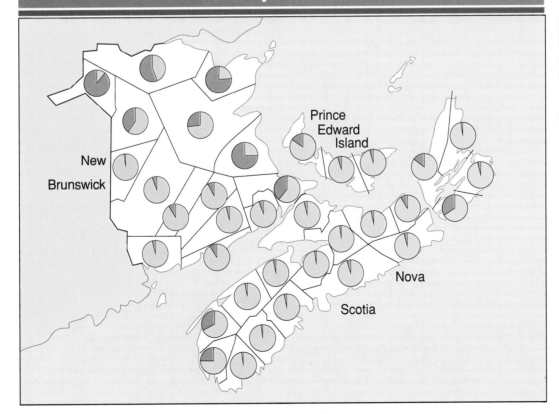

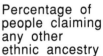 Percentage of people claiming French only ancestry by county

 Percentage of people claiming any other ethnic ancestry

Deportation of the Acadians This painting of the removal of the Acadians from their land was made in 1893. It shows the Acadians being rounded up at Grand Pré in 1755. Between then and 1762, some 10 000 Acadians were uprooted and shipped to far-off places. Many died on the way (courtesy Musée acadien, Université de Moncton).

Acadian Population in Atlantic Canada	
Year	Population
1671	about 400
1701	about 1400
1750	about 13 000
1800	about 8000
1871	87 000
1901	139 000
1961	331 000
1981	337 000
1986	297 000

ilies became hopelessly separated. Many Acadians died during the deportation. Some fled to French territory or hid in the woods, but many of these fugitives were seized in the next few years. The British continued to deport Acadians until 1762. The Acadian farmlands were given to settlers from Britain and New England.

Acadia Rebuilt When the Seven Years' War between Britain and France ended in 1763, a few Acadians were still hiding in the woods of Atlantic Canada. Others began to slip back from exile; but their land had been taken by English settlers, and they were not welcome in the old Acadia. They built new communities around the edges of the Gulf of St Lawrence: on the Gaspé peninsula, in the region that later became New Brunswick, and in the Magdalen Islands, Prince Edward Island, and Cape Breton Island. They also settled in southwestern Nova Scotia and on the islands of St Pierre and Miquelon. Some Acadian exiles who had gone to live in France went to Louisiana, where they founded the "Cajun" population of the southern United States.

In their new lands, the people of the new Acadia had to make a living by fishing, sailing, and wood cutting instead of farming. They were poor and they had to struggle to survive, with their priests as their only leaders. Acadian novelist Antonine Maillet calls this time in Acadian history "one hundred years in the woods." But Acadia continued to grow. There were only about 8000 Acadians in the Maritimes in 1800. Around Confederation, there were 87 000. The Acadians had preserved their communities, their language and folklore, and their memories of what had happened to them. In 1847 the American poet Longfellow wrote "Evangeline," a long poem about the deportation of 1755, and this helped make the Acadian story famous.

By the 1880s, the growing Acadian community began to speak out. In New Brunswick, Acadians founded the Société nationale des acadiens (National Society of Acadians) and other organizations in order to maintain their identity. Gradually, the Acadians established schools, colleges, and newspapers, and they developed their arts and culture. They were no longer quite so poor. The development of co-operatives in the early 1900s gradually improved life in the fishing communities, and Acadians began to enter a wider range of careers.

ACADIA TODAY

Since the 1960s, the Acadians have asserted themselves as a vital element in a bilingual Canada. They have been particularly influential in New Brunswick, where they form more than 30% of the population. They elect one-third of all the members of the New Brunswick legislature. An Acadian politician, Louis Robichaud, served as premier of New Brunswick from 1960 to 1970, and there have been two Acadian lieutenant-governors. New Brunswick has been officially bilingual since 1969, and in 1981 it guaranteed equal status to its English and French communities. In the 1970s and early 1980s, amid French-English tensions in Moncton, N.B., and elsewhere, there was talk of forming an Acadian political movement and of Acadian separatism

Acadians also live in Prince Edward Island and Nova Scotia, and in the American state of Maine, but they form a smaller proportion of the population there than in New Brunswick, and there is greater pressure from the surrounding English-language society. Acadian communities are also found in Quebec on the Gaspé peninsula and the Magdalen Islands.

Despite the influence of the English-language majority, Acadian cultural life is stronger than ever. Theatre, music, dance, painting, sculpture, and literature all thrive in Acadia, and there is renewed interest in Acadian language, folklore, genealogy, and history. Antonine Maillet's novel *Pélagie-la-Charrette* (1979), about the deportation and return of the Acadians, won France's prestigious Prix Goncourt. The Acadian Historical Village at Caraquet, N.B., is a living museum of Acadian history and culture.

▷ RELATED ARTICLES: **Charles Lawrence; Jean-Louis Le Loutre; Antonine Maillet; Maritimes 1713-1900; Micmac; Order of Good Cheer; Port-Royal; Louis Robichaud.**

▷ SUGGESTED READING: René Babineau, *Brief History of Acadie* (2nd ed. 1988); Marion Davison and A. Marsh, *Smoke Over Grand Pré* (1988); Melvin Gallant, *The Country of Acadia* (2nd ed. 1986); Barry M. Moody, *The Acadians* (1981); Rosemary Neering, *Life in Acadia* (1976).

■ Acadia University

Acadia University is located in Wolfville, Nova Scotia. Its three faculties are arts, pure and applied science, and management and education. There are also schools of computer science, nutrition and home economics, business administration, music, recreation and physical education, engineering, education, secretarial science, and graduate studies.

The university began in 1828 as Horton Academy. It received a charter under its present name in 1891. The Acadia Divinity School is an affiliate founded in 1968. Its purpose is to train Baptist clergy.

Acadia University has about 3800 undergraduate and 220 graduate students. For further information, write to the Registrar's Office, Acadia University, Wolfville, N.S., B0P 1X0.

■ Accounting

Accounting is a process of organizing and reporting complex, mainly financial, information about the economic activities of individuals and organizations. It consists of concepts, rules, and procedures that are generally accepted by those who prepare and use the information. Accountants assist various interested parties, such as owners, lenders, and managers, in making decisions about their own or an enterprise's financial welfare.

Accounting traces its origin to the 15th century. Many of the significant developments in the field, however, can be connected to the economic instability of the 1930s, to changing financial markets, and to the emphasis by accountants on preparing formal guidelines and standards during the past three decades. Computers have also affected the field by speeding the managing and processing of large quantities of routine information in the bookkeeping process, which is a part of the accounting field.

There are two sub-divisions of accounting. One, often called "financial accounting," stresses financial reports and the needs of those outside a company. The other, "managerial," emphasizes information which is mainly useful to the internal managers of an organization. Financial accounting reports information in four main financial statements. A *balance sheet* describes finances at a certain time. It reports *assets* (what an enterprise owns), *liabilities* (what an enterprise owes), and *equity* (the owners' rights to

Wars and Battles of Acadia

1613	Samuel Argall of Virginia attacks and burns Port-Royal
1629-32	English occupy Acadia, which they call Nova Scotia
1636-45	Feud between d'Aulnay and La Tour
1654	English expedition under Robert Sedgwick captures Port-Royal. England rules Acadia until 1670
1670	France recovers Acadia by the 1667 Treaty of Breda with England
1690	William Phips of Boston plunders Port-Royal
1696	Benjamin Church of New England burns Beaubassin
1710	Francis Nicholson captures Acadia
1713	Treaty of Utrecht confirms British possession of Acadia (Nova Scotia). The islands in the Gulf of St Lawrence remain part of New France
1744	French troops from Louisbourg capture Canso
1750	Beaubassin is abandoned by the French. Both the British and French build forts on the Isthmus of Chignecto
1755	The British capture the French forts on the isthmus. Charles Lawrence orders the deportation of the Acadians
1760	At Restigouche, on Chaleur Bay, the British capture the last French ships and troops still fighting in Acadia

Careers in Accounting

There are three kinds of accounting occupations in Canada: chartered, certified general, and certified management accounting. Accounting can be studied at community colleges and major universities across the country. Applicants must have graduated from high school and are usually expected to have some post-secondary education. In the case of chartered accountants, a university degree is required. To qualify for professional status, an accounting student must pass examinations before obtaining a licence. A few years of additional training are usually required.

Some accountants work in government and industry, while others prefer to set up their own offices to provide accounting services to the general public. There are more than 84 000 accountants in Canada. About 4300 graduate each year.

the difference between the assets and the liabilities). An *income statement* discloses an enterprise's *revenues* (resource inflows) and *expenses* (resource outflows) for a period of time. If the revenues are greater than the expenses, the result is *income*. If expenses are greater than revenues, the result is a *loss*. Another report, the statement of *retained earnings*, reconciles the changes in equity in the balance sheet. These changes result mainly from income, loss, or dividend payments. A fourth report, called a statement of *changes in Financial Position*, indicates how an enterprise's operating, financing, and investing activities change its cash resources.

Management accounting offers significant scope for assisting decision makers in matters of operating an enterprise economically, efficiently, and effectively. It employs many approaches to do this. These include analysing an enterprise's capital and its production costs, and examining the choices and possible results associated with changes to an enterprise, for example, expanding or reducing its operations.

Some key ideas in financial accounting include measuring resources by their *actual cost*; assuming that economic change takes place only when a market *transaction* occurs between unrelated parties; and appropriately *matching* only related inflows and outflows to compare accomplishment with effort. Important ideas in management accounting include *relationships*, such as those of costs, lev-

The pH Scale measures the degree of acidity. A drop of 1 in pH value means a ten-fold increase in acidity (artwork by Michael Lee).

els of activity, and income; *planning and budgeting*; and ways of *transferring* costs within an enterprise when it has several divisions. It is the appropriate use of these and many other ideas in the accounting field that require skill and judgement in working with accounting information.

■ Acid Rain

Acid rain is one of the most serious threats to the environment. It turns lakes acidic, kills fish and other life in lakes, destroys forests, makes soil less fertile, and destroys buildings made of marble and sandstone. It puts toxic metals, freed from metal pipes, into the water that people drink.

WHAT IS ACID RAIN?

Acid rain consists of chemical pollutants that fall to the ground from the air. It falls as rain, snow, fog, sleet, dew, and as dry particles. The chemicals are mainly oxides of sulphur dioxide plus oxides of nitrogen. Smelters, which extract nickel, copper and other metals from ores contaminated with sulphur, release this poisonous gas into the air. The Inco smelter in Sudbury, Ont., produces more sulphur dioxide than any other single source in North America.

Power plants which burn sulphurous coal to generate electricity also release this gas. Ontario Hydro runs five such plants. There are more than 60 large coal-burning power plants along the valley of the Ohio River in the United States, which produce about 70% of the acid rain in North America.

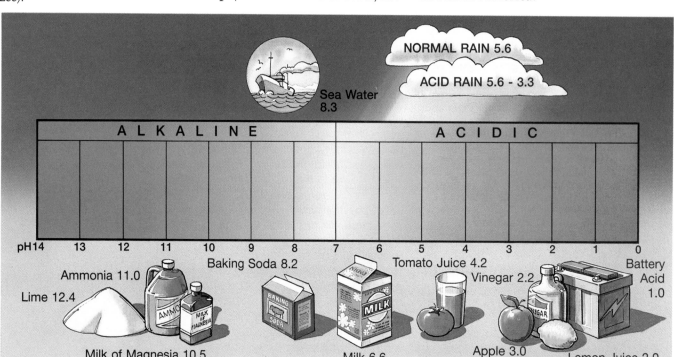

NORMAL RAIN 5.6

ACID RAIN 5.6 - 3.3

Sea Water 8.3

ALKALINE							ACIDIC						

pH14 13 12 11 10 9 8 7 6 5 4 3 2 1 0

Ammonia 11.0

Baking Soda 8.2

Tomato Juice 4.2

Vinegar 2.2

Battery Acid 1.0

Lime 12.4

Milk of Magnesia 10.5

Milk 6.6

Apple 3.0

Lemon Juice 2.0

Oxides of nitrogen also come from coal-burning power plants, but their main source is motor vehicles.

In order to reduce the damage it does locally, most of this pollution is released into the air from tall smokestacks. Because sulphur dioxide had killed all the green plants near its Sudbury smelter, for instance, Inco built the tallest chimney in the world, the Superstack, in the 1970s.

Once in the air, sulphur and nitrogen oxides combine with water and gradually turn into sulphuric acid and nitric acid. Blown by the winds, these acids may remain airborne for days and travel thousands of kilometres before falling from the sky.

Not all acid rain is man-made. A minor but dramatic natural source is the Smoking Hills in Canada's western Arctic. These sea cliffs contain sulphur-rich rocks which have been burning for centuries, producing poisonous fumes. The ponds in the region are among the most polluted in the world.

Where it Falls Where acid rain falls on limestone, a rock that neutralizes acid (that "buffers" it, the chemists say), it is relatively harmless. But much of eastern Canada is part of the Canadian Shield. Its granite rocks are naturally acidic. For this reason, and because winds carry a good deal of the acid pollution from the Ohio Valley and other industrial regions of the United States to Ontario, Quebec, and the Atlantic Provinces, this region is particularly vulnerable to damage by acid rain.

Acid rain from smelters, transportation, and other industrial plants also pollutes parts of the Prairie provinces and British Columbia.

The pH Scale The degree of acidity is measured by the pH scale, which ranges from 0 to 14. Substances that are highly acidic, such as lemon juice and vinegar, are at the low end of the scale (see diagram). A pH of 7.0 is neutral. A drop of 1 in pH value means a ten-fold increase in acidity.

Pure rain, which is naturally mildly acidic, has a pH of 5.6. The rain that falls in eastern Canada often has a pH of 4.6 and lower. Such rain is at least 10 times more acidic than normal. One sample of rain taken in the United States had a pH of 1.5 — the same strength as battery acid!

THE EFFECTS OF ACID RAIN

Lakes and Rivers The effects of acid rain were first noticed in fish. In the late 1960s, Canadian zoologists began reporting that fish had died in lakes deep in the northern Ontario wilderness, far from any polluting industry, and that the water of these lakes was acidic.

As water grows more acidic, scientists now know, fish fail to lay eggs, and they slowly suffocate because metals leached from the soil choke their gills. The young fish are the first to die, then the old. More than 14 000 lakes in eastern North America are acidic — their pH has dropped below 4.5. They have no fish, and their waters are crystal clear and lifeless. At the present rate, tens of thousands of lakes in Ontario and Quebec will be destroyed by the year 2000.

In many cases, the damage done by acid rain cannot be undone. Atlantic salmon, for instance, inherit the instinct to return from the sea to spawn in a particular river. Acid rain kills not only salmon in such rivers, but also the salmon run. At least a dozen Nova Scotia rivers have lost their salmon runs. Others are on the brink of destruction. If acid rain is stopped, however, the water quality could be restored by using lime. Other salmon runs could then be introduced.

Forests Acid rain upsets the chemical balance of the soil by, among other things, releasing metals such as aluminum from soil minerals. Aluminum poisons tree roots, thus choking off the supply of water and nutrients to leaves and branches. Even though there is water in acid rain, trees begin to die of thirst. Sections of the bark and branches die, then, gradually, the whole tree. Already,

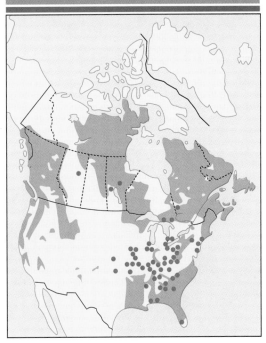

Acid Rain

Areas most sensitive to acid rain

Major source areas of Sulphur Dioxide

many sugar maples in Quebec are dying or dead.

Since forestry is one of Canada's most important industries, acid rain is a threat to Canada's economy. Acid rain has also been shown to harm birds and other wildlife. There is concern that acid rain is harmful to crops.

Buildings and People Acid rain dissolves limestone, marble, and other materials, destroying buildings and statues. It has already damaged the Parliament Buildings in Ottawa.

Acid rain can cause copper, lead, and other poisonous metals to get from pipes into drinking water. There is evidence that acid rain hurts and kills humans, especially people with breathing disorders such as asthma.

FIGHTING ACID RAIN

Reducing acid rain is not a technical problem but a political one.

It is possible to generate electricity and smelt nickel and copper without generating nearly as much acid rain as we now do. It is possible, for instance, to remove sulphur from coal or to "scrub" sulphur dioxide from the gases given off by the burning coal.

Though such control measures are costly, the economic benefits to everyone of reducing acid rain are greater than the overall costs of control. The problem is deciding who should bear these costs. Polluting companies are reluctant to pay for control measures from which they will not benefit directly.

Scientists cannot prove that what comes out of a particular smokestack affects what happens in a particular lake or forest. Specific polluters cannot be blamed for damaging specific parts of the environment and charged with cleaning them up.

The politics of acid rain are complicated because it is an international problem. Most of the acid rain falling on Canada comes from the United States. Eastern Canada receives three to four times more acid rain from the United States than the United States receives from Canada.

Under government pressure and with government funding, polluting companies in Canada have been reducing the emissions that lead to acid rain. The goal of the government is to reduce these by 1994 to half their 1980 level. (More than 50 million tons of sulphur and nitrogen oxides were released into the air in North America in 1980.)

Acid rain is a major source of political friction between Canada and the United States. Scrubbing equipment, which reduces the amount of pollutants emitted, is required by law in all new coal-burning power plants in the United States. But such equipment is not required on old plants, such as those in the Ohio Valley, where coal is the major source of electricity. In 1989 President George Bush announced a plan to clean up acid rain. Even if the plan becomes law, it will be many years before the pollution stops.

▷ RELATED ARTICLES: **Air Pollution; Pollution.**

Acid Rain Gases are shown rising from industry and automobiles. They mix with oxygen to form new gases and are carried by the wind. The chemicals fall to earth as acid rain (right). The acid rain releases toxic metals from rocks and soils into the lakes and rivers. The environment is thus under attack from above and below (artwork courtesy National Research Council).

▷ SUGGESTED READING: Ellen MacGregor and D. Pantell, *Miss Pickerell on the Trail* (1982); Laurence Pringle, *Rain of Troubles* (1988).

■ Act of Union

The Act of Union, 1841, joined Upper Canada and Lower Canada, making them a single colony called the Province of Canada. The Act was passed in Britain in 1840 and came into effect when it was proclaimed in Montreal on February 10, 1841.

▷ RELATED ARTICLE: **Province of Canada.**

■ Action française

L'Action française was a monthly magazine published in Montreal from 1917 to 1928 by a group of French-Canadian nationalists. The group was called the Ligue des droits du français, later the Ligue d'Action française. Members, several of whom were priests, promoted the use of the French language and the rights of French Canadians in Confederation.

■ Action libérale nationale

The ALN was a political party in Quebec in the 1930s. It was founded in 1934 by discontented Liberals, and was led by Paul Gouin. It joined with the Conservatives to form the Union Nationale (UN), led by Maurice Duplessis. However, once the UN was elected in 1936, Duplessis ignored the policies of the ALN and the party drifted into oblivion.

■ Adams, Bryan Guy

Singer, songwriter (*born in 1959 at Kingston, Ont.*). At age 16 he got a job as a singer in a rock band. He wanted to write songs as well as sing. He bought a piano with the money that had been saved for his education and began writing songs. His third album, called *Cuts Like a Knife*, made him a star. A later album, *Reckless*, sold over 8 million copies and made him known around the world. In one year he performed 150 concerts in front of over 1.5 million fans. He writes songs for other performers as well, and he helped to write the song "Tears Are Not Enough," to raise money for Africans suffering from famine. With his gruff voice and exciting way of performing, he is the best-known Canadian rock musician of his time.

▷ SUGGESTED READING: Jane O'Hara, *Bryan Adams* (1989).

■ Adams, David

Ballet dancer (*born in 1928 at Winnipeg, Man.*). Adams was Canada's first principal male dancer. He trained with the Winnipeg Ballet, the forerunner of the Royal

David Adams rehearsing with Lois Smith. The two dancers were the National Ballet's first stars (photo by John de Visser).

Winnipeg Ballet. Like many Canadian dancers of his generation, he went abroad to make his career and danced with some of the major companies in England. When the National Ballet of Canada was formed in 1951, Celia Franca hired him as a lead dancer and choreographer. He excelled in the great classical male roles. He married Lois Smith, the company's principal ballerina, and they were frequently paired together on stage. They became the National Ballet's first "stars." Adams went back to England and joined the London Festival Ballet (1961-69) and the Royal Ballet (1970-76). Since his return to Canada, he has been ballet master of the Alberta Ballet (1977-79), a teacher at the Edmonton School of Ballet (1984-86), and choreographer and coach of Ballet North in Edmonton.

■ Adams, Thomas

Town planner (*born in 1871 near Edinburgh, Scotland; died in 1940 in Sussex, England*). In the early 20th century, Adams was one of the leading planning experts in the world. He spent nine years in Canada, during which he had a vital influence on the laws, institutions, and development of both urban and rural planning in this country.

In Britain, Adams had been associated with groups that were concerned about planning attractive, efficient, and healthy

Bryan Adams is the best-known Canadian rock musician of his time (photo by Ken Regan/Camera 5).

cities. In 1914, he was invited to Canada by the government as a planning adviser.

Adams made several trips across Canada, studying land-use and settlement problems. He drew up model planning laws for both rural and urban areas, and tried to persuade the provincial governments to act on them. He thought that cities should be divided into different areas and that each part should have the services it needed: schools in residential areas, railways in industrial areas, shops and offices in business areas. Private and public development should be co-ordinated to avoid costly mistakes.

Adams published many books and articles on planning. He founded an organization for citizens concerned about the quality of their cities, and an institute for professionals who were interested in research.

In 1917, following the explosion which destroyed large areas around the harbour in Halifax, Adams drew up an urban-renewal plan for the city. He also planned the town of Témiscaming in Quebec. The government, however, was slow to act on his advice on other matters. Adams left Canada in 1923 for New York City. His ideas were taken up again in the years after World War II.

■ Adaskin Brothers

The three Adaskin brothers have been talented, enthusiastic promoters of music in Canada for over 50 years. The eldest is **Harry Adaskin** (*born in 1901 at Riga, Latvia*). He is a widely travelled violinist who has often given the first performances of Canadian works. He also set up the music program of the University of British Columbia in 1946, teaching there until 1973. **Murray Adaskin** (*born in 1906 at Toronto, Ont.*) is a composer and conductor. The youngest brother was **John Adaskin** (*born in 1908 at Toronto; died in 1964 at Toronto*). As a radio producer on the Canadian Broadcasting Corp. (CBC), he was an enthusiastic supporter of Canadian music. Harry and Murray are Officers of the Order of Canada.

▷ SUGGESTED READING: Gordana Lazarevich, *The Musical World of Frances James and Murray Adaskin* (1988).

■ Adoption

By adoption, parents take a child who was not born to them and raise him or her as part of their family. The parents assume the same legal responsibilities as if the child had been born to them. Adoption is a legal process in Canada. Because it is the responsibility of the provinces, the rules of adoption vary from province to province.

There are usually several stages in the process of adoption. The applicants are screened to make sure that they will care for the child. This may be a long process because the investigation is very detailed. Also, there are more parents wanting children than there are children available to be adopted. In addition, some provinces have particular rules which must be followed, such as a limit on the age of prospective parents or on the number of children already in their care. There follows a trial period in which the child is brought to the parents' home.

The formal adoption is done through a court order. After an adoption order is made, the parents become the legal parents of the child. The process usually requires the consent of the natural parents. If the child is old enough (often 12 years), his or her consent is also necessary.

Because of social changes over the past 20 or 30 years, the process of adoption has changed. The identity of natural parents is usually kept secret. Recently, there has been more pressure from adopted persons for the right to contact their birth parents. Some provinces have a system in which adopted persons can register their wish to contact their birth parents. If the birth parents have registered the same request, the connection will be made.

Another issue is how old a child can be before he or she has the right to agree to the adoption. This varies from province to province. In Ontario, for example, a child of seven years must consent, while in Alberta, a child of 12 years must approve. Yet other questions have arisen as to whether unmarried or single people or couples of the same sex should be allowed to adopt.

■ Adult Education

Adult education refers to the education of people who are over the legal age for having to attend school, usually people over 16. It can be provided publicly (by governments, school boards, universities, etc.), privately (by industry, unions, churches, etc.), or voluntarily (by clubs, etc.). Adult education serves at least five purposes: 1) basic education, as in the case of literacy or learning an official language; 2) academic study, as in obtaining a high-school diploma or university degree; 3) job training, as in learning skills that will lead to a job or to improve existing skills; 4) general interest, as with courses in current affairs, carpentry, and so on; and 5) the pursuit of hobbies, for example, photography and stamp collecting.

Examples of adult education can be found throughout Canadian history. In the early 19th century, working men formed Mechanics' Institutes where they could broaden their knowledge in subjects such as science or religion. Churches ran many classes for adults. Classes were organized to prepare immigrants for life in Canada. Women's Institutes provided many kinds of adult education, including lectures, discussion groups, and reading programs. After the two world wars, courses were offered to veterans. In the 1940s, radio was used intensively, as in the Citizen's Forum and the Farm Radio Forum.

In recent years, adult education has become increasingly popular. Older people take classes in subjects that interest them. Universities have major programs in continuing education. Employers are providing more and more training programs. It is now generally accepted that formal education does not end when people stop being full-time students. Today about one in every five Canadians over the age of 17 has taken at least one adult education course.

■ Advertising

Advertising is the promotion of goods, services, and ideas by a sponsor. Advertising is very big business in Canada. In 1988, advertisers in Canada spent an estimated $8.5 billion in the various media — a significant increase from the $4.3 billion spent in 1981.

As communications have become more common and more sophisticated, so has advertising. Today, we are surrounded by advertisements — on television and radio, in newspapers and magazines, on posters and billboards, and by catalogues and direct mail. Advertising has become a deeply rooted part of our culture. In both style and content, it reflects and even shapes the society in which we live.

The role of advertising is to influence people to view a product or service in a favourable light. Advertising alone does not persuade a consumer to buy. It works with other factors, such as the quality of a product, its price, and the place it is sold.

There are two main types of advertising. The first is advertising to consumers. This type of advertising may be a national campaign to make people recognize a brand name. It may take place in stores or through the mail. The second type is business-to-business advertising. Much of

this advertising is done through special magazines, called "trade magazines," read by doctors or lawyers, for instance.

The industry includes three main groups: advertisers, agencies, and media. There are also many other supporting players.

ADVERTISERS
Canadian advertisers include manufacturers, retailers, service firms, governments, and non-profit organizations. The largest advertiser, by far, is the federal government. In 1988 it spent $91 million. The Ontario government was the tenth largest, with $38 million. Because advertising is so effective, there are legal limits on the amount of money candidates can spend on advertising during elections.

Advocacy Advertising Corporations, labour unions, political parties, social organizations, and special-interest groups all use advertising to promote their ideas and to win the public over to their point of view. The Canadian Cancer Society, for example, has mounted a successful campaign against smoking. Different cities across Canada are using clever advertising to support their recycling schemes for glass bottles, tin cans, and newsprint.

AGENCIES
Many large companies have their own advertising departments, but most national advertising in Canada is organized by ad agencies. Agencies plan advertising campaigns. They research the market, create and produce the ads, place them in the different media, track their effect, and manage the account. There are over 600 agencies in Canada, ranging in size from one-person operations to companies with staffs of over 300 based in several cities.

MEDIA
There are two broad categories of media: broadcasting (television, radio) and print (newspapers, magazines, outdoor, direct mail). There are also other forms of less importance, such as aerial advertising and the yellow pages in phone books.

Newspapers are one of the oldest means of advertising. They still receive the largest share of the advertising budget. Together, the daily and weekly newspapers sell about 60% of their space to advertisers. In return, they derive about 75% of their revenue from this source. Since most newspapers serve a limited market, the bulk of their advertising is from local suppliers.

Catalogues, Direct Mail, and Flyers make up the second-largest advertising

Careers in Advertising
A career in advertising may begin in a number of places, from special departments of large corporations to advertising agencies that serve a variety of clients.

Success in advertising requires imagination and an understanding of the way people think. Some skills can be learned at community colleges or universities in programs leading to degrees, for example, in business administration, sociology, or psychology.

Net Advertising Revenue by Media 1988 (%)

Electronic Media

Radio	8.5
Television	15.5

Print Media

Newspapers	24.4
General magazines	3.4
Catalogue, direct mail	22.6
Outdoor	8.2
Other*	17.4

*Includes business papers, farm papers, directories, newspapers and supplements

Source: Maclean Hunter Research Bureau

medium. Local advertisers generally blanket every house in their neighbourhood with promotional material. National advertisers select a target audience, buy the appropriate mailing lists, and contact their potential customers through the postal service. Either method is relatively inexpensive to the advertiser.

Television accounts for the third-largest advertising expenditure. The sight, sound, and action offered by television advertising are very effective. Both the Canadian Broadcasting Corporation (CBC) and privately owned stations sell advertising. The private stations derive 90% of their revenue from commercials. Television advertising is expensive. For example, in 1988, a 30-second commercial on the CTV network's 16 stations could cost up to $20 250. Since most stations are connected to one of the networks, television carries more national than local advertising.

Radio has a more select audience than either newspapers or television, since different stations cater to different segments of the population. Radio advertising is also relatively inexpensive. A 30-second commercial on CFRB Toronto cost approximately $400 in 1989. Radio commercials can be repeated frequently. They can also be very imaginative in their use of dramatic skits, songs, and jingles. By 1975, advertising had been dropped from CBC radio stations, but the private stations depend on commercials for 97% of their revenue. Because most stations broadcast to a small area, radio attracts local rather than national advertisers.

Magazines have been declining in advertising revenue in recent years. Canada's 1400 consumer, trade, and business magazines are usually aimed at a particular group of people who share the same interests or profession. For this reason, most magazine advertising is of national brand-name products. Only lifestyle magazines directed at a single city or region carry local advertising. Of all the print media, magazine advertising is the most attractive to look at and is also the most expensive. This is because magazines offer better quality paper, printing, and colour reproduction. Advertising represents about 60% of magazine revenues.

Outdoor Advertising takes many different forms and reaches great numbers of people. It includes signs on buses and subway trains, posters on billboards and in shopping malls, and flashing neon signs on busy streets. As people have become more concerned with the environment,

The 15 Largest Buyers of Advertising Space and Time in 1988

	Advertisers	$ millions
1.	Government of Canada	91.3
2.	Proctor & Gamble	58.6
3.	General Motors of Canada	52.5
4.	Gulf & Western	44.6
5.	RJR	42.3
6.	John Labatt Limited	42.1
7.	The Molson Companies	41.2
8.	The Thomson Group	40.2
9.	Cineplex Odeon Corporation	38.9
10.	Ontario Government	37.9
11.	Unilever	36.3
12.	McDonald's Restaurants of Canada	32.2
13.	Chrysler Canada	32.1
14.	Bell Canada Enterprises	31.8
15.	PepsiCo	29.8

advertisers in outdoor spaces have had to modify their products to conform to public taste.

LAWS AND REGULATIONS

Advertising is regulated by both the federal and provincial governments and within the industry itself. Canadian consumers are among the best-protected buyers of goods and services in the world. Advertisements for food, drugs, alcoholic beverages, and cosmetics must be cleared by government agencies. In some media, advertisements for cigarettes and tobacco are banned altogether. Advertisements are watched for misleading information or for bad taste. In recent years there has been a campaign against certain portrayals of women in advertisements. People have objected to housewives always being shown in the kitchen or laundry, endorsing cleaning products, while glamorous women are used to sell expensive items such as cars.

EFFECTS OF ADVERTISING

Critics complain that advertising persuades people to buy goods they neither want nor need. It has an enormous influence in shaping people's attitudes and feelings about themselves and the world around them. Defenders reply that advertising is only meant to sell products, that mass marketing helps to keep prices down, and that competition is healthy for the economy. The media also depend on advertising to a great extent. Without advertising we would have to pay far more for our newspapers and magazines, and our television and radio.

▷ SUGGESTED READING: Keith Tuckswell, *Canadian Advertising in Action* (1988).

■ **Aerodynamics,** *see* **Aviation.**

■ Aerospace Industry

The aerospace industry designs, makes, and repairs aircraft and spacecraft. In Canada it employs about 60 000 people, of whom about 10% are engineers and other highly skilled workers.

There are about 200 companies in Canada's aerospace industry. Most are based in Montreal, Toronto, or Winnipeg. A few companies design and make complete aircraft. Some make aircraft parts, such as wings or landing gear, for other companies. Some make and repair aircraft engines. Many make equipment for military purposes, such as rockets. Still other companies make satellites and equipment for use in space vehicles.

Canada's aerospace industry is the fifth largest in the Western World, after those of the United States, Great Britain, France, and West Germany. Canadian firms lead the world in certain areas of aerospace technology, such as flight simulators, small gas turbines, and communications satellites.

The aerospace industry demands products which must be exceptionally light, strong, and reliable. The development of this technology requires a great deal of research. Much of the design and production is aided by computers.

Role of Government The Canadian aerospace industry sells most of its products to other countries. About one-third of what it produces it sells to armed forces, mainly those of the United States. About one-eighth of what it produces it sells to the Canadian government.

The Canadian government supports the industry in a number of ways. It provides services, such as the National Research Council's wind tunnels, in which aircraft designs can be tested. It pays for expensive projects, such as the designing and building of Canadarm, the robot mechanical arm made for the space shuttle. It provides money for the industry, and it has owned many of the major firms.

HISTORY

Alexander Graham Bell is best known as the inventor of the telephone. He was also fascinated by flying machines. In 1909 he encouraged two young men to form the Canadian Aerodrome Company. One of these men, John McCurdy, had just made the first powered flight in Canada. In February 1909, he had taken off from the frozen lake in front of Bell's summer home near Baddeck, N.S., in an aircraft called the *Silver Dart*. Later that year, the company built the *Baddeck I*, the first

Dash 8 Series 300 *production line in Downsview, Ont. (courtesy de Havilland Aircraft of Canada, Ltd).*

aircraft designed and made in Canada.

World Wars I and II During World War I (1914-18) aircraft developed from primitive to practical machines, and the aerospace industry grew rapidly in Canada. British and American companies opened plants in Canada. De Havilland, for instance, began selling and repairing aircraft designed in Britain, and Pratt and Whitney sold and repaired engines made in the United States.

The Canadian industry flourished during World War II (1939-45). Canada was far from the battlefields and bombers that damaged the industries of its allies. Canada produced more than 16 000 military planes during the war. Most of them were trainers, but they included fighters, bombers, and seaplanes.

After the war, a number of Canadian companies began to design and make their own equipment. De Havilland Aircraft of Canada Ltd, for example, designed the Chipmunk trainer. In 1947, it designed a rugged, single-engine plane called the Beaver. The Beaver was designed especially to operate in Canada's North. It was reliable and could take off and land in tight spots. Over 1600 Beavers were made and sold to over 60 countries. A lake, glacier, and island in Antarctica have been named for this aircraft. De Havilland followed the Beaver with other, similar aircraft: the Otter, Caribou, Buffalo, and Twin Otter.

Like de Havilland, A.V. Roe, Canada, was also a subsidiary of a British company. It had produced Lancaster bombers in World War II. After the war, it designed and built jet engines. It also designed Canada's first jet fighter, the CF-100. A total of 692 were built and the CF-100 served for ten years in the Canadian air force. A.V. Roe also designed the Jetliner, only the second jet transport in the world. However, the aircraft did not sell and was scrapped.

Avro Lancaster, *1941. This bomber was produced at Malton, Ont., during World War II (courtesy Canada Post Corporation).*

The de Havilland Beaver *was designed and built in Canada. It could take off and land in a very short space. It was therefore very useful in remote areas of the Canadian bush (courtesy de Havilland Aircraft of Canada, Ltd).*

Challenger is a successful business jet built by Canadair (courtesy Canadair).

Computer Design *Much of the design and production of aircraft is now aided by computers (© James Sugar/First Light).*

Canada's most celebrated military aircraft was the Avro Arrow (CF-105), a supersonic jet fighter. The Arrow was the world's fastest and most advanced fighter. Nevertheless, in 1959, when only a few Arrows had been built, the Canadian government scrapped the aircraft. The reason given was its high cost, but the decision was controversial. Over 14 000 employees at A.V. Roe were fired. In the future, Canada would be forced to buy or build American military aircraft. Canadair manufactured the American fighters CF-104 and CF-5 under licence.

In 1962 Canada became the third country — following the U.S.S.R. and the U.S. — with a satellite in space. A number of Canadian companies excel at designing the satellites from which television and other communication signals can be bounced, and the Earth stations which send and receive such signals.

SOME CANADIAN AEROSPACE COMPANIES

Canadian Aircraft Electronics (CAE) Ltd of Montreal is expert in designing and making flight simulators. Simulators use computers to recreate the experience of flying many different kinds of aircraft. They enable future pilots to train without leaving the ground. Canadian Aircraft Electronics makes about one-half of all the world's jet aircraft simulators.

Canadair Ltd of Montreal makes water bombers and business jets. The company was formed in 1923 and began making aircraft designed in other countries. Its first

Avro Arrow on its last flight. The Arrow was Canadian aviation's greatest success and failure. It was the world's fastest and most advanced fighter. It was scrapped by the politicians before it went into production (courtesy Len Wilkinson).

all-Canadian aircraft was the CL-215 water bomber, the only aircraft in the world designed to fight forest fires. It can scoop up water while flying over a lake, and then drop it on a fire. In 1978 Canadair launched the Challenger, a long-range, wide-bodied business jet. Despite some troubles, including the crash of the first Challenger, the company had sold more than 184 of these aircraft by 1989. The Government of Canada sold Canadair to Bombardier Inc. in 1986.

de Havilland Aircraft of Canada Ltd, based in Toronto, began operations in 1928. This company is known for its Short Take-Off and Landing (STOL) aircraft: the Beaver, Otter, Caribou, Buffalo, and Twin Otter. The company now produces the very successful Dash airliners. These aircraft have highly specialized wings which enable them to take off and land in a short distance. Over 300 Dash 8 aircraft have been ordered to date. In 1986 the Canadian government sold de Havilland to Boeing Commercial Aircraft Co. of Seattle, Washington.

Pratt and Whitney Aircraft of Canada, based outside Montreal, is the largest company in the Canadian aerospace industry. It began operations in Canada in 1929, repairing the engines made by its parent in the United States. After World War II, Pratt and Whitney Canada designed a small gas turbine engine. These engines now power many small aircraft and helicopters around the world. The company is the world's largest producer of small gas turbine aircraft engines.

Spar Aerospace Ltd, located in Toronto, Ottawa, and Montreal, has been designing satellites since the 1960s. In the mid-1970s the company led a team of firms working on a robot mechanical arm, later known as Canadarm. This machine was used in space for the first time in 1981, on the U.S. space shuttle *Columbia*. Spar, with a number of other Canadian aerospace companies, is now designing

a more advanced robot to perform many tasks on board the international space station, which will be launched in the 1990s.

Examples of many of the aircraft and satellites made in Canada can be seen at the National Aviation Museum, which is located in Ottawa.

▷ RELATED ARTICLES: **Aviation; F.W. Baldwin; Alexander Graham Bell; John Alexander Douglas McCurdy; Space Technology.**

▷ SUGGESTED READING: F.W. Hotson, *The de Havilland Story* (1983); Greig Stewart, *Shutting Down the National Dream: A.V. Roe and the Tragedy of the Avro Arrow* (1988).

■ Affleck, Raymond Tait

Architect (*born in 1922 at Penticton, B.C.*). Affleck studied architecture at McGill University and in Europe. With several other architects he formed a company later called Arcop Associates. His firm designed many important projects, including the Queen Elizabeth Theatre (1955) in Vancouver, Place Ville Marie (1965) in Montreal, the Arts and Culture Centre (1967) in St John's, and Market Square (1983) in Saint John.

Place Bonaventure, completed in Montreal in 1968, is one of Affleck's most important works. It is a large, multi-purpose development which is well suited to the cold Canadian climate. Place Bonaventure combines many different activities with indoor streets and several atria.

The Maison Alcan (1983) in Montreal combines a modern glass and aluminum headquarters building and a restored historic hotel and stone houses. Affleck's sensitivity in combining the old and the new won him the Prix d'excellence in 1984.

■ Agar, Carlyle Clare

Helicopter pioneer (*born in 1901 at Lion's Head, Ont.; died in 1968 at Victoria,*

Maison Alcan, designed by Raymond Affleck, combines historic buildings with the modern headquarters of Alcan (courtesy Alcan Aluminum Ltd).

Carl Agar was Canada's helicopter pioneer (courtesy NAC/C-60002/photo by Antray, Vancouver).

B.C.). It was largely because of Carl Agar that helicopters came into widespread use in Canada. He proved how valuable they could be as a means of transport in remote regions.

Agar served in the RCAF during World War II and then formed Okanagan Air Services Ltd. This small company operated Canada's first non-military helicopter, which was used to spray British Columbian orchards with insecticide. Agar and his partners proved that since helicopters could land in a very small space, they would be useful in remote mountain areas. In 1949 the helicopter proved its worth during the building of British Columbia's Palisade Lake Dam when heavy equipment, including concrete mixers, was flown to the site. It took more than 1000 trips, of which Agar himself flew about 250.

In 1955 Agar's company carried dog teams and sleds on a government surve﹐ of the arctic islands. People from as f away as Indonesia called on Agar for ﹐ services or advice, and his company g﹐ to be one of the largest of its kind in world.

■ Agawa Bay

Agawa Bay, 90 km north of Sa﹐ Marie, Ont., is a broad bay on th﹐ eastern shore of Lake Superior. T﹐ nificent sand beaches are part of ﹐ perior Provincial Park. On the ﹐ are famous pictographs, drawi﹐

ochre and grease done by the native people over 200 years ago. The name comes from an Ojibwa word for "sacred place."

■ Agricultural Education and Research

A century ago, 80% of the population worked on farms. Agricultural education was then, for many people, part of the experience of growing up. Yet even then, some people recognized that specialized training could be helpful. As early as 1670 in New France, an industrial school at St-Joachim provided some training in agriculture. Other courses were later started, both in French and English Canada.

Education Today, agricultural education in Canada occurs at four levels: in the school system, at the diploma level, at the degree level, and at the postgraduate level. As well, there are informal opportunities for acquiring knowledge (for example, through radio programs on farming). There is also on-the-job training.

At elementary and secondary schools, agriculture is seldom taught as a separate science. Often it is part of a biology or environmental course. It may include a visit to a farm or agricultural fair. One of the aims is to make students aware of the important role agriculture plays in providing the world with food.

At the diploma level, there are two-year programs in agriculture to prepare students for a career on the farm or in agribusiness. Today, agriculture is far more than farming. "Agribusiness" includes marketing, processing, and distributing food, as well as producing it.

The graduate and postgraduate courses provide specialized training, which can lead to degrees in a wide range of subjects. These include general agriculture, agricultural engineering, animal science, plant science, soil science, and many other areas, ranging from agricultural economics to rural sociology.

Canada has eight degree-granting schools of agriculture: Nova Scotia Agricultural College; Laval University; Macdonald College (McGill University); Ontario Agricultural College (University of Guelph); Manitoba Agricultural College; the Faculty of Agriculture and Forestry, University of Alberta; and the faculties of agriculture at the universities of Saskatchewan and British Columbia.

Research Agricultural research is carried out by three main groups: private industry, the universities, and Agriculture Canada. Industries conduct research for their own particular needs and usually do not make their findings public.

Research in the universities dates back to 1874, when the Ontario School of Agriculture was founded. Today, university research includes a wide range of researchers: chemists, biotechnologists, geneticists, and many other specialists.

Research in Agriculture Canada is conducted through a nation-wide network of research stations, funded through the Research Branch of the federal Department of Agriculture. The first such research station was the Dominion Experimental Farm in Ottawa, which was established in 1886, along with four branch stations. Today, there are some 46 stations.

Agricultural research includes plant-breeding and animal-breeding programs to develop improved strains of field crops, fruit trees, cattle, hogs, and so on. Well-known Canadian successes in these areas include Marquis wheat, canola, and the Lacombe breed of hogs. Some researchers concentrate on ways of controlling plant diseases, insect pests and weeds, and on developing safe herbicides and insecticides. Others specialize in soil and water conservation or in improved systems of crop management. Much recent research has been aimed at ways of preserving and storing foodstuffs, and increasing the safety and quality of food.

▷ RELATED ARTICLES: **Agriculture, History of; Food; Veterinary Medicine.**

■ Agricultural Fairs and Exhibitions

Fairs and exhibitions have always been a part of farming communities. Before radio, television, and high-speed roads, when most communities were isolated from one another, these fairs provided farm families with a reason to gather in town for several days. They gave farmers a chance to compare their success with

Computer Control *helps to regulate light, temperature, and humidity in a greenhouse in Campbellville, Ont. (courtesy Agriculture Canada).*

others, and they brought entertainment from far away. Even though modern communications and transportation have greatly reduced this isolation, agricultural fairs remain popular throughout the country.

Location of Fairs In 1988, there were 813 agricultural fairs and exhibitions held in Canada. These were spread across the entire country.

Many of our largest exhibitions, such as the Canadian National Exhibition in Toronto, Ont., the Pacific National Exhibition in Vancouver, the Calgary Stampede, and Klondike Days in Edmonton, began as agricultural fairs and still include agricultural activities. The Royal Agricultural Winter Fair in Toronto (330 000 visitors) is the largest agricultural fair in Canada. Most of the rest draw fewer than 10 000 visitors. Many, in small towns, draw fewer than 2000.

Competitions and Judging The most "agricultural" part of a fair is the showing and judging of farm and home produce. These competitions are usually organized into four areas: livestock, crops, horticulture, and home arts.

There are two kinds of livestock competition. In *conformation trials*, competing animals are compared to a breed standard which describes the ideal size, shape, weight, colour, and so on for an animal of that type. Points are awarded for each characteristic, and the competitor that comes closest to the ideal is the winner. Contests and standards exist for all types of farm animals. In *performance trials*, competitors must complete tasks typical of their farm work. For example, sheep dogs compete to see which can most quickly and calmly gather loose sheep into a flock and move them into a pen. Similarly, draft horses compete in pulling weighted sleds, and saddle horses compete on trail ride courses or jumping courses.

Draft horses *competing in pulling weighted sleds -- a popular trial at agricultural fairs (photo by Allan Browarny/Browarny Photographics Ltd).*

Crop and horticulture competitions are similar to animal conformation trials. Standards of colour, size, and weight have been set for all types of field crops (*crop competition*) and garden produce (*horticulture competition*). Each plant or produce sample is rated against the standard, and the one that is closest to the ideal wins.

The home-arts competitions include food preparation, sewing, and arts and crafts. The largest categories in the food sections are baking and preserving. In both cases, points are awarded for appearance and taste. Sewing competitions usually focus on clothing and quilt making. Entries are judged for their technical quality, their appearance, and the originality of their design.

Arts and crafts can include any creative endeavours. Painting, ceramics, woodwork, and photography are most common. As in the sewing competitions, technical quality, appearance, and originality are the main aspects judged.

Gathering and Entertainment The midway provides much of the entertainment at an agricultural fair. Midways offer a mixture of rides, games, and sideshows that attract both farming and non-farming visitors.

Many fairs, especially the large ones, also feature daily or evening stage shows as entertainment. Other common forms of entertainment at agricultural fairs include horse races, ploughing matches, rodeos, and tractor pulls. All combine entertainment and a celebration of historic or modern agricultural skills.

▷ RELATED ARTICLE: **Calgary Stampede.**

■ Agricultural Marketing

Agricultural marketing includes the many activities that transform farm products into the food that we consume. Farm products pass through many stages: from farmers to assemblers, processors, wholesalers, retailers, and finally to consumers. Thus, they are bought and sold many times. Most farm products must be processed, and most are produced in a certain season. They are often produced far away from where they are processed or purchased. Therefore, transportation and storage are also important parts of agricultural marketing.

Because most farm products vary greatly in quality, they must be graded. A grading system reduces the costs of agricultural marketing. Graded products can be bought and sold based on grade description, rather than on inspection. Agricultural marketing. Graded products can be bought and sold based on grade description, rather than on inspection. Agricultural marketing is also aided by reliable market information. It costs a great deal of money to assemble, process, and distribute farm products. These costs tie up large amounts of money, much of which must be borrowed. Agricultural marketing can be very risky. The products may spoil or drop in price.

Agricultural marketing adds a great deal to the value of farm products. It makes the products available in the form, time, and place preferred by consumers. Partly because of efficient agricultural marketing, Canadians spend a lower percentage of their income on food, compared to other countries. The food system plays an important role in the Canadian economy.

Agricultural marketing boards and co-operatives, as well as private firms, are involved in marketing farm products. Producers' co-operatives and marketing boards perform some marketing activities on behalf of groups of farmers. These co-operatives often sell the farmers' products to processors. The co-operative Saskatchewan, Alberta, and Manitoba wheat pools handle 60% of western Canadian wheat. There are also large co-operative dairy processors in Quebec and in the Prairies.

Agricultural marketing boards are set up by federal or provincial governments. There are many differences in boards' powers and activities. Unlike a co-operative, once a board has been set up, all farmers must market their produce through it. Sometimes the boards pool (average) producers' prices for sales of a product of similar quality. The Canadian

Holland Marsh is a low, fertile area north of Toronto (photo by J.A. Kraulis).

Wheat Board is responsible for the export marketing of western Canadian wheat and barley. The sale of hogs from farmers to slaughtering plants is made through marketing boards in most provinces. Boards for eggs, chickens, and turkeys regulate the quantities and prices of these products.

About one-half of Canadian farm output is exported. The United States, Japan, the Soviet Union, Europe, and China are the leading markets for Canada's agricultural exports. Grains and grain products are the largest exports. Meat, livestock, and oilseeds are also important exports. Fruits and vegetables are major agricultural imports.

Farm south of Stony Plain, Alberta, from the air. There are 293 000 farms in Canada — less than one-half as many as there were in 1941 (photo by John Kitsco).

■ Agriculture

Agriculture is the science, the art, and the process of raising products from the soil. The products include a wide variety of plants and livestock. Most crops are used for human food and animal feed. However, tobacco, decorative plants and shrubs, pedigreed seeds, and plants for fibres (such as flax) are a few of the exceptions. Most livestock is used directly for human food, but some have special purposes; for example, dairy cows and laying hens, riding horses, and pedigreed breeding stock.

Canada's climate and geography, local economic conditions, and government policy all affect agriculture in the regions of Canada. However, several nationwide trends are apparent. Since the Depression of the 1930s, the number of farms has decreased and the average size of farms has increased. In 1986 there were 293 000 farms in Canada, compared to 733 000 in 1941. The relative numbers of different types of farms have also changed. Fruit and vegetable farms have increased and livestock farms have decreased.

Of the total land area of Canada, only 7% (about 68 million hectares) is farmland. Only two-thirds of the farmland is actually used; it is called *improved land*. Sixty-two percent of the improved land is in the Prairie provinces, 9% is in Ontario, 5% is in Quebec, and the rest in the other provinces.

This land supports Canadian farms, which can be classified into four types: livestock, field crop, fruit and vegetable, and mixed. Livestock, which provides roughly 50% of the total of farm cash receipts, and cereals and oilseeds which provide about one-third, are by far the most important. In 1988 farm produce amounted to nearly $22 billion.

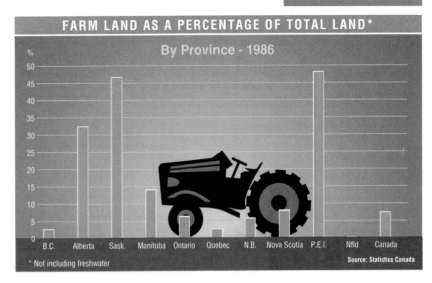

FARM LAND AS A PERCENTAGE OF TOTAL LAND*
By Province - 1986
B.C. Alberta Sask. Manitoba Ontario Quebec N.B. Nova Scotia P.E.I. Nfld Canada
* Not including freshwater
Source: Statistics Canada

CROPS

Crops can be classified as to general trade use, as cereal crops, forages, oilseeds, orchard crops, berries, vegetables and specialty crops.

Cereals are grown for the dried seeds they produce at maturity. The major Canadian cereal crops are wheat, barley, oats, rye, and corn. Cereals are Canada's main agricultural export.

Forage Crops can be grazed or harvested and stored for later use. The major Canadian forages are grasses (hay), legumes (alfalfa), and corn (considered a forage when the whole plant is chopped into silage).

Oilseed Crops Oil-bearing seeds of such crops as soybeans, canola, flax, and sunflowers are the major Canadian oilseed crops. Oilseeds are another important Canadian export crop.

Orchard and Berry Crops Canadian orchard crops include apples, peaches, pears, and cherries. The major Canadian

berry crops are strawberries, raspberries, blueberries, and grapes.

Vegetable Crops Canadian vegetable crops include carrots, turnips, peas, tomatoes, corn, onions, potatoes (these can be considered a field crop when acreages are large), peppers, the cabbage family, cucumbers, vegetable marrow, zucchini, pumpkins, and rhubarb, as well as many others. The limited growing season in Canada restricts the harvest of most vegetables to a very short period, so most vegetable production is for small local markets, such as "pick your own" farms, farm stands, farmers' markets, and the canning and freezing industry, which contracts acreages for processing fruits and vegetables in Ontario, Quebec, B.C., and the Maritimes. Consumers' desire for fresh produce dictates tht most Canadian table vegetables are imports.

Specialty Crops This is a category for

Harvesting Wax Beans, P.E.I. *Harvesting still requires manual labour for some crops (photo by Malak, Ottawa).*

Harvesting Tomatoes, Niagara Peninsula, Ontario (photo by Malak, Ottawa).

Farm Cash Receipts by Region (1988)	
% of Region	Total
Atlantic Canada	3.7
Quebec	15.6
Ontario	26.4
Prairie Regions	49.1
British Columbia	5.2
The North	0.0

Tractors are among the most useful farm machinery. Here a tractor in P.E.I. hauls a potato crop (photo by Malak, Ottawa).

crops that are hard to fit anywhere else, such as mint, mustard, maple syrup, tobacco, and dried legumes (beans, peas, and lentils), which are grown as field crops but marketed like cereals.

AGRICULTURE POLICY

Agriculture is subject to many influences. Policies of the federal and provincial governments must deal with rapidly changing conditions. Such issues as trade agreements, subsidies, and production and price controls provoke heated opinions from consumers and producers, who have different stakes in the outcome. These issues are influenced by external factors, and opinions and arguments change according to perceived needs. Therefore, Canadian agricultural policy is fluid, and responds to the needs of the times. The overall objective of agricultural policy has been to promote the growth, stability,

and competitiveness of the agricultural sector of Canada's economy.

MECHANIZATION

Canadian farmers purchase over $2 billion worth of farm equipment annually. Tractors, swathers, hay balers, combines, and tillage tools comprise the majority of the machines. Canada is part of a worldwide farm machinery industry. Canadian farmers use machinery imported from all over the world: small tractors from Japan, medium-size tractors from Europe, and large tractors and combines from the United States. Machinery manufactured in Canada is shipped to the United States, Australia, Saudi Arabia, and many other countries.

Harvesting Carrots in southern Ontario (courtesy Agriculture Canada).

Canadian farmers have access to the most advanced farm machinery in the world. This machinery has allowed farmers to produce more and better products with less labour. An individual working in Canadian agriculture now produces 2.5 times as much output as in the early 1960s.

Tractors have evolved rapidly in the past 25 years. Diesel powered, averaging 90 horsepower (the range is from 10 to 500), the new tractors are equipped with computers, which provide operating information, advice on gear changes, fuel consumption, and efficiency.

Tillage and Seeding Equipment In response to the wide variety of soils and growing conditions found in a large country like Canada, several different soil preparation and seeding systems have been developed. Many of the ideas for these systems come from the farmers themselves. Over the last 50 years a prairie farm machinery industry has developed, producing equipment especially suited to the dryland conditions found on the prairies. With increasing concerns about drought and soil erosion, machin-

AGRICULTURE AS A PERCENTAGE
OF GROSS DOMESTIC PRODUCT - 1928-1988

%

20

18

16

14

12

10

8

6

4

2

0

1928 1932 1936 1940 1944 1948 1952 1956 1960 1964 1968 1972 1976 1980 1984 1988

Source: Statistics Canada

Harvesting, Mount Agassiz, Manitoba. Harvesters can cut and harvest a swath of wheat as much as 10 metres wide (photo by Malak, Ottawa).

Aberdeen Angus is a Scottish breed used in beef production (photo by Walt Browarny).

Shorthorn cattle were brought to Canada from Britain in 1832 (photo by Walt Browarny).

ery manufacturers have developed minimum tillage and seeding machinery that allows farmers to minimize soil disturbance and leave crop residues on top of the soil, conserving moisture and reducing erosion.

Combine Harvesters New combine harvesters are capable of handling several different crops such as wheat, barley, soybeans, corn, and canola. In addition, the newer harvesters are capable of cutting and harvesting a swath as much as 10 m wide.

Hay and Forage Equipment capable of handling forages in round bales (over 600 kg each), has saved much labour in beef feedlots and on dairy farms.

Computers Farm buildings are equipped with automatic feeders, stable cleaners, and pipeline milking machines that do most of the heavy work in the daily chores on livestock farms. Computers are used to plan rations, keep track of breeding cycles, and even to control the amount of feed each animal receives.

LIVESTOCK AND POULTRY

Livestock are those classes of mammals that are farmed to provide food, clothing, or draft power for humans. Birds that are farmed are normally referred to as poultry. In Canada, the most important livestock are beef cattle, dairy cattle, pigs, horses, and sheep; and the most important poultry are meat-producing chickens (broilers), egg-producing chickens (layers), and turkeys. However, many other species of animals are farmed in Canada, such as ducks, geese, goats, rabbits, mink, and foxes. The farming of other native

and imported wild species is also growing in Canada (for example, bison, elk, fallow and red deer, wild boar, reindeer, and pheasants).

The feeding of livestock and poultry to meet their nutritional needs has developed to a precise science. Canadian foodstuffs such as pasture, hay, straw, cereal grains, and protein supplements (canola meal and meat meal) form the bulk of diets for livestock. Beef and dairy cattle are ruminants whose digestive systems have four compartments. One of these compartments is called a rumen. It acts as a large fermentation vat where bacteria and protozoa digest coarse feeds, making them available to their host. These micro-organisms also synthesize amino acids and vitamins essential for cattle. Hogs and poultry are single-stomached animals and require more digestible feeds such as processed cereal grains. Supplements, providing essential nutrients, such as amino acids and vitamins, must also be supplied in the right proportions for these species.

Hygiene and health are important in successful animal agriculture. Sanitation, good management, and prescribed disease control practices are followed to keep herds and flocks healthy.

Canadian research in animal genetics has had a major impact on the productivity and market acceptability of Canadian farm animals and their food products. The Lacombe breed of pigs, developed in the 1950s by Dr Howard Fredeen at the Agriculture Research Station at Lacombe, Alta, was the first livestock breed developed in Canada. The Lacombe is now propagated in over 20 countries. Following extensive introduction of a number of European breeds of cattle beginning in the 1960s, Canada has become a prime sup-

Horned Hereford The Hereford is western Canada's main breed of beef cattle. It is a hardy animal that can forage in difficult conditions (courtesy Walter Browarny/Browarny Photographics Ltd).

Lacombe Pig was developed in Alberta by Canadian scientists. The breed is known for its excellence (photo by Walter Preugschas).

plier of breeding stock to many countries around the world. Commercial cross-breeding of beef cattle, hogs, and sheep allowed producers to make significant improvements in animal productivity on Canadian farms during the last three decades.

Research pioneered by Dr Fredeen and Dr Roy Berg of the University of Alberta led to modern grading systems for beef and hog carcasses where measurements of fatness determine grade and influence prices. Hence, Canadian beef and pork have developed a reputation for leanness and are very desirable in export markets.

The healthfulness of Canadian meat products is assured by a thorough inspection system of live animals and carcasses at abattoirs; inspectors from Agriculture Canada and provincial agriculture departments thoroughly inspect the animals for health, as well as conducting tests to see if there are any drug residues.

ANIMAL WELFARE

In recent years there has been an increasing protest around the world regarding the inhumane treatment of animals. The protest gained great momentum after World War II, when medical research expanded dramatically and many more animals began to be used in such research. The official Canadian response to this movement came in 1968, when the Canadian Council on Animal Care (CCAC) began to monitor the ethical use of animals for research purposes. The CCAC's pioneer efforts in enforcing humane experimental animal care are just now being copied in other countries.

Those concerned with animal welfare also look for abuses in the way livestock is raised, in the use of animals for entertainment in zoos, circuses, and rodeos, and animals which are hunted or trapped, for sport or fur. Agriculture Canada ensures that livestock within Canada and for export are treated in a humane manner. In animal agriculture, proper management results in the best quality, which means high profits. Mishandling results in decreased yields and poor quality, which means no profits. It does not make good economic sense to mistreat livestock, and those few who do so usually do not remain in business for very long.

EXPORT MARKETS

Red meats, cereals, and oilseeds, and their products, are Canada's major agricultural exports. In 1988, over 7% of all exports were agricultural products. The United States, Japan, and other Pacific Rim countries, and the European Economic Community (EEC) are athe most important markets. Wheat is the most important comprising over 40% of all agricultural exports. In 1987 Canada was the world's sixth-largest producer and second-largest exporter (next to the U.S.), with 90% of total production destined for export markets. About one-half of the marketplace is made up of centrally planned governments such as China and the Soviet Union. Another one-quarter is exported to developing countries. In addition, a substantial amount is sent as food aid to countries in need.

Canola is the major oilseed exported, with exports approaching 1.6 million tonnes of seed, over half of Canadian production. The remainder is processed domestically. Major markets are Japan and Mexico. Flaxseed is another important oilseed export, with 0.6 million tonnes. Canada is the leading exporter of linseed, the oil from flaxseed. In 1987, 90% of the linseed exported in the world came from Canada. Major markets of flaxseed are the U.S., Japan, and the EEC.

Red meats are fresh or frozen beef, pork, and horse, and processed meat products. They comprise about 6% of total export sales. Export markets exist in many countries, but the U.S. marketplace takes most of the exports.

Other agricultural products that are exported wherever markets can be found include honey, potato seeds, alfalfa pellets, cattle for breeding, furs, maple products, and a wide variety of processed foods including frozen french-fried potatoes, cookies, baked goods, and other ingredients for the food-processing industry. It is hoped that these exports will help diversify Canadian agricultural exports, thereby making it less dependent on just a few products.

CONSERVATION

Conservation in Canadian agriculture is the attempt to manage land and water resources for maximum sustainable yields, minimum soil losses, and control of pollution. Throughout Canada, erosion of topsoil is increasing and this represents a loss of one of Canada's basic resources. Water and wind erosion are caused by climatic factors which are often uncontrollable, but conservation tillage and cropping systems, crop rotations, and wind barriers such as shelter belts on farms can dramatically reduce the amount of erosion. A second point of loss of agricultural soils is urbanization. Unfortunately, there is a high rate of conversion of agricultural land to urban expansion. Parking lots and highways, as well as highrises and rural non-farming populations, are reducing the agricultural land base. B.C. and Quebec have enacted zoning legislation to conserve agricultural land. The third point of loss of soils is through deteriorating quality or soil degradation. Factors such as depletion of soil organic matter, and salt deposition (salinization), render soils useless for sustained agriculture. Management techniques are available to minimize many of these factors; however, in some cases costs are high and improved educational programs or incentives are needed to teach farmers the new techniques.

Water and land pollution through agricultural and chemical mismanagement were among the first types of pollution to capture public attention in the early 1960s. By the 1980s realization that general industrial chemical pollution posed a vastly greater hazard to the environment changed the emphasis of legislation and public attitudes. However, agriculture management programs in Canada continues to focus on minimizing soil and water contamination.

RURAL SOCIETY
Rural society is characterized by a shrinking population of agricultural producers, and an increasing population of non-farm residents. In 1900, nearly 80% of Canada's population lived on farms. By 1986, about 24% of Canadians lived in rural areas; however, less than 4% live on farms. The move away from cities by non-farmers is encouraged by the widely held romantic notion (less of a fact and more of a legend) that since the rural population formed the backbone of the country in the past, it is good to have rural roots.

In reality, the infrastructure support (businesses involved in goods and services) and municipal services network (water supply, sewage disposal, hospitals, schools, and communication networks) in rural Canada are far less diverse and of a different nature than in the urban areas. Hence, people in rural communities have a greater reliance on each other than people in urban areas. The lack of infrastructure leads to greater co-operation and interactions in economic and social organization. Durable rural organizations such as 4H, and co-operatives are examples of associations with rural roots. Farm organizations such as Unifarm and the Wheat Board in the West and the Canadian Federation of Agriculture in the East play an important part in rural society. These organizations have been fostered and encouraged as part of the government's agricultural policy.

GOVERNMENT SERVICES
The short and harsh agricultural environment in Canada has influenced the policy of the Canadian government to stabilizing production and prices for domestically consumed commodities, in order to create income stability for farmers. Therefore, Canadian government services are very highly developed at both the provincial and federal levels. Dozens of programs exist at both levels to assist the economic well-being of the agricultural producing sector now and in the future. A few examples are credit subsidies, land conservation programs, research to improve crop yields, marketing boards for orderly marketing of commodities, crop insurance, supply quotas, and stabilization and transportation programs. The intention of all of these programs is either to offset the cost of production or to increase farm revenues.

Provincial and federal government services and programs cost over $7 billion per year. Farm profits are vulnerable to the many changes that are occurring, so rapidly, in Canadian and world agriculture. If government services were not available to soften the economic hardships caused by weather, declining markets, and increased competition for markets by providing some degree of income stability to farmers, Canadian agriculture would suffer.

PLANT PESTS AND DISEASES
Plant pests and diseases cause millions of dollars of losses every year in Canada. Insect pests in Canada are generally restricted to one generation annually because of the cold weather. Insect pests cause crop losses in two ways. The first is by eating parts of plants; for example, seed grains and potatoes are destroyed by wireworms; seedlings of most crops are eaten by cutworms, flea beetles, attack canola seedlings; other plants are food for army worms, aphids, potato beetles, and numerous others. Even harvested grains can be attacked by certain beetles. Second, sucking insects (such as aphids, leaf hoppers, thrips, whiteflies, mealiebugs, and mites) can act as vectors, transmitting infectious agents which cause parasitic diseases to healthy plants.

The parasitic plant diseases are caused by viruses, bacteria fungi, and nematodes

Careers in Agriculture
Agriculture specialists include 1) *agronomists* whose speciality is crops (for example, increasing yield and controlling diseases); 2) *horticulturalists* who develop better vegetables and fruit; 3) *soil scientists* who try to find ways to increase soil productivity and solve problems of soil (for example, erosion); and 4) *animal scientists* who study animal breeding.

Programs that teach these skills are offered in community colleges in most provinces. The program usually takes two years. About 1400 students graduate each year. Similar courses are offered at universities in every province except Newfoundland, Prince Edward Island, and New Brunswick.

About 950 students graduate each year, and about 200 complete master's degrees.

(worms). Fungi (molds) cause nearly 100 000 diseases in plants, including rusts, smuts, mildews, blights, scabs, and damping-off of seedlings.

Viruses cause a wide variety of fruit, vegetable, and certain cereal diseases, including mosaics, ring spots, and others. Bacterial diseases are less well known. Nematodes cause root galls, rots, and lesions, and they can be vectors for virus diseases.

A second disturbance to plant growth (noninfectious) is caused by mineral malnutrition or poor environmental conditions. Most of the mineral deficiency diseases can be corrected by addition of nutrients (fertilizers and soil supplement sprays) before or during seeding. Environmental pollutants such as sulphur dioxide (acid rain) can only be fought through legislation.

Protection against pests and infectious diseases is attained by use of pesticide chemicals such as fungicides, nematocides, fumigants, and insecticides. Plant breeding for *disease resistance* is an important control measure, but infectious agents can develop new properties and damage new varieties, given time. *Exclusion* of pathogenic agents by quarantine or other methods prevents diseases from spreading. *Biological control* and *integrated pest management* offer potentially safe and effective means of control, but few of these systems have been perfected so far.

PLANT BREEDING

Canadian agriculture has several unique aspects, which have created plant breeding programs with unusual objectives. First the short, harsh agricultural environment in Canada means that only certain crops can be grown. The first settlers needed early (fast ripening) varieties of wheat and other food and feed grains in order to survive. The government has long supported plant breeding research programs to identify and select these desirable early crops, because we cannot always obtain these varieties from anywhere else in the world. Second, the early varieties must be protected from rusts and other pests, so disease resistant types must also be selected. After these two features are stabilized, the plant breeder can seek enhanced quality characteristics. For example, six-row barley was selected because it was early maturing and disease resistant, but a nice surprise was that this variety also had superior malting quality.

Canada leads the world in plant breeding programs for cereals and oilseeds. Canadian Durum wheat was tailored by plant breeders specifically for macaroni production. In just three decades plant breeders perfected canola oilseed varieties, by removing undesirable quality defects from the early varieties imported from Poland and Argentina.

Forage breeders have increased yields and quality in alfalfa and other forages, while other breeders have developed

Harvesting Wheat
Saskatchewan is one of the great wheat-growing areas of the world (photo by Brian Milne/ First Light).

Major Farming Types

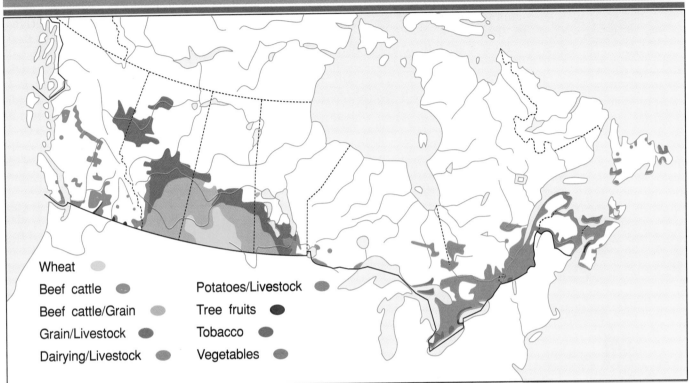

Wheat
Beef cattle
Beef cattle/Grain
Grain/Livestock
Dairying/Livestock

Potatoes/Livestock
Tree fruits
Tobacco
Vegetables

fruits, vegetables, and ornamentals which are adapted to northern climates. Canada's unique environment has required that the breeding expertise be developed here in Canada.

Genetic engineering research has provided many new tools for the scientists in plant breeding specializing in DNA and control of gene expression. These researchers are working steadily to improve older varieties and perhaps create entirely new species. However, the development of these new crops still requires systems to segregate plants with desirable characteristics in order to get optimum varieties, and then evaluating them under Canadian field conditions.

AGRICULTURAL AID

Canada has played a vital role in the world by providing agricultural and food aid to developing nations. The Canadian International Development Agency (CIDA) was created in 1968. The International Development Research Centre (IDRC) was formed in 1970. These two agencies distribute about 80% of Canada's total foreign aid, of which about 25% is directed towards programs related to agriculture and food. The aid is in several forms: through the advice of technical experts and the sending of agricultural inputs such as tools, equipment, and fertilizers; through food aid (mostly via the

United Nations World Food Program); by training the farmers, agricultural instructors, scientists, and administrators in developing countries; by supporting international agricultural research centres; and by funding non-governmental organizations like CARE, OXFAM Canada, and the Canadian Hunger Foundation.

For further information write to the Communications Branch, Agriculture Canada, 930 Carling Avenue, Ottawa, Ont., K1A 0C5.

▷ RELATED ARTICLES: **Agricultural Education and Research; Agricultural Fairs and Exhibitions; Agricultural Marketing; Agriculture, History of; Livestock and Poultry;** and "Agriculture" section of entries on the provinces.

▷ SUGGESTED READING: Keith Bowman, *Agriculture* (1985); Dean Walker, *Canada's Agriculture* (1970).

■ Agriculture, History of

Farmers provide most of the food found in grocery stores: from flour, bread, and breakfast foods to vegetables, meat, and fruit, not to mention the potato chips and other items commonly known as "junk food." Without agriculture, civilization as we know it could not exist. There would be neither industries nor cities. Both of these are possible only because food is provided for others by the farmers.

Agriculture began long ago when wild animals were first domesticated. Humans thus became the keepers of animals, re-

Huron Agriculture in 1615

Describing a Huron village in 1615, Samuel de Champlain wrote:

"They plant a great quantity of Indian corn, which grows there finely. They plant likewise squashes, and sunflowers, from the seed of which they make oil, with which they anoint the head. The region has numerous brooks, emptying into the lake. There are many very good vines and plums, raspberries, strawberries, little wild apples, nuts, and a kind of fruit of the form and colour of small lemons."
Samuel de Champlain, *Voyages*, 1615

Combine Harvester
Massey-Harris advertised this self-propelled combine in the 1930s (courtesy Varity Corp.).

Changing Farm Techniques *The top photo (1900) shows a ploughman breaking the prairie sod with oxen (PAA/H. Pollard/P451). Within a few years, animal power was replaced by steam power, as shown in the bottom photo, taken in Alberta around 1918 (courtesy PAA/H. Pollard/P579).*

Palliser's Triangle ●

sponsible for their welfare, their shelter, their food and water. This responsibility involved providing pasture for the animals, and harvesting and storing fodder for their winter feed.

Early Agriculture of the Native People

Archaeological evidence shows that, as long as 2000 years ago, the native people had established successful agricultural practices in America. Their crops included maize (corn), beans, and squash. Some native communities, such as those in Central America, developed very advanced irrigation systems to provide water and nourishment for their crops.

When the Europeans arrived in what we now know as Canada, they found the native people of the St Lawrence and Great Lakes region cultivating crops of maize, beans, and squash, using seeds and technology acquired from their southern neighbours. Surplus produce was traded for skins and meat, provided by the hunting tribes of the region. This native agriculture later provided food for European fur traders, missionaries, and soldiers.

Agriculture in New France, 1604 to 1763

Early European agriculture in Canada consisted of little more than gardens tended within trading forts and missions. The first real attempt to begin a farming settlement in Canada was in 1606 at the French trading post of Port-Royal in Acadia (Nova Scotia). As the years passed, more French settlers arrived in Acadia. Besides bringing livestock and seed, they brought their agricultural practices to the Maritimes. They tamed the marshlands of the Annapolis Valley by dyking. They tilled the land by hand, using shovels, hoes, and rakes. Seed was spread by hand from the pocket of a large apron. Crops were harvested by scythe or sickle. Grain was threshed with a hand-held flail or by being trampled under foot by oxen, who walked in an endless circle around a fixed post. Hay crops were harvested by scythe or sickle, raked by hand, and stacked with a pitchfork.

In the St Lawrence region, the first farm was begun in 1617 at the fur-trading post of Quebec. It took eight years to bring the first six hectares under cultivation, for a great deal of work was required to clear and cultivate land with the hand tools of the time. To establish a food source for this new colony, the French government took steps to increase the number of settlers, and by the 1640s the colony was raising enough to feed itself. In the 1660s there was even a surplus of food and the beginning of a small export

trade. But this was an exception; for most of its history, the French colony on the St Lawrence barely managed to be self-sufficient in food production.

Agriculture in British North America, 1760s to 1867

Large-scale settlement of what is now Ontario began in 1784. The soil along the lakes and rivers was rich and, by about 1800, wheat was being exported to Lower Canada (Quebec) and to Great Britain.

The first farming attempted west of the Great Lakes was in the Red River Colony, settled in 1812 in what is now Manitoba. Farming techniques followed the same pattern as those used by the Acadians 200 years earlier. It was not until 1824 that land was tilled using oxen with walking ploughs made of wood and harrows made of timbers with spikes driven through as teeth. The first 12 years produced more crop failures than successes. Unfavourable weather and grasshoppers were the two main hazards, but mice and flooding took their toll.

The Hudson's Bay Company (HBC) wanted to restrict settlement to the Red River area. The HBC argued that the land elsewhere was poor and would doom any attempt at farming. To examine this claim, the British government sent a scientific expedition to western Canada (1857-60). Captain John Palliser, the leader of this mission, reported that the vast central area of the plains was arid and generally unfit for agriculture. This judgement of what has become known as "Palliser's Triangle" was upheld in another survey, made by Professor Henry Hind of Toronto. Hind noted, however, that the aridness of the area could be countered by irrigation if a dam was built near the elbow in the South Saskatchewan River.

These reports helped to discourage settlement in the West. In contrast, eastern agriculture continued to progress with the advent of the cast-iron plough, horse-powered seeders and reapers, and stationary threshing machines. In the Quebec region and the Maritimes, grain farming was being phased out in favour of livestock, principally dairying. In the Ontario region, there was a great increase in both wheat and dairy production.

Agriculture After Confederation, 1867 to the 1940s

Agriculture in western Canada began in earnest after 1870, when the federal government bought the former HBC territories, which included the prairies. In 1872 the government passed the Dominion Lands Act, which estab-

Harvesting, 1892 near Brandon, Manitoba. The harvest required a great deal of hand labour before machinery became common (NAC/PA-31489/photo by J.A. Brock & Co.).

lished homestead rights for new settlers and set in motion the orderly survey of the area west of the Great Lakes. The government also promised financial assistance and gifts of land to individuals and companies in return for promoting settlement. Completion of the Canadian Pacific Railway in 1885 provided a link between eastern and western Canada. All this led to farms being started throughout the prairies, with a massive influx of settlers in the late 1890s and early 1900s.

The settlers of the late 19th century used oxen, horses, and sometimes steam engines to break the prairie sod. Once the sod was broken, horses provided the major source of farm power. Wheat was the chief grain crop, and the West quickly became Canada's bread basket. The steam engine, capable of pulling 16-furrow ploughs but usually used for powering huge threshing machines, helped revolutionize agriculture on the prairies in the period from 1900 to 1920. Cattle ranching spread on grasslands that were considered unsuitable for cultivation because of climate or topography.

World War I brought a temporary boom to agriculture, which helped to finance the purchase of more machinery. But the boom waned after 1920, and by 1929 the entire world was gripped in an economic slump, the Great Depression. On the prairies, the economic woes were made worse by the great drought of 1929 to 1937. So vast was the affected area, and so persistent the strong winds and lack of moisture, that clouds of prairie dust were reported to darken the skies as far away as New York City. As if this was not enough, the prairies during these years were plagued by hordes of grasshoppers

and by marching legions of army caterpillars. Particularly hard hit was the dry Palliser's Triangle. Total loss of income, coupled with the cost of trying to crop the parched land, drove thousands of farm families out of their homes.

World War II erupted shortly after the close of this dismal period. Once again there was a boom in prices, and once again young men left the farm to join the armed forces. Because of the preceding drought and depression, few farmers had been able to buy tractors and other new machinery. The labour shortage continued after the war, for many of the returning servicemen did not go back to farming. To replace this lost labour force, costly new machinery was needed, so farms were consolidated into larger units so that they could afford the mechanization. The direct result was that fewer people were involved in agriculture. Today, less than 4% of the Canadian population is engaged in farming, compared with more than 33% in 1931.

Modern Agriculture The importance of farming to the Canadian economy can-

Prairie Homestead, around 1920. The homestead often began with a sod hut before a wooden shack could be built (courtesy PAA/H. Pollard Coll./P592).

not be overstated. In 1988 its products generated cash receipts of $22 billion. Most of this was pumped back into the Canadian economy by purchases of goods and services. For example, the amount spent that year for purchases of farm equipment was more than $2 billion. This production in turn generated business for a host of agribusiness operations, including food processing, which provided employment to a large number of Canadians.

Some of the new technologies spawned by World War II have found a place in the farming industry. These include herbicides and pesticides. Other developments that have helped increase production include the widespread use of chemical fertilizers; the continual genetic upgrading of plant and animal resources, made possible by research; new technologies for seeding (to conserve moisture) and harvesting (to minimize losses in quantity or quality of product).

Vast tracts of Palliser's Triangle in the prairies have now been brought under irrigation. The earliest portion of this system is fed from a dam that was built in the early 1940s on the St Mary River in southern Alberta. The second portion was initiated by construction of Gardiner Dam on the South Saskatchewan River at the site envisioned by Professor Hind some 130 years ago. A dam on the Oldman River in southern Alberta is under construction, but is very controversial. Some users of these systems employ computer-controlled irrigation booms that are capable of watering a quarter-section field at one time without intervention by the operator.

Agricultural Implements Canadian agricultural implements were dominated by the hoe and sickle and similar hand tools for about 350 years. Starting about 1850, there was a gradual transition to cast-iron and wrought-iron implements, all designed to be powered by oxen or horses. Two leaders among the Canadian manufacturers of these implements — the seeders, the reapers, and the grain separators — were Massey and Harris of Ontario. In 1891 they merged under the name Massey-Harris. By 1900 they were manufacturing large ploughs and grain separators suited to the immense power (for that time) of the steam engine as well as horse-drawn implements.

Gasoline tractors made their debut during the first two decades of this century. Early models were large and clumsy, but later models, because of their small size

and easy handling, quickly replaced the big steamers. Nevertheless, horses remained the most common form of farm power until the late 1940s. After World War II, large four-wheel-drive tractors appeared on the scene.

Subterranean cultivators (which till without noticeably disturbing the soil surface) and air seeders (which drive the seed grain to the desired depth, using pneumatic pressure) were designed to reduce the likelihood of soil erosion. Harvesting equipment, both grain and forage, also increased in scale and complexity. Self-propelled combine harvesters, an innovation in the 1930s, now come with computerized control systems designed to monitor and control the efficiency of grain separation. During the same 50-year period, forage harvesting equipment has evolved to include automatic twine tie balers that deliver bales weighing over 600 kg; silage-making equipment; and engineered storage units for silage (the familiar "blue tubes" that stand on many farm sites).

▷ RELATED ARTICLES: **Agriculture; Dominion Lands Act; Louis Hébert; Homesteading; Livestock; New France; Ranching; Western Settlement.**

■ **Ahearn, Thomas**
Inventor, electrical engineer (*born in 1885 at Ottawa, Ont.; died there in 1938*). Ahearn is said to be the inventor of the electric cooking range. This was in 1892, when a meal was cooked at the Windsor Hotel in Ottawa, using electrical devices he had invented.

Ahearn had begun work at age 14 as a telegraph operator. By the age of 25 he was Ottawa branch manager of the telegraph and telephone companies. He then started an electric light company in Ottawa. His firm, Ahearn and Soper, grew into a network of companies dealing with electricity. Among other projects, the company established Ottawa's electric streetcar system in the 1890s. Ahearn invented an electrical heating system for the streetcars, as well as an electric sweeper that removed snow from the streetcar tracks.

Fascinated by the possibilities of electricity, Ahearn enjoyed other people's inventions as well as his own. At the turn of the century he drove the first automobile in Ottawa. It was, of course, run by electricity.

■ **Aid to (or of) the Civil Power**
Aid to (or of) the Civil Power (ACP) is a legal process used by civil governments. It enables them to call out the military to

5.6% 0.9%
2.8% 1.5%
4.3% 5.0%

79.9%

Homosexual or Bisexual Men
Persons from Endemic Areas*
Blood Products
Heterosexual Partners
Pediatric Cases
Other or Unknown
Intravenous Drug Abusers
*Ie: Haiti, French Guiana
Source: Federal Centre for AIDS

help maintain public order when their local police forces are unable to do so. In Canada since 1870, ACP has been used 140 times to quell public disturbances (such as during labour strikes or in times of political, religious, or racial unrest). It has been used 20 times to repress penitentiary riots.

In 1924 the power to call out the troops was transferred from local governments to the attorney general in each province. Nowadays in Canada, most local police forces are able to maintain order.

■ AIDS

AIDS stands for Acquired Immunodeficiency Syndrome, the full name of a deadly disease.

AIDS is caused by a virus called HIV which stands for Human Immunodeficiency Virus. HIV can multiply inside the living cells of humans and chimpanzees. It attacks and kills the cells that defend the body against disease, the cells of the immune system. AIDS is the final stage in the process of HIV infection.

FROM INFECTION TO DEATH

Being infected with HIV does not necessarily mean getting sick, at least not right away. Some infected people remain healthy for months, or even years. As their immune systems weaken, however, infected people show symptoms of common illnesses. For instance, they may be tired, lose weight, and have night sweats or fevers. Finally, up to ten years after being infected, half of the infected people will develop AIDS. They suffer and die from infections and cancers not normally seen in persons with healthy immune systems, from unusual infections of the lung and brain, for instance, or from a rare cancer of the skin.

AIDS IN CANADA

AIDS was first recognized in the United States in 1981. The first AIDS case in Canada was reported in 1982. By 1989, over 2850 people had AIDS in Canada and more than half of them had died. Several hundred people are killed every year. By comparison, cancer and heart disease are each killing over 50 000 Canadians a year. Most of the people these two diseases kill are at, or near, the end of a normal lifespan. The tragedy of AIDS is that it kills young people, people who might otherwise have lived for many more years.

HOW YOU BECOME INFECTED

Worldwide, AIDS is a leading cause of death for people who participate in two specific activities. The first high-risk activity is anal intercourse, in which a man puts his penis into the anus of another person and releases semen. The second high-risk activity is sharing intravenous drug needles or syringes. In Canada, the first high-risk activity is by far the main cause of the AIDS cases.

You cannot catch AIDS by shaking hands, sharing food, kissing, or other casual contact with an infected person. There must be contact between your blood and the infected person's blood, semen, or vaginal fluids, where the HIV is found. There are three ways in which this can happen.

Having Sex The most common way to get AIDS is by having sex with an infected person. As in other industrialized countries, more than three-quarters of AIDS victims in Canada are homosexual men; that is, men who have sex with other men. AIDS can also be caught during sex between men and women.

Receiving Infected Blood Some people have got AIDS from blood transfusions. Many of them were people who require lots of blood transfusions, such as those suffering from hemophilia, an inherited disease which causes excessive bleeding. The risk of becoming infected this way is now very low. Since 1985, all the blood given in Canada has been tested for AIDS antibodies.

The people most at risk of receiving infected blood are addicts who share dirty needles when they inject drugs such as heroin into their blood.

Babies Mothers infected with the AIDS virus may pass it to their babies before or during birth, or through breastmilk.

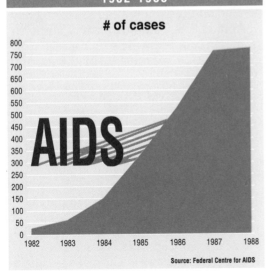

NUMBER OF NEW CASES OF AIDS 1982-1988

# of cases

800
750
700
650
600
550
500
450
400
350
300
250
200
150
100
50
0

1982 1983 1984 1985 1986 1987 1988

Source: Federal Centre for AIDS

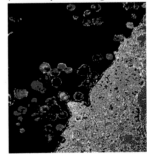

AIDS Virus, *shown in a computer-generated image. The viruses are the red-coloured circles (courtesy First Light).*

AN EPIDEMIC

AIDS is spreading rapidly. In North America the number of cases reported has been doubling every year. In Canada the figure doubles about every 16 months. AIDS is already widespread and still spreading in other parts of the world, es-pecially in central Africa.

There is no way, as yet, to stop HIV in-fection or to repair immune systems dam-aged by HIV.

There are new drugs to strengthen the immune system in order to prolong the lifespan of an AIDS patient and to help prevent someone with the virus from ac-quiring full-blown AIDS.

Avoiding sex with people who may be infected, and properly using condoms, are the best-known ways to avoid getting AIDS and to slow its spread.

▷ SUGGESTED READING: Margaret O. Hyde and others, *Know About AIDS* (1987); David Suzuki and others, *David Suzuki Talks About AIDS* (1987).

■ Air Pollution

A breath of air in any Canadian city may contain dozens of pollutants. Most are in quantities too small to be harmful. How-ever, some pollution occurs in large enough quantities to harm people and the environment.

Sources Air pollution comes from five main sources: transportation (48%), in-dustry (27%), stationary fuel burners (14%), forest fires (6%), and the burning of solid wastes (2%). The remainder are sources such as cigarette smoking and dry cleaning.

Most pollution results from the burn-ing of fossil fuels: coal, oil, natural gas, and gasoline. Fossil fuels consist of car-bon and hydrogen atoms. The burning of these fuels produces heat. Automobile engines, the furnaces that produce metals, and some plants that generate electricity, burn fossil fuels. The burning does not completely use up the com-pounds made up of carbon and hydrogen, which are released into the air. If sulphur and nitrogen are present in the fuel, they combine with oxygen in the air and form harmful gases.

Some of these gases are harmful in themselves. Others combine with other gases in the presence of sunshine to form ozone. Ozone irritates lungs and damages plants. It combines with other pollutants to form a greyish-yellow smog over cities. Smog is especially severe in cities with many factories, such as Vancouver, To-ronto, and Montreal.

Inco's Stack at Sudbury, Ont. Inco built the world's tallest chimney hoping that it would di-lute the air pollution. However, it simply spread it over a wider area (photo by J.A. Kraulis).

Wind carries air pollution over hun-dreds and sometimes thousands of kilo-metres. Usually, air pollution rises with the warm air near the ground and thins out. If warmer air above the ground traps the pollution, it can reach dangerous lev-els. In November 1962, these conditions produced a blanket of heavy smog in To-ronto. It made many people sick. Players could not see the ball during the Grey Cup football game and the game was sus-pended and completed the following day.

Acid rain is a serious form of air pollu-tion. It is caused by the sulphur and nitro-gen gases that are released by the burning of fossil fuels.

Effects of Air Pollution High levels of air pollution can irritate the nose and throat. People caught in traffic jams suffer headaches from automobile fumes. Expo-sure to air pollution over long periods may cause more serious problems.

Air pollution harms plants, crops, and flowers. Acid rain is destroying areas of Canada's forests, especially in the eastern part of the country. It is also killing fish and plants in Canada's lakes.

Air pollution also causes damage to

metals, and stone. Acid rain is destroying many beautiful buildings and statues around the world.

Perhaps the greatest danger of air pollution is its effect on climate. The burning of fossil fuels releases carbon dioxide into the air. This gas acts like the glass of a greenhouse. It slows down the escape of heat from the Earth, slowly warming the atmosphere. This "Greenhouse Effect" may raise the Earth's temperature enough to alter the climate. It is possible that the Greenhouse Effect could cause serious changes in agriculture.

Reducing Air Pollution There are three ways to control air pollution: technical changes, laws, and changes in human behaviour. In the 1970s, the Inco plant at Sudbury, Ont., built the world's tallest chimney. Inco believed that the chimney would dilute the air pollution. As a result the area around Sudbury became green again, but the pollution spread over a wider area.

Other technical solutions have been more successful. Car engines now contain a converter in the exhaust system to reduce the emission of harmful gases. Automobile owners can help by keeping their engines well tuned.

Industries could reduce pollution by switching to sources of energy that pollute less. For example, gas burns more cleanly than coal. Better equipment can reduce pollution. In Arvida, Que., Alcan replaced its old equipment and cut pollution by two-thirds. However, such changes are very expensive.

We could reduce the pollution produced by cars by using public transportation and fewer cars. If people did not all work the same hours, it would reduce the traffic jams which add so much pollution to the atmosphere.

In Canada, the provincial governments are mainly responsible for controlling air pollution. They and the federal government have passed laws to try to limit the amount of pollution. The governments measure air quality in stations across Canada. They can fine or shut down industries that fail to stop polluting.

Because of government action, the air in Canadian cities is cleaner now than it was ten years ago. However, ozone levels are as high, and the Greenhouse Effect and acid rain are growing problems. Some scientists predict that the air would become clean again within a few days if humans suddenly stopped polluting it.

▷ RELATED ARTICLES: **Acid Rain; Environment; Greenhouse Effect; Pollution.**

Air Pollution: Sources, Causes, and Effects

Substance	Sources	Causes	Effects
Carbon Monoxide	gasoline-powered vehicles (63%), industry (6%), forest fires (10%)	insufficient oxygen present during burning of fuels	headaches, dizziness
Particles	industry (64%), burning fuel (16%), forest fires (11%)	industrial processes	lung disease
Sulphur Oxides	industry (67%), especially copper and nickel industry; burning fuel (30%)	industry processes, combustion of fossil fuels which contain sulphur	acid rain, damage to vegetation, buildings
Nitrogen Oxide and Hydrocarbons	motor vehicles (43%), burning fuel (18%), industry (17%), forest fires (12%)	mixing of the two substances with sunlight produces ozone	smog, lung irritation

■ **Aircraft,** *see* **Aviation**

■ **Airport**

An airport is a place at which aircraft can land and take off. Most airports have runways and buildings. In 1989 there were about 900 airports certified by the federal government in Canada. They handle millions of landings and take-offs every year.

Towns, private corporations, and individuals own and run Canada's airports, most of which are relatively small. As well as handling passengers and freight, many of these airports house flying clubs where people can learn to fly. Some have companies offering services such as aerial photography or crop dusting — spraying insecticides from the air.

The federal government owns and operates 90 of the certified airports. Some of these are smaller airports. Many of them scattered across the Arctic where air travel is the only link to the outside world.

All the big airports in Canada are government operated. Cities such as Vancouver, Calgary, Edmonton, Winnipeg, Ottawa, Toronto, Montreal, and Halifax have international airports. They receive planes from all over the world.

The busiest airport in Canada is Lester B. Pearson International in Toronto. Over 16 million people either landed or took off from there in 1987.

Big airports are expensive to establish and complex to run. They use a lot of land for car parking lots, for hangers, for fuel storage, for terminal buildings, and, especially for runways. They also employ tens of thousands of people and are important to the local economy.

▷ RELATED ARTICLE: **Aviation.**

Canada's Largest Airports, 1987

Airport	Flights
Lester B. Pearson (Toronto)	171 300
Vancouver	76 600
Dorval (Montreal)	74 900
Calgary	66 000
Winnipeg	34 000
Ottawa	31 500
Edmonton (International)	31 000
Halifax	26 400
Mirabel (Montreal)	17 900
Saskatoon	15 300

Air Traffic Controllers in the Toronto area control centre (courtesy Transport Canada).

■ Aitken, Robert Morris

Flutist, composer (*born in 1939 at Kentville, N.S.*). Aitken was the principal flute player with the Vancouver Symphony Orchestra at the age of 19. He was widely sought after as a soloist all over the world.

Aitken's compositions are highly original, often combining Oriental techniques and modern electronics. He was appointed director of advanced music studies at the Banff Centre in 1985, a position he held until 1989.

■ Aitken, William Maxwell

First Baron Beaverbrook, newspaper tycoon and businessman (*born in 1879 at Maple, Ont.; died in 1964 at Mickleham, England*). Max Aitken gained international fame as a man who could "get things done" on a big scale. He was the friend and adviser of world leaders, including British Prime Minister Sir Winston Churchill and Canadian Prime Minister R.B. Bennett, whom he met when they were both young men in New Brunswick.

Aitken was the son of a Presbyterian minister and grew up in Newcastle, N.B. At first he thought he might train as a lawyer, like his friend Bennett, but long-drawn-out studies did not suit the character of the dynamic Max Aitken. He liked to see quick results. To get them, he was prepared to use all his energy and inventiveness.

Success in Business Aitken began as an insurance salesman in the Maritimes and soon moved on to other ventures. In 1903 he formed the Royal Securities Corporation, which bought small businesses and reorganized them to make them prof-

itable. This so suited Aitken's talents and passion for making money that he was a millionaire by 1907 — and still only 28 years old. He moved to Montreal; he then risked another experiment: buying failing companies that sold similar products and merging them to form large companies. One of his greatest successes here was the formation of the Steel Company of Canada (Stelco).

In 1910 Aitken took his business skills to England, where he became involved in politics and was elected a Conservative member of parliament in 1910. His tactics later helped Lloyd George become prime minister of Britain. During World War I, Aitken served as Canada's military representative in Britain and then as Britain's minister of information. He had been awarded a knighthood in 1911, and in 1917 he was made Lord Beaverbrook. He took the name of the title from a stream near his Canadian home.

Newspaper Baron After the war, Beaverbrook built up his British newspaper empire, which he had begun in 1917 by buying the *Express* of London. Beaverbrook's newspapers strongly reflected his own views. He championed the defence of the British Empire, as well as many other causes which were not as popular among his Conservative friends. In 1940, early in World War II, Beaverbrook was appointed minister of aircraft production in Britain. It was a vital post because

Max Aitken's passion for making money made him a millionaire in his late twenties. He went on to play a major role in Britain's effort in World War II (NAC/PA-6467).

Britain urgently needed planes to fight off the German bombers. Beaverbrook rose to the challenge so effectively that the fighter pilots never lacked planes. Later in the war, Beaverbrook performed much the same service as minister of supply, ensuring there were enough food and war supplies.

When the war ended in 1945, Beaverbrook retired from politics and concentrated on his newspapers and on writing books. Churchill considered him "a man of exceptional genius, who is at his very best when things are at their very worst."

▷ SUGGESTED READING: William A. Hayes, *Beaverbrook* (1979); A.J.P. Taylor, *Beaverbrook* (1972).

■ Aklavik

Aklavik, N.W.T., is a hamlet in the delta of the Mackenzie River, about 100 km from the Arctic Ocean. In the 1950s Aklavik was the most important community in the Beaufort Sea-Mackenzie Delta region.

As a result of spring flooding and erosion, the community of Aklavik was supposed to be moved to a new town built to replace it. Inuvik was built in 1961. Aklavik did not die, and today its motto is "Never Say Die." Aklavik means "place where there are grizzly bears" in the Inuit language. In 1986 the population of Aklavik was 763.

■ Alaska Boundary Dispute

The Alaska Boundary Dispute was a disagreement between Canada and the United States over the boundary of the Alaska Panhandle — the southern strip of Alaska that runs south to 54°40′ on the British Columbia coast.

Alaska was owned by Russia until 1867 when the tsar sold it to the United States. According to the Anglo-Russian treaty of 1825, the border lay along the "summit of the mountains which extend in a direction parallel to the coast." This vague description was good enough when there was little interest in the region. But during the Klondike gold rush of 1897-98, both Canada and the United States needed to know exactly where the boundary lay. In particular, Canada needed access to the Pacific, with a port on one of the fjords, so that gold miners could bring in supplies without paying American customs duties.

Since Canada and the United States could not agree on the boundary, a tribunal was set up to settle the matter. The tribunal met in 1903 and was composed

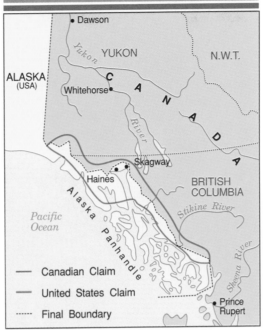

Alaska Boundary Dispute

- — Canadian Claim
- — United States Claim
- ----- Final Boundary

of three Americans, two Canadians, and one Englishman (the lord chief justice of England, Lord Alverstone). Alverstone sided with the Americans, and thus the dispute was decided 4-2 in favour of the American claim. This caused great anger among Canadians, and it increased the feeling that Canada should have full control of its foreign affairs, without Britain having a say in arranging treaties.

■ Albani, Dame Emma

Opera singer (*born Marie-Emma Lajeunesse in 1847 at Chambly, Canada East [Quebec]; died in 1930 at London, England*). Lajeunesse took the stage name Emma Albani at a time when people thought an Italian name was necessary for a singing career. She was hailed across the world as "the queen of song."

Albani first sang in public at the age of nine, at the Mechanics' Hall in Montreal. Her family moved to the United States so that Emma could have a career in music and raise money to study in Europe. She made her debut in Italy in 1869 and went on to sing on all the great opera stages. During her career, Albani sang 43 leading opera roles.

Albani returned to Canada about 12 times. On her first Canadian tour in 1883, she was greeted by more than 10 000 fans when she arrived in Montreal. She retired from the opera stage in 1896. Her voice was recorded in the very early days of the phonograph.

▷ SUGGESTED READING: Cheryl E. MacDonald, *Emma Albani* (1984).

Emma Albani, 17¢ stamp issued July 4, 1980 (courtesy of Canada Post Corporation).

Alberta

Facts about the Province of Alberta

Created as a Province:	September 1, 1905
Motto:	*Fortis et Liber* (Strong and Free)
Origin of Name:	Named after Princess Louise Caroline Alberta, 4th daughter of Queen Victoria and wife of the Marquis of Lorne, Governor General of Canada from 1878 to 1883
Capital City:	Edmonton
Government:	*Provincial:* Lieutenant-Governor, Executive Council (premier and cabinet), Legislative Assembly. The number of members of the Legislative Assembly (MLAs) is 83
	Federal: Represented in the Senate of Canada by 6 senators; in the House of Commons by 26 members of Parliament (MPs)
Population:	2 375 278 (1986 census), 9.3% of total population of Canada. Alberta's population is 79.1% urban, 19.7% rural, 1.2% Indian Reserves.
Main Products:	*Resource Extraction and Mining:* oil and gas, coal
	Agriculture: beef cattle, feed grain, wheat, oilseed, barley
	Manufacturing: food products, oil and gas products (including petrochemicals), wood products
Time Zone:	Mountain Standard Time
Parks:	*National:* Banff, Jasper, Elk Island, Waterton Lakes, Wood Buffalo
	Provincial: There are more than 60 provincial parks, including Cypress Hills, Dinosaur, Lesser Slave Lake, and Writing-on-Stone
	Land and Water Reserved for Conservation: With some logging, mining, hunting allowed: 9.4%; with no logging, mining, hunting allowed: 8.5%
Highest Points:	Mount Columbia 3747 m
	The Twins 3733 m
	Mount Alberta 3620 m
	Mount Assiniboine 3618 m
Lowest Points:	Slave River 152 m
	Lake Athabasca 213 m
Largest Lakes:	(Entirely within Alberta)
	Lake Claire 1436 km²
	Lesser Slave Lake 1168 km²

■ Alberta

Alberta is the farthest west of Canada's prairie provinces. It is a province that has depended on its natural resources for its wealth: the furs of the northern forests, the prairie soil, and lately, its oil and gas.

The province has seen great surges of growth, as well as hard times. The discovery of large deposits of oil and gas in the late 1940s made Alberta Canada's fastest-growing province until the early 1980s, helping to shift Canada's power and wealth westward. Nevertheless, Albertans have often felt that they are too far from the centre of power and that their fate is too much in the hands of forces that are not in their control.

LAND AND WATER

Alberta's land was created by 2.5 billion years of geological activity. Alberta is now in a cool, dry, northern location, but 100 million years ago it was covered with rich, tropical forests. The Pacific and Arctic oceans and the Gulf of Mexico all reached Alberta's shores millions of years ago.

Today, the land surface of Alberta can be divided into four major regions.

Rocky Mountains The ranges of the Rocky Mountains form a spectacular border on the southwest. They were created by the action of the great plates which make up the surface of the Earth. The oceanic plate of the Pacific is pushed under the continental plate, causing the edge of the plate to lift and fracture.

Foothills Similar, but less powerful, pressure also created the second region, the foothills, which are next to the mountains. These forces are still alive beneath the Earth in the famous hot springs of Banff and Jasper, which attract visitors from all over the world.

Shield The Canadian Shield is found only in a small area on the extreme northeastern corner of the province.

Plains The rest of the province is a great flat plain, which once formed the floor of ancient seas. It is thought that the plant and animal life that lived in this ancient sea is the source of the deposits of oil, which are the basis of so much of Alberta's wealth. The plains are not totally flat. Their surface has been gouged and twisted by the action of massive glaciers which once covered the province. At one time most of Alberta lay under some 2000 m of ice.

Rivers Alberta has two major river systems, both of which have their origin in the western mountains. The rivers of northern Alberta — the Hay, Athabasca, Peace, and Slave rivers — flow northward towards the Arctic into the Mackenzie River. Central and southern Alberta are drained by the Saskatchewan River system. The North Saskatchewan River cuts

Peyto Lake in Banff National Park is typical of the magnificent scenery of the Rocky Mountains of Alberta (courtesy Colour Library Books Ltd).

a broad valley in the northern prairie, part of which provides Edmonton with its beautiful parkland. The South Saskatchewan River drains most of southern Alberta. The Red Deer River has carved a deep valley through the Badlands and created some of Alberta's most unusual scenery. Unfortunately, the greatest flow of water through these rivers is in the north, while the greatest need for water is in the south, where almost all the farming takes place.

Lakes Alberta's largest lakes are in the north: Lake Athabasca, which it shares with Saskatchewan, Lake Claire (the largest lake entirely in Alberta), and Lesser Slave Lake, in the centre of the province.

CLIMATE AND WEATHER

Alberta's climate is affected by its northern location, by the cold arctic air masses to the north, and by the position of the Rocky Mountains along its western border. The low-lying sun and the arctic air make for short, very cold days in the winter. Some warmer air enters Alberta from the south, or from the west, making temperatures in southern Alberta as much as 10° to 15°C higher than in the north. Because of this flow of air, Alberta is also warmer than areas farther east; for example, it is about 7° warmer on average in winter than Manitoba.

The prairie region has some of the most violent extremes of weather found anywhere. The city of Medicine Hat, for example, has had a range in temperature from -46.1°C in January to 42.2°C in July.

The Rocky Mountains cast a "rain shadow" over much of Alberta. As the moist air from the Pacific Ocean rises to pass over the mountains on its way to Alberta, it is cooled and precipitation falls on the Pacific side of the mountains. As the air descends into Alberta, it gains heat and produces warm, dry winds. The driest area is the southeast, which receives only 30 cm of precipitation per year; the north receives about 45 cm, while the foothills get about 60 cm.

Fortunately, two-thirds of Alberta's precipitation falls in the summer, when it is most needed for agriculture. Nevertheless, some areas, especially the southeast, are much too dry for farming. Most of the agriculture is located in central and western Alberta. It is still fairly dry in this region but is moist enough for some crops. Northern Alberta is both too cool and too wet, except for a small area in the northwest, called Peace River Country, which receives warm, moist air from British Columbia. The Peace River Country is the farthest north that grain is grown in North America.

The best-known feature of Alberta's weather is the chinook wind, which sweeps into southern Alberta several times each winter. This dry, warm wind can rapidly lift Alberta out of a deep freeze. During one chinook, which reached Pincher Creek on January 27, 1962, temperatures soared from -18.9°C to +3.3°C in one hour.

The main climate hazards in Alberta are droughts in summer and blizzards in

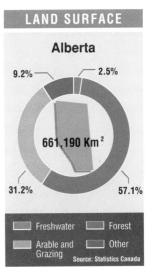

LAND SURFACE

Alberta

9.2%
2.5%

661,190 Km²

31.2%
57.1%

☐ Freshwater ☐ Forest
☐ Arable and ☐ Other
Grazing
Source: Statistics Canada

Alberta's Record Temperatures
Highest: 43.3°C on July 23, 1931, at Bassano and on July 18, 1941, at Fort Macleod

Lowest: -61.1°C on January 11, 1911, at Fort Vermilion

Alberta

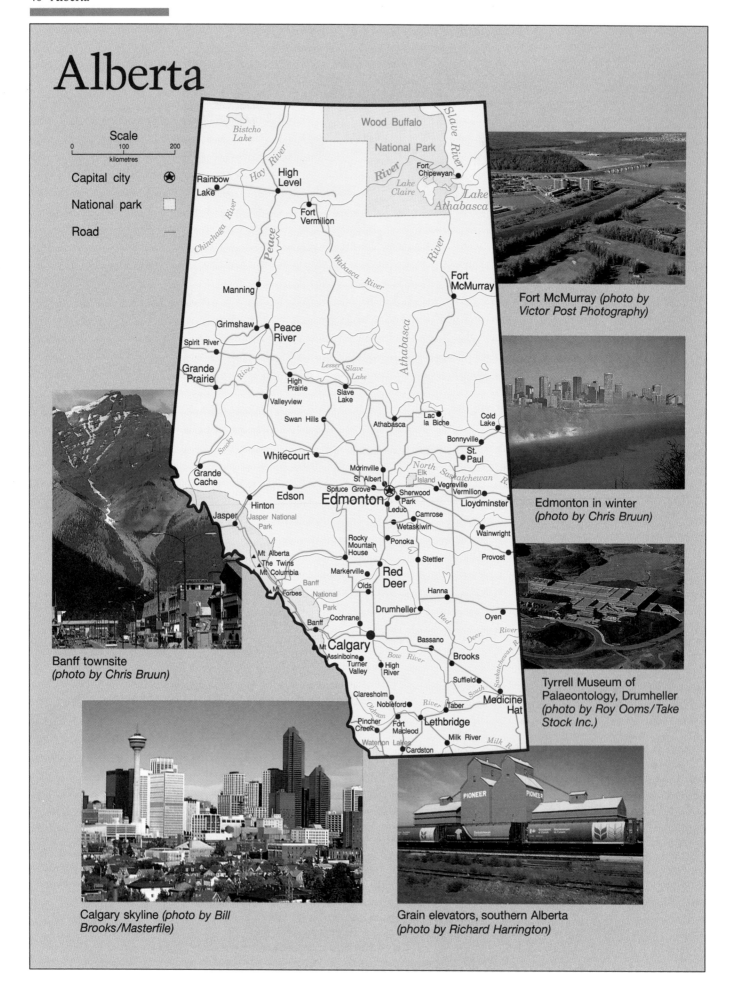

Scale
0   100   200
kilometres

Capital city   ✪

National park   ☐

Road   —

Bistcho Lake

Wood Buffalo National Park

Rainbow Lake

High Level

Hay River

Fort Chipewyan

Slave River

River

Lake Claire

Lake Athabasca

Chinchaga River

Fort Vermilion

Peace River

Manning

Grimshaw

Peace River

Spirit River

Wabasca River

Fort McMurray

Grande Prairie

River

Lesser Slave Lake

High Prairie

Valleyview

Slave Lake

Swan Hills

Athabasca

Lac la Biche

Cold Lake

Bonnyville

Whitecourt

St. Paul

Grande Cache

North Saskatchewan R.

Elk Island

Vegreville

Vermilion

Lloydminster

Edson

Morinville
St Albert
Spruce Grove

Sherwood Park

Hinton

Edmonton

Leduc

Camrose

Jasper

Jasper National Park

Wetaskiwin

Wainwright

Ponoka

Provost

Mt Alberta
The Twins
Mt Columbia

Rocky Mountain House

Markerville

Stettler

Mt Forbes

Banff National Park

Olds

Red Deer

Hanna

Oyen

Drumheller

Cochrane

Banff

Red Deer River

Calgary

Assiniboine
Turner Valley

Bassano

Brooks

High River

Suffield

Bow River

Claresholm

Nobleford

Saskatchewan R.

Medicine Hat

Pincher Creek

Fort Macleod

Taber

Lethbridge

South Saskatchewan R.

Waterton Lakes

Cardston

Milk River

Oldman River

Milk R.

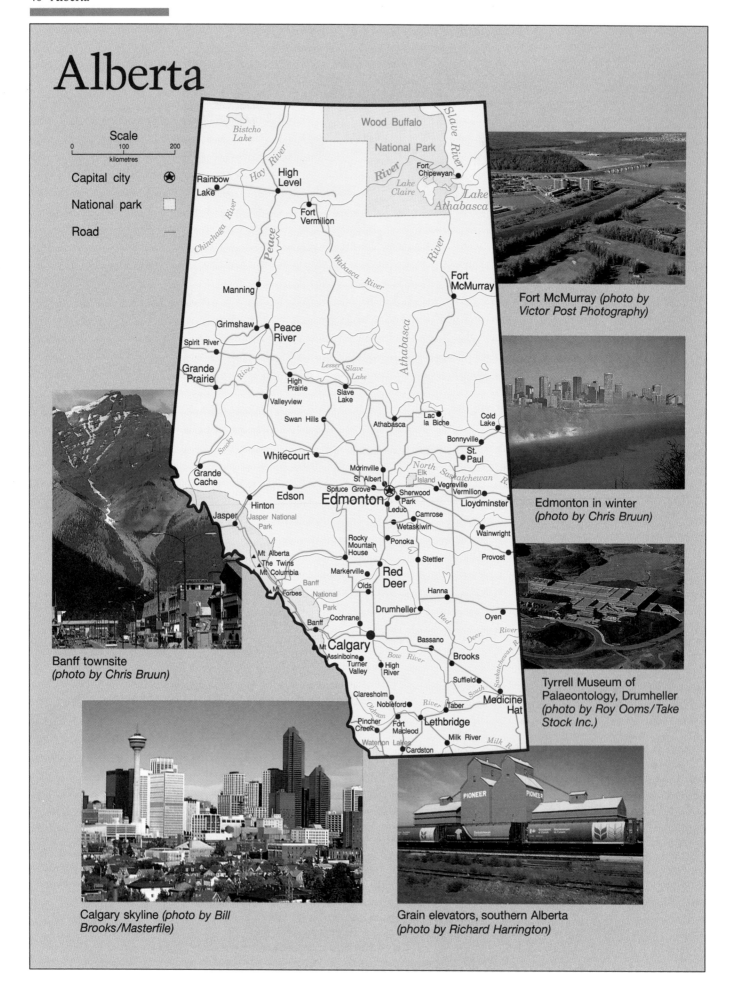
Fort McMurray (*photo by Victor Post Photography*)

Edmonton in winter (*photo by Chris Bruun*)

Tyrrell Museum of Palaeontology, Drumheller (*photo by Roy Ooms/Take Stock Inc.*)

Banff townsite (*photo by Chris Bruun*)

Calgary skyline (*photo by Bill Brooks/Masterfile*)

Grain elevators, southern Alberta (*photo by Richard Harrington*)

Porcupine Hills, Alberta, are a forested outer region of the foothills. The view, through morning fog, looks west to Whaleback Ridge (photo by Cliff Wallis).

winter. Droughts almost destroyed agriculture in the 1930s and have caused real hardship in other years. A prairie blizzard is a storm with very high winds, bitter temperatures, and driving snow, which lasts for many hours and can severely disrupt transportation.

During the summer, showers and thunderstorms are common in the south and central areas. Occasionally, the storms develop into tornadoes. Most of these rage for brief periods in open areas, doing little damage, but in 1987 a tornado tore through the outskirts of Edmonton, killing 27 people.

NATURAL REGIONS

Alberta offers perhaps the greatest variety of natural beauty found in any province. Four main natural areas are easily recognized: the Prairie, the Montane Cordillera, the Boreal Plains, and the Taiga Plains. A fifth, small area, called the Badlands, has some of the most unusual scenery in Canada.

Prairie The Prairie, or grasslands, region of Alberta is part of an enormous area which stretches from Calgary to Winnipeg. The prairie region of Alberta varies from dry areas in the southeast, which in places look like desert, to moister areas to the north and west, which are the basis for much of Alberta's agriculture and ranching.

The prairie has few trees, except for those planted around farms to break the wind, or those found along streams where there is adequate water.

The prairie has been utterly changed by settlement. Most of the original grasses have disappeared, as have the herds of millions of bison, and the many black bears, grizzlies, wolves, and coyotes which once lived on the grasslands.

In the 19th century, it was not known

if the prairie was a desert or a wonderful garden. The prairie did turn out to be one of the greatest farming areas of the world, but its dryness and extreme winters are a constant challenge to its farmers.

Only two of Alberta's cities are situated on the grasslands: Lethbridge and Medicine Hat. Calgary is in the zone between the grasslands and aspen parkland.

The aspen parkland is a transition zone between the prairie and the Boreal Plains region to the north. It is a wide belt located along the northern fringe of the prairie,

Photos by Cliff Wallis (Taiga Plain), Cleve Wershler (Boreal Plain), Thomas Kitchin (Montane Cordillera), Tim Fitzharris (Aspen Parkland), and Cleve Wershler (Prairie).

Natural Regions of Alberta

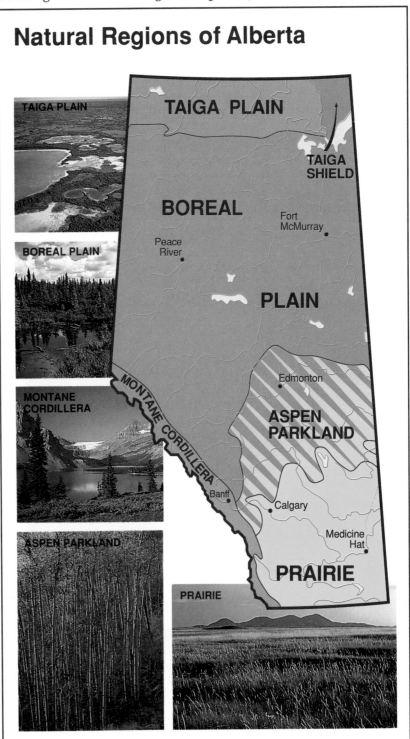

across south-central Alberta. The trembling aspen tree, which gives the region its name, was called trembling because its heart-shaped leaves flutter continually in the wind. Aspen groves were common before the Europeans arrived, and many settlers were drawn to them in preference to the treeless prairie. Today, about 75% of the parkland is cultivated, and it has Alberta's best arable land as well as the most cattle. Alberta's two largest cities are on the parkland: Edmonton and Calgary.

Montane Cordillera The mountain regions of Alberta contain some of the province's greatest beauty, with majestic peaks, stands of forest, sparkling rivers, and wildflowers. They attract many of the tourists who come to Alberta, but the only settlements are resource towns or tourist centres, located in small valleys or mountain passes.

The vegetation and wildlife in this region vary with altitude. Above 1500 m the *alpine* environment contains lichen and shrubs, as well as some trees. At lower elevations the forest grows thicker and taller.

Much of this region has been set aside for recreation and wildlife in Banff and Jasper national parks.

Boreal Plains The boreal forest covers a vast northern area of Alberta. Here, moist, cool conditions favour coniferous trees, especially spruce and pine. The soil is very poor and huge areas are covered in muskeg.

The only renewable resource is timber. There are few towns in this area, except near the great oil sands, for example, Fort McMurray.

Taiga Plains This area of northern Alberta is low and waterlogged over large areas. Much of it is underlain with permafrost. The drier areas are covered with trees. The wetter areas are covered with moss and sedge. The region is largely uninhabited.

Badlands The famous badlands are a unique area in southeastern Alberta. They are very dry and have little vegetation. Streams and rain have eroded the soft rocks, leaving bluffs, gullies, and multicoloured layers of stone. The Red Deer River has cut a deep, wide valley through the badlands, exposing the fossils of plants and animals which lived in Alberta millions of years ago, including the famous dinosaurs.

WILDLIFE

Because of its northern location, Alberta

Dinosaur Provincial Park Erosion has exposed layers of sandstone and shale in scenery typical of Alberta's badlands. The badlands are one of the most valuable sources of dinosaur fossils in the world (photo by Cleve Wershler).

has few reptiles. There are only eight species, including the prairie rattlesnake and the red-sided garter snake, which is the most northerly reptile in North America.

There are also only around 50 species of fish native to Alberta, but they include many that are favourites of sports fishermen, such as sturgeon, pike, and goldeye.

In contrast, the province is known for its great variety of waterfowl and shorebirds, as its wetlands provide excellent stopover points for migrating birds. There are loons, grebes, pelicans, herons, swans, geese, and ducks, as well as cranes and whooping cranes.

Among birds of prey are the peregrine falcon and the great horned owl, Alberta's provincial bird. The striking black and white magpie, which is a familiar sight in Alberta's cities, once followed the bison across the prairie.

Alberta has an unusual richness of mammals. On the grasslands are mule deer, coyote, fox, gopher, weasel, and the rare pronghorn antelope. In the parkland area the snowshoe hare is common, along with beaver, fox, lynx, and mink. Elk Island Park contains many of these mammals, including herds of wood bison and plains bison, moose, wapiti, and the pygmy shrew, which is the world's smallest mammal.

NATURAL RESOURCES

Alberta's economy has always depended on its natural resources, beginning with the fur trade in the early days and continuing with the discovery of oil and gas. Today, Alberta's energy resources are of overwhelming importance, not only to the province, but to the whole country.

Energy The first important oil strike was made in 1914 in Turner Valley, near

Bison *Elk Island National Park is one of the few refuges for the bison in their former range on the prairie (photo by Cliff Wallis).*

Grande Cache *Coal lies under huge areas of Alberta. The photo shows a coal-preparation plant at Grande Cache, on the Smoky River (photo by Jack Deenik).*

Calgary, but the real boom did not begin until discovery of the Leduc field, near Edmonton, in 1947. Today, oil is found throughout the province, particularly in the south. Alberta produces most of Canada's oil, and has increased its share of total production, from 75% in 1971 to 83% in 1988. Nearly 40% is exported to other countries. Alberta's oil is limited and will one day run out — as early as 20 years from now by some guesses. However, the great oil sands near Fort McMurray are said to contain more oil than Saudi Arabia, although it is at present very expensive to mine this oil.

Natural gas was discovered as early as 1883, near Medicine Hat. Alberta now produces from 80% to over 85% of Canada's natural gas. About 20% of it is used in the province.

Coal underlies a huge area of the province, over some 300 000 km². The coal was used long before the oil and gas; it was first mined near Lethbridge in 1872. Alberta now produces over 40% of Canada's coal, and coal is used to produce about 80% of the province's electricity. Because most of its rivers are slow-moving prairie rivers, Alberta produces little hydroelectricity.

Forestry About one-half of Alberta is covered by trees, but not all the forests can be harvested. In much of the north, for example, muskeg makes it almost impossible to move the trees. Large quantities of lumber are shipped from Alberta to markets in Canada and the United States. About 100 000 railway ties are made each

Syncrude Plant, *Fort McMurray, Alta. Alberta produces over 80% of Canada's oil. The oil sands near Fort McMurray contain huge deposits of oil, but it is very expensive to produce (photo by Victor Post Photography).*

year in Alberta. There are three large pulp mills in operation, one at Hinton, one at Grande Prairie, and one at Whitecourt.

Alberta is turning to the forest industry in order to diversify its economy. Unlike petroleum and coal, the forests are renewable if they are carefully managed. There are four new proposed pulp mills, a proposed paper mill, and a proposed newspaper mill. All of these will be located in northern Alberta.

Wetlands, *such as these in Waterton Lakes National Park, are home to a variety of wildlife (photo by Cliff Wallis).*

Tourism and Recreation Hundreds of thousands of tourists are attracted to Alberta each year, especially to the spectacular mountain scenery of Banff and Jasper national parks. Special attractions, such as the Calgary Stampede or West Edmonton Mall, bring tourists to the main cities as well. Tourism brings about $2 billion a year to Alberta's economy—almost as much as agriculture—and it provides around 75 000 jobs.

There are five national parks: Banff, Jasper, Waterton Lakes, Elk Island, and Wood Buffalo. These parks make up about 9% of the area of the province.

Chateau Lake Louise, *one of the most popular tourist stops in Alberta (photo by John Dean/Take Stock Inc.).*

These parks are shared with visitors from all over the world in summer and winter. Some provincial wilderness reserves have been left untouched, with no access by automobiles.

Conservation The use of Alberta's resources has often resulted in damage to its environment. Coal mining, for example, leaves open gashes in the land, with damage to wildlife and to the beauty of the wilderness. The petroleum industry requires roads and pipelines and the clearing of large areas of forest, which cannot then be used for forestry or recreation. Runaway gas wells may spread sour gas over long distances. The forest industry has left ugly bare patches; this was particularly so in its early days, when the trees were "clean cut," with no care for replanting. The pulp mills cause some pollution of nearby rivers. Even the tourists and campers, enjoying the scenic beauty, leave garbage and overcrowd areas such as Banff. Campers set some 60% of forest fires. Tourist towns, such as Banff, permanently change the wilderness and damage the soil and plants.

By holding back the development of the parks, the government hopes to preserve their beauty for future generations. Open-pit coal mines have been partly filled and reshaped in some areas, and the forest industry has begun to replant the forests.

THE ECONOMY

Alberta's economy once depended almost entirely on agriculture. Agriculture remains important, but it now produces only 3% of the province's income. Almost

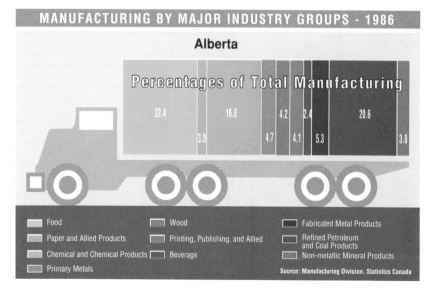

MANUFACTURING BY MAJOR INDUSTRY GROUPS - 1986

Alberta

Percentages of Total Manufacturing

22.4   16.8   4.2   2.4   20.6

3.0   4.7   4.1   5.3   3.8

Food
Paper and Allied Products
Chemical and Chemical Products
Primary Metals
Wood
Printing, Publishing, and Allied
Beverage
Fabricated Metal Products
Refined Petroleum and Coal Products
Non-metallic Mineral Products

Source: Manufacturing Division, Statistics Canada

50% is produced by the two sectors of the economy, finance and mining (including oil and gas). Next in importance are service industries, retail and wholesale trade, manufacturing, and transportation.

Agriculture Ranching and grain growing were the reasons for Alberta's origin. They are still very important to the province, to Canada, and to the world. Alberta produces about 20% of Canada's food. About one-third of the total is made up of cattle ranching; the rest is crops, led by wheat, canola, and barley. Potatoes, sugar beets, and vegetables are also important.

Dairy, poultry, cattle, hog, and sheep farming are concentrated around Edmonton and Calgary, and between Camrose and Lloydminster.

Although Alberta has a great deal of land that can still be developed for farming, the most fertile land has all been settled. In fact, some of the best land lies within the city borders of Edmonton and Calgary. As these cities expand, they destroy this land forever.

Industry Alberta's industries tend to produce raw materials, such as petroleum or food products, or equipment used in the resource industries.

Construction has always been important in Alberta, beginning with the railways and the building of the grain elevators. Huge energy projects, such as the oil-sands development, require massive construction. Edmonton and Calgary, which were Canada's fastest-growing cities in the 1970s and early 1980s, were known as "cities of cranes."

The manufacturing industry is heavily concentrated in the two main cities of Edmonton and Calgary.

POPULATION

Alberta already had a mixture of cultures by the time that the first European settlers arrived over 100 years ago. Nine different tribes of native people, belonging to three very different language groups, occupied the area: Athapaskan, Algonqian, and Siouan. The native people had two different ways of life. The plains tribes hunted the bison that once numbered in the tens of millions. The bison provided food, clothing, and shelter. In the northern forests the Indians lived by hunting game, such as moose and deer, and they fished and gathered berries and wild plants. Unlike the Plains Indians, whose way of life was completely destroyed 100 years ago, a few northern communities still support themselves in the traditional ways of hunting and fishing.

In 1986, Alberta's native people numbered around 61 000. Some 49 000 of these are official "status" Indians; the rest are Metis (people of mixed Indian and non-Indian ancestry). Indian reserves make up about 1% of Alberta's lands.

The settling of the prairies brought a rapid influx of people from Ontario, Great Britain, and the United States, making the population mainly English speaking. Germans and Scandinavians added to the mix, and then large numbers of central and eastern Europeans, such as the Ukrainians. A number of persecuted religious groups, including Mormons, Hutterites, Mennonites, and Doukhobors, also came to Alberta. From the late 1960s to the early 1980s, immigrants came to Alberta from all over the world.

Alberta: Population of Cities (1986)

Edmonton	785 465
Calgary	671 326
Lethbridge	58 841
Red Deer	54 425
Medicine Hat	50 734
Ft McMurray	48 497
St Albert[1]	36 710
Grande Prairie	26 471
Leduc[1]	13 126
Camrose	12 968
Ft Saskatchewan[1]	11 983
Airdrie[2]	10 390
Lloydminster	10 201
Wetaskiwin	10 071
Drumheller	6 366

[1] Included as part of Edmonton
[2] Included as part of Calgary

Alberta: Major Religious Groups (1981*)

	% of pop.
Roman Catholic	25.9
United Church	23.7
Anglican	9.1
Lutheran	6.5
Baptist	3.0
Presbyterian	2.9
Eastern Orthodox	2.2
Greek Orthodox	2.1
Mormons	1.9
Church of Latterday Saints	1.9

* Last figures available. Religion was not counted in the 1986 census.

Alberta Farm Agriculture is still very important to the economy and life of Alberta (photo by Ken A. Meisner/Take Stock Inc.).

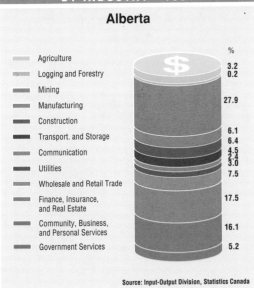

GROSS DOMESTIC PRODUCT BY INDUSTRY - 1984

Alberta

	%
Agriculture	3.2
Logging and Forestry	0.2
Mining	27.9
Manufacturing	6.1
Construction	6.4
Transport. and Storage	4.5
Communication	2.4
Utilities	3.0
Wholesale and Retail Trade	7.5
Finance, Insurance, and Real Estate	17.5
Community, Business, and Personal Services	16.1
Government Services	5.2

Source: Input-Output Division, Statistics Canada

especially in the 1930s, when 42 000 more people left than entered. The 1950s, however, saw a gain of 127 000. From 1961 to 1981, 1.6 million people came to Alberta and 1.2 million left. Since the downturn of the economy in the early 1980s, 34 000 more people left the province than entered.

The number of people of British origin is still the largest, but it has declined from as high as 60% early this century, down to 25.3% (1986). Over the years, the number of immigrants from Europe and the U.S. has declined, and the numbers from Africa, Asia, and Latin America have increased greatly. Over 80% learn English as their first language.

The native people remain a small but unique part of the population. In 1901, they were about 9% of Alberta's population; now they are over 2%, including the Metis. The largest number live around Cardston, Calgary, Edmonton, and Pincher Creek, but the largest reserves by area are in the south, around Calgary and in the southwest corner of the province.

TRANSPORTATION AND COMMUNICATIONS

Transportation has been of vital importance to Alberta since the early days of the fur trade, when the main routes followed the rivers. The railways made possible the settlement of the prairie, bringing the settlers west and returning the grain east to market.

The Canadian Pacific Railway reached Calgary in 1883. The Canadian Northern (later Canadian National) reached Edmonton in 1905. The two separate rail routes are one of the reasons that Alberta has two major cities. During the early 20th century, rail lines spread like veins

Alberta: Languages (1986)	
English	80.9%
German	3.2%
French	2.0%
Ukrainian	2.0%
Chinese	1.5%
Dutch	0.8%
Polish	0.6%
Other	9.0%

Russian Orthodox Church at Smoky Lake. The cross-topped churches with onion-shaped domes are found throughout Alberta (courtesy PAA/UV16).

Immigrants have had a lasting influence on Alberta, especially where a particular area was settled by a single group: for example, the Mormons in Cardston; the Icelanders in Markerville; the Dutch in Nobleford; the French Canadians in Morinville and St Paul; and the Ukrainians in Vegreville. Each group has left traces of its old culture on the local speech, architecture, and customs.

During the past 85 years, Alberta's population has increased 30 times and it has spread over the province.

Alberta has grown at a greater rate than Canada, and its share of the total population of Canada has grown from 1.4% in 1901 to 9.3% in 1986. In recent times, the population has shifted from rural areas to the cities.

There have been periods in which more people left the province than entered it,

Alberta: Major Ethnic Origins (1986) (ranked by size)

1. British
2. German
3. Ukrainian
4. French
5. Dutch
6. Aboriginal
7. Chinese
8. Scandinavian
9. South Asian
10. Polish

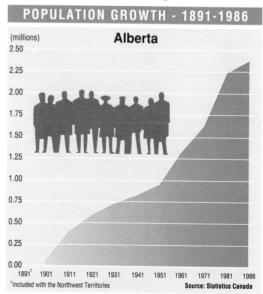

POPULATION GROWTH - 1891-1986

Alberta

(millions)

2.50	
2.25	
2.00	
1.75	
1.50	
1.25	
1.00	
0.75	
0.50	
0.25	
0.00	

1891¹ 1901 1911 1921 1931 1941 1951 1961 1971 1981 1986

¹Included with the Northwest Territories

Source: Statistics Canada

of a plant leaf across the prairie, creating most of the present-day cities and towns of Alberta.

There have been two major rail projects in modern times: the Great Slave Lake Railway and the Alberta Resources Railway. Both were built in the 1960s to open the resources of the North. The railways still ship many of Alberta's products, particularly its grain and coal.

Trucks have become increasingly important in moving goods in Alberta, especially cement and petroleum products.

Alberta has over 150 000 km of pipelines which move its oil and gas to refineries and to markets in eastern Canada and the United States.

Communications There are more than 140 weekly newspapers published in Alberta, as well as several monthlies and nine dailies. There are 15 television stations, 170 cable systems, 62 AM radio stations, and 18 FM radio stations. Albertans watch the same programs and listen to the same music as people in the rest of Canada. *Alberta Report* and the *NeWest Review* are two of the 20 commercial magazines published in Alberta.

EDUCATION

The first schools in Alberta were founded by missionaries in the 19th century. Some were Protestant. Others were Roman Catholic. When Alberta became a province in 1905, a single system of public schooling was set up, with "separate" schools for Roman Catholics. The school system is similar to those in most provinces, with high school ending in Grade 12.

The University of Alberta was the province's first university. Located in Edmonton, it was founded in 1906 and opened in 1908. Today, there are five universities, including Athabasca University, which specializes in distance learning. The world-renowned Banff Centre for Continuing Education is not a true university, but it is usually included in this category. It offers special programs in the arts. There are also three technical schools and a number of public colleges. The Alberta College of Art is located in Calgary.

CULTURE

Alberta's culture has been enriched by its many groups and by the beauty of the land, which has inspired artists and writers.

The performing arts are centered in Edmonton and Calgary. Each city has a symphony orchestra and an opera company.

Alberta's Universities and Technical Institutions	
Universities	*Location*
Athabasca University	Athabasca
University of Alberta	Edmonton
Banff Centre for Continuing Education	Banff
University of Calgary	Calgary
University of Lethbridge	Lethbridge
Technical Institutions	*Location*
Northern Alberta Institute of Technology (NAIT)	Edmonton
Southern Alberta Institute of Technology (SAIT)	Calgary
Westerra Institute of Technology	Stony Plain

Edmonton has two ballet companies and a very active theatre community. The Citadel Theatre operates year-round in Edmonton, while the Fringe, a ten-day festival which takes place in many settings, is the largest theatre festival in North America.

Artists, sculptors, and actors study at the University of Alberta at Edmonton. The Alberta College of Art in Calgary has long been a centre of painting. The Banff Centre is a renowned centre for young artists, actors, dancers, and musicians. Alberta's young artists and musicians include cellist Shauna Ralston and pianist Angela Cheng, who won the prestigious Montreal International Competition in 1988.

Writers W.O. Mitchell, Rudy Wiebe, and Myrna Kostash are based in Alberta and have written about prairie life. Young writers are encouraged by the government's annual Search-for-a-New-Alberta-Novelist competition.

Alberta's main museums are the Provincial Museum of Alberta, in Edmonton;

Alberta's Daily Newspapers
Calgary
 Calgary Herald
 The Calgary Sun
Edmonton
 The Edmonton Journal
 The Edmonton Sun
Fort McMurray
 Fort McMurray Today
Grande Prairie
 Daily Herald-Tribune
Lethbridge
 The Lethbridge Herald
Medicine Hat
 News
Red Deer
 The Advocate

The Glenbow Museum *in Calgary has an outstanding collection of displays and paintings relating to western Canada (photo by Bilodeau/Preston Ltd/Take Stock Inc.).*

the Glenbow Museum, in Calgary, which has an outstanding collection of articles, displays, and paintings relating to western Canada; and the Edmonton Art Gallery. Of special interest is the Tyrrell Museum of Palaeontology, near Drumheller, with its collection of dinosaur fossils and its displays of life at the time of the dinosaurs.

Historic sites in Alberta include Head-Smashed-In Buffalo Jump, which is a World Heritage Site; Rocky Mountain House, from the fur trade days; Cochrane Ranch, from the early days of ranching; and the Ukrainian Cultural Heritage Village, from the early pioneer days of farming settlement.

SPORT AND RECREATION

Alberta has participated in sports from its earliest days. The ranchers brought cricket, which was Alberta's favourite sport for a while, and polo. American cowboys brought their rodeo skills. Alberta's love affair with the horse continues with horse racing, equestrian sports, and the famous Calgary Stampede.

Alberta's first well-known sports team was the world-famous Edmonton Grads women's basketball team, which was active from 1915 to 1940. Today, Edmonton and Calgary have professional hockey, football, baseball, and soccer teams. Edmonton teams in particular have enjoyed success: the Edmonton Eskimos are perennial Grey Cup champions in football, and the Edmonton Oilers won the Stanley Cup in hockey four times.

Edmonton has hosted the Commonwealth Games (1978) and the World University Games (1983), and Calgary hosted the Winter Olympics in 1988. The great success of these events was largely due to the volunteer spirit in each city.

Popular recreation sports that take advantage of Alberta's natural riches include fishing in the lakes and rivers, mountaineering, horseback riding, ski-ing, hiking, and canoeing. Numerous facilities are available for swimming, hockey, baseball, tennis, and golf. One of Canada's most spectacular settings for golf is Kananaskis Country, west of Calgary. As a result of the Olympics, Calgary now has nearby facilities for ski-jumping, bobsled, and other events.

Calgary is the home of the Alberta Sports Hall of Fame which has, among its displays, mountaineering equipment from the 1982 Canadian Mount Everest Expedition. Calgary-born Laurie Skreslet was the first Canadian to scale Mount Everest. Sharon Wood, of Canmore, was the first woman from the Western Hemisphere to climb Mount Everest (1986). Other Alberta sports champions include Susan Nattrass (shooting), Betty Cole (golf), Tom Three Persons (bronco riding), Kurt Browning (skating), and Gail Greenough (equestrian).

GOVERNMENT AND POLITICS

Government Like the people of other Canadian provinces, Albertans take part in three levels of government: federal, provincial, and local. At the federal level, they elect members to the House of Commons in Ottawa. As well, they are represented by six members in the Senate of Canada; the senators are appointed by the federal government.

At the provincial level, Albertans elect members to the Legislative Assembly of Alberta (the Alberta legislature). At the local level, Albertans elect councillors who administer their city, town, village, or district.

The number of members was increased over the years as the population increased. In Alberta's first years as a province, the people could elect 25 members to the provincial legislature and seven members to the House of Commons. By 1989 the numbers had risen to 83 provincial members and 26 federal. Similarly, four appointed senators in 1905 had been increased to six by the late 1980s. As well, Alberta was pressing for an elected Senate.

The Government of Alberta operates by the same laws, rules, and traditions as the federal government and the other provinces. These are described in the entries **Government** and **Parliament**. The legislative building is in Edmonton.

Politics Since the formation of the province in 1905, Albertans have followed a pattern of voting the same party into office election after election. The Liberals held power until 1921, when the

Celebration, Edmonton, as Alberta becomes a province in 1905 (by permission of the British Library).

United Farmers of Alberta (UFA) gained majority support. Albertans voted for the UFA because they thought the party would protect their interests against those of the big grain companies and railway companies.

During the hard times of the Great Depression, Albertans turned to the Social Credit Party to solve their problems. In 1935, William Aberhart, who was known to Albertans for his religious radio show, became premier at the head of a Social Credit government. Social Credit remained in power until the 1971 elections, when Peter Lougheed led the Progressive Conservatives to victory, winning 49 of the 75 seats in the Alberta legislature. Lougheed won his next 3 elections with overwhelming majorities partly because he, like Aberhart, seemed to stand up for Alberta's interests in Canada.

Premiers of Alberta 1905-89

	Party*	Term
Alexander Rutherford	Lib	1905-10
Arthur Lewis Sifton	Lib	1910-17
Charles Stewart	Lib	1917-21
Herbert Greenfield	UFA	1921-25
John Edward Brownlee	UFA	1925-34
Richard Gavin Reid	UFA	1934-35
William Aberhart	Socred	1935-43
Ernest Charles Manning	Socred	1943-68
Harry Edwin Strom	Socred	1968-71
Peter Lougheed	PC	1971-86
Donald Ross Getty	PC	1986-

*Abbreviations:
Lib=Liberal Party
UFA=United Farmers of Alberta
Socred=Social Credit Party
PC=Progressive Conservative Party

HISTORY

Alberta's history can be seen as four very different phases. The first was that of the native people, who settled in Alberta several thousand years ago. The second was that of the fur trade, which brought the first Europeans to the region. The third was the great settling of the prairie by farmers in the late 19th and early 20th century. The fourth was brought on by the discovery of immense oil reserves around Leduc in 1947.

The first European to reach Alberta was the fur trader Anthony Henday, who likely explored the vicinity of present-day Red Deer and Edmonton in 1754-55. He spent the winter with a group of Blackfoot, with whom he traded and went buffalo hunting.

The routes that the traders took into

Head-Smashed-In Buffalo Jump is a World Heritage Site. The Plains Indians of Alberta drove the bison herds over these cliffs (photo by Thomas Kitchin).

Alberta followed the rivers. The northern route came by Lake Athabasca. Its main depot was Fort Chipewyan, built near the mouth of the Athabasca River in 1788 for the North West Company (NWC). The second route came by the Saskatchewan River to Fort Edmonton, at the site of the future city of the same name. A third centre was set up at Rocky Mountain House in 1799, near the mountain pass that led to British Columbia.

The fur trade opened Alberta and made it known to Europeans. In the 1790s and early 1800s, David Thompson made the first good maps of the Alberta region as he explored and surveyed for the NWC. However, the fur trade brought very few permanent settlers to Alberta.

The Missionaries In 1821 the NWC merged with the Hudson's Bay Company (HBC), and the HBC took control of the whole Northwest. The company tried to keep out settlers, but it allowed missionaries to move in. Alberta's first missionary was Robert Rundle, a Methodist, who arrived at Fort Edmonton in 1840. The first Roman Catholic missionary was Jean-Baptiste Thibault, who arrived at Lac Sainte Anne in 1842. Some of Alberta's future towns were built at mission sites; for example, Albert Lacombe's mis-

Thatched Cottage *near Hilliard, Alberta, 1917. John Gavinchuk sits reading a newspaper outside his plastered cottage. These cottages were common in Alberta until a larger, wooden house could be built (courtesy PAA/UV4).*

Alberta: Time Line

1754　Anthony Henday is the first European to reach Alberta

1788　Fort Chipewyan is established as a fur trade post

1821　Hudson's Bay Co (HBC) gains control of the whole Northwest

1872　After the Northwest is turned over to Canada in 1870, the area is opened for settlement

1876　First ranchers arrived

1882　Alberta, part of the North-West Territories, is divided into the district of Athabasca in the north and the district of Alberta in the south

1897　Clifford Sifton begins his successful "Last Best West" campaign to attract settlers to the region

1905　Alberta is made a province

1914　The first oil strike

1930s　Great Depression causes great hardship in the province, which relies heavily on agriculture

1947　Major oil discovery at Leduc

1950-
1980　More oil is found bringing prosperity to the province

1982-
1986　Oil prices collapse ending the period of growth

1988　Calgary hosts the Winter Olympics

sion at St Albert, which is now a historic site.

Law and Order In 1870 the entire Northwest was turned over to Canada by the HBC. In 1872, the region was opened for settlement. To support its claim to the Northwest and to keep law and order in the region, the Canadian government formed the North-West Mounted Police (NWMP) in 1873. The Mounties established their first post in Alberta in 1874 at Fort Macleod.

American whisky traders had moved into the region to sell whisky to the native people. One of the first tasks the Mounties faced was to control this trade. The way of life of the plains tribes had virtually been destroyed by the overhunting of the buffalo, largely brought on by the fur trade. In a series of treaties, the original inhabitants gave up almost all their land and moved onto their reserves, where government agents provided food.

Settlement and Growth Settlement remained slow even after the railway arrived in Calgary in 1883. In 1881 there were only about 1000 non-native settlers; ten years later there were still only 17 500. The most successful settlers were the ranchers, who found the foothills ideal ranching country. The first cattle were brought in by American cowboys in 1876. The federal government opened the land to ranchers at the very time when American ranchers were losing their land to wheat farmers. Most of the big ranchers were English, but the American cowboys brought their skills — and their sometimes riotous behaviour. Many early ranchers were former members of the NWMP.

Settling the prairie was more difficult. Large-scale settlement did not occur until land was no longer available in the American West and immigrants began to look

north. In 1897, Canada's minister of the interior, Clifford Sifton, began a massive advertising campaign in Europe to encourage people to come to the West. The result was spectacular. Alberta's population grew to 73 000 in 1901; to 374 000 in 1911; and to 588 000 in 1921!

Roughing it out through bitter winters in sod huts or flimsy frame shacks, the newcomers transformed the open grassland. Hamlets popped up at crossroads and were strung along the railway lines like beads on a necklace. Edmonton won out over Calgary for the provincial capital, but both towns grew rapidly. The new province had an early taste of bitterness against the federal government, because when Alberta was made a province in 1905, it was not given control of its own resources, as had been the case with the older provinces. Alberta finally was given control 25 years later, but the anger remained. Meanwhile, the farmers resented the railways and the banks, which controlled their lives but were centered in the East.

Alberta suffered particularly in the Great Depression of the 1930s. Droughts, grasshopper plagues, and soil erosion drove many farmers from the land. Even harder to bear were the falling prices of wheat, which left many farmers bankrupt.

Alberta's destiny was changed forever in 1947, when a major oil discovery was made at Leduc, near Edmonton. As more and more discoveries were made, royalties flowed to the provincial government. Jobs were created in the petrochemical industry and in surveying, construction, transportation, and other areas. Edmonton and Calgary emerged as prosperous centres of business and finance, dwarfing their prairie neighbours.

The Alberta boom lasted into the 1980s, when falling oil prices brought business to a halt. Unemployment rose and people began to leave the province. Once again Albertans felt the weakness of relying on resources, which could disappear or lose their value. The Alberta Heritage Savings Trust Fund was set up in the boom time to deal with such a rainy day. Only time would tell if it would be enough.

For information about Alberta, contact the Alberta Public Affairs Bureau, 10044 - 108 Street (2nd floor), Edmonton, Alta, T5J 3S7. For questions about agriculture, contact Agriculture in the Classroom, J.G. O'Donoghue Building (2nd floor), 7000 - 113 Street, Edmonton, Alta, T6H 5T6.

▷ SUGGESTED READING: Dave Cunningham, *Alberta Album: The Living Past* (1985); W.G. Hardy, *Alberta: A Natural History* (1967); James G. MacGregor, *A History of Alberta* (1981); Rosemary Neering, *Historic Alberta* (1987).

■ Alberta, District of

This was the name, between 1882 and 1905, for most of the southern portion of what is now the province of Alberta. Since 1870, the region had been part of the North-West Territories. When four new "provisional districts" were formed in the territories in 1882, Governor General the Marquis of Lorne was asked to name one of them. He chose Alberta after his wife, Princess Louise Caroline Alberta. The name was retained when the province of Alberta was formed in 1905. *See* **North-West Territories.**

■ Alcoholic Drinks

Alcoholic drinks, such as beer, wine, and whisky, contain a chemical known as ethyl alcohol or, simply, alcohol.

Producing alcoholic drinks, especially beer, is a major industry in Canada. Taxes on alcoholic drinks and on their sales are important sources of money for the provincial and federal governments.

Consumption of Alcohol Alcoholic drinks have been popular for thousands of years. Alcohol is a drug that acts on the brain, giving a feeling of well-being.

Most alcohol is drunk in small quantities from time to time. It is taken with meals or at parties. If it is taken in excessive amounts, alcohol is addictive and causes a great deal of pain and often death.

Beer is the alcoholic drink Canadians prefer. On average, an adult Canadian drinks about 8 litres of spirits, 12 litres of wine, and more than 100 litres of beer every year. This is a lot of beer, but much less than the nearly 150 litres per year that the world's leading beer drinkers, the Germans, drink.

The combined alcoholic consumption by Canadians amounts to about 10 litres of pure alcohol per adult each year. About half of this is consumed in the form of beer. About a third is consumed in the form of spirits.

BEER

Beer is one of the oldest known man-made drinks. The ancient Egyptians drank it.

Beer is made from barley. First the starch in this grain is converted to sugar and mixed with water. This sweet solution is then boiled with hops, the flowers of a climbing plant, which give the beer its smell and flavour. Then yeast is added, and the mixture is left for about seven days.

During this time, the mixture ferments. That is, the tiny, living organisms we know as yeast turn sugar into alcohol. Alcohol comprises about 5% of the volume of most beers.

The kind of yeast used determines the kind of beer produced. Most beers are lagers, which are light in taste. Lager beer is produced by yeast that sinks to the bottom of a liquid. Ale, which is stronger in flavour, is made with a kind of yeast that floats. In Nova Scotia and Quebec, ale is the preferred drink. In the rest of Canada, lager is preferred.

The Brewing Industry Many of the early settlers of Canada drank "firewater," strong alcoholic drinks such as rum from the West Indies. French officials built Canada's first commercial brewery in 1668 in Quebec City. One of their reasons for doing so was to make a mild alcoholic drink generally available.

Making beer is one of the oldest industries in Canada. Breweries, such as the Montreal brewery of John Molson, were the foundation of some of the greatest fortunes made in Canada.

Gradually, during the 19th and 20th centuries, the large firms swallowed up the small independent breweries. Today, Canada's brewing industry is dominated by two main firms. The largest of these is Molson Breweries of Canada Ltd, with Labatt Brewing Company Ltd a close rival.

Beer is a large industry in Canada. Some 20 000 people work directly for the brewing industry. As well, an estimated 160 000 people work at jobs that depend on beer. These people include farmers who grow barley, truckers who distribute beer, and bartenders who serve it.

Canada is one of the largest exporters of beer in the world. Eight percent of Canadian production is exported each year, particularly to the United States.

In the mid-1980s a number of small breweries were established to serve local markets.

WINE

Wine is likely the oldest form of alcoholic drink. It is primarily made from grapes, which require very special conditions for growing. These conditions of climate and soil are found in only three small regions of Canada: the Niagara Peninsula of Ontario, the Okanagan Valley of British Co-

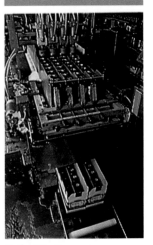

Labatt's Brewery, *London, Ont. (photo by Peter Christopher/Masterfile).*

lumbia, and the Annapolis Valley of Nova Scotia.

The most important area is the Niagara Peninsula, where wine has been made since 1800. Canada's largest winery, T.G. Bright and Company Ltd, was founded here in 1874. The British Columbia wine industry is centered in the Okanagan Valley. Production began here in the late 1920s. Grapes are also grown in the Annapolis Valley, but the wine industry there is very small.

Consumption of wine has increased in Canada since the 1960s. Most of this wine is imported, but Canadian wines have steadily improved in quality. Today, the industry employs 2000 people and supports 4000 grape growers.

Canadian winemakers are unlikely to be able to survive when tariffs are eliminated on American wines. Areas such as California produce excellent wines for a lower cost.

SPIRITS

Spirits, such as whisky, are made by distilling fermented drinks. To distill a liquid means to boil it and then turn the steam back to liquid. This concentrates the alcohol content. Most spirits contain between 40% and 50% alcohol by volume, compared to wine, which contains between 8% and 14%.

Distilled drinks popular in Canada include rum, made from sugar cane, and whisky, made from barley and other grains.

In the 19th century, millers began to make whisky from grain for which they had no other use. Some of the main distilling firms in Canada, such as Hiram Walker, began operation in the middle of the 19th century.

Canadian whisky became popular in the U.S., particularly during and after the period of Prohibition. During and after World War I, laws in both Canada and the U.S. prohibited making or selling alcohol. In the U.S., Prohibition was stricter and lasted longer than in Canada. Along the borders between "wet" Canada and "dry" U.S., alcohol smugglers, or "rum runners," carried liquor to the U.S.

A Canadian distilling firm, The Seagram Company Ltd, made enormous amounts of money selling its stocks of aged whisky in the U.S. Seagram's profits laid the foundation for one of the largest financial empires in Canada, that of the Bronfman family. Seagram is one of the ten largest companies in Canada, and the largest distilling firm in the world.

Distilleries in Canada employ about 4400 workers directly, and support about another 17 600 jobs.

The Canadian distilling industry sells over 40% of what it produces, particularly whisky, in other countries, mainly in the United States. During the 1980s, sales of distilled spirits in Canada have declined steadily.

Government and the Alcoholic Drinks Industry Governments in Canada tax alcoholic drinks heavily. They also profit from selling it through stores owned by provincial governments. The provincial and federal governments earn several billion dollars from taxes on alcoholic drinks.

The federal government restricts the amount and the kind of advertising of alcoholic drinks. Companies advertise their products mainly by sponsoring sporting events.

▷ RELATED ARTICLES: **Alcoholism; Bronfman Family; Sir John Carling; Drug Abuse; John Sackville Labatt; John Molson; Eugene O'Keefe.**

■ Alcoholism

Alcoholism is a set of problems resulting from a person regularly drinking too much alcohol.

Alcohol is found in beer, wine, and distilled spirits such as rum and whisky. It is absorbed rapidly into the bloodstream through the stomach wall and small intestine. From the blood, alcohol is distributed to all parts of the body. The effects of the alcohol vary from person to person, but they can generally be measured by its concentration in the blood. This measurement is called the "blood alcohol level."

After three typical drinks of an alcoholic beverage, an average adult male would have a blood alcohol level of 0.06%. The effect of this may vary from a mild sense of well-being to slight depression. In larger doses, alcohol has more serious effects. A level of 0.1% affects some motor areas of the brain. Speech is slurred, balance is unsteady, and reflexes are slow. A level of 0.2% depresses all the motor centres and has a serious effect on the emotions. A blood alcohol level of 0.45% may result in a coma, and 0.7% in death.

Alcohol taken in moderate amounts has no adverse effect on health. However, long-term heavy drinking can lead to addiction, to serious health problems, and even death. A change occurs in a person's body cells, which have become adapted to alcohol. A heavy drinker who tries to stop may suffer craving, shakiness, intense worry, nausea, seizures, and even hallucinations.

Several serious problems result from long-term heavy drinking. These include malnutrition, anemia, and a liver disease called cirrhosis. Drinking by pregnant women may also harm an unborn child, causing mental defects or physical deformities. Alcohol abuse probably costs industry over $2 billion per year in lost production.

One of the most serious effects of heavy drinking is drunk driving. About 3000 Canadians die each year in accidents involving drunk drivers. Alcohol is also frequently a factor in deaths from falls, fires, and drowning, and in crime.

About 80% of Canadian adults drink alcoholic beverages at least once in a while. Canadians consume relatively little wine compared to countries such as Italy and France, or beer compared to the Germans, but are among the leaders in drinking spirits.

About 2.5% of adult drinkers are alcoholics. This amounts to at least 500 000 people. Alcoholics are widely spread among the regions of Canada and among various groups.

Treatment The government tries to regulate the use of alcohol. It controls all the distribution and licensing. It restricts advertising. It is against the law to drive with blood alcohol levels above a certain point. Police have the power to stop drivers and demand breath samples. However, governments also reap a huge amount of money from taxing the sale of alcohol.

A variety of programs are available to treat alcoholism. Patients are treated in hospitals to get them through withdrawal, which can be very painful. They are later treated in clinics or halfway houses and retreats. It is estimated that the costs of alcoholism to the health-care system are about $6 billion per year.

Some treatments use a drug, such as Antabuse, which causes unpleasant reactions in the drinker. A group called Alcoholics Anonymous (AA) is a self-help group in which alcoholics help one another. Local Alcoholics Anonymous offices welcome inquiries from the public. Nevertheless, only about 10% of alcoholics receive treatment. Alcoholism is one of the most serious health problems in the modern world.

▷ RELATED ARTICLES: **Alcoholic Drinks; Drug Abuse.**

▷ SUGGESTED READING: Reginald G. Smart and A.C. Ogborne, *Northern Spirits: Drinking in Canada Then and Now* (1986); Rob Stepney, *Alcohol* (1987).

■ Alder

Alders (*Alnus*) belong to the birch family (Betulaceae). Except for the red alder (*A. rubra*), which grows to the size of a regular tree, alders are shrubs. They have outspread branches and a trunk that sometimes divides right from ground level. The large leaves, single- or double-toothed according to the species, have prominent veins. The male flowers form elongated, hanging spikes called "catkins." Female flowers are grouped into cone-shaped structures. These woody little cones, full of winged seeds, cling for a long time to the twigs. Alders usually grow near water, such as rivers, pools, or bogs. Since they need a great deal of light, they are often the first to appear in areas that have been cleared by a forest fire or logging. Alders seldom live very long but they are still useful since, wherever they grow, they prevent soil erosion and add nitrogen thanks to bacteria found in their roots. Wildlife also benefit from alders. Deer and moose graze their leaves and branches, while birds eat their seeds.

Speckled Alder, with male flowers (left), female flowers (centre), and cones (right). Alder wood is resistant to water and is used for bridge foundations (artwork by Claire Tremblay).

■ Alderdice, Frederick Charles

Politician (*born in 1872 at Belfast, Ireland; died in 1936 at St John's, Nfld*). Alderdice was twice prime minister of Newfoundland before it joined Canada in 1949. He served briefly in 1928, and again from 1932 to 1934. When he took office in 1932, as prime minister for the second time, Newfoundland was in deep economic distress and facing bankruptcy. He appealed to Britain for help. As a result, the independent government of Newfoundland was suspended, and Britain established a commission in its place. Alderdice was one of the three Newfoundlanders appointed to the commission, on which he served until his death.

▷ RELATED ARTICLE: **Commission of Government.**

■ Alderfly

Alderflies (family Sialidae) are cousins to Dobsonflies, with whom they form a small insect order called Megaloptera. (*Megale* means "large," and *pteron* means "wing.") Some 10 species are known in Canada, the most widespread being the *Sialis velata*, found from Quebec to British Columbia. These insects undergo a complete metamorphosis. They are usually less than 2.5 cm long. Adults have two pairs of strongly veined, membranous wings that fold over their bodies like a kind of roof when they are at rest.

Alderflies may be blackish or greyish in colour, sometimes with white spots. Their front wings have the same form and texture as their rear wings. They lay their eggs on vegetation overhanging water. Once hatched, the little larvae fall into the water. Aquatic and carnivorous, the larvae hunt tiny organisms in the water. In our temperate climates, they take two to three years to grow. They are the prey of both fish and fishermen (who use them for bait). The pupal stage is passed in a cell on land, but near water. Some species are found along moving water, some along still water. Adults do not feed. They live for a few days only, just long enough for reproduction.

■ Alderson, Sue Ann

Author, professor (*born in 1940 at New York City, U.S.*). Alderson attended Ohio State University before moving to Canada. Since 1980 she has taught creative writing at the University of British Columbia.

Her first book, *Bonnie McSmithers, You're Driving Me Dithers* (1975), describes the conflicts between a mother and her little girl. There are two sequels, *Hurry Up, Bonnie!* (1977) and *Bonnie McSmithers Is at it Again!* (1979). In *Comet's Tale* (1983), a novel, a zany family has a visit from a bossy aunt, tries to help a pound keeper who likes standing

Alderfly is a small insect found in freshwater near alder trees (artwork by Jan Sovak).

***Illustration** by Fiona Garrick of* Bonnie McSmithers, You're Driving Me Dithers, *by Sue Alderson. Fiona Garrick's pen and ink sketch is made to look like a child's drawing. She depicts the mess Bonnie has made of her dress while playing in a mud puddle, and the frustration and annoyed feelings of her mother (courtesy Fiona Garrick).*

on his head, and awaits the appearance of Hartley's comet. *The Not Impossible Summer* (1983) recounts how Jenny learns to respect herself and her mother. The heroine of *Ida and the Wool Smugglers* (1987) bravely rescues a sheep and its two lambs. Alderson's stories are notable for their humorous incidents and understanding of conflicts between children and parents.

■ Alert

Alert is a military base at the northern tip of Ellesmere Island in the High Arctic region of the Northwest Territories. The base opened in 1958 when the military took over a government weather station. Alert is the most northerly permanent settlement in the world. It can only be reached by air.

■ Alexander, Lincoln MacCauley

Lawyer, politician, lieutenant-governor of Ontario (*born in 1922 at Toronto, Ont.*). Born of West Indian parents, Lincoln Alexander grew up in Ontario and served in the Royal Canadian Air Force during World War II. He then practised law before being elected to Parliament in 1968. He sat in the House of Commons as a Conservative (1968-80) and was minister of labour in Joe Clark's government (1979-80). He then served as chairman of the Workers' Compensation Board of Ontario until 1985, when he was appointed lieutenant-governor of Ontario.

Lincoln Alexander was appointed lieutenant-governor of Ontario in 1985 (courtesy Office of the Lieutenant-Governor).

Algae are found wherever light and water are present. These algae are on the rocky B.C. coast (photo by J.A. Kraulis).

During his life of public service, Lincoln Alexander has worked to build harmony among Canada's many cultural groups.

■ Algae

The first algae appeared in the ocean about three billion years ago, and were at the origin of the entire Plantae kingdom. Some unicellular algae are visible only under a microscope; others, such as giant kelp, form organisms up to 100 m long.

Algae are divided, according to their pigment and cell structure, into Rhodophyta, Chromophyta, and Chlorophyta. The Cyanophyta (blue-green algae) are not, strictly speaking, algae: like bacteria, they belong to the Monera kingdom.

The membranes of some red algae (Rhodophyta) contain calcium carbonate and build up into living coral reefs.

Chromophyta, which are yellow-brown in colour, include diatoms (an important part of phytoplankton), *Fucus* (rockweed), and *Laminaria* (kelp).

The Chlorophyta, or green algae, are the most varied: some are unicellular (for example, *Chlamydomonas*); others have filaments (for example, *Spirogyra*); others form colonies (for example, *Volvox*); others are leafy (for example, *Ulva*).

Algae play an important role in maintaining life on this planet by absorbing carbon dioxide and releasing oxygen through the process of *photosynthesis*. In both freshwater and saltwater, algae are the first link in the food chain.

Common places where you can find al-
gae are in a fish tank (either green or brown depending on the amount of light); in seaweeds along Canada's coastline, particularly the west coast; and in quiet lakes or ponds as a blue or green tinge of the water or a green covering on rocks.

Red Tide near Vancouver Island. Phytoplankton is a kind of algae which can form a "red tide." It produces a toxin that may be harmful if shellfish feed on the algae and are then eaten by birds or mammals (photo by Janet Dwyer/First Light).

Algae *The three main types of algae are brown (left), red (middle), and green (right) (artwork by Claire Tremblay).*

■ Algonquin

The word Algonquin is applied, in different spellings, to a native language (Algonquian), to a broad cultural group (Algonkian), and to a particular tribe (Algonquin).

The Algonquin tribe live in western Quebec and nearby Ontario. They were nomadic hunters who lived in bands, consisting of related families. They were early allies of the French in the fur trade. In the 19th century they moved onto reserves. They have recently joined with the Cree and others to work for the survival of their traditional way of life. *See* **Native People: Eastern Woodlands.**

Algonquin Portage The birchbark canoe of the Algonquin was ideal for travelling rivers and lakes separated by narrow watersheds (by permission of Gerald Lazare and Lewis Parker and the National Wildlife Federation).

■ Algonquin Provincial Park

Algonquin Park is the oldest provincial park and one of the largest parks in Canada. Its 7653 km² lie on the southern edge of the Canadian Shield, between Georgian Bay and the Ottawa River. It is a huge tract of forest, lake, and rivers larger than the province of Prince Edward Island. It takes its name from the Algonquin Indians, who lived there for over 1000 years.

Loggers moved into the area in the 1830s to cut down the great pine trees. By the time the park was created in 1893, most of the pine trees had been cut. Fires had ravaged huge areas. The park was not created, therefore, to preserve the original environment. Rather, it serves as a wildlife sanctuary and recreation area. Despite opposition from conservationists, logging continues today in the park.

Algonquin lies in a zone between northern and southern forests. It is therefore home to both northern animals, such as wolves, moose, and fishers, and southern animals, such as raccoons and white-tailed deer. Other animals include beavers, squirrels, bears, and porcupines. The park is a delight for birdwatching and sportfishing. Zoologist Douglas Pimlott was almost single-handedly responsible for saving the park's wolves. More people have likely heard the wolves' famous howl in Algonquin than anywhere else.

The park has two packing trails and several shorter walking trails. There is a vast network of canoe routes among the park's many rivers and lakes.

■ Allan, Sir Hugh

Shipowner, businessman (*born in 1810 at Saltcoats, Scotland; died in 1882 at Edinburgh, Scotland*). Allan immigrated to Montreal at the age of 16 and found employment with the help of relatives. In the 1850s, with money from Scotland, he established a shipping company in Montreal, which in 1856 gained the contract to carry mail across the Atlantic. Quick to adopt technological improvements, such as steam engines (instead of sails) and screw propellers (instead of paddle wheels), the shipping line was a great success. Allan's ships were well known until after the turn of the century, with their characteristic names, *Sardinian, Sarmatian,* and *Hungarian.*

Allan also invested in railways. He wanted the contract to build the Canadian Pacific Railway, which the Canadian government had promised British Columbia when it joined Canada in 1871. Allan was not very scrupulous about how he got the contract, and during the 1872 elections he gave about $350 000 in campaign funds to Sir John A. Macdonald and other Conservatives. This brought on the Pacific Scandal, which caused the Macdonald government to fall from office. It also lost Allan the railway contract. But Allan was hurt only a little by the affair. He had so many other financial interests that he could ride out political storms.

Allan's financial network included the Montreal Telegraph Company and the Merchants' Bank of Canada. In his time he was the richest man in Montreal. He lived in a huge house on the slopes of Mount Royal. He called the house Ravenscrag, and for many years it dominated the Montreal landscape as he had dominated the city's finances.

▷ RELATED ARTICLES: **Pacific Scandal; Shipbuilding.**

■ Allen, Bruce

Rock promoter, manager (*born in 1945 at Vancouver, B.C.*). Allen is probably the most successful manager in the history of Canadian rock music. He has been responsible for the careers of Prism, Red Ryder, Bachman-Turner Overdrive, Powder Blues, and others. He co-manages Loverboy and is the sole manager of Bryan Adams. Allen's strategy is to tour new performers with better-known acts. He helped co-ordinate "Tears Are Not Enough," Canada's famine relief record.

■ Allergy

An allergy is an abnormally sensitive reaction of the body to substances such as pollen from ragweed, grass and other plants, dander from a pet's fur, household dust, some industrial chemicals, some medicines, insect venom, and certain foods. Common allergic reactions include itching and other kinds of skin irritation, breathing difficulties, coughing, sneezing, and watering of the eyes. In an allergic reaction, the immune system — whose job it is to defend our bodies against infection — overreacts, attacking substances that most people tolerate.

About 17% of all Canadians suffer from allergic diseases such as hay fever and asthma. Allergies to ragweed pollen occur mainly in the eastern provinces of Canada; allergies to grass pollens occur throughout Canada; allergies to western red cedar occur mainly in B.C.

If the substance that causes the allergic reaction (it is known as an allergen) cannot be avoided, the treatment usually involves drugs, which help but do not cure

the allergic person. Allergy injections may be helpful to reduce the sensitivity to allergies.

By learning more about the mechanisms of allergy, medical researchers are striving to improve treatment.

■ Alligator Pie

When Dennis Lee, an editor and poet, began reading nursery rhymes to his children, he wished there were some about Toronto in the 1960s, a place and time to which his children could relate. There were none, so he decided to create some. After he had written several rhymes, he put them together in a book, *Wiggle to the Laundromat* (1970). He wrote many more which he added to the collection and published them as *Alligator Pie* (1974), considered to be the best-selling Canadian children's poetry book of all time. Children like the strong rhythms and enjoy hearing poems about things they know, such as hockey sticks and highrises. There are rhymes about Canadian towns, songs, a former prime minister, and Ookpik, the Arctic owl, as well as skipping songs with Canadian references in them. Frank Newfeld, a well-known artist and book designer, created illustrations, and he and the author toured Canada, reading and drawing pictures of the poems for thousands of children and parents. Newfeld and Lee collaborated on two other books of children's poetry,

Sir Hugh Allan's *business empire included steamship lines, railways, telegraph companies, and a bank (courtesy NAC/C-26668).*

The poem "In Kamloops" *from* Alligator Pie, *by Dennis Lee, illustrated by Frank Newfeld, 1974 (used by permission of Macmillan of Canada).*

In Kamloops

In Kamloops
I'll eat your boots.

In the Gatineaus
I'll eat your toes.

In Napanee
I'll eat your knee.

In Winnipeg
I'll eat your leg.

In Charlottetown
I'll eat your gown.

In Crysler's Farm
I'll eat your arm.

In Aklavik
I'll eat your neck.

In Red Deer
I'll eat your ear.

In Trois Rivières
I'll eat your hair.

In Kitimat
I'll eat your hat.

And I'll eat your nose
And I'll eat your toes
In Medicine Hat and
Moose Jaw.

Almighty Voice died in a shootout after a 19-month manhunt. He was wanted for killing a North-West Mounted Police sergeant (courtesy Glenbow Archives/ NA-2310-1).

Characteristics of Aluminum
Formula: Al
Appearance: A silvery metal when refined
Properties: non-magnetic, light, strongly resistant to corrosion, good conductor of heat and electricity, has a density one-third that of steel; melting point is 660°C
Atomic weight: 26.981
Uses: in manufactured products include doors, window frames, house siding, beverage cans, foil, cooking utensils, and electrical wiring; it is the principal metal in aircraft

Nicholas Knock and Other People (1974), and *Garbage Delight* (1977).

Alline, Henry

Preacher and evangelist (*born in 1748 at Newport, Rhode Island; died in 1784 at North Hampton, New Hampshire, U.S.*). Between 1776 and 1783, Henry Alline led a religious revival in the Maritimes, known as the New Light movement.

Alline was the son of New Englanders who in 1760 had moved to Falmouth, Nova Scotia. Deeply religious, Alline believed that he had been personally called by God to inspire others with his faith and thus bring them the "New Light." Travelling by boat, horse, or snowshoes, depending on the season, he preached in almost every pioneer community of the Maritimes, often holding his services out of doors. His stirring sermons were accompanied by hymns, many of which he had written himself.

The New Light movement was very popular with the settlers; but the clergy disapproved, for Alline had no official qualifications. Nor did he follow any church doctrine. Instead, he stressed personal experience — that people should feel "born again" with a new commitment to Jesus. The movement relied greatly on Alline's personal magnetism, and it lost its impetus after he died of tuberculosis at the age of 36.

▷ SUGGESTED READING: J.M. Bumsted, *Henry Alline 1748-1784* (1984).

Alma

Alma, Que., lies beside the Saguenay River near Lac Saint-Jean, north of Quebec City. Lumbering and farming began in 1860. The town really boomed in the 1920s when a new hydro station provided power for a local paper mill and the aluminum plant at nearby Arvida. Since World War II, Alma has had its own aluminum works as well. The city is an important business and government centre in the Saguenay-Lac Saint-Jean region. In July a rowing festival, Festirame, attracts tourists. The 1986 population was 25 923.

Almighty Voice

Cree warrior (*born in 1874 near Batoche [Saskatchewan]; died there in 1897*). Almighty Voice grew up on One Arrow Reserve, near Batoche. In 1895 he was arrested for stealing a steer or a cow (the stories vary). Soon afterwards he escaped, but he shot and killed Sergeant Colebrook, the Mountie who came after him. This started a major manhunt, which continued for 19 months. Almighty Voice

was eventually traced to a small poplar bluff near his reserve. There, along with two relatives (one of whom was only 13), he held out for two days. The Mounties brought in more than 100 police and local volunteers, as well as two heavy guns. They bombarded the woods with cannon fire for four hours. Two Mounties and the local postmaster were killed before the battle was over. Almighty Voice and his companions lay dead.

Almonte

Almonte, Ont., is a town beside the Mississippi River, 48 km southwest of Ottawa. A scenic waterfall has provided power for flour, lumber, and textile mills since the town was founded in 1819. The origin of the name is very unusual. It was chosen in 1856 to honour a Mexican general, Juan Almonte, who was a well-known champion of Mexican independence at the time. Almonte grew as a centre for producing woolen textiles. Its population in 1986 was 4122.

Altman, Sidney, *see* Nobel Prize

Aluminum

Aluminum is a silvery metal with many useful properties. Though light in weight, it is strong. It does not rust. It is a good conductor of electricity and heat. Aluminum is used in storm doors and windows, cans, aircraft, wires, pots and pans, and many other things. Next to iron and steel, it is the most widely used metal in the world. Canada is a leading producer of aluminum, but the metal is not found in Canada. Aluminum is the most common metal in the Earth's crust, but it is always mixed with other things. The main source of aluminum is bauxite, which is found in tropical countries.

Canada has the abundant electricity

Aluminum The white powder (called alumina) shown here is produced from bauxite. Alumina is reduced to aluminum metal through a powerful electrical process (courtesy Alcan Aluminum Ltd).

needed to extract aluminum from bauxite. First, pure aluminum is separated from the bauxite in a refinery. Then the metal is produced by passing an electric current through it. Pure aluminum is soft. It may be hardened by the addition of alloys such as copper. There are seven aluminum smelters in Quebec, and one in British Columbia. All are located near large hydroelectric power dams.

In 1987, Canada produced about 12% of all the world's aluminum. About three-quarters of the aluminum Canada produces is shipped to other countries, mainly to the United States. Canada exports more aluminum than any other country in the world.

The main company producing aluminum is Alcan Aluminum Ltd.

▷ RELATED ARTICLE: **Hydroelectricity.**

■ Ambassadors and Embassies

Ambassadors are the senior representatives (diplomats) of a government in foreign countries. Embassies are the places where they live and work. Ambassadors represent the interests of their country abroad.

They provide information to the government at home about what is going on in the country to which they have been sent. They also protect the property and rights of Canadian citizens travelling or living abroad. Ambassadors are normally "accredited" by the head of state of a foreign country. This means that they are officially recognized as having special status and duties.

The exchange of ambassadors is a way in which one country accepts another country's independence and international rights. To ensure the freedom of the ambassador and staff in carrying out their business, the embassy is considered not to be on foreign soil but to be part of the diplomat's own country. The ambassador can give someone refuge (called "diplomatic asylum") in the embassy when there is public unrest or when lives are threatened.

Canada has ambassadors in foreign capitals and at certain international bodies, such as the United Nations in New York and at NATO in Brussels, Belgium. Because of the special relationship among Commonwealth countries, they have high commissioners rather than ambassadors. Canada set up a high commission in London, England, in 1880. Canada exchanged ministers — a junior form of ambassador — with the United States (1927), France (1928), and Japan (1929). In those

The New Canadian Embassy *occupies a favoured site in Washington, D.C., to reflect Canada's special relationship with the United States. The building was designed by Canadian architect Arthur Erickson (courtesy Arthur Erickson Architects).*

days, the top jobs usually went to the rich (who were able to help out with funds for diplomatic buildings) and to the well-connected. However, the Department of External Affairs also hired young professional diplomats, such as L.B. Pearson, who would themselves be ambassadors in the future. During World War II, with Canada's independence and importance in the world increasing, the minister in Washington, D.C., became a full-fledged ambassador (1943), Canada's first such appointment.

■ American Civil War

The northern and southern states of the United States fought a terrible civil war from 1861 to 1865. The southern states broke away from the United States and formed the Confederacy. The conflict had many causes, one of which was the use of slaves in the South. The North was victorious.

The war played an important part in the development of Canada. Britain and its North American colonies remained neutral throughout the conflict, although Canadians, while not approving of slavery, generally hoped for a Southern victory. The Northern government, in Washington, knew of these sympathies, and was angered by them. Some Canadians feared that Northern armies would invade Canada to punish its citizens for their apparent support for the Southern cause. Washington did not deny the possibility. Suspicions on both sides led to four serious incidents.

The Alabama Incident A Confederate ship, the *Alabama*, was built in Britain. This angered the government of the North, particularly because the *Alabama* sank many Northern ships. The Ameri-

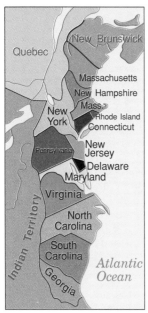

The American Colonies, 1775

Death of General Montgomery This engraving shows the American attack on Quebec on New Year's Eve, 1775. The attack failed and cost the life of the American general (courtesy NAC/C-46334).

cans demanded compensation from Britain. At one point, Americans suggested that the compensation be paid by giving Canadian territory to the U.S. The dispute was settled in 1872, with Britain paying the U.S. $15.5 million.

The Trent Incident The most serious crisis of the war occurred in November 1861. Sailors from the American ship *San Jacinto* boarded the British merchant ship *Trent* in neutral waters. They removed two Confederate commissioners who were on their way to Europe. Britain was outraged at this breach of neutrality. It prepared for war and sent troops to reinforce the border garrisons in Canada and the Maritime colonies. The U.S. returned the two men, and the crisis passed.

The Chesapeake Incident In December 1863, 16 Confederates seized the American steamer *Chesapeake* off Cape Cod. They took it to Saint John, N.B., and then tried to get to Halifax, N.S. When the U.S. navy recaptured the ship — in Sambro Harbour, just south of Halifax — there were two Nova Scotians on board. The incident showed the hostility that many Maritimers felt towards the North.

The St Albans Raid In October 1864 a group of Confederates, who had taken refuge in Canada East, raided St Albans in Vermont. They then fled back over the border. Northern troops followed the Confederates onto Canadian soil. The raiders were arrested by Canadian police. However, the Montreal magistrate found a reason for releasing them.

THE EFFECTS ON CANADIAN CONFEDERATION

These four incidents left a feeling of distrust between the Northern states and

Britain. This tense atmosphere contributed to the cancellation of the Reciprocity Treaty in 1866. This agreement had encouraged trade between the Canadian colonies and the U.S. The colonies now had to look to one another to make up for the lost trade.

Many Canadians feared that the victorious Northern armies would be turned against Canada. If the colonies were united, they would be better able to defend themselves. These fears were strongest after the war ended in 1865 and therefore played an important part in the timing of Confederation.

The leaders who drew up the Canadian Constitution regarded the Civil War as a lesson. John A. Macdonald, for example, believed that the American Constitution gave too much power to the states, and that this had caused the war. He argued for a stronger central government in Canada to prevent such a break-up. Thus, the Civil War influenced Canada's system of government.

▷ RELATED ARTICLES: **Confederation; Reciprocity Treaty.**

■ American Colonies

The American Colonies, also known as the Thirteen Colonies, were the British colonies that broke away from Britain during the American Revolution and formed the United States.

■ American Revolution

The American Revolution (1775-83) was the war by which the Thirteen Colonies won independence from Great Britain and became the United States of America. The Canadian colonies (Quebec, Nova Scotia, and Prince Edward Island) were deeply affected by the war, which had a lasting influence on their future.

By the 1770s, Britain's American colonies were large prosperous communities with a strong tradition of running their own affairs. They also had a growing sense of separateness from the country that had founded them. Britain's conquest of New France in 1759-60 had removed the threat of French invasion. Meanwhile, the American colonists had serious disputes with the British government over their rights and the rights of their legislatures. The Quebec Act of 1774 was a further cause of anger. By enlarging the boundaries of Quebec, the Act prevented the Thirteen Colonies from expanding inland into the Ohio Valley.

THE REVOLUTIONARY WAR

In 1775 the arguments turned into fight-

The American Revolution

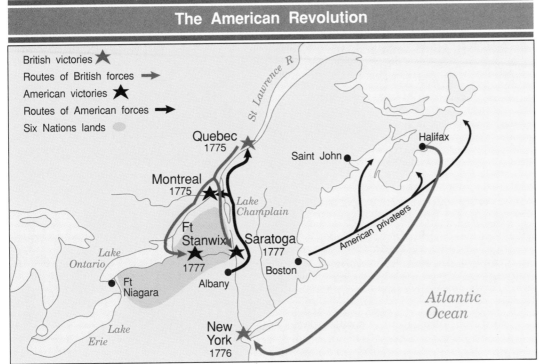

British victories ★
Routes of British forces →
American victories ★
Routes of American forces →
Six Nations lands ▮

St Lawrence R.

Quebec 1775
Montreal 1775
Lake Champlain
Ft Stanwix 1777
Saratoga 1777
Lake Ontario
Ft Niagara
Albany
Boston
Saint John
Halifax
American privateers
Lake Erie
New York 1776
Atlantic Ocean

ing. The Americans formed the Continental Congress and renounced their allegiance to Parliament. On July 4, 1776 (now celebrated as Independence Day in the U.S.), Congress approved the Declaration of Independence.

As soon as the fighting began, the American colonists (or Patriots, as they called themselves) tried to include the Canadian colonies in their revolution, both by persuasion and by invasion. In 1775 an army sent by Congress captured Montreal and laid siege to Quebec. On New Year's Eve, the Americans were defeated when they attempted to seize Quebec, and they were driven back to New York State early in 1776. They had expected to be welcomed by the people of Quebec, but most French Canadians, led by their seigneurs and the Church, remained neutral or were opposed to the rebellion.

In 1776 New England Patriots attempted to invade Nova Scotia. In spite of the close ties between Nova Scotians and New Englanders, most of the colonists remained loyal to Britain. Again the invaders were driven out. In the following years, American privateers raided the Nova Scotia coast and the Gulf of St Lawrence. Nova Scotian privateers fought back.

From Halifax, the Royal Navy directed naval warfare against the rebels. Halifax was an important British garrison and naval base throughout the war. Similarly, Montreal was the starting place for a British invasion of New York State in 1777. When the invasion failed disastrously, France joined the war on the side of the Americans. Commanders in Canada feared that France might use the war to regain possession of Quebec. British troops were therefore stationed at Quebec, Montreal, and all along the borders with the rebellious colonies.

From 1775 on, American Loyalists began coming to the Canadian colonies. Some sought safety. Others came to join loyal militia regiments and companies of rangers, such as Butler's Rangers. From Halifax, Saint John, Montreal, Niagara, and other cities and forts, these soldiers, along with native allies and British troops, defended the Canadian colonies and launched many raids into the rebel territory.

The Iroquois of northern New York were an important British ally in the fighting. They had originally intended to remain neutral; but Molly and Joseph Brant helped persuade most of the Six Nations of Iroquois to fight for the British in order to preserve their lands. In reprisal, American troops burned Six Nations towns and cornfields in 1779. For the rest of the war, most of the Iroquois were refugees around Fort Niagara.

RESULTS OF THE REVOLUTION

By 1781, after being beaten at Yorktown, Virginia, Britain admitted it could not defeat the rebellion. Negotiations began, and in the Treaty of Paris (1783) Britain recognized the independence of the United States. Thousands of Loyalists then had to leave the United States. About 40 000 of them, along with almost 2000 Iroquois, settled in Canada. So many settled in Nova Scotia that parts of the colony were divided off to form two new colonies: New Brunswick and Cape Breton (though Cape Breton again became part of Nova Scotia in 1820). In Quebec, the Loyalists were the first large group of English-speaking settlers. Most settled in the west of the colony, in the region which in 1791 became Upper Canada.

The American Revolution introduced powerful new ideas into the world. As a republic, the United States proclaimed that people could rule themselves without kings or princes. Even though they kept slaves, the revolutionaries proclaimed liberty and equality for all people. Few Americans could vote in the early republic, but the revolutionaries pointed the way towards democracy by arguing that the people could govern themselves.

Many Americans expected that Canada would accept these ideas and would either join the United States or be annexed by it. Preserving Canada from American invasion was a vital concern of Canadian political leaders until the mid-1800s.

▷ RELATED ARTICLES: **Loyalists; Quebec Act; Province of Quebec; Paris, Treaty of, 1783.**

▷ SUGGESTED READING: Alan Skeoch, *United Empire Loyalists and the American Revolution* (1982).

■ Amherst

Amherst, N.S., is a town at the head of the Cumberland Basin, on the narrow neck of land that separates Nova Scotia and New Brunswick. Shortly before World War I, Amherst developed into an important centre of industry, producing railway cars, pianos, footwear, and woolen goods. After the war, much of this industry left, and thousands of residents left to look elsewhere for jobs. Today, Amherst is the centre of a farming district and has some light industry. Tourism is also important. In 1986 the population was 9671. For information, contact the Town Clerk, P.O. Box 516, Amherst, N.S., B4H 4A1.

■ Amherst, Jeffery

British army officer (*born in 1717 near Sevenoaks, England; died near there in 1797*). Amherst was the British general who completed the conquest of New France during the Seven Years' War. He was sent to North America in the spring of 1758 with orders to capture Louisbourg, the French fortress on Île Royale (Cape Breton Island). "Slow but sure" was Amherst's policy. He planned the assault on Louisbourg with typical thoroughness, and the fortress fell to his forces on July 27, 1758. Promoted to commander-in-chief in America, Amherst later organized the three-pronged attack on Montreal (1760), which led to the city's surrender and the end of French rule. In 1763 he returned to England, where he rose to the rank of field marshal as well as being made a lord, 1st Baron Amherst.

▷ RELATED ARTICLE: **Seven Years' War.**

■ Amherstburg

Amherstburg, Ont., is a town on the Detroit River, across from the U.S., near Lake Erie. It was first settled in 1784. In 1796 Fort Malden was established here. During the War of 1812, it was captured by the Americans, and it was attacked and bombarded in the Rebellion of 1837. The fort has been partly restored and is a national historic park. Among other historic buildings are a beautiful mansion, built in 1819, and Christ Church, built in 1818. The population in 1986 was 8413.

■ Amiens, Battle of

The Battle of Amiens occurred at the end of World War I near Amiens, France. From August 8 to 11, 1918, Canadian soldiers led an attack which shattered the German forces. The battle began a period known as the One Hundred Days, during which the Germans suffered defeat after defeat and finally agreed to make peace. About 9000 Canadians were killed and wounded at Amiens.

▷ RELATED ARTICLE: **World War I.**

■ Amos

Amos, Que., lies at the heart of the Abitibi region of northwestern Quebec. The town was founded in 1914 although the influx of new settlers into the region had begun a few years earlier. Situated where the National Transcontinental Railway (now part of the CN system) crosses the Rivière Harricana, Amos has relied on farming and logging for its prosperity. It is also the site of a major paper mill. In 1986 the population was 9261.

■ Amphibian

Amphibians are a class of vertebrates consisting of the anura (frogs and toads), the caudata (salamanders and newts), and the gymnophiona (tropical worm-like burrowers). Their skin is naked, moist, and glandular, and in some amphibians it is poisonous as a defence against predators. They go through *metamorphosis* (change)

Green Frog in a pond. Frogs hatch as tadpoles with gills and without legs. A small mouth and hind legs appear and the tadpole lives on plants. Later the gills move inside, the tail disappears, and the mouth grows large to gulp whole creatures (artwork by Claire Tremblay).

Norwegian Explorer Roald Amundsen with some of the dogs he used in his explorations (by permission of the British Library).

The Maud made several voyages in Canada's Arctic under Amundsen's command from 1918 to 1925. It had especially heavy construction to survive the pressures of arctic ice (photo by H.R. Rokeby-Thomas).

from a larval, gill-breathing tadpole stage, into an adult stage when they breathe through their lungs and richly veined skin. Most live in moist surroundings since, unlike reptiles, they have little protection from dehydration. Amphibians are "cold-blooded"; their body temperature is determined by the surrounding environment. Some frogs are able to survive a freezing. Many anura come together in the water for mating purposes. The males have a distinctive song, which they use to attract females or to defend their territory. Salamanders, on the other hand, are silent but have complex courting rituals. Amphibians' eggs are usually laid in the water or in very moist places on land, but some tropical anura carry their eggs on their backs. Canada has 21 species of frogs and 19 of salamanders. Their sometimes large populations are an important part of the ecosystem. Anura tadpoles eat aquatic vegetation while the adults are carnivorous (and in turn fall prey to other predators). Amphibians are important to research and as an indicator of the quality of the environment.

▷ SUGGESTED READING: Francis R. Cook, *Introduction to Canadian Amphibians and Reptiles* (1984).

Amund Ringnes Island

Amund Ringnes Island is one of the Sverdrup Islands at the top of the Arctic Archipelago. Flat and windswept, it was discovered in 1900 by a member of the Norwegian Sverdrup expedition and named for a sponsor of the expedition. It is 5255 km² in area.

Amundsen, Roald

Explorer (*born in 1872 at Sarpsborg, Norway; died on a rescue mission to the North Pole in 1928*). Amundsen aban-

doned his medical studies for a life at sea. His real ambition was to be a polar explorer. As a young man in Norway, he ran, cycled, and skied to ready himself for the hard life he had chosen.

Explorers had searched for almost 300 years for the Northwest Passage through the arctic islands. In 1903 Amundsen set off in the small fishing boat, *Gjoa*, with six others to make the attempt. Travelling east to west, the explorers spent three winters in the ice before the *Gjoa* emerged safely on the other side of the Arctic in 1906. Amundsen had succeeded where so many others had failed.

Amundsen was also the first person to reach the South Pole (1911), after a long, exhausting trek across the wind-swept ice. In 1926, he took to the air and commanded the first airplane to fly over the North Pole. In 1928 he died at sea, flying to assist the search for an aviator who had crashed near the Pole.

▷ RELATED ARTICLE: **Northwest Passage.**

Amyot, Francis

Canoeist (*born in 1904 at Toronto, Ont.; died in 1962 at Ottawa, Ont.*). Amyot was a large man who needed a custom-made *shell* (racing canoe) and paddle. He paddled with a long, powerful stroke. He won a gold medal in the 1000 metre race at the 1936 Olympics in Berlin, Germany. He served in the Royal Canadian Navy in World War II.

Ancaster Assizes

The Ancaster Assizes were treason trials held at Ancaster, Upper Canada, in May and June of 1814. This was during the War of 1812. Nineteen men were tried, all settlers accused of siding with the Americans during the war. John Beverley Robinson was in charge of the prosecution, which led to eight of the men being hanged. The purpose of the trials was to set an example and prevent other settlers from going over to the Americans.

■ Anderson, Doris Hilda

Editor, author, broadcaster (*born in 1925 at Calgary, Alta*). Anderson was raised in Alberta and briefly taught school before becoming an editor. From 1958 to 1977 she was editor of *Chatelaine* magazine, which she changed dramatically. It had formerly been a "women's magazine," concentrating on beauty tips and recipes. With Anderson as editor, *Chatelaine* included a wide range of topics that were of interest to businesswomen as well as homemakers. The monthly sales of the magazine soared from 46 000 to one million.

After leaving *Chatelaine*, Anderson was president of the Canadian Advisory Council on the Status of Women (1979-81) and the National Action Committee on the Status of Women (1982-84). Meanwhile, she wrote two novels: *Two Women* (1978) and *Rough Layout* (1981). She has since continued to promote the cause of women, both as a broadcaster and a newspaper columnist. Her most recent book is *Affairs of State* (1988).

▷ Related Article: **Magazines.**

■ André, Brother

Roman Catholic religious figure, faith healer (*born Alfred Bessette in 1845 at St-Grégoire, Canada East [Quebec]; died in 1937 at Montreal, Que.*). Brother André was the son of a very poor Quebec family. Both his parents died before he was 12. He lacked money and education and he suffered from poor health. But he was very religious, and in 1870 the Brothers of the Holy Cross of Montreal accepted him as a novice. Four years later, he took his vows as a brother.

Brother André was given the position of doorkeeper at the Holy Cross school for boys in Montreal, the Collège Notre-Dame. This remained his position in the years that followed, even when he was the most famous religious figure in Quebec. Around 1877, he prayed to St Joseph in a ward where some schoolboys and priests were sick with smallpox. All of them recovered. This was attributed to Brother André's prayers.

As word of Brother André's faith heal-

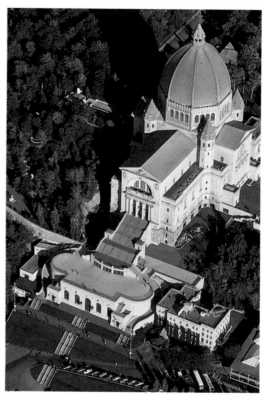

St Joseph's Oratory, *Montreal, attracts many pilgrims to where Brother André built a chapel to pray for the sick (photo by Aerocamera Services Inc., Orangeville, Ont.).*

ing spread, people came flocking to him for cures. "I do not cure," he told them. "St Joseph cures." In 1904 he built a small wooden chapel to St Joseph on the slopes of Mount Royal so that he could pray for the sick there. This was the beginning of the building that became St Joseph's Oratory. It is now a major pilgrimage site, visited by people seeking cures. About half a million pilgrims pray at the shrine each year.

In 1978 the Pope declared Brother André "Venerable," and this was followed by Brother André's beatification in 1982. These are the first two of three stages towards making someone a saint of the Roman Catholic Church.

■ Anemone

Anemone are herbaceous plants of the Ranunculaceae (buttercup) family. Most of the 120 to 150 anemone species are found in northern or arctic zones. Their common name, windflower, may refer to the windy locations where they grow, or to the origins of their name, *anemos*, which means "stroked by the wind." The pretty and usually solitary flower of the anemone is cup-shaped and without petals. The 5 to 20 sepals take a variety of colours. The fruit, carried on rounded heads, has a single seed. Of the American

Anemone, also called windflower, is found in subarctic areas across Canada (artwork by Claire Tremblay).

anemones, the Canada anemone (*A. canadensis*), with white flowers, is most widespread in moist locations and found everywhere in Canada except Newfoundland. The anemone popularly but incorrectly known as the prairie crocus (*A. patens*) has been Manitoba's official flower since 1906. Its lavender-tinted spread is a beautiful early sign of spring across the prairies. Japanese anemone (*A. hupehensis*) bloom in fall. Legend has it that the bright red of the florist's anemone (*A. coronaria*) comes from the drops of blood shed by Adonis (who was loved by Aphrodite, goddess of love) at his death. Anemones grow in well-drained, partially shaded spots. They are propagated by seed or by division.

■ Anglicanism

Anglicanism is one of the world's major Protestant religions. It stems from the Church of England, which was formed when King Henry VIII broke with the Roman Catholic Church during the Protestant Reformation of the 1500s. Until 1955, the Anglican Church of Canada was called the Church of England in Canada.

Unlike most other Protestant churches, the Anglican church has kept much of the ancient Catholic tradition. For example, it has a ministry of bishops, priests, and deacons, who are viewed as part of a spiritually linked chain of command dating back to the Apostles. In the United States and some other countries, Anglicans are called Episcopalians (which means "with bishops"). There are Anglicans throughout the world. Although each national Anglican Church is largely independent, all look to the Archbishop of Canterbury in England for leadership and guidance.

The first Anglican ministries in Canada were established at British outposts on the Atlantic seaboard in the early 1700s. (In fact, Canada's first Anglican church was built at St John's, Nfld, in 1712.) However, historians mark the real beginning of Anglicanism in Canada with the British conquest of Quebec (1759-60) and then the arrival of Loyalists in the 1780s, following the American Revolution.

The Rev. Charles Inglis, a prominent clergyman in New York before the American Revolution, was Canada's first Anglican bishop. In 1787 he was named Bishop of Nova Scotia, where he established King's College. His diocese included all of what are now the Atlantic Provinces, Quebec, and Ontario.

Today, Anglicans in Canada number about 2.4 million. Since the days of Bishop Inglis, the church has been active in education and has established or helped sponsor numerous schools and colleges.

▷ RELATED ARTICLES: **Clergy Reserves; Missionaries; John Strachan.**

■ Anglin, Margaret

Actress (*born in 1876 at Ottawa, Ont.; died in 1958 at Toronto, Ont.*). Anglin was for many years one of the most famous actresses in North America. Even her birth was dramatic. She was born in the Parliament Buildings, where her father, Timothy Anglin, was Speaker of the House of Commons. Like most Canadian actors of her day, she went to New York to establish her career. When she was only 22, she enjoyed great success there in *Cyrano de Bergerac*. Her stage career lasted for more than 50 years. At one time she had her own classical company, which specialized in plays by Shakespeare. She often performed in Canada, and her international reputation was so great that she made one tour to Australia.

▷ SUGGESTED READING: John Le Voy, *Margaret Anglin, A Stage Life* (1988).

■ Animal Stories

Stories in which animals are the main characters are of two types. In animal fantasies, animals can act, talk, and dress like human beings. By contrast, realistic animal stories are based on careful observation of wild animals.

Animals played important parts in the myths, legends, and folktales of the native people. These people believed that all created beings were equal because animals, as well as human beings, possessed spirits. Thus, the animals in the stories often acted like human beings. Christie Harris, in *Mouse Woman and the Vanished Princesses* (1976), and Kay Hill, in *Glooscap and His Magic* (1963), retell many native Indian animal myths and legends.

The first great animal fantasies were written in England around the end of the 19th century. Rudyard Kipling's *The Jungle Book*, Beatrix Potter's *The Tale of Peter Rabbit*, and Kenneth Grahame's *The Wind in the Willows* are stories about animals who have personalities like people. *Charlotte's Web*, by American writer E.B. White, is considered by many people to be the greatest of all animal fantasies.

There have been few Canadian animal fantasies. *Jason's Quest* (1970), by Margaret Laurence, is about a mole who seeks a cure for a mysterious sickness. *Hug Me* (1977), by Patti Stren, is the story of a lonely porcupine. *Zoom at Sea* (1983), by Tim Wynne-Jones, is about a water-loving cat. *Clyde* (1986), by Lindee Climo, is about a horse who feels neglected when his owner buys a new tractor.

Canadian authors were the first important writers of realistic animal stories. Ernest Thompson Seton, in *Wild Animals I Have Known* (1898), and Sir Charles G.D. Roberts, in *The Kindred of the Wild* (1902), carefully observed the habits of wild animals. They then wrote about strong, intelligent creatures who could almost be considered heroes. Later writers of realistic animal stories include Roderick Haig-Brown (*Ki-yu: A Story of Panthers*, 1934), Fred Bodsworth (*Last of the Curlews*, 1955), and Farley Mowat (*Never Cry Wolf*, 1963).

Pets have also been the subject of realistic novels. Margaret Marshall Saunders's *Beautiful Joe* (1894) is the "autobiography" of a dog who is rescued from a cruel master. The hero of Farley Mowat's *The Dog Who Wouldn't Be* (1957) seems to think that he is human. Sheila Burnford's *The Incredible Journey* (1961) is an account of the 400 km trek made across northern Ontario by two dogs and a cat.
▷ Suggested Reading: Muriel Whitaker, editor, *Great Canadian Animal Stories* (1982).

■ Animals

Animals are living things that can move about as they choose. Plants, the other major group of living things, cannot do this. (*See* entry on **Plants**.)

Evolution of Animals Over the three billion years since life began, plants and animals have slowly changed. The forms they take have become ever more varied and complex. Life has spread out to occupy most zones on Earth. For example, there are algae living in frigid arctic waters and in steaming hot springs.

Life began in the sea. There were plants long before there were any animals. The first kinds of animals to evolve were invertebrates — soft-bodied animals without backbones but with an external skeleton or shell, such as insects and shellfish.

Much later, animals with backbones evolved. These are called vertebrates. The first vertebrates were fish. Some fish developed lungs and left the water to live on land as amphibians. Then reptiles, birds, and mammals — including humans — evolved.

There are many millions of different kinds of animals on Earth. Thousands of species are discovered every year.

ANIMALS IN CANADA

Canadians share land, water, and air with some 200 other species of mammals, with some 600 kinds of birds, with over 80 kinds of amphibians and reptiles, with about 200 species of freshwater fish, and with about 100 000 kinds of insects and other invertebrate animals.

Some of these animals — fish such as the northern pike and the walleye, birds such as the Canada goose, mammals such as the beaver, the moose, muskrat, and black bear, insects such as the mosquito and the black fly — live nearly everywhere in Canada.

Other animals live only in limited areas, such as the forest, the tundra, the prairies, the coasts, the mountains, or the Great Lakes. Each of these areas has its own characteristic communities of animals and plants. Each of these areas, in other words, is an *ecosystem*.

North of the forest, in the treeless tundra, roam muskoxen (an animal found almost nowhere else but in Canada), as well as polar bears and the snowy owl.

Mountain goats, bighorn sheep, grizzly bears, and cougars are among the animals that are well adapted to the climate, shelter, and food available in the mountains of western Canada.

Life in A Cold Climate Animals that live in Canada have bodies or behaviour adapted to cope with the cold and snow of winter. For instance, the thickly feath-

The Ptarmigan's thickly feathered feet help it to cope with life in a cold climate (photo by Harry Savage).

ered feet of the ptarmigan, the densely furred paws of snowshoe hare and lynx, and the splayed hoof of the caribou all serve as snowshoes.

Many cold-blooded animals, those that cannot regulate their body temperature from within, such as insects and reptiles, go into a stupor in winter. Some insects even produce a kind of antifreeze to protect their cells.

Shrews and other small rodents keep warm in tunnels they dig beneath the snow.

A number of small, warm-blooded animals hibernate. Squirrels and bats, for instance, store fat in the fall, then enter into a kind of sleep. They breathe slowly, and their hearts pump slowly, saving their energy.

Only a few kinds of animals can survive the severe conditions in the Far North. Most are relatively large mammals, such as polar bear, which have thick insulating fur. Those that cannot adapt, such as some birds, migrate to warmer climates for the winter.

ENDANGERED ANIMALS

Humans are a threat to other animals. In Canada, hunters exterminated or endangered the existence of several animals in the last century. In our time, activities such as clearing land for farms, cutting down forests for wood, and polluting the air and water threaten to wipe out a number of animal species by destroying the plants and the environment on which they depend.

Organizations, such as the World Wildlife Fund, work to conserve endangered species such as the peregrine falcon and the wolverine.

USES OF ANIMALS

We use animals for, among other things, their fur, food, wool, leather, and feathers. We also get animals to work for us. Dogs,

Canada Goose *defends its nest from a striped skunk trying to steal its eggs (photo by Thomas Kitchin).*

for instance, have been used to pull sleds and guide blind people. Animals serve us as pets, as entertainers — in rodeos, circuses, and zoos — and as subjects for scientific experiments.

Wild Animals Canada's native people depended on wild animals for food, their skins for clothing and shelter, and their bones, antlers, etc. for tools and other uses.

Beaver furs and cod fish were the basis of the economy of the early European settlers in Canada. Wild animals are still being harvested for fur and for food. Every year, Canadian trappers kill about 3 million fur-bearing animals, such as beaver, fox, and muskrat, for their furs.

Wild animals, such as moose, deer, and birds, are hunted for sport. Sportfishing is a popular outdoor recreation in Canada.

Ruffed Grouse *"drumming" during its mating dance (photo by Thomas Kitchin).*

White-tailed Deer *flashes its tail to warn others of danger (photo by Thomas Kitchin).*

Domesticated Animals Each Canadian consumes an average of 100 kg of meat every year. Most of the meat produced in Canada comes from domesticated animals, such as cattle, chickens, and hogs.

Horses are also domesticated animals. Once they were the main source of power in Canada. Now they are used for riding, racing, and ranching.

Pets The most popular pets in Canada are cats, dogs, and horses. Pets provide companionship for humans. Dogs help handicapped people, such as the blind, to get around.

Humane societies exist in most Canadian cities. They help to protect animals by investigating complaints of cruelty. They operate shelters for lost and abandoned animals, mostly cats and dogs. Every year, they have to kill about 500 000 unwanted pets, mainly dogs and cats.

Animals and Science Because many of the diseases from which humans suffer are similar to those of animals, some scientists conduct medical experiments on animals. Insulin, which saves the lives of thousands of people by controlling diabetes, was discovered by giving the disease to dogs. Rabbits, rats, mice, and a number of other animals are used for research such as testing drugs and vaccines.

▷ RELATED ARTICLES: **Biology; Birds; Cats; Diabetes; Dogs; Endangered Wildlife; Fish; Horses; Invertebrates; Insects; Wildlife Conservation; Zoology.** There are also separate articles on most of Canada's animals.

▷ SUGGESTED READING: A.W.F. Banfield, *The Mammals of Canada* (1974); Adrian Forsyth, *Mammals of the Canadian Wild* (1985); the magazines *Ranger Rick* and *National Wildlife* are a good source of information about animals and current issues concerning them.

■ Anka, Paul

Singer, songwriter (*born in 1941 at Ottawa, Ont.*). He began performing at age 10 in amateur shows and on radio. His first hit single, "Diana," was released when he was only 15. It was one of the most successful records in pop music history, selling over 20 million copies. He continued with another 20 hit singles from 1957 to 1962. His singing career waned with changing tastes and he concentrated on writing songs. Over 400 of his songs have been recorded, including "My Way" by Frank Sinatra. He has sold over 100 million records, and continues to perform all over the world.

■ Anna Wyman Dance Theatre

The Anna Wyman Dance Theatre is one of Canada's most important modern dance companies. It was launched in Vancouver in 1973 by Anna Wyman, an Austrian dancer, choreographer, and teacher. Wyman, who trained in ballet and contemporary movement techniques, does her own choreography, although the company occasionally invites guest choreographers to do pieces.

Wyman's style is highly theatrical and often uses dramatic technical effects. The company runs its own dance school and has toured extensively in Canada and abroad.

▷ RELATED ARTICLE: **Dance.**

■ Annapolis Royal

Annapolis Royal, N.S., is a town on the Annapolis River in western Nova Scotia. The French built Port-Royal nearby in 1605. Acadian settlement spread slowly up the river.

The English also claimed the area, and several forts were built and destroyed over the years. The English captured Fort Anne there in 1710 and renamed it Annapolis, in honour of Queen Anne. The old and new names gradually merged to become Annapolis Royal.

Annapolis was the capital of Nova Scotia until Halifax was founded in 1749. In the 19th century, the town was an important port. Today, it is a shipping centre for apple growers in the Annapolis Valley. Many historical attractions recall the area's colourful history. Fort Anne became Canada's first national historic park. The town's population in 1986 was 631.

▷ RELATED ARTICLE: **Port-Royal.**

■ Annapolis Valley

Annapolis Valley is a fertile farming area on the northwest shore of Nova Scotia. It extends 155 km from St Mary's Bay on the west to the Minas Basin on the east, and is flanked to the north and south by rocky cliffs. The large salt marshes at each end of the valley were the site of the earliest settlement in Canada. The French built Port-Royal here in 1605. Acadian farmers built dykes to drain the marshes for use as rich hayfields.

The French were later expelled by the English. Farther inland, the rich soil and mild climate promote apple growing and dairy farming. Principal towns in the valley include Kentville, the fishing port of Digby, and Wolfville, home of Acadia University.

▷ RELATED ARTICLES: **Acadians; Fruit Farming; Nova Scotia.**

Anne of Green Gables is performed every year at the Charlottetown Festival. The heroine is Anne Shirley, an orphan with red hair (courtesy Gord Johnston Photography).

■ Anne of Green Gables

As a young woman, Lucy Maud Montgomery earned money by writing for children's magazines. In a notebook, she jotted down ideas she had for new stories, articles, and poems. One idea — "Elderly couple apply to an orphan asylum for a boy. By mistake a girl is sent them" — grew into her first and most famous novel, *Anne of Green Gables*. It was first published in 1908.

The heroine is Anne Shirley, an orphan with red hair, a freckled face, and a vivid imagination. As she grows up on Prince Edward Island, she makes many mistakes, such as accidentally dying her hair green. She learns from them to become a responsible young lady. She also influences her lonely guardians, Matthew and Marilla Cuthbert, with her lively and loving ways. The novel has been translated into many languages and made into a television special and a musical stage play. Montgomery wrote many other novels about Anne and her family but none was as popular as her first book. In it, she created memorable characters, vividly and accurately described the Prince Edward Island setting, and brought to life events in Anne's life which are at times funny and at times sad, but are important steps in her process of growing up.

■ Annelida

Annelida are a phylum of invertebrates whose body consists of segments or rings. (The name comes from the Latin word for "ring.") Annelids are divided into three major classes. One is the Oligochaeta (the word means "few bristles"), which includes earthworms. Members of this class generally live in damp soil or fresh water. The second class is the Polychaeta (meaning "many bristles"). Polychaetes live on seashores and some are known as beach worms. These two classes are well known to fishermen, who use them as bait. The third class is the Hirudinea, or leeches, that live in fresh water and have no bristles at all. Some scientists include a fourth class, the Archiannelidae, but not all scientists agree that this is correct.

Most Annelids live in tunnels or burrows. There are some 5300 species of Polychaetes, most of which live in maritime environments. The main characteristic of Annelids is that they are composed of nearly identical segments. With the Oligochaetes, the leeches, and many Polychaetes, each creature is both male and female at the same time, but some Polychaetes are one sex or the other. The largest earthworms (*Megascolides australis*) are more than 2 m long, and the *Eunice gigantea*, a Polychaete, is almost 3 m long. Neither is found in Canada.

■ Anse aux Meadows

L'Anse aux Meadows, on the northern tip of Newfoundland, is the earliest known European settlement in North America. Around 1000 AD the site was occupied for just a few years by groups of Norse settlers. They built large sod houses and workshops for carpenters and blacksmiths. The houses had wooden frames, but the walls and roof were made entirely of turf. The biggest house measured 28.8 by 15.6 metres and had several rooms. It was heated by open fires and there were wooden sleeping platforms around the walls. Archaeologists have found a bronze pin, part of a bone needle, and a tool for spinning wool among the remains.

The site was discovered by the Norwegian explorer and writer Helge Ingstad in 1960 and was excavated by his wife, archaeologist Anne Stine Ingstad, between 1961 and 1968 and by the Canadian Parks Service between 1973 and 1976. The Ingstads had been searching along the coast of eastern North America for a possible location for Vinland, the Viking settlement described in Norse stories which date from about 1000 AD. Both the *Green-*

L'Anse aux Meadows, Nfld. This Viking site was discovered in 1960. Sod houses like these were built by Vikings about 1000 years ago (photo by Malak, Ottawa).

landers' Saga and the *Saga of Eric the Red* tell of a land many days' sail to the west of the Norse colonies in Iceland and Greenland. While it is impossible to tell whether this Newfoundland cove is indeed in Vinland, it is certain that a group of Norse colonists came here some 500 years before Columbus "discovered" the New World.

L'Anse aux Meadows is now a National Historic Park and a United Nations World Heritage Site. The settlement has been reconstructed by Parks Canada, so visitors can get a clear impression of the way the first Europeans lived in North America.

▷ RELATED ARTICLES: **Archaeology; Vikings.**

■ Anse du Cap des Rosiers

Anse du Cap des Rosiers, Que., is a steep point at the end of the Gaspé Peninsula. A line drawn from the north shore to this point traditionally marks where the St Lawrence River ends and the Gulf of St Lawrence begins. There were many shipwrecks in the nearby waters until a lighthouse was built. The cape is named for the many wild roses that grow there.

■ Ant

Ants (family Formicidae) are the well-known social insects belonging to the or-

Ants with Larvae The ant larvae are tended by workers (artwork by Claire Tremblay).

der Hymenoptera. This abundant, widespread order also includes other insects such as wasps and bees. In Canada we have about 186 species. Ant colonies are usually divided into three social classes. The males have wings, small heads, and long antennae.

The sterile females, or workers, form the majority of the colony's population. They are responsible for bringing food to the anthill, for caring for the eggs, larvae, and pupae, and for cleaning and defending the colony against other colonies. The third caste consists of fertile females: the queen, who is wingless and about twice as large as the workers; and future queens, who have wings and do not spend more than two weeks in the colony. They leave with the males, with whom they couple and form new colonies, where they will be the queens.

When this happens, the new queens pull off their wings. If you disturb an anthill, you will often see the workers hurrying to move about some small, off-white objects: the eggs, larvae, and pupae. Ants may be either vegetarian or carnivorous. Some cultivate mushrooms or raise aphids for nourishment.

▷ RELATED ARTICLE: **Insects.**

■ Anthony Island Provincial Park

Anthony Island Provincial Park is on one of the smallest of the Queen Charlotte Islands, off the north coast of British Columbia. The densely wooded island is the site of the Haida village of Ninstints. Archaeologists have found remains of totem poles and houses going back 2000 years. Most of the inhabitants were killed by disease, and the village was abandoned by the late 1800s. Because the site contains so many remains of the rich Haida culture, it was made a provincial park in 1958.

In 1981 the United Nations declared Ninstints a World Heritage Site, "of importance to the History of Mankind."

▷ RELATED ARTICLES: **Haida; Queen Charlotte Islands.**

■ Anthropology

Anthropology is the study of the origin, development, and culture of human beings, both in the past and in the present day.

Anthropologists are interested in every aspect of the life of the groups they are investigating — from the biology and anatomy of the people, to the utensils and artworks they make, to their social organization, language, and beliefs.

Shaman's Mask *Anthropologists study all aspects of culture, including religion. This mask would have been used by a native shaman in a religious ritual (courtesy NMC/CMC/S71-3830).*

HOW ANTHROPOLOGISTS WORK

Anthropology is a relatively new area of study, but it has already developed its own theories and techniques. These methods are usually learned at university. Anthropologists do much of their research by staying among the people they are investigating for several months. This is known as fieldwork. They observe the everyday activities of the people. They collect examples of their tools, clothing, songs, and stories. They interview people who can explain things they want to know. They make detailed notes about their subjects' way of life, and they write systematic reports of their findings.

Some anthropologists are interested in only one group of people, and they study them in considerable depth over several years. Others are interested in comparing one group with another, or in finding general patterns in human behaviour.

BRANCHES OF ANTHROPOLOGY

There are several branches of anthropology, each specializing in different aspects of human life. As more information is collected, new sub-disciplines develop within anthropology. In recent years, for example, there has been an interest in women's anthropology and in medical anthropology, the study of women and of health and disease, respectively, in various societies. In Canada, there are five main branches of anthropology: physical anthropology, linguistic anthropology, social-cultural anthropology (also called ethnology), applied anthropology, and archaeology.

Physical Anthropology is concerned with the origins and evolution of human beings. Anthropologists interested in this area usually work in universities, and they come from such backgrounds as anatomy, dentistry, zoology, and biochemistry. The most famous Canadian in this branch of anthropology was Davidson Black, who identified a new species of ancient human from the fossil remains of "Peking Man" in 1927 and suggested a new theory about the evolution of prehistoric people.

Other physical anthropologists in Canada have studied the skeletal remains of early Indians and Inuit, as well as the distribution patterns of past populations. They have investigated the effects of nutrition, disease, climate, and genetics on people in past and present societies. They have recognized that human beings have developed as they have because of the interaction between human biology and human culture.

Linguistic Anthropology is concerned with the organization of language. In Canada, this has been a particularly important branch of anthropology because of Edward Sapir. A great linguist, Sapir was director of the first anthropology department organized by the federal government within the Geological Survey of Canada. He held the position from 1910 to 1925. During his term as director, he encouraged fieldwork on different native languages and dialects. He was also able to trace the movements of early native people by analysing the language of their descendants. In this way, he showed that the Navajo and Apache who live in the American southwest originally came from Alaska and northwestern Canada.

Today, linguistic anthropologists often work with native communities to help them preserve their language. Although a few native tribes have made use of spelling systems introduced by European missionaries in the contact period, native languages have remained primarily oral. Now, anthropologists and linguists are developing additional writing systems for a variety of them. Some of these systems are based, like English and French, on the

Careers in Anthropology
Anthropologists are employed by museums, universities, businesses, and government departments.

A master's degree is usually the minimum requirement for employment.

Advanced positions in teaching or research are usually open only to persons with a PhD.

Graduate programs in anthropology are offered by the universities of Alberta, British Columbia, Laval, McGill, McMaster, Manitoba, Montreal, Simon Fraser, and Toronto.

Roman alphabet, while others are based on syllabics, a phonetic system of writing which combines consonants and vowels in each symbol.

Social and Cultural Anthropology is concerned with the relationship between behaviour and culture. This has been the most common branch of anthropology in Canada, particularly because of the influence of Franz Boas, Edward Sapir, Charles Marius Barbeau, and Diamond Jenness, the first professional anthropologists in the country. They did their fieldwork with small, isolated native groups in the Arctic and on the Northwest Coast. They collected examples of native artwork, utensils, and myths for the museum in Ottawa. Barbeau also made a fine collection of folklore and songs in French Cana-

Dorset House *Anthropologists try to piece together past cultures from evidence such as this house. It was built 700 years ago by the Dorset people in Canada's Arctic (courtesy NMC/CMC/J-14879).*

da. They established a model, by which the anthropologist observed and reported on the whole way of life of a particular community — its social organization, technology, value systems, and beliefs. This tradition has continued to the present day. In English Canada, most anthropologists have studied different native groups, while in French Canada anthropologists have concentrated on rural and small-town studies in Quebec.

In recent years, native leaders as well as anthropologists have been concerned that some aspects of native culture in Canada might be lost unless special efforts are made to record and preserve them. About 37 of Canada's 53 native languages, for instance, are spoken by 1000 people or less. Many could easily be extinct within 50 years. From the late 1960s to the mid-1980s, the National Museum in Ottawa ran what was called the Urgent Ethnology Program, which was an attempt to record the culture of those groups that were considered particularly vulnerable in all areas of Canada. Anthropologists were hired on contract to go out into the field and preserve on film and sound tapes, in writing, and in photographs, whatever they could of the groups they were studying. Changing priorities as a result of the new museum building in Ottawa led to the decline of the program.

Applied Anthropology uses the knowledge and techniques of anthropology to help solve problems and to achieve practical goals. Anthropologists who work in this area try to develop ways to help people cope with certain situations, instead of merely describing what they find.

Early anthropologists such as Boas and Sapir were sometimes asked by the government to comment on different aspects of Indian policy. Their successor, Jenness, wrote a detailed report on Eskimo administration in the Arctic. In more recent years, the federal government commissioned anthropologists H.B. Hawthorn (University of British Columbia) and M.A. Tremblay (Université Laval) to recommend improvements in Indian policy in their report, *A Survey of Contemporary Indians of Canada* (1967).

Since the 1970s, the number of anthropologists who are involved on commissions and practical projects has greatly increased. Many anthropologists work with native groups on land-claims research, advising them on the best way to present their claims to the government. A team from McGill University helped to negotiate the James Bay and Northern Quebec

Agreement (1975), the first comprehensive land claim to be settled. Other anthropologists worked on the Mackenzie Valley Pipeline inquiry (1975-76), assessing the possible effects of an oil and natural gas pipeline on native people in the North.

Anthropologists have also moved on to areas other than native policy. They work with different ethnic groups, particularly over questions of language, family life, and health. They also advise communities that are experiencing difficulties, such as fishing and mining villages in Newfoundland and rural villages in Quebec, as to whether they should resettle in other parts of the province or try to attract new industries to their towns. And as cities become more complex, anthropologists are asked to work with immigrants, with the elderly, and with industrial and professional groups.

Archaeology studies the material remains of past cultures, especially in the prehistoric period before there were any written records. *See* separate entry.

ANTHROPOLOGY IN CANADA

Although anthropology did not become formalized in Canada until 1910, many of the early missionaries, traders, and explorers left descriptions and drawings of the native people which have been extremely useful to anthropologists. The Jesuit missionary Paul Le Jeune established the custom of writing a report each year for his superiors in Paris, and these documents, which covered the years 1632 to 1672, were later published as the *Jesuit Relations*. In the West, explorers such as Sir Alexander Mackenzie left valuable accounts of the groups they met in their travels. Often these are the only descriptions we have of the natives' customs before they were heavily influenced by contact with Europeans.

After about 1870, scientists who worked for the Geological Survey of Canada began to collect native artifacts as well as rock specimens for their museum. Then, in 1910, Prime Minister Wilfrid Laurier established a Division of Anthropology within the Geological Survey, with Sapir as director. Sapir attracted a brilliant group of anthropologists to the department, including Barbeau and Jenness. These men had a great influence on the direction anthropology would take in Canada.

Museums have played an important role in Canadian anthropology. In 1910 the Geological Survey moved its museum, including the artifacts it had collected from native groups across Canada, into the new Victoria Memorial Museum in Ottawa. This collection is now part of the Canadian Museum of Civilization. Over the years, excellent museums have been established in every province. They all have collections of native artworks and utensils. They also employ trained anthropologists to carry out research, organize exhibitions, publish books and pamphlets about their work, and to answer requests for information from the public.

Universities lagged behind museums in establishing departments of anthropology. It was not until 1925 that the University of Toronto set up the first department, under Thomas McIlwraith. But growth was slow, and the next universities to hire anthropologists, McGill University in Montreal and University of British Columbia in Vancouver, did not do so until 1947. Finally, during the 1960s the number of universities and anthropology departments suddenly increased. At the same time, anthropologists began to broaden their interest beyond native studies and rural Quebec. Today, Canadian anthropologists are employed by museums, by private firms as consultants, and by universities to research and consult on a wide range of topics both within Canada and abroad.

▷ RELATED ARTICLES: **Archaeology; C. Marius Barbeau; Davidson Black; Franz Boas; Culture; Diamond Jenness; L'Anse aux Meadows; Native People: Pre-Contact; Potlatch; Edward Sapir.**

▷ SUGGESTED READING: Look for books and pamphlets published by the Canadian Museum of Civilization, the Royal Ontario Museum, or the museum in your province.

■ Anticosti Island

Anticosti Island, 7941 km², lies at the entrance to the St Lawrence River. The coastline is dominated by steep limestone cliffs and the eastern end is a huge bog. Larger than Prince Edward Island, Anticosti has a population of only about 300. The first recorded sighting was by Jacques Cartier in 1534. Several private owners have attempted to develop the island. These include millionaire French chocolate maker, Henri Menier, who bought it in 1895. Menier developed Baie-Ste-Claire as a model town and imported Virginia white-tailed deer for hunting. Deer hunting is still an attraction. But Menier failed and in 1926 the island was sold to Consolidated Bathurst Inc., which developed a pulpwood industry that existed

Aphids are major insect pests that stunt or kill plants. They may be red, pink, brown, yellow, green, purple, or black (artwork by Jan Sovak).

until the end of 1971. The Quebec government expropriated the island in 1974. The island is now divided into seven regions: one is reserved for hunting and fishing, and the other six are divided among six outfitters.

Most residents now make their living fishing, trapping, and logging. At the turn of the century there were many farms, but none remain. Port-Menier, or Baie Ellis, is the only settlement. Thousands of ships pass each year and about 400 have foundered on the outlying reefs. The name probably comes from an Indian word meaning "where bears are hunted."

■ Antigonish

Antigonish is a town near St Georges Bay, on Nova Scotia's North Shore. It is about halfway between Halifax and Sydney. It was founded in 1784 by a party of British soldier-settlers. The community attracted many Scottish farm settlers, and the nearby harbour grew as a timber port. In 1855 St Francis Xavier University opened, and today Antigonish is a quiet college town with no major industry. The name comes from a Micmac word. Its population in 1986 was 5291.

■ Antigonish Movement

Antigonish Movement was a movement for social and economic reform which began at St Francis Xavier University in Antigonish, N.S., in 1928.

Led by a Catholic priest, Father Moses Coady, the movement relied on adult education to carry its message to the community. Organizers formed study clubs, which held meetings to work out a program of local self-help. This usually led to the creation of one or more co-operatives, which helped people obtain housing, consumer goods, and medical care at a cost they could afford. Co-operatives were also set up to sell fish and farm produce at fair prices. "Co-operation," said Coady, "is the only means in our day through which the masses of the people can again have a say in the economic processes."

In Atlantic Canada the Antigonish Movement had its greatest influence in the 1930s and 1940s. Since that time, television, improved transportation, and a better standard of living have forced the movement to change its emphasis. The message of co-operation spread to poorer countries around the world, and in 1959 the Coady International Institute began training community workers from developing countries in Asia, Africa, and Latin America.

■ Anti-Semitism, *see* Prejudice and Discrimination.

■ Aphids

Aphids (family Aphididae) are insects which belong, like cicadas and hoppers, to the order Homoptera. They are very small, with a soft body that may be yellow, red, green, pink, brown, mauve, or black. Some 600 species are known in Canada.

Aphids live on the sap of plants and reproduce very quickly. Sometimes they cause great damage to the plants, not only because they suck the sap but also because they transmit disease and inject their saliva which is toxic to the plants. In spring the eggs hatch, producing females only. Some of them fly off to begin new colonies.

During the spring and summer, these females reproduce without the help of a male. A female can give birth to a new female every half-hour. They grow rapidly, and within a few hours reach maturity and can themselves reproduce. In one day, in other words, each female may become the grandmother of several hundred insects! As winter approaches, generations of males and females appear. They mate and the females lay eggs, which pass the winter in a protected state. Aphids have various enemies, including syrphid flies, green lacewings, and, most important of all, the coccinella. They also have some friends in the insect world: ants, in exchange for their sugary secretions (honeydew), protect them from their enemies.

■ Applebaum, Louis

Composer, conductor (*born in 1918 at Toronto, Ont.*). Applebaum studied music at Toronto and New York. He moved to Hollywood in the mid-1940s where he wrote film scores. He returned to Canada in 1949 and has been one of Canada's busiest composers ever since. He has written scores for film, theatre, radio, television, and ballet.

Applebaum has also been active in many Canadian arts organizations, including the National Film Board, the Canada Council, the Canadian Broadcasting Corp. (CBC), the Stratford Festival, and others. He was the co-chairman, with Jacques Hébert, of a committee to review the role of the federal government in the arts. It reported in 1982. The report recommended that arts agencies, such as the CBC, be independent of interference from government. It called for support for book publishing and the film industry.

Apprentice

An apprentice is a young person who learns a skilled trade from an expert. It used to be the way in which boys — rarely girls — learned to become skilled craftsmen, such as carpenters, mechanics, and tailors. Apprenticeship usually lasted three or five years and took the form of a legal contract. An apprentice was "articled" or "indentured" to a master. He promised to be faithful and obedient, to avoid drinking and gambling, and to be a good student and worker. The master promised to provide food and shelter, to teach the skills of the trade, and to look after the apprentice. However, apprentices were sometimes mistreated. When an apprentice completed his apprenticeship, he became a skilled worker or "journeyman," so called because he was paid by the journée (a French word for "day").

Apprenticeship was the standard way to learn a trade in 17th- and 18th-century Canada. Towards the end of the 19th century, it was replaced by vocational training in schools. Even so, apprenticeship still exists today, as a combination of on-the-job training and classroom learning, in such trades as plumbing, electrical work, hairdressing, and so on.

Apprenticeship of Duddy Kravitz, The

The fourth novel by Montreal author Mordecai Richler is about a tough, clever boy who wants to escape his working-class neighbourhood. To become successful, he often betrays the people who have loved and helped him. He finally gains the land he wants, but loses love and friendship. Richler was praised for his successful characterization of Duddy and his vivid portrayal of life in a poor Jewish neighbourhood in the Montreal of the 1950s. The book made Richler one of Canada's most respected novelists. It was published in 1959, made into a motion picture in 1974, and into a musical stage play in 1984.

Aquaculture

Aquaculture is the farming of fish, lobsters and other shellfish, and other water-dwelling creatures and plants. Aquaculture is a means of replacing stocks of fish in the oceans, which are depleted by overfishing and pollution. It may become an important source of food for the world's growing population.

Fish farming has an ancient history. It probably began in China. China, Japan, and Indonesia are the major fish-farming countries in the world today. Norway, which has a coastline similar to Canada's east coast, has recently and successfully become a fish-farming country.

A salmon farm is an example of aquaculture. A salmon farmer hatches the salmon eggs. Once the fish reach a certain size, they are released into the waters of a protected fjord. The farmer feeds them and watches for disease. In two or three years, when the fish are fully grown, the farmer harvests them.

Fish Farming in Canada Canada has waters suitable for aquaculture along both the Atlantic and Pacific coasts, and in its freshwater streams, lakes, and prairie sloughs.

Government fish farms produce young fish for release in the wild. For example, they stock lakes and streams with young trout for sportfishing.

On the prairies, several thousand farmers stock small lakes with rainbow trout each spring, and harvest the fish in the fall. They rarely sell the fish, but keep them to feed their families.

Some privately owned fish farms produce fish and shellfish for sale. Since 1960, this business has been growing. On Canada's east coast, for instance, mussels are grown on ropes and nets which are suspended from floating rafts. There are now salmon farms on both the east and west coasts. The industry now employs over 4000 people.

▷ RELATED ARTICLES: **Fish; Fisheries.**

Aquin, Hubert

Novelist (*born in 1929 at Montreal, Que.; died there in 1977*). Aquin was educated in philosophy and politics. He worked in radio and film in the 1950s and 1960s. A member of Quebec's first independentist political party, he announced in 1964 that he was going "underground" to fight for the cause of Quebec independence as a terrorist. A short time later, he was arrested and held for four months in a psychiatric hospital. There he wrote his first novel, *Prochain épisode* (1965).

After his release, Aquin remained in the political spotlight. In 1969 he refused to accept a Governor General's Award for his second novel, *Blackout* (1968). He continued to write, producing two more novels, but his life was increasingly tormented until it ended in suicide.

Arabs

There are over 100 000 Canadians with some Arab ancestry. Most are from Syria, Lebanon, and Egypt. Others are from a

Denys Arcand began as a documentary filmmaker and later moved to fiction. His films are among the most highly praised of all Canadian filmmakers (photo by Daniel Dutka).

wide variety of countries in West Asia and North Africa, including Algeria, Kuwait, Iraq, Jordan, Morocco, Saudi Arabia, and Tunisia.

Apart from about 7000 Syrians who settled in Canada before World War I, nearly all Arabs have arrived since the 1940s. Most are highly educated people. Most live and work in Quebec, Ontario, and Nova Scotia, especially in the cities of Montreal and Toronto. They have a number of social and cultural clubs, the main one being the Canadian Arab Foundation.

Arabs do not all have the same religion. Some belong to Christian churches, such as the Coptic Orthodox Church. Others are Muslims. The first Canadian mosque was built in Edmonton in 1938, and nearly all the large cities now have mosques. Most of the larger universities give courses in Islamic studies. Although many Arabs no longer speak or read Arabic, they are proud to be descended from the ancient Arab civilizations. They are interested in studying their history and in keeping up aspects of the Arab culture such as traditional food, music, and dance.

Joe Ghiz, elected premier of Prince Edward Island in 1986, is of Arab (Lebanese) origin.

▷ RELATED ARTICLE: **Ethnic Group.**

■ Arachnida

Arachnids are a large class of arthropods (segmented animals). They consist of spiders (Araneae), scorpions (Scorpionida), ticks and mites (Acarina), and some other, smaller groups. Their body is divided into two parts: the cephalothorax, with four pairs of legs, and the abdomen. Almost all of them live on land. Several species have poison glands which they use to paralyse their prey.

Arachnids are second only to insects in the number of species. There are more than 300 000 species in the world. They are found everywhere, from sea level to the highest mountain ranges, throughout the world. In Canada we have more than 12 000 species.

Scorpions have elongated bodies with large pincers at the front and a poisonous stinger at the tip of the abdomen. Ticks and mites are extremely small animals, often less than a millimetre long, but even so they can cause human beings serious injury. Some are parasites, feeding on people or domesticated animals, or on their organic matter. Ticks live on the blood of reptiles, birds, and mammals.

Some can live more than a year without feeding. Mites live on plants or animals, or suck the plants' sap.

▷ RELATED ARTICLES: **Scorpion; Spider; Tick.**

■ Arcand, Denys

Filmmaker (*born in 1941 at Deschambault, Que.*). Arcand's first surviving film, *Seul ou avec d'autres* (1962), was made with Denis Heroux while they were students at Université de Montréal. From 1963 to 1971, Arcand worked at the National Film Board (NFB), where he built a reputation for understanding the political and social changes in Quebec. His film *On est au coton* (1970), a documentary on textile industry workers, was considered too political and was banned for six years.

Arcand then left the NFB to make privately financed feature films, such as *Réjeanne Padovani* (1973). They show a witty and original view of Quebec society. Arcand's television work includes writing the script for Radio-Canada's "Duplessis" series and directing three episodes of "Empire Inc."

Le Déclin de l'empire américain (1986), a cynical comedy about modern sexual attitudes, brought Arcand international fame. It received prizes from the Cannes Film Festival and the New York film critics, and swept the Canadian Genie awards.

Arcand's film *Jésus de Montréal* (1989) won the highest prize ever awarded to a Canadian filmmaker at Cannes in 1989. The controversial film is about an actor who plays Jesus and begins to think he is Jesus.

■ Archaeological Survey of Canada

The Archaeological Survey of Canada (ASC) is a division of the Canadian Museum of Civilization. As a museum, it collects and preserves archaeological specimens. It also manages archaeological sites across Canada, and informs the public through exhibitions and publications. The ASC took its present name in 1971.

■ Archaeology

Archaeology is the study of the remains of past cultures. It is closely related to anthropology, which studies the origin and development of human beings and their societies. Archaeologists do not work with written records but with objects that have survived from previous cultures. Most often they excavate pits in the ground, called digs, in search of bones and hand-made objects known as artifacts. They can tell a lot about the people who lived in the area from the seeds, tools, religious relics, and human and animal skeletons that they find. They can even tell the age of an object through a process called radiocarbon dating.

In Canada, the earliest human inhabitants arrived some time before 12 000 years ago. None of the native people developed a system of writing, so it is up to archaeologists and anthropologists to find out whatever they can about the people who lived in Canada until the early 1500s, when the Europeans arrived and began to leave records. The historic period in Canada, then, is very short compared with the prehistoric period.

HOW ARCHAEOLOGISTS WORK

Archaeologists have two main goals: to collect objects and samples from the sites they are excavating, and to make detailed notes about the site as they work. Since the site is usually destroyed during the excavation, archaeologists want to be able to reconstruct it through diagrams and photographs at any time in the future. They have developed precise methods for excavating different kinds of sites.

Early archaeologists worked mainly by chance, as erosion uncovered piles of bones or as farmers ploughed up long-buried objects. Today, however, archaeologists look at aerial photographs, maps, and local surveys before they decide where they will dig. The local landscape and patterns in the vegetation often give them clues that an area was once a village, a burial ground, or an animal killing site.

Once they have decided where they will dig, archaeologists divide the site into a grid of uniform squares, usually one metre a side. They dig within each square, using small trowels, shovels, buckets, and screens for sifting the soil. Every object they find and every seed or soil sample they take is carefully labelled, showing its exact location in the excavation.

Archaeologists know that the materials that have been preserved over hundreds or thousands of years are only a small portion of the culture they are investigating. They must be able to interpret the maximum information from the few objects they find.

One of the first clues archaeologists look for are strata (or layers) in the excavation. If the site was occupied by several different groups over a period of time, each group will have left its own layer of remains. The archaeologist can assume that the lowest level represents the oldest culture, while the most recent culture

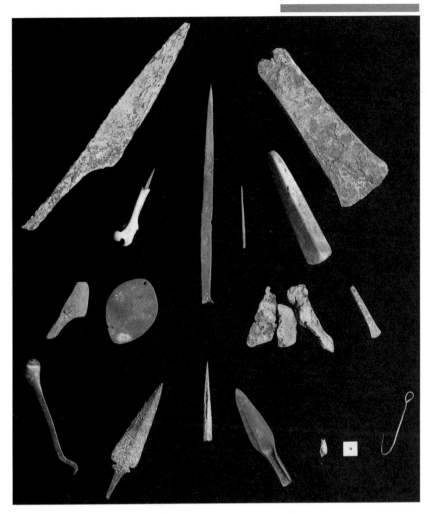

will be on top. The objects are usually dated by radiocarbon dating or by comparing them with similar objects found in other sites.

The archaeologist also watches for such features as house sites, garbage pits, and hearths. Most native houses in Canada were built of wood, brush, or animal skins, none of which have survived over time. But the stains from the houseposts remain in the soil, along with the stones that surrounded the tipis or built up the

Copper Tools These copper tools were likely all made from copper found near Lake Superior. They range in age from 600 to 6000 years old. They include a fish hook (lower right), three dart heads (lower middle), a knife (upper left), and an axe (upper right) (courtesy NMC/CMC/K75-588).

Oxbow Site, near Red Bank, on the Miramichi River, N.B. The site was occupied from 3000 BC until the historic period (photo by David Keenlyside/ASC/CMC).

Radiocarbon Dating

All living things — whether people, animals, or plants — contain a substance called radiocarbon.

When living things die, the radiocarbon begins to decay at a constant rate.

Scientists can measure how much radiocarbon is left, and thus estimate the date of the object. In the early 1980s, scientists in both Canada and the United States developed a more accurate method of radiocarbon dating known as accelerator mass spectrometry (AMS). It can measure blood smears on stone tools in samples weighing less than one human hair.

When a caribou leg scraper (above) was discovered in the Old Crow River valley in the Yukon in 1966, it was estimated by radiocarbon dating to have been made 27 000 years ago. AMS dating now puts it at a mere 1350 years old (photo courtesy CMC/J-19221-7).

Prehistory

Prehistory is the time before there were any written records.

The historic period is the time that is recorded in written documents.

hearths. The charcoal from the fireplaces has been preserved, together with food that was burned by mistake. Corn, for instance, was cultivated and eaten in what is now southern Ontario by 500 AD, though beans did not arrive until around 1400 AD.

Bones and artifacts tell the most dramatic story. Human skeletons show how tall people were, whether they suffered from diseases such as arthritis, and how old they were when they died. Broken bones and crushed skulls indicate violent deaths and warfare. If the skeleton is surrounded by objects known as grave goods, they can reveal a lot about the culture and status of the person in life.

Animal bones and the remains of shellfish are a good indication of what the people ate, how they butchered their meat, and how they cooked their food. If the bones are not burnt, it is obvious that they boiled their meat in containers rather than roasting it over an open fire. If only the bones of migratory animals or fish are found at a particular site, that is evidence that the people spent just one season of the year at the camp. Sometimes the absence of bones tells something about the religious beliefs of the people. On several sites on the Northwest Coast, for instance, fishhooks and barbs are found in abundance, but there are no fish bones. Evidently, these early fishermen did not throw the bones of their catch into the fire or the garbage pit but returned them to the river, in order to show respect for the fish spirits.

Archaeologists find tools, weapons, household utensils, religious relics, and personal ornaments, all of which tell a great deal about how the people who occupied the site lived and worked. They also look for objects such as copper and shells which are not found in the area around the site. Obviously, these items were brought in from another location. They indicate either trade routes or conquests in war. If a large number of Cayuga clay pots are unearthed in a Huron village, for instance, it is safe to assume that a group of Cayuga women hostages must have been brought back by a Huron military expedition.

Unfortunately, most soils in Canada are high in acid and they destroy bones and other natural products over time. Archaeologists are most likely to find bones and antlers in a state of good preservation in shell middens — garbage pits made up of shellfish — since the calcium in the shells neutralizes the acid in the soil. Water-saturated soil is also free from the bacteria that attacks wood and vegetable fibres, so wooden boxes, arrow shafts, and baskets can sometimes be found buried in the beds of slow-moving streams.

ARCHAEOLOGICAL SITES

Archaeologists have excavated hundreds of sites in all parts of Canada. Together, these digs give some idea of past settlement on this continent. They provide a few clues about the first people who crossed over from Siberia more than 12 000 years ago. They uncover a variety of native villages, burial grounds, and animal killing sites in different areas and periods. They prove that there was a Viking colony in Newfoundland around 1000 years ago. And they reveal the foundations of early European missions, forts, trading posts, and towns. Two examples give some idea of how archaeological sites fill out our history from earliest times.

Lachane Site, near Prince Rupert, B.C. This site was excavated in 1973. About 4000 artifacts were recovered, including arrow shafts and spears (photo by Richard Inglis/ASC/CMC).

L'Anse Amour Burial Site in southern Labrador is one of the oldest known ceremonial burial mounds in the world. It was built 2000 years before the pyramids in Egypt. The grave was dug between 5500 BC and 5000 BC by Indian hunters who came to the area each summer to catch walrus and seals. When the mound was discovered in 1973, it measured 8 metres across and was covered with large boulders. About 1.5 metres below the surface, archaeologists found the skeleton of a young teenager lying chest down with his head turned to the west. The bones were stained with red ochre and a flat rock rested on the back. There were several stone and bone spearpoints and knives in the grave, as well as a walrus tusk, a harpoon head, an ivory carving, and a bone whistle. On either side of the body were small piles of charcoal, where fires had been built at the bottom of the pit. Since it would have taken a band of hunters about a week to build a grave of this size, this adolescent must have been very special, or else very fearful, to the group who buried him.

Cliff at Head-Smashed-In Buffalo Jump. The native people stampeded the bison over this cliff to their death (photo by Thomas Kitchin).

Head-Smashed-In Buffalo Jump is one of hundreds of animal killing sites on the Canadian plains. It is in the Porcupine Hills in southern Alberta. The site consists of a cliff 10 metres high, with a large natural basin to the west, surrounded by hills and crisscrossed by streams. For over 5000 years (3500 BC to 1750 AD), groups of native people used the site to stampede large numbers of bison to their death. They built several rock cairns among the streams in the basin to make a network of drive lanes leading up to the cliff. Then they herded the bison into the lanes and drove them forward over the cliff. Many bison were killed outright in the fall, and those that were wounded were quickly killed off by hunters waiting below with clubs, arrows, and spears. Archaeologists

Bison Jump found at Head-Smashed-In Buffalo Jump. Archaeologists have uncovered bones and some 5000 arrow and spear points at the site (photo by Thomas Kitchin).

have excavated butchered bones and stone tools to a depth of 11 metres at the base of the cliff and have recovered over 5000 arrow and spear points. Some of the rock used to make the knives and arrowheads came from as far away as Wyoming and North Dakota, which shows the extent of trade among native groups. Because it is one of the oldest and best-preserved jump sites, Head-Smashed-In has been named both an Alberta Historical Resource Site and a United Nations World Heritage Site.

ARCHAEOLOGY IN CANADA

The history of archaeology in Canada can be divided into three main periods: early collectors, professional archaeologists, and compulsory legislation.

Early Collectors The first "archaeologists" in Canada were amateur collectors who enjoyed looking for relics or curiosities in old Indian cemeteries. Unfortunately, their hasty and unscientific methods probably destroyed more evidence of native culture than was found. Gradually, collections of artifacts were put together, which became the basis for many new museums in cities in central and eastern Canada after 1850. The most important collection was made by scientists employed by the Geological Survey of Canada. In 1911 their museum became the Victoria Memorial Museum in Ottawa, and today their archaeological collection is part of the Canadian Museum of Civilization.

Professional Archaeologists In 1925 the first anthropology department was established at the University of Toronto, with offices located in the Royal Ontario Museum. Gradually, other universities across Canada set up similar departments, where archaeology was taught as part of the anthropology program. It was not until 1964 that the University of Calgary organized the first separate archaeology department.

Archaeologists employed by both universities and the major museums excavated sites in many parts of Canada, though they were often hampered by lack of money. In 1961 the Canada Council began to fund archaeological research. The Quiet Revolution in Quebec in the 1960s and Centennial Year in 1967 also made the public much more aware of its heritage, including what archaeologists have found out about the past. As a result, there has been a tremendous expansion in the field. The Archaeological Survey of Canada was founded in 1971, and there

Abitibi Lake, *Quebec. Artifacts found at this site date from as early as 4200*BC *(over 6000 years ago) (photo by Roger Marois/ASC/CMC).*

are numerous publications and exhibitions related to archaeology. Canadian archaeologists are also involved in excavations and research in other countries, particularly in Italy, Greece, Egypt, and Central and South America.

Compulsory Legislation Since 1975, most provincial governments have insisted that lands must be investigated by archaeologists before they are developed or disturbed in any way. This legislation has produced a new profession known as salvage archaeology. When a shipping terminal was planned for the harbour at Prince Rupert, B.C., for example, archaeologists were called in to excavate the 2000-year-old Lachane site before it was inundated by water.

Another expanding area is industrial archaeology. Here, people trained as historians, museum curators, architects, and archaeologists work together to investigate the sites of early industries, including mining, logging, fishing, brewing, and ironmaking. As a result, there are now hundreds of historical sites and industrial and transportation museums in Canada.

▷ RELATED ARTICLES: **Anse aux Meadows; Anthropology; Archaeological Survey of Canada; C. Marius Barbeau; Franz Boas; Diamond Jenness; Prehistory; Edward Sapir; V. Stefansson.**

▷ SUGGESTED READING: Welwyn Katz, *False Face* (1987); W.A. Kenyon, *The History of James Bay 1610-1686: A Study in Historical Archaeology* (1986); George F. MacDonald and Richard I. Inglis, *The Dig* (1976); Robert McGhee, *The Burial at L'Anse-Amour* (1976); David L. Newlands and C. Breede, *An Introduction to Canadian Archaeology* (1976).

■ Archer, Violet

Composer, educator (*born in 1913 at Montreal, Que.*). Archer studied composition in Montreal and New York. Among her teachers were Béla Bartók, one of the great composers of the 20th century.

Archer has written a wide variety of music, including an opera (*Sganarelle*, 1973), a film score, and a piano concerto. She taught music in the United States and at the University of Alberta (1962-78). Archer uses musical ideas from the past as well as modern electronic sounds in her music.

■ Archibald, Sir Adams George

Politician (*born in 1814 at Truro, N.S.; died there in 1892*). Archibald was chosen in 1870 as the first lieutenant-governor of Manitoba because he was a man of moderate views, was bilingual, and was from the Maritimes.

In the wake of the Red River Rebellion, Archibald could not be identified with either of the opposing groups: the pro-Metis people of Quebec or the anti-Metis people of Ontario.

Since the 1850s, Archibald had been one of Nova Scotia's leading politicians. He had taken part in all three Confederation conferences. After Confederation, John A. Macdonald appointed him to the Cabinet (secretary of state, 1867-70).

Archibald served as lieutenant-governor of Manitoba and the North-West Territories from 1870 to 1872. This was a very difficult role, for the West was seething with hatred aroused during the rebellion. Acting with tact, Archibald gradually lessened the tensions. He made sure that Metis as well as Protestant settlers from Ontario had a say in government policy. His final appointment was as lieutenant-governor of Nova Scotia, from 1873 to 1883.

Sir Adams Archibald was a tactful politician who took part in the conferences leading up to Confederation. As the first lieutenant-governor of Manitoba, he lessened tensions between the Metis and white settlers (courtesy PAM).

> RELATED ARTICLE: **Fathers of Confederation; Red River Rebellion.**

■ Archibald, Edward William

Surgeon, educator (*born in 1872 at Montreal, Que.; died there in 1945*). As professor of surgery at McGill University and surgeon-in-chief at the Royal Victoria Hospital, Edward Archibald made radical changes in the way surgeons were trained. Like William Gallie in Toronto, he brought in reforms early in this century that laid the foundation for today's high standard of surgery in Canada.

Archibald was one of the first to realize that advances in surgery could only be made through research. A gifted surgeon himself, he was a pioneer in thoracic surgery. (The thorax is the part of the body between the neck and the abdomen.) He also played a key role in the early history of brain surgery by bringing Wilder Penfield to Montreal in 1928.

> RELATED ARTICLES: **William Gallie; Medicine; Wilder Penfield.**

■ Architecture

Architecture is the art of designing buildings. An architect designs churches, banks, stadiums, government buildings, or other structures to be useful, convenient, and durable.

The aim of building as an *art*, is also to achieve beauty or to create places that express our most important values. Architecture, therefore, requires that an architect show imagination as well as having skill as a builder.

Architecture is one of the most familiar forms of art. Those who live in cities are surrounded by a great variety of buildings, from skyscrapers to shopping malls and neighbourhood houses. Architecture shapes the environment around us. It also

Canadian Centre for Architecture, interior, designed by Peter Rose. The Centre will collect information on Canadian and world architecture (courtesy Canadian Centre for Architecture, Montreal).

gives pleasure, expresses our values, and leaves a heritage for future generations.

ARCHITECTURE IN NEW FRANCE

The French began settling in Canada in the 1600s. The buildings they erected copied the styles that were familiar to them in their homeland. The farm houses were simple wood and stone structures, similar to those of rural France. More important buildings were constructed of stone in an ornate style, called *Baroque*. They called to mind the great palaces of France, though much smaller and less richly detailed.

Two important buildings in the Baroque style were the Archbishop's palace in Quebec City and the Château de Vaudreuil in Montreal. They included in their designs columns, sweeping double staircases, and steep roofs alive with tiny windows and tall chimneys.

Churches in New France The church was the most important patron of architecture in New France. (A *patron* is one who orders and pays for a building.) The earliest churches in New France were simple wood and stone chapels. As skilled builders and craftsmen arrived in the colony from France, more ambitious churches were built in Quebec City and Montreal. The largest by far was the Jesuit church in Quebec City (1666), which recreated the style of the Jesuit churches of Europe. For over 150 years, this church, with its tall spire, dominated the centre of the city.

In 1669 Bishop Laval set in motion a plan to build a series of churches to serve the people of the countryside. By 1700, about 15 had been built. They were smaller than the town churches. These parish churches were plainer than the churches in Quebec. They also had to make use of local materials, such as fieldstone.

One of the grander churches is Ste-Famille on Île d'Orleans, near Quebec. First built by Laval in 1669 it was replaced in 1745 and is still standing. It has two towers in the front and a spire atop the steeply pitched roof. Inside, these parish churches were full of colourful and richly carved decorations.

EARLY 19TH-CENTURY ARCHITECTURE

The British Tradition Canada passed from French to British rule in 1763. The change was naturally reflected in architecture, as settlers from Britain brought their traditions to Canada. Because the

Ste-Famille, on the Île d'Orleans, Quebec, is a typical parish church in the French style (photo by John de Visser).

Colborne Lodge, Toronto, 1836, is a surviving example of the Picturesque. With its verandah, chimneys, and lovely setting, the house made a dramatic impression (photo by J.H. Marsh).

English-speaking settlers had different origins, they brought several different architectural traditions. Many houses and churches, for example, showed the strong influence of architectural style in the United States.

The gentlemen immigrants from England, on the other hand, preferred a colourful movement called the *Picturesque*. Inherited from England, the Picturesque was not really a style. Rather, it showed itself in a taste for dramatic natural settings and unusual houses, built to be viewed as if they were Romantic paintings. A surviving example is Colborne Lodge in High Park, Toronto (1836). The house was placed to command a fine view. Its tall chimneys and verandah give it an exotic look.

The most popular architecture in Britain for government buildings and churches was the *Palladian* style. It took its name from the 16th-century Italian architect Andrea Palladio. It is also called *Georgian*, after the four British kings named George who ruled England from 1714 to 1830.

The principles of Palladian architecture were balance and harmony. It included such features as a central pediment, columns, and well-proportioned windows and doors. A good example of Palladian architecture in Canada is Province House (1818), in Halifax, N.S. Its carefully arranged columns and windows give a sense of balance and order.

St Paul's Church (1750) in Halifax was one of the first churches in Canada to be built in the Palladian style. In 1804, Holy Trinity, the Anglican cathedral in Quebec City, was also built in this style. It was a symbol of the law, customs, and religion of Quebec's new rulers.

The Palladian style did not influence French-Canadian architecture until the 1820s and 1830s. Thomas Baillairgé, who was Quebec's greatest church architect, successfully combined the French and Palladian traditions, as in his St Joseph parish church (1832) in Lauzon, Que. The main doorway, with its stone columns, resembled the Palladian style. By this time, however, Palladian was being abandoned by English Canada for several new styles.

In the 18th and 19th centuries, interest in ancient architecture was sparked by archaeological discoveries in Greece and Italy. Buildings in "the Greek style" or "the Roman style" became very popular in Europe. The style was later called *Neoclassical*, "Neo" meaning new, and "classical" referring to the time of ancient Greece and Rome.

The Neoclassical style was first brought to Canada by architects who had trained in Britain. Typical of this style was its love of columns. Its smooth stone walls, monumental domes, well-proportioned windows, and stately columns recalled the harmony and beauty of ancient temples.

These new buildings were grander and more sophisticated because of the presence of trained architects in Canada after

Columns and Pediment of the Neoclassical style are shown in this Nova Scotia house. The pediment is the triangular shape above the columns. The style copies temples from the time of ancient Greece and Rome (courtesy SSC Photocentre/photo by S. Homer).

St Paul's Anglican Church, Halifax, is an excellent example of Palladian architecture in Canada (courtesy Environment Canada/Parks).

Colonial Building, *St John's, Nfld, is one of the best-preserved Neoclassical buildings in Canada. It was built from 1847 to 1850 (courtesy Environment Canada/Parks).*

1830. A larger population meant that more buildings had to be constructed, and communities were willing to pay more money for impressive new buildings. This is true, for example, for the outstanding Neoclassical building in Canada — the City Hall in Kingston, Ont. It was built (1844) on a large scale, in the hope that Kingston would become the capital of Canada. It displayed the columns and round dome of the "Roman style."

Other Neoclassical buildings, such as St Andrew's Church at Niagara-on-the-Lake, Ont. (1831), were more in the "Greek style." Bonsecours market, in Montreal (1852) is decorated in the Greek style.

The Neoclassical style was very popular among bankers. They liked to think of their banks as "temples of commerce," which would inspire confidence in their customers. One of the most influential banks in the Neoclassical style was the Bank of Montreal (1848) at the Place d'Armes in Montreal, which was the financial heart of Canada. The Neoclassical style remained popular for banks for almost 100 years.

MID-TO-LATE 19TH-CENTURY ARCHITECTURE

Late 19th-century architecture (called the Victorian Era, after Queen Victoria of Britain) was a confusing array of styles. There was increasing interest in rediscovering the architecture of the past and using it as a model for new design. Architects felt free to borrow and blend elements from several different styles. A continued interest in the Picturesque was shown in the flair for drama, colour, and irregular designs.

These tastes were first introduced in a style called *Gothic Revival*, which took as its model the Gothic architecture of Europe during the Middle Ages.

The first important building in the new Gothic style was Notre-Dame Cathedral in Montreal (1829). Its pointed arches and soaring towers were in stark contrast to the pure, restrained taste of the Palladian and Neoclassical.

Because many of the magnificent cathedrals of Europe were erected in the Gothic style, it was considered to be appropriate to the Christian faith. Gothic architecture sought to instil a sense of awe with its towers, high ceilings, and pinnacles. The Gothic also tried to astonish and delight with detail and ornament. It was brought to Canada by a number of architects trained in Britain, such as the Irish architect James O'Donnell, who designed Notre-Dame. (This angered many French Canadians, who considered the style too English and too Protestant.)

Gothic Revival quickly became the favourite style for church architecture in Canada, especially for Anglican churches. Gothic features, such as pointed arches, spires, and a variety of ornaments, are found in Christ Church Cathedral in Fredericton, N.B. (1853), designed by two well-known British architects. It was the largest church in North America when it was completed.

A humbler version of Gothic Revival, called "Carpenter's Gothic," was also

Notre-Dame, *Montreal. The soaring towers and pointed arches of this cathedral (built 1823-29) announced the Gothic Revival style in Canada (courtesy Environment Canada/Parks).*

Gothic Tower and Spire, *St James Cathedral, Toronto (1849-53). The tower is the highest in Canada and second highest in North America. By carefully copying English Gothic tastes, St James proclaimed its ties with Britain (courtesy Environment Canada/Parks).*

Beaux-arts Style *is shown in the simple forms, dome, and columns of the Alberta Legislature Building (courtesy Government of Alberta).*

Canadian Pacific Building, Toronto (1912), left, and the Traders Bank (1905) were two early skyscrapers. They were similar in style, with a solid base, repetitive floors above, and an ornamental top (courtesy NAC/PA-60392).

Skyscraper The Canadian Imperial Bank of Commerce (1929-31) was for many years the tallest building in Canada. Though soaring, it still has a rock-solid appearance unlike modern glass-and-steel towers (courtesy Herb Nott and Co. Ltd, Photographers).

adapted for churches in wood, as in St John's Church (1753) in Lunenburg, N.S.

The Gothic Revival style was also used for the first Parliament Buildings, constructed in Ottawa between 1859 and 1866. The new Houses of Parliament in London, England, had been built in this style a few years before. In choosing the same style, Canada declared its strong ties with Great Britain. The liveliness of the Canadian Parliament Buildings was unmatched even in Britain. Unfortunately, the buildings burned down in 1916. The buildings which replaced them are far less flamboyant. Only the original library remains.

Gothic Revival was also used for many early university buildings in Canada. University College in Toronto (1859), for example, was designed by F.W. Cumberland, who had come out from England in 1847. Gothic features were also found in Ontario farm houses and in homes of the wealthy in Montreal and Toronto. The style later spread to western Canada (for example, in St Paul's Cathedral in Regina, 1895).

A number of other styles, also modelled on the past, reflected the Victorian taste. The *Second Empire* style originated in France and took Canada by storm in the 1870s. It was named for the "second empire" of Napoleon III and is also called "the French style," although many of its elements may be traced to Renaissance Italy. Its main feature is the mansardt roof, named for François Mansardt, the 17th-century French architect. The mansardt roof begins with a steeply sloping section with dormer windows, then rises to a flat or more gently sloped top section. It included columns and elaborate decorations. The Montreal City Hall (1878) is built in this style. Second Empire was the preferred style for public buildings in the 1870s and early 1880s, as shown in the Legislative Building at Fredericton, N.B. (1882), and the Custom House at Saint John, N.B. (1881).

In the mid-1880s, Canadian architecture began to take its lead from the United States, rather than from Britain or France. For example, the rugged wall surfaces, huge rounded arches, square or rounded towers, and squat columns of Toronto City Hall (1890) were strongly influenced by the work of the well-known American architect Henry H. Richardson. Richardson's style was inspired by yet another past era, the Romanesque.

An American architect was directly re-

Chateau Frontenac, built in 1892, was inspired by French castles. The chateau style was a continuation of the ideas of the Picturesque (courtesy Environment Canada/Parks).

sponsible for a style that is considered particularly Canadian, the *Château* style. The Canadian Pacific Railway invited architect Bruce Price to design the new Banff Springs Hotel (1888). His design drew inspiration from 16th-century French castles, or *châteaux*, with their steeply pitched roofs and numerous towers and turrets. Several other hotels were built across Canada in this style. The most dramatic example is the Château Frontenac, perched atop the cliff overlooking the St Lawrence River at Quebec City (1892).

MODERN ARCHITECTURE

Modern architecture is inspired by modern materials and technology, and by the function of the building itself. It rejects the use of historical forms and details. It emerged in Europe early in the 20th century, spread to the U.S. and eventually to Canada. Within modernism, a variety of approaches have emerged. Some of these are clearly defined styles.

Beaux-Arts In the early years of the 20th century, architects began to reject the excesses of 19th-century design. They were influenced by the *Beaux-Arts* movement from Paris, which urged a return to more clearly organized designs. The details, such as domes, columns, and pediments, were drawn from history and were usually classical in origin. The Beaux-Arts style resulted in several imposing railway stations in Winnipeg, Vancouver, and Ottawa. Most impressive of all was Toronto's Union Station (1920, designed by Canadian John Lyle and others), with its massive vaulted hall, classical columns, and sculptured decorations on Canadian themes. The legislature buildings in Saskatchewan, Alberta, and Mani-

toba were all designed in the Beaux-Arts style. Each included an impressive portico and a massive central dome.

The Skyscraper The greatest change in architecture in the 19th century was the raising of office buildings to a status once held only by palaces and churches. Business replaced the church and government as the chief patrons of architecture. This new type of building first emerged in Chicago and New York in the 1890s. For several years, these buildings were limited to four or five storeys. Then several technical advances, such as steel beams, reinforced concrete, and the Otis elevator made it possible to build these office buildings higher and higher, giving them their familiar name "skyscraper." The skyscraper also helped a business get the most profit from expensive downtown real estate.

Skyscrapers had an important effect on architectural style. Tall, multi-storey buildings had no historical precedent. At first, architects continued to try to adopt historical styles to clothe them. Later, the remnants of the old styles were simply used as decoration (such as "pillars" carved into the stone wall but serving no purpose).

The Canadian Imperial Bank of Commerce building, in Toronto (1931), was for over 30 years the tallest building in Canada at 34 storeys. Designed by New York architects, it has a massive, solid base. Like other tall buildings of the time, its tower is stepped back at the top. The arches and sculptures are in a Romanesque style.

Some of the early skyscrapers were built in a style called Art Deco, which was popular in the 1920s and 1930s. Art deco buildings usually had stepped storeys — creating a "wedding cake" effect — and geometric decoration that was often bold and jarring. The lobby of the Marine Building in Vancouver (1930) is one of the best examples with its rich ornamentation.

Few large buildings were erected during the Depression years of the 1930s and the war years of the 1940s. The houses of this era, from 1925 to 1945, were modelled on various styles of the past. The Neo-Tudor home looked like picturesque mansions of Elizabethan England. Other styles copied Spanish villas; still others went back to the Georgian style of the early 19th century.

Along with the birth of the skyscraper came a new generation of architects in Europe and the United States who transformed the shape of our cities. In many ways, they returned to the principles of the architecture of the early 1800s. They preferred simple, geometric forms. They wanted their buildings to stand alone, like the temples of earlier days. They avoided details and ornament. They rejected direct references to the past, such as pointed arches or columns. They relied on basic materials, such as steel, concrete, and glass. By the 1940s, their work was so widespread that it was known as the *International* style.

Peacetime brought prosperity in the 1950s and a building boom. Countless buildings rose in Canadian cities, more and more of them in the International style. The Toronto Dominion Centre (1968) in Toronto, for example, was designed by the German architect Mies van der Rohe, one of the foremost designers in the International style. The dark, imposing towers rely for their effect on precise detail and simple shape. Among other notable skyscrapers are Place Ville Marie (1965) in Montreal, as well as Canada's tallest building at 72 storeys, First Canadian Place (1975) in Toronto. The International style was used for high-rise office towers, apartment buildings, hospitals, airports, and schools in every city in Canada. While many of these buildings were "boring boxes," some were more imaginative. The new Toronto City Hall (1965), for example, is a daring design, with two tall curved towers cradling the council chambers. The architect was Viljo Revell of Finland, who won an international competition for the design.

Centennial Year in 1967 and Expo 67 gave a tremendous boost to architecture in Canada. All across the country, governments commissioned cultural buildings

Romanesque Style *(shown here in Toronto's Old City Hall) featured solid shapes, round arches, and roughly cut stone (photo by J.H. Marsh).*

Second Empire Style *The steeply sloping mansardt roofs of the Montreal City Hall (1878) are typical of the Second Empire style. They recall the style of French castles (courtesy NAC/C-16468B).*

Toronto City Hall (1965) The daring design was chosen in an international competition. The bold lines of the building are set off by a sweeping plaza and reflecting pool (photo by J.H. Marsh).

International Style *(1968) The simple, repeated patterns of the Toronto Dominion Centre are typical of the International style (photo by J.H. Marsh).*

Heritage Conservation

Many buildings of historic interest have suffered the same fate as the Tegler Building in Edmonton, Dec. 12, 1982, shown above.

The building boom of the 1950s was often accomplished at great cost to the architectural heritage of the past. Governments and businesses paid little heed to the cries of small groups of conservationists, who pleaded on behalf of many beautiful buildings. The demolished buildings were often replaced by mediocre office towers, or worse, by parking garages.

The Centennial celebrations helped Canadians to focus attention on Canada's architectural heritage. As a result, there was a new interest in conserving historic buildings. In 1970, the federal government began to survey historic buildings across Canada. Heritage Canada Foundation has some 12 000 members dedicated to the preservation of important buildings. The federal government and most provincial and city governments are now active in conserving their architectural heritage (photo courtesy of City of Edmonton Archives/Ellen Edwards Coll.).

to commemorate the occasion. Among these buildings were the Fathers of Confederation Memorial Building in Charlottetown, the Grand Théâtre in Quebec City, the Ontario Science Centre and Ontario Place in Toronto, the National Arts Centre in Ottawa, and the Centennial Planetarium in Calgary. In Montreal, the Expo 67 site was studded with original and exuberant pavilions in the shapes of domes, tents, building blocks, and mirrored boxes. Many of these buildings were designed by Canadian architects, such as Arthur Erickson, who went on to an illustrious career in Canada and abroad. One of the most interesting projects connected with Expo 67 was Moshe Safdie's Habitat, a modular housing scheme which was intended as a model for housing developments in the future.

The 1960s and 1970s were also years of prosperity and optimism in Canada. In architecture, this was reflected in the highrise development of the downtown core of the large cities. Some of these were complex structures which served many purposes. In Montreal, for example, Raymond Affleck designed Place Bonaven-

Royal Bank Plaza, Toronto (1973-77). The lively, golden glass towers enclose a 12-storey high atrium. The late, modern style is a contrast to the simpler, more sombre feeling of the International Style (courtesy Webb Zerafa Menkes Housden Partnership/photo by Derek Griffiths).

Mississauga Civic Centre includes the shapes of a tower, pyramid, and drum (courtesy City of Mississauga).

ture (1968) as a self-contained city block which housed offices, shops, restaurants, a trade centre, and a hotel, all connected internally with parking garages and the subway system. The building boom was also seen in the expansion of universities across the country. Architects Ronald Thom and Arthur Erickson, in particular, planned university campuses which are among the best modern works in Canada.

In the midst of this activity and enthusiasm, several architects turned away from the International style, which many people found impersonal and boring.

The buildings of the recent past show so much variety that they cannot be categorized under any one style. Their most common characteristic is that they have rejected the International style; hence, they are often called *Post-Modern*. Some architects, especially in western Canada, work in a sculptured style of building, in wood, concrete, and brick. The moulded shape of Douglas Cardinal's St Mary's Church in Red Deer, Alta (1968), stands in bold contrast to the flat suburban landscape around it. The curves of his Canadian Museum of Civilization (1989) in Hull, Que., blend with the banks of the nearby Ottawa River.

J. Michael Kirkland and Edward Jones included buildings in the shape of a pediment, a pyramid, a tower, and a drum in their design for the Mississauga Civic Centre near Toronto (1986). Robson Square (1979) in Vancouver, designed by Arthur Erickson, includes the provincial art gallery and law courts, as well as a government office building and several restaurants. The raised square creates a separate landscape from the neighbouring streets by its tiers of staircases and waterfalls. In Edmonton, the Muttart Conservatory (1976) provides a colourful botanical garden all year round. Four glass pyramids of varying size have been designed by Peter Hemingway to cover a series of buried concrete chambers which house plants from tropical, temperate, and arid zones.

Finally, some Post-Modern architects have turned back to the past. In his design for the Canadian Centre for Architecture (1989), in Montreal, architect Peter Rose showed a renewed interest in the Beaux-Arts. The Royal Architectural Institute of Canada, 328 Somerset Street, West, Ottawa, Ont., K2P 0J9, can be contacted for more information.

▷ RELATED ARTICLES: **Barns; Grain Elevators; Heritage Conservation; House; Parliament Buildings;** and biographies of **Raymond Affleck; Baillairgé Family; Douglas Cardinal; Arthur Erickson; John Lyle; Raymond Moriyama; John B. Parkin; Francis Rattenbury; Moshe Safdie; Ronald Thom; Eberhard Zeidler.** *See also* entries on individual buildings: **Canadian Museum of Civilization; Christ Church Cathedral; CN Tower; Kingston City Hall; Province House.**

▷ SUGGESTED READING: Ruth Cawker and William Bernstein, *Contemporary Canadian Architecture* (1988); Alan Gowans, *Building Canada* (1966); Ron MacGregor and others, *Canadian Art: Building a Heritage* (1987); Moshe Safdie, *Form and Purpose* (1982); Leon Whiteson, *Modern Canadian Architecture* (1983).

■ Archives

Archives are places where permanent

St Mary's Catholic Church, Red Deer, Alta. Architect Douglas Cardinal's moulded shapes are a sharp contrast to the rigid lines of the International style (photo by Roy Ooms/Take Stock Inc.).

Paris Opera House Canadian architects' fame and work are spreading to other countries. Canadian architect Carlos Ott designed the new Paris Opera House, one of the most important new buildings in Paris (courtesy NORR Partnership Ltd).

records are kept. The word *archives* also refers to the records themselves. Governments, institutions, corporations, clubs, and individuals all produce records of their everyday activities. Most of these records are thrown away almost immediately, but others have value as a history of the particular organization or person. It is these significant records that are collected in archives. The people who look after them are called archivists.

Many institutions keep their own archives, but the largest archives in Canada are maintained by the federal and provincial governments. Several cities also have archives, including Toronto, Vancouver, Edmonton, Calgary, and Ottawa.

The National Archives of Canada in Ottawa is the most important archives in Canada. It traces its roots back to 1872. From 1912 to 1987 it was called the Public Archives of Canada. It keeps records from all federal government departments, as well as maps, paintings, books, photographs, films, sound recordings, music scores, architectural drawings, medals, and other objects. It also collects letters and diaries from politicians, scientists, writers, and other individuals who are of national interest.

What Archives Do Archivists collect

Architecture Styles

● Palladian was a classical style based on the architecture of the Renaissance in Italy.
Characteristics: balance and harmony; columns
Period: 1800 to 1875

● Neoclassical was inspired by the architecture of ancient Greece and Rome ("Classical Era").
Characteristics: classical columns, smooth stone walls, domes
Period: 1825 to 1860

● Gothic Revival was a Picturesque style inspired by the late Middle Ages.
Characteristics: soaring towers, pinnacles, pointed arches, spires, ornament
Period: 1845 to 1890

● Second Empire style was based on 17th-century French castles.
Characteristics: the mansardt roof, elaborate decorations
Period: 1870 to 1885

● Romanesque Revival was a Picturesque style that looked back to the late Middle Ages.
Characteristics: massive and sombre; rugged walls, rounded arches, squat columns
Period: 1880 to 1900

● Beaux-Arts was a Classical style.
Characteristics: balance, restraint, domes, columns
Period: 1900 to 1930

● Art Deco was influenced by streamlined technology.
Characteristics: smooth forms, colourful details, round curves
Period: 1925 to 1955

● International style is based on the idea that a building's form should reflect its function.
Characteristics: simple, geometric forms, lack of decoration
Period: 1945 to 1975

● Neo-Expressionist is a variation of the International style.
Characteristics: dramatic and striking; sculpted forms, sweeping curves
Period: 1950 to present

● Post-Modern is a tendency away from the International style.
Characteristics: new materials, references to the past; arches, pitched roofs
Period: 1975 to present

Archives are storage spaces for objects that have value as a history of a person or organization. Objects shown above include a rare book, photograph, cassette, watercolour, and government documents (courtesy NAC/PPB/K-0000004).

records, preserve them, and open them to the public. Before records even arrive at the archives, archivists help institutions and individuals with record management. They advise them on which documents can be destroyed and which should be kept. Once the selected records are transferred to the archives, they are carefully preserved in a secure, fireproof, and appropriate environment. Archivists catalogue the records and arrange them in files where they are accessible to researchers. Most archives publish guides to their collections. Staff assist readers in finding the information they want. Copies of photographs and papers held in the archives are available for a small fee to cover costs.

Archives also arrange exhibitions and publish books and pamphlets related to their collections. Archives have kept pace with new technologies. The early records at the National Archives, for example, were transcribed by hand from archives in Britain, France, and various parts of Canada. By the late 1980s the archives were equipped with laser disc recorders and machine-readable files.

Archives are used by researchers from government and universities, as well as by journalists and people interested in history and genealogy. The records in the archives can solve problems ranging from international boundary disputes to individual family trees. For everyone, they are our most direct link with our past.

■ Arctic

The Arctic is the Earth's most northern region. It surrounds the North Pole. It is sometimes defined as the area north of the treeline, or north of a line where the temperature in the warmest month is 10°C. This would include all Canada's arctic islands, the northern tip of Quebec, and a large area of the mainland of the Northwest Territories. Another definition of the Arctic is that it is everything north of the Arctic Circle.

The Arctic is very cold. It is one of the world's most sparsely populated areas. It receives very little precipitation, mostly in the form of snow. The length of days and nights varies greatly, ranging from 24 hours of daylight to 24 hours of darkness.

▷ RELATED ARTICLE: **Arctic Circle.**

▷ SUGGESTED READING: Pierre Berton, *The Arctic Grail* (1988); Normee Ekoomiak, *Arctic Memories* (1988); Janet Foster, *Journey to the Top of the World* (1987); Dan Francis, *Discovery of the North* (1986).

■ Arctic Archipelago

The Arctic Archipelago is a group of islands lying north of mainland Canada. It is the largest group of islands in the world, covering over 1.3 million km².

Some of the islands, especially in the east, have high mountain ranges which are covered in ice all the time. Canada's largest glaciers flow from these icecaps. Mount Barbeau in northern Ellesmere Island is the highest peak on the islands at 2616 m. It is the highest peak east of the Rockies.

The central and western islands are flat. The climate is very cold and the region is one of the driest in the world. The annual average temperature in the north, where the sun disappears completely for three to four months, is below -20°C. Summer temperatures may rise above freezing for only one or two months. The islands are treeless. Mosses, grasses, and low bush are the most common plant life. In the brief summer, vegetation can be quite lush in some areas. Animal life includes caribou, muskoxen, fox, wolf, lemming, white arctic hare, polar bear, walrus, seal, whale, and several species of

Ellesmere Island is the most northerly island in the Arctic Archipelago (photo by Stephen J. Krasemann/DRK Photo).

birds. The channels between the islands are almost always covered in ice during the winter.

Inuit have lived on the islands for thousands of years. Today, Inuit live in coastal villages throughout the islands. The non-Inuit population is mainly government and military personnel.

Europeans were first attracted to the High Arctic in search of the Northwest Passage, a sea-route around the top of North America. The quest for the passage began in the 16th century. It was finally navigated by Roald Amundsen and the crew of the *Gjoa* from 1903 to 1906. Whalers were active in the region until World War I.

Trapping furs still provides some income for the Inuit. Following World War II, mining became important at Nanisivik on Baffin Island and Polaris on Little Cornwallis Island. The islands may also prove to be a valuable source of oil and natural gas. The world's first arctic national park, Auyuittuq, was established in 1972 on Baffin Island. A second park, Ellesmere Island, was created in 1986.

■ Arctic Circle

The Arctic Circle is a line drawn parallel to the equator at latitude 66° 32'N. If you were to stand on the Arctic Circle on June 21, which is usually the longest day of the year, you would not see the sun set; it would remain above the horizon, even at midnight. Similarly, on December 22, usually the shortest day of the year, you would not see the sun rise at all; it would remain below the horizon, even at noon.

As you go north from the Arctic Circle, the number of summer days when you can see the sun at midnight increases, as do the number of winter days when it is dark at noon. At the North Pole, the sun never sets during the six months of summer; and once it has set, it does not rise again until the six months of winter are over.

▷ RELATED ARTICLES: **Arctic; North Pole.**

■ Arctic Ocean

The Arctic Ocean is one of the three oceans on which Canada has a coast. It is the smallest of the world's oceans. It is shaped roughly like a circle, with the North Pole at its centre. The ocean is connected to the Pacific Ocean by the Bering Strait. A much larger passage, the Greenland Sea, connects it with the Atlantic Ocean.

Once called the Frozen Sea, the Arctic Ocean's waters are covered with ice for most of the year. This ice drifts southward and westward, pushed by wind, waves, and a current. This moving ice has been used by explorers.

Much of the Arctic Ocean remained unexplored until the 20th century. During this century, scientists from Holland, the United States, and other countries began to explore the Arctic. Only a handful of Canadians, such as the ocean scientist Max Dunbar, had ever explored this ocean.

After World War II, the Government of Canada began supporting Arctic exploration. It was prompted to do so by the recognition of its military importance. Canada also realized that the Arctic Ocean might hold valuable resources, such as oil and natural gas. Doing research in the Arctic Ocean is one of the ways in which Canada stakes a claim to control the waters north of its northern coast.

The waters of the Arctic are relatively poor in nutrients. This is because there is little mixing of its waters to stir up food from its floor, as happens in other oceans. As well, the Arctic's ice cover limits the amount of sunshine (essential to life) getting into the upper layers of water. Nevertheless, the ocean is home to fish, such as

Icebreaker The Arctic Ocean was once called the Frozen Sea because it is covered with ice for most of the year. Here the icebreaker Terry Fox *keeps open a sea lane (photo by Ranson Photographers, Edmonton, for Gulf Canada).*

the Arctic char, and to a number of mammals. These include seals, walrus, a variety of whales, hares, and polar bears.

▷ RELATED ARTICLES: **Maxwell Dunbar; North; North Pole; Ocean; Oceanography; Sea Ice.**

■ Arctic Red River

Arctic Red River, N.W.T., is a small arctic community. It is located where the Arctic Red River meets the Mackenzie River. The site has been a native fishing camp for centuries. The river was the main means of communication until the arrival of the Dempster Highway in the late 1970s. Its population in 1986 was 108.

■ Arctic Sovereignty, *see* Sovereignty

■ Arctic Winter Games

The Arctic Winter Games are held in a northern community every two years. They provide northern athletes with a chance to train and compete in events such as skiing, curling, snowshoeing, and skating. The most unusual events are sports developed by the Inuit to test stamina and strength, such as the high kick. The games include participants from Alaska and Greenland, as well as from northern Canada. In 1990 performers and observers from the Soviet Union will attend the games for the first time.

■ Arden, Elizabeth

Beautician (*born in 1878 at Woodbridge, Ont.; died in 1966 at New York City, New York, U.S.*). Arden was the founder of the well-known cosmetics firm. She grew up in Ontario, the daughter of

The SkyDome in Toronto is Canada's newest stadium. The dome closes to cover the field during bad weather (courtesy Aerocamera Services Inc./ Orangeville, Ont.).

The High Kick is one of the unique events at the Arctic Winter Games (photo by Jim Merrithew).

British settlers. Her real name was Florence Nightingale Graham. She first worked as an apprentice nurse. When she was in her late twenties, she moved from Toronto to New York. She took a job in a beauty salon, where she learned how to prepare cosmetics. She borrowed money from her brother and opened her own salon in 1910, calling herself Elizabeth Arden. Her salon was a success from the beginning. She made new and improved skin creams and was the first to introduce eye make-up to North America. Her business grew into a multimillion-dollar empire which sold clothes as well as make-up. It had branches across the world. Arden had an equally successful hobby as the owner of racehorses, which won her more than $2 million in prize money.

■ Arenas and Stadiums

The first covered ice rink in Canada was built in 1852 in Quebec City. Over the next 20 years others opened across Canada. The most famous of these was Montreal's Victoria Rink, built in 1862. It was at the time considered to be the largest arena in the world, holding some 2000 spectators. The first recorded indoor game of hockey took place in this arena in 1875. All the early arenas used natural ice. The first artificial ice surface was built in 1911 in Victoria, B.C.

Canada's best-known arenas were built as homes for National Hockey League teams. The Montreal Forum (1924) and Toronto's Maple Leaf Gardens (1931) are still home to the Montreal Canadiens and Toronto Maple Leafs. Other NHL rinks include the Saddledome in Calgary, Pacific Coliseum in Vancouver, Northlands Coliseum in Edmonton, Winnipeg Arena in Winnipeg, and the Colisée in Quebec City. Each of these holds from 15 000 to 20 000 spectators; as does the Victor Copps Coliseum in Hamilton, Ont.

Canada's outdoor stadiums were built as Canadian football gained popularity. Varsity Stadium in Toronto opened in 1911 and was enlarged to hold 19 000 spectators by 1930. It was home to the Toronto Argonauts football team and held many Grey Cup games. The first stadium in Canada designed to offer both an open and covered field was Montreal's Olympic Stadium. Its controversial design caused huge cost overruns, and though opened in 1976, its soft, retractable roof was not in place until 1987. The stadium cost over $1 billion. The first covered stadium, B.C. Place in Vancouver, opened in 1983 at a cost of $126 million. The most recent is Toronto's SkyDome, which has a unique retractable roof. It cost $532 million and holds 53 000 fans for baseball and 52 000 for football. Other large outdoor stadiums include Commonwealth Stadium in Edmonton, which holds 60 000 people.

Canada's arenas and stadiums are part of all its major cities and many of its towns. They are part of its sporting life and are used for many other purposes as well.

■ Argentia

Argentia, Nfld., is a village on the west coast of the Avalon Peninsula in Placentia Bay. It was founded as a French fishing village in the late 1600s. First called Little Placentia, the name changed to Argentia around 1900 after the opening of a silver-lead mine. During World War II the community was taken over to form an American military base. At one point the base had over 12 000 residents. It closed in 1975, and today the site is a small research station. It had a population of 50 in 1986.

■ Armaments

Armaments are weapons used for attack or defence. In earliest days, armaments were made out of readily available and easily used stone or wood. Now they can be complex, computer-controlled weapons, such as missiles capable of hitting a target thousands of kilometres away.

Before European settlement, the native people were armed with clubs, axes, bows and arrows, and spears. They also carried protective shields. These simple weapons were no match for the guns that Europeans introduced to North America.

The early guns were rather difficult to use. Samuel de Champlain's gun, for instance, was called an arquebus. It was a muzzle-loader. Gunpowder and a ball were thrust down the barrel, and the gun was fired by igniting the gunpowder with a burning wick. It was not very accurate at any distance, but it impressed the Indians very much.

Guns developed in later years were better. The long barrelled flintlock was a favourite weapon among hunters in the 1700s because it was accurate over long distances. It was fired by striking a spark into the gunpowder. Soldiers used short barrelled muskets. They were not very accurate, but could have a devastating effect when a number of them were fired together. These were the weapons used at Quebec in 1759, where a few murderous volleys from British muskets scattered the French forces.

The breech-loading rifle replaced the muzzle-loader in the mid-19th-century. It was vastly more efficient. A metal cartridge holding both the bullet and the gunpowder were inserted into the barrel at the breech, just above the trigger. Rifles were sent to Canada in 1866 when the Fenians threatened to invade. A Gatling gun, a type of machine gun, was used against the Metis during the North-West Rebellion in 1885. A young Scot who grew up in Ontario, James Paris Lee, helped develop a new rifle called the Lee-Enfield, which was used by Canadian soldiers until 1950. Less successful was the Canadian-made Ross rifle, which proved very unreliable during World War I. In that war, Canada produced shells and ammunition for its allies. The machine gun proved so deadly during World War I that it became almost impossible to overcome a defensive position. As a result, millions of soldiers died on the battlefield in futile attempts to push back enemy lines. Furthermore, the pounding of heavy artillery churned the battlefield into a sea of mud and rained death on the soldiers huddled in trenches. By World War II, soldiers were far more mobile as a result of tanks, trucks, and armoured personnel carriers. Military aircraft, which had been introduced in World War I, now not only threatened soldiers; they also carried war, indiscriminately, to the cities of the enemy. Many European cities, especially in Germany, were devastated by air attacks. At sea, the submarine revolutionized warfare. Much of Canada's role in World War II was fighting German submarines. Canadian industry expanded greatly during World War II to build these new weapons.

During the two world wars, the Canadian Armed Forces required vast numbers

Canadian Soldier on patrol as part of the United Nations forces keeping the peace in Cyprus. The soldier is carrying a C-7 rifle (Canadian Forces Photo/photo by Sgt John Smith).

HMCS Iroquois *A Sea King helicopter approaches to land aboard the deck of the* Iroquois *(Canadian Forces Photo).*

Northern Terrain Vehicle *is capable of operations in all climates and on all terrains (Canadian Forces Photo/photo by Sgt Dick Brackele).*

of weapons. At the end of World War II, for example, the forces had 368 ships, almost 5000 aircraft, hundreds of tanks, and countless rifles. After World War I Canada disarmed almost completely. AFter World War II it maintained armed forces appropriate to the role it set for itself in international affairs. Ground forces have required tanks, armoured personnel carriers, artillery, and sophisticated communications equipment to meet Canadian commitments as a member of NATO and as a UN peacekeeper. The air forces require jet fighters and transport aircraft. The navy still concentrates on anti-submarine defence.

Most of these weapons are designed and built in foreign countries. Some weapons, or parts, are manufactured in Canada, and Canadian companies also sell arms to other countries. The Avro CF-100 fighter aircraft and the Tribal and St Laurent class destroyers for the navy were both designed and built in Canada in the 1950s. A turning point came when the Avro Arrow, the world's most advanced jet fighter, was cancelled in 1959. The Americans refused to buy the Canadian-designed Arrow and Canada replaced it with American planes and the Bomarc missile, which had a nuclear warhead.

The most fearsome weapon ever devised is the nuclear bomb. Carried thousands of kilometres by guided missile or dropped from an aircraft, a single bomb could annihilate an entire city. The government of Pierre Trudeau decided in the 1970s that it would not have nuclear weapons on Canadian soil. The last of these was phased out in July 1984. Nevertheless, like the rest of the world, Canada lives under the terrifying threat of nuclear war.

■ Armed Forces

The armed forces of Canada protect Canadians from enemy attack, help allies in time of international crisis, and keep order within Canada during emergencies. Until 1968, the armed forces were made up of three separate arms: navy, army, and air force. In that year they were combined into the unified Canadian Armed Forces.

In 1988 there were 87 393 regular force members, as well as 58 331 reserve personnel in the armed forces.

ARMY

In the 17th and 18th centuries, both in New France and in the British colonies, defence was provided by military units raised in times of crisis. Called "militias," these forces were made up of all able-bodied men (usually between the ages of 16 and 60). The militias were not well trained, but were available quickly in every community. They were therefore adequate for the small clashes that occurred on the frontiers of settlement.

Professional soldiers from Britain and France were sent to North America in small numbers until the 1750s. These forces of regular soldiers, called "garrisons," were increased during the Seven Years' War of 1756 to 1763. Later, the British army and Royal Navy were vital in saving Canada from being taken over by the United States in the War of 1812.

The Americans were still a threat to Canada after the War of 1812. When Britain was unable to keep a large garrison in North America because of its cost, the Canadian colonies had a reason for creating their own regular army. But Canadians never really warmed to the idea of a professional army, even after Confederation in 1867.

There were three main reasons for this. A regular army would have been more expensive than the militia. Canadians preferred the militia's informal way of doing things to the rigid discipline of a professional army. Just as important, Canadians had developed a myth about the War of 1812, which claimed that the militia, not the British army, had held off the Americans. The part-time volunteer militia thus came to be seen as a symbol of solid Canadian values, an institution that made them different from and better than the Americans and even their British mother country.

Regular regiments of infantry and cavalry were created in 1883, joining artillery units formed 10 years before, but they

were very small, and their role was restricted to teaching the militia. In 1885, these permanent soldiers were only a tiny part of the 8000-man army sent to fight Louis Riel in the North-West Rebellion. The rest were mainly militia volunteers, called out with their regiments.

World War I After 1885, the regular army grew somewhat larger, numbering 3000 men in 1914. However, this was still small compared to the part-time militia, which numbered 60 000. When World War I broke out in August 1914, the Canadian government decided to contribute one infantry division as well as cavalry units (about 25 000 men in all) to fight alongside the British and the French. Later, second, third, and fourth divisions were sent to the front. These four divisions were organized in the Canadian Corps. The corps initially came under the command of British officers, Generals E.A. Alderson and Sir Julian Byng, but from June 1917 it was led by a Canadian, General Sir Arthur Currie.

The Canadian troops won the respect of all the Allies as well as the Germans for their performance under all three commanders. At Ypres, in April 1915, the 1st Division held firm during the first German attack using poison gas. At Vimy Ridge, in April 1917, the four Canadian divisions, fighting alongside each other for the first time, captured a strong German position that had resisted previous British and French attacks. At Amiens, in August 1918, the Canadian Corps under Currie led the way in smashing through the German line in what proved to be the Allies' victorious final offensive.

Over 600 000 Canadian men served in the army during World War I. About 60 000 were killed. The majority of these men came straight from civilian life and had never put a uniform on before they joined up. This was the largest army so far in Canadian history, and it could have been the nucleus of a large peacetime army. But when the war was over, the government chose again to maintain only a small army of about 4000 regulars, backed by part-time militiamen. It also bought very little equipment. When a major war started again in September 1939, neither the regulars nor the volunteers were really prepared for battle.

World War II Because conscription (compulsory service in the forces) had caused a political crisis in World War I, the government at first wanted to limit the size of Canada's army in World War II. It decided to send only one division over-

seas. By the end of the war, however, there were five divisions and two armoured brigades in Europe. In addition, two infantry battalions (about 2000 men) were sent to help defend Hong Kong in 1941, where they were overrun by the Japanese. On August 19, 1942, the 2nd Canadian Division took part in the disastrous raid on Dieppe, France. Of the nearly 5000 Canadian soldiers who left England on the raid, only 2211 returned, the rest being killed or captured.

The Canadian Army was led by Canadians from the beginning of World War II, coming first under General A.G.L. McNaughton and then under General H.D.G. Crerar. Unlike World War I, when the Canadian Corps was kept together, the Canadian Army was split up in World War II. About half took part in the Sicilian and Italian campaigns from July 1943 to February 1945, as part of the British Eighth Army. The other half fought in northwestern Europe from June 6, 1944, to May 8, 1945, under Canadian command in the First Canadian Army. Both halves were finally united in the last months of the war, when they were largely responsible for liberating Holland from the Germans.

The Post-War Period Over 700 000 Canadians served in the army in World War II, and the majority, as before, had no

Canadian Soldiers on a NATO exercise in West Germany (Canadian Forces Photo/photo by Sgt Margaret Reid).

Canadian Military Organization

Navy
Ships are usually commanded by Lieutenant Commanders, or Commanders

Army

Unit	Size	Commanded by
Section	10 men	Master Corporal or Sergeant
Platoon	3 sections	Lieutenant
Company	3 platoons	Major
Battalion/Regiment	6 companies*	Lieutenant Colonel
Brigade	3-4 battalions	Brigadier General
Division	2-3 brigades	Major General
Corps	2+ divisions	Lieutenant General
Army	2+ corps	General

* Counting necessary administrative and supply personnel, battalions number about 800 to 1000 men

Air Force

Unit	Size	Commanded by
Flight	4 aircraft	Captain or Major
Squadron	3+ flights	Lieutenant Colonel
Wing	2+ squadrons	Colonel
Air Group*	2+ wings	Brigadier General
Air Division	2+ groups	Major General

* In WWII, the RCAF's No. 6 Bomber Group comprised nine operational squadrons, three training units, and was commanded by an Air Vice-Marshal (Major General equivalent)

Training Exercise in B.C. *Canadian soldiers attack from a Grizzly armoured personnel carrier during a training exercise (Canadian Forces Photo/photo by Sgt Mac Johnson).*

prior military experience. Twenty-three thousand were killed. The government had another nucleus for a large peacetime army when World War II came to a close, but it chose to keep the military small. However, with the creation of NATO and the start of the Korean War (in which 22 000 soldiers were involved, fighting alongside other members of the United Nations), Canada realized that it needed to have a larger and better-trained regular army.

The army's size was increased gradually to 52 000 men and women in 1962. The part-time militia or reserve, which was once the most important element of the army, was now seen to be less useful for fighting a modern war, and its strength gradually decreased.

When the army, navy, and air force were unified in 1968, the strength of the regular army was 37 000, while the effective strength of the reserve was probably less than 10 000.

Canadian Destroyers *(left and right) take on fuel from a support ship (centre). The role of the destroyers is to search and destroy enemy submarines (Canadian Forces Photo/photo by M/Cpl Attilio Sartori).*

NAVY

The idea of a Canadian navy separate from Britain's powerful Royal Navy (RN) can be traced to a collection of small, armed civilian ships, assembled in 1886. These ships patrolled Canadian waters because the Royal Navy refused to arrest American fishermen who were doing business in Canadian waters. Canada, therefore, realized that some sort of presence at sea was part of what went with being an independent country.

The Royal Canadian Navy (RCN) was founded on May 4, 1910, at a time of intense naval rivalry between Germany and Great Britain. English Canadians hoped that, by defending its own coasts and trade, Canada could also contribute to the British Empire by relieving the Royal Navy of these responsibilities. Most French Canadians, however, had no interest in British affairs and approved the formation of a separate navy. When war broke out between Britain and Germany in August 1914, the RCN had only 350 men and two old training cruisers, the *Niobe* and *Rainbow*.

World War I In World War I, Canada was a vital shipper of supplies and men to the war effort of Britain and its allies. Canadian waters had to be defended against an entirely new weapon, the German long-range submarine (U-boat). Because the British did not have enough small, maneuverable ships, the RCN used the private yachts and crafts built by Canadian industry to create a navy of about 130 anti-submarine vessels. These patrol ships did valuable work in protecting convoys headed towards Great Britain, although the Royal Navy's warships were needed when heavily armed German U-boats marauded off Canada in 1918. They sank only three steamers and about 24 fishing boats in Canadian waters.

After the war, funds were short, regular personnel few, and equipment limited. In 1923 the navy formed a reserve like the army's militia: the Royal Canadian Naval Reserve. It was made up of veteran sailors and the Royal Canadian Naval Volunteer Reserve. (The RCNVR was an organization for enthusiastic amateurs.) The navy came close to being shut down during the Great Depression of the 1930s. The most influential soldier of the time, A.G.L. McNaughton, favoured the air force and thought no navy was necessary. The RCN survived, however, and was strengthened as Canada slowly rearmed to meet the threat of Germany and Japan in the late

1930s. There were 3000 men, six destroyers, and five minesweepers in 1939 (still a meagre force).

World War II In World War II, the RCN again expanded greatly and again protected convoys as its major role. This time, however, the challenge of the German U-boat was much greater. By the end of 1942, half the ships which escorted the convoys carrying men and materials overseas across the North Atlantic were Canadian, many of them built in Canada for that purpose. The navy's contribution to the Battle of the Atlantic was crucial. The RCN had command of the northwest Atlantic theatre of operations from early 1943 on, and also made appearances in many other parts of the world, including the D-Day landings in Normandy in June 1944. About 100 000 men and 6500 women served in the World War II navy.

The Post-War Period Financial restraints and morale problems followed the outbreak of peace in 1945. There were complaints about low pay and poor leadership. Membership in NATO and a commitment to the Korean War gave the navy a new life, a role in the defence of the Western World, and a reason for having more people and better equipment. Three destroyers and 3600 officers and men of the RCN served in Korea, 1950 to 1953. A destroyer escort program began in 1949. In the next 10 years, 14 anti-submarine vessels were commissioned, and six similar ships came on duty in the 1960s. The RCN also established a naval aviation branch, and kept one aircraft carrier on service from 1946 until 1970.

When the RCN celebrated its 50th birthday in 1960, it had 62 ships. This was a high point, because by the end of 1965, the RCN had been reduced to one aircraft carrier, 21 destroyer escorts, and 10 ocean escorts. Personnel levels had gone from less than 5000 in March 1945 to more than 21 500 in 1963, but the RCN always had difficulty in finding and training people with the necessary technical skills to help run a modern navy.

AIR FORCE

World War I Canada did not have an air force until almost the end of World War I. Over 20 000 Canadians served with the British flying services in World War I, among them some of the great names of early military aviation, such as W.A. (Billy) Bishop, Raymond Collishaw, W.G. Barker, and D.R. MacLaren. The contribution of Canadians to their allies' air effort was extraordinary, especially for a country of Canada's size. In addition, two-thirds of the Canadians in the British air forces were trained in Canada.

Formation of the Royal Canadian Air Force (RCAF) A small air reserve was formed in Canada in 1920. A permanent, professional air force followed in 1923. It became the RCAF on April 1, 1924, the date that is celebrated as the air force's birthday. At first, the RCAF's main task was non-military, civil air operations, such as making surveys, crop-dusting, medical rescue, and fighting forest fires. As one of the RCAF pioneers remembered it, "We were bush pilots in uniform." In 1939 the 4000-strong Royal Canadian Air Force was in no way prepared to fight a modern war.

World War II Prime Minister W.L. Mackenzie King hoped to concentrate as much as possible of the country's war effort in Canada. He therefore took the opportunity to give the RCAF charge of a Canada-based scheme to instruct air crews for the war overseas. This British Commonwealth Air Training Plan (BCATP), which was agreed to in late 1939, was a major contribution to Allied air superiority in World War II. It trained over 131 000 pilots, navigators, bomb aimers, wireless operators, air gunners, and flight engineers from all over the Commonwealth, the United States, and the countries of occupied Europe. Canada paid $1.6 billion, three-quarters of the total BCATP cost.

Once trained, a great many of the 72 835 Canadian graduates went overseas. At first, almost all Canadian air crew were posted to units of the British Royal Air Force (RAF). After RCAF squadrons began to be formed overseas in March 1941, there were Canadian units to which Canadian trainees could be sent. By the end of the war, 48 RCAF squadrons had served overseas. Even so, most RCAF personnel outside Canada went to British units, not those of their own national air force. These large numbers led to a great many casualties, quite the opposite of Mackenzie King's original aim of keeping Canadians away from the fighting.

About 250 000 men and women served in the RCAF in World War II. Most served in the BCATP and in the air commands which defended Canada (not, as it happened, a pressing need) and which reached out into the Atlantic to protect convoys and watch for submarines. Those outside Canada saw duty in the Battle of Britain, 1940, in North Africa and Italy, in the northwestern Europe campaign of

Women in the Forces

During World War I, more than 3000 nurses and a few women doctors served with the armed forces, many in front-line positions of great danger. However, it was not possible for women to join the armed forces as such until World War II, when separate corps were established for them: the Canadian Women's Army Corps (formed 1941), the Royal Canadian Air Force (Women's Division) (formed later in 1941), and the Royal Canadian Naval Women's Service (1942). None of these women were given combat roles. In general, they were assigned to secretarial or nursing duties. Today, the more than 8000 women in the Canadian Armed Forces have the same opportunities as men and can become pilots, vehicle technicians, and so on.

1944 to 1945, and in India and Burma at the end of the war against Japan. Canadians played a special role — and paid a special price — in the RAF's bomber offensive against Germany, in which 10 000 Canadian airmen were killed (more than half of the 17 000 killed in the whole war). The RCAF had its own formation, No. 6 Group, in RAF Bomber Command, led by Air Vice-Marshals G.E. Brookes and C.M. "Black Mike" McEwen. J.E. "Johnny" Fauquier and G.F. "Buzz" Beurling, who both flew with RAF and RCAF squadrons, were among the best-known and most-decorated individual Canadians of the air war.

The Post-War Period The RCAF demobilized to a force of 13 000 all ranks in 1946 and returned to duties not unlike those of the 1920s: search and rescue, air survey, and transport. But the peace was soon a bitter one. The RCAF sent a transport unit, No. 426 (Thunderbird) Squadron, to the Korean War (1950-53). In 1951 it contributed an air division of 12 fighter squadrons to NATO in Europe. The RCAF also trained almost 6000 pilots and navigators from NATO countries (1950-58). By the 1950s, Canada was clearly vulnerable to an air attack from the Soviet Union.

The RCAF co-operated closely with the American air force in the defence of North America. Early Warning Systems were constructed, and a joint Canada-US air defence command, NORAD, was established (1958).

By the mid-1950s, the RCAF had grown to more than 50 000 regular personnel. It played an important role in the air defence of North America, and in NATO forces in Europe. It was equipped with the CF-100, the first successful military aircraft completely designed and built in Canada, and the F-86 Sabre, built by Canadair in Montreal. However, the 1959 cancellation of the CF-105 Avro Arrow, an all-Canadian supersonic jet, was a blow to the pride of the RCAF, which despite the CF-100 got most of its equipment from foreigners.

1964 TO THE PRESENT

The year 1964 marked the beginning of a new phase in the history of Canada's armed forces. The minister of national defence, Paul Hellyer, pushed forward, despite several resignations from senior military staff, with the complete "unification" of the three services into a single "Canadian Armed Forces." The Royal Canadian Navy, the Canadian Army, and

CF-18 Fighter *flies over the clouds in southern Germany (Canadian Forces Photo/photo by W.O. Vic Johnson).*

the Royal Canadian Air Force all disappeared, along with their distinctive uniforms on May 1, 1966. This became law in February 1968. Among Hellyer's aims were cost-cutting and efficiency. No other country in the world had such a unified structure, and it was much criticized. In addition, many disliked the new, green uniforms which would be worn by sailors, soldiers, and airmen. As time went on, however, it was clear that the sea, land, and air elements remained separate for the purposes of co-operation in NATO and NORAD, and they were able to maintain many of their old customs and traditions.

The government of Pierre Trudeau, in power from 1968, at first questioned NORAD, NATO, and the value of some peacekeeping operations. Numbers were reduced from about 99 000 in 1968 to 78 000 in 1976. Canada's NATO contingent of 10 000, based in Germany, was slashed in half in 1969. Trudeau believed that the Canadian Armed Forces should serve interests at home, such as protecting the coastlines, and he did not hesitate to use them during the October Crisis in 1970. Yet Canada also remained firmly a member of NATO and NORAD. Peacekeeping commitments continued and even increased. In the late 1970s and early 1980s, the Liberal government began slowly to upgrade the forces, with recruitment and equipment such as the Leopard tank and the CF-18 fighter aircraft. In addition, Trudeau made the Canadian forces a model for his government's policy of insisting that its employees be able to function and serve the public in both English and French.

The Conservative Party was critical of the Liberals for not doing enough for the armed forces, and during the brief period in 1979-80 when Joe Clark was prime minister, a study was made to see if unification remained a good idea. The Mulroney government, elected in 1984, did not question the overall policy of unification, but it brought back versions of the three old uniforms. The Mulroney government has found it more difficult to implement other real changes, especially the building of a "three-ocean navy" with 10 to 12 nuclear-powered attack submarines. The reason is the same one that has faced governments since the early 1960s: too much to do and not enough money to do it with. Accordingly, in 1989 the submarines were cancelled and millions of dollars were cut from the defence budget.

These recent cuts echoed a common theme in Canadian history. When money is tight, and Canadians do not feel threatened, the armed forces will always be one of the first candidates for restraint.

▷ RELATED ARTICLES: **Aviation; Carignan-Salières Regiment; Conscription; Defence; Dieppe; Militia; NATO; North-West Rebellion; October Crisis; Seven Years' War; Voltigeurs Canadiens; War of 1812; Wars; World War I; World War II.**

■ Arnprior

Arnprior, Ont., is a town nestled in the Ottawa Valley, 56 km west of Ottawa. It was founded as a colony of Scots pioneers by Archibald McNab in 1823. He named the site for his family home in Scotland. After 1850 logging became important and later still the textile industry. Its population in 1986 was 6022.

▷ RELATED ARTICLE: **Archibald McNab.**

■ Arpent

The arpent was a French measurement that was used in New France for dividing up land. One arpent was equal to 58.5 m. A square arpent was 0.342 ha.

▷ RELATED ARTICLE: **Seigneurial System.**

■ Arsenault, Aubin E.

Premier of Prince Edward Island (*born in 1870 at Abrams Village, P.E.I.; died in 1968 at Charlottetown, P.E.I.*). Arsenault was the first Acadian to become premier of P.E.I. He was proud of his Acadian heritage and was active in preserving its culture. Trained as a lawyer, Arsenault was first elected in 1908. He served as premier from 1917 to 1919. Arsenault was one of the first to recognize the important role that tourism could play in the economy of the Island. From 1921 to 1946 he was a judge of the Supreme Court.

■ Art

The word art has many different mean-ings. It can describe a special skill in performing an ordinary task, as in "the art of cooking." It can describe those activities, such as painting or music, which inspire in us a sense of beauty or wonder.

Not all cultures consider art to be separate from other activities. The concept of art, for example, was most likely alien to the Northwest Coast Indian people. Yet they created objects that are known around the world for their beauty and imagination.

Today, we make a distinction between two forms of art, depending on their main purpose. The applied arts apply artistic principles to the making of practical objects. These include furniture, glass, jewellery, weaving, graphic design, and many others. The fine arts and performing arts have as their main purpose the sense of beauty or the understanding of human experience. The fine arts include painting, drawing, printmaking, film, and sculpture. They sometimes include architecture, or the two are spoken of together, as in "art and architecture." The performing arts include dance, music, and drama.

ART TERMS

Art Conservation Art objects are among the most highly valued in society. Their preservation requires care and expertise. Art galleries, for example, must control the temperature, humidity, light, air pollution, insects, and moulds which are dangers to paintings. They must also try to minimize human error, such as careless handling, cleaning, storage, and transportation.

The first Canadian institutions to set up conservation units were the National

Red Bear, *by native artist Jackson Beardy, whose art expressed the great myths of his people (courtesy DIAND).*

Gallery of Canada and the Royal Ontario Museum in the 1950s. Other art galleries and museums, libraries, archives, and historic sites were restricted by a lack of funds and of trained staff. In 1972 the federal government set up the Canadian Conservation Institute to provide research, treatment, and training in conservation for all these institutions. In the years since, the institute has developed new methods of environmental control, specifically over humidity and temperature. It has responded to fire and flooding disasters in museums and archives. It has sent its mobile laboratory to visit institutions across the country, and it has trained staff from other institutions in conservation techniques. In the 1970s, a few Canadian universities and community colleges began to offer courses in art conservation to their students.

Art Critics are people who express their opinions about artists and exhibitions in the media. Most major newspapers review art shows and gallery openings. The Canadian Broadcasting Corporation in particular carries art reports on both radio and television. Art critics also write articles and reviews for news and lifestyle magazines, and for an increasing number of specialized art magazines such as *Camera Canada, Canadian Art,* and *Parachute*.

Art Dealers are the link between artists and the people who buy art. Dealers usually run commercial art galleries, where they hold exhibitions of works by artists they represent. Most artists need a dealer to be successful. The dealer arranges group shows of several artist's work or solo exhibitions of one artists' work, in exchange for 30% to 50% of the selling price. Costs for advertising, framing, and catalogues are usually shared between the artist and the dealer.

Since dealers have to make money to

Art Dealers *Gallery owner Kathleen Laverty (left) and artist Francine Gravel. Most artists need a dealer to be successful (photo by J.H. Marsh).*

survive, they must respond to public taste. In the years before 1950, most collectors bought European art. It was difficult for a gallery to make a profit if it sold only Canadian art. Dealers can have a strong influence in shaping public attitudes towards particular artists. The Roberts Gallery in Toronto gave Painters Eleven, the first group of abstract artists in that city, their first exhibitions in 1954 and 1955. Although sales were small, public interest was great, and the group went on to success in both Canada and New York. Some dealers gamble on the eventual success of promising young artists. They may buy up their works in advance, keeping them for sale for a few years. The Dominion Gallery in Montreal helped Emily Carr when she was unknown and was later rewarded for the risk it had taken.

In recent years, the highest prices for Canadian art have been paid, not through dealers but at auction. In 1986 a painting by Lawren Harris sold at Sotheby's in Toronto for $450 000, not including tax and commission.

Art Historians are people who study and teach art. Most art historians teach in universities or are curators in art galleries. They write books on art and catalogues for exhibitions. Sometimes, they are asked to identify a work by an unknown artist or to decide whether a particular artwork is genuine or a fake.

Art Organizations Over the years, Canadian artists have grouped together in several organizations. Some were clubs associated with a particular form of art, such as painting, sketching, or printmaking. Some were geared to artists in one province or in one city. Others promoted a particular idea about art, lobbied for artists' rights, or served the needs of a group, such as women artists.

Art Conservation at Work in the National Gallery of Canada. Art objects are highly valued and require care (courtesy NGC).

Art Auction The highest prices for art have been paid at auctions, such as this one at Sotheby's (courtesy Sotheby's (Canada) Inc./photo by Brian Boyle).

In the years after 1850, artists began to set up associations to exhibit and market their work. They also provided courses in art for the public. The Art Association of Montreal was set up with these goals in 1860, followed by the Ontario Society of Artists in 1872. In 1880, Governor General the Marquis of Lorne founded the Royal Canadian Academy of Arts (RCA). It served a select group of artists working in various areas and from all parts of Canada. The annual exhibitions run by the RCA were very popular, and the collection of artworks donated by its members formed the basis of the National Gallery of Canada. Many artists felt that the RCA was too dominant in shaping public taste. They organized smaller associations with fellow artists in their own areas.

The most vibrant associations were those formed by small groups of artists to promote a particular kind of art. The best known is the Group of Seven (1920-33), who painted the landscape as an expression of Canadian nationalism. They were followed by the Canadian Group of Painters, a larger group of both men and women from across Canada who were interested in figure painting as well as in landscape. In 1939, John Lyman, who had spent time in Europe, set up the Contemporary Arts Society to encourage modern art in Canada. Within ten years, members of this group began to split into different factions. In 1948 the Automatistes, led by Paul-Émile Borduas, demanded the right to paint spontaneously as their subconscious directed them. In 1955 the Plasticiens returned to a more formal style of abstract art, as in the structured series of paintings by Guido Molinari. Abstract art came to Toronto in the 1950s with Painters Eleven, who got together so they could hold exhibits and create a market for their work. The group included Jack Bush and Harold Town.

Since the 1960s, some artists have formed tight-knit groups which act as a unit in creating their art. The N.E. Thing Co. in Vancouver and General Idea in Toronto, for instance, are known by their group name rather than as individuals. Other organizations, such as Western Front in Vancouver and Art Metropole in Toronto, run what are known as "parallel galleries" to provide exhibition space for experimental artwork and for performance art and large installations that are impossible to sell.

In 1967, artists led by painter Jack Chambers formed an organization called Canadian Artists Representation / Front des artistes canadiens (CAR / FAC), to fight for certain rights. They forced galleries to pay artists a fee for reproducing their works on postcards and calendars, and for exhibiting their works in exhibitions. However, they have made little progress in other areas of concern to artists, including those of tax reform and social security.

Arts Funding Canadian arts organizations get their money from three main sources: from government, from individuals and corporations, and from the sale of tickets, memberships, and similar activities.

All levels of government provide support for the arts through grants and loans.

Young Indians Hunting, by Albert Laliberté, displayed in the National Gallery of Canada, Ottawa (photo by Malak, Ottawa).

Other money is channelled through provincial arts councils or such federal programs as the Canada Council, the Canadian Broadcasting Corporation, the National Film Board, and Telefilm Canada. Since 1972, the Canada Council Art Bank has bought thousands of pieces of art from Canadian artists and rented them out to government offices, businesses, and individuals. In the late 1980s, the federal government alone was spending more than $2.6 billion a year on culture.

Arts companies cannot survive without private support as well. In 1987-88, more than $77 million was donated to the arts, according to surveys by the Council for Business and the Arts in Canada. Of this amount, about $33.7 million went to the performing arts, while the visual arts received about $43.5 million. Although not all donations were classified under types of contributors, individuals gave at least $13.6 million to the arts, while corporations and foundations contributed at least $31 million. Altogether, however, only a small percentage of businesses donate money to the arts. Most of this money goes to individual programs and new buildings. Both individuals and corporations prefer to support established companies, rather than new and experimental groups. In 1987-88, for example, the "top twenty" arts organization received three-quarters of the money from private donations. Some companies and the major banks have also put together impressive collections of Canadian art. The Toronto Dominion Bank, in particular, has excellent collections of both Inuit and contemporary art.

Public Art is art that is commissioned for a particular public space, such as sculpture outside an office tower, murals for a hotel lobby, or paintings on the side of a building. The art is usually designed to blend in with and complement its surroundings.

Canada has a long tradition of public art. For centuries before the arrival of Europeans, the native people of the Northwest Coast carved totem poles and painted the fronts of their houses. These artworks had a ritual significance as crests, tracing the lineage of the people who lived in the village back to a time of their ancestors. They were also important as a public display of power and wealth, and brought prestige to the people who erected them.

In New France, sculpture was the most common form of public art. Churches were decorated with statues, both on the inside and out. The area behind the altar was often a harmonious blend of architecture, gilded sculpture, and richly coloured paintings. Ships built in naval shipyards were decorated with carved figureheads of women, animals, and other emblems.

Under the British regime, and particularly after Confederation, statues of politicians, explorers, and war heroes were mounted in public squares and on government buildings. Over the years, the Parliament Buildings in Ottawa have been surrounded by sculptures of some of the prime ministers. In the 1890s, Louis-Philippe Hébert produced a dynamic series of sculptures for the Quebec legislative building. In Canada, there are also war memorials commemorating the War of 1812, the South African War, and both World War I and World War II.

In recent years, hotels, banks, office buildings, airports, and subway stations have all been designed to include works of public art. In 1965, the federal Department of Public Works set aside up to 1% of all construction budgets to go towards artworks in new government buildings. The program was cancelled by budget cuts after 13 years. As a result, private developers are left to decide whether they will include works of art in their buildings. The result is often "plop art," art which is dropped into position as an afterthought and not integrated into the overall design of the project.

Some corporations, however, have approached public art with imagination and flare. The Cineplex Odeon Theatre chain, for instance, is including art by contemporary artists in many of its new buildings. In 1987 the Manufacturers Life Insurance Co. sponsored Painting the Town, a display of billboard art created by five Canadian artists who travelled to nine cities across Canada.

Cineplex Odeon Theatre, Toronto. The Cineplex chain includes works of art in many of its new theatres (courtesy Cineplex Odeon).

▷ RELATED ARTICLES: FINE ARTS: **Architecture, Contemporary Arts; Drawing; Painting; Printmaking; Sculpture; Folk Art; Indian Art; Inuit Art.**
APPLIED ARTS: **Cartoons; Ceramics; Crafts; Furniture; Glass; Leatherwork; Quilts; Rugs; Silver; Weaving; Woodenware.**
PERFORMING ARTS: **Ballet; Dance; Drama; Theatre.**
GENERAL: **Art Gallery of Ontario; Canadian Museum of Civilization; Glenbow Museum; Musée d'art contemporain de Montréal; Musée du Québec; Musée des beaux-arts de Montréal; National Gallery of Canada; National Museum of Natural Sciences; National Museum of Science and Technology; Ontario Science Centre; Royal Ontario Museum; Tyrrell Museum of Palaeontology; Vancouver Art Gallery.**

▷ SUGGESTED READING: Gerald F. Brommer, *Discovering Art History* (2nd ed. 1988); H.W. Janson with S. Cauman, *History of Art* (2nd ed. 1988); Ron MacGregor and others, *Canadian Art: Building a Heritage* (1987).

■ Art Education

The training of artists is part of that larger debate over whether an artist is born or trained. The role of the art school — whether it should simply teach the techniques which allow innate talent to develop or should actively redefine the nature of a work of art — remains an open question. Early art education in Canada was based mostly on the apprenticeship system. Most of the artists received their training before they arrived. In the apprenticeship system, a master artist trained a young apprentice in exchange for assistance. Apprenticeship first appeared in the woodcraft and decorative art fields, such as woodworking, cabinet-making, tinsmithing, ironmongery, and silversmithing. These were fields for which the demand was greatest. In apprenticeship, knowledge and methods in the arts and crafts are passed on through several generations.

Some of the most important early centres of creativity owed their existence to the apprenticeship system, especially in sculpture and architecture. The Levasseur and Baillairgé family dynasties dominated art activity in Quebec and passed on a tradition.

A system of private art instruction developed throughout the 19th century. The number of visiting artists declined and many immigrant artists settled in the colony. It seems that most students were young, cultured, and socially privileged ladies. The students learned to copy various themes and fragments of artistic works.

Private educational establishments also offered courses by local artists. Education officials began art-education programs in the schools. These programs were based on the principle that instruction in drawing is as important as instruction in reading and writing, and should be taught to all children.

In the 19th century, the Industrial Revolution brought a new awareness of the relationship between form and function in manufactured objects. This development led to the creation of schools of art and design which focused on industry. It also led to a renewed interest in arts and crafts. This influence spread to Canada in the 1860s, and in succeeding years, various schools of applied art and technology were established. Consistent efforts were made well into the 20th century to keep strong ties between design and fine arts. Today, numerous schools and university departments, one of which is the Nova Scotia College of Art and Design, offer both programs.

Apprenticeship and private art schools were replaced in the late 19th century by schools founded and directed by societies of artists and amateurs. Their methods taught respect for tradition, and the supremacy of drawing. Some European-trained teachers taught in and led their schools for more than 30 years, thus influencing several generations of students. William Brymner at the Art Association of Montreal school and George Reid at the Ontario College of Art were particularly well known.

Young Canadian artists preparing for a career turned increasingly to the United States, because the range of courses was broader and instruction more specialized.

In the 1940s there was a major reform in the specialized schools. Art and industry were no longer closely linked, and the influence of art from the past was viewed as less important than the development of the artist's own values. Two major reactions followed. One was to return to individualized training. This system took various forms such as workshops and seminars, as at Emma Lake or the Banff Centre School of Fine Arts, where professionals share their beliefs and experience with younger people.

The other major reaction was that the university took responsibility for the training of a large number of artists. Since the first Bachelor of Fine Arts was awarded in 1941 at Mount Allison University in Sackville, N.B., many institutions of higher learning across the country have established their own programs.

Art Gallery of Ontario

The Art Gallery of Ontario was founded in 1900 as the Art Museum of Toronto. It later changed its name to Art Gallery of Toronto (1919) and the Art Gallery of Ontario (1966). There are over 11 000 paintings, sculptures, drawings, and prints in its collection; more than half of them are by Canadian artists.

The gallery arranges about 40 special exhibits each year and also schedules lectures, concerts, film screenings, tours, and programs for children. There is an excellent reference library and audio-visual centre, as well as restaurants and shops. The original gallery building, The Grange, is maintained as a Georgian mansion and as a museum of life in Upper Canada around 1830.

Henry Moore Collection at the Art Gallery of Ontario. The great English sculptor Henry Moore donated much of his work to the AGO (photo by Dawn Goss/First Light).

Nearly one-half million people visit the gallery each year. It is supported by grants from the federal, provincial, and municipal governments, by gifts from individuals and corporations, and by its own admission fees and shop sales.

Arthabaska

Arthabaska, Que., is a town south of the St Lawrence River, halfway between Montreal and Quebec. Founded in 1834, the town was known for potash and maple sugar produced from the surrounding forests. Soon it was a thriving manufacturing and milling centre. Today, dairy farming and lumbering are important to the local economy. Prime Minister Wilfrid Laurier began his law career here and had a summer home here (which is now a museum). Its population in 1986 was 7244. For information, contact Freffier, 841, boul. Bois Frances sud, Arthabaska, Que., G6P 5W3.

Arthritis

Arthritis is an inflammation of the joints of the body. Joints, such as the ankles or knees, are where bones in the body join together. (The word arthritis combines the Greek words for "joint" and "inflammation.")

Arthritis causes swelling, stiffness, soreness, and sharp pains. It afflicts not only humans but all creatures with jointed bones. By the time they have reached the age of 65, one in every eight Canadians may seek medical attention for some form of arthritis. Most of these will have only mild discomfort. More females than males get arthritis.

Arthritis can cripple, particularly old people. One rare form of the disease (known as systemic juvenile rheumatoid arthritis) attacks children between the ages of one and five years. They suffer a high fever, a rash, and pains or swelling in the joints. Rheumatoid arthritis may cause heart trouble, and it may destroy the joints.

The cause of arthritis is unknown. Nor is there any known cure for arthritis. Drugs such as aspirin may help make some of the symptoms less painful. Exercise is also an important part of treatment.

The Arthritis Society supports research into arthritis. Its national office can be contacted by writing to 250 Bloor Street East, Suite 401, Toronto, Ont., M4W 3P2.

▷ SUGGESTED READING: Rebecca C. Jones, *Angie and Me* (1981); Colin Thiele, *Jodie's Journey* (1988).

Asbestos

Asbestos is the name of a group of thread-like minerals found in certain rocks.

Asbestos has many useful properties. The fibres are long and thin. They can be woven into cloth or added to cement for extra strength. They are resistant to fire. Asbestos does not burn and is not damaged by heat. The Romans wrapped their dead in cloth woven with asbestos before cremating them. In Finland, people used asbestos as wicks for their oil lamps, because it would not burn up. Asbestos is now used in thousands of products, such as cement water pipes and brake linings.

Canada, in the late 1980s, produces more asbestos than any other country in the world except the Soviet Union. Most of this asbestos comes from a belt of rocks some 100 km long in eastern Quebec. Thetford-Mines is in the middle of this region. It developed around the first asbestos mine in Canada, which opened in 1878.

Canada sells most of the asbestos it produces to other countries.

Asbestos as a Health Hazard In the 1940s, many places of work, such as shipyards, had high levels of asbestos dust. Workers therefore breathed in this dust, some over several years. Many became sick with lung cancer, with asbestosis (a disease of the lungs), and mesothelioma, a rare cancer of the body cavities. These diseases were caused by asbestos. They killed many workers, particularly those who smoked.

Cigarette smoke and asbestos dust are a bad combination, which together cause lung cancer even more often than either would separately. The risk of dying from continued exposure to a large amount of asbestos dust is about four times greater if you are a smoker than if you are a nonsmoker.

Today, the levels of asbestos dust to which workers in mines, mills, and factories are exposed have been sharply reduced. Products that can release this dust, such as asbestos insulation, are no longer made. Asbestos is now used in Canada only for things that cannot be made of safer materials, or things that do not allow the dust to escape.

Concerns about health risks have made it difficult to sell asbestos. The Environmental Protection Agency of the United States government has proposed banning asbestos completely. Instead, the Government of Quebec, which now owns most of Canada's asbestos mines, and the Government of Canada propose new rules so that asbestos can be mined and used safely. Since Canada sells much of its asbestos to poorer countries, Canadian organizations are working to ensure that it is used safely around the world.

▷ RELATED ARTICLE: **Mining.**

■ Asbestos Strike

The Asbestos Strike was one of the most bitter labour disputes in Quebec history. In February 1949 miners walked off the job at four asbestos mines in the Eastern Townships region. They demanded higher pay and healthier working conditions. The strike was illegal. Owners tried to keep the mines open by hiring strikebreakers. The 5000 strikers fought back and squads of police were brought in.

Strikers had the support of unions in the rest of Canada and of the Catholic Church in Quebec. However, the companies managed to keep the mines operating by hiring replacement workers. Violence flared, especially in the town of Asbestos,

as police and strikers fought on the picket line. Hundreds of workers were arrested before the dispute ended in June. Miners received a small pay increase, but many did not get their jobs back.

■ Ash

Ashes (*Fraxinus*) are trees or shrubs which belong to the olive family (Oleaceae). In Canada, they are found primarily in the eastern provinces. The trees are of medium height, with a generally straight and slender trunk. Ashes have very large leaves consisting of clusters of five to 11 leaflets, depending on the species. These leaves occur in pairs on the twig and are called compound leaves. Flowers appear early in spring. Ashes produce a large quantity of winged fruit (keys, or samara) that look like canoe paddles. Grouped in hanging clusters, they stay on the tree well into winter and provide an important source of food for birds and squirrels. Ashes usually prefer the rich, moist soils of bogs and the banks of waterways, except for the white ash (*F. americana*), which prefers dry soils. The wood of the white ash is hard and resilient and is used for hockey sticks and baseball bats. A red dye can be extracted from the bark of the red ash (*F. pennsylvanica*) and a blue one from that of the blue ash (*F. quadrangulata*). When well-pounded in water, the wood of the black ash (*F. nigra*) separates into thin sheets. It was formerly used to make barrel hoops, baskets, and other such items.

White Ash, *with male flowers and fruit. Ash wood is very hard and strong and is widely used for furniture and sporting goods (artwork by Claire Tremblay).*

> ### Characteristics of Asbestos
> *Appearance:* long, soft, thread-like fibres
> *Properties:* resistant to heat and chemical attack
> *Uses:* asbestos-cement water pipe and sheet, flooring, roofing products, brake linings and clutch linings, coatings and compounds, special papers and fabrics, and insulation.

Ashburton-Webster Treaty

The Ashburton-Webster Treaty, 1842, settled a border dispute between New Brunswick and Maine.

The treaty was named for negotiators Lord Ashburton of Great Britain and U.S. Secretary of State Daniel Webster. It gave much of the disputed territory to Maine, including the Acadian settlements south of the Saint John River. New Brunswickers were not pleased with the decision. They believed that Ashburton had betrayed them in order to promote good relations between Britain and the United States.

The Ashburton-Webster Treaty also set the boundary line between Lake Huron and Lake of the Woods.

▷ RELATED ARTICLE: **Timber Trade.**

Ashcroft

Ashcroft, B.C., is a village nestled on the banks of the Thompson River in the interior of B.C. The Interior Salish built winter homes here. The name comes from Ashcroft Manor, a stopping house built on the old Cariboo Road in 1863. The village began in the 1880s with the arrival of the Canadian Pacific Railway. Transportation and the nearby open-pit copper mines are important to the economy. Its population in 1986 was 1914. For information, contact the Village Clerk, P.O. Box 129, Ashcroft, B.C., V0K 1A0.

▷ SUGGESTED READING: Brian Belton, *Bittersweet Oasis: A History of Ashcroft* (1986).

Aska, Warabé

Author, artist (*born in 1944 in Kagawa, Japan*). Aska established himself as a major artist and children's book illustrator and author in Japan. He moved to Toronto in 1979. In 1984 he published *Who Goes to the Park*, a description in words and pictures of the activities which take place during the year in Toronto's High Park. *Who Hides in the Park* (1986) is set in Vancouver's Stanley Park. In each book, vivid oil paintings capture the many types of people and activities found in a big city park. Aska has said that he likes to look at natural objects and let his imagination "see" all kinds of magical details. Trees contain mysterious faces and blowing leaves become flying geese. Stanley Park, as the picture shows, is haunted by native gods and spirits who wandered freely there long ago.

Aspen

Aspens belong to the genus *Populus* of the willow family (Salicaceae). We have two species in Canada: the large-toothed aspen (*P. grandidentata*) and the trembling aspen (*P. tremuloides*). The large-toothed aspen grows only from Manitoba eastward, and prefers fertile, moist soil. As its name suggests, it is characterized by the prominent teeth on its leaves. The trembling aspen is the most widely distributed tree in Canada; it can be found from east to west and all the way north to the treeline. Its nearly circular leaves have a flattened stalk that makes them quiver in the slightest breeze, giving the tree its name. A light-loving tree, it moves quickly into territory that has been disturbed by forest fire or logging. It therefore pro-

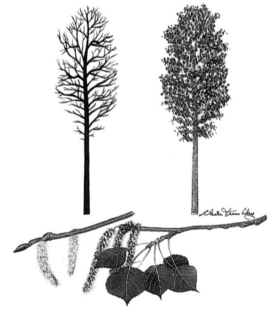

Trembling Aspen, with male flowers (left) and female flowers (right). The flat stalks and circular leaves appear to "tremble" in the wind (artwork by Claire Tremblay).

Killer Whales in Stanley Park, illustration for Warabé Aska's book Who Hides in the Park. Aska shows us that a park is a place where people can enjoy real and imaginary events. The killer whales are real; the flying fish are imaginary (©1986 Warabé Aska/published by Tundra Books).

vides the shade necessary for other deciduous and coniferous trees. The trembling aspen also plays an important role in the life of various animals. Deer and moose graze its branches, beavers use it in their dams, hares eat its bark, and many bird species eat its seeds. Used in combination with conifer fibres, aspen wood can be used to make wood pulp. It is also used for boxes and matches.

Assembly of First Nations

The Assembly of First Nations (AFN) is the organization which represents some 444 000 status Indians across Canada in 1988. It was founded in 1982, replacing the National Indian Brotherhood. The AFN deals with the federal government in discussions about aboriginal rights. The AFN's main objective has been to have the right of Indian self-government placed in the Canadian Constitution. The AFN has made progress in negotiating native people's rights in land, education, health, social services, and economic development. Non-status Indians are represented by the Native Council of Canada.

▷ RELATED ARTICLE: **Native People in Contemporary Society.**

Assiniboia, District of

District of Assiniboia refers to two different regions at different periods of Canada's history. From 1812 to 1870, it was the official name of the Red River Colony, in what is now Manitoba. From 1882 to 1905, it was one of four southern districts in the North-West Territories. The district later became part of the province of Saskatchewan. (See **North-West Territories.**)

Settler's Home in Assiniboia. This area later became part of the province of Manitoba (NAC/C-11030).

Assiniboine

The Assiniboine are a group of native people who now live in Saskatchewan. They are closely related to the Stoney of Alberta. Both groups speak dialects of the Dakota language. Traditionally, they hunted bison, and these and other big-game animals provided their food, clothes, and ti-

Assiniboine Hunting Buffalo, painting by Paul Kane. The bison provided the Assiniboine with food, clothes, and tipis (courtesy NGC).

pis. They were allied with the Cree, and often fought against the Blackfoot. During the fur trade, they acted as middlemen between the Hudson's Bay Company and distant Plains groups to the west. They were particularly important as guides and as suppliers of pemmican. In 1986 there were 1850 Assiniboine and 2643 Stoney in Canada. The band at Morley has invested its natural gas royalties in a variety of commercial enterprises and enjoys a high standard of living. *See* **Native People: Plains.**

Assiniboine River

The Assiniboine River, 1070 km long, rises in southeastern Saskatchewan and winds across the fertile, wheat-growing plains of Manitoba. It joins the Red River at Winnipeg. The region was occupied by Assiniboine Indians, and the name comes from the Indian for "those who cook by placing hot stones in water." The river was well travelled by fur traders. After 1850, farm settlement moved westward along its banks. Before the railway came, steamboats plied the 500 km stretch from Winnipeg to Fort Ellice.

Aster

Aster (meaning "star") is the common name for plants belonging to genus *Aster* of the daisy family. North America is the kingdom of this plant, which is still evolving. New species are regularly being found in the wild, and many ornamental varieties have been developed. Asters are usually perennials, with straight stalks bearing simple, alternating leaves. In late summer or early autumn, asters explode into many flowering heads, which usually resemble tiny daisies. Each head consists of several flowers: tube-shaped ones at the centre forming a yellow disc, surrounded by tongue-shaped rays. The ray flowers may be blue, pink, purple, mauve, or white, depending on the species. Wild

New England Aster
Asters are late season flowers and range in colour from purple (shown here) to blue, pink, or white (artwork by Claire Tremblay).

asters are found in both dry and moist fields, bogs, forests, rocky land, and maritime shores. The roots and sometimes the stems, leaves, or flowers, were used as medicine to cure a number of ailments by Indians. The Iroquois, for example, used the roots to bring down fever. The heart-shaped leaves of the large leaved aster (*A. macrophyllus*) carpet the forests of eastern Canada. The young leaves of this plant have a pleasant taste when cooked, and are eaten like spinach. Indians smoked the leaves like tobacco. The symbol of refinement, asters are also a lucky charm in affairs of the heart.

■ Asthma

Asthma is a disease in which breathing becomes difficult. The word "asthma" comes from the ancient Greek word for "panting." During an asthma attack, muscles tightly squeeze the airways and glands plug them with mucus. The victim then cannot take in enough oxygen. In a severe attack, the person begins to suffocate.

The cause of asthma is not known. Colds caused by viruses often trigger attacks in young children. Vigorous activity, such as running, is another common trigger. So is emotional stress. Allergies to foods, pets, dust, or other substances also cause attacks, especially in older children.

Almost one in every 40 Canadians suffers from asthma. In more than half of all cases, the asthma first appears when the asthmatic person is a child. Asthma is the leading cause of children missing school. In general, though, as a child grows older, his or her asthma becomes less severe.

The frequency and severity of asthma have been increasing during the 1980s in Canada. Asthma can kill; 478 Canadians died of asthma in 1987.

Though there is no cure for asthma, it is relatively easy to treat its symptoms by spraying medicines that relax muscles into the airways. Such treatment allows asthmatic children to exercise and to live relatively normal lives.

■ Astronaut

An astronaut is a person who travels in space. The word "astronaut" comes from the Greek for "sailor among the stars."

Yuri Gagarin, a Russian, was the first astronaut. In April 1961 he became the first person to travel outside Earth's atmosphere. Only eight years later, in 1969, American astronauts landed on the Moon. By the mid-1980s, about 200 people had travelled in space. The United States built the space shuttle to ferry people and equipment into space and back again. Canada built a robot arm, the Canadarm, for the space shuttle. In return, the United States invited Canadian astronauts to fly on board two space shuttle flights.

In December 1983, the Canadian government selected six people to become Canada's first astronauts. They were chosen on the basis of their education, their technical expertise, and their physical fitness.

Only one of Canada's astronauts, Marc Garneau, has actually travelled in space. Garneau is an electrical engineer. He is also a military officer. He was one of seven astronauts on board the space shuttle named *Challenger* when it took off in October 1984. During his eight days in space, he carried out several experiments. He tested a machine designed to judge the position of objects moving and turning in space. He studied how the human body responds to weightlessness.

Weightlessness Weightlessness is a remarkable experience of space flight. The astronaut is "weightless" because the spacecraft is "falling" at the same rate as the astronaut. "Weightlessness" would be experienced in an elevator if the cables were cut and the elevator fell freely. When he wanted to sleep, Marc Garneau did not lie down. He simply shut his eyes and allowed his body to float around inside the space shuttle.

Space travel is difficult and dangerous. Astronauts must be protected from extreme temperature and deadly radiation. The powerful rockets that lift the astronauts into space can explode. A year and a half after Marc Garneau's flight, on January 28, 1986, the space shuttle *Challenger* exploded, killing all seven crew members. Future shuttle flights were postponed, including the second planned flight of a Canadian astronaut. The space shuttle *Discovery* was the first flight to resume the program, with a successful mission in September 1988.

Space Station Canada will help the United States build a space station in the late-1990s. Astronauts will use the station for many purposes. It will be a base to study the stars and a laboratory to carry out experiments. Canada is building a spider-like machine for the space station. Its main arm will be bigger and stronger than the Canadarm. It will help assemble and repair the space station. Canadian astronauts will be among the station's crew.

▷ Related Articles: **Canadarm; Marc Garneau; Space Technology.**

▷ Suggested Reading: Lydia Dotto, *Canada in Space* (1987); Sally Ride, *To Space and Back* (1986).

■ Astronomy

Astronomy is the science of the universe. The term "astronomy" is formed from the ancient Greek words for "star" and "law." Professional astronomers make a career of astronomy. Those who make a hobby of astronomy can also make useful contributions to research in astronomy.

ASTRONOMY BECOMES A PURE SCIENCE

People have always felt wonder and awe looking at the stars in the vast night sky. Their curiosity gave birth to the oldest of the sciences, astronomy. At first, astronomers watched the stars for practical reasons. They made calendars and predicted when the Nile would flood. In the early days of Canada, explorers used star sightings to determine their position, or to tell time with accuracy.

In the late 19th century, astronomers came to Canada to observe total eclipses of the Sun. Today, astronomy's usefulness is taken for granted, and it is mainly studied as a pure science. Astronomers try to discover truths about the stars and the universe.

Astronomers study the Solar System. At the centre of the Solar System is the Sun, our neighbourhood star. The Earth, our Moon, the other planets and their moons, the asteroids, and comets (chunks of ice as big as cities) orbit around the Sun. Astronomers also study stars and galaxies, including the Milky Way, the vast wheel-shaped, spinning family of stars to which our Sun belongs.

THE TOOLS OF ASTRONOMY

The moon and planets can now be studied by spacecraft. The stars, however, are enormous distances from Earth, far beyond the range of spacecraft. To get information from stars, astronomers study electromagnetic waves, such as light and radio waves. They use optical telescopes to gather light, and radio telescopes to gather radio waves. The radio waves are produced by the clouds of gas between the stars.

Spectroscopy is one of the astronomer's most important tools. An instrument breaks light into colours or wavelengths. In this way, astronomers can see the "fingerprint," or spectrum, of light. The spectrum reveals the chemicals that make up a star or the gases through which the light passed on its journey to Earth. Spectra give astronomers clues about the temperature and other properties of stars. Spectra enable astronomers to estimate how fast stars are moving towards Earth or away from it.

Dr Gerhard Herzberg of Ottawa won the 1971 Nobel Prize for Chemistry for his work in spectroscopy.

Telescopes and other tools are housed in observatories. The Dominion Observatory opened in Ottawa in 1905. The main purpose of this observatory was to gather data to help make accurate maps. In 1918, the Dominion Astrophysical Observatory opened in Victoria, B.C. At the time, its telescope was the largest in the world. The Victoria observatory was used to observe the spectra of faint stars. Here, Canadian astronomers J.S. Plaskett and Joseph Pearce conducted a classic study of the Milky Way. A generation of astronomers took their ideas about the size, shape, and movement of our galaxy from this study. Today, astronomers study, among other things, the age and size of the universe.

Observatories which are built near cities can do useful work. However, the bright city lights may interfere with the light of the stars. Distant mountain tops, where the air is thin and clear, are excellent locations. In 1904, the University of Toronto set up the first department of astronomy in any Canadian university. In 1971, it became the first Canadian university to build an observatory in another country. The Las Campanas Observatory is built on a mountain in Chile. It is one of the best sites in the Southern Hemisphere to view the sky. In 1987, Ian Shelton, a young Canadian astronomer working at this observatory, discovered a bright supernova. These massive, exploding stars are a very rare sight. Shelton's supernova was the first to be seen with the unaided eye since 1604.

Another Canadian observatory, shared with France, is built on a mountain peak called Mauna Kea, in Hawaii. Its 3.6 m telescope is the most powerful optical telescope that Canadian astronomers use. It began operation in 1979. Mauna Kea is the best site for astronomy in the Northern Hemisphere. With this telescope, astronomers can collect light which has been travelling for thousands of millions of years from stars at the edge of the known universe.

Three Canadian astronomers working at Mauna Kea believe that they have dis-

Careers as an Astronaut
Astronauts carry out technical and scientific projects in space. They are selected on the basis of their academic background, technical expertise, and physical fitness.

Competition for the few positions available is fierce and standards are high. A postgraduate degree with proven research skills in such fields as medicine, science, or engineering are the minimum requirements for success.

Canada-France-Hawaii Telescope on *Mauna Kea in Hawaii is located above 40% of the Earth's atmosphere. It is the best site for an observatory in the Northern Hemisphere (courtesy National Research Council).*

Artist's Depiction of the Winter Sky The diagram (far right) names the constellations and stars shown in the painting.

Orion and the Stars of Winter (courtesy Canada House Publishing/John Bianchi).

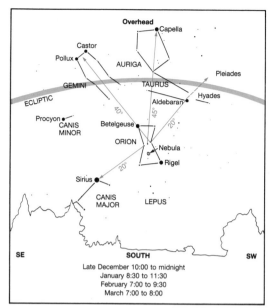

Late December 10:00 to midnight
January 8:30 to 11:30
February 7:00 to 9:30
March 7:00 to 8:00

covered planets orbiting around other stars. It is the best evidence yet that stars other than our Sun may have planetary companions.

RADIO TELESCOPES

Scientists at the National Research Council used surplus radar equipment to build Canada's first radio telescope. This work led to Canada's two national radio observatories: the Algonquin Radio Observatory in Ontario's Algonquin Park and the Dominion Radio Astrophysical Observatory, near Penticton, B.C. Both began operation in 1960. The National Research Council administers both observatories. The dish-shaped antenna of the Algonquin observatory is as big as half a football field and is the largest in Canada. In 1987, the observatory was closed although the antenna is sometimes used by other scientists.

Space between the stars is not completely empty. It contains thin clouds of gas and dust. Using the Algonquin radio telescope, some Canadian astronomers searched the dust clouds of the Milky Way for chemical compounds. They discovered the heaviest molecules known to exist in space.

A STRANGE UNIVERSE

In probing space, Canadian astronomers contribute to the international effort to answer such big questions as: How are stars born and how do they die? How big is the universe? When and how did the universe begin?

The answers astronomers provide to such questions are not always comforting. They reveal that the universe is a place of mystery, where violent events often occur.

For example, a massive star explodes at the end of its life. It flares as a supernova, and then it shrinks. As it shrinks, it becomes super-dense and exerts a force of gravity that is extremely strong. The star may even shrink out of existence. What remains is a "hole in space." Its force of gravity may suck everything nearby into the hole, even light. Because no light can escape from it, it is called a black hole. Black holes are invisible, but astronomers use other evidence to detect them. For example, black holes exert a force on stars which orbit around them. In 1972, a University of Toronto astronomer found evidence for a black hole in the direction of the constellation Cygnus. It may be the nearest black hole to Earth. Some astronomers believe that a bigger black hole exists at the centre of our own galaxy — the Milky Way.

▷ RELATED ARTICLES: **Gerhard Herzberg; Helen Hogg-Priestley; Meteorites and Craters; Stars.**

▷ SUGGESTED READING: Terence Dickinson, *Exploring the Night Sky* (1987); *The Universe and Beyond* (1988); Christopher Lampton, *Astronomy* (1987); the magazine, *Odyssey*, is a good source of information.

■ Athabasca

Athabasca, Alta, is a town on the Athabasca River, 150 km north of Edmonton. The Hudson's Bay Company built a post on the site in 1877. It was then called Athabasca Landing because it was the terminus of the Athabasca Landing Trail. Goods were moved overland to the post, where they were loaded onto steamships and taken by river to the North. From

1877 to 1912, the trail was the busiest northern route in Canada. The town was known as the "Gateway to the North."

Athabasca Landing became a town in 1911 and changed its name to Athabasca. The town's importance dropped after 1912. The railways bypassed the town, ending its days as an inland port. Today, Athabasca is a service centre for the surrounding area. It is the location of Athabasca University, moved here from Edmonton in 1984. The population in 1986 was 1970.

■ Athabasca, District of

This was the name of the region around Lake Athabasca. Before 1870 it was a Hudson's Bay Company district. It then became part of Canada's North-West Territories. In 1882, when four "provisional districts" were established in the Territories, one of them was named District of Athabasca. In 1895 the District of Athabasca was enlarged to include all the northern part of what in 1905 became the provinces of Alberta and Saskatchewan.

■ Athabasca Pass

The Athabasca Pass lies on the British Columbia-Alberta border, south of Jasper. After David Thompson crossed in 1811, the pass became a favoured route through the Rocky Mountains for fur traders. Today, it is an isolated spot visited rarely by hikers and climbers. Its elevation is 1748 metres.

■ Athabasca River

The Athabasca River rises in the Columbia Icefield and flows northeast across Alberta to Lake Athabasca. In northeastern Alberta it passes through large deposits of oil sands. It was part of the first freight route west to the Rockies and another route north from Edmonton. It is 1231 km long.

■ Athabasca University

Athabasca University is in Athabasca, Alta. It specializes in distance education. Students learn at home, using course materials such as study manuals, workbooks, and textbooks mailed to them. Each student has a telephone tutor who answers questions about the course and marks term papers. Some courses include workshops, labs, seminars, radio and television programs, and audio and video-cassettes.

The university has an open admissions policy: a student has to be 18 years or older and a Canadian resident. Athabasca University began in Edmonton in 1972

and was moved to Athabasca in 1984. It has about 8000 students. For further information, write to Student Services, Athabasca University, Box 10 000, Athabasca, Alta, T0G 2R0.

■ Atikokan

Atikokan, Ont., is a northern mining centre, located about 200 km west of Thunder Bay. It was a division point on the railway line in the early 1900s, surrounded by gold mines and lumber camps. In the 1940s iron-ore mining began at nearby Steep Rock Lake. The mines closed by 1980, and the town's economy now relies on the forest industry. The name is an Ojibwa word for caribou bones. The population in 1986 was 4345. For information, contact the Clerk, 204 Main Street, East, P.O. Box 1330, Atikokan, Ont., P0T 1C0.

■ Atlantic, Battle of the

The Battle of the Atlantic was the struggle to protect Allied ships in the North Atlantic from marauding German submarines during World War II. Vessels crossing the Atlantic carried crucial supplies to Britain from Halifax and other North American ports.

Canadian forces played an important role in protecting the convoys of merchant ships from enemy submarines. The air force gave air cover to the vessels. Warships escorted the merchant ships across the ocean. At first, Canada shared these duties with the United States and Britain. After the bombing of Pearl Harbor by the Japanese in late 1941, the U.S. moved most of its ships to the Pacific Ocean. The Royal Canadian Navy was then forced to carry out much of the escort work in the northwest Atlantic.

In all, 24 Canadian warships were sunk, and nearly 2000 Canadians died protecting shipping lanes during the Battle of the Atlantic.

▷ RELATED ARTICLES: **Armed Forces; World War II.**

■ Atlantic Ocean

The Atlantic Ocean is the world's second-largest ocean, next to the Pacific Ocean. It extends in a huge "S" shape from the Arctic to the Antarctic. It connects with the Arctic Ocean by the Greenland Sea. The Atlantic forms the eastern coast of Canada. Two great extensions of the ocean form Hudson Bay and Baffin Bay in northern Canada.

Beneath the Atlantic Ocean is a long submarine mountain range, called the Mid-Atlantic Ridge. The ridge is a centre of volcanic activity and is constantly widening and filling with molten rock from beneath the earth. As a result, the continents of the Americas are slowly moving away from Europe and Africa.

The Atlantic Ocean has played a big role in the history and economy of Canada. It was thought, before Columbus, to be an endless sea from which ships would plunge off the end of the Earth. Columbus crossed it in 1492. John Cabot followed a more northerly route, sighting Canada in 1497.

Ship traffic on the North Atlantic, that portion of the Atlantic lying north of the equator, is very busy. Many major ports are located on North Atlantic coasts. Canada's major Atlantic port is Halifax.

The Atlantic coast of Canada is one of the world's greatest fishing grounds. The Grand Banks off Newfoundland, for instance, contain shallow waters which are stirred by currents, providing nutrients for enormous numbers of fish. Within a few years after Cabot discovered that the fish were so plentiful that they could be hauled in with a basket, scores of fishing boats were visiting the coast. The industry continues to support the people of Atlantic Canada.

▷ RELATED ARTICLES: **Fishery; Grand Banks; Oceans; Plate Tectonics; Water Transport.**

■ Atlantic Provinces

The Atlantic Provinces are the four provinces of Canada which lie along the coast of the Atlantic Ocean: Newfoundland, Prince Edward Island, Nova Scotia, and New Brunswick. The last three are also called the Maritime Provinces. The Atlantic Provinces are 540 300 km², or about 5.5% of the land area of Canada.

The Atlantic Provinces were the first area encountered by Europeans when they crossed the North Atlantic Ocean. The Grand Banks, off southeastern Newfoundland, are one of the world's richest fishing grounds. The Atlantic region still produces nearly three-quarters of Canada's fish catch.

About 9% of Canada's population live in the Atlantic Provinces. In 1986 the combined population was 2 278 600. About 14% are of French origin; another 1% are native Indian. Each of the four provinces has a single large city: Halifax, N.S., St John's, Nfld, Saint John, N.B., and Charlottetown, P.E.I. Other cities include Moncton, N.B., Sydney, N.S., and Corner Brook, Nfld.

The Atlantic Provinces have a similar rugged landscape, with numerous bays

Cap Rouge on the Cabot Trail, Nova Scotia. The ocean forms the eastern coast of Canada, shaping the way of life of the people of Atlantic Canada (photo by Roland Weber/Masterfile).

and inlets along the coast. All except Prince Edward Island have forested upland areas. The island of P.E.I. is mostly flat, as is southeastern New Brunswick, the Annapolis Valley of Nova Scotia, and the Saint John River valley of N.B. Most of the area's agriculture is carried on in the lowlands.

Fishing, mining, and forestry are important in all four provinces. Agriculture is important in all but Newfoundland. Manufacturing is of growing importance, but does not play the large role in the economy that it does in Ontario or Quebec. The service industries and government are the most important parts of the economy in the Atlantic Provinces, making up one-third of the gross domestic product (the total value of goods and services). Many tourists come to the area, drawn by the beauty of the coast and the opportunities for recreation.

The Atlantic Provinces are linked by ferry lines as well as air, rail, and roads. Halifax has an international airport.

The Beothuk, Maliseet, Micmac, and Montagnais-Naskapi Indians lived in the area before the Europeans came. The Norse discovered the area around the year 1000. They built a small settlement in Newfoundland at L'Anse aux Meadows, which is now an archaeological site. Explorers arrived from England, France, and Portugal 500 years later. On June 24, 1497, John Cabot landed somewhere on the coast, claiming the land for England. The Corte-Real family of Portugal explored the area in 1500 to 1502. In 1534 Jacques Cartier of France explored the Gulf of St Lawrence.

The English formally claimed the harbour of St John's in 1583, and settlement gradually began there. The French first settled at Port-Royal (now Annapolis

Fishing Off Nova Scotia
The waters off Atlantic Canada are one of the world's richest fishing grounds (photo by Sherman Hines/Masterfile).

Royal, N.S.), in 1605. The Acadians, as the French settlers in the area became known, slowly spread around the Bay of Fundy area. The French also built a huge fortress at Louisbourg, on Cape Breton Island. But France generally ignored the area in favour of the St Lawrence River valley. In 1749 the English founded Halifax, on the coast of Nova Scotia.

The Atlantic region was a zone of conflict between England and France. Eventually, the English gained control. Doubting the loyalty of the Acadians, the English rounded them up and deported them from 1755 to 1762. The Acadian lands were taken up by settlers from England and New England. Loyalist refugees from the American Revolution arrived in large numbers in 1783 and 1784. Later immigrants arrived from Scotland, Germany, and Ireland. Meanwhile, many of the exiled Acadians returned, although not to their original lands.

The Atlantic colonies enjoyed their greatest economic prosperity in the early 19th century. New Brunswick, in particular benefited from supplying Great Britain with timber. The three Maritime colonies directed their eyes to the sea, concentrating on fishing, trade, and shipbuilding. The era slowly faded, however, with the passing of the age of sail.

In 1864 delegations of the Atlantic Provinces, except Newfoundland, met in Charlottetown, P.E.I., to discuss uniting to form a single province. By 1867, this had evolved into a plan to join Canada. There was opposition as well as support in each colony for Confederation. Both Nova Scotia and New Brunswick had second thoughts, but they joined in 1867. P.E.I. held out until 1873.

Newfoundland developed quite a separate path from the Maritime colonies. It had few ties with the Maritimes or Canada. Rather, it kept its powerful ties with Great Britain and developed its own brand of independence. It rejected Confederation and did not join Canada until 1949.

Despite gains over the past 30 years, the Atlantic Provinces still have a lower level of economic prosperity than other provinces. Wages are lower and unemployment is higher than in the rest of Canada. In 1954 the Atlantic Provinces Economic Council was formed to deal with economic problems in the region.

▷ RELATED ARTICLES: **Acadia; Grand Banks; Bay of Fundy; Gulf of St Lawrence; Natural Regions;** and entries under the names of the four provinces.

■ **Atwood, Margaret Eleanor**

Poet, novelist, critic (*born in 1939 at Ottawa, Ont.*) Atwood grew up in Toronto and was educated at University of Toronto and at Radcliffe College in Cambridge, Mass. Her first published volume was *Double Persephone* (1961), a book of poetry. Atwood's poems, which are collected in several other volumes, are written in a sharp, straightforward style and simple but startling language. She received the Governor General's Award for poetry for *The Circle Game* (1966).

Atwood has written several novels, which have earned her an international reputation. Her first, *The Edible Woman* (1969), introduces a series of female characters found in her novels. Each is confronted with situations that are at once humorous and horrible. *Surfacing* (1972) follows a woman's passage from madness to a fuller identity. It is also an exploration of a "Canadian," as opposed to "American," state of mind. In *Life Before Man* (1979) several narrators tell the story of a love triangle. In *Bodily Harm* (1981) a food and fashion writer is caught in a brutal Caribbean political uprising. For *The Handmaid's Tale* (1985), a futuristic look at the role of women in a barren society, Atwood won her second Governor General's Award and worldwide acclaim. An-

Margaret Atwood has written a number of children's books as well as the novels that have made her one of Canada's best-known authors (photo by Graeme Gibson).

other novel, *Cat's Eye* (1988), tells the story of Elaine, a painter.

Atwood's short stories are collected in *Dancing Girls* (1977) and *Bluebeard's Egg* (1983). Her book of criticism, *Survival: A Thematic Guide to Canadian Literature* (1972), argued that the main theme of Canadian literature was "grim survival." A second book of criticism is *Second Words* (1982).

Atwood has published several children's books: *Up in the Tree* (1978), and *Anna's Pet* (1980) which have also been adapted for the stage. Atwood has also written film scripts and a history. She edited the *The New Oxford Book of Canadian Verse in English* (1982) and co-edited *The Oxford Book of Canadian Short Stories in English* (1986).

Atwood's versatile writings are among the most powerful influences on Canadian culture. She is an outspoken defender of human rights and an opponent of censorship.

■ Aubert de Gaspé, Philippe-Ignace-François

Author of the first French-Canadian novel (*born in 1814 at Quebec City, Lower Canada [Quebec]; died in 1841 at Halifax, N.S.*). The author of the first French-Canadian novel was an outspoken young journalist. He spent a month in prison in 1835 because of a quarrel with a member of Lower Canada's Legislative Assembly. After leaving prison, he revenged himself by placing a stinkpot in the hall of the Assembly. (The smell was so powerful that all Assembly members had to leave the building.) He then fled to his family's country estate on the Gaspé shore of the St Lawrence River. It was there, during 1836, that he wrote his novel, *L'Influence d'un livre*. The book did not sell well, partly because it was published in 1837, the year of the rebellion in Lower Canada. The young novelist died suddenly a few years later, having been too discouraged to attempt a second book.

■ Aubert de Gaspé, Philippe-Joseph

Novelist (*born in 1786 at Quebec City, Que.; died there in 1871*). He was the father of Philippe-Ignace-François Aubert de Gaspe. He wrote the classical historical novel, *Les anciens canadiens* (1863), which was later translated into English as *The Canadians of Old*. The book was published when he was 77 years old, 26 years after his son's novel.

By profession, Aubert de Gaspé was a lawyer. From 1816 to 1822 he was sheriff of Quebec City, but he went bankrupt and was imprisoned for debt (1838-41). He was still in prison when his son died. After his release, he spent his summers at the family estate at Saint-Jean-Port-Joli on the Gaspé shore of the St Lawrence River. This was the setting of his novel, which describes the lives of two friends doomed to fight each other. It blends history with local legends and folk stories. The book was a great success. Three years later, Aubert de Gaspé published more local stories in his *Mémoires* (1866).

■ Aubry, Claude

Author (*born in 1914 at Morin Heights, Que.; died in 1984 at Montreal*). Aubry was a librarian, and between 1953 and 1979 was director of the Ottawa Public Library.

His first book, *The King of the Thousand Islands* (1960), is a literary folktale about a foolish king who falls in love with a supernatural creature and loses his most precious possession, the love of his subjects. The animal hero of *The Christmas Wolf* (1962) wanders into a village on Christmas Eve and is saved by a priest. The ten traditional French-Canadian legends retold in *The Magic Fiddler* (1968) are about ordinary people experiencing magical events and meeting strange beings. *Agouhanna* (1972) is a novel about the timid son of an Iroquois chief. For all his stories, Aubry carefully researched historical backgrounds and combined facts with his understanding of the strengths and weaknesses of human character.

■ Auditor General

The position of Auditor General was created in 1878. The auditor general is the official appointed by Parliament to examine how the government spends its money. In general terms, the auditor general's task is to judge whether the government spends its money effectively.

The auditor general is independent of the government and thus free from any use of threats or influence. The annual report of the auditor general often contains examples of waste or inefficient use of funds. It is widely publicized by the opposition parties and the media. There is a fine line between judging whether money has been spent honestly and judging whether what it was spent on was worthwhile in the first place. The first is a question of accounting; the second involves political judgement. Sometimes, the au-

Canadians of Old, by Philippe-Joseph Aubert de Gaspé, describes the lives of two friends who are doomed to fight each other (courtesy NAC/C-14250).

ditor general receives criticism for crossing the line between these two tasks. Nonetheless, it is generally accepted that an effective auditor general is an important way to help make governments accountable to the people.

■ Augustyn, Frank

Ballet dancer (*born in 1953 at Hamilton, Ont.*). Augustyn is one of Canada's best-known classical dancers. He was trained at the National Ballet School in Toronto and joined the National Ballet of Canada in 1970. He had immediate success. By 1972 he was a principal dancer with the company, and in 1973 he and his partner Karen Kain won the prize for the best *pas de deux* at the Moscow International Ballet Competition. Later, he and Kain performed in *Giselle* at the famous Bolshoi Theatre in Moscow. In 1980 Augustyn joined the Berlin Opera Ballet, but returned to Toronto after two years. He has toured widely in Europe and North America, and has starred in several dance films produced by Norman Campbell. In 1989 he was appointed artistic director of the Theatre Ballet of Canada.

▷ SUGGESTED READING: Christopher Darling, *Kain and Augustyn* (1977).

■ Auk

Auks are a family (Alcidae) of seabirds which includes auks, razorbills, murres, guillemots, murrelets, auklets, and puffins. There are 11 species of this family in Canada. They come to land only to breed. They are black and white, with a short neck, chunky body, and narrow wings. Their webbed feet are placed well back on the body, which is why they seem to be standing upright when on land. They feed primarily on small fish and invertebrates. They spend the winter at sea and come to breed in colonies on the shoreline or on rocky islands, sheltered from predators. The female usually lays one egg on the

The Great Auk, shown in this painting, became extinct in 1844 (courtesy NMNS/artist John Gould).

bare rock, and then she and the male take turns sitting on it for about 30 days. The couple also shares the work of caring for their offspring during its first 10 weeks of life. Young birds reproduce from their fourth or fifth year.

Common Murres (*Uria aalge*) and Thick-Billed Murres (*U. lomvia*) are found in the Atlantic and Pacific. The Razorbill (*Alca torda*), the Atlantic Puffin (*Fratercula arctica*), and the Black Guillemot (*Cepphus grylle*) are found in the Atlantic and Arctic oceans. The Tufted Puffin (*Lunda cirrhata*), the Rhinoceros Auklet (*Cerorhinca monocerata*), the pigeon Guillemot (*Cepphus columba*), the Marbled Murrelet (*Brachyramphus marmoratus*), the Ancient Murrelet (*Synthliboramphus antiquus*) and the Cassin auklet (*Ptychoramphus aleuticus*) live in the Pacific Ocean. The Great Auk, which became extinct in 1844, lived in the Atlantic Ocean. *See* **Great Auk**.

■ Aurora

Aurora, Ont., is situated 30 km north of Toronto. It was named in 1854 by the local postmaster after the Greek goddess of dawn. In its early years, Aurora was the centre of a farming community. Today, the local economy relies on a variety of manufacturing. Many residents commute to work in Toronto. The town's population in 1986 was 20 905. For information, contact the Town Clerk, 50 Wellington Street West, Aurora, Ont., L4G 3LB.

▷ SUGGESTED READING: W. John McIntyre, *A History in Pictures* (1988).

■ Automation

Automation is the use of machines to perform a series of tasks automatically. In particular, it means the use of devices that take the place of human beings in performing work, or making decisions.

Automation is used in a variety of jobs that are too boring, or too dangerous, for people to do. The most widespread use is on automobile assembly lines, where robots perform the same task over and over. Other examples of automation are home thermostats, which control the temperature, and pacemakers, which regulate the rate of the heart beat. Automation is used in nuclear reactors to handle radioactive materials that would be deadly to humans.

Devices that work automatically have been used for centuries. However, their use has spread since the availability of computers. Computers enable systems to make calculations and decisions that are

Automation *An automatic arm places tires in car trunks at the automobile plant at Oakville, Ont. (courtesy SSC Photocentre).*

impossible for humans. For example, they can monitor and control traffic over a large city. Today, complex robots also use lasers to make very accurate measurements.

Automation now enables us to make telephone calls anywhere in the world without an operator. Mail is sorted automatically. Large cost savings are made because machines perform tasks more cheaply.

However, automation also replaces workers. Unskilled workers are particularly threatened by automation. Some labour unions have had to fight to protect their members from losing their jobs. On the other hand, automation increases the need for highly skilled workers.

▷ RELATED ARTICLES: **Eric Leaver; Robots.**

■ Automobile

The word "automobile" comes from the Greek word auto, meaning "self," and the French word mobile, meaning "moving." Automobiles are generally called "cars" in everyday speech.

Highway on Vancouver Island, around 1912. Automobiles created a need for highways, which in the early days were often little more than cleared paths (courtesy NAC/PA-29916).

The first vehicles that could move on their own were powered by steam. They were noisy and dangerous, and hard to start. In the early 1860s a French inventor installed a gasoline engine in a vehicle. The improvement of the gasoline engine in Germany, France, and the United States led to a safer, quieter vehicle. When the price of gasoline dropped after discovery of huge oil fields in Texas in 1901, the way was clear for the automobile to change the world. Few other inventions have had as great an impact on the world as the automobile — not all of it positive.

Canada's first automobile was built by Henry Taylor in 1867. The automobile industry began in Canada in 1904. Early automobiles were mainly used by the wealthy for amusement and racing. Many of them were hand built. As the methods of production improved, the price dropped. By 1913 there were about 30 000 cars in Canada. Automobiles created a demand for more streets and highways, as well as for large quantities of gas and oil.

While there are an estimated 400 million cars on the road throughout the world, few nations are as dependent on the car as Canada. Canada ranks fifteenth in the world in the number of cars owned per 1000 people. There are about 12 million cars in Canada. People use cars for about 75% of all trips to work, and for almost 90% of all the trips they make. Canada has about 850 000 kilometres of highways, roads, and streets.

The automobile has brought a great deal of freedom and mobility to people. It is also a great source of recreation and sport. The auto industry is one of Canada's largest industries. It also supports numerous other activities, such as repairs and insurance. However, it has also devoured huge amounts of land, much of it precious farmland, and produced serious air pollution. The automobile also kills about 4000 Canadians and injures another 250 000 every year. Concern over the loss of land has led to the cancellation of expressways in various Canadian cities. Pollution controls have led to somewhat lower levels of pollution, and increased safety in the design of cars may lead to lower fatalities.

▷ RELATED ARTICLES: **Air Pollution; Automobile Industry; Road Transportation.**

▷ SUGGESTED READING: Frank Young, *Automobile: From Prototype to Scrapyard* (1982).

■ Automobile Industry

The automobile industry is of major economic importance in Canada. It is especially important in Ontario, which has over 80% of the production. Two Ontario cities, Windsor and Oshawa, depend almost entirely on this industry. The industry is also important to Quebec, with about 10% of the production. The industry sold more than $41 billion worth of products in 1988, more than any other manufacturing industry in Canada. Canada's automobile industry is the seventh largest in the world.

About 150 000 people work in auto firms. This amounts to some 7% of all the people working in manufacturing plants in Canada. Auto firms are major consumers of the products of other industries, such as steel, rubber, aluminum, and glass. Counting the people working at supplying the automobile industry, it supports some 300 000 jobs in Canada.

The automobile industry in Canada consists of some 900 firms. Most of these companies make parts for cars and trucks. More than 10 of them, including the largest (General Motors Corporation, Chrysler Corporation, and Ford Motor Company), also assemble vehicles.

Auto Pact Canada does not have an independent national automobile industry, as do countries such as Japan and Germany. Many of the automobile firms in Canada are owned and controlled by companies based in the United States, and all the cars built here are designed elsewhere. In 1965 Canada and the U.S. signed an agreement known as the Auto Pact. Under its terms, Canada's automobile industry became integrated with that of the U.S.

The Auto Pact made it possible for the Canadian industry to expand and export to the U.S. free of duty. Canadian exports to the U.S. have increased from $2.5 billion in 1965 to $36 billion in 1988.

History In 1867 in Stanstead, Que., Henry Seth Taylor built a carriage powered by a steam engine. His horseless carriage was the first automobile built in Canada.

Such early automobiles were expensive, hand-made toys for the rich. By the beginning of this century, however, a number of Americans invented ways of producing automobiles at a cost that large numbers of people could afford. As Henry Ford, one of the pioneers of the automobile industry, put it, the way to make automobiles was to make one auto exactly like another, with identical parts. This meant perfecting the assembly line. As the cars being assembled roll down the

Robotic Welding at General Motors, Canada. Automobile manufacturing is one of Canada's most important industries. It supports about 300 000 jobs (photo by Mike Dobel/Masterfile).

line, a worker repeats the same operation on identical parts, over and over again.

In 1903 Ford opened his first car plant in Detroit, Michigan. A number of firms there were already making carriages, bicycles, and boat engines. Detroit became the world's largest automobile-making centre. In 1904, a group of Canadian businessmen started the Ford Motor Co. of Canada Ltd in Windsor, Ont., just across the border. This branch plant was the beginning of the automobile industry in Canada.

A number of independent Canadian automobile companies were formed in those early years. None survived, and the rest merged with larger, successful American companies. For instance, Colonel R.S. McLaughlin, who had been making sleighs and carriages in Oshawa, Ont., and who switched to making automobiles in the early 1900s, joined forces with American businessmen to form General Motors of Canada Ltd in 1918.

Automobile manufacturers prospered during World War I as the military discovered the automobile's many uses. In the years following that war, Canada was the second-largest vehicle producer in the world. Many people had cars. Gas stations, billboards, and suburbs began to spring up.

After World War II By the end of World War II, North American cars had become big and fast, though the technology used in them had changed little since the invention of the gasoline engine. They glittered with chrome and burned up lots of cheap gasoline.

In the mid-1970s, the price of gasoline shot upwards. Many people stopped buying North American cars. Instead, they bought smaller, more fuel-efficient cars made in Japan and Europe. North American car companies began to lose their hold on a market they had always dominated. Slowly they have regained the confidence of car buyers. Canada's auto plants have been rebuilt and modernized at a cost of billions of dollars. Computers and robots aid greatly in the production of the modern automobile.

▷ Related Articles: **R.S. McLaughlin; Road Transportation.**

■ Autumn Colours

In fall, the forests of Canada are ablaze with colour. Leaves turn from green to yellow, amber, crimson, and purple. The colours come from chemical substances in the leaves.

The substance that makes leaves green is called chlorophyll. (By converting sunlight into food, chlorophyll makes all plant life possible.) Because leaves need sunlight to make chlorophyll, they are green in spring and summer, when there are many hours of light. In autumn, when the daylight hours grow fewer, chlorophyll production slows down. The green fades, and colours produced by other chemical substances become visible. Some of these chemicals were present in the leaves but were masked by the dominant chlorophyll.

The yellow in autumn leaves comes from chemicals known as carotenoids, which also give corn, carrots, and bananas their colour. The red and purple come from another group of chemicals, called anthocyanins, which also colour apples, plums, cherries, and strawberries. These substances produce the most vivid autumn colours. They occur in trees only in autumn, and only in Japan, Korea, northern China, and North America.

Wind and rain can strip the leaves from trees before they reach their peak of colourfulness. Both dry spells and heavy

Fall Colours in Gatineau Park, Quebec. *Chemical changes in the leaves produce the blazing colours (courtesy SSC Photocentre/photo by A. Holbrook).*

rain make for pale autumn colours. The best weather conditions for vivid fall colours are warm, sunny days and cool nights without frost.

▷ Related Articles: **Climate; Natural Regions.**

■ Auyuittuq National Park

Auyuittuq is the first national park in the world north of the Arctic Circle. It is on the mountainous Cumberland Peninsula of Baffin Island. One-third of the park is covered year-round by the famous Penny Ice Cap. There is little wildlife, except for millions of birds living along the coast or on the tundra. The name of the park is an Inuit word meaning "the place which does not melt." For information, contact the Park Superintendent, Pangnirtung, NWT, X0A 0R0.

Avalanche crosses the highway in Kootenay National Park, B.C. (photo by Jim Davies, Banff).

■ Avalanche

An avalanche is a mass of snow, ice, or other materials moving rapidly down a mountain slope. Avalanches occur frequently in the mountainous areas of Canada. There are two kinds of avalanche. In a "point" avalanche, loose snow spreads out from a single point into a wide V-shape. In a "slab" avalanche, a hard layer of snow slides over a looser layer below.

Most avalanches start high on a steep slope of a mountainside. Something loosens the grip holding the snow to the slope. It may be a loud noise, such as a pistol shot. It may be a yell. It may be weather conditions, such as rain or a warm wind. Once the snow begins to slip, it loosens more snow, as well as ice, rock, and soil. As it tumbles down the slope, the avalanche grows in size and speed. Avalanches of dry snow can fall at speeds as fast as 50 m/sec, accompanied by blasts of wind and spectacular clouds of powdered snow.

Avalanches are a danger to skiers and mountaineers. About seven people are killed each year in Canada. The largest number of deaths occur in British Columbia. Many of the people buried by avalanches are buried in air pockets and remain alive for hours or even, in rare cases, for days. Rescuers search for these victims by probing the snow with poles. Dogs are also helpful.

Avalanches damage buildings and powerlines in their path. They are a hazard to roads and railways. A number of protective measures can be taken. Concrete wedges, which are shaped like the prow of a ship, can deflect falling snow around buildings and over roads. By monitoring snow conditions, specialists can forecast where an avalanche is about to occur. In vulnerable areas, such as Rogers Pass (where the Trans-Canada Highway crosses the Rocky Mountains), authorities use explosives to release the snow before it builds up.

■ Avalon Peninsula

The peninsula forms the southeast corner of the island of Newfoundland and is the most easterly point in North America. It is joined to the rest of the province by the narrow Isthmus of Avalon. It has always been the island's most populous area. Today, about 40% of Newfoundlanders live there, mainly in the capital city, St John's.

The rugged, irregular coastline of the peninsula has four main bays: Trinity, Conception, St Mary's, and Placentia. Each was a centre of the early fishing industry. Settlement began at Cupids, Conception Bay, in 1610. For many years French and English fought over the peninsula. The French established an outpost at Placentia in the 1660s. The name "Avalon" comes from the legendary site where Christianity was introduced into England.

■ Aviation

Canadians have participated in the development of aviation almost from its beginning. Alexander Graham Bell, the inventor of the telephone, was also fascinated by flying machines. He recruited a small team of Canadians and Americans, who built and flew several aircraft. F.W. Baldwin was the first Canadian to fly. He made two successful flights in the *Red Wing* in 1908 before crashing. The flights took place at Hammondsport, New York. On February 23, 1909, John McCurdy flew the *Silver Dart* at Baddeck, N.S., becoming the first person to fly over Canadian soil.

Today, aviation plays a very large role in Canadian life. It provides transportation over the great distances that separate Canadians. It provides services to remote communities. It moves the mail and other valuable cargo. It also has many specialized uses, such as aerial photography, fire fighting, and mining reconnaissance.

COMMERCIAL AVIATION

The first use of an airplane for transportation in Canada took place in October 1913. An aircraft carried newspapers from Montreal to Ottawa. Unfortunately, it crashed on the return flight. The first paying passenger was taken aloft in 1920, when a fur buyer was flown north to The Pas, Man., from Winnipeg. One month later, aircraft began to ferry men and supplies from Edmonton to the new oil fields at Fort Norman in the Northwest Territories. This was the first regular air service in Canada.

Air transport expanded rapidly from 1920 to 1937. In 1924 the first scheduled flights began and the Post Office began to deliver mail by air. In 1936 the federal government created the Department of Transport. C.D. Howe was the first head of the department, and he played a role in the creation of Canada's first airline, Trans-Canada Airlines, in 1937. TCA was owned by Canadian National Railways, which in turn was owned by the government. In 1965 the airline's name was changed to Air Canada, and in 1977 the government took over control from Canadian National. Beginning in 1988, the government sold the airline to private investors. Air Canada is Canada's largest airline, and one of the largest airlines in the world.

The Canadian Pacific Railway was also involved in aviation at an early stage. In 1941 it bought 11 small companies, and in 1942 it gave the new company the name Canadian Pacific Air Lines. The airline was restricted as to the routes it could fly in Canada, but it opened up international routes to the Far East in 1949,

Aerial Experiment Association Alexander Graham Bell is well known as the inventor of the telephone. He also played an important part in Canada's aviation history. He is shown here (centre), with Glenn Curtiss and J.A.D. McCurdy on the left and F.W. Baldwin and Tom Selfridge on the right (courtesy Library of Congress).

Curtiss HS-2L arriving at Rivière du Loup, Quebec, in the driving rain (courtesy National Aviation Museum).

Avro CF-100 Canuck was the first jet fighter plane designed and built in Canada. It served in Canada's air force from 1953 to 1963 (courtesy Canada Post Corporation).

Hawker Hurricane, 1935. This aircraft celebrated in a 35¢ stamp, was Canada's main fighter early in World War II (courtesy Canada Post Corporation).

Curtiss JN-4 Canuck, shown here on a Canadian postage stamp, was typical of Canada's early aircraft (courtesy Canada Post Corporation).

to South America in 1953, and to Europe in 1955. CP Air purchased several other companies in the 1980s, before being taken over itself by Pacific Western Airlines Corp. (PWA Corp.) in 1987. The new company is called Canadian Airlines International Ltd.

A third major airline in Canada was Wardair. It began operations out of Edmonton as a bush charter company in 1953, and expanded in 1962, specializing in charter flights overseas. It began regular scheduled flights in 1986. In 1989 it too was purchased by PWA Corp.

In the late 1960s, air traffic in Canada was growing at about 15% per year. However, because of increased costs and other reasons, the growth per year has now dropped below 5%. The major airlines carry over 20 million passengers each year to points in Canada and abroad.

GENERAL AVIATION

Today, there are about 28 000 civil aircraft operating in Canada. Only about 200 of these are owned by major airlines.

Bush Pilots were the 20th-century pioneers of the North. They flew supplies to remote areas, explored, and prospected. Their hardy planes could land on any lake in summer, and, equipped with skis, on any frozen patch in winter. The bush pilots here are at Great Bear Lake, N.W.T. (City of Edmonton Archives).

About 22 000 are for private use. Most of the the remainder are used commercially for training, crop spraying, fire fighting, construction, aerial photography, and sightseeing.

There are about 60 000 licensed pilots in Canada.

GOVERNMENT REGULATION

Most countries, including Canada, control aviation to make sure that it is safe. Aviation is wholly the responsibility of the federal government. Transport Canada, a federal government department, is responsible for safety regulation. It helps to build and operate the major airports in Canada. It also provides navigation aids, radar surveillance, and approach aids to guide aircraft. It controls the air traffic, and licenses pilots and aircraft. A separate branch of government investigates aviation accidents.

Kiowa Helicopter on patrol from Canadian Forces Base Petawawa, Ont. (Canadian Forces Photo).

MILITARY AVIATION

Aircraft first engaged in air-to-air combat in World War I. When the war began in 1914, the planes were primitive and ineffective. However, by the end of the war in 1918, the major powers had fleets of fighters, bombers, flying boats, and other aircraft. Canada had no air service when it went to war. Nevertheless, over 21 000 Canadians flew with British squadrons in Europe. Among them were some of the leading "aces" of the war, such as William "Billy" Bishop and William Barker.

In 1919 Britain gave Canada over 100 aircraft. These planes formed the basis of the Royal Canadian Air Force, which was created in 1924. The early peacetime activities of the RCAF included topographical surveys, forest and fishery patrols, and anti-smuggling operations. When war broke out again in 1939, Canada had only a few modern fighter aircraft.

Dash-8 *This Canadian-designed aircraft is shown operating over Germany (Canadian Forces Photo/photo by W.O. Vic Johnson).*

CF-18 Fighter *Canada's military aviation has a number of roles, including the air defence of western Europe (Canadian Forces Photo/photo by W.O. Vic Johnson).*

Canada's aircraft industry boomed during World War II. Over 16 000 airplanes were built, most of which were military aircraft. Most of these were of British or American design. The RCAF flew operations in northwest Europe, the Mediterranean, and Southeast Asia. It also took part in the Dieppe Raid, in the Battle of the Atlantic, and in the bombing of Germany.

Since 1948, Canadian military aviation has had a number of roles. It contributes to the air defence of North America. It takes part in United Nations peacekeeping operations, and supports ground and naval forces. It also assists in search-and-rescue missions.

▷ RELATED ARTICLES: **Aerospace Industry; Armed Forces; Bush Flying.**

▷ SUGGESTED READING: E.W. Anderson, *Man the Aviator* (1975); Z. Lewis Leigh, *And I Shall Fly* (1985); Larry Milberry, *Aviation in Canada* (1979).

■ Avison, Margaret

Poet (*born in 1918 at Galt [Cambridge], Ont.*). Avison attended the University of Toronto. She worked as a librarian, a teacher, and, from 1968, as a social worker at the Presbyterian Church mission in Toronto.

Avison's first poems were published in 1939. She won the Governor General's Award for her first book of poems, *Winter Sun* (1960). Two more collections followed. Her complex poems often combine social concerns with religious themes.

■ Avocet

The American avocet (*Recurvirostrata americana*) is a large shorebird of up to 50 cm in length. It is black and white on top, and white underneath. At breeding time, the head and neck take on a rusty colour; in winter, they both turn grey. The bird has long, slender legs and pale blue webbed feet. The Avocet lives in shallow ponds, marshes, and coastal waters, where it feeds on small crustaceans, worms, and other animals. It wades slowly through the water, sweeping its long, curved bill from side to side, stirring its prey from the muddy bottom. Avocets breed in small colonies. The nest is built out of earth and designed to shelter some four eggs. Of the four species in the world, only the American avocet is found in Canada. It breeds in southern Alberta, Saskatchewan, and Manitoba, and winters in Texas, California, and Central America.

■ Axel Heiberg Island

Axel Heiberg is the seventh-largest island in Canada. It is in the far north of the Arctic Archipelago. It was discovered in 1899 by a Norwegian expedition led by Otto Sverdrup. It was named for a Norwegian sponsor of the expedition. About one-third of the island is covered by icefields and glaciers. It is 43 178 km² in area.

■ Aylmer

Aylmer, Que., is a city on the Ottawa River. It is southwest of Hull and looks across the Ottawa River at the city of Ottawa. It was named for Lord Aylmer, who was governor general of British North America from 1831 to 1835. The original town of Aylmer merged with two neighbouring communities in the 1830s. The town has numerous golf courses, a horse race track, and a marina. Most residents work in Ottawa or Hull. In 1986 the population was 28 976. For more information, contact the Greffier, Hôtel de ville, rue Principale, Aylmer, Que., J9H 3M2.

Breeding Range of Avocet ●

Range of Badger ●

Bacteria comes in various shapes. The illustration shows the following: A) cocci in a chain arrangement, B) simple bacillus (rod) with its locomotion organ (flagella), c) cocci in a cubicoidal arrangement, D) spirochite with its filament, E) vibrio, with a stalk, F) bacterium with numerous appendages (artwork by Claire Tremblay).

■ Back River

The Back River, 974 km long, flows northeast across the Barren Lands of the Northwest Territories. It begins in Contwoyto Lake and empties into Chantrey Inlet on the Arctic coast. It is named for George Back who explored the river in 1834. It is one of the most remote rivers in North America.

■ Bacteria

Bacteria are prokaryotic unicellular organisms (that is, consisting of a single cell, even though some live in colonies). They are invisible to the naked eye. It would take 500 000 laid end to end to add up to 1 mm in length. They are usually spherical or rod-shaped. They are found practically everywhere. They survive in places where higher life forms cannot exist, for example, in acid soil, deep ocean waters, and steaming hot pools. There are millions on our skin, even after it has been washed. Most are inoffensive, but some can cause serious illness.

Even though they are so small, bacteria play a very important role in nature. They decompose organic matter into elements that can be assimilated by plants. Some live in association (*symbiosis*) with the roots of plants — with lucerne, for example, which provides bacteria with necessary sugars while the bacteria fix nitrogen necessary to the plant. Bacteria also play an important role in the production of certain foods. They are involved in the creation of cheese and yogurt, for example. Other species can remove pollutants from their environment. Scientists have succeeded in altering some species of bacteria so that they produce useful products, especially in medicine. Bacteria have been used in mining copper and uranium and to help clean up oil spills.

Bacteria cause numerous diseases in

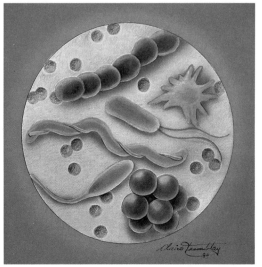

humans, including typhoid fever, cholera, tuberculosis, plague, food poisoning, and venereal disease.

■ Baddeck

Baddeck, N.S., is a picturesque village overlooking the north end of Bras d'Or Lake on Cape Breton Island. It was the summer home of inventor Alexander Graham Bell, and his mansion still stands nearby. In 1909 the first airplane flight in Canada took place on the ice in front of the village. Settlement began in 1819 and the community grew as a mining, milling, and shipbuilding centre. Today the industries are gone, and Baddeck relies on its popularity with summer vacationers. Its population in 1986 was 995. For information, contact the Village Clerk, P.O. Box 370, Baddeck, N.S., B0E 1B0.

■ Badger

The American badger (*Taxidea taxus*) is the only burrowing member of the weasel family. The male may weigh up to 11.4 kg and measure 80 cm in length. The badger's body and head are flattened; the limbs, ears, and tail are short. Its long, sturdy claws enable it to dig a tunnel faster than a human being using a shovel. The coarse fur is a silvery yellow, though longer and paler on the cheeks. A white stripe runs from the nose between the ears to mid-shoulder. The paws are black, the ears white. The badger has a waddling gait and lives in dry, open parts of central and southwestern North America (the Prairies, around Lake Erie, southeastern British Columbia, the western United States, and central Mexico). Except during mating season, it is a solitary animal. Largely nocturnal, its diet consists of small rodents, snakes, and birds.

The badger hunts ground squirrels in a particular way: entering their burrow through its escape route, the badger blocks that exit, positions itself near the main entrance and waits for its victims to flee into it. The enemies of the badger, which defends itself fiercely, are man and the grizzly bear. Young badgers fall prey to the coyote and the golden eagle.

In Canada the badger enters a state of torpor from November to April. Mating takes place during August and September, with one young being born in April to May. Females may start mating when about five months old, males at one year. Badgers live four to five years in the wild, reaching 15 years at most. Overhunting and loss of their habitat have greatly reduced the badger population in some parts of Canada.

The Badger's sturdy claws enable it to dig a tunnel faster than a human being using a shovel (artwork by Jan Sovak).

Badlands

The badlands are bizarre landscapes where streams have cut deeply into a plain of soft rock. The streams carve deep, winding gullies and leave the remnants of the plain in such forms as spires, knobs, ridges, and flat-topped hills. Badlands occur in areas where rocks are soft and where the little rain that falls tends to fall in short, intense rainstorms. The water runs rapidly off the land, eroding the soft rock. The water also makes life almost impossible for plants, which otherwise might anchor the soil and slow erosion.

Badlands are common in the interior plains of western North America. They also occur in China, Israel, and other countries where there are similar conditions. Most of Canada's badlands are in southeastern Alberta and southwestern Saskatchewan. The extensive badlands near Drumheller, Alta, are remarkable for their rugged beauty. They are world famous for the many fossils of dinosaurs which have been exposed by erosion.

▷ RELATED ARTICLES: **Dinosaur; Hoodoo Rock; Natural Regions.**

▷ SUGGESTED READING: Brian Noble, *Alberta: The Badlands* (1981).

Badminton

Badminton is a sport played by two players (or four in doubles) on a court divided by a net 1.5 metres high. Players use racquets to hit a "shuttle," a small piece of cork to which feathers are attached. Players score if the shuttle touches the court, or if the shuttle is hit out of bounds. The game likely originated about 2000 years ago in China. The modern rules were set down in England in 1893. The sport is

Badlands in Dinosaur Provincial Park The badlands' bizarre landscape is carved by streams cutting into the soft rock (courtesy J.A. Walper/Alberta Recreation and Parks).

named for the English country seat of a duke.

Badminton was introduced to Canada by British army officers in the 1890s. The first Canadian club was founded in Montreal in 1907. In 1930 Jack Purcell of Guelph, Ont., defeated the four best players on a touring British team. He went on to be world champion in 1933. Dorothy Walton won the English singles title in 1939. Canadian badminton players compete internationally in the Commonwealth Games and will compete in the 1992 Olympics in Barcelona.

Most badminton is played in school gymnasiums or community centres. There are about 30 facilities in Canada built especially for badminton. Over 1.5 million Canadians play badminton each year for fun. About 85 000 play the sport competitively.

▷ RELATED ARTICLE: **Dorothy Walton.**

Baffin, William

Arctic explorer (*born about 1584 probably at London, England; died in 1622*). Baffin was a veteran of several voyages to northern waters when he sailed as the pilot with Captain Robert Bylot aboard the *Discovery* in 1615. They searched the area around Hudson Bay for the Northwest Passage to Asia, but failed to find it.

The next year, 1616, Baffin made the voyage for which he is chiefly known. Again with Bylot and the *Discovery*, he sailed through Davis Strait to the top of Baffin Bay then back south down the east coast of Baffin Island. No one sailed this far north again for the next 236 years. The expedition saw Lancaster Sound, which we now know to be the entrance to the Northwest Passage.

Baffin was killed in a battle against the Portuguese in the Middle East.

Baffin Bay

Baffin Bay is a wide and deep body of water lying between Baffin Island and Greenland. It empties south through Davis Strait to the Labrador Sea. It is named for British explorer William Baffin who in 1616 was the first to sail through the bay. Icebergs appear year-round and the bay is almost completely covered by pack ice from November to July. In the 19th century it was a route used by explorers heading north towards the Pole.

Baffin Island

Baffin Island (507 451 km² in area), is the largest island in Canada and the fifth-largest island in the world. It is located in the Northwest Territories, off the northern shore of the province of Quebec. It is separated from Greenland by Baffin Bay. The island has a great variety of spectacular scenery, including glaciers, ice-capped mountains, lakes, and waterfalls. The long coastline is indented with many deep bays, called fjords. Admiralty Inlet is perhaps the largest fjord in the world.

Baffin Island was first occupied by the ancestors of the Inuit about 4000 years ago. The first Europeans to visit were probably the Vikings, who came from Greenland in the 10th and 11th centuries. The English explorer Martin Frobisher came in 1576. The island is named for British explorer William Baffin, who charted the east coast in 1616. Whaling began in the surrounding waters in the 19th century and continued until World War I. Today the waters off the coast are home in the winter for beluga and right whales, along with walrus and seals. The island is also a nesting ground for millions of birds, including murres, buntings, and gulls.

Because of its extreme climate, few people live on Baffin Island. Vast areas are covered with ice year-round. The largest settlement, Iqaluit, has a population of

Baffin Island Spectacular view of a glacier and mountains on Canada's largest island (photo by Sherman Hines/Masterfile).

under 3000 people. Lead and zinc are mined at Nanisivik, one of Canada's most northerly mines. In 1972, spectacular Auyuittuq National Park opened, Canada's first Arctic national park.
▷ SUGGESTED READING: James Houston, *Whiteout* (1988).

Bagot, Sir Charles

Governor general of British North America (*born in 1781 at Rugeley, England; died in 1843 at Kingston, Canada West [Ontario]*). Bagot was a British politician and diplomat who was governor general of British North America during the last year of his life. While serving as British ambassador to the United States, he negotiated the Rush-Bagot Agreement, which was signed in 1817. This treaty limited the number of warships that the British and Americans could have on the Great Lakes and Lake Champlain. It was a significant first step towards today's unprotected border between Canada and the United States.

In 1841 Bagot was appointed governor general of British North America, and he arrived in the Province of Canada in 1842. There he appointed the Reform leaders LaFontaine and Baldwin to his Executive Council. Since the Reformers were a majority in the elected Assembly, this was a significant step towards the introduction of responsible government.
▷ RELATED ARTICLES: **Responsible Government; Rush-Bagot Agreement.**

Baha'i Faith

The Baha'i faith is considered a separate religion now, with its own holy scriptures, but its roots are solidly in Islam. In 1844 in Persia "the Bab," the door, announced a new age. He was regarded as a heretic and killed. His teachings were followed by the founder, Baha'u'llah, who is believed to be the most recent messenger of God, but not the last. He was exiled from Persia to a penal fortress in what is now Israel and his burial site on the bay of Haifa has become an important shrine for the Baha'is. His central teaching is that humankind is one race and that this is the time for unification. Baha'is believe in the equality of the sexes, universal education, the end to prejudice, and the establishment of a world government.

The Baha'i faith has no clergy, but democratically elect officials: the Spiritual Assemblies, elected each year, and the Universal House of Justice, every five years. Its world headquarters are in the city of Haifa, Israel, which is said to contain the remains of the Bab. The Baha'i International Community has consultative status as a non-governmental organization at the United Nations. Canada has a special place in the Baha'i faith, along with the United States. The founder's son visited here in 1912 and gave the believers the responsibility for worldwide expansion. The nearly 8000 Canadian believers continue in this central role.

■ **Baie-Comeau**
The town of Baie-Comeau, Que., is on the north shore of the St Lawrence River, at the mouth of the Manicouagan River. In 1936 a Chicago businessman built a paper mill at the site, taking advantage of its deep bay and nearby huge forest resources. A town sprang up and grew rapidly in the 1950s, adding a huge aluminum factory. Nearby power developments harness the vast potential of the Manicouagan and Outardes rivers. The town is named for Napoléon Comeau, a naturalist, and is the birthplace of Brian Mulroney, prime minister of Canada. The population of Baie-Comeau in 1986 was 26 444. For information, contact the Greffier, 19, avenue Marquette, Baie-Comeau, Que., G4Z 1K5.

■ **Baie Verte**
Baie Verte lies near the head of a deep bay on the northeast coast of Newfoundland. Lumbering and mining for copper have been important economic activities of the town since its beginning in about 1870. In 1963, mining for asbestos began. In the early 1980s the copper mine closed, with disastrous results for the economy. However, the discovery of new minerals promises a brighter future. In 1986 the population of Baie Verte was 2049. For information, contact the Town Clerk, P.O. Box 218, Baie Verte, Nfld, A0K 1B0.

■ **Baillairgé Family**
The Baillairgés were famous as architects, sculptors, and painters in Quebec for over 150 years. Their story shows the way in which knowledge was passed down from one generation to another through the apprenticeship system.

Jean Baillairgé (1726-1805) was born in France and received some training as a carpenter and joiner there before he left for New France in 1741. For the next 60 years he worked on public and religious buildings, both as a designer and a craftsman. He was noted for his sculpture and for his decoration of church interiors in Quebec City, including ornately carved and gilded altar walls, pulpits, arches, and columns. Jean Baillairgé's family contin-

ued to live in Quebec City for the next four generations.

François Baillairgé (1759-1830). He showed his artistic talent early, and was sent to Paris to study from 1778 to 1781 by his father Jean. He was trained thoroughly in French classical principles. He owned an extensive library, which he shared with his apprentices in architecture, sculpture, and painting. He worked as designer and craftsman, carving figureheads for ships, and planning and decorating churches.

Thomas Baillairgé (1791-1859) was French Canada's greatest church architect as well as a sculptor and a painter. Unlike his father François, he concentrated solely on design. He successfully blended the traditional style of Quebec church design with new influences from England. Among his most famous churches are Notre-Dame cathedral and St Roch in Quebec City. His designs influenced church architecture in Quebec for over 100 years. True to family tradition, he trained apprentices and built up a magnificent library. A cultured and music-loving bachelor, Thomas often entertained the leaders of Quebec in social evenings at his home.

Charles Baillairgé (1826-1906) was related to Thomas through his father, and trained as his apprentice in architecture, civil engineering, and land surveying. He worked in a variety of architectural styles, and used recent technological developments such as fire-proofing, central heating, and cast iron in his projects. He designed houses, shops, churches, and public buildings, including the Quebec Music Hall, Laval University, and the Quebec prison. In 1863 he went to Ottawa to supervise construction of the Parliament Buildings. From 1866 to 1898, he served as city engineer in Quebec City. He was an intellectual and hard-working man who invented a steam-propelled automobile, designed over 180 buildings, wrote some 250 books and articles in both

François Baillairgé was a skilled painter, architect, and sculptor. This statue, Le Bon Pasteur, is carved in wood and painted (courtesy Musée du Québec).

English and French on architecture, engineering, and mathematics, and fathered 20 children.

▷ RELATED ARTICLE: **Architecture.**

▷ SUGGESTED READING: Christina Cameron, *Charles Baillairgé* (1989).

■ Bait Acts

Because bait is necessary for catching fish by certain methods, having adequate supplies is important to fishermen. In Newfoundland, from the late 1700s, British and Newfoundland laws made it harder for foreign fishermen to use fish as bait. Often, these laws had little effect because they were difficult to enforce around the sparsely populated coasts where some fishermen were quite willing to sell foreigners the bait they wanted.

In 1886 the Newfoundland government passed a bill to restrict the sale of bait to French and U.S. fishermen but allowed access to Canadians. The Americans, however, were to be allowed to buy bait without paying for licences if they removed some duties on Newfoundland products. The French would have to pay an extra fee for bait or else catch their own on the French Shore, a great distance from the preferred fishing grounds, unless France agreed to stop subsidizing its fishermen and allow fairer competition for sales.

Instead, the French fishermen increased their fishing effort and their use of the French Shore. In 1891, claiming that Canadians were selling bait to the French off Newfoundland's west coast, Newfoundland cut off bait sales to Canada. However, the measures were not very successful and the Act was suspended in 1893.

Bait acts, in various forms, continued to be applied by the Newfoundland government from time to time up until Confederation in 1949, when Canada took over bait regulation.

■ Baker, Carroll

Singer, songwriter (*born in 1949 at Bridgewater, N.S.*). Baker began to sing in a choir at the age of four. By the time she was 19, she had started to sing with country bands in Oakville, Ont., where her family had moved. She had a string of hit records in the late 1970s and was voted top female country singer at the 1976, 1977, and 1978 Juno awards.

■ Baker, Edwin Albert

Founder of the Canadian National Institute for the Blind (*born in 1893 at Collins Bay, Ont.; died there in 1968*). Edwin

Edwin Baker *was blinded during World War I. He learned Braille and spent much of the rest of his life helping the blind (courtesy CNIB).*

Baker was blinded by a sniper's bullet in 1915, during World War I. He was 22 years old, an engineering graduate from Queen's University. He thought that his active life had come to an end, but a course at St Dunstan's in England gave him hope. At St Dunstan's he learned Braille, taught himself how to type, and began to go out on his own.

Back home in Canada, Baker got a job as a typist with Ontario Hydro. He also gave public lectures to draw attention to the needs of Canadians blinded in the war. At the time, there were few facilities in Canada to help the blind or people with very poor eyesight.

Baker rallied a group of volunteers and in 1918 they founded the Canadian National Institute for the Blind (CNIB) to help civilians as well as war-wounded. Baker gave up his job with Hydro and spent the rest of his life working for the blind. From 1920 to 1962 he was general secretary and managing director of CNIB. His activities extended beyond Canada. In 1951 he was elected first president of the World Council for the Welfare of the Blind.

■ Baker Lake

Baker Lake is an Inuit community overlooking Baker Lake which is situated inland from the west coast of Hudson Bay in the Northwest Territories. It lies in the Barren Lands, close to the geographic centre of Canada. Residents are mainly Caribou Inuit who rely on hunting caribou and fishing. Since the 1960s the community has become known as a centre for Inuit art. In 1986 the population of Baker Lake was 1009. For information, contact the municipality at Baker Lake, N.W.T., X0L 0A0.

■ **Balance of Payments,** *see* **International Trade**

■ **Baldoon**

Baldoon was a settlement of Highland Scots founded in 1804 on Lake St Clair on the western border of Upper Canada. Organized by Lord Selkirk, Baldoon was Selkirk's second of three attempts to settle landless Scottish families in British North America (his other attempts were Prince Edward Island and the Red River Colony).

The Baldoon settlers were beset by problems from the beginning. Selkirk thought he had chosen a good site, for it was fertile grassland that would not need clearing of trees. Unfortunately it was also swampy ground, made worse by the heavy rains that fell during the summer of 1804. When the first 15 families arrived in September 1804, no houses were ready for them. The mosquitoes, which bred in the swamp, spread malaria among the Highlanders. Within two months, some 15 of them had died of the disease.

The swampy land and "the fever" (as malaria was called) continued to plague the Baldoon settlers. Wolves and disease killed many of their sheep. During the War of 1812 an invading American force overran Baldoon and made off with sheep, cattle, and boatloads of grain and other goods. By 1818 the dismal settlement had come to an end. Many of the surviving Highlanders moved to better land. Laughlin McDougall, son of a Highlander, was the original settler of the nearby community of Wallaceburg.

▷ RELATED ARTICLES: **Scots; Lord Selkirk.**

■ **Baldwin, Frederick Walker (Casey)**

Aircraft pioneer (*born in 1882 at Toronto, Ont.; died in 1948 at Neareagh, N.S.*). An engineering graduate from the University of Toronto, Baldwin was the first Canadian to fly an aircraft. On March 12, 1908, he piloted the *Red Wing* 97 m over the ice of Lake Keuka at Hammondsport, New York State. Flying was still at the experimental stage and was extremely hazardous. Baldwin crashed the *Red Wing* when landing from its second flight on March 17. He then built and tested the *White Wing*, which also had a very brief life.

Baldwin was a friend of J.A.D. McCurdy, who was the first person to fly an aircraft in Canada (the *Silver Dart* in 1909). Both young men were members of the Aerial Experiment Association which Alexander Graham Bell formed in 1907 to build and test flying machines. Together with McCurdy in 1909, Baldwin formed the Canadian Aerodrome Company at Baddeck, N.S., to make airplanes. The company made two planes before closing down in 1910.

Baldwin gave up flying in 1911, but he continued to experiment, specializing in hydrofoils. A grandson of the politician Robert Baldwin, he later became a member of Nova Scotia's House of Assembly.

▷ RELATED ARTICLES: **Aerospace Industry; Aviation; J.A.D. McCurdy.**

Casey Baldwin was one of Canada's pioneers of aviation. Here he is seated in one of the huge kites designed by Alexander Graham Bell (courtesy Alexander Graham Bell National Historical Park).

■ **Baldwin, Robert**

Politician (*born in 1804 at York, Upper Canada [Toronto, Ont.]; died there in 1858*). Baldwin was the son of William Warren Baldwin (1775-1844), who was a strong promoter of the idea of responsible government. Robert took up his father's cause and was first elected to the Assembly in 1829. He was a shy man, devoted to his family. He was thrown into despair by the death of his wife in 1836.

Baldwin remained neutral during the Rebellions of 1837. In 1838 he and his father met with Lord Durham, outlining their demand for responsible government. When the Province of Canada was created in 1841, the Reformers of Canada West rallied around Baldwin. He formed an alliance with Louis LaFontaine, the leader of the French-speaking Reformers of Canada East. The two served as co-premiers of Canada from 1842 to 1843 and from 1848 to 1851. During the latter period, the friends finally saw responsible

Robert Baldwin, 1846. *He was a shy man who was caught up in the stormy politics of the Province of Canada (courtesy Metropolitan Toronto Library).*

government put in place. In his home province, Baldwin's achievements included the founding of the University of Toronto and the planning of a system of local government.

Baldwin was a reluctant leader who served out of a sense of duty. Disillusioned with politics and still tormented by grief, he resigned in 1851.

■ Ballantyne, Robert Michael

Writer (*born in 1825 at Edinburgh, Scotland; died in 1894 at Rome, Italy*). "Ballantyne the brave," as Robert Louis Stevenson called him, wrote over a hundred popular boys' adventure novels. He helped to develop the misleading picture of Canada as a vast wilderness of wild animals and savage Indians.

From 1841 to 1847, he served at a number of Hudson's Bay Company posts in Canada. This experience provided material for his first book, *Hudson's Bay; or, Everyday Life in the Wilds of North America* (1848), and his first adventure novel, *Snowflakes and Sunbeams; or, The Young Fur Traders* (1856). As in later novels, Ballantyne's strength was creating exciting episodes. His weakness was characterization: neither his brave young heroes nor their treacherous Indian enemies are believable. Although most famous for his tropical survival story, *The Coral Island* (1857), Ballantyne used an authentic Canadian wilderness setting in a number of adventures, such as *Ungava: A Tale of Esquimaux Land* (1857).

■ Ballet

Canada did not have its own performing ballet companies until the 1930s. Yet, from the early years of the 19th century on, Canadian audiences could see touring companies perform the best and most innovative ballets from the United States and Europe.

The popular ballet *La Fille mal gardée*, which was performed in France in 1789, was seen in Quebec City in 1816. The famous Russian ballerina Anna Pavlova toured Canada several times after 1910, and Vaslav Nijinsky appeared with Diaghilev's Ballets Russes in Vancouver in 1917. After 1930, the travelling troupe of the Ballets Russes often came to Canada.

Canada was slow to develop its own ballet companies. Talented dancers, such as Lynn Seymour, who had learned ballet in one of the many studios in the country, were forced to leave Canada to pursue a career in dance. Then, in a short period after the mid-1930s, a series of ballet companies and schools were established in Canada.

In a remarkably brief time, these companies gained a world-class reputation and a number of Canadian dancers became international stars.

Four Major Companies The founders of these Canadian ballet companies were all enthusiastic teachers from Britain and Europe.

The first was the Russian, Boris Volkoff, who arrived in Canada in 1929 and, within a year, set up the Volkoff School of Dance. In May 1939 he formed the Volkoff Canadian Ballet, Canada's first ballet company. He commissioned scores from Canadian composers, choreographed his own ballets, and built up a keen and loyal audience. He was also one of the founders of the Canadian Ballet Festival which, from 1948 to 1954, brought dancers and choreographers together in a different city each year. Volkoff's ballet is not one of today's four major companies, but it led the way.

Meanwhile, in Winnipeg, two teachers from England, Gweneth Lloyd and Betty Farrally, opened the Winnipeg Ballet Club in 1938. The club gave its first public appearance in June 1939, and performed two short ballets on prairie themes which had been choreographed by Lloyd. In 1941 the club changed its name to the Winnipeg Ballet and made occasional tours out of town. It went professional in 1949 and received the "royal" title in 1953. The Royal Winnipeg Ballet holds the honour of being Canada's oldest surviving professional ballet company.

By 1950 a group of ballet enthusiasts in Toronto had decided that they, too, wanted to start a classical ballet company in their city. They invited Celia Franca, a dynamic English choreographer and teacher, to head the company, which they called the National Ballet of Canada. She arrived in 1951, took over Volkoff's studio space, and hired her dancers from different parts of Canada.

The fourth major company, Les Grands Ballets Canadiens, was founded in Montreal in 1958 by Ludmilla Chiriaeff, a dancer and teacher from Europe. It began as Les Ballets Chiriaeff in 1952 and performed chiefly on the CBC French television network. Despite opposition from the conservative Roman Catholic Church in Quebec, the company gave its first public performance in 1954.

These last three ballet companies began at a time when there were few well-trained classical dancers in Canada and even fewer suitable stages on which they could perform. They were short of money, had no experienced administration, and made their costumes and scenery from improvised materials. They survived by their enthusiasm, pluck, and optimism for the future. Soon after they were established, they all went on tour both in Canada and the United States, in hopes of earning money and building up experience. They also established their own ballet schools, to train good dancers for their companies.

As a result, the Royal Winnipeg Ballet,

Karen Kain and Frank Augustyn made Canadian excellence in ballet known around the world (courtesy National Ballet of Canada).

Kimberly Glasco in the ballet Sleeping Beauty (courtesy National Ballet of Canada/photo by Barry Gray).

the National Ballet of Canada, and Les Grands Ballets Canadiens are regarded today as major ballet companies of the 20th century. Dancers such as Frank Augustyn, Evelyn Hart, and Karen Kain appear as guest artists around the world and have won coveted prizes in international ballet competitions. Each company has established its own identity. The National Ballet of Canada is known for its lavish, full-length story ballets such as *Swan Lake* and *The Sleeping Beauty*. The Royal Winnipeg Ballet, in contrast, has avoided expensive costumes and sets, and has concentrated on a wide range of shorter ballets which are designed to appeal to a broad audience. Les Grands Ballets Canadiens has also focused on ballets which show off the talents of its particular dancers, and has commissioned several new works from Canadian choreographers, composers, and designers.

Contemporary Scene In the late 1960s and early 1970s there was an explosion of dance activity in Canada. The Canada Council and provincial and municipal arts councils provided the money. Audiences in every city clamoured for more dance performances. As a result, several new ballet companies were formed, including the Alberta Ballet Company in Edmonton, Ballet British Columbia in Vancouver, and the Theatre Ballet of Canada in Ottawa. One of the most exciting developments in the 1980s has been the breakdown in the traditional distinction between classical and modern dance. All the major ballet companies now offer a wide range of ballets, including both classical and contemporary pieces by such

Choreography

Choreography is the art of creating and arranging dances for performance on stage.

Until the 1970s, Canadian choreographers were given little opportunity at home and made no impression abroad. In the 1950s and 1960s the National Ballet Company performed ballets created by David Adams, Celia Franca, Grant Strate, and others. The Royal Winnipeg Ballet performed ballets arranged by its founder Gweneth Lloyd. Brian Macdonald created new works for the Royal Winnipeg and Les Grands Ballets Canadiens. However, Canadian ballet was largely based on dances borrowed from other countries.

In the 1980s a number of talented Canadien choreographers have emerged. They have broken down the traditional barriers between classical ballet and modern dance, and they create works that are innovative and full of personal expression. They have been assisted by dance programs at York University and at the Banff Centre.

James Kudelka

James Kudelka (*born in 1955 at Newmarket, Ont.*) is the leading ballet choreographer of his generation. He trained at the National ballet School, danced with the National Ballet Company (1972-81), and he choreographed many successful ballets for the company, including *Washington Square* and *Dreams of Harmony*. In 1981 he joined Les Grands Ballets Canadiens, and he has also choreographed dances for many other companies in Canada and abroad.

Vanessa Harwood is one of Canada's most graceful dancers (courtesy Jane Corkin Gallery/photo by André Kertèsz).

modern-dance choreographers as Robert Desrosiers, Danny Grossman, Fernand Nault, and Norbert Vesak.

▷ RELATED ARTICLES: **David Adams; Frank Augustyn; Erik Bruhn; Ludmilla Chiriaeff; Dance; Belton Evers; Celia Franca; Grands Ballets Canadiens; Evelyn Hart; Karen Kain; Brian Macdonald; National Ballet of Canada; National Ballet School; Betty Oliphant; Royal Winnipeg Ballet; Lynn Seymour; Lois Smith; Arnold Spohr; Veronica Tennant; Boris Volkoff.**

▷ SUGGESTED READING: K. Bell and C. Franca, *The National Ballet of Canada* (1978); Liliana Cosi, *The Young Ballet Dancer* (1978); Craig Dodd, *A Young Person's Guide to the Ballet* (1980); John H. Martin, *A Day in the Life of a Ballet Dancer* (1985); James Riordan, *Favourite Stories of the Ballet* (1984); A. Whittaker, *Canada's National Ballet* (1967); Max Wyman, *Dance Canada: An Illustrated History* (1989); Meguido Zola, *Karen Kain: Born to Dance* (1983).

■ Balloon

Balloons fly because they are lighter than the air they displace. A balloon may contain hot air, which is lighter and thinner than cold air, or light gases such as hydrogen and helium.

The first manned balloon flight was made over Paris, France, in 1783. Balloons were soon used in war, as observation posts. During World War I (1914-18), large, oblong balloons, called *dirigibles* or *zeppelins*, were used to drop bombs. Dirigibles (the word means "steerable") were used in the 1920s and 1930s to transport passengers. In 1930 the British dirigible R-100 arrived in Montreal. These dirigibles used hydrogen gas, which is highly flammable. In 1937 the airship *Hindenburg* exploded, with the loss of several

lives, ending the age of the dirigible.

Today, large balloons are lifted with helium gas. The modern hot-air balloon was developed in the 1960s and is widely used for recreation and advertising.

Scientific balloons are used to monitor weather conditions at very high altitudes. They are also used for research in pollution studies, astronomy, and observation of wildlife.

▷ SUGGESTED READING: Carole S. Briggs, *Ballooning* (1986).

Recreation Balloons near Barrie, Ont. (photo by J.A. Kraulis).

■ Band, The

The Band was one of the most popular rock groups of the 1960s and 1970s. It formed in southern Ontario around 1960, backing singer Ronnie Hawkins and later Bob Dylan. Its name was originally The Hawks, but in 1967 it was changed simply to The Band. Its hit records include songs such as "The Weight," and "Up on Cripple Creek." Four of the five band members were Canadians: Robbie Robertson, Rick Danko, Garth Hudson, and Richard Manuel. Levon Helm was from Arkansas. The film *The Last Waltz* recorded their farewell concert in 1976.

■ Banff

Banff, Alberta, is a world-famous resort town in the Canadian Rockies. The site, on the Bow River, was chosen in 1883 during construction of the CPR line. It

Town of Banff from the air. The falls on the Bow River are visible to the right of the townsite (photo © Bilodeau/Preston Ltd/Take Stock Inc.).

was named for the town of Banff, Scotland. The town soon began to attract tourists to the local hot springs, which led to the creation of a reserve in 1885, which became Banff National Park. In 1888 the large Banff Springs Hotel opened.

Today, Banff remains the centre of Canada's most heavily visited national park. It has numerous hotels and world-class ski resorts. It is also home to many artists and writers, and the location of the Banff Centre.

Banff was controlled by the federal government until June 1988, because it is located in a national park. The town held its first local election in 1989. For information, contact the Town Manager, P.O. Box 1260, Banff, Alta, T0L 0C0.

▷ Related Articles: **Banff Centre for Continuing Education; Banff National Park.**

■ Banff Centre for Continuing Education

The Banff Centre for Continuing Education offers programs all year round in the arts, management studies, and environmental studies, and is a host to educational conferences. It is known for its arts division, called The Banff Centre for the Arts, which provides training and development for experienced, professional artists in visual arts, drama, dance, music, jazz, opera, singing, musical theatre, theatre production and design, literary arts, and media arts. The school was founded in 1933 by the University of Alberta. It was called the Banff School of Fine Arts until 1978, when it dropped its affiliation with the U of A and changed its name.

The Banff Centre *Musicians in the advanced studies of the music program (photo by Monte Greenshields/The Banff Centre).*

The Banff Centre occupies a beautiful site in the mountains, overlooking the town of Banff, Alta. The Centre has excellent facilities in all branches of the arts, including theatres, galleries, individual studios and practice huts, and modern equipment for video, audio recording, and electronic, computer, and film media. Some of the world's best artists and performers have joined the teaching staff or have spent time at the Centre as artists-in-residence. Students and faculty have the opportunity to perform every summer at the Banff Festival of the Arts.

Scholarships are available to participants, who come from all over the world. There also is the Leighton Artist Colony, which is a working retreat for professional artists. The two other divisions of The Banff Centre are The Banff Centre of Management and The Banff Centre for Conferences.

Every year, about 23 000 people take part in the Centre's programs.

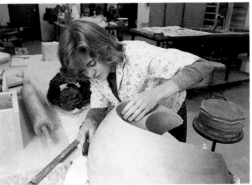

■ Banff National Park

Banff National Park is situated in the Rocky Mountains, 111 km west of Calgary. It is Canada's first national park, created in 1885 to keep the hot springs on Sulphur Mountain for public use. It has since developed into a mecca for skiers, hikers, and campers. Tourists from around the world are attracted by the park's spectacular scenery: snow-capped mountain peaks, deep valleys, and emerald lakes. Many of the park's features

The Banff Centre *Artist at work in the ceramics centre (photo by Monte Greenshields/The Banff Centre).*

Moraine Lake, Valley of the Ten Peaks, Banff National Park (photo by Thomas Kitchin).

have been shaped by glaciers over the past million years. Hundreds of glaciers still exist in the mountains. The park's wildlife includes bear, elk, bighorn sheep, mountain goats, and deer. The Banff Springs Hotel, opened in 1888, looms like a medieval castle over the Bow River valley. The town of Banff is the administrative centre of the park. The park covers an area of over 6600 km². For information, contact the Superintendent, P.O. Box 900, Banff, Alta, T0L 0C0.

▷ SUGGESTED READING: David M. Baird, *Banff National Park* (rev. ed. 1977); Eleanor G. Luxton, *Banff: Canada's First National Park* (1975).

Bow Valley and the Banff townsite viewed from Mount Norquay in Banff National Park (photo by Tom W. Parkin/Pathfinder).

■ Bank of Canada, *see* Banking

■ Banking

Banks are firms which provide financial services to individuals, businesses, and governments. The main service provided by banks is bringing together people who wish to borrow money and people with money to lend. Banks also provide many other services, including making it easy to pay bills, providing financial advice, and safekeeping.

In Canada, there are a number of different kinds of firms which provide services that are similar to banks, including trust and loan companies, credit unions and caisses populaires. A special kind of bank, called a central bank, looks after monetary policy for the economy and issues paper money. In Canada, the central bank is called the Bank of Canada.

Evidence of banking has been found in ancient Babylon as far back as 1750 BC. The word "bank" comes from the Italian word *banco*, which means "bench," and refers to the benches from which Italian moneylenders conducted their business. Later, powerful families like the de Medicis of Florence provided financial services to rich individuals and nobility. In the 1600s, the banks of Amsterdam, Stockholm, and England were formed. These banks provided some of the functions of modern central banks, such as issuing paper money.

The first chartered bank in Canada, the Bank of Montreal, began its operations in 1817. The first Bank Act, which regulates the activities of the chartered banks, was passed in 1871. Banks in Canada have evolved very differently than those in the United States. In Canada, there has tended to be a small number of large banks with branches in all parts of the country. Although there are currently 67 chartered banks in Canada, with total assets of about $516 billion, the largest nine of the banks hold about 90% of these assets. In the U.S., there has tended to be a large number of smaller banks without branches outside a given state.

Role of Banks The primary role of banks is to provide financial services to their customers. Banks provide depositors with a secure place to store their money. They make payments easy by allowing depositors to write cheques on their accounts. These cheques are accepted by many stores and individuals as a substitute for cash.

Banks use some of their depositors' money to make loans to borrowers. A borrower may be an individual who needs money to buy a car or a house, or a large corporation which needs money to build a factory. Borrowers must pay banks to use the money and this is called *interest*. In turn, banks pay interest to their depositors. Banks make some of their profit by charging borrowers a higher rate of interest than they pay to depositors.

The rate of interest banks charge on loans and pay on deposits depends on a number of factors. For example, in the case of loans, banks charge higher interest rates on loans that are less likely to be repaid. This is because if a loan is not repaid, the bank must repay the depositors' money from its profits. To help protect themselves from losses, banks often take *collateral*, that is, something which can be seized and sold by the bank if the loan is not repaid.

For a home mortgage loan, the home acts as collateral. For a car loan, the car acts as collateral. The rate of interest charged on car loans is generally higher than the rate charged on home mortgage loans, since banks consider car loans to be riskier.

The rate of interest paid to depositors also depends on a number of factors. Banks generally pay a higher rate of interest on deposits which cannot be withdrawn on short notice. For example, a *term deposit*, which can be withdrawn only after a specified period, pays a higher rate of interest than a deposit in a savings account, which can be withdrawn with little or no notice. Banks also pay higher rates of interest on larger deposits than on smaller ones.

Banks also charge fees for a number of other services. For example, banks will store customers' valuables in their vaults in safety deposit boxes. Banks allow customers to buy and sell foreign currency, such as U.S. dollars or Japanese yen. Banks will pay customers' regular bills using money from their accounts, and they also provide credit cards, such as Mastercard and Visa, which can be used to purchase different articles and services at many stores. Banks then send one monthly credit card bill to customers, and even lend (at a relatively high rate of interest) them money if they do not wish to pay the whole amount.

Regulation In Canada, chartered banks are regulated by the Bank Act. This federal law states the rules under which banks may be started and must operate. Banks are classified under two separate lists, or schedules, in the Bank Act. Schedule I lists the banks which are mostly owned by Canadians and of which no single individual or group may own more than 10%. Schedule II lists banks which are mostly owned by foreigners and which may be controlled by a single individual or group. Currently, there are ten Schedule I banks and 57 Schedule II banks in Canada. By comparison, there are about 130 trust and loan companies and almost 3100 credit unions and caisses populaires that provide some banking services similar to the banks. To ensure that banks are following the rules of the Bank Act, they are required to provide information to the Office of the Superintendant of Financial Institutions.

Depositing a Cheque *(courtesy Bank of Montreal/photo by J. Marsh).*

Deposit Insurance Many deposits in chartered banks and trust and loan companies are protected by deposit insurance, up to a maximum of $60 000 per person for each institution. This insurance is provided by the Canada Deposit Insurance Corporation (CDIC). The insurance is paid for by contributions from banks and trust and loan companies, and if a bank or a trust or loan company is unable to pay money owed to its depositors, the CDIC reimburses those people who have insured deposits. Institutions that provide deposit insurance display a notice prominently for all depositors to see. Deposits in credit unions and caisses populaires are insured by provincial bodies, for example, the Quebec Deposit Insurance Board.

Changes in Banking The services that banks provide to their customers are changing rapidly. The past ten years have seen the introduction of a number of innovations, such as automated teller machines (ATM). These machines give customers access to their accounts to deposit or withdraw cash or pay bills even when the bank is closed. Some banks in the U.S. (and a few in Canada) provide "drive-through" banking for their customers. Some banks have begun to buy and sell stocks for their customers. The federal government is changing the laws to allow banks and trust and loan companies to offer more services to customers.

Another innovation, currently being tested, is "point-of-sale" debit cards. These cards would allow customers to pay for purchases directly from their bank accounts rather than using credit cards.

▷ SUGGESTED READING: Eve Drobot, *Money: An Amazing Investigation* (1987).

What Happens When You Write a Cheque?

What happens when you receive a cheque drawn on an account in a different bank in another part of the country? The process set in motion when you deposit the cheque in your account is very complicated, but also very fast. Depending on the financial institution, the money is usually transferred within 24 hours, even if the two bank branches are as far apart as British Columbia and Newfoundland.

When you present the cheque for deposit in your account, the cheque is usually credited to your account immediately, although the branch may require that you wait a few days before withdrawing the money. At the end of the business day, the cheque will be sent to the bank's regional "data centre" for electronic processing. At the data centre, the cheque is sorted by a machine which reads the characters written at the bottom in magnetic ink. Bank staff, either at your branch or at the data centre, use the same magnetic ink to type the amount onto the cheque.

At the data centre the cheques are sorted by the banks they are drawn on. They are then given to the appropriate banks. The amounts are then entered into the individual banks' computers to deduct the funds from the appropriate accounts. The actual paper cheques are sent to the right branch by courier the next day. Banks add up the amount they owe, or are owed, by all other banks, and accounts are settled using deposits held by each bank at the Bank of Canada.

■ Bankruptcy

Bankruptcy is not being able to pay one's debts. When people or businesses go bankrupt, an accountant takes control of their assets and distributes them among the people to whom the money is owed (called *creditors*). The person or business owing the money is called the *debtor*.

If the debtor is an individual, the court takes control of all the assets, except those that are exempt under the law. A debtor is allowed to keep, for example, basic clothing, furniture, tools, and sometimes his car and home. A business must turn over all its assets.

Bankruptcies enable a debtor to be released from his debts and make a fresh start. A business cannot begin again, however, unless the debts are paid.

The rate of bankruptcies increases in times of economic problems. In 1986 over 15 000 individuals and over 600 businesses declared bankruptcy.

■ Banks Island

Banks Island, 70 028 km², is the fifth-largest island in Canada. It is the westernmost island in the Arctic Archipelago. The island is a hilly plateau which forms steep cliffs along the coastline. The island was named in 1820 for a British notable, Sir Joseph Banks. Fur-bearing animals, particularly muskox and arctic fox, are abundant. Banks Island was once inhabited by Inuit. Today, aside from an air base at Sachs Harbour, it is occupied only by seasonal trappers.

■ Bannock

Bannock is a type of flat, mainly unleavened, round bread or oatcake that was an important part of the diet of early fur traders and settlers. It originated in Scotland and northern England.

■ Banting, Sir Frederick Grant

One of the discoverers of insulin (*born in 1891 at Alliston, Ont.; died in 1941 near Musgrave Harbour, Nfld*). After studying medicine at the University of Toronto, Fred Banting served as a doctor in France during World War I. On returning to Canada, he became an orthopedic surgeon in London, Ont.

One night in 1920, after reading an article in a medical journal, Banting had an idea about how to look for a mysterious natural substance that helps us get energy from food. People whose bodies do not produce this substance suffer from diabetes, a serious disease. Banting persuaded J.J.R. Macleod, professor of physiology at the University of Toronto, to let him look for the substance by experimenting on dogs at a university laboratory. He was helped by Charles Best, a medical student and, later, by biochemist James B. Collip.

During 1921 and early 1922, this team of researchers discovered what they called insulin. They found that they could get insulin from animals, give it to children who were dying from diabetes, and the children stopped dying. Thanks to their discovery, hundreds of thousands of people with diabetes have since lived long and relatively healthy lives.

Banting did not get on well with Macleod and Collip, the senior members of the research team. When Banting learned that Macleod, as well as himself, was to be awarded the 1923 Nobel Prize for Physiology or Medicine, he gave half his prize money to Best.

He was made Sir Frederick Banting in 1934. During World War II, he did research into the health of pilots. While flying to England in 1941, the plane in which he was travelling crashed, and all aboard died.

▷ RELATED ARTICLES: **Charles Best; James B. Collip; Diabetes; Insulin; John J.R. Macleod.**

▷ SUGGESTED READING: Margaret M. Shaw, *Frederick Banting* (1976).

■ Baptists

Baptists are a religious group who baptize adult believers when they declare their faith. Baptists accept the Bible as the reliable record of God's word to mankind. Every believer has the freedom to interpret the Bible. The local church is a fellowship of believers who have made a commitment to follow Christ.

The pastor's task is to preach, train and

Sir Frederick Banting shared the Nobel Prize for discovery of insulin, which has saved hundreds of thousands of lives (NAC/PA-123481).

counsel all members. Deacons are lay men and women elected by the congregation to assist the pastor.

Baptists in Canada are divided into numerous groups, each with slightly different beliefs. The first Baptist churches in Canada were formed at Sackville (now in New Brunswick) in 1763 and at Horton (now Wolfville, N.S.). The Great Awakening of the late 18th century was a religious movement that led to an increase in the number of believers in the Maritimes. Baptists became the largest Protestant group in New Brunswick.

In Upper Canada, Baptist life was shaped by conflicting traditions. While most Baptists from the U.S. excluded non-Baptists from communion, Baptists from England believed in open communion. Scots Baptists brought a revivalist tradition. Controversy among the groups hindered co-operation.

In the late 1800s, churches in the West were established, at Winnipeg in 1875 and at Victoria in 1876.

Repeated calls for a national fellowship finally led to the formation of the Baptist Federation of Canada in 1944. Its name was changed in 1983 to Canadian Baptist Federation.

Baptists were among the earliest supporters of religious freedom and of separation of church and state. In the 19th century, they fought for equal educational opportunities for all citizens. Baptists founded several colleges, including those that became Acadia University, McMaster University, and Brandon University.

In 1981 there were over 690 000 Baptists in Canada.

■ Barachois Pond Provincial Park

Barachois Pond Provincial Park (established 1962) lies at the head of St George's Bay on the west coast of Newfoundland. The forested hills of the park offer a home to over 100 kinds of birds, as well as snowshoe hare, caribou, beaver, and pine marten. Hunting and logging were once common, but now the parkland is protected for the use of hikers, boaters, and campers. The park is 35 km² in area.

■ Barbeau, Charles Marius

Folklorist (*born in 1883 at Ste-Marie-de-Beauce, Que.; died in 1969 at Ottawa, Ont.*). Barbeau was the founder of folklore studies in Canada. From 1911 until the late 1960s, he worked as an anthropologist at the National Museum in Ottawa. He was particularly interested in French Canada and the culture of the native peo-

ple. He urgently collected as much folk material as he could while there were still people who remembered and before the modern age stamped out traditional ways forever. With great enthusiasm, he travelled across Canada collecting songs and tales, and information about the food, clothing, furniture, utensils, games, beliefs, and art of the groups he studied. He published this material in hundreds of books and articles.

Barbeau collected his information in a scientific and organized manner, noting where he first heard each item and who told him about it. In the days before tape recorders were available, he recorded thousands of songs on Edison wax-cylinders. His collection of songs, texts, and objects is preserved at the Canadian Museum of Civilization, in Hull, Que.

▷ SUGGESTED READING: C. Marius Barbeau and Michael Hornyansky, *The Golden Phoenix and Other Fairy Tales from Quebec* (1980).

Marius Barbeau *recorded ancient folklore from across Canada before it was lost forever (NAC/C-34447).*

■ Barker, William George

World War I fighter pilot, Victoria Cross winner (*born in 1894 at Dauphin, Man.; died in 1930 at Ottawa*). Barker won the Victoria Cross for his one-man fight with about 60 German aircraft near Cambrai, France, on October 27, 1918. Canadian soldiers watched the dogfight with excitement. Brigadier A.G.L. McNaughton, described it as "the most magnificent encounter of any sort which I ever witnessed."

Barker was not even on a combat flight at the time. He was flying to England to become an instructor. After shooting down one plane, he was attacked by wave after wave of German fighters.

Though wounded in both legs and one arm, Barker shot down three more German planes before he crash-landed, weak from loss of blood.

The episode was typical of William Barker, whose boldness and determination was matched by his superb skill as a pilot. Serving in Italy as well as France, he shot down a total of 53 planes during the war. After the war, he joined fellow air ace Billy Bishop in forming a small private air company, but it did not do well financially. In 1922 Barker rejoined the armed forces. He died when his plane crashed at Rockcliffe air station, Ottawa.

Billy Barker *is shown in this painting in his Sopwith Snipe during a World War I "dogfight" with German aircraft (courtesy Canadian War Museum).*

■ **Barkerville**

Barkerville, B.C., is a restored gold-rush town in the Cariboo region of the British Columbia interior. Billy Barker, an English prospector, struck gold there in 1862. A town of mud streets and board shanties immediately sprang up, and by the following summer the population numbered 5000. However, once gold was discovered farther north, the town faded. Mining continued to be the main activity, but it was almost a ghost town when the provincial government made it a historic park in 1959.

For information, contact the Visitor Service Manager, P.O. Box 19, Barkerville, B.C., V0K 1B0.

Main Street, Barkerville, *as it is restored from gold-rush days (photo by Michael Breuer).*

▷ RELATED ARTICLE: **Gold Rushes.**

▷ SUGGESTED READING: Ann Walsh, *Moses, Me and Murder* (1988).

■ **Barley**

Barley is a cereal grass which is grown all over the world. It is a dependable crop where there is drought or summer frost. Barley grain is used as livestock feed, for barley malt, and as human food. A large portion of barley production is used by brewers to produce beer and ale.

In Canada barley is grown mostly on the Prairies. About one-half of Canada's barley is exported.

■ **Barnacle**

Barnacles are a kind of crustacean. They live in the sea in shells attached to rocks and boats, or to living things such as turtles, sharks, and whales. They are the only crustacean that cannot move about on their own.

Barnacles have an odd life-style. They stand on their heads and kick food into their mouths. They have six appendages (called *cirri*) which work like a miniature net, filtering food from the water.

Goose-necked Barnacles *get their name from their resemblance to a bird's neck and head (photo by Tim Fitzharris).*

Barnacles are common on rocks exposed at low tide along Canadian coastlines. They attach themselves with a gluelike substance, which is very strong. In some countries they are thought to be a delicacy, but few people in Canada eat them. Barnacles are a nuisance to ships. They attach themselves in such great numbers that they can slow down a ship's movement through the water.

■ Barns

Barns were among the first buildings constructed by farmers in Canada. In the severe Canadian climate, farm animals and grains had to be sheltered during the winter months, so building a barn was as important as building a house. In a few cases the barn was built first and the family lived there temporarily. They used traditional designs which were familiar to them, and whatever building materials they found locally.

Most barns in early Canada were built of logs, timber, stone, or brick, with wood shingles, slate, and sometimes thatch for the roof. Some farmers filled gaps in the walls with grass, twigs, and mud. Others preferred to leave the gaps open and let the air flow through. In this case, birds, mice, and cats were likely to take up residence in the barn as well.

There are three main styles of barns in Canada: the Pennsylvania, the Dutch, and the English. Pennsylvania barns were the most practical. They were two-storeys high, with a stone foundation on the lower floor. The upper storey extended beyond the dimensions of the floor below. This overhang provided shelter for the animals during the warmer months when they lived outside the barn. In winter, the animals were kept in the lower storey, while the upper floor was used for threshing and storing grain. Since both floors had their own set of doors on the broad side of the building, the barn was often situated on a natural slope to allow easy access to the upper storey. In the Dutch barn, the doors were located at the ends of the building.

The English barn was smaller and only one storey in height. It was found most commonly in wheat-growing areas. It consisted of a central threshing area, with a bay for threshed grain on one side and a bay for unthreshed grain on the other side. If the farmer also kept animals, he simply added a similar barn at right angles to the first. On some farms, four English barns were grouped together around a courtyard, one each to store the wheat,

Pennsylvania Barns were practical barns with a convenient overhang to shelter the animals (courtesy Black Creek Pioneer Village).

the cattle, the horses, and the pigs.

Circular barns are found in some areas of Quebec. They are usually built of smooth, tongue-and-groove timbers and are painted in bright colours. Some farmers even painted scenes of rural activities on the sides of these barns. In other areas, artistic farmers might erect a weathervane on the roof which showed their favourite animal, or they might carve a stone lintel over the door of their barn.

Barns often had a special social significance in rural communities. When a farmer decided to build a new barn, he organized a barn raising. On the appointed day, neighbours would come from near and far and, before nightfall, the barn would be completed.

These traditional barns are doomed to extinction. Many fine barns are patched with galvanized iron roofs, and others are rapidly falling into decay. New barns are almost always constructed in weather-proof aluminum sheeting. They may be efficient, but they lack the cultural and architectural interest of the old Canadian barns.

Modern Barn near Balzac, Alberta (photo by Roy Ooms/Take Stock Inc.).

▷ SUGGESTED READING: Eric Arthur and Dudley Witney, *The Barn* (1972); Bob Hainstock, *Barns of Western Canada* (1985).

■ Barr, Isaac Montgomery

Founder of Barr Colony (*born in 1847 near Hornby, Canada West [Ontario]; died in 1937 at Cohuna, Australia*). Barr was an Anglican clergyman of British origin, who wanted to see the Prairies inhabited by people of British origin. This was why, in 1903, he founded the Barr Colony on a large stretch of empty prairie north and west of Saskatoon.

Barr hoped to become known as a major colonizer, such as Cecil Rhodes of Rhodesia, but he was too difficult a character to be an inspiring leader. As a clergyman in Ontario and then the United States, he had seldom been able to stay in one parish for long. Nor was he an efficient organizer, though he tried hard to provide for his settlers' needs. Because of the many problems, Barr was obliged to leave his prairie colony just as it was getting started. He lived for several years in the United States and eventually immigrated to Australia, where he became a settler.

■ Barr Colony

Barr Colony was a prairie settlement, founded in 1903 in the region of present-day Lloydminster on the Alberta-Saskatchewan border. It was the brainchild of the Reverend Isaac Barr, who signed up for the land in 1902 on behalf of the settlers he was to organize.

Barr recruited almost 2000 settlers in England. In the spring of 1903 he brought them to Canada on the SS *Lake Manitoba*, a ship built to carry only a third of that number. The discomforts of the voyage quickly turned many of the colonists against Barr. After disembarking at Saint John, N.B., a shortage of food and blankets on the train journey to Saskatoon added to their complaints. Part of the problem was that Barr was moving too many people at once. Just getting them and their luggage onto trains bound for the West caused major difficulties.

The colonists arrived in the West in April 1903. Most were from English cities and had no experience in farming. Even the wagon ride from Saskatoon to the colony seemed to them a major hardship. Their feelings against Barr were so strong that he left a few days after arriving at the colony that bore his name. Leadership passed to the Reverend George Lloyd, to whom the settlers had increasingly turned for help during their journey from England. They named their first town after Lloyd, who later became bishop of Saskatchewan.

Some of the colonists soon left, unable to cope with the difficulties of starting a farm on the open prairie. Others persevered, and they formed the basis of many of the rural communities that developed west of Saskatoon.

▷ SUGGESTED READING: Barbara V. Cormack, *Westward Ho!* (1967).

■ Barrett, David

Social worker and politician (*born in 1930 at Vancouver, B.C.*). Dave Barrett was the first and only social democratic premier of British Columbia (1972-75). The son of a Jewish fruit seller, he studied philosophy and social work in the United States before returning to B.C. In 1957 he joined the provincial prison service but lost his job two years later when he criticized the prison system and helped to unionize prison employees.

In 1960 Barrett ran successfully as a Co-operative Commonwealth Federation candidate in the provincial election. After the New Democratic Party (NDP) was formed in 1961, he continued to be re-elected as an NDP member. He became leader of British Columbia's NDP in 1969 and guided it to victory in the 1972 provincial elections.

As premier, Barrett carried out a series of reforms. He made the legal and welfare systems more humane and stopped the sale of valuable farmland to developers. His government took over automobile insurance, but Barrett never carried out his promise to take over the American-owned British Columbia Telephone Company. At the same time, Barrett lost the support of teachers and labour by failing to reform the education system and by legislating the end of strikes. The Social Credit Party easily defeated Barrett's government in 1975. Barrett remained leader of the opposition until 1984. He then be-

Barr Colonists camp on the prairie northwest of Saskatoon (NAC/PA-38667).

David Barrett is shown here as federal MP during Question Period (courtesy Canapress Photo Service).

came the host of a radio talk show in Vancouver. In November 1988 he re-entered politics, winning a seat for the federal NDP in Victoria. He ran a spirited campaign for the NDP leadership in 1989, but came second to Audrey McLaughlin.

■ Barrie

Barrie, Ont., lies at the head of Kempenfelt Bay, an arm of Lake Simcoe, in south-central Ontario. It is 70 km north of Toronto. The first settlers arrived in 1833, but before that time it lay along an important supply route between Lake Ontario and Georgian Bay. Today, the economy relies on manufacturing, with the largest employer being General Tire Canada Ltd. In May 1985 a tornado devastated part of the city and was blamed for eight deaths there. In 1986 the population was 48 287. For information, contact the City Clerk, 70 Collier Street, P.O. Box 400, Barrie, Ont., L4M 4T5.

■ Barry, James Miranda Stuart

Army physician and surgeon (*born around 1795 in England; died in 1865 at London, England*). Dr James Barry was a woman who disguised herself as a man so that she could study medicine and be a doctor. Her real name was probably Miss Bulkeley. Brought up in Britain, she first posed as a male in 1809 so that she could get into Edinburgh University. This was long before universities accepted women students. After graduating in medicine, Barry joined the British army. Serving in South Africa, the Caribbean, and other parts of the world, she gained a reputation as an outstanding surgeon.

In 1857 Barry was posted to Canada as inspector general of military hospitals, the army's senior doctor in Canada. She was still thought to be a man, though a very odd one. Small and slim, and with no hair on her face, she was considered eccentric. She liked to drive around Montreal in a bright red sled, accompanied by a small white dog and a large Black manservant. Nevertheless, the troops appreciated her. She insisted on better food for the soldiers, and she made the hospitals cleaner and more comfortable. She had to return to England in 1859 because she fell sick (though, as usual, she refused to be examined).

Barry's long-kept secret was discovered when she died and was laid out for burial. Some recent scholars still think there is "room for doubt" that Barry really was a woman.

▷ SUGGESTED READING: Carlotta Hacker, *The Indomitable Lady Doctors* (2nd ed. 1984).

Dr James Barry was likely a woman who posed as a man in order to become a doctor (courtesy Federation of Medical Women of Canada).

Robert Bartlett, arctic explorer, learned to navigate ships through the ice around his native Newfoundland (courtesy NAC/C-25962).

Wigwam in the Forest (c1840) by William Henry Bartlett. His accurate pictures are a valuable record of early Canada (courtesy NGC).

■ Barter

Before there was money, people exchanged things they did not want for those they did. Such an exchange is known as "barter."

When Europeans first arrived in North America, they found an economy based on barter. Native tribes controlled the resources in their territory. Permission was needed in order to cross this land. Therefore, if a tribe wanted something found only in another tribe's land, such as copper or furs, they had to barter for it. Many of these goods were transported over hundreds of kilometres.

For many years, trade was carried on between Europeans and the native people by barter. The native people trapped the furs and exchanged them for blankets, hatchets, knives, kettles, guns, and other items.

Today, few Canadians could survive in an economy based on barter. We no longer have the skills needed to make things that could be traded. Nevertheless, there is a thriving "underground economy," in which people exchange goods and services. The extent of this activity is unknown because it occurs away from the watchful eyes of the taxman.

■ Bartlett, Robert

Arctic explorer (*born in 1875 at Brigus, Nfld; died in 1946 at New York City, U.S.*). A fisherman and seal hunter from his youth, Robert Bartlett learned to navigate ships through the ice around his native Newfoundland. He impressed the American explorer Robert Peary with his skills and Peary invited him along on his three expeditions to the North Pole. On the final attempt, Bartlett himself got to within 250 km of the pole.

In 1913 Bartlett took command of the *Karluk*, the supply vessel for the Canadian Arctic Expedition. The ship was wrecked in the ice north of the Russian mainland. Bartlett made a daring sled trip to Siberia and then travelled by ship to Alaska to get help.

After World War I, he commanded a vessel which carried scientists and supplies into the Arctic.

▷ RELATED ARTICLES: **Canadian Arctic Expedition; Robert Peary.**

▷ SUGGESTED READING: Harold A. Horwood, *Bartlett, The Great Canadian Explorer* (1977).

■ Bartlett, William Henry

Artist (*born in 1809 in England; died in 1854 at sea off Malta*). Bartlett travelled extensively in Europe, the Middle East, and North America, making sketches for over 40 illustrated travel books. He also wrote and illustrated 13 books. His paintings were engraved by professional printmakers, and were popular for their accuracy and charm. He visited Canada in 1838, and recorded the falls at Montmorency and Niagara as well as scenes of daily life in the Maritimes and Upper and Lower Canada. These engravings were published in *Canadian Scenery* (1842).

▷ RELATED ARTICLE: **Painting.**

■ Baseball

Baseball was developed in the United States about 150 years ago. It was based on an old English game called "rounders." The basic modern rules were laid down in 1845. The first Canadian team was likely the Young Canadians of Hamilton, formed in 1854. Other early teams were formed in London, St Thomas, and Woodstock, also in Ontario. The first Canadian league was formed in 1876. It had teams in Toronto, Kingston, Hamilton, Guelph, and London.

Baseball soon spread to other parts of Canada. Its growth followed the railway west to Manitoba, Saskatchewan, Alberta, and all the way to the Yukon. There were also leagues in Nova Scotia and Quebec.

The Toronto Maple Leafs and the Montreal Royals teams played in a professional league, called the International League, for many years. There have also been minor league professional teams in Vancouver, Edmonton, and Calgary. A new era in baseball began in 1969 when

the Montreal Expos joined the National League, the first Canadian team in the Major Leagues. The Toronto Blue Jays joined the American League in 1977.

Most of the players on these professional teams were born in the United States or in the Spanish-speaking West Indies. However, several Canadians have played professional baseball. The first was William Phillips, from Saint John, N.B. The best known of these players is Ferguson Jenkins, a pitcher, who is from Chatham, Ont.

In 1987 there were over 250 000 amateur baseball players in Canada.

Softball is a variation of baseball. It is played on a smaller field with a larger ball, which is pitched underhand. The game became popular in Canada early in this century. Over 2 million men and women play softball in Canada on about 150 000 teams. In 1972 the Richmond Hill Dynes of Ontario won the men's world softball championship. Another team, the Victoria Bates, from Victoria, B.C., tied for the men's world championship in 1976. Canada sent a team to the 1988 Olympics at Seoul, Korea, where baseball was a demonstration sport.

▷ RELATED ARTICLES: **Ferguson Jenkins; Montreal Expos; Toronto Blue Jays.**
▷ SUGGESTED READING: William Humber, *Cheering For the Home Team: The Story of Baseball in Canada* (1983).

James Naismith, with the two elements of the game he invented, the "basket" and the "ball" (courtesy NAC/C-80002).

■ Basketball

Basketball is a team sport in which points are scored by throwing a ball into the opponent's hoop, or "basket." Unlike other sports, basketball did not develop slowly over the years. The game was invented as an entirely new game by Canadian James Naismith in 1891. Naismith was an instructor at a school in Springfield, Massachusetts. He wanted to create a game that could be played indoors in the winter. Naismith's original basket really was a wooden basket. His game caught on quickly, and is now played all over the world.

The game of basketball came to Canada before 1900. One of the first teams was the Vancouver YMCA. Canada has sent teams to the Olympic games since 1924.

First Game in the SkyDome Toronto Blue Jay pitcher Jimmy Key delivers a pitch to Paul Molitor of the Milwaukee Brewers (courtesy Canapress Photo Service).

The men's team finished in fourth place in the 1976 and 1984 Olympics and won a gold medal at the World University Games in Edmonton in 1983. The women's team placed fourth at the 1984 Olympics. Canada's greatest basketball team was the Edmonton Grads, a women's team. The Grads ruled basketball in the 1920s and 1930s. From 1915 to 1940, the Grads won four world championships, winning 502 of 522 games that they played.

▷ RELATED ARTICLES: **Edmonton Grads; James Naismith; J. Percy Page.**

■ Basques

Basques are people who live in several provinces along the Atlantic coast of Spain and France. They have long been expert fishermen and sailors. In the 1500s they were among the earliest arrivals on the east coast of Canada. Sailing from Europe each spring, they fished for cod and hunted whales in the harbours of Newfoundland, in the Strait of Belle Isle, and along the north shore of the St Lawrence River. When fall came, the Basques sailed back to Europe.

Basque hunters chased the whales in small boats and killed them with harpoons thrown by hand. They towed the huge carcasses to shore. The blubber was then removed and boiled in large vats to produce the valuable oil, which was used as lamp oil in Europe.

The high point of Basque whaling in Canada was from 1540 to 1590. After that, competition from other European countries forced the Basque whalers to go elsewhere. Cod fishermen from the Basque country still visited North America for many years.

Basque whalers left traces of their activities. Since 1977 archaeologists have discovered a graveyard and many artifacts at Red Bay, Labrador, one of the whaling harbours. The most striking find was the wreck of a Basque ship believed to be the *San Juan*, which sank in a storm in 1565.

▷ RELATED ARTICLES: **Red Bay; Whaling.**

▷ SUGGESTED READING: Jim Tuck and Robert Grenier, *Red Bay Labrador: World Whaling Capital* (1989).

■ Bass

In Canada, the name "bass" applies to three families of fish, with a total of 19 species. All bass have a spiny dorsal fin. The three families are temperate bass, sunfish, and sea bass.

Temperate basses (Percichthyidae) are found in salt water, brackish water, or fresh water in eastern Canada. The striped bass (*Morone saxatilis*) has been introduced into the waters off British Columbia. The spiny part of the dorsal fin on temperate basses is clearly separated from the soft-rayed part.

Sunfish (Centrarchidae) are freshwater fish and are not true basses. This family includes smallmouth bass, largemouth bass, and rock bass, which are all important game fish. They prefer the warmer waters of southern Canada. They are found in lakes, ponds, and slow-moving streams. They are native to eastern Canada but have been introduced in the West. They have bands of teeth on the roof of the mouth, on the tongue, and on the jaws. Sunfish feed on insects, fish, and crayfish.

The largemouth bass (*Micropterus salmoides*) and the smallmouth bass (*Micropterus dolomieu*) are members of the same family. They are highly prized by sportfishers. Their spectacular leaps and aggressiveness make for exciting encounters. Moreover, they are delicious to eat.

Sea bass (Serranidae) are found on the Atlantic coast. Little is known about them.

■ Bassett Family

The Bassett family's business interests are concentrated in communications and sports. **John Bassett** (*1886-1958*) came to Canada from Ireland in 1909. He eventually became president and publisher of the Montreal *Gazette*. In 1952 his son, **John White Hughes Bassett** (*born in 1915 at Ottawa*), purchased part ownership of the Toronto *Telegram*. In 1960 he set up Baton Broadcasting to operate Toronto's first commercial television station, CFTO, and began shifting his attention from newspaper publishing to television. By 1981 he had sold all his newspapers. At one time in the 1960s he was part owner of Maple Leaf Gardens, and in the early 1970s he owned the Toronto Argonauts football club. His son, **Douglas Graeme** (*born in 1940 at Toronto*), now runs Ba-

San Juan, *a Basque ship which sank in a storm in 1565 on the Atlantic coast (courtesy Canadian Parks Service/photo by R. Chan & D. Page).*

ton Broadcasting. Another son, **John Frederick** (*1939-86*) carried on the family's interest in professional sports. His granddaughter **Carling Bassett-Seguso** (*born in 1967 at Toronto*) is an international tennis star. Before turning professional in 1983, Carling Bassett had been ranked first among world juniors and was clearly Canada's best tennis player.

■ Bat

Bats, which comprise the order Chiroptera, are the only mammals capable of true flight. Their wings are formed by folds of skin stretched between the body and hind legs and elongated finger bones. Most bats are active at night (nocturnal). Twenty-two species of bats have been recorded in Canada, one free-tailed bat (family Molossidae) and 21 plain-nosed bats (Vespertilionidae). All Canadian bats eat insects and they occur from the tree-line in the north to the U.S. border in the south. There are about 900 different species of bat in the world. In tropical locations, there are species that feed on fruit, nectar and pollen, fish, bats, birds, frogs, and even blood.

Echolocation Although all bats have vision and see quite well, many of them locate objects in their path by echolocation. These bats use echoes of sounds they produce to locate objects and by this they can detect insects smaller than mosquitoes. In Canada the echolocation sounds of spotted bats are clearly audible to the unaided human ear but these sounds of the other species are beyond the range of human hearing. Many insects such as moths, lacewings, praying mantises, and crickets have ears sensitive to the echolocation calls of bats. Hearing an

approaching bat permits these insects to detect and avoid attacking bats.

Migration and Hibernation In winter the bats in Canada either migrate to more temperate climates or they hibernate, passing the winter in a deep sleep. In summer bats may roost in the foliage of trees or bushes, inside hollow trees, in rock crevices or in buildings.

Reproduction and Feeding Bats have low rates of reproduction and most Canadian species have just one or two young annually. At birth, baby bats are about 25% of their mothers' mass, reflecting the huge investment females make in their young. Little Brown Bats, which weigh 8 to 10 g as adults, are known to live over 30 years in the wild. Insectivorous bats typically consume up to 50% of their body weight in insects every night in summer, making them of great potential benefit to humans.

Like other mammals, bats are susceptible to rabies. Therefore, they should not be handled.

▷ SUGGESTED READING: M. Brock Fenton, *Just Bats* (1983); Alice L. Hopf, *Bats* (1985).

■ Bateman, Robert McLellan

Painter (*born in 1930 at Toronto, Ont.*). Bateman trained as a naturalist and studied painting with Carl Schaefer and others. For about 20 years he taught high school in Toronto and Burlington, Ont., and travelled widely. His early paintings were mostly abstract. In 1963 he began the wildlife painting that has brought him international success. His work is reproduced in Ramsay Derry, *The Art of Robert Bateman* (1981) and *The World of Robert Bateman* (1985), and in S.G. Shetler, *Portraits of Nature: Paintings of Robert Bateman* (1987).

▷ SUGGESTED READING: Ramsay Derry, *The World of Robert Bateman* (1985); Marjorie E. White, *Robert Bateman* (1989).

■ Bates, Maxwell

Artist, architect, writer, poet (*born in 1906 at Calgary, Alta; died in 1980 at Victoria, B.C.*). Bates was an apprentice in his father's architectural firm. He studied painting and lived in London, England, from 1931 to 1939. He wrote a book, *A Wilderness of Days*, about his experiences as a prisoner of war during World War II. He returned to Calgary in 1946 and helped design Calgary's St Mary's Cathedral. A stroke left him partly paralysed in 1961, but he continued to paint landscapes and expressive figure studies in bold colours.

Little Brown Bat
(Macmillan Illustrated Animal Encyclopedia).

Big Brown Bat
(Macmillan Illustrated Animal Encyclopedia).

Bats emit sounds (shown in orange) and use the echoes (blue) to locate insects (artwork by Jan Sovak).

■ Bathurst

Bathurst lies at the mouth of the Nepisiguit River on the shore of Chaleur Bay in northern New Brunswick. In the 19th century, logging and sawmilling were the main activities. The pulp and paper industry has flourished since World War I. In 1953 large mineral finds were made nearby and mining is still important. Settlement was begun in 1652 by the French colonizer, Nicolas Denys. In 1757, displaced Acadians arrived, and the area has had a large French-speaking population ever since. The town was named after Henry Bathurst, a British colonial secretary. In 1986 the population was 14 683. For information, contact the City Clerk, P.O. Drawer D, Bathurst, N.B., E2A 3Z1.

■ Bathurst Island

Bathurst Island, 16 042 km², is located roughly in the middle of Canada's arctic islands. Most of the island is flat and low. Unusual for the Arctic, the island has abundant vegetation and it supports much more wildlife than neighbouring islands. It was first visited in 1819 by the naval explorer Sir William Parry, who named it for Henry Bathurst, a British colonial secretary. Its exact shape was not known until it was explored from the air in 1947. The geomagnetic North Pole is at the northern end of the island.

Polar Bear Pass on Bathurst Island in the Canadian Arctic (photo by Stephen J. Krasemann/DRK Photo).

■ Batoche, Battle of

The Battle of Batoche took place from May 9 to May 12, 1885, at the Metis settlement of Batoche on the South Saskatchewan River. It was the battle that ended the North-West Rebellion. On one side was Louis Riel, with a Metis and Indian force of less than 300 men. Attacking them was General Frederick Middleton, with some 900 men.

The Metis took up a strong position at Batoche. Firing from rifle pits, which they had dug, they held off the larger force for three days. But Middleton's larger army had cannons and a Gatling gun (a type of machine gun). On the fourth day, the Metis were put to flight. Riel surrendered a few days later. The Metis military commander, Gabriel Dumont, escaped to the United States.

▷ RELATED ARTICLE: **North-West Rebellion.**

Battle of Batoche This painting shows the capture of the Metis forces at Batoche (NAC/C-2424).

■ Battleford

Battleford, Sask., lies at the junction of the North Saskatchewan and Battle rivers, 138 km northwest of Saskatoon. It was founded in 1876 as the capital of the North-West Territories. A North-West Mounted Police post was erected nearby. The post is now an historic park. The town did not grow as expected, because the main line of the Canadian Pacific Railway crossed the prairie farther to the south. In 1883, the capital was moved to Regina. Today, Battleford is dwarfed by its larger neighbour, North Battleford. Its population in 1986 was 3833. For information, contact the Town Administrator, P.O. Box 40, Battleford, Sask., S0M 0E0.

■ Battles, see Amiens; Atlantic; Batoche; Beaver Dams; Chateauguay; Crysler's Farm; Cut Knife Hill; Duck Lake; Grand Coteau; Hong Kong; Long Sault; Lundy's Lane; Mont Sorrel; Ortona; Passchendaele; Plains of Abraham; Queenston Heights; Rhineland; Ridgeway; Saint-Charles; Saint-Denis; Saint-Eustache; Ste-Foy; Seven Oaks Incident; Somme; Stoney Creek; Vimy Ridge; Windmill; Ypres. *See also* entries on wars, for example, **War of 1812; World War I; World War II.**

■ Baumann, Alex

Swimmer (*born in 1964 at Prague, Czechoslovakia*). Canada's greatest swimmer arrived in Canada at age nine and soon began setting swimming records for his age group. He set his first world record in

1981 for the 200 m IM (individual medley). This race requires laps in all four styles: butterfly, breaststroke, backstroke, and freestyle. He lowered the record for the 200 m IM at the Commonwealth Games in 1982 and set a world record for the 400 m IM in 1983. He won two gold medals in the 1984 Olympic Games, setting new world records in the 200 m IM and 400 m IM. He is one of only five Canadians to win two Olympic gold medals. He retired in 1987.

▷ SUGGESTED READING: Glynn Leyshon, *Swimmers* (1989).

Alex Baumann holds one of the two gold medals he won at the 1984 Olympic Games (courtesy Athlete Information Bureau).

■ Bay and Gulf
Bays and gulfs are bodies of water partly enclosed by land. Gulfs are generally larger and more enclosed than bays. *See* **Baffin Bay; Bay of Fundy; Bonavista Bay; Chaleur Bay; Chignecto Bay; Frobisher Bay; Georgian Bay; Gulf of St Lawrence; Hudson Bay; James Bay; Passamaquoddy Bay; Placentia Bay; Ungava Bay.**

■ Bay Bulls
Bay Bulls, Nfld, is a fishing port on the east coast of the Avalon Peninsula, south of St John's. Its name may refer to a sea bird common to the area, called the bull bird. The port was first used by the French. The English settled there from about 1635. During the long rivalry be-

tween French and English for Newfoundland's fishery, it was attacked many times. During World War II, Bay Bulls was an important shipbuilding and ship repair facility. Today, the town's main industry is fishing. Its population in 1986 was 1114. For information, contact the Town Clerk, P.O. Box 70, Bay Bulls, Nfld, A0A 1C0.

■ Bay d'Espoir
Bay d'Espoir is a long, narrow, steep-sided arm of Hermitage Bay, on the south coast of Newfoundland. The area is the site of the largest hydroelectric power facility on the island of Newfoundland. Fishing, lumbering, and construction support the local economy.

■ Bay of Fundy
The Bay of Fundy is a large inlet of the Atlantic Ocean that separates New Brunswick and Nova Scotia. It is about 290 km long and about 50 km wide at its mouth. Its name may come from the French word *fendu*, meaning "split." This refers to the two fingerlike channels, Chignecto Bay and Minas Basin, which lie at the head of the bay.

When the last glaciers retreated from the Atlantic Coast about 10 000 years ago, many shallow parts of the coast which are now covered by water were dry land. As the glaciers melted, the sea slowly rose until the coastline took on its present shape and the Bay of Fundy was formed.

High Tides Because of its shape, size, and depth, the Bay of Fundy has the world's largest tides. In the Minas Basin the range from low to high tide can be up to 16 m. The tide results in powerful tidal bores in the rivers around the bay and in the famous Reversing Falls on the Saint John River. The tides also mix the waters of the bay, keeping them rich in nutrients.

At the Annapolis Basin on Fundy's Nova Scotia coastline, the tides are being used to produce electrical power. As the tide recedes, water that has been collected in a large basin while the tide came in, flows back out through a turbine that generates electricity.

Fish and Oil The rich waters of the bay support abundant fish, whales, and seabirds. Fundy is an important fishing ground for boats from Nova Scotia, New Brunswick, and Maine. The boundary of the fishery is the source of a dispute between the United States and Canada. The large mud flats caused by the tides at the head of the bay are feeding grounds for vast numbers of migrating birds.

Bay of Fundy Tides are the highest in the world. The two photos here show high tide (top) and low tide (bottom) at Alma, N.B. (photos by Greg Stott/Masterfile).

Oil companies wish to look for offshore oil, but they are opposed by fishermen who fear that drilling will disturb the area. These problems are most serious on Georges Bank, a fishing area off the mouth of the Bay of Fundy.

▷ RELATED ARTICLES: **Acadia; Georges Bank; New Brunswick; Nova Scotia; Tides.**

Bears The three species of bear found in Canada are the polar bear (Ursus maritimus), shown top; black bear (Ursus americanus), shown centre; and grizzly (Ursus arctos horribilis), bottom (artwork by Jan Sovak).

Bay Roberts

Bay Roberts is a town on the west side of Conception Bay on Newfoundland's Avalon Peninsula. First settled by English fishermen in the late 1600s, it grew as a fishing and seal-hunting centre. Today it is an important business centre for the region, and it produces more salt-fish than any other place in the province. In 1986 its population was 4446. For information, contact the Town Clerk, P.O. Box 114, Bay Roberts, Nfld, A0A 1G0.

Bean

Beans are legumes which belong to the pea family (Leguminosae). They are an important food for humans and livestock. Bean plants may be either bush or vine types, and may have white, yellow, red, or purple flowers. The fruit is a pod that may be straight or curved, round or flat.

Beans are eaten in several forms. Lima beans and snap beans (green or wax) are eaten fresh or may be processed by canning or freezing. Dry beans (kidney or white pea) are used in soups, mixed-bean salads, baked beans, or boiled with meat. All beans are important sources of protein.

Green beans grow well in the warmer regions of Canada. The main areas of production are Quebec, Ontario, and British Columbia. Dry beans are mainly grown in southern Ontario.

Bear

The bear is the largest land carnivore (meat eater). Bears are members of the animal family Ursidae. There are three species in Canada: the black bear (*Ursus americanus*), the grizzly bear (*U. arctos horribilis*), and the polar bear (*U. maritimus*).

All bears are large and heavy bodied, with short tails and short, strong legs. Bears have poor sight, but their hearing and sense of smell are sharp. Bears have paws, each with five toes, bearing powerful claws. They walk on their heels and can also walk upright on their hind legs in an aggressive pose.

The black bear is found throughout the forests of Canada. The grizzly once lived all over the West, but is now limited to the mountains of Alberta, B.C., and the Yukon, and the Barren Grounds of the Northwest Territories. The polar bear's range extends along the Arctic coast from the Yukon to Labrador.

Bears do not really hibernate. In winter they enter a state of lethargic sleep and live off their fatty reserves. Bears are solitary animals, except during mating season. Usually, the female has two cubs during the period of semi-hibernation, whom she raises on her own and accompanies for their first year. Bears have a varied diet of both plants and animals, and will eat grain, vegetables, and farm animals, and will scavenge garbage from dumps or campgrounds.

BEAR ATTACKS

Bears are very powerful animals and they can run very fast. They can seriously injure or even kill humans.

Fortunately, most bears avoid people. They may charge and growl to scare them away. Only rarely will they attack. The grizzly bear is very shy of people, but it will attack if it is encountered suddenly. A grizzly is more dangerous if it has eaten people's food or garbage, or if it is provoked by a dog or a photographer getting too close. Tourists and campers should never feed bears.

Unlike the grizzly, most black bear attacks occur near campgrounds or other areas where bears are trying to get people's food or garbage. A person who encounters a bear should back away when it threatens. Few of these confrontations are serious. Polar bears have been known to stalk people, since this is their nature, but records show few occasions in which they attacked.

▷ RELATED ARTICLES: **Black Bear; Grizzly Bear; Polar Bear.**

▷ SUGGESTED READING: Caroline Greenland, *Nature's Children: Black Bears* (1986); *Nature's Children: Grizzly Bears* (1986); *Nature's Children: Polar Bears* (1985); Charles G.D. Roberts, *Seven Bears* (rev. and abridged ed. 1977); Andy Russell, *Grizzly Country* (1978).

■ Bearberries

The Bearberry (*Arctostaphylos uva-ursi*) belongs to the heath family (Ericacae). Do bears really eat bearberries? The Latin name *uva-ursi* suggests that they do, since *uva* means "grapes" and *ursus* means "bear." In fact, it is usually birds who eat the tasteless red fruit with its large, hard seeds. They help propagate the plant, since the seeds germinate more easily once they have passed through the bird's digestive tract. This plant grows slowly but can live 100 years. It is rarely found near inhabited areas, preferring instead arid terrain such as rocks, gravel, and sand. It is found along with lichens and other trailing plants that can resist such exposed positions, such as the low-bush cranberry (*Vaccinium vitis-idaea*), which looks much like the bearberry.

Bearberries *are rarely seen near inhabited areas. Their tasteless red fruit is eaten by birds (artwork by Claire Tremblay).*

Although lacking more tasty fruit, this trailing shrub is used in a variety of ways. It is known throughout northern regions for its medicinal properties against kidney problems. In North America, dried leaves were mixed with tobacco and then used as a form of money. Depending on the tribe, it is known either as "kinnick-innick" or as "sagakomi," meaning "that which is mixed."

■ Beardy, Jackson

Artist (*born in 1944 on the Garden Hill Reserve at Island Lake, Man.; died in 1984 at Winnipeg, Man.*). In his short life, Beardy made his mark as a fine artist, a passionate collector of Indian myths and legends, and a firm supporter of native culture. He was educated at government residential schools and the University of

Calling the Night, by Jackson Beardy, whose paintings express the harmony and power in nature (courtesy DIAND).

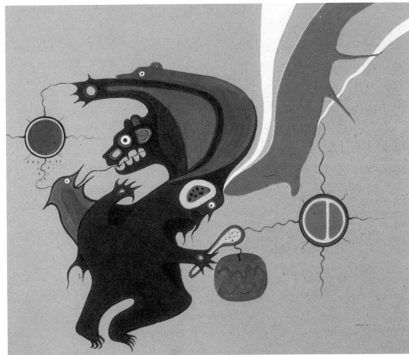

Manitoba. But the greatest influence on his life was his grandmother, who taught him the folklore and traditions of his Cree people. As a young artist he joined with Norval Morrisseau and other legend painters of the Woodlands school. His paintings often portray specific myths, but they also express spiritual concepts such as the harmony and power in nature and the connection between all things. This interdependence is marked by flowing lines joining every figure to another on his canvases. From 1982 to 1983 Beardy was senior arts adviser to the federal Department of Indian Affairs and Northern Development.

▷ SUGGESTED READING: Kenneth J. Hughes, *Jackson Beardy, Life and Art* (1979).

■ Beaufort Sea

Beaufort Sea, about 450 000 km² in area, is the name given to the waters north of Alaska, the Yukon, and the mouth of the Mackenzie River. The Beaufort Sea is actually part of the Arctic Ocean. The term "sea" was given to it early on and has stuck. There is a narrow shelf off the coast, which drops off rapidly to about 4000 m. The sea is largely covered by ice in winter. During the summer, the ice recedes from the coast, leaving a narrow channel of open water for navigation. In 1889 American whalers first used this passage to enter the Beaufort to hunt whales. This activity continued to World War I. Long before this time, Inuit living along the coast hunted mammals and seabirds. In the late 1960s, exploration for oil and gas began in the southern offshore area, although production did not begin until the mid-1980s. The sea is named for Admiral Sir Francis Beaufort.

▷ RELATED ARTICLE: **Arctic Ocean.**

■ Beauharnois Scandal

After the election of 1930 brought the Conservatives to power, the former Liberal government of W.L. Mackenzie King was accused of receiving money from a large utility company in Beauharnois, Que., in return for doing the company certain favours. Two committees of Parliament probed the charges from 1931 to 1932 and failed to connect the money with any government policy. However, the careers of two Liberal Party senators who received money from the company were ruined.

■ Beaulieu, Victor-Lévy

Writer (*born in 1945 at St-Paul-de-la-Croix, Que.*). Beaulieu is a versatile writer who has won many awards, including a Governor General's Award in 1974. He is a leading figure in Quebec literary life. The author of stories, plays, novels, essays, and television series, he also operated his own publishing company, VLB éditeur, from 1976 to 1984.

■ Beaver

The Beaver are an Athapaskan-speaking people of the Peace River area of British Columbia and Alberta. They traditionally lived in small nomadic hunting bands. They lived by hunting bison, moose, caribou, and bears. The hunts were led by religious leaders called "Dreamers." Beaver children were sent into the bush on vision quests to gain supernatural power from the animals. The Beaver now live on reserves in B.C. and Alberta. *See* **Native People: Subarctic.**

■ Beaver

The Latin name for the animal known as the beaver in Canada is *Castor canadensis*. *Castor* refers to the beaver family and *canadensis* recognizes Canada as its home. The beaver is the largest rodent in North America. It can weigh from 13 to 35 kg. Today's beaver is tiny, however, compared to the giant beaver which lived in North America some 10 000 years ago. It could grow as large as a black bear. The mountain beaver (*Aplodontia rufa*), found on the mountains along the Pacific coast, is not a true beaver.

The beaver is well adapted to an aquatic way of life. Its hind feet are large and webbed, and its tail is shaped like a paddle. The beaver has a thick underfur which keeps it warm and dry. The beaver can stay underwater for 15 minutes. Beavers have an elaborate social life, which centres around the female. They communicate with one another with low whines and bellows, by leaving soft mud pies or a musky scent, or by smacking their tails on the water to warn of danger.

Range of Beaver ●

Beaufort Sea This artificial island was built to aid in oil exploration (courtesy Petroleum Resources Communication Foundation).

Habitat Beavers are among the few mammals which change their own habitat. They create ponds by building dams of sticks, roots, sod, mud, and stones. They build a lodge in the riverbank or in the middle of a pond. Beavers do not hibernate, but they cut and store logs and branches in food rafts for the winter. The beaver pond is kept a metre or more deep so that the water will not freeze around the underwater entrance to the lodge. The beaver fells trees with its powerful, ever-growing front teeth. Each colony consists of an adult pair, the newborns (called *kits*), and yearlings.

Enemies The beaver's enemies, besides man, are the bear, wolf, coyote, wolverine, and lynx. The otter is a deadly foe to young beavers because it can swim into the lodge.

Distribution The beaver is found coast to coast in Canada, wherever there are forests or streams. Its thick fur was prized by the native people and, later, by Europeans. For many years the trade in beaver pelts was Canada's most important economic activity. As a result, the beaver was hunted almost to extinction. It has now recovered to the point that it is an occasional nuisance. It may plug culverts, flood roads and bridges, and cut down ornamental trees. Beavers are sometimes blamed for spreading a disease called "beaver fever." However, poor sanitary conditions around campgrounds are the more likely cause of the disease. The beaver is one of our most interesting and valuable animals, and a fitting symbol for Canada. It represents industry, a peaceful nature, strength, and a strong parental concern for its young.

Beaver fur was once so valuable that the animal was hunted almost to extinction (artwork by Jan Sovak).

▷ RELATED ARTICLES: **Beaver Pelts; Fur Trade.**
▷ SUGGESTED READING: Grey Owl, *The Adventures of Sajo and Her Beaver People* (1935).

Beaver Dam The dam (left) keeps the water deep so that it will not freeze around the underwater entrance to the lodge (right). Each colony consists of an adult pair, yearlings, and the newborn kits (artwork by Jan Sovak).

■ Beaver Club

The Beaver Club was a Montreal social club founded in 1785. Members were fur traders and merchants of the North West Company who had spent at least one winter in the western fur country. The club, which was famous for its wild, all-night parties in downtown hotels, stopped meeting in the 1820s.

■ Beaver Dams, Battle of

The Battle of Beaver Dams occurred on June 24, 1813. About 500 American troops planned to attack the British forces, which included 50 British soldiers and about 400 Iroquois warriors. The plan was overheard by Laura Secord, who walked bravely through the American lines to warn the British commander, Lt FitzGibbon.

The British and Iroquois ambushed the Americans at Beaver Dams, near present-day Thorold, Ont. The Americans lost 80 men and surrendered.

▷ RELATED ARTICLE: **War of 1812.**

■ Beaver Pelts

Beaver pelts were the most valuable item in the fur trade in early Canada. Beaver fur is rich and thick because the beaver spends much of its time in the water. The pelt consists of two layers of hair: an outer layer of coarse guard hair, and an undercoat of soft, velvety fur, called the *duvet*. When the guard hairs were still in place, the pelts had to be combed in Europe to remove the duvet, which was used to make felt hats. This type of pelt was called *castor* (meaning "beaver") *sec* (meaning "dry"). A second, more valuable pelt was called "coat beaver," because it had been worn by a native person. As a result, many of the long guard hairs had fallen out, and the duvet was easily removed. This type of pelt was called *castor gras*, referring to the body oils that were absorbed during wearing. After the duvet was removed, the skin could be used as leather.

▷ RELATED ARTICLE: **Fur Trade**.

■ Bécancour

Bécancour, Que., lies on the south shore of the St Lawrence River across from Trois-Rivières at the mouth of the Bécancour River. The town was created in 1965 with the merging of 11 municipalities, which explains its large size (484 km²).

The site originally was in the territory of the Abenaki. Settlement began in 1672 and the community grew as a farming and sawmilling centre. Since the 1960s the economy has relied more on manufacturing, although agriculture is still important. Today, Bécancour has year-round port facilities. In 1986 the population was 10 472. For information, contact the Greffier, 1295, rue Nicolas Perrot, Bécancour, Que., G0X 1B0.

■ Beck, Sir Adam

Businessman and politician (*born in 1857 at Baden, Canada West [Ontario]; died in 1925 at London, Ont.*). Beck was the principal founder of Ontario Hydro, which he built into the world's largest publicly owned power authority. He was a domineering person who tolerated no opposition. The son of German immigrants, he started his career running his family's cigar-box factory in London, Ont. He was mayor of London from 1902 to 1904. In 1902 he was also elected, as a Conservative, to the Ontario legislature, and he became a cabinet minister in 1905.

In 1906 Beck introduced into the legislature a bill to create the Hydro-Electric Power Commission of Ontario. "Power for the People" was his slogan. He wanted to produce electric power cheaply from Niagara Falls so that the people of Ontario would be able to use it at little cost. He led the movement to develop electricity from Niagara Falls, and as head of the power commission he oversaw the project's formation and early growth. Because of Hydro, electricity became available in many towns and villages in Ontario.

▷ SUGGESTED READING: James Sturgis, *Adam Beck* (1978).

■ Becker, Abigail

"The Heroine of Long Point" (*born Abigail Jackson in 1830 at Portland Township, Upper Canada [Ontario]; died in 1905 at Walsingham Centre, Ont.*). Abigail Jackson was married young to a widower, Jeremiah Becker, who already had children, and together they lived in a lonely cabin on Long Point, the narrow spit of land that stretches into Lake Erie.

During a raging storm on the lake in 1854, when Jeremiah was away from home, Abigail saved the lives of seven seamen. Their ship, the *Conductor*, had been wrecked on a sandbar, and all night the men had clung to the rigging, not daring to enter the surf. Abigail saw them in the morning when she went down to the lake to get a pail of water. She called to her stepchildren to bring blankets and build a fire on the beach. Then, although she was unable to swim, she waded shoulder-high into the waves and shouted to the seamen that if they swam towards her, she would help them ashore. One by one they did so. Only the cook remained on board, and he was rescued the next day.

Abigail was 24 years old at the time. She had previously saved a boy who had fallen down a well, and later she saved other shipwrecked sailors. Although honoured for her courage and greatly loved by her 17 children and stepchildren, she had a hard life. Jeremiah was frozen to death in a snowstorm, and she was left to support the children on her own, doing much of the farm work as well as the other chores. She later married a second husband and brought up his children too.

■ Beckwith, John

Composer (*born in 1927 at Victoria, B.C.*). Beckwith studied piano with Alberto Guerrero (Toronto) and composition with Nadia Boulanger (Paris). His career has reflected the breadth of his training. He has done important work as a critic, a scholar (especially of North American music), an educator, and director of the Institute of Canadian Music at the University of Toronto.

Beckwith's three operas — *Night Blooming Cereus* (1953-58), *The Shivaree*

John Beckwith is a scholar and music critic as well as a composer (photo by Walter Curtin).

(1965-78), and *Crazy to Kill* (1987-88) — are all located in the Stratford area of rural Ontario. They are collaborations with the Canadian poet-playwright James Reaney. In his most imaginative music, Beckwith incorporates other music or musical styles in the same way that some painters employ collage. His *Upper Canada Hymn Preludes* (1976-77), based on Ontario hymn tunes, are an obvious example. His *String Quartet* (1977) is surprising in its use of fiddle and banjo effects, and his austere *Études* for piano (1983) include quotes from the 19th-century composer Franz Liszt.

■ Bee

Bees are insects that live almost entirely on pollen and nectar from flowers. Many flowers, in turn, rely on bees to spread their pollen. Bees have hairy bodies, which are usually brownish-yellow, like pollen. They have two pairs of wings, and mouthparts adapted for sucking nectar from flowers. They are part of the order Hymenoptera, which also includes ants and wasps. Unlike wasps, bee larvae feed on honey and pollen rather than animal material.

Honeybees In Canada there is only one species of domestic bee, the honeybee (*Apis mellifera*), which produces honey. They were introduced here from Europe.

The elaborate architecture of the honeycomb, the social behaviour of the colony, and the honey and beeswax they produce make bees among the most fascinating and useful insect friends to humans.

Colonies A colony consists of a queen, sterile females who are the queen's workers, and a small number of male drones. The *queen* may live three years and lay 1500 eggs a day (millions in her lifetime). She produces a substance that makes the workers incapable of reproduction. When the queen leaves the hive to find another, the workers begin to rear a new queen. The *workers* (which may number up to 80 000 in a colony) have a variety of tasks to carry out in the hive. They circulate the air; feed the larvae, the queen, and the future queen; construct honeycombs; gather nectar and pollen; and defend the hive. Honeybees can only sting once because when the barbed stinger is stuck in the victim, it cannot be pulled out. The queen has a stinger that has fewer barbs and can sting a number of times. She uses the stinger to kill off the other queens in the hive. The only function of the *drones* is to mate with the queen. They do no work and have no stingers.

Bee Language Bees have a highly developed language. A worker who has found a source of nectar returns to the hive and performs a dance which tells the other workers the direction and distance of the source. They can tell the type of flower by touching antennae.

Native Bees Bumblebees are black and yellow, and larger in size. They live in the abandoned tunnels of small mammals. They too produce honey, but only in small quantities. There are many species of bees (some 1000) that are native to Canada. Most are solitary and live in tunnels in the soil.

▷ RELATED ARTICLE: **Beekeeping.**

▷ SUGGESTED READING: Elin Kelsey, *Bees* (1985).

■ Beech

Beech trees (*Fagus*), like oaks (*Quercus*) and chestnuts (*Castanea*), belong to the beech family (Fagaceae). In Canada the American beech (*F. grandifolia*) is found only from the Great Lakes eastward. Its long, straight and pointed buds help to identify it in winter. Its bluish-grey bark remains smooth even on very old trees, and is therefore a favourite place for lovers to carve a heart with their initials inside — a bad idea, however, since a tree that has been wounded in this way becomes more vulnerable to insect and fun-

Bumblebee (artwork by Jan Sovak).

American Beech trees are found from the Great Lakes eastward (artwork by Claire Tremblay).

Beekeeping When the beekeeper provides a wooden frame, the bees will use it to store honey. The inset shows the honeybee, which produces the honey (artwork by Claire Tremblay).

gus attacks. The leaves have straight veins which form saw-tooth edges. On young trees, the yellowed leaves often remain on the tree all winter long. The American beech often grows along with sugar maples (*Acer saccharum*). Unfortunately, its leaves, which take a long time to decompose, build up a thick and acidic litter that discourages the growth of maple or other seeds.

Beech wood is hard, and difficult to bend. It is used to make tool handles, furniture, and floors. Its oil-rich seeds are edible. These seeds are also an important food source for several varieties of birds, squirrels, and chipmunks. Even the black bear will climb a beech tree to gather its seeds.

■ Beekeeping

Beekeeping is the art of keeping bees for honey or wax. The honey that is harvested by beekeepers is made from *nectar*, a sweet sugar syrup produced by flowers. Bees help reduce the moisture content of nectar by fanning their wings and add two enzymes which they produce in their bodies.

Beekeeping has been practised for at least 4000 years, using clay pots and other containers as hives.

It was discovered in the 1850s that bees would build a comb in a wooden frame containing a piece of wax. Bees use this wax, or base, to build honeycombs, in which they store honey. When bees are given this frame, they will build the comb where the beekeeper wants it. Each of the frames is removable.

Another discovery, made in 1865, was that honey can be removed from the comb by spinning it in an extractor. If the beekeeper returns the comb to a hive, the bees will fill it again.

Ancient beekeepers knew that smoke calms the bees and modern beekeepers rediscovered this fact to help to remove the frames. As a result of these developments, honey became abundant.

There are about 19 000 beekeepers in Canada and more than 700 000 honeybee colonies.

The colour and flavour of honey depends on the blossoms from which the bees collected nectar. Honey from clover and alfalfa is white, from sunflowers golden, and from buckwheat dark. Most honeys are blends, since the bees visit many different plants.

More and more Canadians are taking up beekeeping as a hobby.

▷ RELATED ARTICLE: **Bee.**

■ Beer, *see* Alcoholic Drinks

■ Beers, William George

Lacrosse player and dentist (*born in 1843 at Montreal, Canada East [Quebec]; died there in 1900*). William Beers wrote the book of standard rules for lacrosse and promoted the game with such enthusiasm that it became a popular sport across Canada. In 1867 he organized a convention in Kingston at which the National Lacrosse Association was formed, with himself as its secretary. Eager to make the

William Beers promoted lacrosse by claiming that it "knocks timidity and nervousness out of a young man" (courtesy Canada's Sports Hall of Fame).

game popular abroad too, he took lacrosse teams to England in 1876 and 1883.

Beers was also a prominent dentist. One of the first Canadians to specialize in the subject, he founded and edited Canada's first dental journal.

▷ RELATED ARTICLE: **Lacrosse.**

■ Beetle

Beetles are insects of the order Coleoptera. Their main characteristics are biting mouth parts and front wings which develop into a hard, protective shell. The rear wings, which alone are used for flying, are folded under the front wings when the insect is at rest. In Canada, 6748 species of beetles are known. They live in almost every kind of habitat, from simple water holes to high mountain streams, from arid deserts to the wettest of forests. They eat practically anything, animal or vegetable: leaves, roots, wood, flowers, honey, hair, feathers, dung, and dead bodies or living prey. Some species are parasites. Their size varies from less than a millimetre to about 75 mm in Canada, and up to 155 mm in the tropics.

In Canada, beetles are usually brown or black, sometimes with vivid touches of colour or a metallic sheen. Like many insects, they undergo a complete *metamorphosis* (passing from egg, to larva, nymph, and adult). The larvae, with soft bodies and differing forms, do not at all resemble the adults they will become. They are whitish in colour, and, in some cases, have three little pairs of legs. They are always found close to their food source. Some species, which live off harvests and stored foods, are serious pests for humans. Like butterflies, beetles are a favourite group of insects for collectors.

■ Begbie, Sir Matthew Baillie

British Columbia judge (*born in 1819 on a British ship off the Cape of Good Hope; died in 1894 at Victoria, B.C.*). Begbie was sent from England in 1858 to be the first judge of British Columbia. The colony had just been formed and thousands of fortune hunters were streaming north from California during the Fraser River gold rush. Begbie quickly made the gold miners realize that they were now on British soil and were subject to British law. His firm action, and the leadership of Governor James Douglas, ensured that the colony remained British and became part of Canada.

Begbie toured the mining camps regularly, setting up court, complete with judge's wig and robes. He was known as "the hanging judge," because of his reputation for sentencing criminals to death by hanging. He once angrily told a jury that he would like to see them all hanged for letting a gunman off too lightly. Despite such ferocious statements, Begbie was no more severe than other judges and he was widely respected. In fact, Begbie was one of the few British Columbians of his day who defended the rights of the Chinese and native people. He remained a judge for 36 years, and was the province of British Columbia's first chief justice after it joined Canada in 1871.

Dung Beetle hauling a load of dung. In all beetles the front wings develop into a hard shell (photo by Brian Milne/ First Light).

Tiger Beetle (artwork by Jan Sovak).

Matthew Begbie was British Columbia's first judge (courtesy PABC/HP-24288)

▷ SUGGESTED READING: Ann Fitzgeorge-Parker, *Gold-rush Justice* (1968); David R. Williams, *Matthew Baillie Begbie* (1980).

■ Bégin, Monique

Politician (*born in 1936 at Rome, Italy*). Monique Bégin was educated in Montreal and Paris, and had a career as a sociologist and administrator before running for office. From 1967 to 1970 she was executive secretary of the Royal Commission on the Status of Women. She was elected to the House of Commons as a Liberal in 1972 and re-elected in 1974, 1979, and 1980 by large majorities. She served as minister of national revenue (1976) and minister of health and welfare (1977-79 and 1980-84). She left political life in 1984, and was appointed to the joint chair in women's studies at Carleton University and the University of Ottawa.

■ Beissel, Henry

Writer and professor (*born in 1929 at Cologne, Germany*). Arriving in Canada from his native Germany in 1951, he attended the University of Toronto, then became a professor of English. His first poetry collection was published in 1963 and was followed by three more books of verse. As well as translating the work of several authors into English, he has written plays and poetry for children.

■ Belaney, Archibald Stansfeld, *see* Grey Owl

■ Belcher Islands

Belcher Islands, N.W.T., 13 000 km², are a group of low-lying islands in southeastern Hudson Bay. The first European explorer to see them was Henry Hudson in 1610. The name probably comes from James

Belcher, a Hudson's Bay Company employee. Today the only settlement is Sanikiluaq — the most southern settlement in the N.W.T. Residents make their living by fishing, trapping, and soapstone carving.

■ Beliveau, Jean

Hockey player (*born in 1931 at Trois-Rivières, Que.*). Beliveau learned to skate in his backyard in Victoriaville, where he grew up. He played junior and senior hockey in Quebec City, where he was idolized by the fans. In 1953 he joined the Montreal Canadiens, where he played for 18 seasons. Although a large man, he played hockey with finesse and a gentlemanly demeanor. He won the NHL scoring championship and the Hart Trophy (most valuable player) in 1956. He scored 507 goals in the regular season and his record of 176 points in playoff games stood until it was broken by Wayne Gretzky in 1987. He became vice-president of the Canadiens in 1971.

■ Bell, Alexander Graham

Inventor (*born in 1847 at Edinburgh, Scotland; died in 1922 at Baddeck, N.S.*). Bell is best known as the inventor of the telephone. He also did major work in two other fields: with the deaf and with some of the world's earliest airplanes.

His father was Professor Alexander Melville Bell, who settled with his family in Brantford, Ont., in 1870. Professor Bell invented "visible speech," a way of teaching the deaf to speak. The younger Bell taught his father's speech methods at Boston University. It was this work with the human voice that gave him the idea of trying to transmit speech electrically.

Invention of the Telephone Bell worked out his ideas for the telephone when he was home on a holiday in Brantford in 1874. On his return to Boston, he recruited Thomas A. Watson to help with his experiments. Together, in Boston, they first transmitted "voice sounds" in 1875, but they could not hear distinct words. On March 10, 1876, the two men tried a new model. Watson waited in Bell's bedroom, with the receiver pressed against his ear. In the laboratory, Bell leaned over the mouthpiece and shouted, "Mr Watson — Come here — I want to see you." They were the first words ever heard on a telephone (Watson's version of these famous words was, "Mr Watson I want you.")

Bell and Watson gradually perfected their invention. In June 1876 they exhib-

Alexander Graham Bell and others at his home in Brantford, Ont., 1906 (by permission of the British Library).

ited the telephone at the Centennial Exposition in Philadelphia. In Brantford that summer they carried out further experiments, stringing up telephone wires on the Bell homestead. In August they made the world's first long-distance call — between Brantford and Paris, Ont.

Like many great inventions, statements about the origins of the telephone are sometimes controversial. In Bell's own words, "the telephone was invented in Canada, but it was made in the United States."

Flying Machines Bell moved to the United States and became an American citizen, but he also bought land at Baddeck, N.S. There, in 1907, he formed the Aerial Experiment Association, a small group of enthusiasts who were dedicated to building flying machines. Among its members were Casey Baldwin, J.A.D. McCurdy, and the American engine builder, Glenn Curtiss.

In December 1907, Bell and his team launched the *Cygnet*, a man-lifting kite. During the next two years they worked in New York State as well as at Baddeck. They successfully designed, built, and tested some of the world's earliest gasoline-powered aircraft. One of these was the *Silver Dart*, which in 1909 became the first airplane to fly in Canada.

Other Work Bell had a far-reaching genius for invention. He developed a way of making phonograph records on wax discs. He worked on the invention of a type of iron lung. He experimented with making fresh water for shipwrecked sailors. He even tried to raise a special breed of supersheep at Baddeck. Meanwhile, throughout his life he continued to work for the deaf.

Bell spent most of his final years on his estate at Baddeck. It is now a national historic site and is the home of the Alexander Graham Bell Museum. The Bell Homestead at Brantford is also a museum with exhibits of his inventions.

▷ Related Articles: **Aviation; Silver Dart; Telephone.**

▷ Suggested Reading: Dorothy Eber, *Genius at Work* (1982); A. Roy Petrie, *Alexander Graham Bell* (1975); Robert M. Quackenbush, *Ahoy! Ahoy! Are You There?* (1981); Florida Town, *Alexander Graham Bell* (1988).

■ Bell, Marilyn

Long-distance swimmer (*born in 1937 at Toronto, Ont.*). Bell was the first person to swim across Lake Ontario. She stepped into the water at Youngstown, New York, just before midnight on September 8,

1954. The following evening she struggled ashore at the CNE grounds in Toronto, having been in the water for nearly 21 hours.

The swim was a competitive event, and an American athlete, Florence Chadwick, had been expected to win. Few people took much notice of Marilyn at first. After Chadwick and another contestant dropped out in exhaustion, news quickly spread about the 16-year-old Canadian schoolgirl who was still swimming. Throughout September 9, the radio broadcast news of Marilyn's progress. An excited crowd of over 100 000 people greeted her arrival in Toronto.

The following year Marilyn made history again when she swam the English Channel. At the time she was the youngest person to have completed this crossing. In 1956 she tried an even more challenging swim — Juan de Fuca Strait in southern B.C. She had to give up after about eight hours, but she was successful two weeks later. Still only 18, she retired from long-distance swimming. Her awards include the Lou Marsh Trophy, 1954, as outstanding Canadian athlete of the year.

Such marathon swims inspire less interest today. Vicki Keith, for example, swam across all five Great Lakes in 1988 but received very little attention from the media.

▷ Suggested Reading: Ron McAllister, *Swim to Glory* (1954).

Alexander Graham Bell, inventor of the telephone (artwork by Irma Coucill).

Marilyn Bell was a 16-year-old student when she swam across Lake Ontario (courtesy Canada's Sports Hall of Fame).

Bell, Robert

Geologist and explorer (*born in 1841 at Toronto, Ont.; died in 1917 at Rathwell, Man.*). As a member of the Geological Survey of Canada, Robert Bell spent 34 years exploring the Canadian north and west. He joined the Geological Survey in 1869 and was sent northwest to map the rivers draining into Hudson Bay. In 1884 and 1885 he was medical and science officer on two expeditions to explore Hudson Strait. In 1897 he explored Baffin Island and in 1899 Great Slave Lake.

Bell felt that far more use could be made of Hudson Bay, which he saw as a natural entranceway to Canada from Europe. He called the bay "the Mediterranean of North America." He was made chief geologist of the Geological Survey in 1906 and retired in 1908.

▷ SUGGESTED READING: Robert G. Blackadar, *The Geological Survey of Canada* (1986).

Bell Island

Bell Island, Nfld, 34 km² in area, was the site of an iron-ore mine which extended beneath the waters of Conception Bay. The mine opened in 1894 and closed in 1966. For a time the mine was the largest iron-ore producer in Canada and the largest underwater iron-mining operation in the world. The island suffered economic problems when the mine closed. Today, many residents work in nearby St John's.

Bella Coola

Bella Coola is a village at the head of a long channel on the British Columbia coast, about 600 km north of Vancouver. It was here that the explorer Alexander Mackenzie emerged on his overland voyage to the Pacific in 1793. The community relies for jobs on mixed farming, logging, and fishing. In 1986 the population was 240. For information, contact the Secretary-Treasurer, P.O. Box 10, Hagensborg, B.C., V0T 1H0.

Range of Beluga Whale

Belleville

Belleville, Ont., overlooks the Bay of Quinte, an arm of Lake Ontario about 180 km east of Toronto. A mission to the native people was established here about 1666. The mission was abandoned and it was not until 1789, when the Loyalists arrived, that Belleville had its real beginning. The settlement was known as Meyers Creek, after Captain John Meyers, who built a gristmill beside the Moira River in 1790. In 1816 the name was changed to Belleville, after Arabella Gore, the wife of Lieutenant-Governor Francis Gore. Logging and sawmilling were important until the 1870s. The city has always been a transportation centre and was also known as a cheesemaking centre. Today, the economy relies on a mix of light manufacturing. In 1986 the population was 36 041. For information, contact the City Clerk, City Hall, 169 Front Street, Belleville, Ont., K8N 2Y8.

Bellingham, Brenda

Writer (*born in 1931 at Liverpool, England*). She came to Canada in 1958, working as a social worker and a teacher before becoming a writer. Although different in plot, her novels share a theme. Young girls in single-parent families overcome problems and discover their identities. Each novel ends happily, with the heroine having a secure place in a two-parent family. In *Joanie's Magic Boots* (1979), Joanie, once caught shoplifting, proves to her policeman stepfather that she is not a thief. Two sisters in the comic *Two Parents Too Many* (1985) try to stop their divorced mother's marriage. They learn that, even though both parents remarry, both still love them. *Storm Child* (1985) is a well-researched historical novel. After her Scots father abandons her native mother, Isobel Macpherson rejects white society for life with her Peigan grandparents. Eventually she accepts a white stepfather, but proud of her Metis identity, she determines to help her people.

Beluga Whale

A member of the suborder Odontoceti (toothed whales), the beluga whale (*Delphinapterus leucas*) can reach 6 m in length and 1400 kg in weight. It is a white-coloured whale with no dorsal fin. The forehead is the shape of a melon. The beluga can change the size of its forehead and make it collapse (like a bagpipe) to make sounds. Adolescents are grey; newborns are brown or blue-grey. Belugas live in arctic and subarctic waters. In summer, they frequent the mouths of the large rivers and swim upstream. In fall they scatter, migrating to the colder pack-ice areas. However, a small beluga population lives year-round in the estuary of the St Lawrence River. The beluga lives on fish, shrimp, seaworms, and squid. Its main enemies are humans, the killer whale, and the polar bear. Belugas mate in May, with gestation lasting about 14 months. Every two or three years, near the end of June, the female gives birth to a single baby, which she nurses for about two years. The males are mature at eight or nine; the females at four to seven years. Belugas have been nicknamed the "sea canary" because they make a sound similar to that of a bird. The numbers of belugas have greatly diminished as a result of hunting, but more importantly because of the destruction and pollution of its waters through dams, tankers, and poisonous chemicals.

■ Bengough, John Wilson

Cartoonist (*born in 1851 at Toronto, Canada West [Ontario]; died in 1923 at Toronto, Ont.*). Bengough is best remembered as the brilliant cartoonist of the era of John A. Macdonald. He came to prominence through his satirical magazine *Grip*, which he launched when he was 22. This was in 1873, the year John A. Macdonald had to resign because of the Pacific Scandal. Bengough took full advantage of the scandal in *Grip*, with his unflattering caricatures of a scrawny and bulbous-nosed Macdonald.

Bengough remained editor and cartoonist of *Grip* until 1892. He was later a cartoonist for the *Montreal Star* and Toronto's *Globe*. He was also a poet and a popular lecturer.

▷ RELATED ARTICLE: **Pacific Scandal.**

■ Bennett, Richard Bedford

Bennett was very successful in his personal business affairs, but he found Canada's affairs far harder to handle. His efforts to solve the many problems of the

Richard Bedford Bennett
11TH PRIME MINISTER OF CANADA

Born: July 3, 1870, Hopewell Hill, N.B.
Died: June 26, 1947, Mickleham, England
Political Party: Conservative
First Elected: 1898
Chosen Leader: 1927
Period as Prime Minister: August 7, 1930, to October 23, 1935
(PHOTO COURTESY JOHN EVANS).

Cartoonist J.W. Bengough put words into the mouth of John A. Macdonald at the time of the Pacific Scandal (courtesy NAC/C-78604).

"WE IN CANADA SEEM TO HAVE LOST ALL IDEA OF JUSTICE, HONOR AND INTEGRITY."—THE MAIL, 26TH SEPTEMBER.

Great Depression had little effect. Nevertheless, his government gave Canada two important institutions: the Canadian Broadcasting Corporation (CBC), whose forerunner he formed in 1932, and the Bank of Canada, created in 1935. Both have had long-lasting effects on the way Canada has grown.

Early Life Raised in New Brunswick, Bennett earned a law degree at Dalhousie and then became a lawyer at Chatham, N.B. There he began his friendship with Max Aitken, the future Lord Beaverbrook. Aitken showed a talent for making money, and he shared his ideas with Bennett, helping to make him a millionaire.

Bennett had great ambitions, and he showed such promise as a lawyer that he was invited to be a partner in the Calgary law firm of Senator James Lougheed. Bennett moved to Calgary in 1897 and quickly built Lougheed and Bennett into one of the most important law firms in the West. At the same time, his business interests, guided by his friend Max Aitken, made him very wealthy.

Meanwhile, he was also making his mark in politics. Soon after arriving in

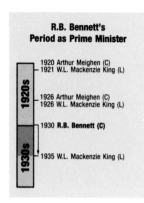

**R.B. Bennett's
Period as Prime Minister**

1920s

1920 Arthur Meighen (C)
1921 W.L. Mackenzie King (L)

1926 Arthur Meighen (C)
1926 W.L. Mackenzie King (L)

1930 R.B. Bennett (C)

1930s

1935 W.L. Mackenzie King (L)

Calgary he was elected to the legislature of the North-West Territories (1898-1905), and after Alberta was created from part of the territories he sat for two years in the Alberta legislature (1909-11). In 1911 he moved to federal politics, becoming a Member of Parliament (MP) for Calgary in the House of Commons in Ottawa. Bennett made a strong impression in Ottawa and in 1927 was chosen leader of the Conservative Party.

Prime Minister In 1930, early in the Great Depression, R.B. Bennett persuaded the Canadian people that he would make things better, and they voted the Conservatives into power in the 1930 election.

As prime minister, Bennett soon found the poverty and unemployment caused by the Depression as hard to deal with as other leaders around the world. He tried various measures, including relief camps where out-of-work men lived in bunkhouses and were paid 20 cents a day in return for a 44-hour week of hard labour. The camps were very unpopular. So, increasingly, was Bennett.

Canadians had hoped for so much from Bennett because of his wealth and success. When he failed to help them, the disappointed people came to view the prime minister as out of touch with their problems. A portly bachelor who lived in style at the Château Laurier Hotel — how could he possibly understand their worries, their hunger, their misery?

In early 1935, realizing he was heading for defeat in the upcoming election, Bennett announced a program which he called the "New Deal." It included promises for a shorter work week, a minimum wage, unemployment and health insurance, and a revised old-age pension. Nevertheless, he lost the election. Canadians had come to see Bennett himself as responsible for their problems.

Later Life Bennett remained leader of the Conservative Party until he retired from Canadian politics in 1938 and moved to England. For most of his adult life he had lived in hotels, but now he bought an estate, next door to Lord Beaverbrook. In 1942 he was himself made a lord: Viscount Bennett of Mickleham, Hopewell and Calgary.

▷ RELATED ARTICLE: **Great Depression.**

▷ SUGGESTED READING: Robert Saunders, *R.B. Bennett* (1979); Donald Swainson, "A Lost Leader: R.B. Bennett," *Horizon Canada*, Number 100 (1987).

■ **Bennett, William Andrew Cecil**
Merchant, politician, premier of B.C.

(born in 1900 at Hastings, N.B.; died in 1979 at Kelowna, B.C.). As premier of British Columbia from 1952 to 1972, W.A.C. Bennett changed the face of B.C. politics. He had wandered west in the 1920s and in 1930 bought a hardware store in Kelowna. He became a notable local figure and in 1941 was elected to the provincial legislature as a Conservative. Discontented with being passed over when cabinets were formed and with failing twice to win party leadership, he became an independent in 1951. In 1952 he was named leader of the tiny Social Credit Party, which had won only 1.5% of the votes in the 1949 election.

British Columbians were discontented with old-line Liberals and Conservatives, and in the 1952 election Social Credit and the Co-operative Commonwealth Federation (CCF) shared 64% of the vote. Bennett had enough seats to form a minority government, and when he called another election in 1953 he won by a landslide. Bennett's aggressive self-confidence suited the expanding economy of British Columbia. He ran a government dedicated to free enterprise. Yet two of his measures, taking over BC Electric (which became BC Hydro) and establishing a publicly owned ferry fleet to Vancouver Island, were pure socialism. He also modernized the road system, extended the publicly owned Pacific Great Eastern Railway to the Yukon border, and created major hydroelectric projects on the Columbia and

W.A.C. Bennett took over the tiny Social Credit Party in 1952, took it to power within the year, and remained premier of B.C. for 20 years (courtesy Canapress Photo Service).

Peace rivers. He expanded universities, created an effective provincial health system, eased the municipal tax burden for the poor and the old, and fought the federal government over many issues, using talk of separation as a bargaining point. In the 1972 election Social Credit was finally defeated by the New Democratic Party (NDP). Bennett was unhappy as leader of the opposition after so many years in power. He retired in 1973.

▷ SUGGESTED READING: Rosemary Neering, *W.A.C. Bennett* (1981).

■ Bennett, William Richards

Premier of British Columbia (*born in 1932 at Kelowna, B.C.*). Bill Bennett is the son of W.A.C. Bennett and was Social Credit premier of British Columbia from 1975 to 1986. He was educated in Kelowna, and became a businessman and real-estate investor there. In 1973 he was elected to his father's seat of Okanagan South, and was also elected leader of the Social Credit Party. He worked to rebuild the party, and in 1975 defeated the New Democratic Party (NDP) government, becoming premier. He was elected to a second term in 1983.

In his second term, Bennett attempted to control rising government costs by a program of restraint. This involved cuts in social services and education, and lay-offs in the civil service. This plan was strongly opposed by the "Solidarity" coalition of labour and other groups, but with limited success. Bennett's government also began several controversial "megaprojects," such as the Coquihalla Highway and coal mining in the province's northeast. In 1986 Bennett resigned from political life to pursue private business interests.

▷ SUGGESTED READING: Allen Garr, *Tough Guy* (1985).

■ Beothuk

Beothuk were the native people who once lived in Newfoundland. They have been extinct since the early 19th century. Word lists compiled from the last few survivors indicate that they spoke an Algonquian language. Their culture was similar to that of other Subarctic groups on the mainland of Canada.

The Beothuk lived in small bands led by chiefs who were skilled hunters. In the warmer months they lived around the coast. They hunted whales, seals, and water birds; they fished, and they collected berries, eggs, and shellfish. In the fall they joined in larger groups and moved inland to hunt caribou. Their bows and arrows, harpoons, spears, traps, and clubs were all made from wood, stone, bone, sinew, and other natural products. Their wigwams were particularly sturdy in winter, with upstanding tree trunks at the base and three layers of birchbark forming a cone above. For transportation, they used birchbark canoes in summer and snowshoes in winter. Their clothing was simple, made from two caribou hides sewn together and tied at the waist. In cold

Bill Bennett *served two terms as premier of B.C. (courtesy Canapress Photo Service).*

Shawnadithit

When Shawnadithit was captured in 1823, she was about 22 years old and starving. The authorities hoped to use her to make contact with her people, but when she returned to the forest with presents, no other Beothuk could be found. She lived with a family, who called her Nancy, and helped around the house with the children. Fortunately, William Cormack, an explorer who had tried to find the Beothuk, took an interest in her and encouraged her to make lists of words in her language and to draw pictures and tell stories of Beothuk life. In 1829 she died from tuberculosis in St John's.

Shawnadithit, *who died in 1829, was likely the last survivor of the Beothuk (NAC/C-38862).*

weather they added sleeves, leggings, moccasins, and mitts. The many carved bones and ivory pieces found buried in their graves suggest that the Beothuk believed in a spirit world.

By the early 17th century, when European settlers arrived, there were probably around 1000 Beothuk. The Beothuk and the Europeans never established a trading relationship.

Gradually the Beothuk were driven inland where, cut off from their main food supplies, they often starved. Many were killed in skirmishes with the settlers. Others died from European diseases to which they had no immunity. In the 18th century, the Micmac, a native group from the mainland, began to move into Newfoundland. Because they had guns and the Beothuk did not, they were usually victorious in battles against the Beothuk. By the late 18th century, there were hardly any left. Shawnadithit, the last of the Beothuk, died in 1829.

The Beothuk covered their bodies and their belongings with red ochre. For this reason, early Europeans called them "Red Indians." This term was later applied to all the native people in North America.

▷ RELATED ARTICLES: **Native People: Subarctic; Wigwam.**

▷ SUGGESTED READING: Kevin Major, *Blood Red Ochre* (1989); Ingeborg Marshall, *The Beothuk of Newfoundland: A Vanished People* (1989).

■ Berczy, William

Painter, architect (*born Johann Moll in 1744 at Wallerstein, Germany; died in 1813 at New York City, New York, U.S.A.*). In 1794, Berczy brought settlers to Markham, Upper Canada. From 1805 on he relied mainly on painting for his living, although he also designed and decorated churches. He was a very popular portrait painter. His well-known portrait of Joseph Brant shows the Indian leader in colourful costume. His painting *The Woolsey Family* (1808-09) is one of the masterpieces of early Canadian art.

■ Berger, Thomas Rodney

Lawyer, judge (*born in 1933 at Victoria, B.C.*). Berger practised law in Vancouver from 1957 to 1971. As a member of the New Democratic Party, he served as federal MP from 1962 to 1963 and provincial MLA and leader of the party from 1966 to 1969. Berger became known to many Canadians as the head of an inquiry dealing with a proposed pipeline down the Mackenzie Valley in the Northwest Territories. His report recommended that no pipeline should be built across the fragile environment of the northern Yukon. It also recommended a ten-year delay on a pipeline in the Mackenzie Valley to permit time to settle the land claims of native people. Berger later argued strongly that aboriginal rights be included in the Canadian Constitution. Many of his views are described in his book *Fragile Freedoms* (1982).

▷ SUGGESTED READING: Carolyn Swayze, *Hard Choices* (1987).

■ Bering, Vitus Jonassen

Explorer (*born in 1680 at Horsens, Denmark; died in 1741 on Bering Island*). Vitus Bering was an officer in the Russian navy. As a reward for his bravery he was appointed by the Emperor of Russia to explore the coast of Siberia. In 1728 he sailed through Bering Strait, proving for the first time that Asia and America are separate continents.

On a second expedition in 1741, Bering became the first European navigator to see mainland Alaska. Sickness and storms forced him to return and he put in for the winter on Bering Island, where he died of scurvy.

▷ SUGGESTED READING: Raymond H. Fisher, *Bering's Voyages* (1977).

■ Bernardi, Mario

Conductor (*born in 1930 at Kirkland Lake, Ont.*). Bernardi is Canada's foremost Canadian-born conductor. He was sent at age six to Italy and graduated at 15 with highest honours from the Venice Conservatory. He returned to Canada in 1947 and continued his piano and conducting studies in Toronto. His career developed first as a solo pianist. He began conducting at the Royal Conservatory

William Berczy painted the fashionable Woolsey Family in 1809 (courtesy NGC).

Mario Bernardi *is the music director of the Calgary Philharmonic Orchestra (courtesy Gold Photography).*

Opera School, Toronto, in 1953. In 1963, he made his London, England, conducting debut in *Hansel and Gretel*. He was appointed music director of an English opera company in 1966. He returned to Canada in 1968 to form the National Arts Centre Orchestra in Ottawa.

During his 14 years with the NAC Orchestra, Bernardi made it one of the best in the country. It won high praise during its numerous tours in Canada and abroad. Bernardi was responsible also for the music program of Festival Canada/Ottawa, summers at the arts centre, and for the succession of stylish opera productions from 1971 to 1979 which highlighted the festival.

Bernardi announced in 1980 that he would not renew his contract with the NAC Orchestra when his contract expired in 1982. In 1983 he was appointed principal conductor of the CBC Vancouver Orchestra and in 1984 he became the artistic director of the Calgary Philharmonic Orchestra. With both of these orchestras he proved again his remarkable skills as an orchestral trainer and interpretive musician. Under his disciplined and buoyant leadership they moved in the mid-1980s into the top rank of Canada's orchestras.

■ Bernier, Joseph-Elzéar

Arctic sailor (*born in 1852 at L'Islet, Canada East [Quebec]; died in 1934 at Lévis, Que.*). Joseph Bernier went to sea when he was 14 years old, and for 25 years he sailed merchant vessels all over the world. In 1904 Captain Bernier was sent by the government into the arctic islands to collect customs from the whalers and traders who were active there. This was the first of several expeditions to the Arctic which Bernier made on his ship, *Arctic*. In July 1909, he erected a plaque on one of the islands, officially claiming the region for Canada.

Captain Bernier later became a private trader, and during World War I he was in charge of a convoy ship protecting supply vessels from enemy submarines. By the time he retired from the sea in 1925, he had commanded over 100 ships and crossed the Atlantic Ocean 269 times. He was the leading arctic sailor of his day.

J.E. Bernier *commanded over 100 ships in his life and was the leading arctic sailor of his day (NAC/C-6672).*

■ Berries, Wild

In botanical terms, the word "berry" refers to a fleshy fruit containing a number of seeds within its pulp, such as grapes and red currants. More loosely, the word is used to describe any fleshy fruit, edible or not, so as to avoid using such scientific terms as drupe and arillus.

In today's usage, berry means any small fruit, but preferably sweet and edible ones. Small fruit with seeds are among the strategies developed by some plants to improve their own propagation. The fruit attract birds and mammals with their appealing colours and flavours. They play an important role in the diet of animals and birds, since they are found

everywhere, in all sorts of habitats and climates. In many cases, the seeds are indigestible and reappear ready to germinate, surrounded by a bit of fertilizer. Of all these wild berries, humans cultivate several of the species which are tastiest and easiest to domesticate. The most important crops are strawberries, raspberries, blueberries, and cranberries. As long as you can recognize and avoid the poisonous ones, all the berries which grow in the wild enrich our lives.

▷ RELATED ARTICLES: **Bearberries; Blackberry; Blueberry; Cranberries; Gooseberries; Poisonous Plants; Raspberries; Saskatoon Berries; Strawberries.**

■ Berton, Pierre

Writer (*born in 1920 at Whitehorse, Yukon*). Berton has had a long and distinguished career as a journalist and author of history books. Since the 1950s, he has also appeared regularly on television. He has written over 30 books about Canada, three of which won the Governor General's Award for nonfiction: *The Mysterious North* (1956); *Klondike: the Life and Death of the Last Gold Rush* (1958); and *The Last Spike* (1971). These books have been praised for their vivid characterization and their clear and lively presenta-

Wild Berries are very important to wild animals and birds, since they are found in all sorts of habitats and climates. The illustration shows (left, top to bottom) blueberry, strawberry, chokecherry, and saskatoon berry; and (right, top to bottom) gooseberry, raspberry, cranberry, and buffaloberry (artwork by Claire Tremblay).

Pierre Berton's many books on Canada include The National Dream *and* The Last Spike, *the epic tale of the building of the CPR. Berton is also the author of* The Secret World of Og, *a children's book in which the characters discover little green people living under their playhouse (photo by Michael Bedford).*

tion of important historical events. *The Secret World of Og* (1961) is Berton's only book for children. It features his own sons and daughters, who discover little green people living in a huge cavern under their playhouse. During the humorous and exciting adventure, the children learn about courage, unselfishness, and prejudice.

▷ SUGGESTED READING: Pierre Berton, *Starting Out* (1987).

■ Bertrand, Jean-Jacques

Premier of Quebec (*born in 1916 at Ste-Agathe-des-Monts, Que.; died in 1973 at Montreal*). Bertrand was premier of Quebec from 1968 to 1970. He was first elected to Quebec's legislature in 1948 as a member of the Union Nationale Party. He was a leading member of the Cabinet during the 1950s, and ran for the party leadership in 1961, losing to Daniel Johnson. In 1966 the Union Nationale returned to power. Bertrand became minister of education. Two years later, when Johnson died, he became premier.

Bertrand was a strong defender of Quebec rights within Canada, but his party was not popular with voters and it lost the election of 1970. He was leader of the opposition until 1971.

■ Bertrand, Pierre

Singer (*born in 1948 at Montreal, Que.*). Since the early 1970s, Pierre Bertrand's warm tones have been a constant fixture on Quebec radio.

Following four smash albums and world tours as bass guitarist and singer/songwriter of Beau Dommage, Bertrand spent some time away from the spotlight before returning in 1981 with his celebrated solo debut album, simply called *Pierre Bertrand*. In 1983 he released the album *Ciel Variable*, from which he had three chart-topping singles.

More critical acclaim followed with the 1985 release of the soundtrack to the hit film *Le Matou* and the 1987 release of his third solo album *Esperance*, which contains five hit singles.

■ Bessette, Gérard

Writer (*born in 1920 at Ste-Anne-de-Sabrevois, Que.*). Educated in French literature at the University of Montreal, Bessette combined a career as poet, novelist, and literary critic with a distinguished teaching career at several universities. The author of more than a dozen books, he won the Governor General's Award twice (1965, 1971) and in 1980 received Quebec's highest literary prize, the Prix David, for his entire body of work.

■ Best, Charles Herbert

One of the discoverers of insulin (*born in 1899 at West Pembroke, Maine, U.S.; died in 1978 at Toronto, Ont.*). Best was studying physiology and biochemistry at the University of Toronto in 1921 when his professor, J.J.R. Macleod, gave him the job of helping a young researcher, Frederick Banting.

Banting was trying to find a mysterious substance produced in the bodies of healthy people that helps them get energy from food. People whose bodies do not produce this substance suffer from diabetes, a serious disease.

Banting and Best's experiments were promising, and they were joined in their research by Macleod and by the biochemist James Collip. During the winter of 1921-22, this team isolated the substance, which they named insulin. Insulin does not cure diabetes, but it saves the lives of people who otherwise would die from the disease.

Banting and Macleod were awarded the Nobel Prize for Physiology or Medicine in 1923, but Banting split his share of the prize money with Best.

Best became a professor at the University of Toronto and continued to make contributions as a teacher and researcher.

▷ RELATED ARTICLES: **Sir Frederick Grant Banting; Diabetes.**

Charles Best's role in the discovery of insulin was recognized by Frederick Banting, who split his share of the Nobel Prize with him (NAC/PA-112972).

■ Bethune, Henry Norman

Surgeon, political activist (*born in 1890 at Gravenhurst, Ont.; died in 1939 at Huang Shiko, China*). Bethune studied medicine at Toronto and served as a stretcher bearer in World War I. He was wounded in the leg and sent home.

After the war, Bethune practised as a doctor in Detroit, where in 1926 he fell ill with tuberculosis, which was generally fatal in those days. He volunteered for an experimental treatment which involved collapsing the diseased lung. It cured him, and in 1928 he moved to Montreal, deter-

Norman Bethune's tireless work on behalf of the Chinese made him a national hero in China (NAC/PA-114788).

mined to help other victims of the disease. In Montreal, Bethune became a well-known surgeon at the Royal Victoria Hospital. Between 1929 and 1936, he invented or redesigned a number of surgical instruments. He became critical of the medical profession and wrote articles suggesting reform.

After a visit to the Soviet Union in 1935, he joined the Communist Party. In 1936 he went to Spain to support the communists. There he organized a mobile blood-transfusion service, which was the first of its kind. In 1938 his beliefs led him to China, where he worked tirelessly as a surgeon and teacher for the Chinese, who were trying to fight off the Japanese invasion. He accidentally cut himself during an operation and died of blood poisoning. The Chinese leader Mao Zedong wrote an essay, "In Memory of Norman Bethune," which urged his people to follow Bethune's example of devotion to others. Bethune is a national hero in China and is being increasingly recognized in Canada.
▷ SUGGESTED READING: Roderick Stewart, *Norman Bethune* (1974).

■ Betula Lake
Betula Lake is a vacation resort area in Whiteshell Provincial Park, 145 km northeast of Winnipeg, Man. It is the site of a group of famous rock outlines (called *petroforms*) made by prehistoric people about 2000 years ago. The rocks are laid out on open ground in the shape of ani-mals, ellipses, and other geometric patterns, and probably had some religious meaning. The largest outline is a long, undulating line which probably represents a snake.

■ Beurling, George Frederick (Buzz)
World War II fighter pilot (*born in 1921 at Verdun, Que.; died in 1948 at Rome, Italy*). Known as "The Falcon of Malta" because of his air victories there, Buzz Beurling had a passion for planes from early childhood. As a boy, he spent so much time hanging around Montreal's Cartierville airport that a former bush pilot taught him to fly. His school work suffered and when he applied for the Royal Canadian Air Force (RCAF) at the beginning of World War II, he was turned down.

In 1940 Beurling joined the crew of a cargo ship and worked his way to Britain so that he could join the Royal Air Force, which was in great need of pilots. He proved to be a brilliant fighter pilot and played a major role in the defence of Malta in 1942. During the massed German and Italian attack on the island, he shot down 26 planes. His total by the end of the war was 31, making him one of the ten top Allied fighter pilots of the war.

Hailed in Canada as a hero, Beurling transferred to the RCAF in 1943. But he had never been an easy character — he was too independent-minded — and he was released from the RCAF in 1944. Four years later, Beurling joined the Israeli air force. He died on his way to Israel when his plane caught fire and crashed.
▷ SUGGESTED READING: Hugh Halliday, *The Tumbling Sky* (1978).

"Buzz" Beurling shot down 31 enemy planes during World War II (courtesy Canadian War Museum).

■ Bianchi, John
Writer, illustrator (*born in 1947 at Rochester, New York, U.S.*). Bianchi served with the United States Navy in

The Four Cowboys *above the banner* "Last of the Tree Ranchers" *on John Bianchi's cartoon-like cover for* The Bungalo Boys *helps the reader to predict that the story which follows will be unusual and humorous (courtesy John Bianchi/Bungalo Books).*

Vietnam before moving to Canada in 1969. He sold drawings on the street, worked for a film animator, and illustrated magazine articles. The first picture book he illustrated was Helen Levchuk's *The Dingles* (1985). The first book he wrote and illustrated himself, *The Bungalo Boys* (1986), is a humorous western adventure and is filled with funny, cartoon-like drawings. *Princess Frownsalot* (1987) and *The Swine Snafu* (1988) are also silly stories. Bianchi combined his interest in science and nature with his artistic skills to provide colour illustrations for Terence Dickinson's *Exploring the Night Sky: The Equinox Astronomy Guide for Beginners* (1987).

Biculturalism

Biculturalism means "having two cultures." In Canada, this refers to French and English, the two European cultures from which the majority of Canadians trace their roots.

The term "biculturalism" became common in the 1960s, when Prime Minister Lester Pearson launched the Royal Commission on Bilingualism and Biculturalism to try and improve relations between French and English Canadians. Bilingualism means "having two languages." The commission studied to what extent the French and English languages were used across Canada. One of the results of the commission was the Official Languages Act of 1969, which made both French and English official languages to be used in the federal government and federal law courts.

The description of Canada as having two cultures has been challenged by those who point out that the Canadian people trace their roots to many nations, not just two. Nevertheless, the people who are not of French or English origin tend to associate with one or the other. Canada remains a nation with two principal cultures — one associated with the English language, and one associated with French. The relations between the two continue to be a major political challenge for Canada.

▷ RELATED ARTICLES: **Bilingualism; French-English Relations; Multiculturalism.**

Bicycling

The bicycle began with a two-wheel contraption called the "boneshaker," so named for the ride it gave over rough ground. The fad was short-lived until the appearance of the "high wheel," named for its huge front wheel. Though it was expensive and hard to ride, the high wheel became popular, especially among well-to-do young men.

The bicycle as we know it arrived in the 1890s. It had two wheels of the same size, gears and a chain, and soft tires. It was the rage with both men and women. It was a means of getting around as well as a source of fun.

By 1898 there were more than 25 companies making bicycles in Canada. The following year the huge company Canada Cycle and Motor Company (CCM) was formed. It made about 40 000 bikes a year. The bicycle was used everywhere, even in the Yukon during the gold rush of the late 1890s. By 1900, the 400 km trail from Dawson to Whitehorse was the busiest "bicycle path" in the world.

Bicycle racing began in the 1880s and 1890s on outdoor tracks. The sport attracted large crowds across Canada. Many cities had road races and the world championship was held in Montreal in 1899. The most famous Canadian racer of his

Jocelyn Lovell
Jocelyn Lovell (*born in 1950 at Norwich, England*) of Toronto was almost unbeatable in bicycle racing in the 1970s. He won gold medals in the Commonwealth Games and Pan-American Games. His career ended tragically in 1983, when he was hit by a truck near Toronto. He was paralysed from the neck down (*photo by Ron Watts/First Light*).

day was William "Torchy" Peden, who won 38 races.

Bicycling suffered a setback when the automobile became popular in the 1920s. Bicycling became an activity for children. Only in the 1960s did the bicycle become popular again. The renewed interest was sparked by the concern for fitness and for the environment. By the 1970s, at least one in four households had a bicycle. Racing also revived. In Canada, the success of racer Jocelyn Lovell inspired other Canadians such as Sylvia Burka, Gord Singleton, and Steve Bauer, who have all done well in international events. Bauer has worn the "yellow jersey" in the world's most famous race, the Tour de France. The jersey is worn by the leader of the race on each of its sections.

▷ SUGGESTED READING: Mary F. Coady, *Champion on Wheels* (1987).

■ Biencourt de Poutrincourt, Jean de

Fur-trader, colonizer (*born in 1557 in France; died in 1615 at Méry-sur-Seine, France*). Jean de Biencourt de Poutrincourt and his son **Charles de Biencourt de Saint-Just** (*born in 1591 or 1592 at Champagne, France; died in 1623 or 1624 at Port-Royal*) were early colonizers of Acadia. Jean was in the original party led by de Monts in 1604. After returning to France, he went back to Acadia with his son Charles in 1606 to serve as governor on behalf of de Monts. He led a further expedition to Acadia in 1610, leaving Charles in charge when he returned to France the following year.

Charles was still in Acadia in 1613 when the British attacked and destroyed Port-Royal. He took refuge among the native people. Over the following years, he returned to the settlement. He built up a profitable fishing and fur-trading business, and he succeeded his father as commander of the colony in 1614.

▷ RELATED ARTICLE: **Acadia.**

■ Big Bang

The Big Bang theory is the most widely accepted scientific theory of the origin of the universe. According to the theory, the universe was compressed to infinite density 10 to 20 billion years ago. At that time the "big bang" began. It was the origin of space and time. As the universe expanded, it cooled, and protons, neutrons, and electrons suddenly combined to make atoms. The theory originated in the 1920s, when it was discovered that the universe is expanding.

Big Bear *tried to promote the welfare of his people peacefully. Nevertheless, he was hunted down by the Mounties and imprisoned for treason (NAC/C-1873).*

■ Big Bear

Plains Cree chief (*born as Mistahimaskwa, about 1825 near Fort Carlton [Saskatchewan]; died in 1888 on the Poundmaker Reserve [Saskatchewan]*). Big Bear was the first major chief on the prairies to refuse to sign a treaty with the Canadian government. He believed that the conditions of the treaties would condemn his people to poverty and the destruction of their way of life. He refused to join other chiefs in the signing of Treaty No. 6 in 1876. However, the bison were rapidly disappearing from the western plains and by 1882 his people faced starvation.

Big Bear tried to gain better terms before signing the treaty. The government refused to negotiate and he lost the support of his more extreme followers, who preferred a more violent course. Led by Little Bad Man and Wandering Spirit, they killed nine whites at Frog Lake and burned Fort Pitt. Big Bear took no part in these events, and tried to prevent bloodshed. Nevertheless, he was hunted by the soldiers and Mounties, and gave himself up at Fort Carlton in July 1885. He was convicted of treason and imprisoned for two years. Ill, and broken in spirit, he died shortly after his release.

▷ RELATED ARTICLE: **North-West Rebellion.**

Bigelow, Wilfred Gordon

Heart surgeon (*born in 1913 at Brandon, Man.*). Dr Bigelow headed the division of heart surgery at Toronto General Hospital for more than 20 years. There he led the medical world into a new type of Ice Age by developing a procedure called hypothermia. This is a system of making a patient's body very cold before an operation in order to reduce the amount of oxygen required. One of its advantages is that it makes long and complex operations far safer. It has led to great advances in heart and brain surgery.

Bigelow's research into hypothermia spread over eight years in the 1940s and early 1950s. It involved a large team who made a study of groundhogs. They were trying to discover the cooling agent that makes it possible for groundhogs to hibernate in winter. During the research, Bigelow developed the idea of a heart pacemaker. This is a small electrical device that can start a stopped heart and then keep it beating regularly. Bigelow worked on this project with John Callaghan and J.A. Hopps. By 1950 they had made the world's first pacemaker. Pacemakers have saved thousands of lives throughout the world since they were first implanted in patients in the 1960s.

Dr Wilfred Bigelow was a world pioneer in the treatment of heart disease (courtesy Museum of Cardiovascular Surgery, Toronto General Hospital/painting by Irma Coucill).

Biggar

Biggar, Sask., is situated 100 km west of Saskatoon. It was created just before World War I as a railway construction town. The town was named for W.H. Biggar, an official of the Grand Trunk Pacific Railway. Biggar's economy is based on agriculture and transportation. Its population in 1986 was 2626. For information, contact the Town Administrator, P.O. Box 489, Biggar, Sask., S0K 0M0.

Bigot, François

Intendant of New France (*born in 1703 in Bordeaux, France; died in 1778 in Neuchâtel, Switzerland*). François Bigot was the last intendant of New France. He was originally posted to the colony in 1739 with the position of financial commissary at Louisbourg, where he was in charge of supplies and payments to the soldiers. After the British captured Louisbourg in 1745, Bigot returned to France. Three years later he was sent to Quebec, against his wishes, to serve as intendant.

Bigot made numerous enemies at Quebec. Merchants complained that he hired only his friends to supply the government. He was summoned to France in 1754 to answer these charges and was sent back to Canada the next year. Government spending skyrocketed in New France during the Seven Years' War. The French believed that Bigot stole much of the money meant for supplies and sentenced him to repay 1.5 million *livres*. His property was seized and sold and he spent his last days in disgrace in exile in Switzerland.

Bigot's defenders claim that Bigot was made a scapegoat after the fall of New France and that he was, in fact, an able administrator. However, his case was not helped by reports of the magnificent banquets and balls he held or of his bouts of gambling.

▷ RELATED ARTICLES: **Money; New France.**

François Bigot was intendant of New France during its last days. He was convicted by a French court of stealing money and was exiled (NAC/C-3715).

Bilingualism

Bilingualism is being able to speak or write fluently in two languages. In Canada, the languages referred to are English and French. These are Canada's two official languages.

Why Canada Has Two Official Languages. Most Canadians are either of French or British origin. In the 1600s and early 1700s, there was a French empire in North America. Its core was along the St Lawrence River in the region of today's province of Quebec. When this region became a British colony in 1763, the population was about 76 000.

After the Conquest, about 10 000 French and Canadians moved to France. In 1765, two years after the region became a British colony, the population had grown again to 69 800. All but a few thousand of these people were *francophones* (French speakers). The new British rulers had to take these facts into account. Early laws, such as Quebec Act of 1774, allowed French as well as English to be used in official matters so that francophones could deal with the government in their own language.

There were francophones in other regions too, wherever the French had traded or explored or settled. This included the Maritimes, the region of today's Ontario, and the Prairies. But francophones gradually became a minority. Between 1763 and Confederation in 1867, so many British settlers arrived that French Canadians were outnumbered. At Confederation, the population of Canada was two-thirds anglophone, one-third francophone.

The British government hoped that the people of French origin would assimilate, that is, that they would become British in language and customs. Although many French Canadians did learn English, they had no wish to give up speaking French. It was an essential part of their culture: their character, their history, and their literature. Any threat to it aroused widespread fear and anger.

When agreeing to join Confederation, the people of French Canada therefore insisted that they must have control over language, including the right to educate their children in French. Section 133 of the Constitution Act, 1867, established that federal and Quebec institutions would be bilingual.

In spite of these precautions, the use of French was often restricted in the years following Confederation. Some provinces passed laws, such as the Manitoba Schools Act (1890), which made it very difficult for francophones to send their children to French-language schools in Manitoba. Even in Quebec, francophones faced difficulties. Most of the large businesses were run by anglophones who did not speak French. Some had lived in the province for generations and had not taken the trouble to learn the language. Quebecois generally had to learn English to get a good job.

The dissatisfaction caused by this treatment of French reached a peak in the 1960s. The situation was considered so serious that royal commissions were set up, both at the federal level (Royal Commission on Bilingualism and Biculturalism) and in Quebec (Commission of Inquiry on the Position of the French Language and on Language Rights in Quebec) to investigate the matter.

The Royal Commission on Bilingualism and Biculturalism The B&B Commission was set up by Prime Minister Lester Pearson in 1963 to look into relations between French and English Canadians. Pearson appointed André Laurendeau and Arnold Davidson Dunton as co-chairmen. Their aim was to establish a more comfortable partnership between French and English Canadians, and to make sure that Canadians of both language groups had equal opportunities in all provinces. The recommendations of their report led to the Official Languages Act.

Official Languages Act, 1969 This Act stated that both French and English were to be official languages throughout Canada. This does not mean that every Canadian has to be fluent in both languages. But it does mean that all federal offices and courts must be able to offer services in both languages. The Act led to an increase in bilingualism across Canada, since many anglophones who worked for the federal government were obliged to learn French. It also led to an increase in bilingual printed matter. For instance, the labelling and packaging of pre-packaged goods had to be done in both languages.

This 1969 Act was, in effect, merely an enlargement of Section 133 of the Constitution Act of 1867 in that it confirmed that English and French are Canada's two official languages, but also extended their use to all federal services.

The Commission of Inquiry on the Position of the French Language and on Language Rights in Quebec This commission was set up by Quebec in 1968 to study these matters from a provincial perspective. Since then, Quebec has passed three major laws dealing with the situation of French in that province: An Act to Promote the French Language in Quebec (1969), The Official Language Act (1974), and the Charter of the French Language (1977).

The Canadian Charter of Rights and Freedoms, passed in 1982, proclaims that French and English are the two official languages of Canada and that minority communities have the right to educate their children in their language throughout Canada. New Brunswick, Manitoba, Ontario, Saskatchewan, and Alberta have also passed laws dealing with the use of English and French. New Brunswick also became a bilingual province. In two historic decisions in 1979 and 1985, the Supreme Court reinstated bilingualism in Manitoba, which had been put aside in 1890. The Canadian Charter applies to Quebec, which, however, did not endorse it. In 1986, Ontario passed laws recognizing the right to obtain all provincial services in French in certain regions of the province. Both the Northwest Territories and the Yukon have recently adopted the principle of bilingualism in their language legislation. Saskatchewan has given support to this principle. Alberta has not. These two provinces in 1988 had to enact legislation on language following a decision (the Mercure case) by the Supreme Court of Canada. They chose to do away with some bilingual services.

The 1988 Official Languages Act improved upon the 1969 Act. It deals with the following areas of federal policy: language of service, language of work, and the equal participation of both English- and French-speaking Canadians in all federal institutions.

Bilingualism and Its Critics There have been opponents to the federal government's policy of bilingualism. Native people feel that it is discriminatory to have French and English as the only two official languages. They were in North America first. They feel that their languages should also be respected as official languages. Similarly, Ukrainians and other major cultural groups would like their languages to be officially recognized.

In addition, there are critics of bilingualism within the French and English communities. Some francophones feel that the laws do not go far enough, that the use of French should be made compulsory in more areas. Some anglophones feel the exact opposite, that there should be only one official language in Canada, namely English.

In most parts of the world it is considered an advantage to be able to speak more than one language, but in Canada language has always had a political aspect because of its connections with the two major cultural groups. Consequently, many people have resisted learning the "other" language rather than being pleased that they have the chance of doing so.

Yet this has changed during the past 20 years. Since the Official Languages Act was passed, some provinces (for example, Ontario) have made major efforts to provide far more French-language teaching. Individuals across the country have made the effort to become bilingual and to encourage their children to become bilingual. A public opinion poll taken in 1989 showed that two-thirds of Canadians were in favour of bilingualism.

▷ RELATED ARTICLES: **Ethnic Languages; English Language; French Language; Native People: Language.**

■ **Bill,** *see* **Parliament**

■ **Billiards**

Billiard games became popular in Canada over 100 years ago. All are played on a table with balls and a cue, but there are many variations of the game. The most popular is called "snooker." In this game, 22 balls are used: a white, 15 red, and six other coloured balls. A player must sink a red ball and then may choose one of the other coloured balls. If a player cannot hit the ball that he must hit, because it is blocked by other balls, he is said to be "snookered." Several Canadians have excelled at billiards. In 1980, Cliff Thorburn, of Victoria, B.C., was the first player born outside the United Kingdom to win the world championship.

Billiard games are played in private clubs, homes, and in about 2500 public "pool halls" across Canada. There are about 250 000 regular players.

■ **Bilson, Geoffrey**

Professor, writer (*born in 1938 in Cardiff, Wales; died in 1987 in Saskatoon, Sask.*). Bilson earned a doctorate in history from Stanford University and taught at the University of Saskatchewan.

His three novels portray ordinary children involved in important, but not well-known, events of Canadian history. The heroine of *Goodbye Sarah* (1981) loses her best friend because her own father is a leader in the Winnipeg General Strike of 1919. In *Death Over Montreal* (1982), Jamie and his family arrive in Montreal during a 19th-century cholera epidemic. *Hockeybat Harris* (1984) describes the unhappiness of an English boy sent to live in Saskatoon to escape the bombings of London during World War II. Bilson's careful, accurate research is vividly presented. Living in difficult times, the characters of his novels must develop courage and understanding.

■ **Biochemistry**

Biochemistry is the study of the chemical processes that occur in living organisms. Biochemists study the tiny components of cells, such as genes, the master chemi-

Computer-generated Pictures of the atoms that make up the insulin molecule help scientists understand how it works (courtesy Michael James/U of A).

cals which control what happens in these miniature chemical workshops. Some processes of special interest are the conversion of food to energy, respiration, and the regulation of the chemical activity of cells.

Biochemistry borrows its methods and ideas from biology, chemistry, and a number of other scientific disciplines. It emerged as an independent branch of science in Germany late in the 19th century.

Medical schools first introduced the new science of biochemistry to Canada. Then, beginning at the University of Toronto in 1908, several Canadian universities organized departments of biochemistry. During the early decades of the 20th century most biochemistry research in Canada was carried out at universities.

The outstanding achievement of biochemistry in Canada was the discovery of insulin. Insulin is a hormone produced by the body which regulates the use and storage of food. A lack of it causes a serious condition called diabetes. Working at the University of Toronto, Frederick Banting and his co-workers, including J.R. Macleod, isolated this chemical. Their discovery saved the lives of millions of people suffering from diabetes. Banting and Macleod shared the Nobel Prize for Medicine in 1923, the first Nobel Prize awarded for scientific work in Canada.

From the universities, biochemistry spread to industry and special research institutes. There are now biochemical laboratories in the federal and provincial government departments responsible for agriculture, fisheries, forests, health, and more. Most companies in the Canadian food industry depend on these government laboratories for the techniques they apply in processing food. Breweries and distilleries have biochemical laboratories to test the quality of the drinks that they produce.

Research institutions in which hospitals and universities combine forces, such as the McGill-Montreal General Hospital Research Institute, and the Banting Institute of the University of Toronto, also conduct biochemical research.

Biochemistry is the main scientific base of the drug manufacturing industry.

Through its Medical Research Council, the federal government funds most biochemical research in Canada.

▷ RELATED ARTICLES: **Sir Frederick Grant Banting; Charles Herbert Best; Chemistry; James Collip; Drugs; Insulin; Archibald Macallum.**

■ **Biogeography**

Biogeography studies the distribution of plants and animals around the world, the causes of this pattern and the adaptations that allow living organisms to survive in a given habitat. This science developed rapidly at the beginning of the 18th century because of the exploration of the world then taking place and the discovery of many new species. Alexander von Humboldt is usually considered the father of biogeography. He was the first to recognize the key role played by climate in the distribution of plants. From temperature and humidity alone, one can account for some 20 different vegetative formations. For example, the tropical rain forest exists in hot and wet places; the desert, in hot and dry; boreal forest, in cold and wet; the tundra, in very cold and typically dry.

All species interact in an ecosystem. If there is a change in one species (for example, its abundance) it can affect another species in the ecosystem which relies on it for food or is itself food for the species undergoing change.

Each vegetative formation assures food and shelter to a host of animals who, in return, contribute greatly to the plants' survival by furthering pollination, the transportation of fruit and seeds, and the decomposition of organic material that returns to the soil nutritive elements needed by the plants.

Man has significantly altered the distribution of plant and animal species. Sometimes his impact has been beneficial; for example, the raven thrives on our garbage. More often it has been destructive; for example, the draining of marshland destroys the breeding grounds of many birds.

▷ RELATED ARTICLE: **Ecosystem.**

■ **Biography**

Biography is the written record of a person's life. The word comes from the Greek word *bios*, meaning "life," and *graphein*, "to write."

The earliest biographies were probably orations spoken at funerals and, later, remembrances of deceased people. Famous heroes' lives frequently became the subject of legends, in which great deeds were exaggerated and exciting incidents were invented to make their lives seem even greater.

Some of the earliest written biographies are found in the Bible, particularly in the Old Testament. The four gospels of the New Testament can be called biographies of Christ. Around AD 100, Plutarch, a Greek, wrote *Parallel Lives*. During the Middle Ages, stories of the lives of saints were very popular.

None of these stories, however, could be called biography in the modern sense. Modern biographies are usually based on careful, detailed research, accurate reporting of facts, and balanced analysis of the subject's life. Often biographers spend years reading diaries, letters by and about the subject, and histories of the times in which he or she lived. Frequently they visit the places in which the subject lived. They try to understand the facts of the subject's life and times as completely as possible.

Biographers must carefully select those details which they feel are most important in the subject's life. Too many details result in an unreadable mass of facts. A biographer is expected to include material which shows the subject in an unfavourable, as well as a favourable, light.

A biography is also an interpretation of the subject's life. The writer may offer explanations of why the subject acted in the way he or she did.

Biography in Canada It has been estimated that over 2000 volumes of Canadian biography have been written in English. These include books about the early explorers, native leaders, fur traders, political leaders, and important people in business, science, sports, and the arts.

The earliest Canadian biographies appeared in the middle of the 19th century. They were memorials of important public figures. In 1862, *Sketches of Celebrated Canadians* by Henry James Morgan appeared. It was a collection of shorter biographies and was the first of many books which collected biographies of Canadians. Others include the *Dictionary of Canadian Biography*, edited by W. Stewart Wallace, which first appeared in 1926, and the Dictionary of Canadian Biography, a multi-volumed work published in both English and French. When completed, the first 12 volumes will include articles on the lives of over 6000 Canadians in every field of endeavour.

Important biographies of individual Canadians have been published throughout the 20th century. Up until the middle of the century, the majority of these dealt with explorers and politicians. Since then, important native leaders, scientists, artists, and writers have been written about. With the increased awareness of the important role of women in Canada's history, more biographies of women have appeared.

Many biographies written for younger readers have been written in Canada since 1950. Many of these were volumes in series bearing such names as Canadian Lives, Canadian Pageant Series, Great Stories of Canada, and Canadian Portraits Series. Some of the books can still be found in libraries but many of them are no longer available. Although a few were very good, many were either very dull or inaccurate. New biographies are still being published in series such as Fitzhenry and Whiteside's The Canadians, Grolier's Canadian Pathfinders Series, and Methuen's Canadians All: Portraits of Our People.

Some of the finest Canadian biographies written specifically for younger readers are R.S. Lambert's *Franklin of the Arctic* (1949); Roderick Haig-Brown's *Captain of the Discovery* (1956), the story of explorer George Vancouver; Kay Hill's *And Tomorrow the Stars: The Story of John Cabot* (1968); and Roy Daniells's *Alexander Mackenzie and the North West* (1969).

▷ SUGGESTED READING: Karen Ford, J. MacLean, and B. Wansbrough, *Great Canadian Lives* (1985); Carlotta Hacker, *The Book of Canadians* (1983); Robert Livesay, *Footprints in the Snow: The Heroes and Heroines of Canada* (1978). The volumes of this encyclopedia include some 2000 biographies of Canadians.

■ Biology

Biology is the science of life. The most familiar forms of life are plants and animals. There may be as many as ten million different kinds of living things in the world. Studying this bewildering variety, biologists have discovered a pattern of underlying unity.

Principles of Biology Biologists discovered that all living things are made of tiny units called *cells*. Cells can usually only be seen under a microscope, although some are very large, for example, an ostrich egg.

Also, they have discovered that life evolves, that animals and plants change over time, becoming different from their ancestors. Horses, for example, were once animals the size of dogs. Humans and chimpanzees share a common ancestor. Charles Darwin first put forward the concept of evolution in the 19th century. It was widely opposed at the time, but is now accepted by most scientists.

Biologists also discovered how the characteristics of living things are passed from one generation to another. What does a puppy get from its parents that

Careers in Biology

Biologists find work in many places, from educational institutions to hospitals and government departments.

For most positions, an undergraduate degree in biology, zoology, or botany is needed, but some require only a two-year community college diploma in a related field. Undergraduate university programs last three or four years. About 2600 students graduate every year, and find careers as research assistants and laboratory technicians.

About 225 students graduate with a master's degree each year. Some students continue through a PhD program. They become university professors, consultants, or senior research scientists in government or private industry.

makes it a dog and not a cat? The answer is genes. These are made of DNA sequences found in the nucleus of the cell. All living things have genes.

Kinds of Biology Because the science of life is so broad in scope, no one person can cover the whole field. Biology is divided into three major areas: botany, zoology, and microbiology. Each of these has a large number of branches. Some biologists study whole plants or animals. Some are experts on a particular species, such as caribou. Ecologists study how living things interact with each other and with their environment. Ethologists study how animals behave. Palaeontologists work from the fossil remains of past living creatures.

Biology is a challenging science which asks questions that are harder to answer than the questions raised by physical sciences, such as physics and chemistry. This is so because of the great complexity of its subject: life.

Among the many areas in which biology is put to practical use are animal and plant breeding, medical research, and wildlife conservation.

Biology in Canada Biological exploration began early in the history of the settlement of Canada. A number of collectors gathered specimens of plants and animals, which were studied in Europe.

Early in the 20th century, Canada began to establish its own universities and research institutes.

Most research biologists in Canada now work in universities, in national or provincial museums, or for government agencies such as Agriculture Canada, the Fisheries Board, the Forestry Service, the National Research Council, and the Canadian Wildlife Service.

There are a number of Canadian journals in which biologists publish their results. These include *Canadian Entomologist*, *Canadian Field Naturalist*, *Canadian Journal of Botany* and *Canadian Journal of Zoology*.

▷ RELATED ARTICLES: **Biochemistry; Botany; Zoology.**

▷ SUGGESTED READING: David Attenborough, *Discovering Life on Earth: A Natural History* (rev. ed. 1981); Donald M. Silver, *Life on Earth: Biology Today* (1983); David Suzuki and Barbara Hehner, *Looking at the Body* (1987).

■ Biomass Energy

Biomass is the name for the material of which living things, animals and plants, are made. Biomass contains energy that living plants capture from the Sun by the process of photosynthesis. Biomass energy provides about 7% of Canada's total energy.

Using energy from sunlight, green plants break down carbon dioxide and water, and recombine their constituents to form living tissue. We, in turn, use this material as food and as fuel. Bread and wood are two common sources of biomass energy. When you eat bread, you get energy which a growing wheat plant got, in turn, from sunshine. As you read these words, your brain is being powered by biomass energy. Similarly, when you burn a log of wood, you get energy which a living tree got from sunshine.

We use coal, oil, and natural gas, the main sources of energy in most industrialized countries, far faster than nature produces them. These are non-renewable sources of energy; once pumped dry, an oil well stays dry.

But as long as nutrients are replaced in the soil, a woodlot can provide wood for heating a home year after year. Biomass, in other words, is a renewable source of energy.

BIOMASS RESOURCES IN CANADA

The solar energy stored by all the trees in Canada exceeds twice the energy Canadians use in a year. Because of our enormous forests, Canadians have more raw biomass energy than any other people in the world, except the U.S.S.R. and Brazil.

In practice, Canada's largest practical source of biomass energy is the wastes at pulp and paper mills and at sawmills. The sawdust, bark, and other wastes that are now burned at such mills contribute more to Canada's energy diet than nuclear power plants do. The forest industries have been increasing their use of wood that previously was thrown away, burned as waste, or left on the forest floor. This can cause environmental problems. If debris off the forest floor is burned, there will be no nutrients available for future forests.

The biomass wastes that accumulate on farms are also an energy resource. Straw can be burned; manure can be fermented to produce a combustible gas like natural gas. And since about one-third of the garbage that we throw out every year is paper and cardboard, garbage burners can provide steam or electricity from biomass in cities.

Peat is vegetation that, if left for ages, would eventually be buried and turned into coal. As much as 12% of Canada is covered by peat bogs from which fuel could be mined, as it is in peat bogs in other countries.

The amount of biomass energy available in Canada could be increased by growing trees on energy plantations. Researchers in Canada, for instance, are experimenting with fast-growing poplar trees.

FROM BIOMASS TO ENERGY

The simplest way to convert biomass energy into a useful form of energy is to burn a biomass fuel, such as wood. It may make sense to use the heat thus obtained to produce steam, which in turn drives an electrical generator.

It is also possible, using cooking and brewing techniques, to break down biomass into gases that resemble natural gas, or into fluids that resemble oil. Plants that are rich in sugars or starch can be fermented to produce ethanol (grain alcohol). Wood chips can be baked to yield charcoal, flammable gas, and methanol (wood alcohol). Either ethanol or methanol can be mixed with gasoline. The result, called gasohol, is 10% ethanol and 90% gasoline. It is now sold at gas stations in parts of Canada. Methanol, which can be made from a source that is renewable, reasonably inexpensive, relatively easy on the environment, and available in abundance in Canada, could provide an alternative to oil. While supplies of oil are expected to grow scarce and expensive in coming years, there are sources of biomass energy in most parts of Canada.

▷ RELATED ARTICLES: **Coal; Energy; Forests; Natural Gas; Oil; Petroleum; Pulp and Paper; Solar Energy.**

■ Biotechnology

Biotechnology is the use of living organisms to provide food, medicine, and other goods. The new science and technology of biotechnology is dramatically changing how we grow food, how we make drugs to treat diseases, and many other areas. These changes are the result of recent discoveries in a number of areas, including biology, chemistry, biochemistry, genetics, medicine, and others. Using genetic engineering, one of the key techniques of biotechnology, we can actually redesign living things to meet human needs.

Biotechnology is likely to cause changes in the 1990s as great as those caused by computers in the 1980s.

Early Biotechnology Humans have always made use of other living organisms. The ancient Egyptians, for instance, used tiny organisms known as yeast to make the first bread and beer. Farmers have always used a kind of biotechnology. Every year they have taken the seeds for the next year's crop from the best plants. Thus, gradually, they have selectively bred the most productive plants.

Genetic Engineering Recently, scientists have developed techniques to combine and alter genes. Genes, found in the heart of cells, are actually tiny bits of the molecule known as DNA (for deoxyribonucleic acid). Each gene contains coded instructions. Together, these instructions form the essential blueprints of life, telling cells what to do.

Scientists have learned not only how to "read" genes but also how to "edit" them. From a human cell, for instance, they can cut out the gene that carries instructions for making insulin. They can splice this molecular fragment into the genes of a tiny bacterium. The bacterium now has what is called recombinant DNA: its original genes, and the human gene. Obeying the instructions in its genes, it will now produce human insulin. Many of these genetically engineered bacteria can be grown in a vat, like beer. From these bacterial factories, human insulin, for use in treating diabetes, is now produced.

APPLICATIONS OF BIOTECHNOLOGY

Growing Food Biotechnology is leading to more productive and hardier crops. Scientists are designing plants to grow in inhospitable areas, areas that are dry, salty, or — and this is of significance in Canada — cold.

Some scientists are developing plants that do not need pesticides, but can defend themselves against pests. They take a bacterial gene that causes disease in caterpillars. They splice this gene into a plant's genes. The leaves of the modified plant kill feeding caterpillars, but do no harm to humans.

By such means, Canadian scientists have made a hardy new kind of canola, formerly known as rapeseed. Their new plant resists both pests and cold.

Similarly, some scientists are taking bacterial genes for getting nitrogen directly from the air. They are splicing these genes into plants. The modified plants do not need expensive nitrogen fertilizer, but can fertilize themselves.

Mining Certain bacteria can recover minerals such as copper and iron from rock containing very small quantities of these metals. Sprinkled on the rock, the bacteria "harvest" the minerals and form mineral-rich pools. This new way of mining is low in cost and energy consumption, and creates little pollution.

Waste Treatment Biotechnology may help in cleaning up pollution. Scientists are finding and designing organisms that can digest pollutants such as PCBs and crude oil sludge.

Medicine Biotechnology research has led to new ways of detecting diseases such as lung cancer, and has also led to the development of new cancer treatment drugs, new ways of making vaccines, and more. It is providing more efficient ways of getting drugs which, up to now, have been taken mostly from living plants and micro-organisms. Biotechnology may also make it possible to remove or change defective genes in order to end inherited diseases such as cystic fibrosis.

Energy By developing trees that grow quickly and that resist disease, pests, and cold, biotechnology could help produce wood. A genetically engineered forest could provide both fuel and chemicals that now come from petroleum and coal.

Biotechnology in Canada Major federal government facilities include the National Research Council's Biotechnology Research Institute in Montreal, and its Plant Biotechnology Institute in Saskatoon, Sask. Most of the provincial government research agencies also do biotechnology research.

During the 1980s there has been a sharp increase in the number of students graduating from Canadian universities with degrees in biotechnology disciplines, such as chemical engineering, biochemistry, microbiology, and genetics.

By the late 1980s, more than 200 companies were working in the biotechnology field in Canada. The majority of these were established during the 1980s. The two main areas in which Canadian biotechnology companies concentrate are health-care products and agriculture.

For instance, Connaught Laboratories Limited of Toronto, Canada's oldest biotechnology company, is Canada's largest manufacturer of vaccines and other health-care products.

Allelix Inc., which is located in Malton, Ont., is developing new strains of canola and other biotechnology products for use in agriculture.

CONCERNS

To prevent experimental organisms carrying dangerous new traits from escaping from the laboratory, scientists conduct genetic engineering experiments with bacteria that can only survive in the laboratory. Critics of biotechnology fear that these bacteria, or larger genetically altered organisms — such as fish designed to grow fast and big — might escape. Once in the wild, there would be no way to retrieve such organisms, to prevent their genes spreading through the gene pool. Such an event might dramatically, perhaps even catastrophically, upset natural processes.

While scientists and biotechnology companies describe the benefits of leaner meat, chickens resistant to disease, and other positive results of biotechnologically altered organisms, critics suggest that people other than the scientists and companies should have a say in whether our food is altered in this way.

▷ RELATED ARTICLES: **Genetic Diseases; Genetics.**

■ Birch

Birches (*Betula*) belong to the birch family (Betulaceae). Birches can be recognized by the colour and structure of their bark — yellow and divided into little curly-edged strips on the yellow birch (*B. alleghaniensis*); creamy to pinkish white on the Alaska birch (*B. neoalaskana*); smooth and reddish brown on the water birch (*B. occidentalis*); white with triangular black splashes on the grey birch (*B. populifolia*); white and easily stripped on the paper birch (*B. papyrifera*). It is tempting to collect the beautiful bark, but if

Paper Birch (B. papyrifera) *played an important role in the life of the native people, who used its bark to make canoes (artwork by Claire Tremblay).*

sections are cut from the tree, the circulation of its sap is cut off and the tree may die. However, one can happily collect strips from the trunks of dead trees, which decompose very slowly and thus last a long time on the forest floor.

The European birch (*B. pendula*), with white bark and drooping branches, and the hairy birch (*B. pubescens*) were introduced from Europe. The paper birch played an important role in the life of the native people, who used its bark for their canoes (hence the tree's nickname of "canoe birch"). Today, it is the yellow birch that is most important to the economy: its wood is used for floors, parquetry, and woodworking.

▷ RELATED ARTICLE: **Canoe.**

■ Bird, Florence Bayard

Broadcaster, journalist (*born Florence B. Rhein in 1908 in Philadelphia, U.S.*). Florence Bird came to Canada in 1931, and she moved to Winnipeg in 1937. During World War II she formed a volunteer organization for Winnipeg women who wanted to do war work. Using the pen name Anne Francis, she began to write newspaper articles about the women's work and to give talks on the local radio station. Then, in 1942, she began broadcasting for the CBC, launching a career that would make the name Anne Francis known throughout Canada.

For 20 years after the war, "Anne Francis" was a news commentator for the CBC. In 1967 she was appointed chairperson of the Royal Commission on the Status of Women in Canada, an enormous task involving public hearings that at-tracted hundreds of women from across the country. The commission's landmark report, completed in 1970, made 167 recommendations aimed at equality between men and women.

Bird was appointed to the Senate in 1978 and served there until reaching retirement age in 1983. She then served two years on the government's Advisory Committee on the Status of Refugees. She has written two books, *Anne Francis: An Autobiography* (1974) and *Holiday in the Woods* (1976). She received the Persons Award in 1983 in recognition of her contribution to the cause of women.

▷ RELATED ARTICLE: **Women's Movement.**

■ Birds

Birds have certain features which make them different from all other animals. They have a horny bill and feathers, which are made up of keratin, the same substance we humans have in our fingernails. Most birds can fly, but a few species are not capable of flight. The bones of most birds are light to help them fly.

BIRD HABITAT

Birds are adapted to survive and reproduce within a certain habitat. Their feet and bills are adapted to gather available food. Their feathers protect them from cold in cold climates and heat in hot climates. Feathers protect them from injury, and their colour makes it difficult for enemies to find them. For example, many birds of the southern prairie are adapted for the short, sparse grassland. Their feet are made for walking, not hopping. Their bills clip the vegetation, crush seeds, or pick up insects. Their plumage is dull and helps them to blend in with their surroundings.

The power of flight has enabled birds to overcome barriers, such as mountains, oceans, and deserts. Most of Canada's birds are believed to have evolved else-

Florence Bird amid some of the mountains of reports made for the Royal Commission on the Status of Women (NAC/PA-135131).

East Coast Horned Puffin (photo by Stephen J. Krasemann/DRK Photo).

Bird Feeders

Bird feeders help birds through the winter and encourage birds to "come to you" so they are easier to observe.

A bird feeder can be made by putting bird feed into an upside-down plunger.

Use two pie plates on a pole for a high-rise feeder. To make hanging feeders, suspend milk cartons or plastic bottles from a tree.

For a unique feeder, tie a string around a pine cone and smear it with unsalted peanut butter and roll it in seeds. Hang the cone from a branch.

Feathers

Feathers are unique to birds. They help maintain the bird's body temperature, act as a water-resistant barrier. They enable it to fly, and help to conceal it through camouflage. In flight, feathers provide power, lift, steering, and braking.

Feathers contain a single, long vane which supports a row of barbs (branches) along each side. Barbules branch out from the barbs and contain small hooks which attach to the barbules of the next barb. This structure is very strong and very light.

Great Cormorant *is one of five species of pelican found in Canada (Macmillan Illustrated Animal Encyclopedia).*

where. They later colonized Canada from the south or from Asia or Europe. Some, such as blackbirds, apparently came from tropical South America. Others, such as grouse and finches, likely came to North America from Asia. The number of species decreases towards the Far North, on mountain tops, and on distant islands.

BIRD CLASSIFICATION

Birds are vertebrates (having backbones) of the class Aves (capable of flight). They are distant relatives of reptiles and their feathers likely evolved from reptilian scales.

There are over 9050 species of birds, and occasionally new ones are discovered. Birds which share certain characteristics are grouped into 28 orders. The orders are, in turn, broken down into families, genera, and species. All but eight of the 28 orders are represented in Canada.

Running Birds consist of five orders, with six families. They are large birds with muscular legs. Most, like the ostrich, cannot fly. None of these birds are found in Canada.

Penguins (order Sphenisciformes) are flightless birds which are adapted to the water. Their wings are modified into flippers. The emperor penguin is an example. Penguins are only found in the southern hemisphere.

Grebes (order Podicipediformes) breed in fresh water, making a nest of floating plants. Their legs are set back on their bodies and they are fast swimmers. They dive to catch fish with their pointed bills. There are five breeding species in Canada.

Loons (order Gaviiformes) are diving birds, similar to grebes. They propel themselves with webbed feet. Four species breed in Canada.

the oceans. Most store a foul-smelling stomach oil which is secreted for defence or preening. Three species of these seabirds breed in Canada.

Pelicans (order Pelecaniformes) are medium-sized to large aquatic birds. They have webbed feet, hooked bills, and large throat pouches. The order also includes gannets and cormorants. Pelicans generally nest in large colonies. Five breeding species are found in Canada.

Wading Birds (order Ciconiiformes) are fairly large birds with slim bodies, long legs and necks. They grab their prey with dagger-shaped bills. Many have patches of downy feathers used in preening the feathers. This order includes herons, storks, and bitterns. There are six breeding species in Canada.

Flamingos (order Phoenicopteriformes) are large wading birds. None are found in Canada.

Mallard Duck *Ducks live on the water and feed on plants or animals (Macmillan Illustrated Animal Encyclopedia).*

Ducks (order Anseriformes) are a highly diverse group of birds, found all over the world. All live on the water and feed on plant or animal life on the surface or beneath it. They are broad-bodied with short legs and webbed feet. Their bills are broad and flat. There are 36 species in Canada, including ducks, geese, and swans.

Birds of Prey (order Falconiformes) are small to large birds that hunt live prey or feed on dead animals. They have hooked bills and powerful claws, and generally hunt by day. There are 19 species in Canada, including hawks, eagles, falcons, and ospreys.

White Throated Swift *Swifts are the most expert flyers of all birds. They even sleep in the air (Macmillan Illustrated Animal Encyclopedia).*

Red-throated Loon *All four species of loon are found in Canada (Macmillan Illustrated Animal Encyclopedia).*

Petrels and Albatrosses (order Procellariiformes) are seabirds with webbed feet and hooked bills. They are found over all

Game Birds (order Galliformes) live mostly on the ground. They are plump, round birds which scratch the ground for buds, seeds, and bugs. They are capable of strong, but short, flight and may roost at night in trees. There are 15 breeding species in Canada, including grouse, bobwhite, and quail. The Greater Prairie Chicken is endangered.

Cranes (order Gruiformes) are splendid, long-legged birds with long necks. They often display bright colours on their face or in plumes above their head. They may be up to 1.5 m tall. Cranes migrate in large flocks. Rails are smaller and are adapted for life in dense vegetation. There are seven breeding species in Canada, including the endangered Whooping Crane.

Shorebirds (order Charadriiformes). Some shorebirds, such as sandpipers and plovers, find their food in water, through which they wade with long legs. Others have webbed feet and dive for food. Gulls and terns have powerful bills and dive for fish or catch insects in flight. There are 71 breeding species in Canada, including puffins, snipes, avocets, and auks.

Pigeons (order Columbiformes) can be fairly large birds. Their relatives, the doves, are smaller. They have an unusual reproduction feature. They feed their young for the first few days with milk secreted from the lining of the crop. As adults they feed on seeds, buds, and small insects. They are strong fliers. The Passenger Pigeon, once very common across Canada, was hunted to extinction. There are at present three breeding species in Canada.

Parrots (order Psittaciformes) are brightly coloured tree-dwelling birds. They are vocal birds, renowned for mimicking human speech. None are native to Canada. The budgerigar (budgie) is a popular cage bird.

Yellow-billed Cuckoo *Cuckoos are named for their loud, unmusical call (Macmillan Illustrated Animal Encyclopedia).*

Cuckoos (order Cuculiformes) are known for their habit of laying their eggs in the nests of other birds, which then rear their young. North American species make very unstable nests. They are named for their loud, unmusical call.

There are two breeding species in Canada.

Owls (order Strigiformes) are soft-feathered birds of prey. Most hunt at night, silently. They have enormous eyes, facing forward, and very keen eyesight. All have hooked bills and they kill with their talons. They generally swallow their prey whole and regurgitate the bones and fur. There are 14 breeding species of owls in Canada.

Nighthawks (order Caprimulgiformes) are medium-sized, dumpy birds. They usually have a wide mouth surrounded with bristles, possibly to help catch insects. They feed on insects and fruit. There are three breeding species in Canada, including the whippoorwill.

Swifts and Hummingbirds (order Apodiformes) have very special flying abilities. Swifts are the most adept flyers, performing almost all their activities — even sleeping — in the air. Hummingbirds are named for the sound produced by the rapid beating of their wings. They are very small. They can fly in all directions, including backwards. There are seven breeding species in Canada.

Colies (order Coliiformes) are small African birds with long tails.

Trogons (order Trogoniformes) are spectacular, colourful birds found in tropical and sub-tropical zones. There are none in Canada.

Belted Kingfisher *dives headlong into the water to seize its prey (Macmillan Illustrated Animal Encyclopedia).*

Kingfishers (order Caraciiformes) live mostly in hotter regions. There is one breeding species in Canada. It has a stocky body, large head, and a straight bill. It dives headlong into the water to seize its prey, but cannot swim.

Woodpeckers (order Piciformes) are tree-dwelling birds well known for their hammer-like pecking of trees. Most have

Snowy Owl *Owls form a separate order, called Strigiformes, among birds (Macmillan Illustrated Animal Encyclopedia).*

Bobwhite *Like all pheasants, these birds are plump and round (Macmillan Illustrated Animal Encyclopedia).*

Whooping Crane, *typical of the long-legged birds of the crane family, is an endangered bird (Macmillan Illustrated Animal Encyclopedia).*

Common Flicker, *like most woodpeckers, has two toes facing backward, to help it climb trees (Macmillan Illustrated Animal Encyclopedia).*

Northern Oriole, *a colourful member of the perching family (Macmillan Illustrated Animal Encyclopedia).*

Eastern Meadowlark *is a perching bird, whose call is a short, clear whistle (Macmillan Illustrated Animal Encyclopedia).*

two toes pointing forward and two backward, to help the bird climb up tree trunks. There are 14 breeding species in Canada.

Perching Birds (order Passeriformes) are by far the most numerous birds. There are 60 different families and over 5270 species worldwide, of which there are over 180 species in Canada. They are named for their ability to perch on any thin support, such as twigs or stems of grass. Many are songbirds that sing to defend territory or court mates. They include such diverse species as flycatchers, larks, swallows, pipits, shrikes, wrens, waxwings, dippers, thrushes, warblers, finches, crows, orioles, and starlings.

Bobolink *is one of the order of perching birds, called Passeriformes (Macmillan Illustrated Animal Encyclopedia).*

BIRD MIGRATION

In summertime, many of the birds of Canada nest on the tundra. Only a hardy handful of these birds — such as the Common Raven, chickadees, the Snowy Owl, and some species of ptarmigan — stay in Canada during the winter.

Most migrate. When fall comes they leave Canada, flying south to spend the winter in warmer climates. When spring comes, they fly north again to Canada.

The longest of all such migrations is that of the Arctic Tern. Every year this bird flies from the Canadian Arctic to Antarctica and back again, a round trip of some 35 000 km.

BIRDS AND PEOPLE

Birds as Food Birds are an important source of food for humans. Most of the birds we eat are domesticated: chickens, turkeys, ducks, and geese. There are more than three times more chickens than people in Canada.

Hunting birds is popular in Canada. Among the birds that hunters now shoot are ducks and geese, grouse and pheasants, and snipe and woodcocks. Laws govern the kind and number of birds that

sport hunters can kill, and the times of the year during which they can hunt. Such laws are important, for several species of birds have been hunted to excess in Canada.

Conservation Thousands of great auks once bred off Canada's east coast. Passenger Pigeons were once so numerous they darkened the skies of Canada when they flocked overhead. Both these birds are now extinct, wiped out by hunters and trappers.

Today, the threat to birds is no longer from hunters but from the side effects of industry and urban life. By cutting down forests and draining swamps, and by building cities and roads, we destroy the habitats of birds. Acid rain destroys forests and lakes and their inhabitants. Pesticides, poisons designed to kill insects, also kill the birds that eat the insects. At least 30 species of bird are considered to be in danger of extinction now in Canada.

Birds and their habitats are protected in Canada's national and provincial parks. Canada also has over 95 bird sanctuaries, covering over 112 000 km^2, which are set aside by the Canadian Wildlife Service. Among the best known of these is Last Mountain Lake, Sask., which is the oldest bird sanctuary in North America. Established in 1887, it hosts ducks, swans, cranes, and many other species of birds. The largest bird sanctuary is Queen Maud Gulf, N.W.T., which is nearly 63 000 km^2. Bonaventure Island, Que., has spectacular concentrations of gannets, kittiwakes, murres, and others.

Cap-Tourmente, Que., hosts a large population of the world's Greater Snow Geese. Wood Buffalo National Park is the only remaining nesting area of the rare Whooping Crane. Some provinces have their own protected areas.

Cities, private agencies such as Ducks Unlimited, bird clubs, and individuals have also taken steps to protect important areas.

BIRD WATCHING

Bird watching is a very popular hobby in Canada. There are bird clubs in most cities. "Birders" provide useful information as to the distribution of birds. Some become highly efficient at identifying birds and compete with one another. One of the most popular bird-watching sights in North America is Point Pelée National Park, a sand spit jutting into Lake Erie.

▷ RELATED ARTICLES: **Auk; Avocet; Blackbird; Bluebird; Chickadee; Coot; Cormorant;**

Crane; Creeper; Crow; Cuckoo; Dipper; Dove; Duck; Eagle; Falcon; Finch; Flycatcher; Fulmar; Gallinule; Gannet; Gnatcatcher; Goose; Great Auk; Grebe; Grosbeak; Grouse; Gull; Hawk; Heron; House Sparrow; Hummingbird; Jaeger; Jay; Kingfisher; Kinglet; Lark; Loon; Magpie; Meadowlark; Mockingbird; Murre; Nighthawk; Nuthatch; Oriole; Osprey; Owl; Oyster Catcher; Passenger Pigeon; Pelican; Peregrine Falcon; Phalarope; Pheasant; Pigeon; Pipit; Plover; Ptarmigan; Puffin; Purple Martin; Quail; Rail; Raven; Razorbill; Robin; Sandpiper; Shrike; Snipe; Solitaire; Sparrow; Starling; Storm-petrel; Swallow; Swan; Swift; Tanager; Tern; Thrasher; Thrush; Vireo; Vulture; Warbler; Waterfowl; Waxwing; Whooping Crane; Woodcock; Woodpecker; Wren. *See also* **Birds of Prey; Game Birds; J.T. Miner; Shorebirds; Waterfowl.**

▷ SUGGESTED READING: J.C. Finlay, *Bird-Finding Guide to Canada* (1984); W. Earl Godfrey, *The Birds of Canada* (1979); Pamela M. Hickman, *Birdwise* (1988); Bobbie Kalman, *Birds at My Feeder* (1987); Louise de Kiriline Lawrence, *The Loghouse Nest* (1988); Mary MacPherson, *Birdwatch: A Young Person's Introduction to Birding* (1988); John Rodgers, *Birdwatching: An Introductory Guide for Young Canadians* (1982).

■ Birds of Prey

Birds of prey belong to two separate orders. The Falconiformes include the eagles, falcons, hawks, vultures, kites, and the osprey. The Strigiformes are the owls.

Great Grey Owl Owls are birds of prey that hunt at night (photo by Wayne Lankinen/DRK Photo).

Members of both groups have similar bills, for tearing the flesh of their prey. They also have strong claws (called talons) for seizing their victims.

Most birds of prey feed on warm-blooded animals, such as rabbits and mice, but some feed on dead animals, and others prefer fish or amphibians.

Species that hunt by day, such as eagles and hawks, have long, powerful wings for extended flights. They are large, fierce, and strong, and have very keen vision.

Falcons also hunt by day but fly much faster. They are very specialized because they destroy large numbers of animal pests but do not overkill.

Owls hunt at night. Unlike the species that hunt by day, owls are silent fliers. They have soft feathers which in some species reach down to their toes. Unlike other birds, the owl's eyes are located in the front of its head. They have a very keen sense of hearing.

■ Birney, Alfred Earle

Author (*born in 1904 at Calgary, Alta*). Birney received a PhD from the University of Toronto in 1938. After serving as a personnel officer during World War II, he became a professor of medieval literature at the University of British Columbia.

Two collections by Birney have won the Governor General's Award for poetry, *David and Other Poems* (1942) and *Now Is Time* (1945). He has written two nov-

Earle Birney is one of Canada's best-known poets (courtesy Plum Studios/Bruce Cole).

Yellow-bellied Sapsucker Woodpeckers hammer their beaks into trees in search of bugs (Macmillan Illustrated Animal Encyclopedia).

Rock Dove Doves are somewhat smaller birds than their cousins, the pigeons (Macmillan Illustrated Animal Encyclopedia).

Herring Gulls, like most shorebirds, have webbed feet and dive for food (Macmillan Illustrated Animal Encyclopedia).

Peregrine Falcon All birds of prey have powerful claws for clutching their victims (Macmillan Illustrated Animal Encyclopedia).

els, *Turvey* (1949), winner of the Leacock Medal for humour, and *Down the Long Table* (1955).

Birney experiments with many styles. For example, the satiric "Anglosaxon Street" uses the devices of Old English poetry. "Like an Eddy," written in the spiral shape of an eddy, is intended to be a mobile.

His most famous poem is the controversial narrative "David." It is about two characters who form a close friendship. Crippled when he falls during a mountain climb, David begs Bob to kill him so he will not have to suffer. Although the difficulty of Bob's choice is one theme, another major theme is the loss of the narrator's youthful illusions about the goodness of nature.

■ Birth Control

Birth control includes various methods used to prevent pregnancy. It is more accurately called "contraception" or family planning. Some groups in society oppose birth control and consider some methods immoral. It is estimated, however, that at least 30% of Canadians practise birth control. Couples may want to limit the number of children in their family, or to have no children at all. Others may want to postpone having children.

In Canada, until the 1920s, most methods of birth control were illegal. The first organized groups supporting birth control appeared in Canada after World War I. They argued that parents should want, and be able to look after, every child born to them. Birth-control advocates also argued that birth control could prevent abortions and unplanned pregnancies, especially among teenaged girls, but support was not widespread.

By about World War II, the attitudes of many Canadians to birth control had changed, and methods became more available. The change was partly accelerated by reports that the world was becoming overpopulated. It was also partly the result of the invention and improvement of two new methods of birth control: the Pill and the intrauterine device (I.U.D.). In 1969, Canada changed its laws, making any method of contraception legal. Many volunteer organizations worked to provide birth-control information and services.

Birth control continues to be a controversial issue. Some religious groups, notably the Roman Catholic Church and some Fundamentalist churches, believe that only certain types of birth control should be used. They strongly oppose such methods as the Pill. Other groups, including most Protestant churches, believe that full information should be available to all Canadians. Birth-control advocates now argue that the lack of reliable information will lead to an increase in the number of teenaged girls who become pregnant, and in the number of unwanted children. The idea of birth control is partly determined by an individual's religion and moral beliefs, and by his or her idea of sexuality.

Birth-Control Methods An ovum is normally released by one of a woman's ovaries once a month. Pregnancy begins after a man's sperm fertilizes a woman's ovum and travels through the fallopian tubes to be implanted in her uterus. Birth control methods are designed to prevent the meeting of ovum and sperm.

The most certain way to prevent pregnancy is not to have sexual intercourse. This method, called "abstinence," is a voluntary decision. It may be taken for a range of personal or moral reasons.

A woman is fertile only for a short time each month. These times can be identified by monitoring her body temperature or other changes in her body. Couples can then arrange intercourse according to their desire to conceive.

Birth-control pills are prescribed by a doctor. They contain hormones which prevent the monthly release of the ovum. They are reliable and convenient. However, they have adverse effects on some women.

The intrauterine device (I.U.D.) is a small plastic device which a doctor places in the woman's uterus. It is not fully understood how it works. There are various kinds of I.U.D.'s, some of which may have side effects in some women.

The condom is a protective sheath, worn over a man's penis, which prevents semen released in intercourse from entering the woman's cervix. Condoms also provide protection against sexually transmitted diseases. They can be bought in drugstores and elsewhere. Condoms are not always a completely effective means of birth control because they may break or slip off.

Voluntary sterilization is a permanent method of birth control for men or women. In a woman, the fallopian tubes, by which an ovum reaches the uterus, are cut and tied. In a man, the tubes through which the sperm travel are cut and tied.

Other methods of birth control include the diaphragm, which is fitted by a doctor, and inserted in the vagina by the woman before intercourse. Used with a diaphragm, spermicides form a chemical barrier to prevent sperm from entering the cervix.

The attempt by a man to pull out his penis during intercourse or *coitus interruptus*, also called withdrawal, is *not* a reliable method of birth control. Semen may have already escaped without the man's knowledge.

Those who support birth control believe that a firm understanding of it is necessary before a person engages in sexual intercourse. Each form of contraception has certain advantages and disadvantages, risks and benefits. Reliable information about birth control can be obtained from a doctor, hospital, clinic, or family planning centre.

▷ SUGGESTED READING: Marjorie Wild, *Elizabeth Bagshaw* (1984).

■ Bishop, William Avery

World War I fighter pilot and winner of the Victoria Cross (*born in 1894 at Owen Sound, Ont.; died in 1956 at Palm Beach, U.S.*). Billy Bishop was one of the most celebrated air aces of World War I. A fellow pilot called him "a fantastic shot but a terrible pilot." At a time when a pilot's score was a measure of his fame, Bishop claimed that he shot down 72 enemy planes — more than any other Allied airman.

Bishop's most famous exploit is also his most controversial. On June 2, 1917, he claimed that he attacked a German airfield which was more than 25 km inside enemy territory and shot down three enemy aircraft. His plane was in tatters when he landed almost an hour later. Bishop had already won several medals, including the Military Cross, but the account of this daring, one-man raid won him the highest of all British honours for bravery in battle, the Victoria Cross.

After the war, Bishop and a partner ran a small air service for a while, and then he took a post with an oil company. He was an honorary air marshal with the Royal Canadian Air Force during World War II, and helped recruit young airmen.

Bishop's victories were an inspiration to the troops during World War I, but some critics have suggested that his famous raid never took place. There were no eyewitnesses and no German record of the event. Those who support Bishop charge that these accusations are an insult to a national hero. A film that questioned Bishop's claims caused a furor in

Billy Bishop *was awarded the Victoria Cross for bravery for a daring raid on a German airfield during World War I (NAC/PA-1651).*

Parliament and led to a Senate investigation, which was not conclusive. Bishop was also the subject of the popular play *Billy Bishop Goes to War*, by John Gray. A hero or not, Bishop seems destined to remain part of the Canadian imagination.

▷ SUGGESTED READING: Dan McCaffery, *Billy Bishop: Canadian Hero* (1988).

■ Bishop's University

Bishop's University is located in Lennoxville, Que. It offers undergraduate and graduate degrees in a variety of subjects, taught in English. The university was founded in 1843 by the Anglican bishop of Quebec, in part to train Anglican clergy. It has not had a religious connection since 1947.

Bishop's has over 1300 full-time undergraduate students (1987). For further information, write to the Registrar's Office, Bishop's University, Lennoxville, Que., J1M 1Z7.

■ Bison

The bison (*Bison bison*) belongs to the cattle family Bovidae. There are two subspecies: wood bison and plains bison. It is the largest of our land mammals, reaching 2 m in height at the shoulder blades and weighing almost 1000 kg. The name "buffalo" is incorrectly applied to the bison. The head, shoulders, and front legs are covered by a shaggy, woolly, chocolate-coloured mane. The rest of the fur is short, smooth, and a coppery colour. The head and beard are almost black and the tail is adorned with a tuft of hair. The bison's shoulders have a massive hump and its short, black horns have inward-curving tips.

A social animal, bison form into bands of up to 20 beasts. These bands may join to form herds numbering thousands. Bison are suspicious and may charge with little warning. The bison can be easily frightened and stampede. The native hunters used this trait to their advantage,

Bison, *often incorrectly called "buffalo," can weigh up to 1000 kg. It once numbered up to 60 million on the western prairie (Macmillan Illustrated Animal Encyclopedia).*

Stalking the Bison *The native hunters coaxed the bison herd towards the cliff (artwork by Lewis Parker and Gerald Lazare).*

Driving the Bison over the Cliff *(artwork by Lewis Parker and Gerald Lazare).*

▷ SUGGESTED READING: Laima Dingwall, *Nature's Children: Bison* (1985).

Historic range of Bison ●

Present range of Bison ●
Park herds •

stampeding them towards a cliff. Bison have a keen sense of smell and can distinguish odours as much as 2 km away. It can spot a moving object at up to 1 km. Bison are migratory, and may range over several hundred kilometres searching for better grazing land. Some of the old bison routes are still visible from the air. Bison feed on grass, sedge, lichens, and berries.

Before human hunters the bison's only predators were the grizzly bear, cougar, and wolf, which could only take the young, old, or sick. Mating takes place from July to September. Bulls engage in shoving matches, which are often violent. A single baby is born between mid-April and early June. A bare half-hour after birth, the calf will struggle up on wobbly legs to nurse.

The plains bison once inhabited the great grasslands from Lake Winnipeg to the Rocky Mountains. Before European settlement moved westward, they numbered between 40 and 60 million. Their herds thundered over the open prairie. By the 1860s, they had almost been wiped out in the east. By the late 1870s, the western herds were also very scarce. The native people, whose lives depended upon the bison, were left starving and destitute. In 1906, in an effort to save the bison, the Canadian government purchased over 700 plains bison from a rancher in Montana. Most of the bison were shipped to a new park, near Wainwright, Alta. Because of disease, this herd was completely destroyed in 1938 and 1939. The 50 bison left at Elk Island National Park, east of Edmonton, grew into a healthy population. Today, there are roughly 80 000 to 100 000 bison in Canada and the United States. In 1922 the government set aside Wood Buffalo National Park to preserve the wood bison.

■ Bison Hunt

The bison hunt was carried on by the Plains Indians and their early ancestors for thousands of years. It was later also taken up by the Metis. The hunt was the basis for the way of life on the western plains. It provided meat for food, sinew and bones for tools and weapons, and skins for clothing and shelter.

Early peoples hunted the bison by creeping up on them and stampeding them over cliffs (buffalo jumps) or into corrals (pounds). About 1730, the horse arrived on the plains and Indians began using it to hunt the bison.

During the fur trade, pemmican, made from dried bison meat, was a staple item in the diet of traders. It was collected at forts on the plains and carried by canoe and boat to trading posts farther north. As well, after 1850 hides went to make drive belts for machinery.

Before 1800, bison herds roamed the plains in vast numbers. During the next 80 years the animals were hunted almost to extinction. The disappearance of the bison brought enormous changes in the

Slaughtering the Bison *The hunters made sure the bison were dead, then stripped the meat and hides (artwork by Lewis Parker and Gerald Lazare).*

way of life of the Plains Indians and Metis.

▷ RELATED ARTICLES: **Bison; Metis; Native People: Plains.**

▷ SUGGESTED READING: Beatrice Culleton, *Spirit of the White Bison* (1985).

■ Bitumen

Bitumen is a dark, tar-like form of crude oil. Unlike conventional crude oil, bitumen is too thick and heavy to flow. It is the thickest and heaviest of all forms of petroleum. An enormous amount of bitumen occurs along the banks of the Athabasca River and in several other parts of northern Alberta. It is mixed with sand, in what are known as tar sands or oil sands. These Athabasca oil sands are the largest known deposits in the world. Though these petroleum deposits contain vast quantities of energy, the costs of harnessing this energy — that is, of extracting bitumen and processing it to make a synthetic oil — are very high.

▷ RELATED ARTICLES: **Energy; Fossil Fuels; Oil; Oil Sands; Petroleum.**

■ Bjarni Herjolfsson

Apparently the first European to see the coast of North America (*birth and death dates unknown*). A Norseman, Bjarni traded in Scandinavia each summer. Each autumn he returned to Iceland to spend the winter with his father, who had settled there. About the year 986, Bjarni learned that his father had accompanied Erik the Red to Greenland to found a colony there. Bjarni set out to join them. He was blown off course in stormy weather. He came in sight of land that was hilly and wooded. Sailing north, he saw a land that was level and wooded. Still farther north, he saw a mountainous land covered with snow. These three lands are thought to have been Newfoundland, Labrador, and Baffin Island. Bjarni did not land on any of them, but he described them when he reached Greenland. A few years later Eric the Red's son, Leif Ericsson, followed up on Bjarni's explorations and the lands became known to history as Vinland, Markland, and Helluland.

■ Black, Conrad Moffat

Businessman (*born in 1944 at Montreal, Que.*). Toronto millionaire Conrad Black inherited a large fortune and in 1978 he used it in a brilliant financial maneuvre to gain control of the Argus Corporation. Argus controls a large number of Canadian corporations. After taking it over, Black reorganized the company, making it a more tightly knit operation.

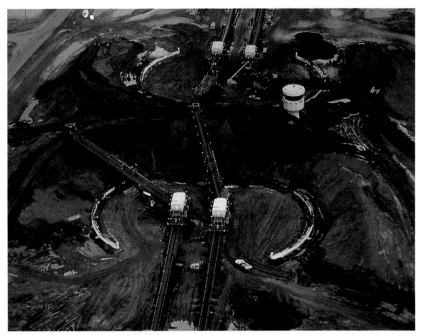

In 1985 Black bought the *Daily Telegraph*, one of the leading newspapers in Britain. He also bought newspapers in the United States and Canada, and in 1987 he took over Canada's prestigious magazine, *Saturday Night*. Black extended his British newspaper interests in 1989 by buying into United Newspapers. This chain's papers include the *Daily Express* and *Sunday Express*, which were once owned by another Canadian businessman, Lord Beaverbrook.

Black's activities include writing, and

Bitumen Very heavy equipment is required to dig the bitumen from the earth so that it can be refined to make oil (courtesy A.O.S.T.R.A.).

Conrad Black's *financial interests include newspapers in Canada, Britain, and the U.S.*

he has contributed articles on political and economic matters to the *Globe and Mail*. He is the author of *Duplessis* (1977), a biography of the controversial Quebec premier.

■ Black, Davidson

Anthropologist (*born in 1884 at Toronto, Ont.; died in 1934 at Beijing [Peking], China*). Black's discovery of "Peking Man" in 1927 changed accepted ideas about human evolution. He studied anatomy at the University of Toronto and, while he was in Britain with the Canadian army during World War I, he became interested in the origins of man. He went to China, where he became a professor at Peking Union Medical College, and began searching for the remains of early man. In 1927 he was shown the fossil of an unusual tooth. He identified it as a new species of ancient man, which he called *Sinanthropus pekinensis*, or Chinese man of Peking.

Black and other scientists later found the partial remains of over 30 of these prehistoric people, as well as stone tools and the bones of animals they had killed. "Peking Man" lived about 375 000 years ago and belonged to a species of early human beings called *homo erectus*. He was about 1.5 m tall, with heavy bones, a protruding forehead, and large jaws.

■ Black, Martha Louise

Yukon pioneer (*born Martha Louise Munger in 1866 at Chicago, Illinois, U.S.; died in 1957 at Whitehorse, Yukon*). She joined the gold rush to the Klondike in 1898. Unlike most of the gold seekers, she stayed on in the Yukon after the rush was over. In 1901 she started a sawmilling business near Dawson and in 1904 married a Dawson lawyer, George Black (*born in 1873 at Woodstock, N.B.; died in 1965 at Vancouver, B.C.*). George was appointed commissioner of the Yukon in 1912.

Martha accompanied her husband to England during World War I and helped to look after the needs of wounded Yukoners. In 1921 George was elected the Yukon's member of Parliament and was Speaker of the House of Commons from 1930 to 1935.

In 1935, when George was too sick to run for election, Martha ran instead. She was elected and in 1936 became the second woman to sit in the Commons (the first being Agnes Macphail). Martha was 70 at the time. She lived another 21 years, a keen Yukon enthusiast to the end.

■ Black Bear

The black bear (*Ursus americanus*) is the most familiar of Canada's three species of bear. It has small black eyes, rounded ears, a short neck, and thick, powerful legs. Its fur is coarse and long and is most commonly black, except for an occasional white V on the chest. However, some black bears are cinnamon or honey coloured. The average weight of an adult male is 169 kg; of a female, 136 kg.

The black bear is found all across the forested areas of Canada, from Newfoundland to the Pacific coast. Black bears are bold and may become roadside beggars in parks. They climb trees to feed on young shoots, buds, and fruit. A young bear cries when afraid and hums when contented. The bear has the peculiar habit of clawing the bark of trees, perhaps in order to mark its territory.

In autumn the black bear finds shelter in a cave, rock crevice, or hollow log. It collects branches for its winter den and enters a sleepy state. (It is not true hibernation.)

Black bears eat a huge variety of food, including twigs, leaves, spruce needles, ants, grubs, carrion, grass, fruit, berries, nuts, mice, fish, and farm animals. They have a sweet tooth and love honey and corn.

Range of Black Bear ●

Martha Louise Black lived an eventful life in the rugged conditions of the Yukon (courtesy Yukon Archives).

Black Bear in a salmon stream on the Pacific coast (photo by Thomas Kitchin).

Black bears can be a considerable nuisance around garbage dumps and as camp robbers. They can be very dangerous and unpredictable.

▷ RELATED ARTICLE: **Bear.**

■ Black Creek Pioneer Village

Black Creek Pioneer Village is a group of pioneer buildings located in a suburb of Toronto. They show visitors what daily life was like in Ontario before 1867. A museum contains a large collection of toys and games from the 19th and early 20th centuries in Canada. For information, contact the Black Creek Pioneer Village, 1000 Murray Ross Parkway, Downsview, Ont., M3J 2P3.

▷ SUGGESTED READING: N. Mika, H. Mika, and G. Thomson, *Black Creek Pioneer Village* (1988).

■ Black Fly

Black flies, also called "buffalo gnats," are part of the family Simuliidae, order Diptera. This order includes all other flies as well. They are very small (under 5 mm), and brown or black. Their wings are large, in proportion to their bodies (which in profile look quite hunchbacked). At least 100 species are known in Canada. They are particularly abundant in the boreal forest. Females are very familiar to us since they bite in order to feed on blood. They need blood to complete the development of their eggs (150 to 600). Like all stinging insects, the males do not sting and are rarely seen. At dusk they fly in swarms over water. Their life span is about three weeks.

In Africa and Central America, black flies may transmit a disease known as "river blindness," caused by a small worm which forms a nodule under the skin and can even, as the name suggests, cause blindness.

The larvae live in fast-running streams and rivers. They cling, by means of a kind of sucker on the abdomen, to submerged debris such as branches, plants, and large, flat stones. They feed on suspended particles carried along by the current. They therefore help to filter the water and also serve as food for the fish.

Black flies are a scourge to livestock, causing weight loss and even death. They are also a great irritation to humans in northern areas. Forest workers in northern B.C. and Quebec demand extra pay during black-fly season.

■ Black Hole

A black hole is a region of the universe from which nothing, not even light, can

Black Hole, *artist's impression (artwork by Helmut K. Wimmer).*

escape because its gravity is so strong. The theory of black holes was worked out mathematically before evidence for their existence was found.

Since black holes cannot be seen (they emit no light), their existence must be suggested by other means. A Canadian astronomer, Thomas Bolton, has located the best candidate so far. It is a star orbiting around an unseen companion — possibly a black hole. Important work on black holes is being done at the observatory in Victoria, B.C., and by Werner Israel of the University of Alberta.

▷ SUGGESTED READING: Stephen Hawking, *A Brief History of Time: From the Big Bang to Black Holes* (1988).

■ Blackberry

Blackberries, like raspberries, belong to the genus *Rubus* of the rose family (Rosaceae). These bushes grow 1 to 2 m high, with two types of stems: those of the current year, non-branching, with large leaves of five leaflets each; and branching stems from the previous year. These stems have smaller leaves, consisting of only three leaflets, and flowers which turn into fruit. The blackberry stems have fierce thorns.

The blackberry often grows on the edge of a wood, a road, or a field, on disturbed soil. A colony of blackberry bushes with

Black Fly *females need blood to complete the development of their eggs (artwork by Jan Sovak).*

entangled branches is just like an enclosure of barbed wire. It is absolutely impossible to penetrate unless you are willing to leave behind some flesh and some clothing. Fortunately, the fruit is found at the end of the branches. It is used to make excellent pies, preserves, jellies, and even wine. The thorny and bent branches make a much-sought-after refuge for birds, hares, and several other small mammals. The black raspberry (*R. occidentalis*) has thorns like the blackberry but black fruit resembling raspberries. It has more delicate stems than the blackberry. The tips of the bent-over stalks can take root and produce a new plant.

Blackbird

Blackbird is the common name for different species of birds belonging to the subfamily Icterinae.

These birds have a pointed bill, and usually have black feathers with splashes of yellow and red. The female, however, is not as brilliantly marked as the male. This group of blackbirds includes the red-winged blackbird (*Agelaius phoeniceus*), the most common blackbird in Canada and undoubtedly the best-known bird in North America; the yellow-headed blackbird (*Xanthocephalus xanthocephalus*); the rusty blackbird (*Euphagus carolinus*); and the brewer's blackbird (*Euphagus cyanocephalus*).

Red-winged and yellow-headed blackbirds nest in colonies in the thick vegetation of freshwater swamps and fields. The male very forcefully defends his territory against intruders. The female usually lays four eggs, with incubation lasting 11 to 12 days. Though they may eat some crops, these birds also eat a great many destructive insects during their nesting period. The rusty blackbird nests near water, in conifers and sometimes in bushes. The

Breeding Range of:
Red-winged
Blackbird ●

brewer's blackbird nests in small colonies in bushes bordering roads and waterways. Sometimes two other species are included in the blackbird group: the brown-headed cowbird (*Molothrus ater*), metallic green-black with a brown head, and the common grackle (*Quiscalus quiscula*), a large black bird with an iridescent blue-green head. In fall, to glean the crops in the fields, they often join forces with other members of the blackbird family.

Blackfoot

The Blackfoot are one of three Indian groups which, together with the Blood and the Peigan, make up the Blackfoot Nation. They all speak an Algonquian language. Their traditional culture was based on bison hunting, and this animal provided their food, clothing, and tipis. Around 1730 they obtained horses from Spanish traders to the south and guns from Cree middlemen who traded with the Hudson's Bay Company (HBC). In turn, they too began to trade with the HBC and the North West Company. They were great warriors, and frequently fought against the Cree, Assiniboine, and Kootenay. Chief Crowfoot was their best-known leader and played a dominant role in the signing of a treaty in 1877 with the Canadian government. In 1988 the population of the Blackfoot Nation was about 13 000. Most reserves are involved in farming, ranching, and small industries. *See* **Native People: Plains.**

▷ SUGGESTED READING: Cliff Faulknor, *The White Calf* (1965); Madeline A. Freeman, *A Horse for Running Buffalo* (1972).

Blacks

There are well over 300 000 Canadian Blacks. About one in four are West Indians who have immigrated since the 1960s, but some belong to families who have lived in Canada for more than 300 years. Blacks were among the earliest non-natives to live in Canada.

The Pioneers About 1000 Blacks were taken to New France as slaves during the 17th and early 18th centuries. Some were brought directly from Africa, and some were from New England or the West Indies. A number of the slaves were children, who became pages to rich French families or who waited at table, dressed in fine clothes. Most of the Blacks in New France were household servants.

Much the same system continued under the British after the Conquest of 1760, for slavery was still legal in Britain's colonies. Loyalists who fled from the

Red-Winged Blackbirds nest in the thick vegetation of freshwater swamps (courtesy NMNS/artist Allan Brooks).

American colonies because of the American Revolution (1775-83) brought approximately 2000 slaves with them. About 3500 free Blacks also immigrated to British North America at that time. They too were Loyalists, having fought for the British during the revolution.

More free Blacks arrived during the following years. They included a group of people called Maroons, who arrived from Jamaica in 1796. There was another large influx during the War of 1812, for the British offered grants of land in Nova Scotia to any American slaves who escaped and joined the British side. There was thus already a large community of free Blacks in Canada even before 1834, when slavery was abolished throughout the British Empire.

Most of the Black immigrants settled in Nova Scotia and the newly formed colony of New Brunswick. But they had a tough time there. They expected the rewards promised to all Loyalists: a grant of land and food rations for three years. But little land was given to the Blacks, and their food rations only lasted three months. They were not allowed to vote and did not have access to the law courts.

The Blacks lived in separate communities from other Maritimers, some of whom were former slave owners. Unable to support themselves by farming, because of their small plots of land, they were forced to take low-paying jobs. Some left the Maritimes. Between 1792 and 1800, about 1700 Blacks sailed for Sierra Leone in West Africa. In 1820 a further 95 went to Trinidad in the Caribbean. However, many others stayed, and they formed the basis of today's Black community in the Maritimes.

During the 19th century, at least 30 000 escaped slaves from the southern U.S. states found a safe haven in British North America. Most made their way to Ontario via an escape route known as the Underground Railroad. Some went as far west as the Prairies and Vancouver Island.

Most of the early Blacks faced considerable prejudice from other Canadians. Some were attacked physically or had their property damaged. A few gained widespread affection and respect. There was William Hall, for example, who was the first Nova Scotian and first Canadian sailor to win the Victoria Cross. There were boxers such as George Dixon, teachers and ministers such as Josiah Henson, and two much-admired pioneers in the West: John Ware, the famous Black cowboy, and Alfred Shadd, western Canada's

Thomas Peters
Thomas Peters (c 1738-92) was an early civil rights leader in Nova Scotia.

He escaped slavery in North Carolina and joined the Black Pioneers, a Loyalist regiment. He arrived in Nova Scotia in 1784, and became the spokesman for the Black Loyalists. He petitioned the governor to fulfil Britain's promises and treat them the same as other Nova Scotians. He had little success, so in 1790 he took his grievances to England. He had little success there either. Thus he helped to organize a group of Blacks who left Halifax to start a colony in Sierra Leone in 1792. He died of fever soon after his arrival in Africa.

first Black doctor.

The Modern Era During the latter half of the 19th century and the first half of the 20th century, Canadian immigration laws made it very difficult, if not impossible, for Blacks to enter Canada. Restrictions based on race were not lifted until the 1960s. Since then, thousands of Blacks have come to Canada. By far the largest number of these came from the West Indies. In the 1970s alone, approximately 130 000 West Indian Blacks immigrated to Canada.

Canada's West Indians come from more than 20 different islands and territories in the Caribbean. The largest group is from Jamaica, followed by Trinidad-Tobago. There are also French-speaking West Indians from Haiti, most of whom have settled in Montreal. Most English-speaking West Indians have made their home in Ontario, especially Toronto. It has been estimated that more than half of Canada's West Indian population lives in Toronto. Each August, the Caribana festival is celebrated there, attracting crowds of spectators with its colourful street parade and entertainments.

Today, Blacks are employed in almost every type of work throughout Canada. They have a high level of education and participate in all areas of Canadian life.

▷ RELATED ARTICLES: **Ethnic Origin; Prejudice and Discrimination; Slavery; Underground Railroad.**

▷ SUGGESTED READING: Barbara C. Smucker, *Underground to Canada* (1977).

Blacksmith Shop *in Innisfail, Alta, in 1910. The horseshoe was heated red hot and shaped by pounding it on the anvil with hammers (courtesy Glenbow Archives/NA-1709-52).*

■ Blacksmithing

Blacksmithing is the craft of turning crude iron into useful or decorative items. The metal is heated in a *forge* (very hot fireplace), then hammered into shape, and finally *tempered* (cooled) in a bucket of water.

Blacksmiths were among the first settlers in Canada because their skills were needed by soldiers, farmers, and ordinary citizens. They were locksmiths, nailmakers, gunsmiths, cutlers (blade makers), farriers (shoemakers for farm animals), and more. French smiths had to apprentice three years before they qualified as skilled craftsmen. In English Canada, some of the first blacksmiths were brought from Britain in the 1670s by the Hudson's Bay Company to help build trading posts and to repair goods and machinery. Blacksmiths had already been working in Newfoundland since the early 1600s.

Early blacksmiths specialized in one type of ironwork and produced work of a very high quality. They often formed a small community within the towns in which they lived. In the mid-1800s, these specialized artisans were increasingly replaced by blacksmiths who did many kinds of work.

Blacksmiths were especially important in the towns founded along the newly built railway lines. They shoed horses, repaired tools and wagon wheels, and made and repaired parts for farm machinery.

The local blacksmith was an important man in his village. He might also be the banker, veterinarian, or doctor. He kept the horses to draw the hearse. His smithy was a centre of social life. Blacksmiths were also the heroes of many folk songs and stories.

Industrialization made tools cheaper and machines replaced horses. Throughout the early 20th century, the number of blacksmiths shrank. Today, few blacksmiths maintain the old craft. Most shoe horses and farm animals. Some can be seen at work in recreated pioneer villages.

■ Blackwood, David Lloyd

Printmaker (*born in 1941 at Wesleyville, Nfld*). Blackwood is one of Canada's most popular and skilled printmakers. He also teaches art at Trinity College School in Port Hope, Ont. His etchings are based on the history and folklore of Newfoundland, particularly the fishermen and sailors who worked the rocky shores. He sees his pictures as part of the local storytelling tradition. His early prints were in black and white, but he is increasingly using colour in his finely detailed works.

▷ RELATED ARTICLE: **Printmaking.**

■ Blades, Ann

Writer, illustrator (*born in 1947 at Vancouver, B.C.*). Blades taught for two years in northern British Columbia and then studied to become a Registered Nurse. She nursed for several years before devoting herself full-time to illustrating children's books.

Her first two books, *Mary of Mile 18* (1971) and *A Boy of Taché* (1973), are based on real people and settings in British Columbia. Mary Fehr can keep the wolf pup she has found after it proves its usefulness to her poor, hard-working family. Charlie, a young native boy, must travel alone to Taché to get medical help for his grandfather. Blades's other two books, *The Cottage at Crescent Beach* (1977) and *By the Sea: An Alphabet Book* (1985), are realistic presentations of summer activities on the West Coast.

Blades has illustrated several books for other authors: *Jacques the Woodcutter* (1977), a French-Canadian folktale retold by Michael Mecklam; *A Salmon for Simon* (1978) and *Pettranella* (1980), both by Betty Waterton; *Anna's Pet* (1980), by Margaret Atwood; *A Candle for Christmas* (1986), by Jean Speare; and *Ida and the Wool Smugglers* (1987), by Sue Ann Alderson.

In her own stories and those illustrated for others, Blades's watercolour paintings present character and settings and communicate emotions. When Mary Fehr must give up the pup and Simon cannot catch a fish, their shoulders slump in dejection. Houses are warm and cosy, with members of the family enjoying activities together. Rugged outdoor scenes show the harshness of the wild in which some of the characters live.

▷ RELATED ARTICLE: **Mary of Mile 18.**

■ Blais, Marie-Claire

Writer (*born in 1939 at Quebec City, Que.*). Marie-Claire Blais grew up in poverty and was educated by nuns at a convent school. This childhood of distress and strict discipline served as the background for her early writing.

She left school at age 15 to work in a shoe factory. She wrote her first novel, *La Belle Bête* (1959), translated as *Mad Shadows*, when she was just 19 years old. For many years, she lived in New England and France before returning to live and write in Montreal. Probably her best-

His Father Dreams, *an etching by David Blackwood (courtesy Madison Gallery/artist's collection).*

Ida *claps and shouts at a mother sheep and her lambs so that they will not be caught by the wool smugglers. Her face shows how anxious she is and her body leans forward in the direction she is driving the sheep. From* Ida and the Wool Smugglers, *illustrated by Ann Blades (©1987 by Ann Blades, published by Douglas & McIntryre).*

known novel is *Une Saison dans la vie d'Emmanuel* (1965), translated as *A Season in the Life of Emmanuel*, which brought her worldwide fame.

Blais has written more than two dozen books. She has received the Governor General's Award twice (1968, 1979). In 1982 she won the Prix David, Quebec's highest literary award. She is a Companion of the Order of Canada.

■ Blake, Edward

Politician (*born in 1833 near London, Upper Canada [Ontario]; died in 1912 at Toronto, Ont.*). Blake was one of the most prominent Liberal politicians in Parliament in the years following Confederation. An outstanding equity lawyer, he had been the senior partner of his firm at the age of 34. He was premier of Ontario from 1871 to 1872, but opted for the House of Commons in Ottawa, where he was a member of Parliament from 1867 until 1891. He was leader of the Liberal Party from 1880 to 1887.

In a strictly political sense, Blake can be thought of as one of the great failures in Canadian history. He was never prime minister. During his leadership, the Liberals lost two elections, 1882 and 1887. Although Blake was blessed with a brilliant mind, he was cursed with too much sincerity. To him, every issue was a moral issue. Consequently, he agonized over decisions. Similarly, he knew that every issue was complicated. Therefore, to simplify issues was dangerous, because it distorted the truth. Blake's speeches in Parliament were thus long recitals of facts, which put his fellow politicians to sleep, rather than giving them simple, clear answers. Yet Blake was the conscience of the House of Commons. He was also something of a nationalist. He showed interest in the Canada First movement in the mid-1870s. Judged by what he stood for, he still towers over many of his contemporaries.

■ Blakeney, Allan Emrys

Premier of Saskatchewan (*born in 1925 at Bridgewater, N.S.*). Blakeney attended Dalhousie and then Oxford University, where he was a Rhodes scholar. He came to Saskatchewan in 1950 as a young lawyer to work in the provincial civil service. He was later a legal adviser and practised law privately. In 1960 he was elected to the legislature as the Co-operative Commonwealth Federation (CCF) member for Regina. He served as minister of education, finance, and health in the governments of T.C. Douglas and W.S. Lloyd, then as an important member of the opposition from 1964 to 1970.

In 1970 Blakeney was elected leader of the provincial New Democratic Party (NDP). In 1971 the NDP won the provincial election, and Blakeney became premier. He was re-elected in 1975 and 1978, but was defeated by the Conservatives in

Edward Blake's long speeches often put his fellow politicians to sleep (courtesy NAC/PA-27030).

Allan Blakeney was premier of Saskatchewan from 1970 to 1982 (courtesy Canapress Photo Service).

1982 and again in 1986. In 1987 he resigned as leader of his party. As premier, he was known for a competent and well-run provincial administration, and for giving a strong voice for Saskatchewan at the federal level.

■ Blakeslee, Mary

Writer (*born in 1938 at Calgary, Alta*). Blakeslee studied at the University of British Columbia, where she graduated as a social worker. Soon after, a bout of polio left her "in a wheelchair, with a lot of time to rehabilitate." This turned her thoughts to writing. Her various experiences as manager of the Calgary Volunteer Bureau, director of a poverty project in Texas, and media consultant for the Manitoba Department of Education, all deepened her interest in writing.

Her writing career was launched with *Wheelchair Gourmet* (1981), a recipe book for the disabled. Since 1985, she has focused on writing novels for children and young adults. Her more than a dozen books include *It's Tough To Be A Kid* (1983), *Halfbacks Don't Wear Pearls* (1986), *Outta Sight* (1987), *Chocolate Pie for Breakfast* (1988), *Will to Win* (1988), *Museum Mayhem* (1988), *It's Still Tough To Be A Kid* (1988), and *Stampede* (1989).

■ Bland, Salem

Church leader (*born in 1859 at Lachute, Canada East [Quebec]; died in 1950 at Toronto, Ont.*). Bland was a leading Methodist minister and a well-known supporter of social reform in the 1920s and 1930s. Like other followers of the Social Gospel movement, Bland believed that the church should be involved in solving social and economic problems. He preached this message to his students at Wesley College, in Winnipeg, where he taught from 1903 until he was dismissed from his job in 1917, because of his outspoken views.

For two years Bland was a popular public speaker and journalist in the West. Then he moved to Toronto, where he served as a church minister and also wrote a regular newspaper column.

In 1920 Bland published his most important book, *The New Christianity*. It argued for a church which should be involved in social and political action. The RCMP declared the book "subversive" (that is, politically dangerous).

During the 1930s Bland helped to found the Co-operative Commonwealth Federation, the forerunner of today's New Democratic Party.

Bland was respected by the labour movement and farmers in the West. He was less popular with business leaders and church officials, who thought that the church should not be meddling in social reform.

▷ RELATED ARTICLE: **Social Gospel.**

■ Bleus

The Bleus were followers of Louis LaFontaine and other moderate politicians in Canada East from the 1850s on, that is, French-Canadian Conservatives. *See* **Parti Bleu.**

■ Blind River

Blind River, Ont., is a town on the north shore of Lake Huron, 136 km southeast of Sault Ste Marie. The first sawmill was built in 1853 and lumbering was important until 1969. More recently, uranium mining nearby and tourism have helped the local economy. In 1986 the population of Blind River was 3553. For information, contact the Town Clerk, 11 Hudson Street, P.O. Box 640, Blind River, Ont., P0R 1B0.

■ Blindness

Blindness generally means that a person has 10% or less of normal vision. At least 60 000 Canadians are blind. By far the major cause of blindness is disease. The most common, accounting for some 40% of all cases, is degeneration of the centre of the retina, called the *macula*. Much of this degeneration is caused by aging or hardening of the arteries. Diabetes mellitus may cause the blood vessels nourishing the retina to become fragile and prone to bleed.

Glaucoma is a disease in which pressure builds up in the eye, damaging the optic nerve. Cataracts are a clouding of the lens of the eye. Blindness occurs if the lens becomes opaque. A much smaller number of people are blinded by injuries, such as blows to the head, cuts, infections, and burns.

Sharpness of vision deteriorates with age in all people. Degeneration of the macula cannot, as yet, be treated. However, many of the other causes of blindness can be prevented or treated. Glaucoma is treated with eye drops. Cataracts can be removed with surgery. Injuries can be prevented by the use of protective glasses or masks.

In Canada, the Canadian National Institute for the Blind (CNIB) and other agencies provide services for the blind. Some blind students attend special classes, but most attend regular schools and

Mary Blakeslee Describes her Work
"My main purpose in writing for children is to entertain — to bring the joy that only reading can bring into their lives. Many of my books have underlying themes that probably could be considered to have a 'moral' — it's stupid to lie, friends are more important than material things, that sort of thing. But I don't make an effort to incorporate this into my writing. It just happens."

universities. With the help of braille and tape recordings, they train to be lawyers, engineers, etc. Information on blindness can be obtained from any of the 55 CNIB local offices. Another source of information is the CNIB Sherman Swift Reference Library, 1929 Bayview Avenue, Toronto, Ont., M4G 3E8.

▷ RELATED ARTICLES: **Edwin Albert Baker; Sir C.F. Fraser.**

■ Blizzard

A blizzard, according to Canadian weather officials, is a snowstorm that lasts at least four hours, with temperatures less than -10°C, wind speeds greater than 40 km/h, and visibility less than 1 km. Blizzards block roads with drifting snow and kill animals and people with extreme windchill. Like most weather systems in Canada, they tend to sweep across the country from west to east. They may occur almost anywhere, but are most severe and frequent in the Prairie and Maritime provinces and in the lee of the Great Lakes.

▷ RELATED ARTICLES: **Climate and Man; Precipitation; Wind.**

■ Bloc populaire canadien

The Bloc populaire canadien began in September 1942, as an alliance of Quebec nationalist politicians who opposed conscription (compulsory military service). At the federal level in Ottawa, several members of Parliament supported the Bloc, but it was most successful in Quebec where members formed a third party. Led by journalist André Laurendeau, the party elected several members to the legislature. It ceased to exist in 1949.

■ Bloore, Ronald

Painter (*born in 1925 at Brampton, Ont.*). Bloore changed the art scene in Regina by teaching and exhibiting abstract art. In 1960 he organized an exhibition of five artists, including himself, called the Regina Five. Their work had a lasting effect on painting in the West. Bloore often creates

Blue Rodeo Bazil Donovan, Bob Wiseman, Greg Keelor, Mark French, and Jim Cuddy (courtesy The Artist Consulting Team Inc.).

a texture on the surface of his canvasses. This helps his muted colours come alive through the play of light and shadow.

■ Blue Jay, *see* Jay

■ Blue Rodeo

Blue Rodeo is a popular music band made up of Robert Wiseman (piano, organ; *born in 1961 at Winnipeg*), Greg Keelor (vocals, guitar, songwriter; *born in 1954 at Toronto*), James Cuddy (vocals, guitar, songwriter; *born in 1955 at Toronto*), Mark French (drums; *born in 1958 at Toronto*), and Bazil Donovan (bass; *born in 1955 at Halifax*). The band was formed in 1984 by Keelor and Cuddy and made its name performing in Toronto. Its first album, *Outskirts* (1987), sold over 200 000 copies, and its first single, "Try," went gold. Appearances in the United States and Europe have helped spread its popularity beyond Canada, where it has won numerous awards. The band has its own blend of country, rock, and jazz. Its second album, *Diamond Mine*, was released in 1989.

■ Bluebell

Bluebell is the common name for several plants with blue, bell-shaped flowers. These plants belong either to the Boraginaceae family or the Campanulaceae family. The best-known Canadian species is the *Campanula rotundifolia*, which is found from the Yukon to the Atlantic Provinces. It earns its name "bluebell" from the shape of its flowers, which hang from a long stalk. As the stalk is flattened and twisted under the flowers, they flutter at the slightest breeze. Moreover, this plant grows in very windy areas, such as cliffs and gravelly beaches. If the bells of the bluebell really rang, the areas they colonize would be deafening!

When the plant is in fruit, these frantic movements help to spread the tiny and numerous seeds, sometimes into places where only the most experienced climbers can venture. Some seeds manage to colonize still-open rock crevasses. Despite their delicate appearance, bluebells can withstand the roughest weather. They survive in spots which apparently have no soil, thanks to their ability to reach into the tiniest crack. The plant contains a milky, sour juice. Add some alum to the juice of bluebells and you will have ink — of a lovely green colour! Several species of annuals, biennials, and perennials are cultivated as ornamental flowers.

Blueberry (artwork by Claire Tremblay).

Blueberry

The blueberry (*Vaccinium*) belongs to the heath family (Ericaceae). These are shrubs, with alternating, non-notched leaves, which are quite small and thick. Blueberries flourish in vast, uninhabited regions, especially in areas of boreal forest which have been thinned by forest fires. These inaccessible blueberries are not lost, since bears, birds, squirrels, and other animals eat them, not to mention bees, which gather nectar from the flowers.

The big, cultivated blueberries come primarily from New Jersey, where a large species, the highbush blueberry (*V. corrymbosum*), has been improved for commercial purposes. In Quebec, the Lac Saint-Jean region has boasted so much about its blueberries ("It only takes three to make a pie") that people from the area call themselves "blueberries from Lac Saint-Jean." The quantity of wild fruit varies from year to year, depending on the thickness of snow the preceding winter. As is the case with various fruit shrubs, old branches produce little. During a winter with little snow, the branches which protrude from the snow freeze. Fire can work an even more effective rejuvenation — assuming, of course, that the shrub survives it. The native people gathered blueberries widely and knew how to preserve them (without sugar or refrigeration) through a slow drying process.

Bluebird

Bluebirds belong to the Turdidae (thrush) subfamily of birds. Three species are found in Canada: the eastern bluebird (*Sialia sialis*), the western bluebird (*Sialia mexicana*), and the mountain bluebird (*Sialia currucoides*). They can be distinguished from other species of thrush by the bluish cast to their head, back, tail, and wings. They are a little larger than the house sparrow.

Bluebirds live on a wide variety of insects. They nest in holes in trees or fenceposts, or use human-built birdhouses. The parents take turns sitting on the four, five, or six eggs for the incubation period of 13 or 14 days. Both eastern and western bluebirds choose open woods, farms, and orchards. Their population has dropped sharply; the bluebird is more timid than the house sparrow or starling and tends to yield nesting spots to them. People can help save this lovely bird by providing it with birdhouses. The mountain bluebird lives above 1500 m in high-altitude fields and meadows, and winters in the United States.

Blue-green Algae

Blue-green algae are usually aquatic organisms. They were long thought to be true algae, but certain cell characteristics cause them now to be placed in the Monera kingdom, along with bacteria. Unlike bacteria, however, blue-green algae can *photosynthesize* their food and release oxygen. They appeared at least 3 billion years ago and may be the first organism in the atmosphere to produce oxygen. Blue-green algae are found in widely differing habitats: on desert rocks, on the bark of trees, in mud, in salt and fresh water, in hotsprings, and in frigid settings such as mountain lakes and snow. In warm, nutrient-rich waters, the algae can multiply so rapidly as to cause a phenomenon known as "bloom." Some species are resistant to drought and are able to live a slowed-down life for dozens of years. They are very useful when present in soil, for they can transform gaseous nitrogen into the nitrates that the plants need. Blue-green algae form close partnerships with other organisms, such as fungi, mosses, and animals, for which they supply nitrogen.

Bluenose

The *Bluenose* was Canada's most famous sailing ship and the pride of Nova Scotia. It was designed by William J. Roue to recover the International Fisherman's Trophy, which was lost to an American ship in 1920. Unlike other sailing races, both the ships and the crew members had to have fished one full season on the Grand Banks.

Bluenose was launched at Lunenburg in 1921. Angus Walters, who had started going to sea at age 13, took over as captain. The first race was held on a 65 km course off Halifax in October 1921. *Bluenose* defeated the American ship *Elsie* handily. The victory was trumpeted in Nova Scotia and across Canada.

In 1922 *Bluenose* lost the first race to *Henry Ford*, but recovered to win the next two. *Bluenose* defended the trophy in 1923. Its only defeat was to the Boston schooner *Gertrude L. Thebaud* in the Lipton Cup in 1930. However, *Bluenose* outraced the *Thebaud* in the Fisherman's Trophy the following year. The rematch did not take place until 1938 and it was *Bluenose*'s last race. In a best of five, *Bluenose* broke a mast and lost the first race. It won the second and third races to lead 2-1, but *Thebaud* won the fourth to tie the series. The fifth and last race ever took place on October 26. *Bluenose* won

Eastern Bluebirds are timid and yield their nesting spots to aggressive sparrows and starlings (Macmillan Illustrated Animal Encyclopedia).

Breeding Range of:
Eastern Bluebird
Western Bluebird

Breeding Range of:
Mountain Bluebird

Bluenose was Canada's most famous racing ship of any era (courtesy Wilfred Eisnor, Knickle's Studio & Gallery).

Captain Angus Walters is celebrated here on a 37¢ stamp, which also shows the famous Bluenose, which he led to victory (courtesy Canada Post Corporation).

"going away," finishing almost three hours ahead of its rival.

Bluenose came to a sad end. Walters sold it to a West Indies trading company in 1942. It hit a reef and sank off Haiti in 1946. *Bluenose*'s races captured the imagination of Canadians and are a source of pride to Nova Scotians. Its profile appears on the Canadian 10¢ piece. A replica, *Bluenose II*, was built in the same shipyards in Lunenburg in 1963. It sails out of Halifax harbour, bringing back memories of the golden age of the sailing ship.

■ **BNA Act**

BNA Act is the popular name for the British North America Act of 1867, now called the Constitution Act, 1867. *See* **Constitution Act, 1867.**

■ **Boas, Franz**

Anthropologist, folklorist (*born in 1858 at Minden, Germany; died in 1942 at New York City, U.S.*). When Boas arrived in North America, the study of anthropology was still in its early stages. He, more than any other individual, shaped the direction anthropology would take both in Canada and the United States.

Boas began his career by living among the Inuit of Baffin Island (1883-84). He then switched his interest to Indians on the Northwest Coast. This fieldwork convinced him that the best way to study anthropology was to observe and record the whole culture of a particular group of people — their language, food, clothing, tools, housing, transportation, social organization, art, myths, and religious beliefs. Each culture was distinctive, and it was culture, not race, that explained the basic differences among human beings.

Boas joined the American Museum of Natural History in 1895. In 1899 he be-

Bluenose II is a reconstruction of the original schooner. It is shown here at its berth in Halifax (photo by J.H. Marsh).

Range of Bobcat

came the first professor of anthropology at Columbia University, a post he held for 37 years. Most of his fieldwork was done in Canada, and he contributed more to our knowledge of Northwest Coast groups than any other individual. Many of the men and women who worked with him, including Edward Sapir in Canada and Margaret Mead in the U.S., went on to have illustrious careers of their own in anthropology. In the 1930s the Nazis in Germany burned one of his books, *The Mind of Primitive Man*, because it conflicted with their theories of race. The same book was used to support the civil rights movement in the U.S. during the 1950s.

▷ RELATED ARTICLES: **Anthropology; Edward Sapir.**

■ Boat People

Boat people were refugees uprooted from Vietnam, Laos, and Cambodia in the aftermath of the Vietnam War. They escaped in overcrowded ships in the late 1970s and early 1980s. About 75 000 found new homes in Canada. Most arrived under a "matching" program by which the government brought in one refugee for each refugee who was privately sponsored by a group or individual.

Across Canada, many community groups, churches, schools, and other groups of people joined together to raise money for the Boat People, which helped to bring them to Canada and to give them the support they needed on arrival.

▷ RELATED ARTICLES: **Ethnic Group; Indochinese; Refugees.**

■ Bobcat

A member of the Felidae (cat) family, the bobcat (*Lynx rufus*) can reach 1 m and weigh from 6.4 to 18 kg. The bobcat can be distinguished from the lynx by its smaller feet, barred tail, and shorter tufts on its ears. Bobcats live farther south than the lynx, in scrubland, open forests, swamps, thickets, agricultural land, and even areas close to cities. The bobcat is a solitary animal. It lives primarily on hare and rabbit but will also eat squirrels, shrews, mice, birds, and sometimes deer. It has a distinctive way of hunting, lying in wait for its prey, hidden in the brush, or occasionally in lower branches of a tree overhanging a path. It usually hunts at night, alone, and is active all winter. Trappers value the bobcat for its fur. Other enemies include the cougar, coyote, and wolf. Sometimes the red fox and the great horned owl will attack bobcat

Bobcat is so-named for its "bobbed" tail. It lives in southern Canada in woodlands, farmlands, and thickets (artwork by Jan Sovak).

young. The kittens (usually two or three) are usually born between late April and mid-May. Gestation lasts 50 to 70 days. The bobcat helps control the population of small rodents. It lives 12 to 15 years. Bobcats may purr or mew, like the domestic house cat.

■ Bobsledding

Bobsledding is a winter sport in which a sled races down a course of ice with sharp turns and steep curves. The sled may reach dangerously high speeds of up to 150 km/h. The crew (two or four people) must be strong in order to push the heavy sled from a dead start at the top of the course.

The first Canadian bobsled team entered competition in 1959. Although there was nowhere in Canada to practise, a Canadian team won the gold medal here. The team was made up of Victor and John Emery, Douglas Anakin, and Peter Kirby. The Emerys also won the world championship in 1965.

Luge Luge racing began in 1879. The

Bobsled on the track during the 1988 Olympic Games at Calgary, Alta (photo by Rick Rudnicki/ Take Stock Inc.).

luge sled is smaller than a bobsled. The rider lies on his or her back and slides down the course feet first, reaching speeds of up to 135 km/h. There are sleds for one or two riders. Canada first competed internationally in luge in 1964. In 1983, Czech-born Miroslav Zajonc, racing for Canada, won the world luge championship.

A world-class bobsled and luge run was built at Calgary for the 1988 Olympic Games.

■ Bodsworth, Frederick

Writer (*born in 1918 at Port Burwell, Ont.*). After working for newspapers and for *Maclean's*, Bodsworth became a freelance writer, specializing in articles about nature. He is also a naturalist who has led many bird-watching tours.

Bodsworth's major theme, that "man is an inescapable part of all nature," is evident in his first novel, *Last of the Curlews* (1954). It alternates fiction and non-fiction. Fictional chapters trace the life of the last two Eskimo curlews. Non-fictional chapters document how men, for no reason at all, slaughtered these once-abundant birds.

■ Boer War

The Boer War (1899-1902) was a war in southern Africa, in which Canadian forces fought for the British. *See* **South African War.**

■ Bomarc Missile Crisis

A controversy over whether Canada's Bomarc anti-aircraft missiles should be armed with nuclear weapons led to the defeat of John Diefenbaker's government in 1963. The government had agreed to purchase Bomarcs from the United States in 1958. The missiles needed nuclear warheads to be effective, but some members of Diefenbaker's Cabinet were opposed to nuclear weapons. Diefenbaker refused to make a decision, and in early 1963 the government broke apart over the issue. An election followed. Diefenbaker narrowly lost, and the new prime minister, Lester B. Pearson, immediately accepted nuclear warheads. Bomarcs were in service in Canada until 1971.

■ Bombardier, Joseph Armand

Inventor of the snowmobile (*born in 1907 at Valcourt, Que.; died in 1964 at Sherbrooke, Que.*). In 1922 when Bombardier was 15, he designed, built, and tested his first snow vehicle. It had a propeller at the rear and looked very unlike the modern snowmobile. Working in a garage on his father's farm, Bombardier improved the design over the years, substituting a drive wheel and track at the rear while using skis at the front for steering. By the late 1930s he was selling these vehicles, which included a type of snow bus.

As the years passed, Bombardier invented and produced a variety of other snow vehicles. In 1959 he produced the first model of the Ski-Doo, the motorbike of snow machines. From the first, the Ski-Doo was immensely popular. In the North, it offered the Inuit far wider freedom of travel; and it provided southern Canadians with a new sport.

Exhibits of Bombardier's many inventions, together with documents and illustrations, may be viewed at the J. Armand Bombardier Museum in Valcourt, Que.
▷ RELATED ARTICLES: **Invention; Snowmobile.**

■ Bonavista

Bonavista is one of the oldest towns in North America. It is situated on the east coast of Newfoundland, at the tip of the Bonavista Peninsula. Cape Bonavista, in the northeastern part of the town, was likely the point of land first sighted by John Cabot in 1497. The town was settled by English fishermen in the late 1500s. Bonavista is still entirely dependent on fishing. A modern plant processes fish caught by longliners and inshore fishermen. In 1986 the population was 4605. For information, contact the Town Clerk, P.O. Box 279, Bonavista, Nfld, A0C 1B0.

■ Bonavista Bay

Bonavista Bay is a broad inlet on the Atlantic coast of Newfoundland. It is about 65 km across, from Cape Freels in the north to Cape Bonavista in the south. Fishing for lobster and cod is the most important activity in the villages which lie around its rugged shoreline. Terra Nova National Park is located on Bonavista Bay. Six of Canada's nine species of seal, as well as pilot whales, are among the bay's wildlife.

■ Bond, Sir Robert

Politician (*born in 1857 at St John's, Nfld; died in 1927 at Whitbourne, Nfld*). During his career in Newfoundland politics Bond supported the trans-island railway and economic independence, and was involved in Confederation negotiations with Canada.

Bond was a lawyer who was first elected to the House of Assembly in 1882 as a Liberal. In 1889 Bond was appointed to the important office of Colonial Secre-

J.A. Bombardier was the inventor of the snowmobile (artwork by Irma Coucill).

tary. In this position he negotiated the Bond-Blaine Treaty to increase trade with the U.S., but this fell through when Canada objected.

With Newfoundland in the midst of a severe financial crisis, Bond went to both Britain and Canada for financial help. In Canada he discussed entering the Canadian confederation but, dissatisfied with the terms offered, he borrowed money in Britain instead. The Liberals were briefly out of power again, but Bond became premier in 1900.

As premier, Bond continued his unsuccessful trade negotiations with the U.S., negotiations with the Newfoundland railway, and the dispute over the French Shore, which was settled in 1904. He failed to receive a majority in a tie election in 1908 and resigned as premier in 1909. He retired from politics in 1914.

■ Bonhomme, *see* Folklore

■ Book Awards
Each year, many awards are presented to outstanding Canadian authors and their books.

The most prestigious of these are the Governor General's Literary Awards. Seven awards in English and seven in French are given, one in each of the following categories: children's literature (illustration), children's literature (text), translation, nonfiction, poetry, drama, and fiction. The winners receive a copy of their books, specially bound by a master bookbinder, and $10 000.

The awards were first given in 1937 for the year 1936. At that time only two prizes were awarded, for English fiction and nonfiction. A prize for poetry or drama was added the next year, and a separate category for drama was created in 1981. French awards have been given since 1959. From 1949 to 1958, a prize for juvenile literature was given. In 1988, the awards for children's literature were first presented.

Of the many prizes given to English-Canadian children's books and authors, the Governor General's Awards and two prizes of the Canadian Library Association are most important. From 1975 to 1986, the Governor General's Awards were known as the Canada Council Children's Literature Prizes. The first winner was Bill Freeman, for *Shantymen of Cache Lake*. Beginning in 1978, two prizes were awarded, one for writing and one for illustration. Only three people, Marie-Louise Gay, Laszlo Gal, and Monica Hughes have won two Canada Council/Governor General's Awards in these categories.

Since 1947, the Canadian Library Association has presented a bronze medal (CLA Award) to the author of the best English-Canadian children's book. The first award was given to Roderick Haig-Brown for *Starbuck Valley Winter*. He won again in 1964 for *The Whale People*. James Houston has won the prize three times. Other double winners have been Christie Harris, William Toye, Dennis Lee, and Janet Lunn.

The Canadian Library Association also awards the Amelia Frances Howard-Gibbon Medal for the best English-Canadian illustrated book of the year. The first award was presented in 1971 to Elizabeth Cleaver for *The Wind Has Wings*. She has won the award twice, as have William Kurelek, Ken Nutt, and Marie-Louise Gay.

Three books have won both the Canada Council/Governor General's and CLA awards: Jan Hudson's *Sweetgrass*, Cora Taylor's *Julie*, and Marie-Louise Gay's *Rainy Day Magic*.

Another important book award to Canadian children's authors is the Vicky Metcalf Award, given annually since 1963 to a person who has written at least three excellent books for children.

■ Book Publishing
Books are an ancient invention and are still the most convenient way to store and present the written word. Books were produced at least 4000 years ago in Egypt. These ancient books were written on *papyrus*, from which we get our word "paper." The long pieces of papyrus were rolled up in scrolls. Scrolls were used by the Greeks and Romans and continued in use until about 300 AD, when the papyrus was replaced by parchment, which could be cut into sheets and sewed together along the fold. This method of folding and sewing is still used today.

All the early books were copied out by hand. They were therefore rare and very expensive. The Chinese made the first printed book in 868 AD. They carved each page from a block of wood. By spreading ink on the block and pressing paper to the ink, they could make many copies. Many years later, this system was invented separately in Europe during the 1300s. The Chinese also invented *movable type*, in which each letter is carved into a separate piece of metal. Printers can arrange the type to produce the text, and make many

Booksellers
The value of books sold in Canada every year is over $1.3 billion. Most are sold through bookstores, though many are sold through the mail or door to door.

There are two main categories of books: educational (textbooks), and general, or *trade*, books, which include everything from novels and cookbooks to self-help manuals.

About 70% of English-language books in Canada come from the U.S. Canadian books account for only 20%; the others are mostly British.

Much of the power of bookselling is in the hands of large chains, which offer discounts that independent booksellers cannot match. The independent booksellers usually offer the widest variety of books as well as the largest selection of books published in Canada.

Publishing a Book

A book begins as an idea, which may have come from an author, a publisher, or an agent. After, a writer will prepare a manuscript and send it to a publisher, who decides whether or not to publish it. Frequently, a writer must send an outline, chapter, or entire manuscript to one publisher after another before one accepts it. Once the decision is made, author and publisher sign a contract. The publisher undertakes to pay to produce and sell the book. The author usually receives a *royalty*, or payment, of about 10% of each sale.

Editors deal with the author, suggesting improvements, editing for spelling and grammar, and checking the facts.

A designer chooses the typeface, paper, and cover. Most type is now set by computer and is sent to a printer along with illustrations.

Books are marketed in a similar way to other products. The publisher determines the number of copies to be printed and the selling price. Books are advertised in newspapers, magazines, and in book stores. Larger publishing houses have sales representatives who visit the booksellers. Despite a great deal of experience, publishers seldom know which books will succeed and which will fail.

Courses in book publishing are offered at the Banff Centre, Simon Fraser University, and Ryerson and Centennial College in Toronto.

copies. The first books printed in Europe by movable type appeared in the 1450s. The sheets were printed by pressing the type against the paper, hence the modern word printing "press." Printing spread throughout Europe by 1500, the eve of the discovery of the New World. By the time Samuel de Champlain produced accounts of his travels in New France, after 1610, books looked much like they do today.

Book production was revolutionized by inventions during the 19th century. Machines set type and steam-powered presses printed large numbers of copies at lower prices. Canadians played a part in these developments. For example, W.A. Leggo and G.E. Desbarats of Montreal played important roles in inventing a method to print photographs.

Book publishing began in Canada in the mid-18th century when newspaper and government printing offices were set up. Among the first publishers were William Brown and Thomas Gilmore, who set up a press in Quebec City and published a newspaper, the *Quebec Gazette*. They also published a school primer, books on the law, and a volume of poetry. In Kingston, Upper Canada, Hugh Thomson published the first book of fiction by a Canadian-born author, *St. Ursula's Convent* (1824), by Julia Beckwith Hart. In Halifax, N.S., Joseph Howe published *The Clockmaker* (1836), by Thomas Haliburton. The book sold rapidly in the United States and Great Britain, as well as Nova Scotia. Haliburton was the first Canadian author to achieve international success.

During the 19th century most books were imported from Britain, the U.S., and France. Children had to attend school, by law, which increased the need for textbooks. In Quebec, the church was responsible for education and also controlled the production of textbooks. The earliest English school books were imported from the U.S. or Britain. Ontario began to produce its own readers in the 1880s. In a pattern that has been repeated to the present day, many of these early texts were Canadian versions of foreign books.

Publishing expanded greatly in the period from 1880 to 1914. Numerous new publishing houses were founded, including University of Toronto Press (1901), Oxford University Press (1904), Macmillan of Canada (1905), and McClelland and Goodchild (1906, later McClelland and Stewart). The industry suffered from poor sales in the Great Depression of the 1930s.

World War II led to a turning point in Quebec publishing. Germany defeated France in 1940 and many French writers fled to Montreal. New publishing houses sprang up, and 21 million books came off the Montreal presses between 1940 and 1946.

The years after World War II were difficult for publishers in both English and French Canada. A flood of cheap British and American paperbacks hit Canada. Canadian publishers struggled to gain a share of the growing school market.

By the 1960s a new era of literature emerged in French and English Canada. The growth of publishing and the emergence of writers such as Marie-Claire Blais, Michel Tremblay, Margaret Laurence, Margaret Atwood, and Leonard Cohen went hand in hand. Farley Mowat wrote bestsellers about the Canadian wilderness, and Pierre Berton about Canadian history. In Quebec, publishers played a major role in the new development of ideas that is called the Quiet Revolution.

Most of the publishing industry today is centered in Toronto and Montreal. In the 1960s and 1970s numerous new publishers were set up across the country; for example, Fiddlehead Books in Fredericton, N.B.; Western Producer Prairie Books in Saskatoon, Sask.; Hurtig Publishers in Edmonton, Alta; and Douglas & McIntyre in Vancouver, B.C. There were also dramatic changes in the way books were produced, with metal type being replaced by computers.

The publishing industry accounts for about $1.4 billion in sales each year in Canada. Nevertheless, it faces serious problems. The market in Canada is small compared to Britain, the U.S., or France, and books from these places compete in the Canadian market. Furthermore, the market in Canada is dominated by foreign-owned publishers. In Quebec, publishers based in France bought out a leading chain of book stores in the province and tried to force all Quebec stores to buy French books only from them. Despite these problems, Canadian-owned publishers continued to produce the majority of new books written by Canadians.

By 1970 the problems of the Canadian-owned companies were serious. Ryerson Press, one of the oldest and largest Canadian firms, was sold to an American company in 1970. McClelland and Stewart, the most important publisher of Canadian literature, was deep in debt. Government inquiries were held both in Quebec and Ontario, and both provinces promised aid to its publishers. The federal government and the Canada Council also provided support. Nevertheless, the Canadian publishing industry is still dominated by foreign companies that continue to take most of the profits from the sale of books while devoting only a small percentage to publishing books by Canadian writers.

▷ RELATED ARTICLES: **Bookselling; Printing Industry**.

▷ SUGGESTED READING: Douglas C. McMurtrie, *The Book* (1943).

■ Bookkeeping, *see* Accounting

■ Booth, John Rudolphus

Lumberman, railway builder (*born in 1827 near Waterloo, Lower Canada [Quebec]; died in 1925 at Ottawa, Ont.*). Booth came to Ottawa at the age of 21 with $9 in his pocket. He had worked as a carpenter and labourer, but in a short time he proved himself a keen and honest businessman.

Booth convinced the banks to lend him money on the strength of his reputation. He leased a small shingle mill and went on to build the biggest timber empire in the Ottawa Valley. One of his major contracts was for supplying lumber to the new Parliament Buildings in Ottawa.

At the height of his career, Booth controlled 10 000 km² of forest land and employed 4000 men. He built a railway to carry his timber from his Georgian Bay camps to his Ottawa mills, and to take finished lumber to the United States. Canada Atlantic Railway, over 1000 km long, was the largest railway ever financed by one man.

Unlike most of the timber barons of his day, Booth was concerned that wasteful cutting methods were ruining the pine forests. He was one of the founders of the Canadian Forestry Association, which advocated proper forest management. Unfortunately, these efforts came too late. The last square timber pine raft came down the Ottawa River from Booth's Coulonge River camps in 1908.

Booth lived to be almost 100. In old age, this short old gentleman, with a white beard and sparkling eyes, could be seen on the streets of Ottawa or out in the woods, inspecting the lumber camps that had made him rich and famous.

■ Boothia Peninsula

The Boothia Peninsula (32 300 km²) is the most northerly point of mainland North America. A desolate, treeless peninsula about 250 km long, it is named for Sir Fe-

lix Booth, a British distiller who financed an expedition to the area in 1829. There is an airfield at Spence Bay on the west coast. Residents rely on carving, and on traditional fishing, hunting, and trapping.

■ Borden, Sir Robert Laird

Robert Borden was prime minister of Canada during the difficult years of World War I. He was a reluctant politician. Several times during his 19 years as leader of the Conservative Party, he came close to retiring and returning to the private life of lawyer and businessman. But he was an effective leader, who is best remembered for his success at gaining an independent status for Canada in world affairs.

Legal Career Robert Borden was raised on a farm in rural Nova Scotia. He briefly taught school before becoming a lawyer in Halifax. His legal practice grew, and by the 1890s it was the largest in the Maritimes. Borden himself was one of Halifax's leading citizens.

Sir Robert Laird Borden
8TH PRIME MINISTER OF CANADA

Born: June 26, 1854, Grand Pré, N.S.
Died: June 10, 1937, Ottawa, Ont.
Political Party: Conservative
First Elected: 1896
Chosen Leader: 1901
Period as Prime Minister: October 10, 1911, to July 10, 1920
(PHOTO COURTESY NAC/C-81453).

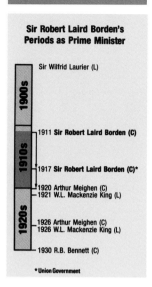

In 1896 Prime Minister Sir Charles Tupper convinced Borden to run in the upcoming federal election as a Conservative. Though Borden won, his party did not. He went to Ottawa as a member of the opposition to Wilfrid Laurier's Liberal government.

Borden was not ambitious for power. There was much about politics that he did not like. But he was quick to learn the issues, and he handled himself well in debate. After just four years, the Conservatives chose him to lead their party.

Leader of the Opposition As leader of the opposition, Borden promoted two main policies. One was "clean government." He wanted to end the system of patronage by which the Liberals appointed their friends to government jobs. He argued that public officials should be hired on merit.

Secondly, Borden believed that the government should own large enterprises, such as railways, which were of crucial importance to the country. The government should also provide essential services, such as telephones and electricity. At the time, these were considered new ideas. Later they were adopted by other governments.

In 1911 Laurier's government struck a deal with the Americans to bring free trade between the two countries. Borden opposed the deal, arguing it would draw Canada too close to the United States. Free trade was the main issue in that year's election, an election won by Borden's Conservatives.

PRIME MINISTER

World War I Borden's time as prime minister was overshadowed by the Great War which broke out in 1914. The country was divided over the conduct of the war. Most English-speaking people supported Canada's participation in the war. They believed that Canada had a duty to support Great Britain. For them, the ties to the British Empire were strong and binding. Many French Canadians, on the other hand, had no strong ties to Britain or to France. Many of their leaders were against taking part in a dispute that did not concern them.

By 1917, the war had lasted longer than anyone had thought possible. It had claimed many thousands of lives and Borden was persuaded that Canadian forces fighting in Europe could not be kept up to strength without conscription. Conscription would mean that many men who had not volunteered would be forced to join

the army, and it raised a storm of protest in Quebec. Borden invited Laurier to join a coalition government to last the war, but the Liberal leader refused. He vehemently opposed conscription. However, many of Laurier's followers in English Canada deserted their leader and joined the coalition, called the Union Government. In the election that followed, Borden's Unionists won a strong victory.

Peace When the war ended, Borden took part in the peace conference in France. He convinced Great Britain to allow Canada to sign the treaty separately and to have its own seat at the League of Nations, formed in 1919. These were important steps on Canada's path to full independence from Britain.

Resignation The post-war world was filled with turmoil. An epidemic of labour unrest swept the country. The government answered with laws banning radical groups. It sent in troops to break up the Winnipeg General Strike in 1919. By this time Borden was withdrawing from the day-to-day business of government. He was ill and spent much of his time out of the country. Finally, in July 1920, he resigned as prime minister. He was succeeded by Arthur Meighen, who tried but failed to preserve the coalition.

Borden devoted his retirement to his business affairs, to supporting the League of Nations, and to writing his memoirs.

▷ RELATED ARTICLES: **Conscription; League of Nations; Union Government.**

▷ SUGGESTED READING: John English, *Borden: His Life and World* (1977); Kathleen Saunders, *Robert Borden* (1978).

■ Borduas, Paul-Émile

Painter (*born in 1905 at St-Hilaire, Que.; died in 1960 at Paris, France*). Borduas had a great influence in the development of modern art in Canada. He also played an important role in changing the way people in the province of Quebec thought about art.

Borduas had little formal education. He trained as a church decorator with the artist Ozias Leduc in St-Hilaire and studied in Paris, France, from 1928 to 1930. In 1937 he became a teacher in a Montreal art college, École du Meuble. He painted in a very traditional style until 1942 when he developed strong new ideas about painting. Like most modern painters in Europe at the time, he came to believe that an artist must be more concerned with the act of painting itself than merely with painting some particular object. Borduas became more interested in the pow-

Black Star (1957) is the kind of abstract painting Borduas fought to have accepted. What interested him was not that a painting look like a photograph but that it explore the power of shapes and colour on the canvas (courtesy Montreal Museum of Fine Arts).

er of colours and shapes on the canvas than with trying to paint the likeness of a person or landscape. This view brought him into conflict with the church and government in Quebec.

Borduas and several of his students formed a group, known as the Automatistes because of their attempts to paint "automatically" in a dream-like trance. Borduas and his group argued that each artist must be free to express his or her art in their own way — not just in a way that was acceptable to the church or other parts of society. In 1948, the group published their views in a pamphlet called *Refus global*. Borduas was severely criticized and was fired from his teaching job.

Borduas moved to New York in 1953 where he was excited by the bold, vibrant work of modern American painters. He moved on to Paris but was lonely and unhappy there. He dreamed of returning to Canada but he died suddenly in Paris in 1960. Borduas's last and most famous paintings were powerful, large canvasses in which simple black areas of thick paint contrasted with areas of white.

■ Boreal Forest
The boreal forest is a broad and vast band of coniferous trees that circles the northern hemisphere.

The word "boreal" comes from the name of "Boreas," who personified the north wind in Greek myth. The Russian word "taiga" is another term for this forest region. Canada has 2.5 million square km of boreal forest, more than any other nation except for the Soviet Union. Canada's boreal forest stretches in an unbroken carpet of green from Alaska to the Atlantic coast. The majority of the trees in Canada's boreal forest are white and black spruces, mixed with broadleaved trees such as white birch and balsam poplar. From these trees comes the wood used to make pulp and paper, lumber, and other forest products. The boreal forest is Canada's most important commercial forest region.

▷ RELATED ARTICLES: **Forest; Forest Industry; Natural Regions.**

Boreal Forest covers 2.5 million km² of Canada (photo by Thomas Kitchin).

■ Botanical Garden
Botanical gardens are museums of living plants. They are wonderful places to learn about the world of plants and their importance to mankind. The gardens are distinct from parks or public gardens (for example, Butchart Gardens, B.C.) in that they contain collections of plants identified and organized to make education, research, and display easier. A botanical garden usually consists of smaller gardens, often organized along thematic lines: perennial plants, aquatic plants, plants with medicinal properties, alpine plants, roses, etc. The trees, bushes and shrubs are found in a section called the arboretum. Greenhouses protect plants that could not withstand the natural climate. For example, the only way to recreate a tropical forest with orchids is in a controlled climate with the necessary heat and humidity. The team of professionals working in a botanical garden includes botanists, horticulturalists (or gardeners), landscape architects, display artists, etc.

The early herbal or physic gardens were created by doctors and students of medicine to grow plants having medicinal or

Dr Sun Yat-Sen Classical Chinese Garden, Vancouver.

pharmaceutical properties. The first botanical garden directly devoted to the study of plants was created in Pisa, Italy, in 1543. In Canada we had to wait until 1861, when George Dawson founded our first botanical garden, attached to Queen's College, in Kingston, Ontario. However, it closed again in the 1870s. In 1887, the Central Experimental Farm in Ottawa opened an arboretum and botanical garden, primarily for research into the ability of plants to withstand cold. Ontario also contains the arboretum (founded in 1970) of the University of Guelph, and the Royal Botanical Gardens.

The Jardin botanique de Montréal, which was founded in 1931, is considered one of the most beautiful in the world. It contains more than 26 000 cultivated species. It consists of 17 theme gardens, including a Japanese one, and display greenhouses showing vegetative diversity ranging from cacti to orchids. The Morgan Arboretum of MacDonald College (McGill University) boasts an imposing collection of native trees. In Vancouver, in 1916, John Davidson founded a botanical garden affiliated with the University of British Columbia. The Ross Arboretum in Saskatchewan specializes in the development of prairie-adapted trees, while the Devonian Botanical Garden of the University of Alberta (Edmonton) concentrates on alpine and native plants. The presentation gardens of the Memorial

University Botanical Park, in Oxen Pond, Nfld, include a peat bog, a rock garden, and a garden designed to attract butterflies. Manitoba has a botanical garden attached to its Morden research station. New Brunswick plans to open a botanical garden in 1991.

Botanical gardens play an important role in protecting nature, by preserving rare plants or ones threatened with extinction. To visit a botanical garden is to undertake, through its plants, a trip around the world.

▷ SUGGESTED READING: Eustella Langdon, *Pioneer Gardens at Black Creek Pioneer Village* (1972).

■ Botany

Botany, or plant biology, is the study of plants and plant life. A botanist (plant biologist) may study the tiniest portion of a plant, such as its molecules or cells, or a large community of plants, such as a forest. Some botanists specialize in a particular group of plants, such as grasses, ferns, or weeds.

Palynology is the study of fossil spores and pollen. In Canada this study has helped botanists trace the history of vegetation, from the time that Canada was covered in ice, up to 12 000 years ago, to the present.

Plant Ecology is the study of how the environment affects plant growth. It includes the study of how plants are affected by water, temperature, energy, and minerals, as well as man-made factors, such as acid rain.

Plant Genetics includes the breeding of plants to improve their yield, beauty, flavour, and structure, and their value as medicines. As a result of plant genetics, Canadian botanists have extended the geographical areas over which wheat, corn, and other crops can be grown.

Applications Botanists have broadened the uses of plants to such areas as forestry, horticulture (growing flowers), agriculture, landscape architecture, and wildlife conservation.

PLANT CLASSIFICATION

Scientists divide living things into five kingdoms: Plantae (plants), Animalia (animals), Fungi (fungi), Protista (protozoa), and Monera (bacteria). Plants contain a green pigment, called *chlorophyll*, which converts sunlight into chemical energy. They are therefore one of the few forms of life that produce their own food. Hence, all life on Earth is dependent on green plants as sources of energy and producers of oxygen.

How White-Bark Pine is Classified		
Classification	Name	Description
Kingdom	Plantae	includes all the plants
Division	Spermatophyta	seed plants
Class	Gymnospermae	non-flowering seed plants
Order	Coniferales	evergreen trees in which seeds are held in cones
Family	Pinaceae	the pine family with 10 genera
Genus	*Pinus*	pine tree, of which there are over 80 species
Species	*albicaulis*	meaning "white bark"

There are about 600 000 different kinds of plants on Earth. These are organized in a system that begins with the most general category and is subdivided until it becomes more and more specific. The table shows how white-bark pine is classified.

In everyday life we refer to plants by their "common names," such as white-bark pine. However, these names vary from language to language and are often imprecise. For example, "yellow pine" refers to several different kinds of pine tree. Thus, botanists use scientific names (taken from Latin), consisting of two words. The first word identifies the *genus* and the second the *species*. Thus, white-bark pine is called *Pinus albicaulis*, or *P. albicaulis* for short.

▷ RELATED ARTICLES: **Plant**, and various articles under the names of plants.

■ Botulism, *see* Food Poisoning

■ Boucher, Gaëtan
Speed skater (*born in 1958 at Charlesbourg, Que.*). Boucher won his first Canadian speed-skating championship at age 14. He was 18 when he placed ninth in the 1000 m race in the 1976 Olympic Games. He became world indoor champion the following year and won a silver medal in the 1000 m race in the 1980 Olympics. He suffered a broken ankle in 1983 but recovered to capture two gold medals (in the 1000 m and 1500 m races) and a bronze (500 m) in the 1984 Olympics at Sarajevo. It was the finest performance by any Canadian at any Olympic Games.

■ Bouctouche
Bouctouche, N.B., lies on the shores of Northumberland Strait, 40 km north of Moncton. Acadian refugees settled here in the 1780s and today the people are mainly French speaking. Fishing, logging, and shipbuilding are the important industries. The name is Micmac for "big bay." In 1986 the population was 2420. For information, contact the Greffier, C.P. 370, Bouctouche, N.B., E0A 1G0.

■ Boulet, Gerry
Singer (*born in 1946 at St Jean-d'Iberville, Que.*). During nearly two decades, Gerry Boulet was the demon-like leader of Quebec hard-rock group Offenbach. The group was often controversial. The break-up of Offenbach in the mid-1980s paved the way for a successful solo career for Gerry Boulet. He wrote new songs with the sole help of a beat-box and a desire to trace back to the rhythm and blues roots of his teens. In 1987 Boulet learned that he had cancer. He increased his already frenetic pace and sought the help of friends to contribute lyrics. The result was Boulet's first solo album, *Rendez-Vous Doux*, a mixture of soul, rhythm and blues, and pop that is at once warm and troubling. Boulet's unique voice continues to caress and shake up Quebec rock into the 1990s.

■ Boundary Waters Treaty
In 1909, this treaty between Canada and the United States set up the International Joint Commission to settle questions about rivers and lakes that form the boundary between the two countries. *See* **International Joint Commission**.

■ Bourassa, Henri
Journalist and politician (*born in 1868 at Montreal, Que.; died there in 1952*). He was the grandson of the celebrated leader of the Lower Canadian Rebellion of 1837, Louis-Joseph Papineau.

Bourassa naturally took an early interest in politics. At 22, he was elected mayor of Montebello. He was an early ally of Wilfrid Laurier and was elected Liberal member of Parliament for Labelle when Laurier became prime minister in 1896.

Bourassa spent the next 11 years in Ottawa. Over that period of time he strongly defended the rights of French Canadians in opposition to many in English Canada who saw Canada primarily as part of the British Empire. Bourassa's nationalism was based on 3 principles: the greatest

Henri Bourassa was the leading spokesman for French-Canadian nationalism in his day (courtesy NAC/C-27360).

possible independence for Canada; respect for both French and English traditions; and French Canadians' control of their own economic and intellectual life. Bourassa's nationalist movement gained strong support in Quebec and shaped Canadian political life for the first two decades of the 20th century at least.

Bourassa's position led him into conflict with Laurier. In 1899 English-Canadian demands forced Laurier to agree to send Canadian volunteers to South Africa in support of British efforts to subdue the Afrikaners. Bourassa resigned his seat in protest, but was immediately returned in the subsequent by-election. In 1905 he defended (in vain) the right of the Roman Catholic minority to have separate schools in the newly created provinces of Alberta and Saskatchewan. In 1906 he attacked the immigration policy of the Laurier government that was changing the face of the country. He feared that the newcomers would soon reduce the French Canadians to a minority in Canada, arguing that the country should be primarily Anglo-French.

A disillusioned Bourassa left federal politics in 1907. He was elected to the Quebec National Assembly in 1908. There he passionately attacked the policies of Premier Lomer Gouin's government. In 1912, he quit the Assembly.

Bourassa founded *Le Devoir* in 1910, which was to become one of the most influential newspapers in Quebec. He expressed his nationalist and Roman Catholic views on the pages of this newspaper until 1932. He bitterly opposed Laurier's plan to build a navy in 1910, and argued in support of French schools in Ontario. In 1917, in the middle of World War I, he joined Laurier in opposing military conscription. At the height of his prestige, Bourassa was one of the most influential men in Quebec public life.

During the 1920s, after the horror of the war, many English Canadians began to agree with Bourassa's views on British imperialism. He returned to the House of Commons in 1925, was re-elected in both 1926 and 1930, but was defeated in 1935. He grew ever more religious, lived in seclusion, and took refuge in prayer. His concept of the dual nature of Canada, as both French and English, endures.

▷ RELATED ARTICLES: **Conscription; South African War; French-Canadian Nationalism.**

■ Bourassa, Robert

Premier of Quebec (*born in 1933 at Montreal, Que.*). After studying law in Montreal, and at the universities of Harvard and Oxford, Bourassa became an expert on taxes. Early in the 1960s he worked in Ottawa as a civil servant and as a university professor.

He returned to Quebec and won a seat in the Quebec National Assembly in the provincial elections of 1966 as a member of the Quebec Liberal Party. Bourassa was seen as a calm, passionless, technically competent politician.

He was elected leader of the Quebec Liberal Party in January 1970. During the general elections of April 1970, he promised to create 100 000 jobs and to fight against separatism. His party won a sweeping victory. At 37, he was the youngest-ever premier of Quebec.

In October 1970 the Front de Libération du Québec, a group that was on the fringe of the independence movement, kidnapped British trade commissioner James Cross and Pierre Laporte, Bourassa's right-hand man in the Cabinet. Bourassa turned to Ottawa for help, and troops were sent to Montreal.

Bourassa and his party were re-elected in 1973. He pressed on with the mammoth James Bay hydroelectric project, but grew unpopular. During the election of 1976 his government was accused of corruption and lost badly to the Parti Québécois (PQ), led by René Lévesque. Bourassa lost his seat in the National Assembly.

Robert Bourassa completed one of the most remarkable comebacks in Canadian history. He was out of office from 1976 to 1985, when he returned as premier of Quebec (courtesy Canapress Photo Service).

He spent the next years at universities in Europe and the United States. He returned in 1980 to support the *Non* side in the PQ campaign to negotiate separation from Canada.

Bourassa was re-elected leader of the Quebec Liberal Party in 1983. In 1985 he led his party to a sweeping defeat of the PQ. He personally failed to gain a seat but was soon elected in another riding, completing his remarkable comeback.

During his second term as premier of Quebec, Bourassa played a leading role in negotiating the Meech Lake Accord and strongly supported free trade with the United States.

▷ RELATED ARTICLES: **Meech Lake Accord; October Crisis.**

■ Bourgeois, Paulette

Writer (*born in 1951 in Winnipeg, Man.*). As a child, Bourgeois lived in Winnipeg, Calgary, Ottawa, and Beaconsfield, Que. Above all, she was a reader, by flashlight under the covers when necessary. She has had various careers, including occupational therapist and journalist. The first taught her to listen, the second to re-

search. Both are useful skills for a writer.

Bourgeois's first book, *Franklin in the Dark* (1986), a picture book, features a turtle who discovers that he is not alone in having fears. Her second picture book, *Big Sarah's Little Boots* (1987), is about the disappointments and pleasures of growing bigger. Bourgeois also writes factual books, *On Your Mark, Get Set. . . : All About the Olympic Games, Then and Now* (1987), and two books of projects, games, history, and science, *The Amazing Apple Book* (1987) and *The Amazing Paper Book* (1989).

■ Bourgeoys, Marguerite

Saint of the Roman Catholic Church (*born in 1620 at Troyes, France; died in 1700 at Montreal, New France [Quebec]*). Marguerite Bourgeoys arrived in Montreal in 1653, when it was still a tiny missionary colony called Ville-Marie. She had hoped to be the colony's school teacher, but there were no children of school age when she arrived so she took on whatever jobs were available. Hard working and very religious, she was a strong support in the hard-pressed community.

In 1658 she opened a small school in a stable, the first of several schools she was to start. The following year, she returned from a visit to France with three young women to help her with her work. This was the beginning of the religious order she founded: the Congrégation de Notre-Dame de Montréal. It was the first religious order founded in Canada. The sisters worked among the community and some lived and taught among the native people on the slopes of Mount Royal.

Meanwhile, Marguerite Bourgeoys continued to give a helping hand wherever it was needed. Among her many concerns were the *filles du roi*, the orphan girls sent from France to be the wives of settlers. She looked after them until they found a husband. She was known affectionately as "the mother of the colony." Her canonization as Saint Marguerite Bourgeoys was announced by Pope John Paul II in 1982.

■ Bourget, Ignace

Roman Catholic bishop of Montreal (*born in 1799 at Lauzon, Que.; died in 1885 at Sault-au-Récollet, Que.*). Bourget was bishop of Montreal from 1840 to 1876. Determined and very dedicated, he was a powerful champion of the Roman Catholic Church, which he felt should be the main influence regulating how people behaved. In Bourget's view, it was the duty of Canadian Roman Catholics to obey

Marguerite Bourgeoys was created a saint by the Catholic Church in 1982. She devoted herself to the care and education of the early colonists of New France (courtesy NAC/C-12340).

Bishop Ignace Bourget was a powerful defender of the Catholic Church in Quebec in the 19th century (courtesy NAC/C-15876).

Sir Mackenzie Bowell's Period as Prime Minister

1870s
Sir John A. Macdonald (C)
1873 Alexander Mackenzie (L)
1878 Sir John A. Macdonald (C)

1880s

1890s
1891 Sir John J.C. Abbott (C)
1892 Sir John S.D. Thompson (C)
1894 **Sir Mackenzie Bowell (C)**
1896 Sir Charles Tupper (C)
1896 Sir Wilfrid Laurier (L)

power, flood control, and irrigation. In 1877, Treaty No. 7, in which the Blackfoot Nation gave up most of its territory in what is now southern Alberta, was signed in a ceremony at Blackfoot Crossing on the Bow River.

■ Bowell, Sir Mackenzie

Bowell was the third of four Conservatives who were prime minister during the five years after Sir John A. Macdonald's death, before Wilfrid Laurier brought the Liberals to power. Bowell had come to Canada with his parents in 1833. He grew up to be an active Orangeman, and became editor and owner of the Belleville *Intelligencer*, a Conservative newspaper.

Bowell was first elected to the House of Commons in 1867, and he remained a member of Parliament until 1892, when he was appointed to the Senate. Macdonald made him minister of customs in 1878, a position he held until 1891. Bowell was a loyal and conscientious member of the team, but he lacked other qualities

their bishops and priests even in such non-religious matters as which party to vote for during elections. This was the "ultramontanist" view — that the church should play a dominant role in everyday life.

Bourget worked hard to build up the power of the church and to strengthen its institutions. In 1842 he brought the Jesuits back to Canada (they had been banned after the Conquest of 1760). In the 1850s and 1860s he launched such a vigorous campaign against the Liberal-oriented Institut Canadien that almost all the Institut's members gave in and resigned. From 1867 to 1870 he headed a successful crusade to enlist Canadians to fight for the pope in Italy. Meanwhile, Bourget encouraged the work of Roman Catholic religious orders and greatly increased the number of church-run schools and hospitals.

▷ RELATED ARTICLES: **Guibord Affair; Institut Canadien; Ultramontanists; Zouaves.**

■ Bow River

The Bow River, 644 km long, rises in Banff National Park, Alta. It flows south and east through Banff and Calgary, and eventually joins the South Saskatchewan River in southeast Alberta. Several dams have been built on the river for electric

Sir Mackenzie Bowell
5TH PRIME MINISTER OF CANADA

Born: December 27, 1823, Rickinghall, England
Died: December 10, 1917, Belleville, Ont.
Political Party: **Conservative**
First Elected: 1867
Chosen Leader: 1894
Period as Prime Minister: December 21, 1894, to April 27, 1896
(PHOTO COURTESY NAC/PA-27161).

needed in Parliament: verve, intelligence, and an expert manner of speaking.

Bowell was 70 years old in 1894 when, on the sudden death of Sir John Thompson, he was asked to take over as prime minister. This proved to be a mistake. Bowell was too weak to handle the role, and there was the added problem that he was in the Senate rather than the House of Commons. Faced with the major problem of the day, the Manitoba Schools Question, he acted so ineptly that he lost support within his own Cabinet. Bowell was obliged to step down in 1896 and let Sir Charles Tupper take over as prime minister.

▷ RELATED ARTICLE: **Manitoba Schools Question.**

■ Bowering, George

Poet, fiction writer, editor, critic (*born in 1935 at Penticton, B.C.*). Bowering served in the Royal Canadian Air Force and then earned BA and MA degrees at the University of British Columbia. During the 1960s, he was one of the founders of the *Tish* group of young experimental poets. He taught in Calgary, London, and Montreal before becoming a professor at Simon Fraser University, where he still teaches. He has published over 40 books of poetry, fiction, and criticism. *The Gangs of Kosmos* (1969) and *Rocky Mountain Foot* (1969) earned him the Governor General's Award for Poetry and are notable for their precise use of language. *Burning Water*

George Bowering reading from his book Burning Water, *which won the Governor General's Award (courtesy Penguin Books Canada Ltd).*

(1980), also a Governor General's Award winner, is a novel about the 18th-century explorer, George Vancouver.

■ Bowling

Bowling is an indoor sport in which the object is to knock down pins with a ball. There are two versions. Ten-pin bowling was developed in the United States in the 19th century. Five-pin bowling was invented in Canada early this century by Thomas Ryan of Toronto. Many of Ryan's customers complained that the ten-pin ball was too large, making the game too strenuous. He used a smaller ball and fewer pins and developed a different scoring system. He also added a rubber band around the pins to make the game quieter. Today, over 2 million Canadians play the game in some 700 bowling centres. More Canadians participate in five-pin bowling than any other indoor sport.

Ten-pin bowling is also popular in Canada. Several Canadians have excelled in international competition. Graydon Robinson won the world championship in ten-pin bowling in 1969.

Lawn Bowling ("bowls") is also played in Canada. This is an outdoor sport played on a flat lawn ("green"). It is one of the world's oldest ball games. Canadian teams have won silver medals in lawn bowling at the Commonwealth Games and the World Championships.

■ Boxing

Boxing is a contest between two opponents who fight with their fists. The rounds are scored by the number of punches landed by each boxer, and the one who wins the most rounds wins the fight. The match is ended if a fighter is knocked out or suffers an injury. In amateur boxing the fighters wear helmets, and the fights are restricted to three rounds. In professional boxing, fights may be ten or fifteen rounds. Boxing is a violent, dangerous, and controversial sport.

Boxing traces its history as far back as the original Olympic games in ancient Greece. The first boxing matches in Canada were fought with bare knuckles. Gloves were later introduced to protect the fists of the boxers. Some early bouts, before the year 1900, were scheduled for 40 rounds. Though they were outlawed in many provinces, boxing matches drew large crowds.

Many famous boxers have come from poor families or underprivileged classes. Sam Langford and George Dixon were Blacks who grew up when there were few opportunities for their race. Dixon was

Sam Langford
Sam Langford (*born in 1886 at Weymouth Falls, N.S.; died 1956*) fought in many different weight classes and was the heavyweight champion of England and Spain. He became champion of Mexico, despite being declared blind at the time! Though he was considered one of the best boxers of all time he was not allowed to fight the great world champion Jack Johnson because it was believed that crowds would not pay to watch two Black boxers.

Lennox Lewis
Lennox Lewis (*born in 1965 at Stratford, England*) moved to Kitchener, Ont., with his family in 1977. His interest in boxing grew out of schoolyard battles with students who laughed at his accent. He won several national and international amateur titles before winning Canada's first gold medal in boxing since 1932 at the 1988 Olympics. Shortly afterward he turned professional and moved to England. He won his first professional bout in 1988 by a knockout.

George Chuvalo (left) takes a punch from world champion Muhammed Ali during their bout in Toronto in 1966 (courtesy Canapress Photo Service).

Ode to Newfoundland*
by
Sir Cavendish Boyle

When sun rays crown
thy pine-clad hills,
   And Summer spreads
her hand,
When silvern voices
tune thy rills,
   We love thee, smil-
ing land.

   We love thee, we
love thee,
   We love thee, smil-
ing land.

When blinding storm-
gusts fret thy shore,
   And wild waves lash
thy strand;
Through   spindrift,
swirl and tempest roar
   We love thee, wind-
swept land.

   We love thee, we
love thee,
   We love thee, wind-
swept land.

When spreads   thy
cloak of shimmering
white
   At winter's   stern
command;
Through shortened day
and star-lit night
   We love thee, frozen
land.

   We love thee, we
love thee,
   We love thee, frozen
land.
* first three verses

---

bantamweight champion of the world in 1890. Two other Canadians, Tommy Burns and Jimmy McLarnin, were also world champions. George Chuvalo of Toronto fought all the best heavyweights of his day in the 1950s and 1960s, and was never knocked off his feet. Matthew Hilton, of Montreal, held the world junior middleweight title from June 1987 to November 1988. Donny Lalonde, originally from Kitchener, Ont., won the 1988 world lightweight championship. He retired after being badly beaten by "Sugar" Ray Leonard.

Canadian boxers have competed in the Olympic games. Bert Schneider and "Lefty" Gwynne won gold medals in 1920 and 1932. Shawn O'Sullivan and Willie de Wit won silver medals at the 1984 Olympics. In 1988, Lennox Lewis won a gold medal, Egerton Marcus the silver, and Raymond Downey the bronze at Seoul, Korea.

Despite the controversy that surrounds the sport because of its violence, boxing is still popular in many Canadian cities.

■ Boxing Day, *see* Holidays

■ Boyd, Liona
Guitarist (*born in 1950 at London, England*). Boyd moved with her family to Canada when she was a child and began guitar studies at 14 with the noted Toronto teacher Eli Kassner. In her twenties she went on to study in Paris with Alexandre Lagoya, and later she took classes with Julian Bream and others. She began recording in 1974, made her New York debut at Carnegie Recital Hall in 1975, and first toured with singer-songwriter Gordon Lightfoot in 1976. She made numerous appearances with symphony orchestras in the 1970s and 1980s. She continues to perform as a classical guitarist, and is known as much for her pale-golden-haired glamour as for her music-making. She has recorded for the Toronto label Boot and also for Columbia.

■ Boyle, Sir Cavendish
Governor of Newfoundland (*born in 1849 in England; died in 1916 at Brighton,*

England). Sir Cavendish Boyle was the author of "Ode to Newfoundland," the province's national song. It is one of many poems he wrote extolling the rugged beauty of Newfoundland.

Boyle was a member of the British Colonial Service, and he was posted to the Leeward Islands, Bermuda, Gibraltar, and British Guiana before serving as governor of Newfoundland (1901-04). He was later governor of Mauritius. While in Newfoundland, he donated the Boyle Challenge Cup to the Newfoundland Hockey League. It is the second-oldest athletic trophy in Canada.

■ Boyle, Joseph Whiteside
Adventurer, gold miner (*born in 1867 at Toronto, Ont.; died in 1923 near London, England*). "Klondike Joe" and "Saviour of Romania" were two of the names given to Joseph Boyle in his heyday. He ran away to sea when he was about 17 and was managing a boxer when he heard of the Klondike Gold Rush in 1897. He was one of the first gold-seekers to cross White Pass. He immediately staked a claim on the Klondike River.

Unlike most Klondikers, Boyle made a fortune in the Yukon, but it was a result of his large gold-dredging operation, not panning by hand. By the outbreak of World War I, he controlled nearly half of Dawson City, owning its electricity and water utilities.

Boyle was determined to get into the action during World War I. He raised his own 50-man machine-gun unit for the war, and went to England in 1916 as an honorary colonel. He ended up in Russia where his great organizing skill and energy helped to improve the railway system, which was a mess. He cleared a blockage of 10 000 railway cars around Moscow. After the Russian Revolution in 1917, he was responsible for the collection and distribution of food. Amid the chaos of the war and revolution, he returned valuable documents and much-needed paper money to Romania. He had to run a Russian blockade to achieve it. His extraordinary adventures continued as he rescued 54 prominent Romanians who were being held hostage in Russia. All the while he was acting as a spy, feeding information to Britain and France.

After the war, Boyle worked tirelessly for the relief of the destitute Romanian people. He became a close friend and adviser of Queen Marie of Romania. Boyle was made a national hero of Romania and received the highest awards from Russia,

Joe Boyle ran away to go to sea when he was 17. He went on to live a life of extraordinary adventures (courtesy Woodstock Museum).

France, and Britain. He left Romania, exhausted to the point of death. He died alone in England. His remarkable career was virtually forgotten until 1983 when his body was brought home and buried at Woodstock, Ont.

■ Bracebridge

Bracebridge, Ont., lies in the cottage country of the Muskoka Lakes, north of Toronto. The first settlers were road builders who were clearing the Muskoka Road in the 1860s. A scenic waterfall provided power for several mills. Today the town is a bustling centre for the surrounding vacation area. In 1986 the population was 9811. Bracebridge's name comes from a book by the American writer Washington Irving. For information, contact the Town Clerk, 23 Dominion Street, P.O. Box 360, Bracebridge, Ont., P0B 1C0.

■ Bracken, John

Premier of Manitoba (*born in 1883 at Ellisville, Ont.; died in 1969 at Ottawa, Ont.*). Born in rural Ontario, John Bracken attended the Ontario Agricultural College in Guelph. He worked as a professional agriculturalist for the Ontario and federal governments. In 1910 he became a professor at the University of Saskatchewan, and in 1920 was appointed president of the Manitoba Agricultural College.

Bracken's interest in political reform for the benefit of farmers led him to join the Progressive movement in Manitoba. He was elected to the provincial legislature, and in 1922 became premier. He served as premier until 1943, a record period of service for the province. As premier, he was noted for providing fair, honest, and efficient government.

In 1942 Bracken agreed to run for the leadership of the federal Conservative Party on the condition that the party change its name to Progressive Conservative (PC). It has kept the name ever since. He led the party from outside the House of Commons until 1945, when he was finally elected. However, he was no match in Parliament for the Liberal leader, Prime Minister Mackenzie King. The PCs lost the election of 1945, and Bracken resigned as leader three years later.

John Bracken was premier of Manitoba from 1922 to 1943, a record, but he was less successful as leader of the federal Conservative Party (photo © Karsh, Ottawa/Miller Comstock/PAM).

■ Bradford, Karleen

Writer (*born in 1936 at Toronto, Ont.*). Karleen Bradford moved to Argentina when she was nine, and returned to Canada to attend the University of Toronto. She graduated in 1959. She has since lived in South America, the Philippines, the United States, England, and Germany.

Bradford's writing focuses on two major themes. Her two realistic problem novels show that both adults and children must try to understand each other if they are to have good family relationships. Rachel Larrimer, in *I Wish There Were Unicorns* (1983), accepts life after her parents' divorce only by having sympathy for her mother's difficulties.

Bradford's second theme is the power of the individual to change things. In her three time-travel fantasies, a girl goes back in time to help someone who is like

her. In *The Other Elizabeth* (1982), for example, Elizabeth goes back to 1813 and saves an ancestor's life.

Bradford's historical novel, *The Nine Days Queen* (1986), is about Lady Jane Grey (a 16th-century Englishwoman).

Brampton

Brampton, Ont., lies beside the Etobicoke River, 32 km northwest of Toronto. It began in the 1820s as a backwoods settlement known as Buffy's Corners. As the community developed, it was renamed Brampton by a Mr Elliott, an immigrant from Brampton, England. Today, with a population in 1986 of 188 498, it is home to a variety of manufacturing industries. Many residents commute the short distance to work in Toronto. Former Ontario premier, William Davis, was born in Brampton. For information, contact the City Clerk, Central Park Drive, Brampton, Ont., L6T 2T9.

Brandon

Brandon, Man., is the second-largest city in Manitoba. It lies beside the Assiniboine River on the prairie, 225 km west of Winnipeg. Fur traders built the first trading post in the area in 1793, and it became one of the network of forts supplying pemmican to the canoe brigades. Permanent settlers did not start arriving until the 1870s. With the arrival of the Canadian Pacific Railway in 1881, a townsite sprang to life. It grew so fast that it bypassed the stages of village and town, becoming a city in 1882.

Two-thirds of Manitoba's farmland is located within 125 km of Brandon and agriculture is the backbone of the local economy. There is also a variety of manufacturing industries. The city is the site of three major agricultural fairs and of Brandon University. Brandon's population in 1986 was 38 708. For information, contact the Executive Director, City Hall, P.O. Box 960, Brandon, Man., R7A 6A2.

▷ SUGGESTED READING: Fred McGuinness, *The Wheat City: A Pictorial History of Brandon* (1988).

Brandon University

Brandon University is located in Brandon, Man. It offers undergraduate courses in arts, sciences, education, and music. It also offers graduate courses in music. Brandon College, established in 1899, was affiliated with either the University of Manitoba or with McMaster University until 1967, when it received its own university charter. It has over 1300 full-time undergraduate students.

For further information, write to the Registrar's Office, Brandon University, Brandon, Man., R7A 6A9.

Brant, Joseph

Mohawk chief (*born around 1742, south of Lake Erie [near Akron, Ohio, U.S.]; died in 1807 at Burlington Bay, Upper Canada [Ontario]*). His native name was Thayendanegea.

When Joseph Brant was a teenager, he fought for the British during the Seven Years' War. He was befriended by the British administrator, Sir William Johnson, who arranged for his education. Brant then worked for the British as an interpreter and translator, gaining great respect for his abilities.

Brant called the Mohawk to the British side during the American Revolution (1775-83). He visited England in 1776 where he was received with great honour. He tried to form an alliance of Iroquois in order to block American expansion westward. The Americans were victorious in the war and claimed the Mohawks' hereditary lands in the Treaty of Paris, 1783. To compensate for the loss, Brant and other native Loyalists were granted a large tract of land on the Grand River, in the region of today's Brantford, Ont.

Brant spent much of his later life trying to obtain for the Grand River native people full control over the land they had been granted. Although his efforts were not successful, he continued to devote

Joseph Brant in a fine painting by William Berczy, around 1807 (courtesy NGC).

himself to the good of his people. He spent his last years in his magnificent house on Burlington Bay. A scholar as well as a statesman and soldier, he translated parts of the Bible into Mohawk.

▷ RELATED ARTICLES: **Brantford; Mary Brant.**

■ Brant, Mary (Molly)

Mohawk politician *(born around 1736; died in 1796 at Kingston, Upper Canada [Ontario]*. Her native name was Konwatsi'tsiaiénni, meaning "someone lends her a flower."

Molly Brant was head of the Six Nations matrons, the powerful group of women who chose the chiefs of the Iroquois Confederacy. She had far greater influence than her better-known younger brother, Joseph Brant. She was consulted by her people on all important matters. Much of her power came from her close relationship with Sir William Johnson, the British superintendent of northern Indians. The Iroquois honoured Johnson as a good friend. Molly became Johnson's live-in companion in her teens.

Johnson died in 1774 but Molly's influence did not lessen. She encouraged the Iroquois to side with the Loyalists during the American Revolution (1775-83). During the war she sheltered Loyalists who had fled to the woods. She warned the British of an American advance and, in revenge, the Americans ravaged her lands. After the revolution she settled at Kingston, where Governor Haldimand had a house built for her. He also awarded her a pension of £100 a year, the largest paid to a native person in that period.

▷ RELATED ARTICLE: **Joseph Brant.**

■ Brantford

Brantford, Ont., lies beside the Grand River, 104 km southwest of Toronto. It is named for Chief Joseph Brant, who brought his people here in 1784. Where they crossed the river became known as "Brant's ford." The name was officially adopted in 1825. The village site was sold to settlers and Brantford became a town in 1847 and a city in 1877.

The town is famous as the part-time home of Alexander Graham Bell, who worked on the invention of the telephone here. The Bell Homestead is preserved as a historic site. Hockey superstar Wayne Gretzky was born here. Manufacturing is the basis of the economy today. In 1986 the population was 76 146. For information, contact the City Clerk, City Hall, 100 Wellington Square, Brantford, Ont., N3T 2M3.

■ Bras d'Or Lake

Bras d'Or Lake, 1099 km^2 in area, is a large body of water on Cape Breton Island, connected to the Atlantic Ocean by two narrow channels in the northeast. It is about 90-95 km long and is surrounded by high hills. At St Peters, site of an early trading post, a 0.8 km long ship canal joins the south end of the lake to the Atlantic Ocean. The name is a variation of "labrador," a term applied by Portuguese explorers to a large part of Nova Scotia.

■ Brault, Jacques

Writer *(born in 1933 at Montreal, Que.)*. Brault is a versatile writer who has produced poetry, novels, plays, and literary criticism. Since the publication of his first collection of poems in 1965, he has received Governor General's Awards as both playwright (1970) and novelist (1984). He is also a professor at the University of Montreal.

■ Brault, Michel

Filmmaker *(born in 1928 at Montreal, Que.)*. After being a professional photographer, Brault joined the National Film Board as a cameraman in 1956. He quickly moved into directing and became known for the high quality of his camera work.

Using a light, portable camera in *Les Raquetteurs* (1958), Brault helped to develop the direct film technique. He made the classic *Pour la suite du monde* (1963) with Pierre Perrault, and has worked with many other great Quebec directors.

Brault's ability to combine the impact of a documentary with the emotion of fiction reached its peak in *Les Ordres* (1974). This "docu-drama" about the 1970 October Crisis in Quebec won first prize at the 1975 Cannes Film Festival in France. Another documentary, *L'Emprise* (1988), about family violence, also won several awards.

In 1986 Brault received a major award recognizing his work as a whole.

■ Breadalbane

Breadalbane is the name of a wooden sailing ship which sank in the Arctic in 1853. A team led by Joseph MacInnis, a Canadian physician, marine scientist, and diver, found the *Breadalbane* in 1980. The northernmost of all known shipwrecks, she has remained in good condition beneath the polar ice.

The *Breadalbane* was a three-masted barque built in 1843. She was carrying supplies for the last of the British Royal Navy expeditions sent out to search for

Molly Brant *The British flag in this postage stamp refers to Molly Brant's loyalty during the American Revolution (courtesy Canada Post Corporation).*

The Huron Carol
by
Jean de Brébeuf

Written for his followers, in the Huron language; English translation by J.E. Middleton

'Twas in the moon of winter time when all the birds had fled
That Mighty Gitchi Manitou sent angel-choirs instead.
Before their light the stars grew dim,
And wandering hunters heard the hymn;
"Jesus, your King, is born,
Jesus is born; in excelsis gloria!"

Within a lodge of broken bark the tender Babe was found.
A ragged robe of rabbit skin enwrapped His beauty 'round.
And as the hunter braves drew nigh,
The Angel song rang loud and high;
"Jesus, your King, is born,
Jesus is born; in excelsis gloria!"

The earliest moon of winter time is not so round and fair
As was the ring of glory on the helpless Infant there,
While Chiefs from far before Him knelt
With gifts of fox and beaver pelt.
"Jesus, your King, is born,
Jesus is born; in excelsis gloria!"

O children of the forest free, O sons of Manitou,
The Holy Child of earth and heav'n is born today for you.
Come, kneel before the radiant Boy
Who brings you beauty, peace and joy.
"Jesus, your King, is born,
Jesus is born; in excelsis gloria!"

the ships and men of the Franklin Expedition, which had disappeared in 1845 while seeking the Northwest Passage. The *Breadalbane* sank in the waters south of Beechey Island when ice pierced her bow. Her crew escaped by scrambling over the ice to a sister ship.

MacInnis wanted to find a shipwreck in Arctic waters in order to improve methods for exploring in cold water. He chose the *Breadalbane* because, from eyewitness accounts of the time, he knew roughly where she sank.

In 1980, the *Breadalbane* was finally spotted as a ghostly image on the roll of paper recording signals from a *sonar*. (A sonar is a device which emits pulses of sounds and gathers echoes to make a picture of the sea floor.) In 1983 the ice that formed on the surface of the water above the wreck was thick and smooth, permitting MacInnis and his team to camp and dive. They thoroughly studied the *Breadalbane* using cameras mounted on a submersible which could be piloted from surface, armoured diving suits, and other sophisticated technology.

▷ RELATED ARTICLES: **Franklin Expedition; Joseph MacInnis.**

▷ SUGGESTED READING: Joseph MacInnis, *The Breadalbane Adventure* (1983).

■ Brébeuf, Jean de

Jesuit missionary, patron saint of Canada (*born in 1593 at Condé-sur-Vire, France; died in 1649 at Saint-Ignace, Huronia [near Midland, Ont.]*). Brébeuf was a Jesuit priest. He arrived in New France in 1625, and the following year he was sent as a missionary to the Huron people who lived near Georgian Bay. Brébeuf learned the Huron language and devoted himself to converting the Huron to Christianity. When Quebec fell to the English in 1629 Brébeuf was forced to return to France. He returned to Huronia in 1634 and supervised the preparation of a Huron dictionary. But the French and Huron were uneasy allies. The Huron blamed the French for a devastating smallpox epidemic in 1640. They attacked Brébeuf and damaged the mission.

Brébeuf began a new mission among the Neutral, but they regarded him as a sorcerer. He returned to Huronia in 1644. In 1649 he was captured by Iroquois warriors and brutally killed. His bones are buried at the Martyrs' Shrine near Midland, Ont. The Roman Catholic Church declared Brébeuf a saint in 1930.

▷ RELATED ARTICLES: **Huronia; Sainte Marie Among the Hurons; Saints.**

Jonquière Bridge, Quebec, was the world's first aluminum bridge (photo by J.A. Kraulis).

■ Bridge

A bridge is a structure that spans a river, canyon, or other obstacle. Bridges are numerous in a country such as Canada, where waterways abound. In early days most bridges were made from logs, which could be cut from nearby forests. Covered bridges were very popular because they keep the roadway free of snow. They were picturesque additions to the landscape, and were called "kissing bridges," for the privacy they provided. By the year 1900 there were more than 1000 covered bridges in Canada. The covered bridge at Hartland, N.B., is 391 m long, the longest covered bridge in the world.

The railway, which began spreading across Canada in the 1850s, required numerous bridges. Many of these were built of timber. The great trestle bridges in the Rocky Mountains, such as the one over Mountain Creek, B.C. (1885), were considered among the wonders of their day. They were often built in haste and were gradually replaced by metal structures. Sir Sandford Fleming insisted that the bridges of the Intercolonial Railway in eastern Canada be built on stone piers. Many of their metal spans were prefabricated in the United States. One of the

Jacques Cartier Bridge across the St Lawrence River at Montreal (courtesy SSC Photocentre/photo by Michel Gagné).

Lion's Gate Bridge, *Vancouver, is an example of a suspension bridge (photo by J.A. Kraulis/ Masterfile).*

Covered Bridge at Gatineau, Quebec. Covered bridges were very popular in early Canada because they kept the roadway free of snow (photo by John deVisser).

great railway bridges was the Victoria Bridge, spanning the St Lawrence River at Montreal. At 1870 m long, it was one of the longest bridges in the world when it opened in 1860. Its original span was a closed iron box which became unbearably hot and polluted with smoke. It was later replaced by open steel trusses. (The *truss* bridge is supported by triangles of steel or wood.)

Steel revolutionized the building of bridges. The Interprovincial Bridge at Ottawa, the Jacques Cartier Bridge at Montreal, and the High Level Bridge at Edmonton are steel bridges that carried the railway over rivers. Construction began on Canada's best-known bridge, the Quebec Bridge, in 1900. It spans the St Lawrence River. It was designed as a *cantilever* bridge, with two independent sections, joined in the middle by a centre span. In 1907 the southern section collapsed in a sickening tangle of steel, killing 75 workmen. In 1916 the centre span plunged into the river, killing another 13 men. When the bridge finally opened in 1919, it was the longest bridge of its kind in the world.

The *suspension* bridge is suspended from long steel cables, which pass over two high towers and are anchored to a firm foundation. It is very useful for spanning long distances or deep canyons. The Lion's Gate Bridge in Vancouver is an example. It links the city of Vancouver with the north shore. The Angus L. Macdonald Bridge links Halifax and Dartmouth, N.S.

In the 20th century most bridges are built to carry automobiles or modern city transportation, such as light rapid transit lines. Many of these are built of reinforced concrete, formed into graceful arches (one of the oldest kinds of bridges). The Ashburnham Bridge, in Peterborough, Ont., with a centre arch of 71.3 m,

showed a daring use of concrete. It was designed by Canadian engineer Frank Barber, who designed over 500 bridges. The Broadway Bridge in Saskatoon, Sask., is a beautiful, multi-arched bridge.

In 1950 work began on the Trans-Canada Highway, which rivals the transcontinental railway as an engineering feat. At over 7800 km, it is the world's longest paved highway. It required many new bridges, including the Port Mann Bridge, in New Westminster, B.C.; the Louis-Hippolyte LaFontaine Bridge, Montreal; and the Hugh John Flemming Bridge, over the Saint John River, N.B.

▷ RELATED ARTICLES: **Engineering; Sir Sandford Fleming; Sir Casimir Gzowski; Samuel Keefer; Quebec Bridge Disaster.**

Alexandria Bridges are a contrast in style. The old suspension bridge (front) was built in 1926. The new, arched bridge was built in 1961 as part of the TransCanada Highway (courtesy Province of B.C./Image Bank).

■ **Bridgewater**

Bridgewater is situated on the east coast of Nova Scotia on the LaHave River, 16 km from its mouth. Bridgewater's life has centered on the river. The early French and German settlers spread by steps up the river. The town took shape very slowly, helped greatly by the first bridge over the river in 1825 (giving the town its name). The river supported fishermen, shipbuilders, and sawmills. Today, the

British Columbia

Facts about the Province of British Columbia

Created as a Province: July 20, 1871

Motto: *Splendor sine occasu* ("Splendour without diminishment")

Origin of Name: Reflects the British nature of the early non-native settlement

Capital City: Victoria

Government: *Provincial:* Lieutenant-Governor, Executive Council (premier and cabinet), Legislative Assembly. The number of members of the Legislative Assembly (MLAs) is 69
Federal: Represented in the Senate of Canada by 6 senators; in the House of Commons by 32 members of parliament (MPs)

Population: 2 889 207 (1986), 11.4% of total population of Canada. British Columbia's population is 78.9% urban, 19.5% rural, 1.6% Indian Reserves.

Main Products: *Forestry:* lumber, wood pulp, plywood
Mining: coal, copper, gold, zinc
Fisheries: salmon, herring, halibut, shellfish
Agriculture: dairy products, fruit, vegetables
Manufacturing: pulp and paper, food processing, metals

Time Zones: Pacific Standard Time, Mountain Standard Time (eastern part)

Parks: *National:* Pacific Rim, Glacier, Yoho, Kootenay, Mount Revelstoke, South Moresby
Provincial: 385 provincial parks, including 36 recreational areas, and 1 wilderness conservancy, 123 ecological reserves
Land and Water Reserved for Conservation: With no logging, mining, or hunting allowed: 2.4%

Highest Points:
Fairweather Mountain (St Elias Mountains)	4663 m
Mount Waddington (Coast Mountains)	4019 m
Mount Robson (Rocky Mountains)	3954 m
Mount Clemenceau (Rocky Mountains)	3642 m

Lowest Point: Sea Level

Largest Lakes: Entirely within British Columbia
Williston Lake	1761 km²
Nechako Lake	847 km²
Babine Lake	497 km²

largest employer is the Michelin Tire Company. The town serves as the shopping centre for some 50 000 people who live in the area. Bridgewater's population in 1986 was 6617. For information, contact the Town Clerk, P.O. Box 9, Bridgewater, N.S., B4V 2W7.

■ British Columbia

Many Canadians believe that there is something different about British Columbia, and most residents of the province agree. Perhaps it is all the mountains which block the province off from the rest of Canada. Perhaps it is the Pacific breezes which give the southwest part of the province the mildest climate in the country. Or perhaps it is the fact that B.C. is a "Pacific Rim" country and looks for much of its trade to Asia. Whatever the reason, the province has a unique and unmistakable identity.

LAND AND WATER

B.C. has a long and complicated geological history of mountain building, erosion, and glaciation. This has left the province with a very diverse landscape. Many people think of B.C. as the land of the "Rockies," but the province contains several mountain systems. The three main mountain ranges are the Coast Mountains in the west, the Columbia Mountains in the centre, and the Rocky Mountains in the east. Some lesser known ranges include the Skeena and the Omineca mountains.

Offshore Islands The coastline of B.C. is dotted with thousands of islands, from

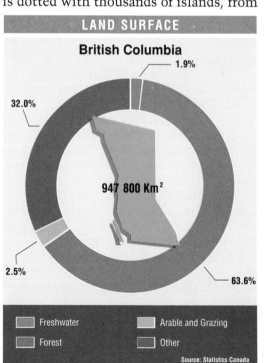

LAND SURFACE

British Columbia

947 800 Km²

1.9%

32.0%

2.5%

63.6%

▢ Freshwater	▢ Arable and Grazing
▢ Forest	▢ Other

Source: Statistics Canada

Port Alberni's setting on a deep inlet on Vancouver Island is typical of the natural beauty of B.C. (courtesy Colour Library Books).

tiny, unnamed reefs to Vancouver Island, which is over 31 000 km² in area. In the north are the Queen Charlotte Islands, 100 km offshore. The Gulf Islands are nestled near the southern end of Vancouver Island.

Coast Mountains The Coast Mountains stretch from the Yukon border almost to the U.S. border in the south.

Because these mountains are the first to encounter the moist air blowing in off the Pacific Ocean, they are among the wettest areas of Canada.

Interior Plateau Sandwiched between the Coast Mountains and the Columbia Mountains is a huge, rugged area called the Interior Plateau. Much of it is mountainous. In the south are several broad river valleys, the Fraser, Thompson, Okanagan, and Chilcotin.

Columbia Mountains This range runs parallel to the southern portion of the Rocky Mountains. The Columbia River flows down its centre. It includes the Monashees, Selkirks, and Purcells.

Rocky Mountains The Rockies are a collection of several ranges. Along the eastern edge is the magnificent Rocky Mountain Trench, one of the world's largest valleys. It runs the entire length of the province. The Columbia, Fraser, and other important rivers have their headwaters in this valley.

Plains In the northeast corner of the province, the border claims a large area of the Great Plains of Alberta and Saskatch-

Coast Mountains, north of Vancouver (photo by J.A. Kraulis).

Upper Fraser River, Mt Robson Provincial Park (photo by Tom W. Parkin/Pathfinder).

B.C.'s Record Temperatures

Highest: 44.4°C on July 16 and 17, 1941, at Lytton, Lillooet, and Chinook Cove.
Lowest: -58.9°C on January 31, 1947, at Smith River.

Record Snowfalls

The heaviest one-day snowfall in Canada was 118.1 cm, at Lakelse Lake, on January 17, 1974. The heaviest seasonal snowfall was 2446.5 cm at Revelstoke during the winter of 1971-72.

W.A.C. Bennett Dam on the Peace River is one of B.C.'s many powerful hydroelectric stations. The dam has created a huge reservoir, called Williston Lake, which is B.C.'s largest body of fresh water (courtesy B.C. Hydro).

ewan. It covers about 10% of the area of British Columbia.

A small area along the Peace River is used for grain farming.

Lower Mainland At the south end of the Coast Mountains, the Fraser River has created a large delta, which supports most of B.C.'s agriculture. It is the most densely populated area in the province.

B.C. is also a land of mighty rivers. The southern half of the province drains into the Pacific by way of the Fraser, the Thompson, and the Columbia rivers. Part of the northern half is drained by the Skeena, Nass, and Stikine rivers, which also flow into the Pacific. The northeast drains by way of the Liard and the Peace

rivers via the Mackenzie system into the Arctic Ocean. B.C.'s rivers have been important as transportation routes, as spawning grounds for fish, and as sources of hydroelectric power.

There are few large lakes in the province. The two biggest are Williston (a man-made lake) and Atlin.

CLIMATE AND WEATHER

B.C. has a wide variety of climates — more than any other area of Canada. The northeast, in the Fort Nelson region, has a cold, Subarctic climate, while the islands in the Strait of Georgia region have the mildest climate in Canada. What makes the difference are the coastal mountains. They protect the Lower Mainland and the coast from the Arctic air masses coming from the north in the winter. Because water holds heat longer than land and also warms up slower, the Pacific Ocean has a strong influence on the climate of the coast. This is why Vancouver and Victoria are warmer in the winter and cooler in the summer than places in the interior of the province. The mean January daily temperature at Victoria is 3°C, the warmest in Canada. The mean July temperature is about 16°C. In the northern interior around Fort Nelson, the January mean is -24°C. In July it is 17°C.

The mountains which give coastal B.C. a mild climate also give it a great deal of rain. The western slopes of the Coast Mountains get 1300 to 3800 mm of precipitation per year. The east side of the mountains, in the Okanagan Valley, receive only 250 to 500 mm of precipitation per year.

NATURAL REGIONS

There are five major natural regions in B.C. In the northeastern corner are the Taiga Plains and a band of Boreal Plains. The remaining two-thirds of the north is covered with Boreal Cordillera. A huge interior area falls under the general term Montane Cordillera, but contains many variations within it. The Pacific Maritime region lies along the coast and some distance inland.

Forest covers about two-thirds of the whole province. Only about 2.5% is suitable for agriculture.

Taiga Plains This area of northeastern B.C. is mainly covered in muskeg, with a ragged forest of spruce. Much of it is permafrost and waterlogged. It forms a mixed zone between the forest to the south and the tundra to the north. Wildlife includes moose, woodland caribou, and black bear.

British Columbia

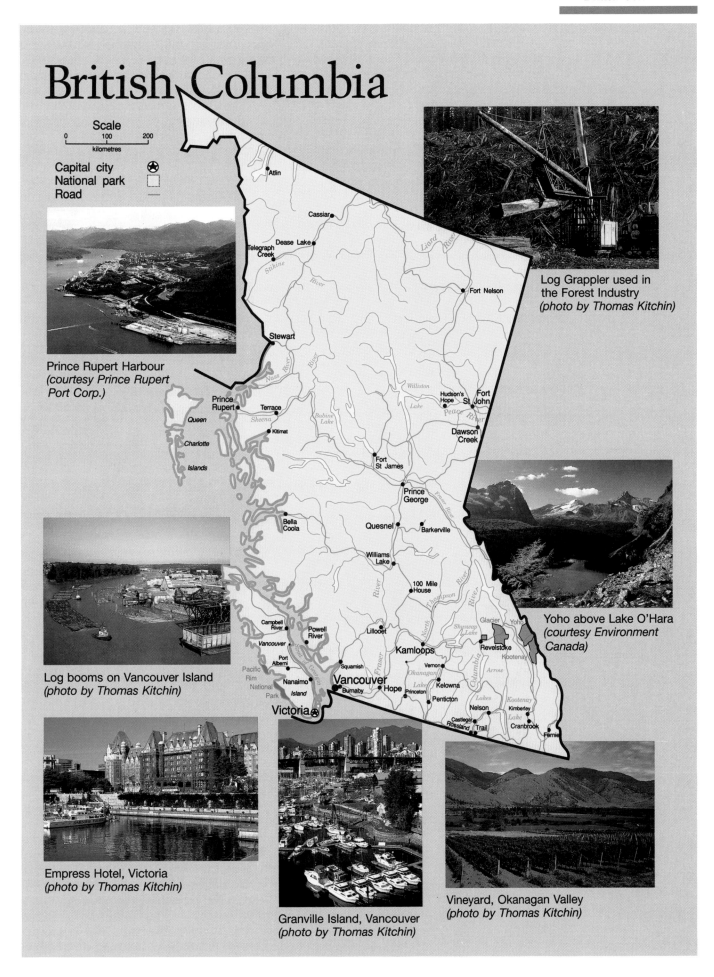

Scale
0   100   200
kilometres

Capital city
National park
Road

Atlin

Cassiar

Telegraph Creek
Dease Lake

Stikine
River

Liard River

Fort Nelson

Stewart

Nass River

Prince Rupert

Terrace

Skeena

Kitimat

Queen

Charlotte

Islands

Babine Lake

Williston Lake

Hudson's Hope

Fort St John

Peace River

Dawson Creek

Fort St James

Prince George

Fraser River

Bella Coola

Quesnel

Barkerville

Williams Lake

100 Mile House

North Thompson River

Glacier

Yoho

Shuswap Lake

Revelstoke

Kootenay

Campbell River

Powell River

Lillooet

Vancouver

Port Alberni

Pacific Rim National Park

Nanaimo

Strait of Georgia

Squamish

Kamloops

Fraser River

Vernon

Okanagan

Kelowna

Columbia River

Arrow

Okanagan Lake

Penticton

Princeton

Nelson

Lakes

Kootenay Lake

Kimberley

Cranbrook

Fernie

Burnaby

Hope

Vancouver

Victoria

Castlegar
Rossland   Trail

Prince Rupert Harbour
(courtesy Prince Rupert Port Corp.)

Log booms on Vancouver Island
(photo by Thomas Kitchin)

Log Grappler used in the Forest Industry
(photo by Thomas Kitchin)

Yoho above Lake O'Hara
(courtesy Environment Canada)

Empress Hotel, Victoria
(photo by Thomas Kitchin)

Granville Island, Vancouver
(photo by Thomas Kitchin)

Vineyard, Okanagan Valley
(photo by Thomas Kitchin)

Boreal Plains This area of the northern plains is covered with a ragged forest, dotted with muskeg, ponds, and moss. Mammals in this area include wolves, black and grizzly bear, and lynx. Most of the forest is not productive in this region.

The northern tip of this plain, along the Peace River, is the most northerly wheat-growing area in North America.

Boreal Cordillera This region, west of the Boreal Plains, spreads into rugged, mountainous country. It receives more rain than the forests to the east. The higher regions are alpine tundra. Animals in this region include moose, Dall's sheep, mountain goat, black and grizzly bear, marten, lynx, American pika, hoary marmot, and squirrels. Human activities in the area are restricted to forestry, mining, and recreation.

Montane Cordillera This region is mountainous like the Boreal Cordillera, but contains very different vegetation. It is shaped by several mountain ranges, each of which produces different local conditions. The valleys between these ranges receive much less rain than the mountain slopes. The southern parts of these valleys are semidesert, with rattlesnakes, lizards, cactus, and sagebrush.

There are four main sub-regions in the Montane Cordillera. The *Columbian* region lies along the Columbia mountain range. The valleys and slopes have thick forests similar to the forests near the coast. This area is home to woodland caribou, living south of their normal habitat.

Farther inland is the *Montane Forest*, which receives less rain. Ducks, moose, wolf, deer, and bear are common here.

At higher altitudes in both these regions is *Subalpine Forest*. The trees are

Photos by Thomas Kitchin (Boreal Cordillera), J.A. Kraulis (Boreal Plains), Tim Fitzharris (Pacific Maritime), Malak (Coastal Region), and Tim Fitzharris (Montane Cordillera).

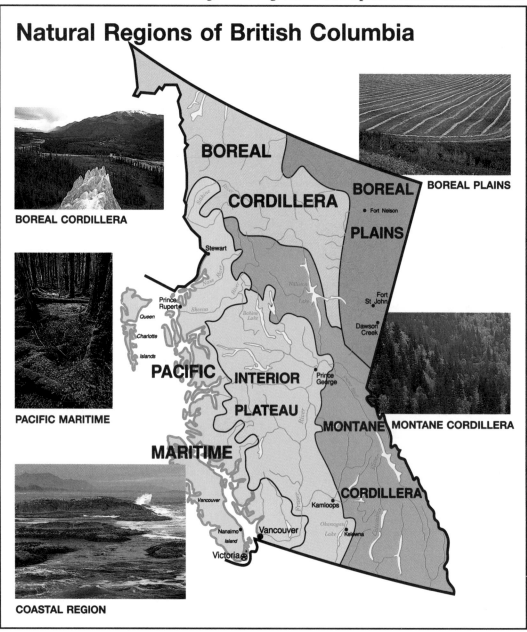

Natural Regions of British Columbia

BOREAL CORDILLERA

PACIFIC MARITIME

COASTAL REGION

BOREAL PLAINS

MONTANE CORDILLERA

stunted in this region, and shrubs are abundant. Porcupine, hare, grizzly bear, and red squirrel are found here. Above the Subalpine Forest is the *Alpine Tundra*, which is cold and dry. Most of the ground cover here are shrubs, moss, and lichen.

Pacific Maritime This is the region people think of most often when they think of B.C. The warm, wet weather supports lush forests. The Coast Mountains provide spectacular scenery. The forest was once dominated by the most majestic trees. Most of the tallest have been cut down. Only a few remnants of the original forest remain, as at Cathedral Grove on Vancouver Island. A sitka spruce, called the Carmanah Giant, is probably Canada's tallest tree. It is 95 m high and 9.5 m in circumference.

The forest is home to Bald Eagle, Stellar's Jay, elk, raccoon, white-tailed deer, black and grizzly bear, mountain lion, fisher, and American pika.

Shoreline B.C. has about 27 000 km of coasts, which has its own pattern of life. Offshore, the abundant food attracts sea lions, seals, killer whales, and sometimes grey whales. The intertidal zone is the part of the shore exposed at low tide. The barnacles, mussels, and limpets survive by anchoring themselves to rocks. When the tide is out, the area is invaded by birds and the occasional bear, raccoon, or mink. The Fraser Delta is rich in vegetation and supports magnificent bird life.

Wildlife Because of the variety of its climatic zones, B.C. has the richest diversity of wildlife in Canada. It has 18 species of amphibians and 15 species of reptiles. In the Pacific coastal waters live animals which are found nowhere else in the country, such as killer whales. As well, the region supports populations of seals, sea lions, and sea otters. The sea otter (a member of the weasel family) has a fur so dense that water cannot penetrate it. It was hunted almost to extinction in the 19th century, but it is now protected, and its numbers are growing.

The land area of the province also supports a rich variety of wildlife, including elk, caribou, black and grizzly bear, mountain goat, mountain sheep, hoary marmot, pika, cougar, and lynx. The mountain goat climbs the steepest rock faces by means of its sturdy legs, non-skid soles, and flexible toes. In winter it migrates to lower elevations.

There are nearly 300 species of birds that breed in B.C., including the ancient Murrelet, Spotted Owl, Mountain Quail, and White-throated Swift, which breed

Helmcken Falls *are preserved in Wells Gray Provincial Park (photo by Valerie J. May).*

nowhere else in Canada. B.C.'s fish are of great economic importance. Its rivers are the spawning grounds for five species of Pacific Salmon. Offshore, red snapper, herring, and halibut are important to the fishery.

Conservation B.C. is a province where conservation is particularly important. Numerous parks and reserves preserve areas of wilderness and protect the habitat of its wildlife. There are six national parks, 385 provincial parks, and 123 ecological reserves.

Many of the province's economic interests conflict with each other. For instance, it would be possible to build hydroelectric dams on the Fraser River to generate large amounts of electricity for industry and for export. But the dams would hinder the salmon from swimming upstream to spawn. Cutting down trees means money for the provincial economy, but it also destroys large areas of wilderness that conservationists want left alone for wildlife or for tourism. The coastal fisheries have been plagued by problems of overfishing, since the fish stocks are limited. The amount of first-class agricultural land in the province is also limited, and must compete with the pressure for land for residential and other construction. Laws have been passed to deal with these problems. Forestry companies are now required to replant forests after cutting the trees, and fishing is

Killer Whales *are one of the most spectacular sights off the coast of B.C. (photo by Barrett & MacKay/Masterfile).*

strictly regulated. In 1973 a law restricted changing the use of agricultural land.

All these measures have proven to be controversial.

NATURAL RESOURCES

Forestry is B.C.'s most important natural resource. About two-thirds of the province is forested. The most important species are hemlock, spruce, balsam, lodgepole pine, red cedar, and Douglas fir. The mild climate and generous rainfall make for tall, straight trees, particularly in the coastal regions. As a result, logs, lumber, and other forest products have been the mainstay of the provincial economy throughout the 20th century.

Lumber for Export in Vancouver Harbour. Forestry is the backbone of B.C.'s economy (photo by Malak, Ottawa).

Communities such as Powell River and Port Alberni grew as a result of the forest industry. Logs are stored in their harbours until they are taken to the sawmills and pulp and paper mills. Ocean-going vessels from all over the world come to pick up the finished products. Forestry has slowly moved inland. Highways and railways opened up large tracts of inland forest. New technology made cutting down the smaller trees more economical.

At present, B.C. produces two-thirds of Canada's sawn lumber, one-quarter of its wood pulp, and most of its plywood.

Energy B.C. has numerous mighty rivers. The province's high rainfall and mountainous terrain produce ideal conditions for power generation. B.C. is the second-largest producer of hydroelectricity in Canada, after Quebec. It still has a great deal of untapped power. The Nechako River produces power for the aluminum smelters at Kitimat. The great development on the Peace River, which flows

The Revelstoke Dam is part of B.C.'s hydroelectric system (courtesy BC Hydro).

northward, is the fourth largest in Canada. The Mica project is one of four major dams on the Columbia River.

On some rivers, such as the Fraser, further developments would interfere with the salmon runs.

The only known reserves of petroleum and natural gas are in the northeastern corner of the province. In 1988, B.C. produced 8081 million m^3 of natural gas (about 9% of Canadian production), and almost 2 million m^3 of petroleum. B.C. must import about 75% of its petroleum needs.

Mining In 1835 coal was discovered on the northern tip of Vancouver Island. Large deposits were later found near Nanaimo and in the Crowsnest Pass area. Coal production declined after World War II, when the railways switched to diesel fuel, and when oil and natural gas became cheaper. In the 1960s, however, B.C. began to export large quantities to Japan. Today, as much as 95% of the coal mined is exported. Much of it is mined near the new community of Tumbler Ridge. Coal production has risen from 765 000 t in 1960 to 24 235 000 t in 1988. B.C. produces more than one-third of Canada's coal. Other important minerals are copper, gold, and zinc.

Fishing Over 20 species of fish and other marine animals are caught in B.C. Salmon is most important, amounting to a catch worth $212 million in 1987. Herring was valued at $107 million. Other important species are halibut, sole, crab, and shrimp.

Fish processing employs about 3000 people in 47 plants (1986). Most of these plants are located in Prince Rupert and Vancouver. There were 6060 licensed fishing vessels in 1987.

Tourism and Recreation The lakes, mountains, forests, islands, and ocean shores of the province, as well as its mild

Vancouver Aquarium Killer whale, Hyak, performs (photo by J.A. Kraulis).

climate, make it a paradise for tourists.

Since the 1970s, the B.C. government has been promoting the mountains and coastline of "Super, Natural B.C." The world fair, Expo 86, helped make B.C. known to many new visitors. In 1988 tourists spent about $3.6 billion in the province.

THE ECONOMY

Gold and then fishing were the mainstays of the economy around the time B.C. became a province of Canada. Coal mining and forestry followed the building of the railway. Today, the economy is dominated by the use of natural resources, especially the forests.

In 1986 the value of goods and services produced in B.C. were as follows:

Value of Goods and Services, B.C., 1984
($millions)

Goods-producing Industries	Value
Manufacturing	6028
Construction	3112
Mining	1844
Utilities	1318
Logging and Forestry	1032
Agriculture	626
Fishing and Trapping	139
Service Industries	
Community, business, and personal services	10 187
Finance, insurance, and real estate	7551
Wholesale and retail trade	5187
Government services	2991
Transportation and storage	2752
Communications	1431

Agriculture B.C. has very little agricultural land. Its land under cultivation as a percentage of its total area is the second lowest in Canada. However, some of this land is so rich that the province still produces 5% of Canada's total agricultural products.

The largest agricultural area in B.C. is

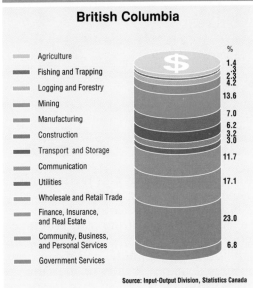

GROSS DOMESTIC PRODUCT BY INDUSTRY - 1984

British Columbia

	%
Agriculture	1.4
Fishing and Trapping	.5
	.3
Logging and Forestry	2.3
Mining	4.2
	13.6
Manufacturing	7.0
Construction	6.2
Transport and Storage	3.2
	3.0
Communication	11.7
Utilities	17.1
Wholesale and Retail Trade	
Finance, Insurance, and Real Estate	23.0
Community, Business, and Personal Services	6.8
Government Services	

Source: Input-Output Division, Statistics Canada

the Peace River District, centered on Dawson Creek and Fort St John. This is chiefly a grain-growing area, and it accounts for 90% of the grain grown in the province. The most valuable agricultural land in the province is in the lower Fraser Valley. Here, dairy and livestock products are produced, as well as vegetables, strawberries, blueberries, raspberries, and specialty crops such as flower bulbs. This is also prime residential land, and by 1970 about 20% of it had been absorbed by Vancouver and the surrounding municipalities. The Agricultural Land Commission Act of 1973 prevented further use of this land for building purposes.

The third important agricultural area in the province is the Okanagan Valley. Hot summers and mild winters make it one of Canada's main fruit-growing regions and one of the few regions where grapes can be

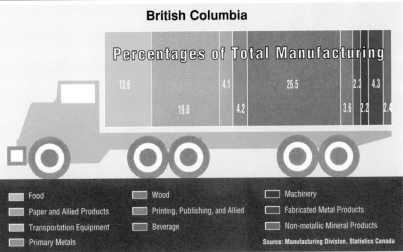

MANUFACTURING BY MAJOR INDUSTRY GROUPS - 1986

British Columbia

Percentages of Total Manufacturing

13.6 19.6 4.1 4.2 26.5 3.6 2.2 2.3 4.3 2.4

Food	Wood	Machinery
Paper and Allied Products	Printing, Publishing, and Allied	Fabricated Metal Products
Transportation Equipment	Beverage	Non-metallic Mineral Products
Primary Metals		

Source: Manufacturing Division, Statistics Canada

Alcan Smelters, *one of the largest in the world, produce over 260 000 t of aluminum each year (photo by Max's Photo).*

Ottertail Bridge, *one of the many spectacular bridges that had to be built to move the rail line across the mountainous terrain of B.C. (courtesy Vancouver Public Library).*

grown. Cattle ranching is practised on the flat grasslands of the interior.

Industry Manufacturing concentrates on products made from the province's natural resources: wood, metal, fish, and agriculture. Wood, pulp, and paper products make up nearly 50% of all manufacturing shipments. Most manufacturing occurs around Vancouver. Other centres include Prince Rupert and Kitimat (fish, aluminum refining), Okanagan (food and beverages, automobiles), and Trail (lead-zinc smelting and refining, fertilizer). Tumbler Ridge, southwest of Dawson Creek, is a new community built for the workers of two coal mines in the area.

TRANSPORTATION AND COMMUNICATIONS

Railways B.C. is served by two transcontinental railways. Both the Canadian Pacific (CPR) and Canadian National (CNR) railways come through mountain passes from Alberta, then wind down opposite sides of the Fraser River valley to Vancouver. VIA Rail now runs passenger service only on the CN line to Vancouver.

The completion of the main line of the CPR in 1885 linked B.C. to the rest of Canada. A branch of the CNR runs from Prince George down the Skeena River valley to the port of Prince Rupert. The province's main north-south railway is the B.C. Railway (originally the Pacific Great Eastern), which links North Vancouver with Prince George and Fort Nelson. The Esquimalt and Nanaimo Railway, a CPR subsidiary, provides freight service for some of the main communities on Vancouver Island. Passenger service on the Island was cut as of January 1990.

Roads The province's mountains have made road building difficult. It was not until 1962 that the first paved highway to run east-west across the province — the Trans-Canada Highway — was completed. Because mountainous terrain and sparse settlement make road building impossibly expensive in some regions, large sections of the province have no roads at all. There are no coastal roads north of Powell River, and only two main roads in the northern half of the province beyond Prince George: the Alaska Highway, running across the northeastern corner, and the Stewart-Cassiar Highway in the northwestern part. A recent major project was the construction of the Coquihalla Highway, completed from Hope to Kamloops in 1987. It cuts several hours off the trip across B.C.

Ferries Ferries are the main transportation link between Vancouver Island and the mainland, carrying freight, passengers, and automobiles. These ferries, as well as ones running to smaller islands in the Strait of Georgia and isolated communities on the coastal islands, are operated by the BC Ferry Corporation. The ferry terminals at Swartz Bay and Nanaimo on Vancouver Island, and Tsawwassen and Horseshoe Bay on the mainland, are

Ferry *passes a tidal marsh. B.C.'s ferry system is among the busiest in North America (photo by Thomas Kitchin).*

Totems *in Kispiox, B.C. (photo by J.A. Kraulis).*

among the busiest in North America. The BC Ferry Corporation also has the four largest double-ended (propellers at each end) ferries in North America, capable of carrying 1500 passengers and 360 cars on three decks, and travelling at speeds of 22 knots.

Airlines All major and many smaller communities in the province are served by commercial airlines. In addition to the major airlines, B.C. is served by two private airlines: Air B.C., based in Vancouver, and Time Air, based in Lethbridge, Alta. There are international airports at Vancouver and Victoria.

Communications The major newspapers in the province are the Vancouver *Sun*, the Vancouver *Province*, and the Victoria *Times-Colonist*. There are 14 other daily newspapers, about 150 weeklies, and over 70 magazines published in the province. The major radio and TV stations are based in Vancouver and Victoria.

POPULATION

The province has the greatest diversity of native people of any region of Canada. They belong to seven distinct language groups, speaking 19 different languages. the major groups are the Tlingit, Tsimshian, Haida, Bella Coola, Kwakiutl, Nootka, and Coast Salish. In 1988 there were 77 153 registered Indians in the province.

Other distinctive ethnic minorities are the Chinese, who came to the province in the 19th century to pan for gold and as labourers on the construction of the CPR and other projects; the Japanese, who came in the late 19th century to work as agricultural labourers and fishermen; and Sikhs and other South Asians who first came at the beginning of the 20th century. Most of B.C.'s population is British in origin.

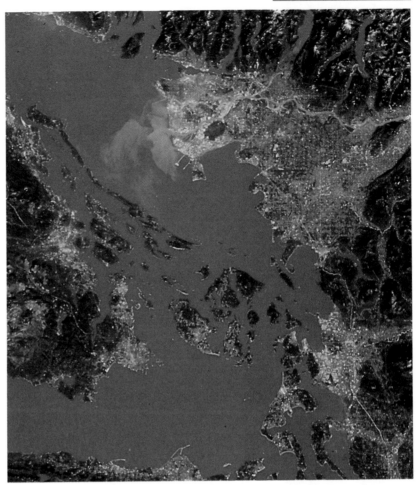

EDUCATION

The first elementary school in the province was established at Victoria in 1852, and the first secondary school in 1876. The Public School Act of 1872 set up a system of free provincial schools. At present there are 75 school districts in B.C., whose schools are administered by local boards of education and are paid for by local property taxes and grants from the provincial government. There are as

Satellite Image of the most populated area of B.C. Vancouver is upper middle, Victoria at the bottom right tip of Vancouver Island (© MacDonald Dettwiler, Advanced Satellite Productions).

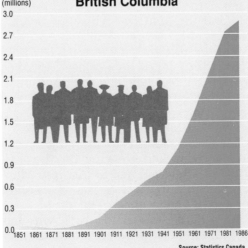

POPULATION GROWTH - 1851-1986

British Columbia

(millions)

3.0 2.7 2.4 2.1 1.8 1.5 1.2 0.9 0.6 0.3 0.0

1851 1861 1871 1881 1891 1901 1911 1921 1931 1941 1951 1961 1971 1981 1986

Source: Statistics Canada

Major Religious Groups (1981*)	
United Church	20.2%
Roman Catholic	19.4%
Anglican	13.8%
Lutheran	4.5%
Presbyterian	3.3%
Baptist	3.0%
Pentecostal	2.0%
Sikh	1.5%
Jehovah's Witnesses	1.2%
Mennonite	1.1%

*Last figures available. Religion was not counted in the 1986 census.

Population of Cities (1986)	
Vancouver	1 380 729
Victoria	255 547
Kelowna	89 730
Matsqui*	88 420
Prince George	67 621
Kamloops	61 773
Nanaimo	60 420
Chilliwack*	50 288
Vernon	42 802
New Westminster [1]	39 972
Penticton	38 966
Courtenay	37 553
North Vancouver [1]	35 698
Williams Lake	33 556
Port Coquitlam [1]	29 115
Campbell River	26 694
Port Alberni	26 134
Duncan	24 062
Quesnel	23 264
Trail	20 257
Powell River	18 374
Prince Rupert	17 581
Terrace	17 390
Langley	16 557
Cranbrook	15 893
Port Moody	15 754
White Rock	14 387
Fort St John	13 355
Colwood [2]	11 546
Kitimat	11 196
Dawson Creek	10 544
Revelstoke	8 279
Nelson	8 113
Kimberley	6 732
Castlegar	6 385
Merritt	6 180
Fernie	5 188
Grand Forks	3 282
Armstrong	2 706
Enderby	1 714
Greenwood	767

* District Municipality
[1] Included in Vancouver population
[2] Included in Victoria population

Languages (1986)	
English	80.9%
Chinese	2.9%
German	2.8%
French	1.3%
Punjabi	1.3%
Italian	0.9%
Dutch	0.8%
Other	9.1%

well a number of private schools, some run by religious groups, and others modelled on the British system. In 1987, 6.9% of the province's students were enrolled in private schools, the highest percentage in Canada outside Quebec.

The province's first university was the University of British Columbia (in Vancouver), founded in 1908 and opened in 1915. There are three other universities: Simon Fraser University, at Burnaby; University of Victoria, at Victoria; and Trinity Western University, at Langley. The province has six technical and vocational colleges, including the B.C. Institute of Technology and the Emily Carr College of Art and Design. There are also 15 community colleges, which offer technical and vocational programs as well as university transfer courses. Royal Roads Military College in Victoria is one of Canada's three military colleges. Lester B. Pearson College of the Pacific, also in Victoria, is part of a chain of international schools and colleges throughout the world.

CULTURE

The province is home to a number of important museums, art galleries, theatrical companies, and archival institutions. It has two major symphony orchestras, the Vancouver Symphony and Victoria Symphony Orchestras.

The provincial museum (Royal British Columbia Museum) in Victoria is one of the best of its kind on the continent. It has particularly good displays of wildlife (the mammoth is a popular tourist attraction), and displays of Indian masks and other artifacts. The University of British Columbia Museum of Anthropology (designed by Arthur Erickson) has a superb collection of Northwest Coast Indian artifacts. There are many other good museums, such as the B.C. Forest Museum in Duncan and the Maritime Museum in Vancouver.

The best-known B.C. artist is Emily Carr (1871-1945) who was born and died in Victoria. She travelled to remote Indian villages to record their houses and totem poles, and her early work was strongly influenced by Indian themes.

There are a number of notable native artists living and working on the B.C. coast. Bill Reid, a Haida, is an internationally recognized carver as well as a worker for native rights. Robert Davidson, a student of Reid's, is a Haida artist who has carved a number of totem poles for various locations in Canada. Tony Hunt is a

Museum of Anthropology, *University of British Columbia (© Kaj Svensson).*

Kwakiutl artist and carver of international reputation. He studied with his grandfather, the famous Mungo Martin, whose totem pole in Victoria's Beacon Hill Park, finished in 1956, is the world's tallest one carved from a single log.

Many of Canada's best-known writers, such as Phyllis Webb and George Bowering, live in B.C.

The province has a number of major historic sites. Fort Langley, established on the Fraser River in 1827, was an important Hudson's Bay Company post. Barkerville is a restored gold-rush town in central B.C. Several of its buildings date from the mid-1860s. Fort Steele, 17 km northeast of Cranbrook, is the site of a Mounted Police post dating from 1887.

SPORT AND RECREATION

The province's major professional sports teams are the Vancouver Canucks (hockey), and the British Columbia Lions (football, winners of the Grey Cup in 1985). The Vancouver Canadians baseball team plays in the Pacific Coast League. In 1954 Vancouver hosted the British Empire Games (now called the Commonwealth Games).

British Columbians take advantage of their natural environment all year round through a wide variety of recreational activities. In summer, these include cycling, swimming, hiking, camping, golfing, and trail riding, as well as sailing, canoeing, kayaking, river rafting, scuba diving, and whale watching. Sportfishing is also popular in the summer months. In winter, activities range from downhill and cross-country skiing to snowshoeing and snowmobiling.

GOVERNMENT AND POLITICS

Government Like the people of other Canadian provinces, British Columbians take part in the three levels of govern-

Legislature, Victoria, B.C. (photo by Malak, Ottawa).

Shoreline, by Emily Carr, one of B.C.'s best-known painters (courtesy McMichael Canadian Collection).

ment: federal, provincial, and local. At the federal level, they elect members to the House of Commons in Ottawa. As well, they are represented by six members in the Senate of Canada; the senators are appointed by the federal government.

At the provincial level, British Columbians elect members to the Legislative Assembly of B.C. (the B.C. legislature). At the local level, British Columbians elect councillors who administer their city, town, village, or district.

The number of provincial and federal members was increased over the years as the population increased. In B.C.'s first years as a province, the people could elect 25 members to the provincial legislature and six members to the House of Commons. By 1989, the number had risen to 69 provincial members and 32 federal. Similarly, three appointed senators in 1871 had been increased to six by the late 1980s.

The government of British Columbia operates by the same laws, rules, and tra-ditions as the federal government and the other provinces. These are described in the entries **Government** and **Parliament**. The legislative building is located in Victoria, facing the inner harbour of the city.

Politics British Columbia has seen the rise and fall of the Liberals and Conservatives as major forces in its provincial political life. But it was not until after the emergence of the Social Credit party in the post-war years, with the New Democrat Party (NDP) as the opposition, that B.C. became known as a province where politics are more polarized than anywhere else in Canada.

Traditional federal party lines were introduced in 1903. The Liberals and Conservatives were successful in the first half of the century. They lost some support during the Great Depression of the 1930s when voters increasingly looked to other parties for solutions to economic troubles. The Liberal and Conservative parties virtually disappeared by the 1960s.

Two members of the same family, W.A.C. Bennett and his son Bill, led the province as Social Credit premiers for all but three years of the period from 1952 to

Government House and Camp, New Westminster, B.C., 1860-65. New Westminster was proclaimed capital of B.C. in 1859 and controlled traffic entering the Fraser River (courtesy PABC/HP15084).

B.C.: Time Line

- **1778** James Cook lands on Vancouver I.
- **1792-94** George Vancouver explores and maps the coast
- **1793** Mackenzie travels overland to the coast
- **1843** Ft Victoria is built on Vancouver I.
- **1849** Vancouver I. made a British colony
- **1858** Fraser River gold rush
- **1858** Mainland B.C. becomes a colony
- **1860** The Cariboo gold rush begins
- **1866** Mainland B.C. and Vancouver I. become a single colony, under the name British Columbia
- **1871** B.C. joins Confederation. It is Canada's seventh province
- **1885** Canadian Pacific Railway is completed
- **1880s to early 1900s** Chinese, Japanese, and Sikhs arrive in B.C.
- **1914** Sikhs on board *Komagata Maru* are denied entry to B.C.
- **1942** Japanese Canadians interned
- **1952-72** W.A.C. Bennett launches projects to expand B.C.'s economy
- **1986** B.C. hosts Expo 86 world fair in Vancouver

1986. The elder Bennett, known as "Wacky" Bennett, was premier from 1952 to 1972. His policies were his own mix of "free enterprise" and government involvement in the economy. After three years in which the NDP under Dave Barrett held power, Bennett's son carried on the family tradition for another 11 years. His successor, Bill Vander Zalm, has continued to keep Social Credit in power since 1986. All of these premiers have faced fierce opposition to their policies. In the case of the Bennetts, much of the opposition came from labour, teachers, and others who experienced budget cuts. In the case of the NDP, it was business. In the case of Vander Zalm, it has focused more on his personal style.

Premiers of British Columbia from 1871

	Party*	Term
John Foster McCreight		1871-72
Amor De Cosmos		1872-74
George Anthony Walkem		1874-76
Andrew Charles Elliott		1876-78
George Anthony Walkem		1878-82
Robert Beaven		1882-83
William Smithe		1883-87
Alexander E.B. Davie	Cons	1887-89
John Robson	Lib	1889-92
Theodore Davie		1892-95
John Herbert Turner		1895-98
Charles Augustus Semlin	Cons	1898-1900
Joseph Martin	Lib	1900
James Dunsmuir		1900-02
Edward Gawler Prior	Cons	1902-03
Richard McBride	Cons	1903-15
William John Bowser	Cons	1915-16
Harlan Carey Brewster	Lib	1916-18
John Oliver	Lib	1918-27
John Duncan MacLean	Lib	1927-28
Simon Fraser Tolmie	Cons	1928-33
Thomas Dufferin Pattullo	Lib	1933-41
John Hart	CG	1941-47
Byron Ingemar Johnson	CG	1947-52
William A.C. Bennett	Socred	1952-72
David Barrett	NDP	1972-75
William R. Bennett	Socred	1975-86
Wilhelmus Vander Zalm	Socred	1986-

*Abbreviations:
CG=Coalition Government
Cons=Conservative Party
Lib=Liberal Party
NDP=New Democratic Party
Socred=Social Credit Party

HISTORY

The earliest human settlement of the Northwest Coast occurred about 10 000 years ago, when people of the "Old Cordilleran" tradition occupied the region. The crude pebble tools that they left behind show that they lived by hunting and fishing.

Northwest Coast Culture About 5000 years ago the patterns of living in the area changed. The earliest inhabitants had lived in small groups, but the remains of the later sites show that these people were living in much larger groups, and for long periods of time. They adapted to harvesting the animals of the sea. Barbed harpoons, fish hooks, weights for fishing nets, knives, and woodworking tools dating from this period have been found by archaeologists.

By 3500 years ago a distinctive society had emerged, one which was to survive until the arrival of Europeans. Part of it still survives. Food was plentiful. Deer, bear, elk, and mountain goat were available to hunters on land, and seals and porpoises in the sea. Huge quantities of seafood and fish, particularly Pacific salmon, were caught. The massive shell middens (piles of shells) mark the living places of these people. The only agricultural crop that was grown was tobacco, which was smoked in stone pipes. Native society in this period was organized on lines of status and wealth, and the goods that have been found in graves show the prosperity that these people achieved. About 2000 years ago they began to build the large plank houses (some of them as long as 500 m) which so astonished the first European explorers.

European Exploration In the year 1774 Spaniards under Juan Pérez Hernández sighted and claimed what is now the coast of B.C. The first European actually to set foot on British Columbia was Captain James Cook, who landed at Nootka Sound on the west coast of Vancouver Island in 1778. His men traded with the native people for otter pelts, and they realized that the land was rich in valuable furs. From 1792 to 1794 Captain George Vancouver explored and mapped the coast, naming many of its main features. This activity gave the British a strong claim to the region, and the Spanish eventually abandoned their claims. The fact that the native people had lived there for thousands of years was of no importance to the Europeans.

The first European to explore the interior was fur trader Alexander Mackenzie, an employee of Montreal's North West Company. He was looking for a trade route from Montreal to the Pacific coast. In 1793 he came via the Peace River and then travelled by way of the upper Fraser River across the Chilcotin Plateau, through the Coast Mountains, to saltwater at Bella Coola Inlet. Two other employees of the company, Simon Fraser and

Two Early Loggers stand on "springboards" which they have inserted in the tree and from which they make their undercut (courtesy British Columbia Archives and Records Service/HP48431)

David Thompson, explored the southern interior, particularly the valleys of the Fraser River (1808), and the Thompson and Columbia rivers (1807-11). Fort McLeod, founded by Simon Fraser in 1805, was the first permanent inland post. He also founded Fort St James in 1806, and Fort George in 1807.

The Fur-Trade Era During the first half of the 19th century there was no agricultural settlement in B.C. Instead, fur traders — first the North West Company, then the Hudson's Bay Company — set up posts on the coast and main river routes of what is now B.C., as well as the present-day American states of Washington and Oregon. The fur trade had a marked effect on the lives of the native people. The abundance of new trade goods meant that the native custom of potlatch (ceremonies at which gifts were given) could become much more lavish. Steel tools made totem poles easier to carve and thus more plentiful. However, European diseases brought death to people who had no resistance to them. Firearms made warfare between tribes much more deadly. The fur trade also reduced the number of wild animals, particularly the sea otter, whose fur was especially prized.

In the 1830s, Americans began to settle in the southern part of this region, in Oregon's Willamette Valley. They resented the Hudson's Bay Company's control, and began to demand that the United States government take over the entire region.

The result was the Oregon Treaty of 1846, which divided the mainland along the 49th parallel, today's boundary, and gave all of Vancouver Island to Britain. The Hudson's Bay Company had already begun to move its operations north, establishing a new headquarters at Fort Victoria on Vancouver Island in 1843.

The Vancouver Island Colony In 1849 the British government made Vancouver Island a colony, and in 1851 James Douglas, chief factor of the Hudson's Bay Company, was made governor. In 1856 the colony was given some self-government when a legislative assembly was set up. A number of settlers arrived to begin farming around Victoria and the other posts, such as Nanaimo and Fort Langley. During this period the mainland remained without organized government.

The Gold Rushes For several years the colony of Vancouver Island remained quiet and little-known by the rest of the world. But in 1856 and 1857 gold was discovered on the Thompson River and on the sandbars of the lower Fraser River. When the news got out in 1858, thousands of people rushed to the region. Many of them were miners who had come to California during the gold rush of 1849, and were now looking for new sources of wealth. In 1858 the town of Yale was founded at the south end of the Fraser Canyon. The gold-seekers fanned out over the watershed of the Fraser River, looking for gold, and found it east of Quesnel and at the western edge of the Cariboo Mountains. There the town of Barkerville was founded in 1862. In 1863 it had as many as 5000 people, making it the largest town in western British North America.

In 1858 a second colony, called British Columbia, was established, made up of the mainland part of today's province (James Douglas was governor of both colonies). Its capital was the settlement of New Westminster. In 1866 it and the older colony of Vancouver Island were united as a single colony, under the name

Population Growth of British Columbia	
1871	36 247
	(native 25 661)
1881	49 459
1891	98 173
1901	178 657
1911	392 480
1921	524 582
1931	694 263
1941	817 861
1951	1 165 210
1961	1 629 082
1966	1 873 674
1971	2 184 621
1976	2 466 608
1981	2 744 465
1986	2 889 207

Prospecting for Gold
This painting by William Hind shows prospectors in central B.C. in the 1860s. Gold played a big part in the fortunes of B.C. in the late 19th century (courtesy B.C. Archives).

British Columbia. From 1866 to 1868 the colonial capital moved about, but in 1868 it was moved permanently to Victoria.

Between 1862 and 1865 the Cariboo Road was built to link the head of river navigation on the Fraser at Yale with the mining town of Barkerville. The road, 650 km long, was built by Royal Engineers, under difficult conditions. Some of it had to be blasted out of the rock of the Fraser Canyon. The present Trans-Canada Highway follows much of its route.

B.C. Joins Canada By 1867 gold production was declining. People were leaving, and the new colony of British Columbia was in economic trouble. The non-native residents, who numbered only about 12 000, debated whether to join the new Dominion of Canada or to join the United States. In 1871 British Columbia joined Canada, lured by the promise that a railway would be completed from Ontario to the West Coast within ten years. The railway project was delayed for several years, causing furious complaints from B.C., but in 1885 it was finished.

Settlers did not rush to live in B.C.'s mild climate at first — by 1881 the population was only 49 000, of whom slightly over half were native people. B.C. had hoped that the completion of the Canadian Pacific Railway (CPR) would bring prosperity, since it was an important link between Europe and Asia; but this prosperity was slow to develop. The railway did, however, change the centre of power and population from Victoria to the new town of Vancouver, which was incorporated in April 1886 as the CPR's Pacific terminus. Within 15 years, in 1901, Vancouver's population had outstripped Victoria's (27 010 to 23 688).

By 1900 a number of businessmen had arrived in B.C. to exploit and develop the province's rich natural resources. Robert Dunsmuir, a Scot who became known as the "coal king of B.C.," came to Vancouver Island in 1851 to work for the Hudson's Bay Co. He discovered a deposit of coal near Nanaimo and set up his own coal mine. By hiring Chinese miners cheaply and keeping trade unions out of his mines he became extremely wealthy and also highly unpopular with his workers. In 1884 he built the Esquimalt and Nanaimo Railway for a payment of one-quarter of all the land on Vancouver Island and $750 000. His son James sold the coal company in 1910 for $11 million.

In the Kootenay district of B.C. around 1900, prospectors and entrepreneurs developed deposits of coal, gold, copper, and other minerals. Towns such as Trail (incorporated in 1901), Rossland (1897), and Fernie (1904) were built as mining towns.

Development of the forest resources of B.C. increased after 1914, when the Panama Canal made it possible to ship timber products cheaply to markets in eastern North America. The great coastal forests of B.C., with their rich stands of Douglas fir, sitka spruce, and western red cedar, produced logs and timber to build the houses for a rapidly expanding Canadian population after 1900, and to provide poles for the telephones and telegraph lines that were spreading across the country. In the early days, business entrepreneurs could get timber rights from the provincial government for one cent per acre and a royalty of 20 cents per thousand board feet. At those prices, thousands of square kilometres of valuable timber were virtually given away.

During the second half of the 19th century, many immigrants from Asia arrived in B.C. The first were Chinese, who came with the gold rushes of the late 1850s and 1860s, and stayed on in service jobs or as labourers. Between 1881 and 1884, more than 14 000 Chinese labourers came to the province, many to work on the building of the CPR. Some went home with their earnings, but others stayed, and prejudice against them by earlier settlers led to discrimination and anti-Chinese riots. In 1886 a "head tax" of $50 was imposed on Chinese immigrants; later it was raised to $500. This temporarily discouraged further immigration. The Chinese Immigration Act, 1923, effectively ended it until 1947.

There was also discrimination against immigrants from Japan, who began to arrive in the 1880s and 1890s. Many of these people worked in the fishing and vegetable-growing industries. An anti-Japanese riot in Vancouver in 1907 was followed by an agreement with the Japanese government which stemmed the flow of immigrants.

Immigrants from India who arrived in the early 1900s were also unwelcome in B.C. In 1914, when the freighter *Komagata Maru* came to Vancouver with 376 mainly Sikh immigrants, all of whom were British subjects, the ship was kept in harbour for two months and then turned away.

The northern half of B.C. was first opened to development by the construction of the Grand Trunk Pacific Railway (now part of the Canadian National Railway) from Edmonton through the Yellowhead Pass to Prince Rupert between 1910 and 1914. Thirty years later the northeastern part of the province was opened up by the construction of the Alaska Highway in 1942.

B.C. suffered serious losses during World War I. From a population of about 400 000, some 55 000 men enlisted, of whom more than 6000 were killed and 13 000 wounded. The Great Depression of the 1930s also was a bad time for the province and its people. By 1933 more than 100 000 people were on "relief" (welfare), about 12% of the entire population, and there were thousands of unemployed men in Vancouver ready to challenge the "system." There were serious public disturbances in the city in 1935 and 1938. The province was rescued from the Depression by World War II, which revived the forest and mining industries.

After the war came the great age of industrial expansion, marked by "megaprojects," such as the aluminum smelter and hydroelectric dam at Kitimat and the Peace River power station near Hudson's Hope. Changes in Canadian immigration laws led to the end of the old racist policies, and a surge of Asian immigration made the province much more multicultural in character. Although B.C. still has many unsolved problems, notably the lack of progress in settling its native people's land claims, it has changed tremendously in the past generation.

For information about B.C., contact the Public Affairs Bureau, Government of B.C., 612 Government Street, Victoria, B.C., V8V 1X4.

▷ SUGGESTED READING: The magazine, *Beautiful British Columbia*; Cecil Clark, *B.C. Provincial Police Stories* (Vol. 1, 1986; Vol. 2, 1989); Harry E. Cullis and David Suzuki, *British Columbia: Frontier for Ideas* (1986); John Macpherson, *This Land: British Columbia* (1986); Derek Pethik and Susan Im Baumgarten, *British Columbia Recalled: A Picture History 1741 to 1871* (1974); J. Lewis Robinson and Walter G. Hardwick, *British Columbia: One Hundred Years of Geographical Change* (1979); George Woodcock, *A Picture History of British Columbia* (1980).

■ British Columbia Hydro

BC Hydro is a company that generates and sells electricity. It supplies power to all of British Columbia, except the southern interior. It was created in 1962 and is owned by the province of British Columbia. It is the third-largest electric utility in Canada.

Most of the electrical power that BC Hydro generates comes from running water. Its major hydroelectric power plants are on the Peace and the Columbia rivers. BC Hydro also distributes natural gas and operates freight services. In 1989 it was being sold to private investors.

▷ RELATED ARTICLES: **Electricity; Electric Utilities.**

■ British Columbia Lions

The B.C. Lions football team played their first game in 1954 (with the slogan "The Lions will roar in '54"). They won only one game in their first season, but improved over the next five years, reaching the playoffs in 1959. Quarterback Joe Kapp led them to their first Grey Cup victory in 1964. They won their second cup in 1985. The Lions play in BC Place, Canada's first domed stadium, which seats 60 000.

■ British Commonwealth Air Training Plan

The British Commonwealth Air Training Plan was a World War II scheme to train military aircrews from Great Britain, Australia, Canada, and New Zealand at training schools in Canada. It was a major Canadian contribution to the war effort, producing 131 553 pilots, bombers, gunners, navigators, and wireless operators for service overseas.

Canada was chosen as host country because it had so much usable air space and because it was far from the battlefields of Europe. Yet it was close enough to ferry planes and crews across the Atlantic to the war-torn areas. The first school opened on April 29, 1940, and by July 1942 the entire plan was in operation. It continued until 1945.

Though it included several countries, Canada controlled the plan and the Canadian air force carried out the training of pilots from around the world.

At its peak, the plan was using 11 000 aircraft and a staff of 104 000 people at more than 100 training schools across the country. It took a huge effort of planning and industry to organize the scheme, at an estimated total cost of $2.23 billion.

Air Training Plan As part of its effort during World War II, Canada trained over 130 000 airmen. Shown here are some of the original officers and staff in 1941 (courtesy PAA/BL-3541).

■ British North America

This is the term that was applied to the British colonies and territories in North America after the American Colonies became independent in 1783. It came to include the colonies of Upper Canada, Lower Canada, Nova Scotia, New Brunswick, Prince Edward Island, and Newfoundland. It also included Rupert's Land and the North-West Territories which were under the control of the Hudson's Bay Company, and the colonies of British Columbia and Vancouver Island on the West Coast. The term was seldom used after Canada became a nation in 1867.

▷ RELATED ARTICLE: **Canada.**

■ British North America Act (BNA Act), see Constitution Act, 1867

■ Brittain, Donald

Filmmaker (*born in 1928 at Ottawa, Ont.; died in 1989 at Montreal, Que.*). Brittain joined the National Film Board in 1955. He soon gained a reputation for his superb documentary films. Using his lively humour and sometimes biting wit he portrayed the lives of Canadian figures such as Leonard Cohen, Lord Thomson, and Norman Bethune. His film on writer Malcolm Lowry's tragic life brought him attention outside Canada. In *The Champions* (1978) he portrayed the relationship between political foes Pierre Trudeau and René Lévesque. He was working on a film on Mackenzie King at the time of his death. Brittain received more than 70 international awards during his career, including three Academy Award nominations.

Donald Brittain received more than 70 awards for his superb documentary films (courtesy National Film Board of Canada).

■ Broadbent, John Edward

Politician, leader of the federal New Democratic Party (NDP) (*born in 1936 at Oshawa, Ont.*). Ed Broadbent was born to a family of auto workers. He studied political science at university and was a professor before choosing politics as a career. First elected to the House of Commons for the NDP in 1968, he was chosen leader of the party in 1975 when David Lewis resigned.

During Broadbent's term as leader, the NDP won more seats in Parliament (43 in 1988) than ever before. During much of the 1980s, his popularity in the polls was higher than the leaders of the other two major parties. A moderate socialist, Broadbent fought for tax reforms, less foreign ownership in the Canadian economy, and measures to improve the lives of working people.

Despite his personal popularity, Broadbent was unable to move the NDP out of its position as the "third party." He retired as party leader in 1989.

▷ SUGGESTED READING: Judy Steed, *Ed Broadbent: The Pursuit of Power* (1988).

■ Broadcasting, see Radio; Television

■ Broadfoot, David

Actor (*born in 1925 at North Vancouver, B.C.*). Broadfoot is one of Canada's best loved and most successful comedians. He was brought up in a strongly religious household, and his three older sisters became missionaries in China. He dropped out of school in Grade 9, joined the Merchant Marine, and later took up acting in Vancouver. In 1952 he moved to Toronto, where he appeared for many years in the popular annual review *Spring Thaw*. He is best known for his many roles in "The Royal Canadian Air Farce," which, since 1973, has been one of CBC's most popular programs, first on radio and then on television. In this show, Broadfoot played The Honourable Member from Kicking Horse Pass; Bobby Clobber, the NHL superstar; Sergeant Renfrew, the Mountie who never gets his man; and others.

Broadfoot is also a popular speaker at conventions and banquets. In 1989 he resigned from the "Air Farce" to open his own one-man show, Dave Broadfoot's Comedy Crusade.

■ Brock, Sir Isaac

Army officer and hero of the War of 1812 (*born in 1769 at St Peter Port, Guernsey; died in 1812 at Queenston Heights, Upper Canada [Ontario]*). Born on the Channel Island of Guernsey, Brock joined the British army when he was 15 and in 1802 was posted to Canada with his regiment, the 49th Foot. In the summer of 1811 he was promoted major-general, and that October he was put in charge of Upper Canada when the lieutenant-governor went to England on leave. Because of his leadership, tact, and hard work, Upper Canada was better prepared than it would otherwise have been when war broke out with the United States in 1812.

In July 1812 an American army invaded Canada at present-day Windsor, Ont. It was repulsed and returned to Detroit. Brock rode to the area, gathering soldiers and volunteers along the way. On August 16, 1812, he crossed the Detroit River and launched an attack. The Americans surrendered. The victory gave an enormous boost to morale in Upper Canada. Brock would not live to receive the news that he had been knighted for his victory.

On October 13 American forces crossed the Niagara River. Brock was awakened by musket fire and rode to rally the men on Queenston Heights. The enemy emerged suddenly from the woods and Brock retreated. He sent for reinforcements and led a bold attack to drive the Americans back before they became too strong. Brock was shot in the wrist and then struck by a bullet near the heart while leading a second charge. He died almost at once. British reinforcements arrived soon after and pinned the Americans at the edge of the bluff, where they surrendered.

Brock's body lies at the base of a monument built in his honour on Queenston Heights. Upper Canadians gave his name to their sons, streets, roads, and the city of Brockville.

▷ RELATED ARTICLES: **Queenston Heights, Battle of; War of 1812.**

■ Brock University

Brock University is located in St Catharines, Ont. It is named for Sir Isaac Brock, famous military commander during the War of 1812. The university offers undergraduate and graduate programs in arts and sciences. It also has schools of administrative studies and physical education and recreation, and a college of education. Founded in 1964, it has about 9300 students. For further information write to the Registrar's Office, Brock University, St Catharines, Ont., L2S 3A1.

■ Brockville

Brockville, Ont., lies beside the St Lawrence River, 80 km east of Kingston. It began as a Loyalist settlement in 1784. First called Elizabethtown, it was renamed in 1812 after the fallen war hero, Sir Isaac Brock. The economy depends on a mix of light manufacturing. It is also a tourist centre for the Thousand Islands. One of Ontario's most historic cities, it features many fine old buildings and Canada's oldest railway tunnel, which was officially opened here in 1860. Brockville became a city in 1962. In 1986 its population was 20 880. For information, contact the City Clerk, Victoria Building, King Street, Brockville, Ont., K6V 3P5.

■ Bronfman Family

The Bronfmans control one of the world's richest business empires, the Seagram Company. They are descended from a Russian tobacco farmer, Ekiel Bronfman, who brought the family to Canada in 1889. Ekiel settled near Wapella, Sask., but soon moved to Brandon, Man., where

Sir Isaac Brock led a bold attack on the American forces on Queenston Heights. He was struck near the heart by a bullet while leading a charge (courtesy NAC/C-36181).

he started a wood-selling business.

Ekiel and his wife Minnie had eight children: Abe, Harry, Laura, Samuel, Jean, Bessie, Allan, and Rose. The three eldest were born in Russia, the younger ones in Canada. Samuel was born either in Russia or at sea on the way to Canada. He was the most famous of Ekiel's children. It was he who laid the basis of the family fortune.

Samuel Bronfman (*1889-1971*). In 1903, when Samuel was a teenager, his father and elder brothers bought a hotel in Manitoba. It did so well that they were able to buy and run other hotels. This led them into the liquor business, making and selling whisky. During the Prohibition era in the United States (1920-33), when Americans were not allowed to manufacture liquor, Samuel and his brothers built up a profitable business by selling Americans Canadian-made liquor. In 1924 Samuel founded a distilling company in Montreal to make quality whisky, and in 1928 he merged the company with a distillers called Joseph E. Seagram & Sons Ltd. As a result of Samuel's energy and business expertise, Seagrams grew to be one of the world's largest distilling firms. He played a leading role in Canadian Jewish affairs. His children have carried on the business.

Edgar Miles Bronfman (*born 1929*), the elder of Samuel's two sons, became chairman of the Seagram Company, working out of the company's head office in New

Samuel Bronfman built the Seagram Company into one of the world's largest distilling firms (artwork by Irma Coucill).

York. He has played an important international role as president of the World Jewish Congress.

Charles Rosner Bronfman (*born 1931*), Samuel's younger son, became Seagrams' deputy chairman, running the Canadian branch of the business in Montreal. In 1968 he bought the Montreal Expos baseball club, and in 1986 he created the CRB Foundation. The foundation sponsors studies on Canadian and Jewish affairs.

Phyllis Lambert (*born 1927*), the younger of Samuel's two daughters, founded the Canadian Centre of Architecture, which includes an architectural museum. Her sister, *Minda, Baroness de Gunzburg* (*1925-86*), married a French nobleman and moved to France, where she became a sponsor of art history.

Edward Bronfman (*born 1927*) and *Peter Bronfman* (*born 1929*) are Samuel Bronfman's nephews, the sons of his brother Allan. They built up a separate financial empire. Called Edper Investments, it includes both Canada's largest forestry company and its largest trust company.

■ Brooke, Frances

Novelist (*born in 1724 in England; died there in 1789*). This English writer lived in Canada from 1763 to 1768. She came with her husband, who was a chaplain (a Christian minister) to the British army stationed at Quebec City. She had written a play and a novel while she lived in England, and when she came to Canada she wrote another novel, *The History of Emily Montague* (1769).

In this novel Brooke showed what life was like in Quebec in the years after the British Conquest. She wrote about the weather, the things that people did to entertain themselves, the landscape, and the way that people dressed. Her novel is therefore read by many Canadians who wish to know more about life in Canada in the 18th century.

■ Brooker, Bertram Richard

Artist (*born in 1888 at Croydon, England; died in 1955 at Toronto, Ont.*). After he immigrated to Manitoba in 1905, Brooker held a variety of jobs in that province and in Saskatchewan before moving to Toronto in 1921 as an advertising executive. In 1927 he became the first painter in Canada to exhibit abstract art. It was not well received by the critics and, influenced by his friend L.L. FitzGerald, he turned to precise, realistic drawings and paintings. Brooker was also a poet and novelist, and

Sounds Assembling, by Bertram Brooker, oil on canvas (1928). Brooker was the first Canadian painter to exhibit abstract art (courtesy Winnipeg Art Gallery).

was the first person to win the Governor General's Award for fiction (for *Think of the Earth*, 1936).

■ Brooks

Brooks, Alta., is a town on the prairie 185 km southeast of Calgary. The surrounding area was home to the Blackfoot Indians. Settlement started with the arrival of the Canadian Pacific Railway in 1883. In the middle of a large irrigation district, Brooks's economy depends upon agriculture and the oil industry. Dinosaur Provincial Park, the Wildlife Centre and the Horticulture Centre, as well as campgrounds in the area, provide attractions for tourists. Brooks, with a 1986 population of 9464, was named for a railway engineer. For information, contact the Town Secretary-Treasurer, P.O. Box 880, Brooks, Alta, T0J 0J0.

■ Brott, Alexander

Conductor, violinist, composer (*born in 1915 at Montreal, Que.*). Brott was a successful violinist and has conducted several Canadian orchestras. His music for voice and several instruments is good humoured and witty. His son **Boris Brott** (*born in 1944 at Montreal*) made his debut as a violinist at age 5. Boris Brott conducted in Toronto and England and has been conductor of the Hamilton Philharmonic Orchestra since 1969. He has also conducted orchestras in Wales, Nova Scotia, and the United States. He is known

Alexander Brott, conducting the Montreal Symphony Orchestra (courtesy SSC Photocentre).

Roy Brown's most famous dogfight was with the German air ace called the Red Baron (courtesy Canadian War Museum).

for his artistic flair and his devotion to Canadian music.

■ Brown, Arthur Roy

World War I fighter pilot (*born in 1893 at Carleton Place, Ont.; died in 1944 at Stouffville, Ont.*). Brown's best-known air battle was in April 1918 when he took on Germany's famed Red Baron, Manfred von Richthofen. This was in France, over the Somme Valley.

At the time, the German air ace was on the tail of Wop May, a greenhorn pilot from Edmonton. Brown gave chase, with a long burst of gunfire. Meanwhile, Australian machine gunners were firing from the ground. The Red Baron went down in flames, but people are still arguing about who killed him — Brown or the Australians. Nevertheless, thanks to Brown's intervention, May survived to fly for many more years.

Brown himself barely survived the war. The strain of battle in the air wore him down, and in July 1918 he fainted while flying and crashed. He was badly wounded but pulled through. Although dogged by ill health, he lived another 25 years and ran his own air company, General Airways, formed in 1928.

▷ RELATED ARTICLE: **Wilfrid Reid May.**

■ Brown, George

Founder of the Toronto *Globe* and Father of Confederation (*born in 1818 at Alloa, Scotland; died in 1880 at Toronto, Ont.*). Brown was raised in Edinburgh and went with his father to New York in 1837. They moved to Toronto six years later. In 1844 George began the *Globe* newspaper, on the Reform side of politics. Brown was a vigorous writer and a strong Presbyterian. These qualities combined with his great energy, made the *Globe* a powerful force in opposing separate schools and Roman Catholic influences.

From 1853 on, as the population of Canada West [Ontario] outstripped that of Canada East [Quebec], Brown was the champion of "rep by pop." This stood for "representation by population," a system that would give Canada West more seats than Canada East in the Legislative Assembly of the Province of Canada. Brown had first been elected to the Assembly in 1851, and in August 1858 he briefly headed the government, in partnership with A.A. Dorion of Canada East.

Towards Confederation In 1862, when Brown was on holiday in Scotland, he met and married Anne Nelson, of the Edinburgh publishing house. Brown was 44 years old, and at that age love, like measles, is apt to hit hard. It was a different George Brown who returned to Canadian politics in 1864. Previously, he had insisted on the Reform Party's solution to the Province of Canada's problems. This involved giving Canada East and West separate assemblies and having a weak central government to deal with common matters, such as the post office and railways. The Conservative Party had never accepted this. If there had to be a change, the Conservatives felt it should take the form of a *federal* union of all the British North American colonies, with a strong central government.

In 1864 Brown conceded this important

George Brown was a fierce defender of the rights of Protestant Ontario. His willingness to compromise was a major boost to the movement towards Confederation (courtesy NAC/C-26415).

frequently consulted by Alexander Mackenzie when Mackenzie was prime minister (1873 to 1878); and he was a Liberal senator from 1874 until his death.

On March 25, 1880, Brown was shot in his office by a former *Globe* employee who had been dismissed for drinking. It was only a flesh wound in the leg, but it became infected, and in those days before sulfa drugs, recovery was at best chancy. Brown was dead from gangrene in six weeks.

Brown had made the *Globe* into a power in Protestant Canada. Indeed, the paper was feared, for it could be a bully. This was a measure of the power of its writing and the range of its circulation. Brown epitomized the best and the worst of Protestant Ontario, its fierce passion for freedom, its hatred of authority (including authority of the churches) and, it must be said, its narrowness and bigotry.

▷ RELATED ARTICLES: **Confederation; Province of Canada; Rep by Pop.**

point and offered to work with the Conservatives in a coalition government to bring about Confederation. Brown's new willingness to compromise meant that the Confederation movement could go forward. As a senior member of the government, Brown played a leading role at the Charlottetown and Quebec conferences in 1864.

After Confederation, Brown largely moved out of politics and concentrated on the Toronto *Globe* and on his livestock farm near Brantford, Ont. Yet he remained a major power in the Reform Party (now called the Liberal Party). He was

■ **Brown, John George ("Kootenai")**
Adventurer and conservationist (*born in 1839 at Ennistymon, Ireland; died in 1916 at Waterton Lakes, Alta*). Educated in England, Kootenai Brown went to India as an officer in the British army. By 1862 he was in British Columbia, drawn there by the Cariboo gold rush. As well as prospecting for gold in B.C., Brown worked as a trapper and police constable. Then, in 1865, he crossed the Rocky Mountains to Kootenay Lakes (now Waterton Lakes), and from there he travelled across the prairies, where he was attacked and wounded by a band of Blackfoot.

Brown spent the following years on the prairies, working as a trader and as a mail carrier for the Americans. In the course of his dispatch riding, he was briefly taken prisoner by the Sioux chief, Sitting Bull. Brown married a Metis woman, and in the early 1870s he lived with his wife's family, joining them in buffalo hunts. He eventually settled down at Kootenay Lakes, where he earned a living as a guide. He served as chief scout for the Rocky Mountain Rangers during the 1885 North-West Rebellion.

Brown was impressed by the beauty of the country around Kootenay Lakes, and it was largely because of his efforts that the area became a national park. In 1895 the Kootenay Forest Reserve was established there. Brown served as fishery officer. In 1910 he was made forest ranger. Then, in 1914, the reserve was enlarged to become Waterton Lakes National Park.

"Kootenai" Brown gained his nickname for his efforts to preserve the wilderness around the Waterton Lakes (courtesy Glenbow Archives/NA-678-1).

■ Bruce Peninsula

The Bruce Peninsula, 100 km long, forms the west side of Georgian Bay in Lake Huron. Part of the Niagara Escarpment which runs through southwest Ontario, it has high, rocky cliffs on its east side which slope away to lowlands in the west. At the tip of the peninsula is Tobermory, a favourite diving spot because of shipwrecks in the area. A number of offshore islands comprise Georgian Bay Islands National Park. Bruce Peninsula and other islands were formed into Bruce Peninsula National Park in 1987. The peninsula contains an unusual variety of plants, including 49 species of orchid and 30 species of fern. The Bruce Trail winds up the Georgian Bay side. For information on the Bruce Peninsula, contact the Superintendent, Bruce Peninsula National Park, P.O. Box 189, Tobermory, Ont., N0H 2R0.

■ Bruce Trail

The Bruce Trail is a 720 km footpath along Ontario's Niagara Escarpment from Queenston, near Niagara Falls, to Tobermory at the tip of the Bruce Peninsula. The idea for a hiking trail across southwest Ontario came from metallurgist Ray Lowes in 1960. This led to the creation of the Bruce Trail Association, a group of volunteers who built and now maintain the trail. It is one of Ontario's major tourist attractions.

■ Bruhn, Erik Belton Evers

Ballet dancer and director (*born in 1928 at Copenhagen, Denmark; died in 1986 at Toronto, Ont.*). When Bruhn first visited Canada in 1964 to stage the ballet *La Sylphide* with the National Ballet Company, he was already a famous dancer in Denmark and Britain. He returned many times as a guest artist, choreographer, and teacher.

In 1983 Bruhn was appointed artistic director of the company. In just three years he had a tremendous impact on the National Ballet. He introduced several new works to the repertoire, most notably works which broke down the traditional barriers between classical ballet and modern dance. He promoted a number of young soloists and inspired everyone by his enthusiasm and drive. Before he died, he arranged for Valerie Wilder and Lynn Wallis to carry on as associate artistic directors and complete his vision for the company. An annual Erik Bruhn international competition for young dancers was established in his memory.

Erik Bruhn introduced many new works to the National Ballet, particularly those that broke down traditional barriers between classical ballet and modern dance (courtesy National Ballet of Canada).

■ Brûlé, Étienne

Explorer, interpreter (*born around 1592 at Champigny-sur-Marne, France; died in 1633 in Huronia*). Brûlé was one of the first *coureurs de bois* (French for "runners of the woods"). As a teenager, in 1610, he was sent to live among the Algonquin. Samuel de Champlain hoped that Brûlé would learn their language and customs, and thereby win their loyalty to the French.

Brûlé went on to live and travel with the Huron, the first European to do so. He left no account of his life and the details of his career are obscure, but he was probably the first outsider to see Lakes Ontario, Erie, Superior, and Huron. He regularly led Huron traders down to Quebec with their furs, and his free lifestyle would later be copied by many young men in the French colony.

Brûlé was admired for his wide travels and many adventures, but some colonists thought that living in the wilderness had made him wild and undependable. Champlain himself expressed disappointment, calling Brûlé "very vicious in character." In 1629 Brûlé deserted to the English Kirke brothers when they attacked Quebec. Champlain called him a traitor. Brûlé went back to live in Huronia, where he was murdered by the Huron, who may have believed he was dealing with their enemies.

▷ RELATED ARTICLES: **Coureurs de bois; New France.**

John Buchanan has served four terms as premier of Nova Scotia (courtesy Canapress Photo Service).

■ Brunette Island

Brunette Island, 20 km², lies at the mouth of Fortune Bay on the south coast of Newfoundland. The main settlement was the fishing village of Mercer's Cove until the 1950s, when residents were moved off the island. It is now a provincial wildlife reserve and an important breeding ground for caribou, arctic hare, and moose.

■ Buchan, Bryan

Writer (*born in 1945 at Aberdeen, Scotland*). Buchan studied at the University of Toronto and, since 1968, has been teaching in Richmond Hill, Ont. His three novels were written to interest his students in reading.

Doug, hero of *The Forgotten World of Uloc* (1970), meets the guardian of a now-polluted pond and helps the creature defeat evil beings. In *Copper Sunrise* (1972), Jamie, a young settler, meets a native boy and discovers that he is not at all like the "savages" believed in by the villagers. *The Dragon Children* (1975) is a mystery-fantasy. In this book John meets Steve, a ghost, and helps him defeat criminals who swindle old people. Doug, Jamie, and John learn about friendship from these unusual characters. Working together with them, the boys also learn about helping other people.

■ Buchan, John (1st Baron Tweedsmuir)

Governor general of Canada (*born in 1875 at Perth, Scotland; died in 1940 at Montreal, Que.*). John Buchan, author of *The Thirty-Nine Steps* and other adventure stories, was governor general of Canada from 1935 to 1940, being created Lord Tweedsmuir on his appointment to the post. The son of a Scottish clergyman, Buchan wrote a vast number of books — biographies and histories as well as his popular novels. By the time he arrived in Canada, he had also held a wide range of jobs. He was a colonial administrator in South Africa; a journalist, lawyer, and publisher in Britain; an intelligence officer in France during World War I; and a member of Parliament in Britain from 1927 to 1935.

As governor general of Canada, Buchan helped establish the Governor General's Literary Awards, and during this period he also wrote his autobiography, *Memory Hold-the-Door* (1940).

■ Buchanan, John MacLennan

Lawyer, politician, premier of Nova Scotia (*born in 1931 at Sydney, N.S.*). After graduating with a degree in law from Dalhousie University, Buchanan practised law in Halifax for several years. He first won election to the Nova Scotia Assembly as a Conservative in 1967, and became leader of the party four years later.

Buchanan led the Conservatives to victory in the provincial election of 1978, and won re-election three times. As premier, he has tried to put life back into the steel industry in Cape Breton, and has sought to develop Nova Scotia's coal and energy industries.

■ Buck, Timothy

Communist leader (*born in 1891 at Beccles, England; died in 1973 at Cuernavaca, Mexico*). An activist for the rights of working people, Tim Buck was leader of the Communist Party of Canada for 32 years.

Buck came to Canada from England in 1910 in search of a better life. A machinist by trade, he got involved in radical politics in Toronto and was a founding member of the Canadian Communist Party at a secret meeting in 1921. At the time of its founding the party was banned, though it became legal in 1924.

In 1929 Buck emerged as general secretary of the party. Under his leadership, it gained support during the 1930s when the Depression left so many people jobless. Because they preached class conflict and demanded dramatic changes to Canadian society, authorities feared the communists and tried to suppress them. Police harassed the party, breaking up its meetings and arresting its members. Buck himself spent more than two years in jail from 1932 to 1934. During that time someone tried to shoot him in his cell.

In 1940, early in World War II, the Communist Party was banned outright. Buck went underground to avoid arrest, and remained in hiding for three years.

After the war, communism in Canada had little support. Buck remained leader of the party until 1962, when he retired. In 1971 the Soviet Union awarded him the Order of the Great October Revolution for his contributions to the party.

■ Bucke, Richard Maurice

Psychiatrist (*born in 1837 at Methwold, England; died in 1902 at London, Ont.*). Richard Bucke introduced important new ways of treating the mentally ill. Rather than keeping them "happy" with alcohol and chaining them up to prevent injury (barbarous methods that were common in his day), he practised a policy of non-restraint. When he judged the cause of a patient's mental illness to be physical, he treated the condition and in some cases performed operations.

All this shocked many of Bucke's contemporaries, who thought it useless to try and help the mentally handicapped. But Bucke had never taken the ordinary approach. As a teenager, he had left home for a life of adventure in the West, and it was only after he had lost a foot from frostbite that he settled down to study medicine.

After a year running the asylum in Hamilton, Ont., Bucke was made superintendent of the asylum at London, Ont., in 1877. He directed the asylum until his death. He offered his patients interesting work to keep them from boredom and arranged concerts, dances, and sports events for them. He was a founder of the medical school at the University of Western Ontario.

Bucke was a friend of the famous American poet Walt Whitman. He visited him frequently and wrote his first biography.

■ Buckler, Ernest

Novelist and short-story writer (*born in 1908 at Dalhousie West, N.S.; died in 1984 at Bridgetown, N.S.*). Buckler's home and inspiration for his writing was Nova Scotia's Annapolis Valley. Living and working on the family farm near Annapolis Royal for most of his life, Buckler wrote two of the most carefully crafted novels in English-Canadian literature, *The Mountain and the Valley* (1952) and *The Cruelest Month* (1963). In his first novel Buckler uses precise language to portray the family relationships surrounding the young artist, David Canaan. The book was beautifully written and influenced a whole generation of young Canadian writers. In *The Cruelest Month*, Buckler explores the personalities and problems brought to a rural Nova Scotia inn by guests who are seeking a retreat from city life.

In Buckler's third major work, *Ox Bells and Fireflies* (1968), he combined fiction with autobiography to write a memoir of his early rural years. In 1973 he provided the fiction and descriptive text for *Nova Scotia: Window on the Sea*. An anthology of short stories, *The Rebellion of Young David and Other Stories*, was pub-

lished in 1975. He received the 1978 Leacock Award for Humour for *Whirligig* (1977), a collection of poetry and stories.
▷ SUGGESTED READING: Claude Bissell, *Ernest Buckler Remembered* (1989).

■ Buddhism

Buddhism is one of the major religions of the world. Within it are many systems of belief and conduct. There are currently more than 52 000 followers in Canada.

Buddhism was founded about 500 BC by Siddhartha Gautama (Gotama Buddha). He was a prince in an area now called Nepal, and although accounts of his life vary, all sects agree on a few essential facts. When he was 29 he turned his back on his privileged life and set off on a journey to attain enlightenment. The concept of enlightenment (knowledge about the truth of life) is central to Buddhist teaching. He led a very pure, self-denying life for six years and after an extended fast attained enlightenment. It is written that he learned that everything is interdependent, that nothing lives forever, that everything eventually becomes dissatisfying, that nothing has a nature of its own, and that when attachment to earthly things is abandoned, bliss is obtained. The Buddha preached these ideas for 45 years. The Buddha is not usually considered divine. The teachings recognize that nothing, including the soul, is eternal. The concept of *bodhisattva* is an exception to this. Believers in this feel that the Buddha was an earthly representation of the eternal.

Buckler's Influence
Margaret Laurence was one of many young writers influenced by Buckler's book *The Mountain and the Valley*. She wrote to him "We, and I mean writers like me and all the young ones as well, owe you so much. You made it all possible. You showed us how to be ourselves. You told us where we really lived."

Altar Shrine to the Buddha of Infinite Life at the Buddhist church in Raymond, Alberta (courtesy PMA).

Budget Leaks

Details of budgets must be kept secret to prevent people from profiting from information that is not known to others. Thus budget "leaks" are a great opportunity for opposition parties to embarrass a minister of finance.

No budget leak ever caused such a furor as that of April 1989. An Ottawa reporter, Doug Small, obtained a copy of the budget summary before Finance Minister Michael Wilson could release it in the House of Commons. Small read details of it on the evening news. Wilson was forced to release the budget a day early. Later, it was revealed that an insurance company had also seen the summary in advance.

The opposition parties screamed for Wilson's resignation day after day. Meanwhile, the RCMP laid charges against five people, including Doug Small. Although it appears no one profited from advanced knowledge of the budget, the whole matter was a great embarrassment to Wilson and the government.

After his death a split occurred. The Therevada sect, based in southern India, emphasized the religious practices that led Buddha to enlightenment. The Mahayana sect, based in northern India, stressed enlightenment itself. These two factions and many more variations are very much in evidence today.

Buddhism was brought to Canada in the late 1800s by Japanese immigrants. Today, we have traditions rooted in Sri Lanka, Thailand, India, Tibet, China, Japan, Korea, Vietnam, Burma, Cambodia, Laos, the United States, and Canada itself. Dominant are the Zen sects from Japan and China and the four Tibetan traditions, which emphasize meditation.

The sects' interpretations of the original teachings vary a great deal. Some say that *Dharma* (insight) is law; others view it as a guiding principle. Some define *Sangha* (congregation) as a group of ordained monks; others include lay people. Many look to their leaders for social leadership more than religious teaching; others see their leaders as guides to their personal spiritual growth.

Believers are asked to follow some basic rules, things not to do in life. These things include three physical acts: the taking of life, taking what has not been given, and sexual excess. Four are speech-related actions: lying, slandering, foolish talk, and harsh talk. Three are mental actions: selfishness, malice, and seeing wrongly.

Sunday has no special meaning in Buddhism, but is used for religious observance to fit into the Canadian culture. Special days are celebrated — New Year's Day, Nirvana or Parinirvana Day (February 18), Wesak (full moon, April-May), Hanamatsuri Day (Flower Festival, April 8), Founder's Day, Organization Day, Bodhi Day (December 8), Special An-

niversary Day, and New Year's Eve. Special occasions in an individual's life are also celebrated: birth, naming, confirmation or ordination, marriage, and death.

A key to Buddha's teaching is the act of meditation, which is part of everyday life. It can be performed while eating or bathing, for example, and this means that Buddhists' religious observances are never far from their minds.

▷ SUGGESTED READING: Anne Bancroft, *The Buddhist World* (1984); John Snelling, *Buddhism* (1986).

Budget

The budget describes what policies a government intends to follow. It states how it intends to pay for them and where it will get the money. The budget is presented to Parliament (or to the Legislature in the case of a province) by the minister of finance every year. The Budget Speech is one of the most important occasions in politics, since it sets out government policies and economic plans. If Parliament (or a Legislature) defeats a budget, the government must resign, as happened with the federal minority governments of 1974 and 1979. Many people are interested in the details of the budget because of what it says about taxes. A budget can also have a great impact on the economy, by increasing or reducing confidence in the government's ability to run the country. For these reasons, the media pay a lot of attention to budgets.

A budget is usually prepared in great secrecy by the minister of finance and his or her advisers. The reason for the secrecy is to prevent anyone from benefiting from inside knowledge of the government's plans. In preparing a budget the minister must consider the government's election promises and goals, the state of the economy, and pressure from various groups.

Once the budget speech has been delivered in Parliament (or the Legislature), the opposition parties debate it. They point out its weaknesses and suggest alternatives, while the government defends it. The budget, however, is almost certain to be approved when the government has a majority in Parliament. The point of the debate, which lasts for six days, is to influence public opinion.

The government presents its Estimates to Parliament separately. These are the plans that each department prepares to show how it will spend the money approved in the budget. This allows the opposition to ask detailed questions about departmental activities. Once again, this

Michael Wilson, finance minister, purchases a new pair of shoes before he delivers his budget in April 1989. No one is certain where this tradition came from (courtesy Canapress Photo Service).

provides a chance to inform and influence public opinion.

The budget, including the Estimates, is a very important part of the political process. It influences voters' decisions as to whether or not to support the government in the next election. It can have a great influence on the economy, thus affecting people's lives and the country's future. For these reasons, the minister of finance is considered to be one of the most important ministers. The budget debate is one of the most valuable aspects of democracy. It forces a government to announce its plans and to defend them against criticism.

▷ RELATED ARTICLES: **Economy; Government; Parliament.**

■ Buffalo, *see* Bison

■ Buffaloberry

The Shepherdia belong to the oleaster family (Elaeagnaceae). In Canada, we have two species: the soapberry (*S. canadensis*), which is found from New-foundland to Alaska, and the silver buffaloberry (*S. argentea*), which grows only along riverbanks in the Prairie provinces. The silvery hairs which cover not only the leaves, but the branches and buds as well, make this shrub particularly attractive, especially when it is covered with fruit. The fruit are not very tasty when raw, but they make a good jelly, especially when they have been harvested after the first autumn frosts. The native people dried them to eat in wintertime; for example, as an accompaniment to buffalo meat. The buffaloberry is *dioecious* (has the male and female reproductive organs on separate plants) and only the female plants produce fruit. Because it is so resistant to drought, the buffaloberry is planted in windbreak hedges between the fields to reduce soil erosion. Among the Canadian buffaloberries (soapberry or russet buffaloberry), only the underside of the leaf is silvery. The floral buttons, which form during the summer, only open the following spring. The orange-red fruit has a sickening odour.

■ Bug

The name "bug" is usually given to insects belonging to order Hemiptera, which is broken down into two groups: Heteroptera, or the true bugs, and Homoptera, which includes cicadas, hoppers, aphids, and others. Some 3080 species are known in Canada. They are widely distributed across the country, in the prairies and forests, with fewer in the more northerly areas. They are different from other insects in that they have piercing and sucking mouthparts housed in a long beak. They are leaden in colour, dull brown, greyish brown or even, in some species, vividly coloured: red, green, blue, or embellished with spots or stripes. The head bears antennae and mouthpieces adapted to pierce and suck liquids. The forewings are thickened over the bottom two-thirds of their surface; the hindwings are completely membranous. These insects undergo an incomplete *metamorphosis*. The larvae very much resemble the adults except that they are smaller, and do not have fully developed wings. Bugs usually feed on the sap of plants. Each species normally concentrates on a particular plant.

Bugs are often serious crop pests (aphids). They can kill or deform seedlings and damage flowers or seeds. Some feed on harmful insects (stinkbugs) and are therefore beneficial. Some (bedbugs) feed on blood. There are also aquatic

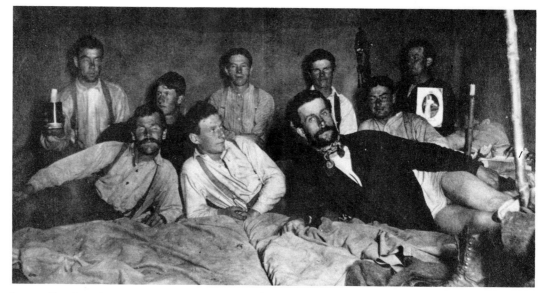

Bunkhouse Men The bunkhouse sheltered the workers who braved the winter and wilderness to build the railways and work in isolated logging and mining camps. This railway survey crew was photographed in northern Ontario in 1905 (courtesy Glenbow Archives/NA-3553-5).

bugs (backswimmers, water scorpions) and semi-aquatic ones (water striders, marsh treaders), which live primarily in stagnant water. Many true bugs are predators and some, such as the giant water bug, can catch prey as large as a frog or a small fish.

▷ SUGGESTED READING: David Suzuki, *Looking at Insects* (1985).

■ Bujold, Geneviève

Actress (*born in 1942 at Montreal, Que.*). The European film *La guerre est finie* (1965) made her famous. She has since made English and French films in Europe, Canada, and the United States. She has spent many years in the U.S., where she now makes most of her films.

Bujold's Canadian films include Michel Brault's *Entre la mer et l'eau douce* (1967), Claude Jutra's *Kamouraska* (1973), and *Murder by Decree* (1979). Between 1968 and 1980, she had a great influence in four films made with Paul Almond, her husband at the time. The best known are *Act of the Heart* (1970), with Donald Sutherland, and *Isabel* (1968). Other films include *Anne of the Thousand Days* (1969), for which she won a Golden Globe award.

Bujold returned to Canada to make David Cronenberg's *Dead Ringers* (1988) and Michel Brault's *L'Emprise* (1988), a film about domestic violence. She won the 1988 Golden Sheaf Award for her role in *L'Emprise*.

■ Bull, Gerald Vincent

Scientist (*born in 1928 at North Bay, Ont.*). Bull studied aerodynamics, and from 1950 to 1964 he worked for the Defence Research Board at Valcartier, Que. There he developed a type of gun that shot packages of instruments into the upper atmosphere. (This was before rockets could be reliably used for this purpose.) Bull's High Altitude Research Project (HARP) was moved to McGill University in 1964, and during the next few years he developed an even more powerful cannon for space research.

In 1971 Bull formed his own research company. As well as offering scientific services, it designed and sold shells and other munitions. In 1980 Bull was convicted by the United States of selling arms to South Africa. After serving a brief prison sentence, he moved to Europe, where he re-established his company as a consulting firm.

■ Bundock

Bundock is the imaginary family name of a Montreal-based rock group. It includes lead vocalist Pierre, bassist Marc, guitarist Dominique, keyboardist Martin, and drummer Alain. All have taken the last name Bundock. They were discovered by a new Canadian record company, Alert, during a Montreal talent contest. They decided to compose and sing in English, because it is "the international language of pop music." Shortly thereafter, Bundock released *Mauve*. Their first single, "American Singer," was a hit in Quebec and earned Bundock a record deal in France. They followed with a full-length album, titled *S.A.* (Société Anonyme), which was also very popular.

■ Bunkhouse Men

The bunkhouse men were loggers, miners, railway builders, and other labourers who worked far from the cities, living in work camps, during the early 1900s. They were named for the bunkhouses in which they slept. Most were single and many were recently arrived immigrants.

■ Bunyan, Paul

Paul Bunyan is a giant lumberjack in 19th-century folktales. The tales describe how Paul ate enormous quantities of food. He could chop down the largest trees with two strokes of his axe. Helped by the mighty blue ox, Babe, he hollowed out the Great Lakes, created the Bay of Fundy tides, and raised up the Rocky Mountains. In one of his adventures, Paul decided to straighten out a crooked river. He tied Babe to a tree on the bend of the river and, with one strong pull, he drew out 15 km of bends.

■ Bureaucracy

The word "bureaucracy" comes from the French word *bureaucratie*, meaning "the power and influence of the staff of government." In a bureaucracy different divisions of an organization carry out separate functions. Within each division, a set of rules, regulations, and procedures covers each activity. The job of each person is carefully defined, and workers report directly to the person above them in the "chain of command." Bureaucracies are found in any large organization, including governments, unions, schools, etc.

Government bureaucracies are divided into departments. The federal government, for example, has about 30 departments, such as Justice, Finance, Agriculture, and Defence. At the head of each department is a deputy minister, who in turn reports to a Cabinet minister, who is an elected member of Parliament. The power to make rules, laws, and policies should lie with the minister, because he or she is elected by the people. However, because these activities require time and expertise, much of the power is left to the bureaucrats.

The purpose of this system of organization is to perform duties as efficiently as possible. Each department has experts to deal with complicated matters. Requests are passed up the chain of command, and decisions come down. This organization, however, also can mean "red tape," or delay and piles of paperwork. Furthermore, much of the work itself is routine and unrewarding. Bureaucrats are often criticized for misusing their power.

Government bureaucracies have expanded greatly since 1945 in order to provide services in many new areas, such as medical care, consumer protection, conservation, etc. By 1989 there were over 1 million employees in government services in Canada, or about 14% of the labour force.

■ Burgeo

Burgeo is a fishing port on the rugged south coast of Newfoundland. Most of the community lies on Grandy Island which is connected to the mainland by a causeway. Accessible only by sea for a long time, it was linked by road to the Trans-Canada Highway in 1979. Its population in 1986 was 2582. For information, contact the Town Clerk, P.O. Box 220, Burgeo, Nfld, A0M 1A0.

■ Burgess Shale

The Burgess Shale is a rock formation in Yoho National Park, in southern British Columbia. The black shale contains the finest collection of Mid-Cambrian fossils in the world. They are 530 million years old and were part of a giant reef of an ancient sea.

The Burgess Shale contributes to our knowledge of a wide variety of animals that would otherwise be unknown. It is a unique look into the very distant past. It was declared a World Heritage Site in 1981.

▷ Related Article: **Fossils.**
▷ Suggested Reading: Stephen Jay Gould, *Wonderful Life: The Burgess Shale and the Nature of History* (1989).

Burgess Shale, *in Yoho National Park, B.C., contains the most important known collection of fossils of very early life on Earth (photo by Thomas Kitchin).*

■ Burka, Petra

Figure skater (*born in 1946 at Amsterdam, Netherlands*). Burka first skated when she was six, having come to Canada with her parents two years earlier. Coached by her mother, the former Dutch champion Ellen Burka, she became a superb figure skater and won the Canadian junior championships in 1961. The following year, at the age of 15, she stunned the skating world by smoothly performing a *triple salchow* during the Canadian championships. In the triple salchow, the skater spins around three times in mid-air. The jump had never be-

Petra Burka won a bronze medal for Canada at the 1964 Olympic Games (courtesy NAC/PA-50342/ © D.G. Newman).

fore been done by a woman during a skating competition.

Encouraged by this success, Burka stepped up her training and in 1964 won the Canadian championships and gained a bronze medal at the Olympic Games. In 1965 she won the Canadian, North American, and world championships. Less successful in 1966, she gave up competitive skating and joined a professional ice show. Burka was chosen Canadian woman athlete of the year in 1964 and 1965, and was awarded the Lou Marsh Trophy as Canada's outstanding athlete of the year, 1965.

■ Burka, Sylvia

Speed skater and cyclist (*born in 1954 at Winnipeg, Man.*). Burka overcame a visual handicap to excel in two sports. Despite losing an eye in a childhood accident she won the world junior speed-skating championships in 1973. She finished fourth at the 1976 Olympics and became world champion two weeks later. She also set two world records.

Burka is also a world-class cyclist. She finished fourth in the pursuit event in 1977 and set a world record in 1982.

■ Burlington

The city of Burlington, Ont., lies at the western end of Lake Ontario. Loyalists settled in the area in the 1790s. The Mohawk leader, Joseph Brant, settled here in a magnificent house that later became a hospital for veterans before it was torn down in the 1930s.

Because there is no natural harbour, wharves were built out into the lake. Small communities grew up around these, the largest of which was Wellington Square. The early economy depended on the shipment of wheat, lumber, and gunpowder. In 1873 Wellington Square and Port Nelson became the village of Burlington. However, growth declined as the forests were cut down and ships bypassed the town for the larger ports of Hamilton and Oakville.

Between the 1890s and World War I, local agriculture shifted to fruit and market gardening. Burlington was given the name "Garden of Canada" and became a town in 1914. Burlington is well connected by highways to Toronto and Hamilton, and many residents commute to work in nearby communities. The city is home to the internationally known Burlington Teen Tour Band, which in 1988 had 209 members. Burlington's population in 1986 was 116 675. For information, contact the City Clerk/Administrator, 426 Brant Street, P.O. Box 5013, Burlington, Ont., L7R 3Z6.

Burlington Bay Skyway connects Burlington with Hamilton (photo by Malak, Ottawa).

■ Burnaby

Burnaby, B.C., lies in the geographical centre of the metropolitan region of Greater Vancouver. It is bordered by Burrard Inlet on the north and the north arm of the Fraser River in the south. Burnaby is both a part of Greater Vancouver and a municipality in its own right. It has its own mayor and eight aldermen. Burnaby began in the 1890s as a logging and agricultural centre. Today it has a diverse economy, which includes high technology and film industries. Many residents work in neighbouring communities.

ONTARIO

Toronto
Burlington

Burnaby is the home of both Simon Fraser University and the British Columbia Institute of Technology. Its population in 1986 was 145 161. For information, contact the District Municipal Clerk, 4949 Canada Way, Burnaby, B.C., V5G 1M2.

■ Burnford, Sheila

Writer (*born in 1918 in Scotland; died in 1984 in England*). Burnford came to Canada with her husband and children in 1948, settling in Port Arthur [Thunder Bay], Ont. There she wrote scripts for a puppetry group and articles for British magazines.

Her first book, *The Incredible Journey* (1961), won many awards and was made into a full-length Walt Disney film. A novel about friendship and determination, it tells of two dogs and a cat who are tested by numerous dangers when they journey across the northern Ontario wilderness. The animals do not talk, but they have distinct, almost human, personalities.

Burnford's other notable books are *Bel Ria* (1977), an adult animal novel about a dog's heroism during war, and *Mr. Noah and the Second Flood* (1973), a satire about men polluting and destroying the world.

■ Burns, Eedson Louis Millard

Soldier, diplomat, writer (*born in 1897 at Westmount, Que.; died in 1985 at Manotick, Ont.*). As career soldier, civil servant, and then soldier-diplomat, General Burns gave a lifetime of service to Canada. He fought on the Western Front during World War I with the Royal Canadian Engineers. He received the Military Cross after he was wounded in the Battle of the Somme in 1916. In World War II, he commanded Canada's most battle-hardened army corps, the 1st Canadian Corps, during the fierce fighting in Italy that led to the capture of Rome. In the late 1940s, Burns became a civil servant with the recently formed Department of Veterans Affairs. There he helped set the generous policy that Canada organized for returning war veterans.

In 1955, Burns transferred to the Department of External Affairs. From 1956 until 1959 he served as commander of the UN Emergency Force in the Middle East, the first peacekeeping force under United Nations direction. In this role, he was respected by both the Israelis and the Arabs. His blunt firmness and even-handed supervision of disputes won him their lasting respect. He continued to be a peacekeeper in the 1960s, when he served as Canada's chief adviser at conferences on disarmament. He wrote several books based on his experiences, including *Between Arab and Israeli* (1962).

In 1981, the United Nations Association of Canada awarded him the Pearson Peace Prize Medal for his peacekeeping work. He was a Companion of the Order of Canada.

▷ RELATED ARTICLE: **Peacekeeping.**

■ Burns, Patrick

Rancher and businessman (*born in 1856 at Oshawa, Canada West [Ontario]; died in 1937 at Calgary, Alta*). Pat Burns, "cattle king of the West," was one of the four Albertans who put up the money for the first Calgary Stampede in 1912. At the time, he owned six huge cattle ranches in Alberta as well as a thriving meat-packing business.

Burns began his career as a penniless homesteader in Manitoba, where he settled in the late 1870s. To earn money, he drove his neighbours' cattle to the Winnipeg market, and by 1885 he was buying and selling cattle full-time. He then became a supplier of beef to the railway-building crews in the West, and in 1897 he sent the first of several herds of cattle 2000 km north to the Yukon for the thousands of miners taking part in the Klondike Gold Rush. This difficult feat brought Burns a large profit, for the miners were willing to pay high prices for fresh beef.

By then, Burns was based in Calgary, where he had set up a small meat-packing plant in 1890. In the next 20 years, P. Burns and Company grew into a major business empire with branches throughout western Canada. In 1931 Burns was made a senator.

Patrick Burns shipped herds of cattle 2000 km north to feed the miners during the Klondike Gold Rush (artwork by Irma Coucill).

■ Burns, Tommy

Boxer (*born Noah Brusso in 1881 at Hanover, Ont.; died in 1955 at Vancouver, B.C.*). In 1906 Burns became the only Canadian ever to hold the world heavyweight boxing title. He defended his title ten times before losing badly to American boxer Jack Johnson in Sydney, Australia, in 1908. The $30 000 he received for the fight with Johnson marked the beginning of "big money" for boxers. He lost only four of 60 fights during his career.

■ Burns Lake

Burns Lake, B.C., is a village in the central interior of the province, 226 km west of Prince George. It was first settled in the

Tommy Burns was the only Canadian boxer ever to hold the world heavyweight boxing title (courtesy NAC/C-14092).

Jack Bush was one of Canada's finest abstract artists. In paintings such as Bridge Passage (1975), shown here, he focused on the simple beauty of colours (courtesy Woltjen/Udell Gallery/© estate of Jack Bush).

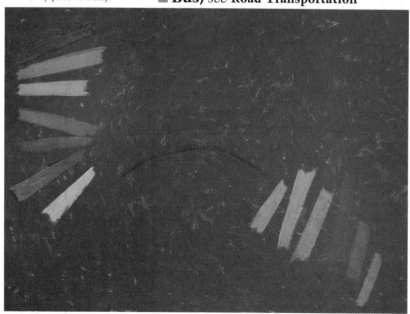

1860s during construction of a telegraph line to Alaska. Farming, forestry, and mining are the important industries in the area today. In 1986 the population was 1723. For information, contact the Village Clerk, P.O. Box 570, Burns Lake, B.C., V0J 1E0.

■ Bus, *see* Road Transportation

■ Bush, John Hamilton (Jack)

Painter (*born in 1909 in Toronto, Ont.; died there in 1977*). Bush was one of Canada's most renowned painters. He worked much of his life in advertising, as a commercial artist. In his early career as a painter, his work was in a style similar to that of the Group of Seven. He became very unhappy with this style of painting in the late 1940s and turned to abstract painting.

In 1954 Bush and a group of other artists formed Painters Eleven. The group showed their work together in Toronto in an attempt to gain support for a new and very different style of painting. Although the reaction to Painters Eleven was at first shock and disgust, the group opened the public's eyes to an exciting new art. Bush's paintings were similar to those of several American painters of the time, but he soon began painting simpler pictures that focused mainly on the beauty of colour.

Many of Bush's paintings contained bold, simple shapes, such as columns or circles, filled with vivid colours. He also experimented with thin colours that seemed to radiate from the canvas. In paintings such as *Tango Accelerando*, countless small slashes of colour brought the canvas to life, like music.

Bush's unique style and wonderful sense of colour made him well known beyond Canada, and he became a major influence on young Canadian painters.

■ Bush Flying

The term "bush flying" refers to the use of aircraft in the North. After World War I, much of southern Canada was linked by railways. The North, however, was as remote as ever. Its countless waterways were barriers to overland travel, but they did offer landing spots for airplanes equipped with floats in the summer and skis in winter. Early aircraft were primitive compared to today's, and weather conditions in the North can be extreme. Bush flying was a supreme challenge to the pilot.

Flights to the North began when a number of forest companies hired pilots to help spot forest fires in northern Quebec and Ontario. They used "flying boats" left over from World War I. In a few years these operations expanded into a regular air service, which carried passengers and mail from Haileybury, Ont., to Rouyn, Que. Ontario set up an air service in 1924.

Flying proved useful in northern mining operations as well. Pilots flew in passengers and freight to the remote area of Red Lake, in northern Ontario, where gold was discovered in 1925. In 1928 bush planes were used to look for minerals in northern Quebec and the Yukon. In 1929 bush pilot Leigh Brintnell dropped off prospector Gilbert LaBine at Great Bear Lake. He then flew to Aklavik on the Arctic coast, then to Edmonton and Winnipeg. It was a round trip of some 15 000 km. Meanwhile, in 1930, LaBine struck it rich, finding radium.

By the mid-1920s, bush pilots were flying in winter as well as summer. In 1926 "Doc" Oaks flew supplies into northern Ontario in winter. He worked out methods of keeping the engine warm in very cold conditions. Two brothers at Sioux Lookout, Ont., worked out how to use skis for landing on snow or ice.

Many of the early planes used in bush flying, such as the Curtiss HS-2L, were adapted sea planes. The first all-Canadian bush plane was the Norseman. It was built by Bob Noorduyn in Montreal and first flew in 1935. Noorduyn designed the rugged plane after talking to several pilots. The most famous bush plane is the Beaver, which was also designed in Canada and built by de Havilland. Its superb ability to take off and land in a very short distance made it the workhorse not only of the Canadian North, but of 60 other countries. Canada continues to excel in building such planes, with the Otter, Dash-7, and Dash-8, among others.

By the mid-1930s more freight was being moved by air in Canada than the rest of the world combined. During the opening of iron ore mines in Quebec and Labrador, the scale of bush flying was greatly expanded. In the 1940s, one company hauled fuel, food, equipment, and even cement. During the building of the line of radar stations (the DEW Line), pilots made some 28 000 flights north.

Bush flying greatly changed life in the North. It became possible by the 1930s to charter a plane and fly almost everywhere. Planes were used by trappers and missionaries. People who were sick or injured could be flown south for medical attention. In 1939 W.E. Catton flew from Winnipeg to Repulse Bay, N.W.T., and brought out a man with frozen hands — a trip of some 4800 km.

Many of the northern settlements now have permanent air strips. There have been improvements in weather forecasting and navigation. Nevertheless, hardy aircraft equipped with skis and floats continue to serve remote areas of the North.

▷ Related Articles: **Aviation** and entries on pilots mentioned.

■ Business

The term *business* is generally applied to (i) profit-seeking activities and (ii) profit-seeking organizations. In the Canadian economy, which relies on the market place to organize production and distribution, the size of profit-seeking activities amounted on average to about 80% of total output in the decade of the 1980s. This figure includes business carried on by federal and provincial crown corporations. Business activities cover an enormous range, all the way from Christmas trees through sound-track videos to the sales of pizza, and from air travel to stainless steel sheeting to the services of a dentist in cleaning teeth.

Organization A business organization may take one of three possible legal forms. In the first, called a *proprietorship*, a business is owned and operated by a single person who is also legally responsible for all debts incurred by the business. The second form is *partnership*, consisting of two or more owners who share responsibilities for operation and management. Nearly all partnerships and individual businesses are small. They are most common in agriculture, for the self-employed, in law, and in medicine. The third is the *corporate* form, under which the business is owned by stockholders who hold shares of stock. Business may assume the corporate form under either federal or provincial law.

A business as a profit-seeking organization is one in which the services of labour are combined with equipment and land or materials to produce something of value to a customer. A business must serve customers effectively in some way if it is to

Bush Flying *These stamps commemorate four of the aircraft that served the northern bush. Each was equipped with skis or floats to land on snow or water. Shown in the stamps are (top to bottom): Fairchild FC-2W1, de Havilland Beaver, Noorduyn Norseman, and Fokker Super Universal (courtesy Canada Post Corporation).*

Robert S. McLaughlin, *businessman, on his 100th birthday, in 1971. McLaughlin entered his father's business making horse-drawn carriages. By 1908 he was producing automobiles. His business was purchased by General Motors in 1918 and McLaughlin remained as president and in other positions until his death (courtesy General Motors of Canada Ltd.).*

Samuel Cunard built a few sailing ships into a shipping empire (courtesy NAC/C-7044).

survive. There is enormous variation in the size of business organizations, which range all the way from one-person operations to huge companies such as Imasco, Canadian Pacific Ltd, and Bell Canada Enterprises. Of the over 435 000 corporations registered in Canada in 1986, some 2200 had assets of more than $25 million while 433 000 had assets of less than this amount. The 2200 accounted for 72% of all assets, 5.3% of all sales, and 65% of all profits. Generally, smaller businesses use more labour hours in what they produce and are therefore important providers of

jobs. In 1986 a special survey by Statistics Canada reported that persons who owned and also operated a business accounted for 44% of Canadian employment.

Competition In a market economy, competition from other Canadian-based businesses and from foreign producers is one important assurance that consumers can acquire the products they desire at reasonable prices. However, since market competition cannot fully protect the welfare of producers and consumers, in the Canadian mixed economy, the federal, provincial, and municipal governments have regulations in place affecting how businesses can operate. Their coverage includes hours of work, minimum wages, health, and occupational safety, the labelling of packages, environmental standards, and government action to maintain competitive conditions in a particular industry. In addition to such generally applicable regulations are specific rules affecting particular types of business, such as telephone companies and electric utilities (in which the rates and terms of service are regulated), banks and insurance companies (financial disclosure requirements), airlines, and radio and television broadcasters.

▷ SUGGESTED READING: *Canadian Business, Guts, Greed and Glory: A Visual History of Modern Canadian Business* (1988).

■ Butler, Sir William Francis
Soldier and writer (*born in 1838 at Ballyslateen, Ireland; died in 1910 at Bansha Castle, Ireland*). Butler was the author of *The Great Lone Land* (1872), a

The Great Lone Land was a book published by William Butler about his adventures in the early West.

Buttercup Tradition says that you can tell if someone likes butter if a buttercup gives off a yellow reflection when it is held under your chin (artwork by Claire Tremblay).

book about his adventures in the Canadian West from 1870 to 1871. As an officer in the British army, Butler was sent to the prairies ahead of the Red River Expedition of 1870 to provide it with information on what was happening at Red River. That fall he went on a similar fact-finding mission to the North Saskatchewan River. This took him on a four months' winter journey of almost 6000 km to Rocky Mountain House and back. All this he described vividly in his book.

At the time, most people in eastern Canada knew very little about the prairies, and Butler's book sparked a great interest in the region. Some people were inspired to go there as settlers. Butler followed up with *The Wild North Land* (1873), about a journey he made to British Columbia early in 1873. He then left Canada, though he continued to write books and to serve the army in many parts of the British Empire.

▷ RELATED ARTICLE: **Red River Expedition.**

■ Buttercup

Buttercup is the common name for various plants of genus *Ranunculus*, of the crowfoot family (Ranunculaceae). The genus name, *Ranunculus*, comes from the Latin word which means "little frog," referring to the wet areas in which most buttercups grow. About 400 species are known worldwide, most of them in temperate and arctic regions. We have over 40 species in Canada. Most buttercups have divided leaves with veins spreading out from the base, giving rise to the name "crowfoot." The Common buttercup (*R. acris*) is abundant in fields and open spaces, where it flowers from June to August. It can reach up to one metre or more in height. The sap of this plant — along with many other species of the crowfoot family — is toxic. It has a bitter taste and can cause skin irritations. Grazing animals avoid it. Tradition says you can tell if someone likes butter, depending on whether a buttercup held under their chin gives off a yellow reflection or not. Native people used it to treat headaches by breathing in the aroma of the fresh or dried plant. Today, it is used in remedies for skin problems and rheumatism.

■ Butterfly

Butterfly is the name given to insects belonging to the order Lepidoptera (*lepidos* meaning "scale," and *pteron* meaning "wing"). The name refers to the bristles and scales on their body, which overlap

Milbert's Tortoise Shell *(Anglais milberti)*

Big Poplar Sphinx *(Pachysphinx modesta)*

Common Buttercup can grow up to one metre in height. Its sap is toxic and can cause skin irritations (artwork by Claire Tremblay).

Butterflies and Moths Butterflies and moths together make up the insect order Lepidoptera. The main difference between the two is seen in the antennae. The butterfly's antennae end in a knob. The moth has antennae of various shapes and forms. The butterfly usually has a long, slender body, while the moth is plump and hairy. Moths are usually active by night, the butterfly by day. Most butterflies rest with their wings upright. Most moths rest with their wings laid out flat. The artwork (left) shows a Milbert's Tortoise Shell butterfly (top) and a Big Poplar Sphinx moth (below) (artwork by Jan Sovak)

Metamorphosis

Metamorphosis is the change of form during the life history of an animal.

In a *complete* metamorphosis, as in the butterfly, there is a middle stage, called the *pupa*.

In *incomplete* metamorphosis, as in a grasshopper, the young resemble the adults.

In some animals, the change is gradual, as from tadpole to frog.

Butterfly Metamorphosis has three stages: caterpillar (or larva), shown above; chrysalis (or pupa), shown centre; and adult butterfly. The striking patterns of caterpillar and butterfly warn predators that they taste bad (photos by Bill Ivy).

like shingles on a roof. There are two general groups of Lepidoptera: the *diurnal* (active by day) ones, and the *nocturnal* (active by night) ones called moths. Butterflies are easily recognized by their usually brilliantly coloured wings which, when the insect is at rest, are lifted and supported against each other, so that only the underside is seen. Their antennae always end in knobs, and they have long, hollow tongues for sipping nectar. They are a diversified group in Canada (272 species), though not to the same extent as moths. Butterflies are found throughout Canada right into the Arctic, where some species exist only there.

The butterfly cycle has four stages: egg, larva (caterpillar), chrysalis, and adult. The *eggs* are usually laid on a particular plant on which the larva feeds after it hatches. The *larvae* (or caterpillars) have well-developed heads, three pairs of true legs in front and usually five pairs of false legs with little hooks on the abdomen. They eat several times their own weight in leaves during their growth period, and molt several times. The caterpillars are eaten by other insects, spiders, and birds. Upon the last molt, the larva becomes a *chrysalis* (which is never enclosed in a cocoon). The *metamorphosis* occurs at this stage. After a period varying from ten days to several months, the skin of the chrysalis splits and the *butterfly* emerges. Many collectors are drawn to this group of insects because of their great beauty.

▷ RELATED ARTICLE: **Moth.**

■ **By, John,** *see* **Engineering.**

■ **Byng of Vimy, Julian Hedworth George, Viscount**

Governor general (*born in 1862 at Wrotham Park, England; died in 1935 at Thorpe-le-Soken, England*). As Lieutenant-General Sir Julian Byng, he was given command of the Canadian Corps (1916), and he directed the victorious Canadian assault on Vimy Ridge in April 1917. Byng was rewarded for his war service by being created a lord. He seemed a popular choice when appointed governor general in 1921. He held the position until 1926.

Byng left Canada under a shadow, because he refused to dissolve Parliament when Prime Minister Mackenzie King requested it. This caused many Canadians to turn against Byng, arguing that he had exceeded his powers as governor general (though in fact most constitutional experts now feel that he acted correctly).

▷ RELATED ARTICLE: **King-Byng Affair.**

Cabinet

The Cabinet is the most powerful part of government, both federal and provincial. Its chairperson is the prime minister (or premier). Its members are the *ministers* in charge of government departments (Finance, Health, Agriculture, etc.). Sometimes, one or two other people are included: they are called *ministers without portfolio*, since they do not have a specific department to control. Cabinet ministers are chosen by the prime minister (or premier) and are members of the governing party and elected members of the House of Commons (or provincial legislature), since they have to explain and defend their policies there. Occasionally, a Cabinet minister may instead be a member of the Senate. The leader of the government party in the Senate is automatically a member of Cabinet.

The word "cabinet" comes from 18th-century England, when the royal council met in a special room, or cabinet, and was called the "cabinet council." The cabinet grew out of the king's or queen's "privy" (or private) council. To this day, the Cabinet is formally a committee of the Queen's Privy Council for Canada. It is the active part of the Privy Council. Cabinet members are entitled to put the letters P.C. (for "privy councillor") after their name for life. At the provincial level, the official name for the Cabinet is the Executive Council.

It is in Cabinet that ministers discuss legislation, prepare policies, plan parliamentary strategy, and generally decide government policy. Thus, the Cabinet is the supreme decision-making body of government. If the Cabinet's decisions are rejected by Parliament in the form of a no-confidence vote, the Cabinet is expected to resign, since it has lost the support and confidence of Parliament. In that case, either the government steps down or an election is called.

Today, the federal Cabinet contains over 40 members. Much of its work is done in special committees and by its permanent officials. Thus, when an issue comes to Cabinet, it has usually already been discussed by those ministers with a special responsibility for it.

The effectiveness of the Cabinet largely depends on the prime minister. The prime minister chairs Cabinet meetings and thus has some influence. He or she chooses Cabinet ministers in the first place and can also ask them to resign. Choosing a Cabinet is usually very difficult: language, ethnic, regional, gender, and other concerns have to be balanced, as do different political views within the party. In addition, Cabinet ministers should have the ability to do their jobs. Ideally, a Cabinet should reflect the diversity of the country, but this may not be easy when a particular region did not vote for the governing party.

Within Cabinet, ministers are expected to speak freely. Once a decision is made, however, everyone is expected to defend it, even those who have private doubts. If these doubts are really strong, a Cabinet minister is expected to resign. The principle that all Cabinet ministers are expected to defend all decisions is known as *Cabinet solidarity*. Its purpose is to show that the government is united and to prevent the opposition parties from taking advantage of internal differences of opinion. To protect Cabinet solidarity and to make sure that discussion within Cabinet is totally open, Cabinet records are kept secret and Cabinet ministers are pledged to secrecy for life.

▷ RELATED ARTICLES: **Government; House of Commons; Parliament; Prime Minister; Privy Council.**

Cabot, John

Explorer (*born about 1449 at Genoa, Italy; died probably in 1498 at sea near Newfoundland*). Cabot was a native of Italy, where he was a merchant and seaman. In 1495 he went to England with a plan to reach China by sailing across the North Atlantic. Christopher Columbus had recently returned from his historic voyage to America, which he believed was the Far East. Cabot thought Columbus was mistaken and that the way to Asia was still undiscovered.

Imaginary portrait of John Cabot on a medallion (courtesy NAC/C-5136).

Cabot received support from merchants in Bristol, England, who sought new fishing grounds in the Atlantic, and he was commissioned by King Henry VII to find new lands. He left Bristol in May 1497 in a ship called the *Matthew*. He reached land on June 24, probably on the east coast of Newfoundland. It was likely the first time Europeans had set foot in North America since the Vikings almost 500 years earlier. Cabot claimed the new land for England, then cruised along the rugged shore for a month before returning to Bristol.

Cabot sailed again in May 1498, with five ships and 300 men, still intending to reach Asia and establish a colony. But he disappeared off the coast of Newfoundland. Almost nothing is known about the fate of the expedition.

The reports that Cabot and his men made about the vast number of fish they saw on their first voyage led to the opening of the rich Atlantic cod fishery.

▷ SUGGESTED READING: Kay Hill, *And Tomorrow the Stars: The Story of John Cabot* (1968).

■ Cabot Strait

Cabot Strait, 110 km wide, is a passage between southwest Newfoundland and Cape Breton Island. Named for explorer John Cabot, it is the main oceangoing route to the Gulf of St Lawrence and central Canada. Ferries connect Nova Scotia and Newfoundland across the strait.

■ Cache Creek

Cache Creek, B.C., is a village in the dry interior of the province on the Trans-Canada Highway, 85 km west of Kamloops. During the fur-trade era, local Shuswap and traders probably *cached* (stored) supplies here. The village began as a stopover on the Cariboo Road to the gold fields in the 1860s. In 1986 its population was 1147. For information, contact the Village Clerk, P.O. Box 7, Cache Creek, B.C., V0K 1H0.

■ Cactus

All members of the cactus family (Cactaceae), have fleshy, often spine-covered stems and branches, and have no leaves. They are *succulents*, which means that they store moisture in their cells. Fewer than 50 of the world's estimated 2000 species are cold-resistant. Only four are found in Canada.

The ball cactus (*Coryphantha vivipara*) looks like a pincushion. The most northerly cactus, the fragile or little prickly pear cactus (*Opuntia fragilis*), is also the smallest Canadian cactus. Its tiny cushions (2-4 cm long), as wide as they are thick, are easily detached and covered with very sharp spines. One of its habitats is Whiteshell Provincial Park in Manitoba, which has among the coldest winters in Canada. The common plains prickly pear (*O. polyacantha*) has larger, more typical cushions (5-10 cm long, 4-10 cm wide, 1 cm thick). It is found in southern B.C., Alberta, and Saskatchewan. Only squirrels and a few rodents can eat cacti without suffering injury from the cactus spines. To survive extremely cold temperatures, some cacti lose a great deal of water in fall, thereby concentrating their sap in an antifreeze solution. Snow also helps protect them from the rigours of winter.

■ Caddisfly

The caddisfly is a small to medium-sized insect, yellowy brown or greyish black in colour, sometimes with spots. Adults look like moths, except that their wings are hairy; hence their scientific name of Trichoptera (*trichos*, meaning "hair" and *pteron*, meaning "wing"). At rest, the wings fold rooflike over the insect's body. The aquatic larvae are eye-catching. They resemble caterpillars, with three pairs of legs emerging from a case that is constructed from grains of sand, some vegetable matter, or even tiny snail shells. The whole thing is cemented together with silk. Often one sees only the case, moving in the water. Since each species builds a case from different materials, it permits the identification of the insect hidden inside. In Canada, we have at least 545 species. The adults are *nocturnal* (active at night). They mate during nuptial flights over the water, and the females lay several hundred eggs on underwater plants and rocks. They start off with gills and feed on debris and aquatic plants. Others spin webs of silk and filter the water, or prey on tiny organisms. In turn, they are preyed upon by fish and other aquatic insects. When in its case, it turns into a pupa. Later it swims to the surface, turns into an adult, and leaves the water for land.

■ Cadets

Cadets are young men and women, 12 to 18 years old, who volunteer for military training. The cadet movement is made up of the Royal Canadian Sea Cadets, the Royal Canadian Army Cadets, and the Royal Canadian Air Cadets. Their aims are to develop good citizenship and physical fitness, and to increase interest in the Canadian Armed Forces. Young women

Caddisfly At rest, the caddisfly's wings fold over its body like a roof (artwork by Jan Sovak).

Ball, or Pincushion, Cactus in bloom in southern Ontario (courtesy Elliot and Nicole Bernshaw).

have been able to join the cadets since 1975.

To join, young men and women must fill out an application form that can be obtained from the cadet corps in their communities. They require parental or guardian approval. There are more than 1000 cadet corps in Canada.

■ Cadieux, Jean

Jean Cadieux is a voyageur in French-Canadian legend who lived on the Ottawa River in the 18th century. When the Iroquois attacked his village, he sent his family down the rapids in a canoe and stayed behind by himself to distract the enemy. The Virgin Mary protected his family and they escaped, but he grew weak from hunger in the woods. He dug his own grave, erected a cross over the head, and wrote a farewell poem in blood on a sheet of birchbark. "Cadieux's Lament" is a well-known ballad in the French-Canadian tradition.

■ Cain, Larry

Canoeist (*born in 1963 at Toronto, Ont.*). In 1981 Cain was the first Canadian canoeist in 45 years to win a championship event at a world level. He won two gold medals at the junior world championships. In 1984, at Los Angeles, he won an Olympic gold medal in the 500 m race and a silver in the 1000 m race.

Larry Cain in action at the 1984 Los Angeles Olympics. He won gold and silver medals in canoeing (courtesy Athlete Information Bureau/Canadian Olympic Assn).

■ Calder, Frank Arthur

Politician and native leader (*born in 1915 at Nass Harbour, B.C.*). A Nishga Indian, Frank Calder was the first native person elected to a provincial legislature. This was in 1949, when he was elected to the British Columbia Legislative Assembly as a member of the Co-operative Commonwealth Federation (CCF). Calder sat in the legislature for 26 years, representing the CCF, then its offspring the New

Democratic Party (NDP), and, after 1975, the Social Credit Party. From 1972 to 1973 he was a minister without portfolio, thus becoming the first Canadian native to be a Cabinet minister.

Calder was also very active in native affairs and was a founder of the Nishga Tribal Council (now the Nishga Nation). He is especially known for the Calder Case of 1973, which he brought before the Supreme Court of Canada. The case concerned Nishga claims to land on which the Nishga people had lived for centuries. It has had a strong influence on negotiations between the government and native groups in the settlement of native land claims.

▷ RELATED ARTICLE: **Land Claims.**

■ Calgary

Calgary is the second-largest city in Alberta after Edmonton. Its population is 671 326 (1986c). It is in the south-central part of the province, about where the flat prairie meets the rolling foothills of the Rocky Mountains. Calgary was once a frontier town of cowboys and Mounted Police. Today, it is the financial centre of Canada's huge oil and gas industries.

Artifacts found nearby show that nomadic hunters occupied the site at least 10 000 years ago. Prehistoric people, and later Indian groups, hunted buffalo in the area. European fur traders reached the western edge of the plains by the late 18th century. Permanent settlement, however, did not take place for another century.

Cadets at the Royal Military College, Kingston (photo by J.A. Kraulis).

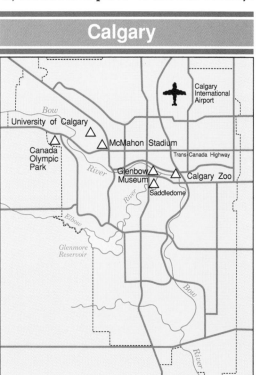

Calgary Municipal Building and City Hall *(photo ©Bilodeau/Preston Ltd/Take Stock Inc.).*

Calgary Skyline, *shown against the beautiful backdrop of the Rocky Mountains. The city and nearby alpine areas hosted the 1988 Winter Olympics (photo by Larry Fisher/Masterfile).*

Early in the 1870s, hunters and whisky traders from the United States moved into the southwest prairies. They slaughtered the buffalo and traded fierce-tasting homemade alcohol with the native people. Stories of drunkenness and bloodshed soon reached eastern Canada. In 1873 the federal government created the North-West Mounted Police (NWMP) and sent a force west to maintain law and order. In 1875 the NWMP built a post at the junction of the Bow and Elbow rivers. This post, which became known as Fort Calgary, is now at the centre of the modern city.

Calgary began to grow with the arrival of the Canadian Pacific Railway in 1883. It was incorporated as a city in 1893. In the early years, ranching was the activity in the area. The Calgary Stampede, an annual exhibition and rodeo first held in 1912, reflects this ranching tradition. Early in the 1900s large numbers of homesteaders began to settle in Alberta. Farming was suddenly important. Calgary enjoyed a prosperous period as a supply centre for this boom.

After ranching and farming, a third important feature in Calgary's growth was the oil and gas industry. The year 1914 marks the discovery of the first major oilfield in Alberta, in Turner Valley. The discovery led to the construction of an oil refinery in nearby Calgary. The city soon became the recognized capital of the Alberta petroleum industry. The industry boomed following World War II and Calgary became one of Canada's fastest-growing, wealthiest cities. Today, so many oil companies have their head offices here that the downtown core has become known as the Oil Patch.

Calgary's nearness to the mountains has made it popular with tourists and outdoor enthusiasts. The city and its nearby alpine areas hosted the 1988 Winter Olympic Games. Educational institutions include the University of Calgary,

Heritage Park *celebrates Calgary's early history as a NWMP post and ranching centre (photo © by Bilodeau/Preston Ltd/Take Stock Inc.).*

EMPLOYMENT BY INDUSTRY - 1988

Calgary

%

Industry	Calgary	Average of top 23 cities
Primary	8.6	0.9
Manufacturing	8.2	17.4
Construction	6.0	5.5
Transportation, Communication, and Other Utilities	7.6	7.6
Trade	19.0	18.1
Finance, Insurance, and Real Estate	7.3	7.1
Services	37.3	35.0
Public Administration	5.7	6.9

Source: Statistics Canada

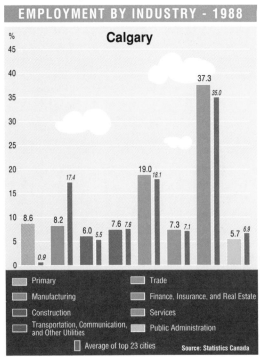

Calgary Centre for the Performing Arts *is home to theatre, symphony, opera, etc. (photo by John Dean/Take Stock Inc.).*

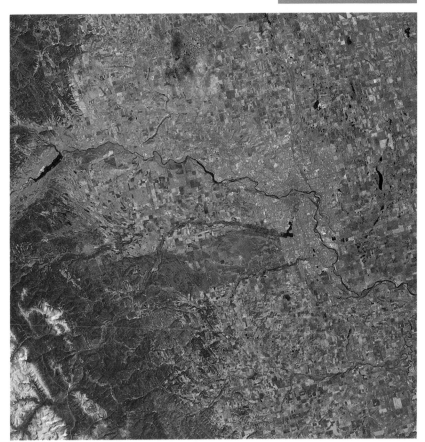

the Southern Alberta Institute of Technology (SAIT), and Mount Royal College. The Calgary Centre for the Performing Arts is home to Theatre Calgary, Alberta Theatre Projects, the Calgary Philharmonic Orchestra, and the Calgary Opera Company. Spruce Meadows, a world-class equestrian facility, is just south of the city. The Glenbow Museum contains excellent collections and archives. The Calgary Stampeders football team plays at McMahon Stadium and the Calgary Flames play professional hockey at the Saddledome. For information, contact the Chief Commissioner, 303 7th Avenue S.E., Calgary, Alta, T2P 2M5.

▷ Suggested Reading: Max Foran and Edward Cavell, *Calgary: An Illustrated History* (1978); Max Foran, et al, eds, *Citymakers: Calgarians After the Frontier* (1987).

■ Calgary Flames

The Flames are Calgary's professional hockey team. They joined the National Hockey League in 1972 as the Atlanta Flames and moved to Calgary in 1980. The Flames quickly built a rivalry with

Calgary Flames *won their first Stanley Cup in 1989 (photo by Brad Watson)*

the Edmonton Oilers. In 1986 the Flames beat the Oilers in the playoffs and went on to lose the Stanley Cup final to the Montreal Canadiens. In 1989 the Flames returned to the final, again against Montreal. This time they were victorious. They play in the 20 100 seat Olympic Saddledome.

■ Calgary Stampede

The Calgary Stampede is a world-famous rodeo and agricultural fair held in Calgary, Alta, each July. Its official name is Calgary Exhibition and Stampede. The Stampede opens with a parade through

Calgary from Space *The city (dark blue) centres on the Bow River. Prairie farms (reddish) and rangeland (green) surround the city. The snow-capped mountains show up as bright blue (lower left) (courtesy Canada Centre for Remote Sensing).*

Steer Wrestling *at the Calgary Stampede (photo by Toby Rankin/Masterfile).*

Bull Riding at the Calgary Stampede (photo by Pat Price/Take Stock Inc.).

downtown Calgary and continues for ten days, with rodeo competitions in bronco riding, steer wrestling, and other traditional cowboy skills. There are exhibits and displays by native people, home and garden exhibitions, agricultural displays, and a midway with sideshows and rides. About one million people visit the Stampede each year.

The first Stampede was held in 1912. Guy Weadick, an American cowboy showman, organized it and advertised it as "The Greatest Outdoor Show on Earth." It attracted 14 000 spectators and cost $100 000 to stage. The money came from Alberta's "Big Four" cattlemen: Pat Burns, A.E. Cross, George Lane, and A.J. McLean. The highlight of the events was a brilliant bronco ride by Tom Three Persons, a Blood Indian from Stand Off, Alta. He was declared world bronco-riding champion.

Despite the success of the first Stampede, another was not held until 1919. The agricultural exhibition became part of the show in 1923. That same year, Guy Weadick introduced chuckwagon racing. These perilous and highly skilled wagon races now draw more crowds than any

Chuckwagon Races at the Calgary Stampede (courtesy The Calgary Exhibition and Stampede).

other event in the Stampede.

▷ RELATED ARTICLES: **Ranching; Rodeo; Tom Three Persons.**

▷ SUGGESTED READING: Mary Blakeslee, *Stampede* (1989); James H. Gray, *A Brand of Its Own: The 100 Year History of the Calgary Exhibition and Stampede* (1985).

■ Calgary Stampeders

The Stampeders football team was formed in 1945. In 1948 they defeated Ottawa in the Grey Cup game. Their exuberant fans celebrated the victory, giving birth to the Grey Cup festival that takes place during the week of the game. The Stamps played, and lost, the Grey Cup game in 1949. They did not win the cup again until 1971. The team has had limited success on the field in the 1980s. It almost folded in 1986 and was only saved at the last minute.

■ Callaghan, Morley Edward

Novelist, short-story writer, broadcaster (*born in 1903 at Toronto, Ont.*). Most of Callaghan's career has been spent in Toronto, except for a brief time when he lived in France, an experience recalled in *That Summer in Paris* (1963). His first novel, *Strange Fugitive*, was published in 1928. Over the next 60 years Callaghan wrote 20 books of fiction, including the novels *They Shall Inherit the Earth* (1935), *The Loved and the Lost* (1951), and *Morley Callaghan's Stories* (1959). *A Wild Old Man on the Road* (1988) was written in his 85th year. Callaghan's stories have centered on the lives of misfits and unfortunates who are at odds with so-

Morley Callaghan's writings center on the lives of misfits who are at odds with society (courtesy Macmillan of Canada/photo by Nigel Dickson).

ciety, on contemporary problems, and on the relationship between spiritual and daily concerns.

Callaghan has received the Governor General's Award (1951), the Molson and Royal Bank awards, and is a Companion of the Order of Canada.

■ Callihoo, Annie Victoria

Writer and spokesperson on Metis culture (*born Annie Victoria Bellcour in 1860 at Lac Ste Anne, northwestern prairies; died in 1965 at St Albert, Alta*). During her long life, Victoria Callihoo saw a complete change in the way of life of the Metis people. When she was young there were still bison roaming the prairies, and people travelled by horseback or Red River cart. She was an authority on Metis culture, and wrote about the customs from her own experiences. In her youth, she took part in bison hunts and in the establishment of Metis settlements. For many years, she and her husband Louis farmed in the Villeneuve district of Alberta. Her published works include "Early Life in Lac Ste Anne and St Albert in the Eighteen Seventies" (published in *Alberta Historical Review*, summer 1953) and "Our Buffalo Hunts" (in *The Best from Alberta History*, 1981).

■ Callwood, June

Journalist and social activist (*born in 1924 at Chatham, Ont.*). After establishing herself as a leading magazine writer in the 1950s, Callwood became a social activist, working on behalf of homeless

June Callwood is a journalist known for her concern for those who have suffered mistreatment (photo by Randy Haunfolder).

youths and drug addicts. She has a fierce social conscience, which is roused when she thinks people are suffering mistreatment. A regular newspaper columnist, she also has written several books on social issues, *The Law is Not for Women* (1976) and most recently *Jim, A Life With AIDS* (1988).

■ Cambridge

The city of Cambridge, Ont., is situated 89 km west of Toronto. It was created in 1973 when the communities of Galt, Preston, and Hespeler amalgamated. The original name of Preston was Cambridge Mills. There are over 400 industries located in the city, including Toyota Motor Corporation's general assembly facility. In 1986 the population was 79 920. For information, contact the City Clerk, 73 Water Street N., P.O. Box 669, Cambridge, Ont., N1R 3B4.

■ Cambridge Bay

Cambridge Bay, N.W.T., is a hamlet on the southeast coast of Victoria Island, looking across at the North American mainland. The residents are mainly Copper Inuit. The community has been the site of a radar station on the DEW Line since 1955. Traditional Inuit hunting and trapping still supports the local economy. The 1986 population was 1002. For information, contact the Senior Administrative Officer, P.O. Box 16, Cambridge Bay, N.W.T., X0E 0C0.

■ Cameron, Agnes Deans

Teacher, writer (*born in 1863 at Victoria, B.C.; died there in 1912*). Cameron is best known for her 16 000 km trip from Chicago to the Arctic Ocean, via Minneapolis, Winnipeg, Calgary, Edmonton, and the Mackenzie River, in 1908. It was a daring venture for a woman at the time. Her book about it, *The New North* (1909), became a classic. She was a popular lecturer and writer both in Canada and abroad.

▷ SUGGESTED READING: Agnes D. Cameron, *The New North: An Account of a Woman's 1908 Journey through Canada to the Arctic* (rev. ed. 1986).

■ Campbell, Alexander Bradshaw

Premier of Prince Edward Island (*born in 1933 at Summerside, P.E.I.*). Campbell, the leader of P.E.I.'s Liberal Party, was premier of the province from 1966 to 1978. When he took office, he was only 33 years old, one of the youngest premiers in Canadian history.

The highlight of Campbell's term as premier was the signing of a Comprehen-

ONTARIO

Toronto

Cambridge ●

sive Development Plan with the federal government. This plan brought federal money into the province to stimulate the economy. Campbell's government also tried to control the sale of Island land to outsiders.

Campbell left politics in 1978 when he was appointed to the Island's Supreme Court.

■ Campbell, James Kenneth

Clarinetist (*born in 1949 at Leduc, Alta*). Campbell is regarded as Canada's outstanding clarinetist. He studied in Toronto and Paris. In 1971 he won both the CBC Talent Festival and the Jeunesses musicales International Clarinet Competition in Yugoslavia. His career developed rapidly as a recitalist, chamber musician, concerto soloist, and as a recording artist.

Campbell has released some 20 recordings. His polished virtuosity and broad tastes (his repertoire includes jazz) have made him popular with both critics and audiences. In 1989 he joined the faculty of the famous music school at Indiana University.

■ Campbell, Maria

Writer (*born in 1940 at Park Valley, Sask.*). Campbell grew up in a Metis family that still respected its heritage.

In her autobiography, *Halfbreed* (1973), Campbell describes her happy childhood, the troubles of the 1970s, and the native peoples' new-found pride in their history. *People of the Buffalo* (1976) and *Riel's People* (1977) are carefully researched histories of the physical and spiritual lives of the Plains Indians and Metis. Her best-known book, *Little Badger and the Fire Spirit* (1977), is a literary folktale describing how people first acquired fire. Campbell says that she wrote this story, as well as her other books, to help native people recover their proud heritage.

■ Campbell, William Bennett

Premier of Prince Edward Island (*born in 1943 at Montague, P.E.I.*). Campbell was P.E.I. premier from 1978 to 1979. He took on the position and leadership of P.E.I.'s Liberal Party when he replaced the former premier, Alexander Campbell (no relation) in mid-term. When voters handed his government a defeat in the election of 1979, he entered federal politics. He was a Liberal member of Parliament for four years, 1980 to 1984, serving in the federal Cabinet as minister of veterans' affairs.

Defeated in two further elections, he was appointed to an official position in the P.E.I. government.

■ Campbell, William Wilfred

Poet and novelist (*born in 1858 at Berlin, Canada West [Kitchener, Ont.]; died in 1918 at Ottawa, Ont.*). For most of his life Campbell worked for the Government of Canada in Ottawa. What he loved to do most, however, was write poetry, plays, and novels. His novels and plays were not very good and are not often read today. But his poems, most of which are about nature, are still well worth reading. They were published in such books as *Lake Lyrics and Other Poems* (1889). Campbell also wrote many poems that praised Great Britain and tried to make Canadians take pride in their British heritage. He was a proud Canadian and wrote the text for a well-known book of paintings called *Canada* (1907). He is remembered as a man who loved his homeland and who tried to make others proud to be citizens of their new nation.

■ Campbell River

Campbell River, B.C., is located about halfway up the east coast of Vancouver Island, about 266 km north of Victoria. First occupied by southern Kwakiutl tribes, it was attracting loggers by 1900.

The major industries are pulp and paper, forestry, mining (coal), fishing, and tourism. It is well known as a salmon-fishing centre.

The District Municipality of Campbell River had a population of 16 986 in 1986. For information, contact the District Municipal Clerk, 301 St. Anns Road, Campbell River, B.C., V9W 4C7.

■ Campbellton

Campbellton lies at the head of Chaleur Bay at the mouth of the Restigouche River in northern New Brunswick. Its population is deeply rooted in both French and English cultures.

In 1757 about 750 Acadians arrived on the Restigouche River, fleeing the British, who had expelled them from their lands on the Bay of Fundy. In 1760 the last naval battle between England and France in North America took place in waters facing the present city. After the battle, about 335 Acadians were rounded up and taken to Halifax. Others escaped down the Gaspé coast. Scottish settlers began arriving in the Restigouche area in the early 1770s.

When the Intercolonial Railway arrived in 1875, Campbellton became the centre of the Restigouche region. The magnificent Restigouche River is renowned for its salmon fishing. An annual salmon celebration in one of New Brunswick's best-known festivals. Fishing, shipbuilding, and lumbering are the main industries, along with a pulp mill at nearby Atholville. In 1986 Campbellton's population was 9073. It is named for a former lieutenant-governor. For information, contact the City Clerk, P.O. Box 100, Campbellton, N.B., E3N 3G1.

■ Campeau, Robert

Businessman (*born in 1923 at Sudbury, Ont.*). Campeau began his career at 15 as a machinist's apprentice at Inco Ltd in Sudbury. In 1949, while working at a paper mill near Ottawa, Campeau built himself a house for $5000. He then sold it for $7300 before he had even moved in. This marked the beginning of his career in real estate, on which he built his fortune. He helped to build Ottawa's skyline, including a series of office towers at Place de Ville. By the 1960s he could boast that he was the federal government's biggest landlord. He owned up to 40% of the buildings that house government departments in the Ottawa-Hull region. His companies built hotels, shopping centres, and condominiums through southern Ontario and Quebec, and in the United States.

Campeau has a reputation as a fighter. In 1980 he aggressively tried to buy Royal Trustco, but failed. He turned his attention to the U.S., where he entered a bitter bidding war for a chain of retail stores, including the famous Bloomingdale's of New York. He won but ended up owing the banks some $10 billion (U.S.). In January 1990, he lost control of his company and faced personal losses of hundreds of millions of dollars.

■ Camping

Camping, or living in a temporary or movable shelter in the outdoors, has a long history in Canada. Most native groups, in the summer at least, moved from place to place in search of food. And the early explorers, trappers, and pioneers had no choice but to live in a variety of lean-tos and tents.

By the latter half of the 19th century, camping was becoming popular as a recreation, especially for people who were interested in hunting and fishing. Because of the weight of camping equipment at the time — canvas tents, sheepskin sleeping bags, sheet-iron stoves — campers usually stayed in one place. Backpacking did not become widely popular until the 1960s, when lightweight equipment made from nylon and polyester became available, along with dehydrated foods.

In the 1890s the Young Men's Christian Association (YMCA) ran its first summer camp for children. Within a few years, the Boy Scouts, Girl Guides, and various churches and labour unions also sponsored camps. They believed that a holiday in the outdoors would make campers more independent and responsible, and would improve their health as well. The children slept in tents, swam, hiked, and canoed. Gradually, permanent wooden buildings were built at the camps; first, dining and recreation rooms, followed by bathrooms and cabins. By the late 1980s, there were approximately 1500 youth camps in Canada, including camps for special groups such as the handicapped or children with particular health problems. Since 1936, the Canadian Camping Association (CCA) has existed to promote youth camping and to encourage standards and training for the many sponsoring organizations. All of the provinces, except P.E.I., have provincial associations affiliated with the CCA.

Car camping became popular in the 1920s and 1930s, as more people bought cars and more roads were constructed throughout the country. At first, travellers simply camped by the roadside, but municipal governments soon felt obliged to provide free camping grounds on the outskirts of cities and towns. There were also private campgrounds, which, for a fee, offered sewage and electrical hookups for motor vehicles and sometimes swimming pools and other recreation activities. As the years passed, campsites were also established in most of the national and provincial parks in Canada. In 1960, the federal government, with the help of the provinces, undertook to provide a

Robert Campeau's ability to seize opportunities made him one of North America's leading businessmen. His business empire soared in 1989 but collapsed in 1990 (photo by Daniel Dutka).

Hikers' Camp in the Purcell Mountains, B.C. (photo by J.A. Kraulis).

campground every 160 km along the Trans-Canada Highway.

The boom in camping led to a profitable industry in Canada supplying outdoor equipment. Several firms make wood and fibreglass canoes; others produce packboards, tents, sleeping bags, gas stoves, ice chests, lanterns, and rugged clothing. Special equipment is also available for winter camping. By 1989 it was estimated that more than one-quarter of Canadian households owned camping equipment, and many people had such expensive items as tent trailers and truck campers. Altogether, there are close to 3000 tent and trailer campgrounds in Canada.

The popularity of camping has put a strain on Canada's remaining wilderness areas. As a result, most national and provincial parks restrict entry by a system of permits, and have strict regulations about where to camp and what kinds of food and equipment can be brought in by campers.

For information about youth camps, contact the Canadian Camping Association, 2077 Dundas Street E., Suite 202, Mississauga, Ont., L4X 1M2, or the Camping Association in your province.

■ Campobello Island

Campobello Island is famous as the summer home of American President Franklin D. Roosevelt. It lies in Passamaquoddy Bay on the south coast of New Brunswick, next to the United States border. The Roosevelt International Bridge links the island to Maine. Fishing has been the major activity.

■ Camrose

Camrose, Alta, lies southeast of Edmonton at the centre of a mixed-farming and oil-producing area. It was settled early in the 1900s, mainly by Scandinavians, though its name refers to a town in Wales. Beautiful Mirror Lake wanders through Camrose and is lined with many parks. In 1986 the population was 12 968. For information, contact the Clerk, City Hall, 5204 50th Avenue, Camrose, Alta, T4V 0S8.

■ Canada

Canada occupies the northern half of the continent of North America and its adjacent islands, except Alaska and Greenland. Canada's boundary with the United States on the south is the 49th degree of latitude between the Pacific Ocean and Lake of the Woods. The border follows a chain of lakes and rivers through the Great Lakes to the St Lawrence River. In

Kaumajet Mountains, on the Labrador Coast. Canada's coastline is the longest in the world. It displays a great variety, from long sandy beaches to rugged mountains (photo by John deVisser).

the east, it takes an irregular course across the state of Maine to the Bay of Fundy. On the Northwest Pacific Coast, a long strip of land belonging to Alaska, called the "Panhandle," cuts northern B.C. off from the ocean.

Canada's coast, the longest in the world, borders on three oceans. Numerous natural harbours on the Atlantic and Pacific coasts provide shelter for ports, such as Halifax and Vancouver. The long Arctic coast, with its large islands, inlets and channels, are too often clogged with ice to be of use for shipping, although Hudson Bay is open to ships for several months of the year. The great waterway of the St Lawrence has been of prime importance to Canada's history and economy. It has funnelled immigration and trade deep into the interior.

Canada is the second-largest country in the world by area, but ranks only 31st in population. Most Canadians live along the southern fringe of the country, within a few hundred kilometres of the U.S. border. One in two Canadians lives in the Great-Lakes/St Lawrence region, where the two largest cities are located: Toronto and Montreal. Much of the rest of Canada is sparsely inhabited.

The vast physical area of Canada is dominated by the Canadian Shield, a massive bed of hard rock. It lies in the heart of Canada, hung around Hudson Bay like a gigantic collar. To the west of the Shield is the Great Plain, a flat, open land famous for its fields of wheat. The plains end abruptly in the west where the Western Cordillera rise. This series of mountain chains stretches from the southwestern U.S. to Alaska. In eastern Canada, the ancient Appalachian range covers much of the Atlantic Provinces. Unlike the younger western mountains,

Nootka House, *with women weaving. Explorers first encountered the native people of the Northwest Coast in the 18th century (courtesy NAC/C-2821).*

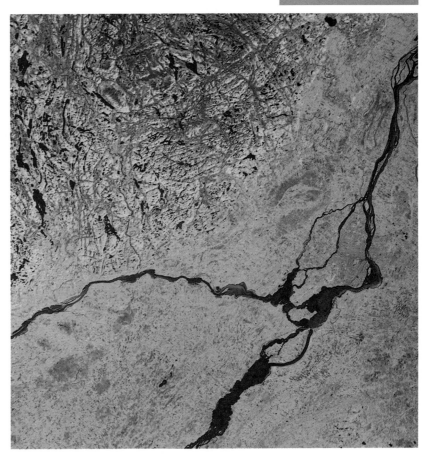

this range has been worn down by erosion into a series of rolling highlands and lowlands. The smallest of Canada's physical areas is the St Lawrence Lowlands, a flat, fertile land which has Canada's heaviest concentration of people.

Many parts of Canada are sprinkled with countless lakes of all sizes. The best known of these are the Great Lakes, but Winnipeg, Great Bear, Great Slave, and others rank among the largest in the world. Many of the lakes spill over from one basin to the next, forming chains. The native people and later the French used these connected waterways to carry on trade for hundreds and thousands of kilometres. *See* **Climate; Economy; Geology; Natural Regions.**

HISTORY TO CONFEDERATION

The original people came to Canada from Asia about 12 000 years ago. They likely came from Asia across a temporary land bridge that joined Siberia and Alaska. By the time the Europeans arrived, over 11 000 years later, these people had developed different cultures across North America, many with their own language.

Exploration The Europeans faced a different challenge in reaching North America: the stormy North Atlantic. The Norse were the first to arrive, around the year 1000. They used the islands of Iceland and Greenland as stepping stones.

After Christopher Columbus discovered the West Indies in 1492, Europeans became more confident about sailing out into the vast open ocean. For a while they believed that somewhere in the region of the Americas was an easy passage to Asia. What is now Canada was discovered in the search for this "Northwest Passage." Even after Jacques Cartier discovered the St Lawrence River and the French had seen the Great Lakes, the search continued. *See* **Exploration; Northwest Passage.**

New France When Samuel de Champlain founded the tiny post at Quebec in 1608, it marked the beginning of New France, and thus the true beginning of Canada. Despite his dedication, France showed little interest in its possession. Almost 60 years after the founding of Quebec, the population of New France was only about 3400. The colony was constantly at war with the Iroquois, who raided the trade routes and threatened the villages.

Joseph DesBarres *was one of the many European sea captains who explored and surveyed the Atlantic coast. DesBarres made this drawing himself (courtesy NAC/C-41599).*

Canadian Shield *is a massive area of rugged terrain covering much of Canada. This satellite photo shows how the Shield (top) contrasts with the St Lawrence Lowland. The city of Montreal is situated on the group of islands where the Ottawa and St Lawrence rivers meet (courtesy Canada Centre for Remote Sensing).*

Mackenzie Mountains,
N.W.T. are one of a series
of mountain ranges that
stretch from the
Canada/U.S. border to
Alaska (photo by Hans
Blohm/Masterfile).

Farmlands along St
Lawrence River,
Trois-Pistoles, Quebec.
The St Lawrence
Lowlands were the first
area to be farmed in
Canada. They still
contain a large
percentage of the
population of Canada
(photo by Thomas
Kitchin).

New France was also in conflict with the English colonies to the south. Partly this was a result of numerous wars between the parent countries, England and France. Partly it resulted from competition for the spoils of the fur trade in the Northwest. It was an uneven contest, in which the French in Canada were greatly outnumbered. Nevertheless, the French colony survived for 150 years. The fur traders of New France spread beyond the Great Lakes to the Great Plains and south down the Mississippi River. *See* **American Colonies; Samuel de Champlain; Fur Trade; New France.**

The Old Province of Quebec New France was a pawn in the larger contest between the empires of Britain and France. During the Seven Years' War (1756-63), a British fleet sailed down the St Lawrence. The British army, led by James Wolfe, was victorious in a brief bat-

tle outside the walls of Quebec in 1759. Within a year the "Conquest" of New France was complete.

In 1774, the British passed a law (the Quebec Act) that guaranteed the French protection of their language and religion. When the American colonies revolted in 1775, they invited the French Canadians to join, but gained little support. In 1775 American soldiers invaded Canada and attacked Quebec, but the fortress held out. The Americans retreated when British reinforcements arrived the following spring.

After the Revolution, American colonists who remained loyal to the British were forced from their land. Many of these Loyalists fled north to Quebec and Nova Scotia. The population of the two colonies grew overnight. As a result, in 1791, by the Constitutional Act, the British divided Quebec into two colonies. Lower Canada was in the area of present-day southern Quebec, along the "lower" section of the St Lawrence River. Upper Canada was farther "up" the river. The boundary between the two was the Ottawa River, which today separates the provinces of Quebec and Ontario.

The Constitutional Act of 1791 gave each of the Canadas a lieutenant-governor, an executive council, a legislative council, and a legislative assembly. Only the assembly was elected by the people.

In Atlantic Canada, the province of New Brunswick was created as a result of Loyalist immigration.

See **American Revolution; Constitutional Act, 1791; Conquest; Loyalists; Maritime History; Province of Quebec 1763-91.**

Lower Canada The French Canadians struggled to preserve their culture and to adapt to a new system of government. In 1826 they formed the Parti Patriote, which was led by Louis-Joseph Papineau. The Patriotes drew up a list of demands for change, which was rejected by the British. In 1837, the Patriotes tried to overthrow the government by force. The rebellion was very quickly put down by British troops. Papineau fled the country and 850 Patriotes were arrested; 12 were hanged. *See* **French-Canadian Nationalism; Lower Canada; Louis-Joseph Papineau; Rebellions of 1837.**

Upper Canada Some 5000 to 6000 Loyalists settled along the St Lawrence River, around present-day Kingston, and on the Niagara Peninsula. They were soon joined by other American immigrants looking for land.

St Lawrence River at Quebec City, Quebec. *The St Lawrence provided European settlers with a corridor into Canada (photo by Thomas Kitchin).*

The first lieutenant-governor of Upper Canada was John Graves Simcoe. He moved the capital to York (the future Toronto), built roads, and set up courts. Politics in the colony became a contest between a small group of powerful men, called the Family Compact, and an opposition group, called Reformers.

During the War of 1812, Upper Canada was invaded by American troops. They burned York, but were turned back at Queenston Heights, near Niagara, by British and Canadian troops led by Sir Isaac Brock.

By the mid-1830s, Reformers, led by William Lyon Mackenzie, were demanding an American form of government and separation from Great Britain. In 1837, Mackenzie led a brief rebellion, which was quickly put down by militia and British soldiers. *See* **Upper Canada; War of 1812**.

Province of Canada Britain sent Lord Durham to Canada to investigate the troubles in the two Canadas. He recommended that Upper Canada and Lower Canada be united and that they be given a system of government that would give more power to the elected members of the Assembly. The Reformers called this "responsible government."

The first suggestion came into effect in 1841 with formation of the Province of Canada. The Province had two sections: Canada East and Canada West. Each had the same number of seats in the government, even though Canada East had a larger population than Canada West (670 000 compared with 480 000). The French Canadians understood that this system was intended to favour the English Canadians. However, their young leaders, such as Louis LaFontaine, soon learned to use the system. LaFontaine joined with Robert Baldwin of Canada West to fight for responsible government. In 1848 LaFontaine became premier of Canada, and Baldwin co-premier. *See* **Province of Canada.**

The Achievement of Responsible Government In 1849 LaFontaine and Baldwin passed a bill in the Assembly and sent it to the governor general, Lord Elgin, for approval. Under the old system, Elgin could veto the bill, even if the Reformers had a majority in the Assembly. Many English Canadians, especially in Montreal where this particular bill was very unpopular, urged Elgin to veto. He did not. This confirmed the principle of responsible government.

The stormy politics of the union continued through the 1850s. Disputes arose over school systems and religion. A new call for reform arose in Protestant Canada West for "representation by population," led by the editor of the Toronto *Globe*, George Brown. This policy would give Canada West, which now outnumbered the East, more seats. The French in Canada East naturally rejected this scheme.

Confederation In the mid-1850s a new partnership emerged, led by John A. Macdonald and George-Étienne Cartier. Each had enemies within his own section. Macdonald's rivalry with Brown was both political and personal. Even with the help of a group of French-Canadian nationalists, under A.A. Dorion, Brown was unable to unseat Macdonald for more than a few days. Neither group was able to stay in power for long and the government fell into chaos. In 1864 Brown and Macdonald buried their differences long enough to

Flag of Canada The new flag was adopted in 1965 (courtesy Canada Post Corporation).

Development of Canada shown in a 1981 series of postage stamps. In 1867, Canada consisted of 4 provinces. By 1873, B.C., P.E.I., and Manitoba had joined (upper right). Alberta and Saskatchewan were added in 1905 (lower left). Newfoundland made the tenth province in 1949 (courtesy Canada Post Corporation).

Dates the Provinces and Territories Entered Confederation

- New Brunswick - 1867
- Nova Scotia - 1867
- Ontario - 1867
- Quebec - 1867
- Manitoba - 1870
- Northwest Territories - 1870
- British Columbia - 1871
- Prince Edward Island - 1873
- Yukon Territory - 1898
- Alberta and Saskatchewan became provinces and entered Confederation in 1905
- Newfoundland - 1949

achieve Confederation with the Maritime provinces in 1867. The new nation of Canada consisted of four provinces: Ontario, Quebec, New Brunswick, and Nova Scotia. *See* **Confederation; Responsible Government; Immigration;** and separate entries on the ten provinces and two territories.

▷ SUGGESTED READING: Craig Brown, editor, *The Illustrated History of Canada* (1987); Tim Fitzharris and John Livingston, *Canada: A Natural History* (1988); R.D. Lawrence, *The Natural History of Canada* (1988); Desmond Morton, *A Short History of Canada* (1983).

■ Canada Act 1982

The Canada Act 1982, was an Act of the British Parliament which, in effect, brought Canada's Constitution to Canada. It ended the power of the British Parliament to make laws for Canada. The Act's second item read as follows:

"2. No Act of the British Parliament of the United Kingdom passed after the *Constitution Act, 1982* comes into force shall extend to Canada as part of its law."

■ Canada Company

The Canada Company was a land company chartered in England in 1825. Its purpose was to attract settlers to Upper Canada. It was the idea of Scottish novelist John Galt, who persuaded a group of British merchants to invest in the project. In 1826 the company bought about 1 million hectares from the government of Upper Canada. The land consisted of the Huron Tract, the Halton Block, and many scattered crown reserves.

Galt's idea was to attract settlers who could pay for their land and put money into developing their homesteads. In return, the company would build roads and other public services. In 1827 the newly formed town of Guelph became the company's headquarters. The company laid out the town of Goderich, in the Huron Tract, hoping that it would become a major port.

During the 1820s and 1830s company lands sold as planned. Wealthy settlers, who arrived with their pianos and their libraries, bought some of the land. But sales were slow. Large-scale settlement did not begin until the 1840s. At that time the company started a leasing system that attracted ordinary settlers who had little or no cash.

Some people said the Canada Company had too much power, that its agents ordered the poorer settlers around. Other settlers complained that promised services were not provided. The Canada Company's posters in Britain were often exaggerated, boasting of "good roads" when the roads had not yet been built. On the other hand, the vigorous advertising helped dispel the British belief that Canada was all ice and snow. Despite its many faults, the Canada Company boosted immigration when Upper Canada really needed the settlers.

■ Canada Council

The Canada Council was created by the Parliament of Canada in 1957. It was funded partly by money from the estates of two wealthy entrepreneurs from the Maritimes who had recently died: Izaak Walton Killam and Sir James Dunn. Its purpose was to encourage the study and enjoyment of the arts, humanities, and social sciences in Canada. In 1978 responsibility for the humanities and social sciences was passed to another organization, leaving the Council responsible for the arts. Initially, the Council financed its operations out of the income from its endowment, but in 1964 the government began to grant additional money to the Council. Today, this grant amounts to over $100 million each year.

The Council is headed by a board of 21 members, named by the government and drawn from all ten provinces. It offers financial assistance to professional artists and arts organizations, including theatre, ballet and opera companies, art galleries, orchestras, film and video organizations, and publishing houses. A number of committees and advisers help the Council decide how the grants should be distributed. Through its Explorations Program it encourages initiatives in areas not covered by traditional disciplines.

The Canada Council has had a strong influence on arts and culture in Canada. Financial support provided by the Council led to a great expansion in the number and quality of full-time artists in the

First Meeting *of the officers of the Canada Council, Ottawa, April 30, 1957 (courtesy NAC/PA-144595).*

country, and in the number and quality of arts institutions. The demands on the Council constantly exceed the money available.

When the Council began its operations, there were very few organizations funding the arts in Canada. Today, provincial governments and municipalities play an increasingly important role in supporting the arts in their jurisdiction.

■ Canada East

Canada East, formerly known as Lower Canada, was the eastern portion of the Province of Canada during the period from 1841 to 1867. It was the nucleus of present-day Quebec.

▷ Related Article: **Province of Canada.**

■ Canada First

Canada First was the name and slogan of a patriotic group founded in Ottawa in 1868 to promote a stronger sense of national pride and purpose among the citizens of the new Dominion. Among their aims were the development of a distinctive Canadian literature and art, and the study of Canadian history. The group was dedicated to Canadian independence from Britain and the United States. It urged the rapid expansion of Canada to the northwest.

With expanded boundaries, enormous resources, and a larger, self-reliant population, the Canada Firsters believed that their country would quickly be able to achieve its destiny as one of the world's great nations.

The movement did not last long. Some English-speaking Canadians attacked the group for suggesting that Canada should become more independent of Britain. A deeper problem was the group's view that Canada's future must be in the hands of Protestant Anglo-Saxons. They believed that the "superior" values of this group would form the basis of Canadian nationhood. During the Red River Rebellion (1869-70), the group helped to provoke a bitter reaction against the Metis, Catholics, and French Canadians.

One of Canada First's aims was that only British Protestants should be allowed to immigrate to Canada. Hence, the movement had very limited appeal outside Ontario. It disappeared around 1875, though its influence continued to be felt into the 20th century. One of the members of the group, Edward Blake, went on to become leader of the federal Liberal Party.

▷ Related Article: **Nationalism.**

■ Canada House

Canada House, an imposing old building on Trafalgar Square in London, England, is Canada's headquarters in Britain. Opened in 1925, it is a centre for promoting Canadian culture and providing information about this country.

■ Canada West

Canada West, formerly known as Upper Canada, was the western portion of the Province of Canada during the period from 1841 to 1867. It was the nucleus of present-day Ontario.

▷ Related Article: **Province of Canada.**

■ Canadarm

Canadarm is the name given to an electro-mechanical arm mounted on the space shuttle. Using the arm from inside their spacecraft, astronauts can handle satellites and other objects floating in space.

The space shuttle is a spacecraft system which the United States, with some help from other countries, built during the 1970s. The goal was to build a kind of space truck that would provide frequent and easy access to space. The key to the space shuttle is the orbiter, a rocket and glider rolled into one. Rockets hurl the chunky orbiter into space. It glides back down to Earth, to be launched again and again.

The orbiter is designed to do work in space. For instance, it can release satellites from its cargo bay, or catch orbiting satellites for repair. To do such work, it needed what its designers called a *remote manipulator system*, that is, a kind of crane or mechanical arm. Canada decided to contribute to the space shuttle by building such an arm, a device later named Canadarm.

Designing Canadarm Hundreds of engineers and technicians joined forces in designing, building, testing, and operating Canadarm. They worked for a team of Canadian industries led by Spar Aerospace Ltd of Toronto, and for the National Research Council of Canada.

The arm had to work reliably in the hostile environment of space: in a near-perfect vacuum, bathed in intense radiation, and subject to extreme fluctuations of temperature.

It had to be strong enough to handle — in space — objects as massive as a bus, with a precise and gentle touch. Yet it had to be as light as possible. Canadarm is made of aluminum, titanium, stainless steel, and graphite epoxy, and weighs under 400 kg. On Earth, where it is subject to

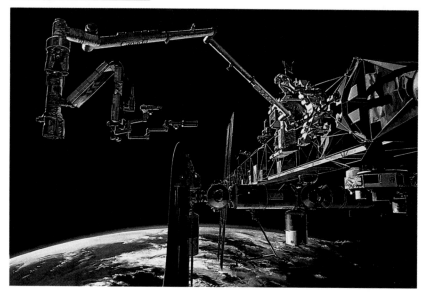

Canadarm A new Canadian robot arm will play a big part in the new space station, to be launched in the mid-1990s. The arm will operate as an extension of the astronauts' own senses. It will react to their voice, sight, and touch (illustration by Paul Fjeld).

the pull of gravity, it cannot even support its own weight. To see how it would work in space, and to train the astronauts who would use it, engineers used computer simulations, similar to video games.

Canadarm looks like and works like a human arm, except it is 15.2 m long. It is attached to the orbiter at a "shoulder" joint. An "elbow" joint divides it into two sections, each about as long as a telephone pole. It ends with a hand which turns in a "wrist" joint and which, thanks to a wire device, can grasp things such as prongs attached to satellites. A white skin of insulation and its internal heaters keep its internal temperature steady.

Using Canadarm In November 1981, Canadarm went into space for the first time. This, the second shuttle mission, was the first real test of Canadarm. From a control panel on the flight deck of the orbiter, named *Columbia*, an astronaut "flew" the end of the arm with hand controls, not unlike those of an aircraft, watching the movements of the arm through windows and on a television system. One of the five computers on board the shuttle served as the brain, translating the astronaut's commands into coordinated movements of the arm. The arm was very easy to control.

The plan was to test Canadarm on that mission, but it turned out to have an unexpected job to do. Some tiles had fallen off the orbiter's nose during the launch. These tiles protect the spacecraft from burning when it re-enters Earth's atmosphere. With the camera mounted on its hand, Canadarm enabled the ground controllers to inspect the orbiter's nose and to determine that the spacecraft could return to Earth with little risk.

On later missions, Canadarm helped launch and retrieve a number of satellites. It came in handy in unplanned ways too. Once, when the solar panels of a satellite being launched from the orbiter refused to unfold, Canadarm shook and turned the satellite so that it faced the Sun. Out popped the panels.

On another mission, the orbiter's astronauts planned to leave the orbiter and catch a satellite in need of repair by attaching connectors to it. The connectors did not fit. The satellite, known as Solar Max (for Solar Maximum), was twisting and turning in space. Maneuvering around it, the orbiter was running out of fuel. The only chance for success was to grab the satellite at the right moment with Canadarm, which is exactly what happened. Solar Max became the first satellite ever repaired in space.

Canada contributed the first Canadarm, which cost $110 million, to the National Aeronautics and Space Administration (NASA), which bought three more Canadarms for $75 million. One of these arms was destroyed in January 1986 when the space shuttle *Challenger* blew up shortly after launch.

Space Station Canada has agreed to provide more robots for use with the space station that the U.S. plans to build with the help of other countries and put into orbit in the late 1990s. Canada's contribution, known as a Mobile Servicing System, will be a roving multi-purpose robot. Its manipulator will be larger than Canadarm's and will be able to handle loads three times more massive than Canadarm can handle. In addition, a smaller, two-armed robot with artificial vision will be produced to do more complicated tasks. Their jobs, like Canadarm's, will include moving equipment and supplies around, catching and releasing satellites, supporting astronauts as they maneuvre outside the station, and more. It will be the main tool used in assembling the space station. Building and operating it will cost Canada an estimated $1.2 billion.

▷ RELATED ARTICLE: **Space Technology.**

■ Canadian-American Relations

The governments and peoples of the United States and Canada touch and affect one another thousands of times every day. These "relations" are sometimes difficult, but are usually friendly. Former Canadian prime minister Pierre Trudeau compared living next door to the United States to sleeping with an elephant. Americans hardly seem to notice Canada, while Canadians are affected by every little movement the U.S. makes. Most Canadians know that the U.S. is by far our biggest trading partner. Very few Americans would guess that Canada is their biggest trading partner. Canada and the U.S. interact in a number of basic ways:

• the Canadian-American border is one of the world's longest; parts of it (Alaska/B.C. and Georges Bank on the Atlantic Ocean) are still in dispute
• that border is frequently crossed by citizens of the two countries (80 million times in 1988)
• each country is the other's biggest trading customer
• individuals and companies in the United States invest many dollars in Canada, and Canadians do likewise
• they are partners in the defence of North America
• they have a mutual responsibility for their fragile shared environment.

History Relations between Canada and the United States have not always been peaceful. Canada was twice invaded (unsuccessfully) by the United States, in 1775-76 and again during the War of 1812. Until the 1860s there were frequent disputes about where the border should be. Canadian Confederation in 1867 was caused in part by the fear of attacks by Fenians based in the U.S. or by the large powerful Northern army that had just won the American Civil War. Some American politicians suggested invading Canada in revenge for Great Britain's support of the South in the Civil War.

The relationship improved by the end of the 19th century. Canadians were often suspicious of the Americans, but they increasingly thought of themselves as North Americans, and of the U.S. as their best friend. The ties that once held Canada so tightly to Great Britain were loosened as more and more immigrants came to Canada from other parts of the world. While Canada's economy once relied almost entirely on trade with Britain, this trade increasingly shifted to the U.S. By 1918 about 30% of Canadian industry was owned by U.S. investors. During the 1920s the U.S. replaced Great Britain as Canada's main trading partner. In these same years, the U.S. was already providing over 60% of Canada's imports.

In World War II Canada and the U.S. were allies after Japan attacked the U.S., although Canadian soldiers still fought alongside the British in Europe. In Canada, Americans and Canadians co-operated in building the Alaska Highway. During

P.M. Lester B. Pearson and U.S. President John F. Kennedy at Hyannis Port, Mass. Canadian-American relations were friendly under Pearson (courtesy NAC/C-90482).

the early 1950s, many Canadians shared the Americans' fear and hatred of the communist Soviet Union.

In the 1960s and 1970s Canadians again became very wary of the U.S., mainly because of its participation in the Vietnam War. The economic, cultural, and military influence of the U.S. in Canada was seriously questioned. The Trudeau government tried a policy, called the Third Option, of reducing our reliance on the U.S. by developing our relations with other nations. The policy was a failure.

Economics Free trade is an important theme of Canadian-American relations. There was a limited free trade (called "reciprocity") treaty from 1854 to 1866. Canadian governments tried to get a similar deal for most of the rest of the 19th century. In 1891, however, the Conservative Prime Minister Sir John A. Macdonald won a stunning election victory by calling on old loyalties (that is, to Great Britain) and on protection of Canadian industries. In the election of 1911, the Liberal Sir Wilfrid Laurier was defeated largely as a result of his support for a new free-trade deal.

Canada and the U.S. signed trade deals in 1935 and 1938. These deals were not only debated as economic issues. They were emotional as well. They raised the question of Canada being too closely tied to the U.S. and losing its independence in the bargain. For this reason, in 1948, Prime Minister Mackenzie King decided against a new trade deal with the U.S.

A new Canada-U.S. Free Trade Agreement was hotly debated in the election of 1988. The Conservatives, under Prime Minister Brian Mulroney, won the elec-

Annexation Manifesto of 1849

The Annexation Manifesto of 1849 was a pamphlet signed and circulated by a group of citizens of the Province of Canada. It was first published in the Montreal *Gazette* on October 11, 1849.

It called for Canada to be annexed (made a part of) to the United States.

It was supported by English-speaking merchants. Some French Canadians also supported the Manifesto. The movement died out after 1854 when the Reciprocity Treaty was signed with the United States.

NDP MPs Howard McCurdy and Steven Langdon, and Liberal MP Herb Gray carrying petitions to the U.S. Embassy protesting the pollution of air over Canada by a U.S. garbage plant (courtesy Canapress Photo Service).

tion and signed the deal later that year. Beginning on January 1, 1989, it provides for the removal of all tariffs between the two countries within ten years. It also gives the U.S. greater access to Canadian resources. It sets up a number of bodies to solve the many trading disputes which crop up in Canada-U.S. relations.

The total trade between Canada and the U.S. is larger than that between any two other countries in the world. Two-way trade in merchandise for 1988 was nearly $190 billion. Canada exported goods worth $101.7 billion to the U.S. and imported U.S. products worth $88 billion. Non-merchandise trade (for example, tourism) is also substantial: Canada paid $32.5 billion to the United States (1988), and the U.S. paid $18.3 billion to Canada.

The U.S. was a customer for 74% of Canadian exports in 1988. Sixty-nine percent of Canada's imports came from the U.S. Twenty-two percent of U.S. exports go to Canada, and Canada supplies 18% of all U.S. imports.

The two countries invest heavily in the other's economy. Canada is the fourth-largest foreign investor in the U.S. (estimated at $42.5 billion in 1988), while the U.S. had invested $136.4 billion in Canada by 1988. The U.S. owns more of the Canadian economy than any other country in the world. Canadian investment in the U.S. makes up 8% of all investment in that country, while American investment makes up 69% of all investment in Canada. Many economists claim that Canada is lucky to have so much money invested. Critics claim that no other nation in the world would allow so much foreign ownership.

Canadians and Americans trade heavily in energy. The value of the trade between the two countries in crude oil, petroleum products, gas, coal, uranium, and electricity amounted to $12.2 billion in 1988. Canada enjoyed a surplus of $8.8 billion in this trade. The 1988 free-trade deal gives Canada better access to American markets, and ensures that the U.S. will be ably to buy Canadian energy at prices no higher than Canadians pay.

The fisheries have always been one of the most difficult problems in Canadian-American relations. There is co-operation, for example, the Canada-U.S. Pacific Salmon Treaty of 1985. However, there are also frequent quarrels over ownership and management of the resource.

There is a good deal of co-operation in the area of science and technology. An example of this is the Canadian contribu-tion of the "Canadarm" to the American space program.

Defence There have been close ties between the Canadian and American military services since World War II. The Permanent Joint Board on Defence (PJBD) was established in 1940 after Hitler had overrun Europe. The PJBD continues to be a place where representatives of the two countries can discuss mutual defence problems and make recommendations to their governments.

After the war, Canada and the U.S. co-operated more and more in the defence against a possible attack by the Soviet Union, which had nuclear weapons and long-range bombers from the late 1940s. In 1957, NORAD, a Canada-US organiza-tion which looks after the air defence of the continent, was established. Canada and the U.S. co-operated in the building of a series of radar stations across northern Canada (the DEW Line) to warn of attack from the north.

The Defence Production Sharing Arrangements (DPSA), begun in 1958, ensured that the U.S. would make some of its defence purchases in Canada. Both NORAD and the DPSA are still active. Both nations are members of the North Atlantic Treaty Organization (NATO).

Canada sometimes helps to test U.S. weapons systems, such as the advanced cruise missile. However, the two nations sometimes disagree on defence matters. Canada has refused to arm with nuclear weapons.

Culture Canadians have always been concerned about the overwhelming influence of U.S. magazines, books, films, radio, and television. While most Canadians enjoy access to these products, many critics believe that they block the access of Canadian artists, writers, and filmmakers to their own market. Large amounts of imported culture may also lead to an Americanization of our view of the world. From time to time, Canadian governments have tried to combat these influences. They created the Canadian Broadcasting Corporation (CBC) to ensure some Canadian control of radio and TV. In 1976, a federal law prevented Canadians from receiving tax deductions for advertisements which are placed on U.S. radio and TV stations, and U.S. magazines aimed at Canadian markets. The U.S. government strongly opposed this law, and passed its own similar bill directed at Canada in 1984. Canadian governments have given subsidies to writers, artists, musicians, book publishers, and others to help them produce Canadian material. While economists argue that culture is just another product, and the free market should decide these matters, others believe that Canada has no future as an independent nation if it cannot support or encourage its own culture.

As of 1988, the foreign (which is mainly U.S.) share of Canada's market for books was 75%; for magazines 60.5%; for English-language television 71%; for screen time 97%; and for recorded music sales 89%.

Environment The environment has become a major issue in Canadian-American relations. The Great Lakes Water Quality Agreement, which aims at cleaning up those bodies of water, is an example of co-operation between the two nations. Attempts at co-operation are sometimes less successful.

Acid rain was one of the biggest areas of disagreement in the relationship in the 1980s. Canada pressed the Americans for a commitment to improve the situation and a set of deadlines for action. The U.S. under President Ronald Reagan resisted. The administration of President George Bush seemed more interested in the problem, and in 1989 asked the Congress to agree to a 10 million metric ton reduction in 502 emissions by the year 2000.

Organization The United States has an ambassador in Ottawa to represent its interests and make Canadians aware of U.S. ideas and policies. Canada has an ambassador in Washington, helped by Consul Generals — also official representatives of the Canadian government — in Atlanta, Boston, Chicago, Cleveland, Dallas, Detroit, Los Angeles, Minneapolis, New York, San Francisco, and Seattle.

Canada is usually the first country visited by an American president after taking office. In 1985 Prime Minister Mulroney and U.S. President Ronald Reagan agreed to get together every year for a "bilateral summit." They had four such meetings from 1985 to 1988. President George Bush and Mulroney met three times in 1989, Bush's first year in power. There are frequent meetings between government ministers, such as the U.S. Secretary of State and the Canadian Secretary of State for External Affairs, and between government officials.

The 1988 Canada-U.S. Free Trade Agreement established a number of bodies and panels to discuss and settle disagreements between the two countries over trading rules and practices. The highest level of these is the Canada-U.S. Free Trade Commission, whose senior Canadian member is the minister of International Trade.

The oldest of the Canada-U.S. joint organizations is the very useful International Joint Commission, which since 1912 has investigated and made decisions about the use and ownership of water resources along the border.

▷ RELATED ARTICLES: **Foreign Relations; Free Trade; Political History; Nationalism.**

■ Canadian Arctic Expedition

The Canadian Arctic Expedition, from 1913 to 1918, was the first major Canadian scientific project in the Arctic.

Tragedy and discord plagued the two-party expedition. On the way into the Arctic, the supply ship *Karluk* sank in the ice. Eventually, 11 members of the expedition died. The rest divided in a dispute over leadership. One party, led by Rudolph Anderson, explored the Arctic coast east of the Mackenzie River. The second party, led by Vilhjalmur Stefansson, travelled in dogsleds out across the sea ice. This second group took important readings from the sea floor and located the last undiscovered islands in the Arctic Archipelago.

▷ RELATED ARTICLE: **Vilhjalmur Stefansson.**

■ Canadian Auto Workers

The Canadian Auto Workers (CAW) is a union of workers in the automobile industry. It began in 1937 as a wing of the United Automobile Workers of America (UAW), which is based in the United States. The UAW was a driving force in several major Canadian strikes, and it won important benefits for its members. In 1985, led by Bob White, the Canadian section broke away from the UAW, forming an independent organization.

■ Canadian Bill of Rights

The Canadian Bill of Rights is a law that was passed by Parliament in 1960, under the leadership of Prime Minister John Diefenbaker. It requires that all federal statutes protect certain rights, such as freedom of speech, freedom of association and assembly, freedom of religion, freedom of the press, and guarantees of equality. In the years since it was passed, the courts have not attached much importance to the Canadian Bill of Rights, mainly because it was not part of the Constitution. Most of the provisions in the Canadian Bill of Rights are now contained in the Canadian Charter of Rights and Freedoms, which *is* entrenched in the Constitution. However, the Canadian

Bill of Rights is still part of our law, and the courts are starting to give it greater attention.

Canadian Brass

The Canadian Brass is a musical group consisting of trumpets, a french horn, a trombone, and a tuba. They were originally members of the Hamilton Philharmonic Orchestra. They toured Europe in 1972 and went on to a very successful international career. They have also performed in China, the Soviet Union, the United States, and Canada. They are lighthearted entertainers as well as superb musicians. They have a long list of recordings. The members of Canadian Brass play on a matched set of gold-plated instruments.

Canadian Broadcasting Corporation (CBC)

The CBC is one of the world's major public broadcasting organizations. With the spread in popularity of radio in the 1930s came the worry that Canada would be drowned in American programs. No privately owned station seemed capable of producing enough Canadian programs. The CBC was formed in 1936 as a public broadcasting system, that is, funded by the government. It began with only eight stations but built transmitters so that it could reach all parts of Canada. Today, the CBC operates radio and television systems in both French and English. It broadcasts in native languages by satellite to the Far North. It runs a shortwave service overseas and broadcasts the proceedings of the House of Commons.

Cross Country Checkup, a CBC Radio open-line program, gives Canadians a chance to discuss issues with public figures (courtesy NAC/PA-139064).

The CBC was also responsible for regulating all broadcasting in Canada. In 1958 this function was turned over to another organization, which later became the Canadian Radio-television and Telecommunications Commission (CRTC).

CBC gradually increased its own programs. Among its early successes were farm programs, women's programs, "Hockey Night in Canada," children's programs, and coverage of news. A separate French-language network was set up. During World War II, the CBC broadcast information about the war. After the war, it increased its coverage of politics. It made an important contribution to the arts by supporting Canadian drama. A repertory of young writers and actors put on hundreds of plays.

The Coming of Television The CBC dealt cautiously with the new medium of TV when it appeared in the late 1940s. It finally began broadcasting in Montreal and Toronto in 1952. In only two years, 60% of all Canadians could receive CBC signals.

With the arrival of TV, the radio audience plummeted. It was revived in the 1970s when CBC shifted its focus from evening (now dominated by TV) to morning and afternoon programming. It concentrated on local information and news. Programs such as "Morningside," "Ideas," and "As It Happens," used radio's ability to respond quickly and to cover topics in greater depth. In 1975 commercials were eliminated from all CBC radio networks.

On television, CBC developed exciting information programs, such as "This Hour Has Seven Days," "Man Alive," and "The Nature of Things." It began popular children's programs such as "Mr Dressup," "The Friendly Giant," and "Chez Hélène." More recently, it has added "The Beachcombers," "the fifth estate," and "Degrassi High." It expanded its nightly news with "The National" and "The Journal," which are scheduled in prime time, at 10:00 PM. In 1989 it began an all-news channel.

The CBC's programming is expensive. It requires more than $1 billion, most of it public money, each year. It is therefore a favourite target for governments looking to trim money off their budgets. In 1989 the Conservative government of Brian Mulroney announced that the CBC's grant would be cut by $140 million over five years. Meanwhile, the CBC is forced to show American programs in order to help pay for its many services. It has many political and creative challenges to face if it is to survive through the 1990s and fulfil its goal of "fostering a national spirit."

▷ RELATED ARTICLES: **Canadian Radio-television and Telecommunications Commission; Radio; Television.**

▷ SUGGESTED READING: Knowlton Nash, *Prime Time at Ten: Behind the Camera Battles of Canadian T.V. Journalism* (1987).

■ Canadian Charter of Rights and Freedoms

The Charter of Rights and Freedoms came into force on April 17, 1982, when it was entrenched in the new Canadian Constitution. The Constitution Act, 1982, states that any law that is inconsistent with the Charter is invalid. Since 1982, various Supreme Court decisions have emphasized the importance of the Charter.

The Charter played an important part in the discussions and negotiations leading up to the Constitution of 1982. The prime minister, Pierre Trudeau, was determined that Canada should have a written Charter of Rights as part of its constitution, in order to protect citizens from unfair government actions. Many provincial governments did not support the Charter. They argued that citizens' rights were well protected under the existing parliamentary system and that nothing more need be done. The basic issue was who would best protect people's rights: judges or politicians. Supporters of the Charter argued that judges were more impartial and objective and were thus not influenced by public opinion. As a result, they would protect human rights better, especially in cases where public opinion was emotionally involved. Opponents of the Charter argued that elected politicians were the best protectors of human rights, since they could be replaced if citizens did not like their decisions and since they would be more in touch with public opinion. Some critics of the Charter feared that it was another step away from Canada's British traditions, which emphasize the supremacy of Parliament, and a step towards American traditions, which emphasize the courts.

The federal and provincial governments agreed to a compromise; they agreed that the Charter would include a "notwithstanding" clause (Article 33), which allows any government to exempt a particular law from the conditions of the Charter. For example, the Saskatchewan government passed a law forcing government employees to end a strike, "notwithstanding" the rights guaranteed by the Charter. The Quebec government passed a law forbidding stores to display signs in any language except French, and similarly included a "notwithstanding" clause. The notwithstanding clause lasts for only five years, but it can be renewed. It is the most controversial item in the Charter. Critics argue that it makes the rest of the Charter meaningless. Supporters argue that, without it, the provinces would never have accepted the Charter.

The Charter guarantees the following kinds of rights: 1) fundamental rights, for example, freedom of speech and of religion; 2) democratic rights, for example, the right to vote, the right to regular elections; 3) mobility rights, for example, the right to move and work anywhere in Canada; 4) legal rights, for example, the right to a fair trial and to freedom from unlawful arrest or punishment; 5) equality rights, for example, freedom from discrimination; 6) language rights, for example, the right to speak either official language in certain circumstances. The Charter also states that women's rights and native rights will be protected, as will Canada's multicultural heritage.

The implications of the Charter are only beginning to become clear as courts begin to interpret it. It is increasingly being used as a defence in legal cases and is certain to become an important part of Canadian life. The text is reprinted below.

▷ RELATED ARTICLES: **Constitution; Law.**

▷ SUGGESTED READING: J. Stuart Langford, *The Law of Your Land* (1982).

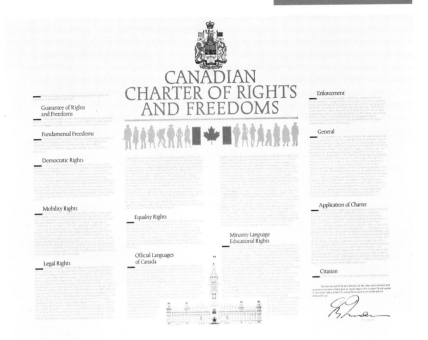

Canadian Charter of Rights and Freedoms (courtesy Department of the Secretary of State of Canada).

Canadian Charter of Rights and Freedoms
Part I

Whereas Canada is founded upon principles that recognize the supremacy of God and the rule of law:

Guarantee of Rights and Freedoms

1. The Canadian Charter of Rights and Free-

doms guarantees the rights and freedoms set out in it subject only to such reasonable limits prescribed by law as can be demonstrably justified in a free and democratic society.

Fundamental Freedoms

2. Everyone has the following fundamental freedoms:

(a) freedom of conscience and religion;

(b) freedom of thought, belief, opinion and expression, including freedom of the press and other media of communication;

(c) freedom of peaceful assembly; and

(d) freedom of association.

Democratic Rights

3. Every citizen of Canada has the right to vote in an election of members of the House of Commons or of a legislative assembly and to be qualified for membership therein.

4. (1) No House of Commons and no legislative assembly shall continue for longer than five years from the date fixed for the return of the writs at a general election of its members.

(2) In time of real or apprehended war, invasion or insurrection, a House of Commons may be continued by Parliament and a legislative assembly may be continued by the legislature beyond five years if such continuation is not opposed by the votes of more than one-third of the members of the House of Commons or the legislative assembly, as the case may be.

5. There shall be a sitting of Parliament and of each legislature at least once every twelve months.

Mobility Rights

6. (1) Every citizen of Canada has the right to enter, remain in and leave Canada.

(2) Every citizen of Canada and every person who has the status of a permanent resident of Canada has the right

(a) to move to and take up residence in any province; and

(b) to pursue the gaining of a livelihood in any province.

(3) The rights specified in subsection (2) are subject to

(a) any laws or practices of general application in force in a province other than those that discriminate among persons primarily on the basis of province of present or previous residence; and

(b) any laws providing for reasonable residency requirements as a qualification for the receipt of publicly provided social services.

(4) Subsections (2) and (3) do not preclude any law, program or activity that has as its object the amelioration in a province of conditions of individuals in that province who are socially or economically disadvantaged if the rate of employment in that province is below the rate of employment in Canada.

Legal Rights

7. Everyone has the right to life, liberty and security of the person and the right not to be deprived thereof except in accordance with the principles of fundamental justice.

8. Everyone has the right to be secure against unreasonable search or seizure.

9. Everyone has the right not to be arbitrarily detained or imprisoned.

10. Everyone has the right on arrest or detention

(a) to be informed promptly of the reasons therefor;

(b) to retain and instruct counsel without delay and to be informed of that right; and

(c) to have the validity of the detention determined by way of habeas corpus and to be released if the detention is not lawful.

11. Any person charged with an offence has the right

(a) to be informed without unreasonable delay of the specific offence;

(b) to be tried within a reasonable time;

(c) not to be compelled to be a witness in proceedings against that person in respect of the offence;

(d) to be presumed innocent until proven guilty according to law in a fair and public hearing by an independent and impartial tribunal;

(e) not to be denied reasonable bail without just cause;

(f) except in the case of an offence under military law tried before a military tribunal, to the benefit of trial by jury where the maximum punishment for the offence is imprisonment for five years or a more severe punishment;

(g) not to be found guilty on account of any act or omission unless, at the time of the act or omission, it constituted an offence under Canadian or international law or was criminal according to the general principles of law recognized by the community of nations;

(h) if finally acquitted of the offence, not to be tried for it again and, if finally found guilty and punished for the offence, not to be tried or punished for it again; and

(i) if found guilty of the offence and if the punishment for the offence has been varied between the time of commission and the time of sentencing, to the benefit of the lesser punishment.

12. Everyone has the right not to be subjected to any cruel and unusual treatment or punishment.

13. A witness who testifies in any proceedings has the right not to have any incriminating evidence so given used to incriminate that witness in any other proceedings, except in a prosecution for perjury or for the giving of contradictory evidence.

14. A party or witness in any proceedings who does not understand or speak the language in which the proceedings are conducted or who is deaf has the right to the assistance of an interpreter.

Equality Rights

15. (1) Every individual is equal before and under the law and has the right to the equal protection and equal benefit of the law without discrimination and, in particular, without discrimination based on race, national or ethnic origin, colour, religion, sex, age or mental or physical disability.

(2) Subsection (1) does not preclude any law, program or activity that has as its object the amelioration of conditions of disadvantaged individuals or groups including those that are disadvantaged because of race, national or ethnic origin, colour, religion, sex, age or mental or physical disability.

Official Languages of Canada

16. (1) English and French are the official languages of Canada and have equality of status and equal rights and privileges as to their use in all institutions of the Parliament and government of Canada.

(2) English and French are the official languages

of New Brunswick and have equality of status and equal rights and privileges as to their use in all institutions of the legislature and government of New Brunswick.

(3) Nothing in this Charter limits the authority of Parliament or a legislature to advance the equality of status or use of English and French.

17. (1) Everyone has the right to use English or French in any debates and other proceedings of Parliament.

(2) Everyone has the right to use English or French in any debates and other proceedings of the legislature of New Brunswick.

18. (1) The statutes, records and journals of Parliament shall be printed and published in English and French and both language versions are equally authoritative.

(2) The statutes, records and journals of the legislature of New Brunswick shall be printed and published in English and French and both language versions are equally authoritative.

19. (1) Either English or French may be used by any person in, or in any pleading in or process issuing from, any court established by Parliament.

(2) Either English or French may be used by any person in, or in any pleading in or process issuing from, any court of New Brunswick.

20. (1) Any member of the public in Canada has the right to communicate with, and to receive available services from, any head or central office of an institution of the Parliament or government of Canada in English or French, and has the same right with respect to any other office of any such institution where (a) there is a significant demand for communications with and services from that office in such language; or

(b) due to the nature of the office, it is reasonable that communications with and services from that office be available in both English and French.

(2) Any member of the public in New Brunswick has the right to communicate with, and to receive available services from, any office of an institution of the legislature or government of New Brunswick in English or French.

21. Nothing in sections 16 to 20 abrogates or derogates from any right, privilege or obligation with respect to the English and French languages, or either of them, that exists or is continued by virtue of any other provision of the Constitution of Canada.

22. Nothing in sections 16 to 20 abrogates or derogates from any legal or customary right or privilege acquired or enjoyed either before or after the coming into force of this Charter with respect to any language that is not English or French.

Minority Language Educational Rights

23. (1) Citizens of Canada

(a) whose first language learned and still understood is that of the English or French linguistic minority population of the province in which they reside, or

(b) who have received their primary school instruction in Canada in English or French and reside in a province where the language in which they received that instruction is the language of the English or French linguistic minority population of the province, have the right to have their children receive primary and secondary school instruction in that language in that province.

(2) Citizens of Canada of whom any child has received or is receiving primary or secondary school instruction in English or French in Canada, have the right to have all their children receive primary and secondary school instruction in the same language.

(3) The right of citizens of Canada under subsections (1) and (2) to have their children receive primary and secondary school instruction in the language of the English or French linguistic minority population of a province

(a) applies wherever in the province the number of children of citizens who have such a right is sufficient to warrant the provision to them out of public funds of minority language instruction; and

(b) includes, where the number of those children so warrants, the right to have them receive that instruction in minority language educational facilities provided out of public funds.

Enforcement

24. (1) Anyone whose rights or freedoms, as guaranteed by this Charter, have been infringed or denied may apply to a court of competent jurisdiction to obtain such remedy as the court considers appropriate and just in the circumstances.

(2) Where, in proceedings under subsection (1), a court concludes that evidence was obtained in a manner that infringed or denied any rights or freedoms guaranteed by this Charter, the evidence shall be excluded if it is established that, having regard to all the circumstances, the admission of it in the proceedings would bring the administration of justice into disrepute.

General

25. The guarantee in this Charter of certain rights and freedoms shall not be construed so as to abrogate or derogate from any aboriginal, treaty or other rights or freedoms that pertain to the aboriginal peoples of Canada including (a) any rights or freedoms that have been recognized by the Royal Proclamation of October 7, 1763; and (b) any rights or freedoms that may be acquired by the aboriginal peoples of Canada by way of land claims settlement.

26. The guarantee in this Charter of certain rights and freedoms shall not be construed as denying the existence of any other rights or freedoms that exist in Canada.

27. This Charter shall be interpreted in a manner consistent with the preservation and enhancement of the multicultural heritage of Canadians.

28. Notwithstanding anything in this Charter, the rights and freedoms referred to in it are guaranteed equally to male and female persons.

29. Nothing in this Charter abrogates or derogates from any rights or privileges guaranteed by or under the Constitution of Canada in respect of denominational, separate or dissentient schools.

30. A reference in this Charter to a province or to the legislative assembly or legislature of a province shall be deemed to include a reference to the Yukon Territory and the Northwest Territories, or to the appropriate legislative authority thereof, as the case may be.

31. Nothing in this Charter extends the legislative powers of any body or authority.

Application of Charter

32. (1) This Charter applies

(a) to the Parliament and government of Canada in respect of all matters within the authority of Parliament including all matters relating to the Yukon Territory and Northwest Territories; and

(b) to the legislature and government of each province in respect of all matters within the authority of the legislature of each province.

(2) Notwithstanding subsection (1), section 15 shall not have effect until three years after this section comes into force.

33. (1) Parliament or the legislature of a province may expressly declare in an Act of Parliament or of the legislature, as the case may be, that the Act or a provision thereof shall operate notwithstanding a provision included in section 2 or sections 7 to 15 of this Charter.

(2) An Act or a provision of an Act in respect of which a declaration made under this section is in effect shall have such operation as it would have but for the provision of this Charter referred to in the declaration.

(3) A declaration made under subsection (1) shall cease to have effect five years after it comes into force or on such earlier date as may be specified in the declaration.

(4) Parliament or the legislature of a province may re-enact a declaration made under subsection (1).

(5) Subsection (3) applies in respect of a re-enactment made under subsection (4).

34. This Part may be cited as the Canadian Charter of Rights and Freedoms.

Part II
Rights of the Aboriginal Peoples of Canada

35. (1) The existing aboriginal and treaty rights of the aboriginal peoples of Canada are hereby recognized and affirmed.

(2) In this Act, "aboriginal peoples of Canada" includes the Indian, Inuit and Metis peoples of Canada.

Part III
Equalization and Regional Disparities

36. (1) Without altering the legislative authority of Parliament or of the provincial legislatures, or the rights of any of them with respect to the exercise of their legislative authority, Parliament and the legislatures, together with the government of Canada and the provincial governments, are committed to

(a) promoting equal opportunities for the well-being of Canadians;

(b) furthering economic development to reduce disparity in opportunities; and

(c) providing essential public services of reasonable quality to all Canadians.

(2) Parliament and the government of Canada are committed to the principle of making equalization payments to ensure that provincial governments have sufficient revenues to provide reasonably comparable levels of public services at reasonably comparable levels of taxation.

◼ Canadian Congress of Labour

The Canadian Congress of Labour (CCL) was a powerful organization of industrial unions. It was founded in 1940. Among its 360 000 members were people who worked in forestry, mines, steel mills, smelters, packinghouses, railways, and automobile and clothing factories. Led by Aaron Mosher, the CCL was very successful at persuading unskilled workers to join a union. In politics, the CCL supported the Co-operative Commonwealth Federation.

In 1956 the CCL merged with another union group, the Trades and Labor Congress, to form the Canadian Labour Congress.

▷ RELATED ARTICLES: **Labour Organizations; Aaron Mosher.**

◼ Canadian Council on Social Development

Canadian Council on Social Development (CCSD) is a group that promotes improvements in social services and government welfare policy. It is based in Ottawa. It began in 1920 as the Canadian Council on Child Welfare. In 1929 its name was changed to the Canadian Council on Child and Family Welfare. During the Great Depression it broadened its concerns to deal with the unemployed. In 1935 it became the Canadian Welfare Council. The group has had its present name since 1970.

◼ Canadian Federation of Labour

Canadian Federation of Labour was an organization of Canadian unions which split from the Trades and Labor Congress in 1902. The Canadian unions had disagreed about the role of American unions in Canada. The federation did not attract many members. In 1927 it became a founding member of the All-Canadian Congress of Labour.

In 1982 several craft unions formed a new organization named the Canadian Federation of Labour. By 1989 it had over 200 000 members.

◼ Canadian Forces Bases

Canadian Forces Bases are centres for Canada's armed forces. There are 36 bases in all: 34 are located across the country, while two are located in Europe as part of Canada's role in NATO. The two in Europe are CFB Lahr and CFB Baden-Soellingen, both in West Germany. Many bases, home to the troops and their families, contain most of the facilities of a small town.

Four bases in Canada have what are known as detachments. These are part of larger units which are located in separate geographic areas and which function as extensions of bases. The detachments are Dundurn, part of CFB Moose Jaw in Saskatchewan; Nanaimo, part of CFB Esquimalt in B.C.; Vancouver, part of CFB Chilliwack in B.C.; and Wainwright, part of CFB Calgary in Alberta.

In addition to bases and detachments, there are 16 Canadian Forces stations in the country. A station is a relatively minor Department of National Defence installation that has a specific and limited function and usually far fewer facilities than a base.

Bases also serve as training centres for the forces. Main training bases in Canada include the following:

CFB Borden, 80 km northwest of Toronto in south-central Ontario. It opened in 1916 as a training facility for the armed forces. The base covers 79 km² and provides housing for up to 10 000 of its residents. It was named for Sir Frederick Borden, Canada's minister of militia and defence from 1896 to 1911.

CFB Cold Lake, 290 km northeast of Edmonton in northern Alberta. Built in the early 1950s, it is a centre for the training of fighter pilots and fighter technicians. It is the main base for flight testing for the Canadian forces. The base also supports Canada's role in NORAD and NATO.

CFB Cornwallis, on the Bay of Fundy shore of western Nova Scotia near Digby. Built in 1942, it was originally a naval training centre, the largest one in the Commonwealth until 1946. Now it is a training centre for all three elements of the forces. The main base site covers about 240 hectares and has all the facilities of a small town.

CFB Gagetown, on the Saint John River between Fredericton and Saint John, N.B. Built in the 1950s, it was originally the home of the Third Canadian Infantry division. Now it is an army combat training centre and is regularly used by NATO troops. Sprawling over 111 000 hectares, it covers 1.4% of the land mass of New Brunswick and is the largest base of its kind in the Commonwealth.

CFB Moose Jaw, 6 km south of the city of the same name in southern Saskatchewan. It is the largest jet training base in Canada.

CFB Trenton, next door to the city of the same name on the Bay of Quinte, in southern Ontario. Construction began in 1931, and the base was completed as a relief project for the unemployed during the Great Depression. CFB Trenton is the largest military air base in Canada.

Other Canadian Forces Bases are located in B.C. at Chilliwack, Comox, and Esquimalt; in Alberta at Calgary, Edmonton, Penhold, and Suffield; in Manitoba at Portage La Prairie, Shilo, and Winnipeg; in Ontario at Kingston, London, North Bay, Ottawa, Petawawa, and Toronto; in Quebec at Bagotville, Montreal, St Jean, and Valcartier; in New Brunswick at Chatham and Moncton; in Nova Scotia at Greenwood, Halifax, and Shearwater; in P.E.I. at Summerside; in Newfoundland at Gander; and in Labrador at Goose Bay.

Because millions of dollars were cut from the defence budget in 1989, fourteen bases and stations will be closed or reduced in size over a period of five years that ends in 1994. Seven bases will have to be closed.

■ Canadian International Stars

Some of the brightest stars of show business were born in Canada but made names for themselves outside the country. Canadians often refer to these personalities as "Canada's own," and take pride in their fame and fortune. Yet in order to further their stage and screen careers, these stars had to leave Canada and settle in the United Kingdom or the United States.

The truth is that in leaving Canada and competing in London's West End, New York's Broadway, and Los Angeles's Hollywood, these "wandering stars" acquired international fame. Thus, they became better known to audiences everywhere, and especially in their native land, than their fellow performing artists who remained in Canada. Here are the names of some of the illustrious ones.

Beatrice Lillie, the Toronto-born comedienne, enjoyed a fabulous career. She was the toast of vaudeville stages in London and New York from the 1920s to the 1960s. Through marriage she became Lady Peel. Another native of Toronto, **Walter Huston,** established himself on the New York stage and then in Hollywood films. He is warmly remembered for his part in *The Treasure of the Sierra Madre*, the 1948 movie directed by his son John Huston. **Marie Dressler,** a feisty stage and screen actress, was born in Cobourg, Ont., and is mainly remembered as the lead in the 1933 movie *Tugboat Annie*.

The distinguished actor **Raymond Massey,** brother of Governor General Vincent Massey, enjoyed stage careers in both London and New York before Hollywood cast him as Abraham Lincoln. In later years he created the part of Dr Gillespie in the TV series "Dr Kildare."

Vaudeville is now a memory, but magic acts remain popular. This is in no small

Marie Dressler (courtesy Phototeque, New York).

William Shatner (courtesy Phototeque, New York).

Mary Pickford (courtesy Phototeque, New York).

Yvonne DeCarlo (courtesy Phototeque, New York).

Glenn Ford (courtesy Phototeque, New York).

Michael J. Fox (courtesy Phototeque, New York).

part due to the smash success of **Doug Henning**'s act called *The Magic Show* which opened on Broadway in 1973. This talented showman and magician was born in Fort Garry, Man. Henning, a "new-wave" magician, specializes in sparkling, fast-moving acts.

A good many television personalities were born in Canada. **Art Linkletter** (Moose Jaw, Sask.) is identified with the long-running series "People Are Funny" and "House Party." **Monty Hall** (Winnipeg, Man.), the smooth host of "Let's Make a Deal," is an originator of the popular game show "Jeopardy," ably hosted by **Alex Trebek** (Sudbury, Ont.). **Robert MacNeil** (Halifax, N.S.) and **Peter Jennings** (Toronto, Ont.) are popular network news anchors.

Raymond Burr (New Westminster, B.C.) attained popularity playing a lawyer in the series "Perry Mason" and a detective in "Ironside." **William Shatner** (Montreal, Que.) created the role of Commander James T. Kirk on "Star Trek" for the TV series and the movie spin-offs. **Lorne Greene** (Ottawa, Ont.) acquired fame, fortune, and a global following as the patriarch Ben Cartwright on "Bonanza." During the period the series was shown, 1959 to 1973, Greene was unquestionably the world's best-known Canadian-born performing artist.

Former Canadians may have glowed on American television, but they shone brightest on Hollywood's silver screen. **Mary Pickford** (Toronto, Ont.) has been rightly called "America's Sweetheart" and "Cinema's First Superstar." She established the United Artists Studio in 1919, along with her director D.W. Griffith, her husband Douglas Fairbanks, and their friend Charles Chaplin. Unable to adapt to the sound screen in 1929, she retired from the world of the movies, a legend in her day.

The list of Canadians who have starred in American and other foreign films is a long one, but among the screen beauties are **Deanna Durbin** (Winnipeg, Man.), **Susan Clark** (Sarnia, Ont.), **Yvonne DeCarlo** (Vancouver, B.C.), **Margot Kidder** (Yellowknife, N.W.T.), **Norma Shearer** (Montreal, Que.), **Alexis Smith** (Penticton, B.C.), and **Fay Wray** (Medicine Hat, Alta) who starred in the original 1933 version of *King Kong*.

Among the male stars are **Dan Akroyd** (Ottawa, Ont.), **Robert Beatty** (Hamilton, Ont.), **Jack Carson** (Carmen, Alta), **Douglass Dumbrille** (Hamilton, Ont.), **Glenn Ford** (Quebec City, Que.), **Michael J. Fox**

(Edmonton, Alta), **Rick Moranis** (Toronto, Ont.), **Leslie Nielsen** (Regina, Sask.), **Walter Pidgeon** (East Saint John, N.B.), and **Christopher Plummer** (Toronto).

Noted movie directors include **Allan Dwan** (Toronto, Ont.), **Edward Dmytryk** (Grand Forks, B.C.), and **Ivan Reitman** (born in Czechoslovakia, raised in Toronto). The creator of the silent screen's Keystone Kops was **Mack Sennett** (Danville, Que.). The famed (and feared) producer, **Louis B. Mayer**, although born in Russia, was raised in Saint John, N.B.

Talent, ambition, and luck are about the only qualities that these stage and screen personalities share. Yet many of them benefited from the varied and professional training they received from Canadian theatres, radio, and television. In some sense, they contributed little if anything to indigenous theatre, broadcasting, and film. Yet, as a group of talented individual performers, "Canada's own" proved that Canadian performing artists, given the opportunity, can shine like "stars."

▷ Suggested Reading: Ed Gould, *Entertaining Canadians* (1988).

■ Canadian Labour Congress

Canadian Labour Congress (CLC) is Canada's largest organization of labour unions. Founded in 1956, it includes over 90 unions and has more than two million members. The three largest member-unions consist of public servants. The fourth-largest is the United Steelworkers of America. In 1961 the CLC helped to launch the New Democratic Party; the link with the NDP continues. The CLC is considered the voice of organized labour in Canada.

▷ Related Article: **Labour Organizations.**

■ Canadian Museum of Civilization, *see* Museums

■ Canadian Museum of Contemporary Photography

The Canadian Museum of Contemporary Photography was founded and affiliated with the National Gallery of Canada in 1985. It was formerly the Still Photography Division of the National Film Board of Canada. Its collection includes over 157 000 artistic and documentary works by Canadian photographers. Its home is a reconstructed railway tunnel between the Chateau Laurier Hotel and the Rideau Canal in Ottawa. Its travelling exhibitions are shown across Canada and abroad. The museum publishes books and catalogues and has a resource centre on photography that responds to enquiries from all over Canada. For more information, write to P.O. Box 465, Station A, Ottawa, Ont., K1N 9N6.

Canadian National Exhibition

The Canadian National Exhibition (CNE) is held in Toronto in late August to early September and is the largest annual exhibition in the world. It began as an agricultural fair in the 1840s. After 1878 it settled permanently in Toronto and became known as the Toronto Industrial Exhibition. In 1904 it was renamed the Canadian National Exhibition. By then the fairgrounds covered 141 ha on the Toronto waterfront, and the old wooden buildings were being replaced with imposing stone and brick structures.

Over the years, exhibits and activities at the "Ex" have changed. At first, agriculture and livestock dominated, though technology has always been important too. In 1882 the grounds were lit by electricity and in 1883 an electric train service was installed. By the early 20th century, there was more emphasis on industry and manufacturing. There were also art exhibits and cultural events. Grandstand shows featured Canadian themes, such as the opening of the West or, during both world wars, patriotism and victory. Entertainment became more important, with rides and sideshows on the midway, and big-name performers in the bandshell. There were special events of all kinds, including a visit by the Dionne quintuplets and, in 1954, a marathon swim by Marilyn Bell across Lake Ontario. In recent years the CNE has become a vast consumer market, displaying the latest cars, computers, and appliances for sale.

In 1989, nearly 2.5 million people attended the "Ex." The fairgrounds are now part of a huge waterfront development in Toronto, which includes Harbourfront and Ontario Place. The buildings are used for a variety of trade shows throughout the year, and for the Royal Agricultural Winter Fair each November.

Canadian National Railways

Canadian National Railways (CNR) combined five other railways that were in financial trouble: the Grand Trunk, the Grand Trunk Pacific, the Intercolonial, the Canadian Northern, and the National Transcontinental. The company was formed over a period of time from 1917, when it was known as Canadian Northern Railway, to 1923.

The new railway was a crown corporation, that is, it was owned by the government. Under its first president, Sir Henry Thornton, the company expanded, even into radio. CN, as it is now called, includes marine operations, hotels, telecommunications, trucking, and resource industries. In 1937, CN organized Trans-Canada Airlines, which in 1964 became Air Canada.

▷ RELATED ARTICLE: **Railway History.**

▷ SUGGESTED READING: Phyllis Bowman, *Whistling through the West* (1980); Patrick C. Dorin, *The Canadian Railway Story* (1975); Keith Wilson, *Railways in Canada: The Iron Link* (1982).

Canadian Nature Federation

The Canadian Nature Federation (CNF) is a national conservation organization. It provides a voice for Canada's naturalists to promote the understanding, awareness, and enjoyment of nature and to conserve the natural environment.

The organization traces its roots to the founding of a children's magazine, *Canadian Nature*, in 1939. The magazine promoted an appreciation of Canada's heritage through popular articles for young readers.

In 1948, the magazine was purchased by the newly formed Audubon Society of Canada, and became more involved in Canadian conservation issues. In 1958, the magazine was renamed *Canadian Audubon* and it shifted its readership to adults. The Audubon Society of Canada became the Canadian Audubon Society, which led to the founding of the Canadian Nature Federation in 1971. The magazine *Canadian Audubon* was then renamed *Nature Canada*, its current title.

CNF members believe that all species have a right to exist, whether or not they are considered useful to humans. They teach that we are a part of the natural world and must be guided by this principle. The CNF deals with numerous environmental issues, such as endangered species, wildlife and fisheries management, and forestry practices. It devotes well over half of its funds to Canada's parks and protected areas.

For more information, write to the Canadian Nature Federation, 453 Sussex Drive, Ottawa, Ont., K1N 6Z4.

Canadian Pacific Railway

When British Columbia joined Canada in 1871, a promise was made that a railway would be built between the new province and Ontario within ten years. Prime Minister John A. Macdonald championed the

Route of the Canadian Pacific Railway

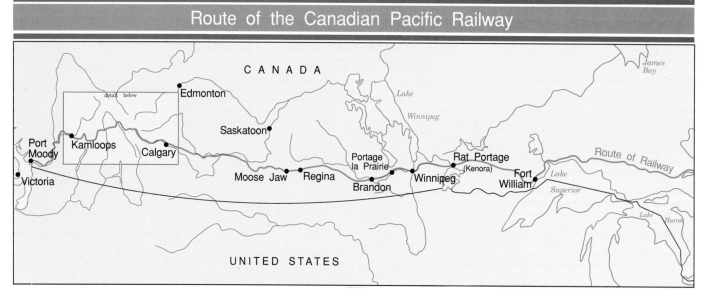

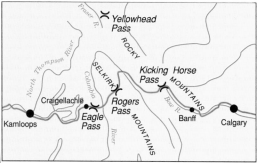

railway. He believed that it was crucial to the future of Canada. Without it, he believed, Canada would lose its claim on the western territories to the United States, which was expanding rapidly westward.

Pacific Scandal The railway was the most important political issue of the day. Its costs, its route, its schedule were points of bitter debate. In 1872, Macdonald ran short of money during a hard-fought election campaign. He asked Sir Hugh Allan for cash, and Allan agreed. Allan was one of the men trying to get the contract to build the railway. After Macdonald won the election, he gave the contract to Allan. When Macdonald's enemies uncovered this conflict of interest in 1873, they raised such a furor that Macdonald had to resign. It was called the "Pacific Scandal" because it involved the Pacific Railway. The new prime minister, Alexander Mackenzie, believed that Canada could not afford the railway, and he moved ahead very cautiously with the project.

Formation of the CPR Work began in 1875 at Fort William, Ont., but there was little headway until after Macdonald regained power in 1878. Finally, in 1881, a group of Montreal financiers formed the Canadian Pacific Railway Company (CPR). They received generous help from the government in the form of land, money, and a monopoly over rail transport between the CPR main line and the U.S. border for 20 years.

The CPR gave the task of building the longest railway in the world to a dynamic American engineer, William Cornelius Van Horne. Van Horne was a brilliant organizer. In the six years before he took over, only 180 km of track had been laid. In his first year as general manager, the CPR laid almost 900 km.

Construction over the flat prairie moved about as fast as the men could drive the spikes. However, in the Canadian Shield, north of Lake Superior, crews had to blast their way with dynamite through the hard rock. In other areas, whole sections of track sank into the spongy muskeg.

In British Columbia, construction crews carved narrow ledges into the mountain sides, tunnelled through solid rock, and erected flimsy bridges across the deep gorges and fast-moving rivers. There were not enough men available for such dangerous and heavy work. To complete the railway on time, the CPR brought thousands of workers from China. The Chinese workers were paid very low wages. Many died from accidents and disease. They were forced to live in squalid conditions in segregated camps. Yet without them the railway probably could not have been built.

By 1885 the CPR was running out of money. Workers went weeks without pay and protested with a strike. Macdonald wanted to help but he could not gain enough support. During the North-West

Rebellion, Van Horne seized the chance to show how important the railway was to Canada. Using the partly completed line, he rushed soldiers to the West. The rebellion was soon over and Macdonald was able to raise the needed cash.

The Last Spike On November 7, 1885, the line moving west met the line moving east at a small siding at Craigellachie, in the mountains of western B.C. Many of the businessmen, contractors, surveyors, and workers responsible for building the railway gathered there, and Donald Smith drove in the "last spike."

On June 28, 1886, the *Pacific Express* left Montreal. It reached Port Moody, B.C., on July 4. It was the first passenger train to travel across Canada.

Beyond Railways The CPR expanded in the 1880s into telegraph services and hotels. It purchased ocean vessels in the 1890s and rapidly expanded its rail lines in the early 20th century. It moved into mining and organized Canadian Pacific Air Lines in 1942 (later called CP Air). In 1987 CP Air was bought by Pacific Western and the two companies became Canadian Airlines International.

Today, Canadian Pacific Ltd controls real estate, hotels, oil and gas, shipping and trucking, as well as railways. It is Canada's second-largest corporation and has over 93 000 employees.

▷ RELATED ARTICLES: **Sir Hugh Allan; Sir Sandford Fleming; Pacific Scandal; Railways to World War I; Donald Alexander Smith; George Stephen; Sir William Cornelius Van Horne.**

▷ SUGGESTED READING: David Cruise and Alison Griffiths, *Lords of the Line* (1988); Stephen Mayles, *William Van Horne* (1976); William C. McKee, *Trail of Iron: The CPR and the Birth of the West, 1880-1930* (1983); Christopher Moore, *William Van Horne* (1987); Keith Wilson, *Donald Smith and the Canadian Pacific Railway* (1978); *Railways in Canada: The Iron Link* (1982).

■ Canadian Radio-television and Telecommunications Commission (CRTC)

The CRTC was established in 1968 to regulate all aspects of broadcasting in Canada. Originally called the Canadian Radio-Television Commission, it was given its present name in 1976. It issues licences to radio, television, and cable systems operators; approves rates charged by telecommunications companies; and supervises the content and quality of programs offered by public and private broadcasters. If a radio or television station fails to maintain its standards, the CRTC can cancel its licence. In general, the CRTC has favoured Canadian ownership of radio and television stations and networks, and has encouraged a high proportion of Canadian content in the programs they air.

■ Canadian Seaman's Union

The Canadian Seaman's Union (CSU) began in 1936, at the height of the Great Depression. Its purpose was to win better wages and working conditions for ordinary seamen. The CSU made important contributions during World War II, but employers did not like the union's communist leaders. In 1949, they brought an American unionist, Hal Banks, to fight the CSU. Banks used violent tactics to break the CSU and replace it with his own Seafarers' International Union.

■ Canadian Shield

The Canadian Shield is an enormous area of flat, low-lying, rocky hills, forest, and tundra that covers much of Canada. The rocks of the Shield are hard and crystalline, commonly granite and gneiss, often marked with coloured streaks and bands of minerals. Some of these rocks are almost as old as the Earth itself.

Geological Origins The Shield formed during the Precambrian Era, which lasted from the birth of our planet, more than 4.5 billion years ago, to some 570 million years ago, when life became abundant. Hence it is also called the Precambrian Shield.

During the Precambrian, the rocks of the Canadian Shield were folded and crumpled, raised into mountains, and injected with molten lava. The mountains of the Shield have long since been worn down to stumps, but the solid core remains. It is the foundation of the continent.

Extent of the Canadian Shield The Canadian Shield occupies 4.6 million square kilometres of Canada. It covers much of Quebec and Ontario, northeastern Manitoba, Saskatchewan, and parts of the Northwest Territories. It is shaped like a shield when viewed from above, and like a basin when viewed from the side. From Hudson Bay, its lowest point and centre, the land generally rises towards the outer edges. The western rim is near the Rocky Mountains. The higher, eastern rim forms the rugged coast of Labrador.

To the north, the Shield also lies under a layer of sedimentary rocks of the arctic islands. To the south, it lies beneath the Great Lakes and the St Lawrence River. It extends far beneath the younger rocks in the interior U.S., but is exposed in places,

Modern Diesel Locomotive in the Crowsnest Pass in southwestern Alberta (courtesy Elliot and Nicole Bernshaw).

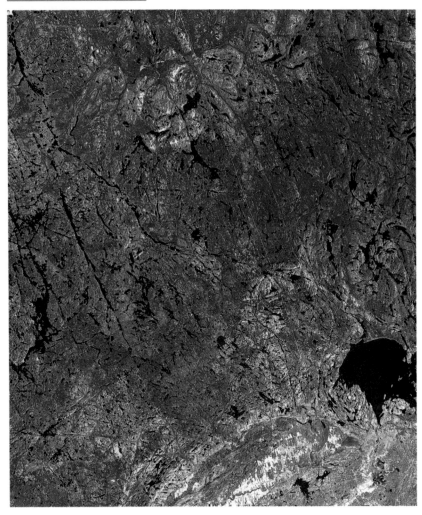

Satellite Image *of the Canadian Shield near Sudbury, Ont. (the purplish area lower right). The image helps us to imagine the rugged rock surface and how it was gouged by the glaciers. The dark areas are water (courtesy Canada Centre for Remote Sensing).*

such as the Adirondack Mountains of New York State. The island of Greenland as well is, geologically, part of the Canadian Shield.

Resources of the Shield Ice sheets gouged out lake basins and dumped their debris from them on the Canadian Shield, creating a lacework of waterways. It is strewn with countless bogs, swamps, ponds, lakes, and rivers. Along its edges lie many of the great lakes and waterways of Canada: Great Bear Lake, Great Slave Lake, Lakes Athabasca and Winnipeg, Lakes Superior and Huron, and the St Lawrence River. Early native people travelled these waterways in their birchbark canoes. Europeans borrowed their invention to explore the northern part of the continent, and to gather its furs.

The Shield presented a formidable obstacle to railway builders. Railway engineers, blasting through Shield rock, were among the first to uncover valuable minerals in the Shield. Most of the Shield's treasure chest of gold, silver, nickel, iron, copper, zinc, and other minerals were found by prospectors and mineral exploration teams. As a result, Canada is among the world's leading producers of these valuable products.

The Shield is far too rocky for agriculture, except in a few areas. However, its southern regions are rich in softwood trees which are the basis of Canada's giant pulp and paper industry. The huge water resources of the Shield are tapped for hydroelectric power.

The stark, wild beauty of the Shield is enjoyed by canoeists, photographers, adventurers, fishermen, cottagers, skiers, hunters, and many others. It is the landscape that most people associate with Canada.

▷ RELATED ARTICLES: **Geology; Manitoba; Natural Regions; Northwest Territories; Ontario; Quebec.**

■ Canadian Wildlife Federation

The Canadian Wildlife Federation (CWF) is a national non-profit organization devoted to conservation. Founded in 1961 and chartered in 1962, it is the largest organization of its kind in Canada. A group of conservationists created it to promote an understanding of the natural world so that people would live in harmony with the environment and to ensure that stocks of wildlife in Canada would be preserved for the use and enjoyment of all Canadians. CWF now has 550 000 members and supporters across the country.

Activities of the organization range from studying long-term effects of projects on the environment to recommending changes to the law to protect wildlife and their habitat. The CWF also sponsors various research projects on, for example, freshwater fisheries and beluga whales. It is also helping to establish a breeding centre for peregrine falcons in Ste-Anne-de-Bellevue, Que.

Its achievements include producing an endangered species list in 1976. In 1988, it took the federal government to court over the Rafferty-Alameda Dam project in southern Saskatchewan. It won its case and forced the government to carry out an environmental review on the effect that the dam would have on local wildlife.

Among school children, the organization is perhaps best known for its public education campaigns. Every year, the CWF sponsors National Wildlife Week in the second week of April. In 1989, a new program called Habitat 2000 was launched to teach conservation and wildlife.

The CWF publishes the following magazines: *Big Back Yard* for ages 3 to 6; *Ranger Rick* for ages 6 to 12; *Internation-*

al *Wildlife*, in English, and *Biosphère*, in French, for adults. Most of its funding, over $9 million in 1989, comes from donations, memberships, the sale of merchandise. For more information, write to Canadian Wildlife Federation, 1673 Carling Avenue, Ottawa, Ont., K2A 3Z1.

■ Canadian Wildlife Service, *see* Conservation

■ Canadiens

Canadiens was a common term for French Canadians in the 18th and 19th centuries. It is carried on today in the name of the hockey team, the Montreal Canadiens.

■ Canal

A canal is an artificial waterway built to allow the passage of watercraft or water for irrigation.

A canal is often built to bypass an obstacle, such as rapids or a waterfall. Canal locks enable ships to move from one water level to another. A ship enters a lock, the watertight doors are closed, and the lock is filled with water (to raise the ship) or emptied (to lower the ship). A rarer form of lock is found at Peterborough, Ont. This lock, which is the largest of its kind in the world, actually lifts by hydraulic force, taking the vessel with it.

Canada's waterways have always played an important role in its economic life. Before the railway, the building of canals was the best way to improve the transportation system. The very first shallow canals in Canada were built by the British military to bypass rapids on the St Lawrence River. Fur traders dug a canal near Sault Ste Marie to bypass the falls and rapids of the St Mary's River at the end of the 18th century.

The first large canal was the Lachine Canal, a narrow route around the Lachine Rapids near Montreal. It was finished in 1825. The Rideau Canal, built by the British to provide a safe military route between Lake Ontario and Montreal, was the greatest engineering feat of the early 19th century. It connects Ottawa and Kingston, following the Rideau River and Rideau Lakes, and required channels, dams, and locks. The Jones Falls Dam was the largest of its kind in the world, and the locks were the highest. Work began in 1826 and ended in 1832. The canal was built to last and is still in use today.

Unlike the Rideau Canal, the first Welland Canal was a private venture. It was built to bypass the Niagara Falls and to draw commerce to the Canadian side of

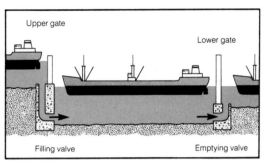

the Great Lakes. It was opened in 1829 but soon had to be enlarged. It was rebuilt in 1845, 1887, and again in 1932. Today, it is 42 km long. Its eight locks raise or lower ships 99.4 m.

The Trent Canal follows an old Indian route from Lake Ontario to Lake Huron, using numerous lakes and rivers. Work on the 388 km waterway began in 1833 but was not completed until 1920. Numerous locks overcome a rise of 181 m to the highest point, and then a 79 m drop to Lake Huron. The hydraulic lock at Peterborough is part of this system. The canal is used today for pleasure craft.

The St Lawrence Seaway is one of the most important waterways in the world. Completed in 1959, it cost about $760 million and was a joint venture of Canada and the U.S. Much of the Seaway is a natural waterway, but canals and locks were needed on the St Lawrence River and between Lakes Huron and Superior. The Welland Canal, Lachine Canal, and St Mary's Canal were all incorporated into the Seaway.

Canal Locks enable ships to move from one water level to another. A ship moving from high to low would enter the centre lock from above (left) and exit to the lower level (right) (artwork by David Shaw).

Welland Canal A ship is shown (top) entering the Welland Canal from Lake Ontario. On its trip westward to Lake Erie, the ship must pass through eight locks (below) and rise a total of 99.4 m (photos by Thomas Kitchin).

▷ RELATED ARTICLES: **Rideau Canal; St Lawrence Seaway; Trent Canal; Welland Canal.**

▷ SUGGESTED READING: R.F. Legget, *Canals of Canada* (1976).

■ Cancer

Cancer is one of the most deadly human diseases. It is second only to heart disease as a cause of death in Canada. One in every four Canadians will die of cancer.

Cells and Tumours Cancer is not one disease but a group of more than 100 diseases. In all these diseases something has gone wrong with the way cells grow.

There are billions of tiny cells in the human body. To replace old or damaged cells, new ones are constantly being formed. Normally, these cells stop forming as soon as the lost cells have been replaced. Sometimes, for reasons no one knows, cells do not stop growing. They form swellings or lumps, called *tumours*.

Some tumours are harmless. They are called *benign*, or non-cancerous tumours. Others, called *malignant* or cancerous tumours, can crowd out healthy cells and destroy them. Like seeds carried by the wind, clumps of cancerous cells may be spread by the blood or other fluids. New tumours begin to grow in other parts of the body.

Cancer of the skin is the most common of all cancers. Most skin cancer can be cured, although there are about 500 reported deaths every year. About 40 000 new cases of skin cancer are detected each year in Canada. Cancer of the lungs, pancreas, stomach, and brain is often fatal.

Deaths from Cancer In 1988, more than 50 000 Canadians died of cancer. About 250 of these were under the age of 15. Cancer is the fourth most frequent cause of the death of children. The most common cancer that children get is leukemia, a cancer of the blood.

The chances of getting cancer increase with age. Now that the infectious diseases, which once killed many people, have been controlled, more people are living to an age at which they get cancer.

What Causes Cancer? The basic cause of cancer remains unknown. Most human cancers probably are caused in part by factors in the environment. Cancer-causing agents, called *carcinogens*, include certain chemicals which may be found in air, water, food, the work place, etc. Cancer-causing agents also include tobacco, sunlight, and X-rays. These agents may alter the information stored in the genes, erasing the instructions that tell normal cells when to stop growing.

Contact with carcinogens may result from individual actions such as smoking or dietary habits. Cancers develop slowly, usually appearing five to 40 years after exposure to a cancer-causing agent.

We know that smoking cigarettes causes lung cancer, for this form of cancer occurs most frequently in smokers. It may take 20 years or more of smoking before the cancer appears. Almost everyone who gets lung cancer dies of it.

Many cancers have occurred following long and continued exposure to small amounts of cancer-causing agents. For example, asbestos brought home on the clothing of asbestos workers has caused fatal cancers in family members. There is evidence that eating fat foods, such as fatty meat, may lead to cancer of the colon and intestine. Repeated exposure to the ultraviolet rays of the sun is the main cause of skin cancer.

There are probably factors which, acting together, cause cancers.

Avoiding Cancer Smoking is the leading cause of cancer deaths in men, and — unless girls who are now starting to smoke do not quit — it will soon be the number-one cause of cancer deaths among women too. It you do not smoke cigarettes, you are unlikely to get lung cancer.

More vegetables, especially cabbage, cauliflower, and broccoli, and more fruit in the diet reduce the chances of getting cancer of the intestine and rectum.

Avoiding repeated exposure to the sun (especially between 10:00 AM and 3:00 PM) and wearing protective clothing and a sunscreen will greatly reduce the risk of skin cancer.

Treating Cancer In the 1940s, only one in every five patients survived for at least five years after getting cancer. Today, because of improved treatments, one in every two patients lives at least this long.

The three most common ways to treat cancer are by radiation, by drugs, and by surgery.

Certain kinds of radiation can destroy certain kinds of cancer cells. In 1951, Harold Johns, a physicist at the University of Saskatchewan, pioneered the use of a radioactive substance called cobalt-60 as a source of radiation for treating cancer. The popular, though inaccurate, name for the machine he developed is the "cobalt bomb." It gives off strong rays similar to X-rays. It is used for killing cancer cells, and bears no relationship to an actual bomb.

Chemotherapy is the use of chemicals to kill cancer cells. As with anti-cancer radiation, such drugs can damage healthy cells as well as cancer cells. Chemotherapy has been especially successful in treating cancer of the blood in children.

Surgery is the most common treatment for cancer. Surgeons cut away malignant cells, and may thus prevent them from spreading.

The best defence doctors have against cancer is early detection. The sooner cancer is found, the sooner it can be treated. The sooner a tumour is destroyed or removed, the better are the chances that it has not yet spread.

Cancer Research More money is spent for research on cancer in Canada than for research on any other disease. A good deal of it is raised in the name of Terry Fox, who lost a leg to cancer and, in 1980, attempted to run across Canada to raise money for cancer research. He died of cancer in 1981.

Cancer researchers are investigating the role of the body's own defence system in the control of cancer. They conduct animal experiments to identify possible cancer-causing agents. The research has helped improve methods of treating cancer with radiation, chemotherapy, and surgery. Nevertheless, cures exist for only a small number of tumours.

For more information, contact your local Canadian Cancer Society office listed in your telephone book.

▷ RELATED ARTICLES: **Terry Fox; Doctors and Medicine; Health; Smoking.**

▷ SUGGESTED READING: Judylaine Fine, *Afraid to Ask: A Book About Cancer* (1984); Monica Hughes, *Hunter in the Dark* (1982).

■ CANDU

The name CANDU stands for Canada Deuterium Uranium. It is a type of nuclear power reactor that was developed in Canada.

All nuclear power reactors are devices for splitting atoms of uranium. This produces heat with which to generate electricity. In order to keep the atom-splitting reaction going, it is necessary to slow down the speeding particles shot out by splitting atoms. The main difference between nuclear reactor types is in how they do this. The CANDU reactor uses *heavy water*, a substance also known by its chemical name, deuterium oxide.

Canadian scientists and engineers began to develop this nuclear power plant technology during World War II. Ontario Hydro operates most of the world's CAN-

DU reactors. The CANDU is more efficient and safer than other types of reactor. Despite worldwide recognition of the efficiency and safety of CANDU, few have been sold to other countries.

▷ RELATED ARTICLE: **Nuclear Power.**

■ Candy, John, *see* SCTV

■ Canoes and Canoeing

Canoes were the means by which the native people travelled the rivers and lakes of Canada. Birchbark is an ideal material for making canoes. It is light, smooth, strong, and waterproof, and it is plentiful in the woods across Canada.

The native people passed the skills needed to build a canoe down through the generations. They made the canoe frames of cedar, which was soaked in water and bent into the shape of the canoe. The women pulled up, split, and boiled pine roots, which the men used to sew the joints together. The seams were covered with spruce or pine resin, which made the canoe waterproof.

The dugout was a different kind of canoe. The Indians of the West Coast made these canoes from gigantic red cedar trees. The builders found suitable logs along the coast as driftwood or cut them down with chisels hit by stone hammers. They shaped and hollowed out the log with other hand tools. The wood was then softened with hot water and spread apart. The men carved the high end pieces separately and attached them to the canoe. These large dugout canoes were propelled by leaf-shaped paddles or sometimes by a square cedar-mat sail. The Haida used these canoes for ocean trading, whaling, and sealing.

The early European explorers quickly adopted the native canoe. Their own rowboats were far too clumsy to be used on

Shooting the Rapids *The great "master" canoes were the basis for the fur trade between Montreal and Lake Superior. Painting by Frances Ann Hopkins (courtesy NAC/C-2774).*

Canoes on the Glenmore Reservoir, Calgary (photo by Mike Keller/Take Stock Inc.).

the rivers of Canada. At first, the Europeans got their canoes from native builders. As the fur trade grew, the French set up a factory to make their own canoes at Trois-Rivières.

The French used the birchbark canoe to haul furs to Montreal from as far as the present area of Manitoba. Later fur traders carried the trade far into the Northwest. Explorers such as Alexander Mackenzie and Simon Fraser used the canoe to reach the Arctic and Pacific oceans. The largest fur-trade canoes were 12 metres long. They carried a crew of 12 and a load of 2300 kg. These "master" canoes were used on the main route from Montreal to Lake Superior. The traders of the Northwest used smaller canoes. The *voyageurs* who manned these canoes paddled about 45 strokes a minute. The man at the head of the canoe, called the *avant*, carried a large paddle for steering through rapids. The fastest canoes could travel up to 130 km in one day.

The Canoe Today Today, the canoe is used for recreation and for competition. There are two types of canoe. The "Canadian" canoe is propelled by a paddle with a single blade. It is known in competition as a C-boat. The kayak, or K-boat, has a closed deck and a paddle with two blades.

The Canadian canoe is the most popular and is widely used for pleasure or fishing. Today, it is made of wood, canvas, fibreglass, aluminum, or plastic. Wooden canoes made in Peterborough, Ont., have

been exported and copied throughout the world for over a hundred years.

Canoe Competition Canoe racing began in the 1870s, and a national championship has been held since the year 1900. When canoeing first became an Olympic sport in 1936, Canadian Francis Amyot won a gold medal in the 1000 m race. Larry Cain won gold and silver medals in the 1984 Olympics.

"White water" racing has become a popular form of competition in recent years. This form of racing takes place on swift rivers or over long distances. It recalls the days when the *voyageurs* rode the rapids with their canoes loaded with furs.

For information about competitive canoeing, you can write to the Canadian Canoe Association, 1600 James Naismith Drive, Gloucester, Ont., K1B 5N4. For information about recreational canoeing, write to the Canadian Recreational Canoeing Association, P.O. Box 500, Hyde Park, Ont., N0M 1Z0.

▷ RELATED ARTICLES: **Francis Amyot; Larry Cain; Fur Trade; Kayak; Native People.**

▷ SUGGESTED READING: Fred Johnston, *The Book of Champions* (1988); Gary McGriffin and Joanie McGriffin, *Where Rivers Run* (1988); James Raffan and Bert Horwood, *Canexus: The Canoe in Canadian Culture* (1988); The Shepardsons, *The Family Canoe Trip* (1985); Don Starkell, *Paddle to the Amazon: The Ultimate 12,000 Mile Canoe Adventure* (1987).

■ Canol Pipeline

The Canol Pipeline was built between 1942 and 1944 to carry oil from Norman Wells, in the Northwest Territories, to a refinery at Whitehorse in the Yukon. It was a major engineering challenge because the line crossed 1000 km of mountainous terrain. The American armed forces built the line to provide a safe supply of oil for its war effort. The pipeline operated only 13 months before it was abandoned in March 1945.

■ Canso

Canso is a town on Chedabucto Bay, at the eastern tip of mainland Nova Scotia. French fishermen knew the port well by the time Champlain visited it in 1604. In the period 1700 to 1750, Canso was one of the busiest ports in North America, and it was frequently destroyed by invaders. Transatlantic cables were landed at Canso between 1881 and 1894. In 1955 the Canso Causeway from nearby Port Hawksbury connected mainland Nova Scotia to Cape Breton Island. Today, Can-

Sport of Canoeing Hugh Fisher and Alwyn Morris at the 1984 Los Angeles Olympics, where they won a gold medal (courtesy Athlete Information Bureau/Canadian Olympic Association).

so's ice-free harbour is home to a fishing fleet. In 1986 the population was 1285. For information, contact the Town Clerk, P.O. Box 189, Canso, N.S., B0H 1H0.

■ Canuck, Johnny, *see* Johnny Canuck

■ Caouette, Joseph-David-Réal
Politician, leader of the Social Credit Party from 1971 to 1976 (*born in 1917 at Amos, Que.; died in 1976 at Ottawa, Ont.*). A car dealer from northern Quebec, Réal Caouette joined the Social Credit movement as a young man. In 1961 he led the Quebec branch of the party, the Ralliement des créditistes, into union with the national Social Credit Party. As deputy leader of the party, he fought a spirited campaign in the election of 1962. The Socreds came out of nowhere to elect 30 members to Parliament; 26 of them were Caouette's followers from Quebec.

A fiery speaker with a large following in rural areas and small towns, Caouette emerged as a major political celebrity in Quebec. He strongly opposed the Quebec independence movement, and blamed the banks for many economic problems.

In 1963 Caouette broke with Socred leader Robert Thompson and became leader once again of his own Ralliement des créditistes, with 12 Quebec members of Parliament. In 1971 Caouette and his followers rejoined the Social Credit Party. He became party leader, a position he held until just before his death in 1976. Without Caouette's forceful leadership,

Réal Caouette, delivering a speech during the 1963 federal election (courtesy NAC/C-87201).

The Shrine at Cap-de-la-Madeleine attracts thousands of pilgrims each year (courtesy SSC Photocentre/photo by Michel Gagnon).

the party faded into political oblivion.

▷ RELATED ARTICLES: **Créditistes; Social Credit.**

■ Cap-de-la-Madeleine
Cap-de-la-Madeleine, Que., lies opposite Trois-Rivières on the north shore of the St Lawrence River, at the mouth of the Rivière St-Maurice. Settled first in the 1600s by French colonists, the site became a centre of industry early in the 20th century. Pulp and paper mills and an aluminum plant provided jobs for a growing population. Industry is less important today, and many residents commute to work in Trois-Rivières. Each year, thousands of pilgrims visit the Shrine of Our Lady of the Cape. In 1986 the population of Cap-de-la-Madeleine was 32 800. For information, contact the Greffier, 10, rue de l'Hôtel-de-ville, C.P. 220, Cap-de-la-Madeleine, Que., G8T 7W4.

■ Cape Blomidon
Cape Blomidon lies on the southeastern shore of the Bay of Fundy at the mouth of the Minas Basin. It is the site of some of the world's highest tides. The Micmac believed it was the home of the powerful man-god Glooscap.

■ Cape Bonavista
Cape Bonavista is the high, rocky tip of the Bonavista Peninsula in eastern Newfoundland. It may have been the landing place of John Cabot (1497). One of the island's first lighthouses, now a museum, was built here in 1843.

■ Cape Breton Highlands National Park
Cape Breton Highlands National Park (950 km^2 in area; established in 1936) stretches across a high plateau on the northern tip of Cape Breton Island. The interior of the park is covered with hardwood forests, ponds, and bogs. Spectacular high cliffs rise straight up from the ocean along parts of the coast. A scenic highway, called the Cabot Trail after the explorer John Cabot, runs around the edge

of the park. For more information, write to the Superintendent, Ingonish Beach, Cape Breton, N.S., B0C 1L0.
▷ SUGGESTED READING: David M. Baird, *Cape Breton Highlands National Park* (1962).

■ Cape Breton Island

Cape Breton Island, 10 311 km² in area, is separated from mainland Nova Scotia by the narrow Strait of Canso. In 1955 the Canso Causeway provided a road link across the strait. Bras d'Or Lake, a saltwater arm of the Atlantic Ocean, nearly splits the island in two. The windswept highlands and rugged coasts proved difficult for settlers. Today, their wild beauty attracts droves of tourists.

History The first inhabitants were Micmac Indians, who fished and hunted in the area. Portuguese and Basque fishermen arrived in the 16th century. In 1713, France ceded most of Acadia to Britain but kept Cape Breton, which it called Île Royale. The French built the massive stone fortress of Louisbourg on the southeast coast to defend the entrance to the St Lawrence River. The fortress was captured by the British and torn apart.

In 1763 the island was ceded to Britain, becoming part of the mainland colony of Nova Scotia. In 1784, the island was made a colony under its present name and was a separate haven for Loyalist refugees. The Loyalists were followed by waves of Scottish immigrants, whose distinctive Scottish folk culture persists today. The island colony was reunited with Nova Scotia in 1820, and it has been part of the province of Nova Scotia since 1867.

Economy Coal mining made Cape Breton one of the more prosperous areas of Atlantic Canada in the late 19th century. By World War II, much of the coal had run out and the steel mills became obsolete. The decline left a legacy of unemployment and unrest. Today, the economy depends on fishing, a renewed interest in coal mining, and manufacturing. Tourists are attracted to beautiful Cape Breton Highlands National Park and to Louisbourg, where the fortress has been rebuilt.

About one-fifth of the population of Nova Scotia lives on the island. The largest city is Sydney.
▷ RELATED ARTICLES: **Acadia; Louisbourg; Nova Scotia.**

■ Cape Breton Strikes

In the early 1920s, coal miners and steel workers around Sydney, N.S., used strikes to protest wage cuts made by their employer, the British Empire Steel Corporation (BESCO). Demand for coal and steel had fallen after World War I. In 1922 BESCO decided to save costs in the mines and steel plants by cutting wages by one-third. Led by their union, the United Mine Workers of America, workers went on strike. Police and soldiers broke up the strikers' protests with clubs and guns, and arrested the strike leaders. Families were turned out of their homes, and company property was smashed.

Workers reluctantly returned to work, but they struck again in 1923 and 1925 as the company tried to reduce wages further. The strike in 1925 lasted five months. It ended in a bloody battle between strikers and police. A miner, William Davis, was killed. (His death is still commemorated each year on June 11, Miners' Memorial Day.)

An era of violence and turmoil drew to a close when a royal commission in 1926 approved the wage cuts. At the same time, the commission criticized BESCO for the treatment of its workers. The company collapsed in bankruptcy soon after.
▷ RELATED ARTICLES: **J.B. McLachlan; Strikes.**

■ Cape Dorset

Cape Dorset is a hamlet on a small island

Cape Breton Island from space clearly shows how Bras d'Or Lake (centre) almost severs the island in two. The Cabot Trail follows the coastline (courtesy Canada Centre for Remote Sensing).

off the southwest end of Baffin Island in the Northwest Territories. Residents are mainly Inuit who rely on traditional hunting and sealing. Since the 1960s, many Inuit artists have been swept up in the enthusiasm for Inuit art in southern Canada and elsewhere. The hamlet supports a famous printmaking shop. In 1986 the population was 872. For information, contact the Municipality, General Delivery, Cape Dorset, N.W.T., X0A 0C0.

■ Cape St Mary's

Cape St Mary's juts into Placentia Bay off the shore of Newfoundland. Its steep, rocky cliff and a nearby island, Bird Island, are a bird sanctuary. It is home to the world's second-largest colony of gannets. The waters surrounding the cape are some of the best fishing grounds in Newfoundland.

Cape St Mary's, Newfoundland, is a haven for colonies of gannets, which dive up to 30 m into the water below to catch fish (photo by J.A. Kraulis).

■ Cape Scott Provincial Park

Cape Scott Provincial Park (151 km²; established in 1973) lies on the northwestern tip of Vancouver Island, B.C. There are no roads into the park. Visitors must come on foot from the nearest highway or by boat. The shoreline is lovely sandy beaches broken by rocky headlands. Rainfall is heavy and inland the forest is thick. Cape Scott is named for a merchant,

David Scott, who sent a trading mission to the coast in 1786.

For information, you can write to the Ministry of Parks, Box 101, 4000 Seymour Place, Victoria, B.C., V8V 1X5.

■ Cape Spear

Cape Spear is the most easterly point in North America. It is a bare, windswept point of land just south of St John's, Nfld. A lighthouse, the first major one in Newfoundland, operated here from 1836 to 1955 and is now restored to its 1840 condition. A second lighthouse, a modern one built in 1955, still operates. The cape was declared a National Historic Park in 1962.

■ Capital City

A capital city is the town or city in which the national or provincial government is situated. The location of a capital may be chosen for various reasons. For example, Samuel de Champlain chose the site of Quebec for its command of Canada's most important river, the St Lawrence. Quebec remained the capital of New France for 150 years, and in 1867 it became the capital of the province of the same name. The site of St John's, Nfld, was chosen for its excellent harbour. In the early days, the captain of the first ship to enter St John's harbour each year was made governor. St John's has been the capital of Newfoundland ever since. The location of Halifax was also selected because of its fine harbour, which sheltered the British navy. It later became the capital of Nova Scotia.

Charlottetown, P.E.I., like many other capitals, had a head start on other towns in its area. When the time came to choose a capital, the largest town was a logical

Legislature, Regina, Sask. The capital building in each province is a symbol of the power and dignity of government (photo by John deVisser).

Capital Cities of Canada

Territory	Capital
Alberta	Edmonton
British Columbia	Victoria
Canada	Ottawa
Manitoba	Winnipeg
New Brunswick	Fredericton
Newfoundland	St John's
Northwest Territories	Yellowknife
Nova Scotia	Halifax
Ontario	Toronto
Prince Edward Island	Charlottetown
Quebec	Quebec
Saskatchewan	Regina
Yukon Territory	Whitehorse

Two Famous Executions

Patrick Whelan was convicted of assassinating Thomas D'Arcy McGee. He was hanged Feb. 11, 1869 at Ottawa in the presence of a large crowd that had to be kept in order by city police. Some people still believe he was innocent.
Louis Riel, Metis leader, was hanged Nov. 16, 1885 at Regina. He was convicted of high treason for his part in the North-West Rebellion. The execution caused a deep rift in Canada. English Canadians considered him a traitor. French Canadians saw him as a defender of his people and French culture.

choice. Victoria was the largest town in British Columbia when that province was formed. It remained the capital of British Columbia even after Vancouver had grown much bigger. Toronto became capital of Upper Canada (which later became Ontario) because the earlier capital of Newark was too close to the American border. Toronto received a big boost over its rival towns by becoming the capital. In a similar way, Fredericton won out over Saint John as capital of New Brunswick because it was a safe distance inland. Saint John is a much bigger city, but it is close to the sea.

Winnipeg was the first large western town. It occupied the site of Upper Fort Garry, which had been a headquarters of the Hudson's Bay Company. It was the logical choice as the capital of Manitoba when the province was created in 1870. Regina became capital of Saskatchewan in 1905 because of its position on the main Canadian Pacific Railway (CPR) line. On the other hand, Edmonton beat out Calgary as capital of Alberta for purely political reasons. Calgary was larger and was on the main line of the CPR.

The National Capital Kingston, Montreal, Toronto, and Quebec had brief turns as the capital of the Province of Canada in the mid-19th century. Each argued vehemently that it should be chosen the permanent capital. Because no compromise could be reached, the government of Canada asked Queen Victoria to decide. In her name, the tiny lumber town of Ottawa was selected in 1857. Ottawa was a safe distance from the United States, and it was on the border between the French and English sections of Canada. It became the national capital when the Dominion of Canada was created in 1867.

A city gains many benefits from being a capital. It gains influence, jobs, and other amenities, such as government buildings, monuments, museums, and parks. Because Ottawa is the national capital, it is important to all Canadians. It is home to Parliament, the governor general's residence, the Supreme Court, and several national museums and galleries.

■ Capital Punishment

Capital punishment is the execution, by the state, of those found guilty of a crime. Canada inherited its legal system from Britain, where the death penalty applied to a large number of crimes. In Canada, however, the penalty was restricted to a small number of very serious crimes, such as treason and murder. The method used was hanging.

In 1976, after two trial periods when there were no executions, Parliament abolished capital punishment for all crimes. The only exception applies to a special case involving someone engaged in military service. To appease those who favour capital punishment, longer prison terms were set up for murder in 1976. In first degree murder, for example, the minimum sentence is life in prison with no eligibility for parole for at least 25 years. Between 1976 and 1987, many people argued for the return of capital punishment. However, in 1987, the House of Commons voted against restoring it.

Between 1867 and 1962, 710 people were executed in Canada. The last hangings in Canada were a double execution in Toronto's Don Jail in 1962.

When a judge imposed a death penalty, the condemned person usually appealed the sentence through all levels of the courts. If this was unsuccessful, the person could ask the federal Cabinet to commute the death sentence (reduce it to a lesser sentence). Historically, the Cabinet had the authority to commute a death sentence to life imprisonment.

■ Caraquet

Caraquet is a town on the shore of Chaleur Bay in northern New Brunswick. French settlers began arriving about 1750, and the town has been a centre of Acadian culture since then. The Acadian Historical Village is just outside Caraquet. Rich fishing grounds are nearby, and fishing and boatbuilding are the main activities. Lumbering and farming are also traditional activities. Its population in 1986 was 4493. For information, contact the Greffier, C.P. 420, Caraquet, N.B., E0B 1K0.

■ Carbonear

Carbonear, on the western shore of Con-

Northern Cardinal, one of the most colourful birds in Canada (Macmillan Illustrated Animal Encyclopedia).

ception Bay, is one of the oldest settlements in Newfoundland. It was first settled by English fishermen in the 1600s. In 1697 Pierre Le Moyne d'Iberville made several attempts to capture Carbonear. He burned the town, but the residents withdrew safely to Carbonear Island. According to legend, Carbonear contains the burial place of the Irish princess, Sheila Na Geira, who was captured by the Newfoundland pirate Gilbert Pike. In the 1800s Carbonear was an important centre of fishing, sealing, and shipbuilding. Fishing is still important, and the town has also grown into a local business and government centre. The population in 1986 was 5337. For information, contact the Town Clerk, P.O. Box 999, Carbonear, Nfld, A0A 1T0.

■ Carcross

Carcross, Y.T., lies at the narrows between Bennett and Nares lakes, 74 km south of the Yukon capital of Whitehorse. It was a national crossing for the caribou herds and a hunting and fishing camp for the Tagish Indians. Originally called Caribou Crossing, it was founded in 1898 during the building of the White Pass and Yukon Railway. Several of the early buildings, including the hotel, were brought to the site by barge. The *S.S. Tutshi,* a sternwheeler, has been restored and operates out of Carcross. In 1986 the population was 209. For information, contact the Secretary, Community and Curling Club, P.O. Box 48, Carcross, Y.T., Y0B 1B0.

■ Cardinal

The Northern Cardinal (*Cardinalis cardinalis*) is a colourful member of the Cardinalinae subfamily, which also includes grosbeaks. It breeds and lives throughout the year in southern Ontario and southwestern Quebec. It is rarely sighted in other parts of Canada.

The adult male is a brilliant red colour with a high crest; the female a duller red. The Cardinal's habitat is deciduous or evergreen forests, bushes, clearings, and bushy areas near dwellings. It is easily drawn to bird feeders filled with sunflower seeds. Its call is a high, sharp note.

■ Cardinal, Douglas Joseph

Architect (*born in 1934 at Calgary, Alta*). Cardinal is the great-grandson of a Blood Indian woman and a European settler. He graduated in architecture from the University of Texas in 1963 and returned to Red Deer, Alta, to practise. His design for St Mary's Church (1968) in Red Deer soon

brought him international attention. The church centers on its altar — a massive block of white limestone. The rest of the church, in Cardinal's words, "grew from the main altar in the manner of a seashell around its soft creature." It has also been compared to the pattern made by the shadow of wheat waving in the wind. Cardinal used the same curved forms in designs for his Grande Prairie Regional College and for his own house in Edmonton.

In 1983 Cardinal began work on the new Canadian Museum of Civilization (completed 1989) in Hull, Que. Again, he designed the building in sweeping circular forms, stacked in terraces and capped in a ribbed copper roof. Constructed in fossil-rich limestone from Manitoba, the building looks as though it has been carved in stone by glaciers, wind, and water. As Cardinal said of his design, "I wanted people to remember that man and nature are related to each other."

▷ Suggested Reading: Trevor Boddy, editor, *The Architecture of Douglas Cardinal* (1989).

■ Cardinal, Harold

Native leader and author (*born in 1945 at High Prairie, Alta*). Harold Cardinal is the author of *The Unjust Society* (1969) and *The Rebirth of Canada's Indians* (1977). Both books are strongly critical of government policy towards the native people. Cardinal has spent most of his life working for the well-being of his people. As president of the Indian Association of Alberta from 1968 to 1977, he launched

Architect Douglas Cardinal standing in front of the Canadian Museum of Civilization, which he designed (photo by Jim Merrithew).

numerous programs to promote Indian culture and traditions, and in 1977 he was the first native person appointed regional director of Indian affairs in Alberta. In 1983 he was appointed vice-chief for the prairie region in the Assembly of First Nations.

■ Cardston

Cardston, Alta, a town southwest of Lethbridge, is famous as the centre of the Mormon religion (Church of Jesus Christ of Latter-Day Saints) in Canada. It was founded in 1887 by a group of Mormons from Utah and named for their leader, Charles Ora Card (1839-1906). Between 1913 and 1923, the Mormons built a magnificent white marble temple, the only one of its kind in Canada. Today, the town is the centre of an agricultural area. It is also the home of the Remington-Alberta Carriage Collection. In 1986 the population was 3497. For information, contact the Town Administrator, P.O. Box 280, Cardston, Alta, T0K 0K0.

■ Careers

A career is an occupation followed as one's life work. A successful career is an important ingredient in a happy life and greatly affects a person's standard of living. Therefore planning a career is one of the most important steps in a person's life. For those whose interests and abilities coincide, planning a career may be easy. However, many young people are expected to choose a direction before their lasting interests have formed. Decisions face most students as they graduate from high school, but it is not unusual for them to change courses during their studies. Even after they have worked in a career for several years, many people quit and take another direction. In Canada, people change careers an average of five times in their lifetime.

Decisions The decision to choose a particular career is based on several elements, including chance. The challenge is greater for those who have chosen beyond their abilities or for those whose families cannot afford the education required. In previous generations, it was more difficult for certain groups in society to enter certain careers. The professions, for example, were generally restricted to those of a high economic standing. Women were discouraged from entering many careers that were open to men, such as law, medicine, engineering, and politics. Today, it can still be harder for women than men to enter certain ca-

reers, but the situation has improved greatly. In fact, the problem for many young people is not a lack of choice but too many choices.

An important factor in making a decision is expectations. Does an individual value high income, fame, leisure, adventure, service to others? Does a person have the skill or aptitude to follow a certain career? Some careers demand exceptional artistic or physical abilities, which few possess. Other careers require an aptitude for a particular subject, such as mathematics or languages. Still others require high ambition and a long period of apprenticeship.

Decisions are made more difficult by constant changes in the work world. New technology, such as computers, influences how work is done. Because of technological changes, fewer people are now needed to produce goods and agricultural products. As a result, jobs in manufacturing, mining, and agriculture are declining. Jobs in the service industries, such as teaching, nursing, and business managing, are increasing.

PREPARING FOR A CAREER

The keys to preparing for a career are education and training. Some of this "education" occurs outside the classroom, including learning to work well with others and to deal with stress and competition. Some jobs require only a high school diploma, but most demand more. Education is required not only to enter a career but often to maintain it.

The range of education required for career training is very broad. Programs and institutions vary from province to province.

Trade or Vocational programs train students in specific occupational skills in areas such as engineering, applied science, or business and commerce. The student does not require a high-school diploma. Programs are offered at community colleges, high schools, technical institutes, and colleges.

An apprenticeship is a combination of on-the-job and technical training that prepares a student for work in the trades, such as carpenter, mechanic, or plumber. Apprenticeships last from two to four years, depending on the occupation.

Colleges are post-secondary institutions that offer certificates (usually in one-year programs) or diplomas (two to four years). They include CEGEPS (in Quebec) hospital schools of nursing, institutes of technology, agricultural col-

Women are entering more and more careers, such as police work, that were once only open to men.

Construction careers range from labourers and skilled trades to engineering and architecture.

Environmental Awareness is leading to more careers such as forest management (all photos courtesy Alberta Career Development).

leges, schools of art, and schools for specialized technical fields. Graduates can expect to enter the labour force at a technical level, as a middle manager, or as a professional assistant. Students generally require high-school diplomas. Over 50% of all college graduates work in one of four areas: clerical jobs; medicine and health; natural sciences, engineering, and mathematics; managerial or administrative.

Universities grant degrees in many different areas, including business, social sciences, humanities, engineering, education, and mathematics and the physical sciences. A bachelor's degree requires three or four years of full-time study. A master's degree requires an additional two or more years, and a doctoral degree at least two or three more. Universities also grant certificates and diplomas. Entrance usually requires a high-school diploma. Over half of the graduates with bachelor degrees work in teaching, managerial/administrative, or natural sciences fields. Master's and PhD graduates work in managerial and administrative fields, or in teaching areas.

Studies show that there is generally lower unemployment among those with higher-education qualifications and that those with higher education can expect higher salaries. At all educational levels, graduates in the health-related fields have the lowest unemployment rates.

CAREER CLASSIFICATIONS

There are thousands of different occupations in Canada today. In order to simplify choice, many of these can be classified according to their goals and activities. For example, jobs in the agribusiness and natural resource sectors often require manual skill as well as knowledge, and they are often carried on outdoors. Within each classification, jobs range according to the level of education and training.

Statistics Canada uses a classification that divides occupations into major groups:
- Arts
- Business, Commerce, Management and Administration
- Education
- Engineering
- Humanities
- Medicine and Health
- Natural Sciences and Primary Industries
- Physical Sciences
- Social Sciences and Services

Each of these major groups can be further subdivided.

Careers in the Arts generally require an artistic ability and a high-school diploma with a good standing in English or French, or mathematics. Educational training ranges from the trade and vocational level to university. Occupations in this category range from hairdressers and barbers to commercial artists and sculptors, dancers, and musicians.

Careers in Business, Commerce, Management, and Administration generally require a high-school diploma, with advanced standing in mathematics, in English or French, and in bookkeeping, business, or secretarial skills. Training is available at the trade and vocational level, at community colleges, and at universities. Occupations range from financial managers, accountants, auditors, hotel managers, and sales and advertising managers, to bookkeepers, clerks, receptionists, legal secretaries, stenographers, and medical secretaries.

Careers in Education require a high-school diploma with good standing in several subjects. Training is available at the community college and university levels. Occupations range from elementary and secondary teachers, child-care workers, education administrators, and counsellors, to welfare and community service workers or managers.

Careers in Engineering and Engineering Technologies usually require a high-school diploma, sometimes with good standing in mathematics, English or French, physics, chemistry, or other subjects. Training is available at the trade and vocational level (including apprenticeships), at community colleges, and at universities.

Occupations vary widely and include architects, skilled construction workers (such as welders, electricians, carpenters, plumbers, etc.), chemical engineers, civil engineers, chemical and medical laboratory technologists and technicians, electrical engineers, electrical/electronic equipment installers, machinists, mechanical engineers, motor vehicle mechanics, heavy equipment mechanics, surveyors, transportation engineers, and pilots.

Careers in the Humanities require a high-school diploma with an advanced standing for university entrance. Training is available at the undergraduate or graduate level. Occupations in this area include teachers, librarians, archivists, translators, interpreters, writers, editors, producers, directors, university professors, and ministers of religion.

Computers have brought about big changes in how jobs are done and have opened new careers.

Child-Care Work is one of many careers in education.

Architecture is a career that requires much advanced education.

Heavy Equipment Operators Careers in the field of engineering and technology vary greatly.

Bricklaying is a trade that requires apprenticeships (all photos courtesy Alberta Career Development).

Careers in Medicine *usually require a high-school diploma and further education.*

Food Service *is one of many occupations in the growing service industries.*

Physical Science *training is usually at the university level (above photos courtesy Alberta Career Development).*

Cariboo Road *above Yale, B.C. in a photo taken around 1867 or 1868 (courtesy NAC/C-8077).*

Careers in Medicine and Health usually but not always require a high-school diploma with good standing in mathematics, biology, chemistry, and perhaps physics. Training occurs at the trade and vocational level, at community colleges, and at universities. Occupations in this area include physicians, surgeons, optometrists, dentists, dental hygienists and dental assistants, pharmacists, physiotherapists, audio and speech therapists, radiological technologists, medical laboratory technologists and technicians, nurses, nursing assistants, and hospital administrators.

Careers in Natural Sciences and Primary Industries normally require a high-school diploma with advanced standing in mathematics, biology, chemistry, and physics. Training occurs at the trade and vocational level, at community colleges, and at universities. Occupations include plant nursery workers, livestock inspectors, farm machinery operators, agriculturalists, biologists, horticulturalists, wildlife and forest conservation officers, dieticians, nutritionists, forest managers and rangers, and veterinarians.

Careers in the Physical Sciences normally require a high-school diploma with above-average standing in the appropriate courses such as chemistry, physics, and mathematics. Training is usually at the university level, although there are some trade and vocational and community college programs available in computer science. Occupations include chemists, computer programmers, data processors, systems analysts, geologists, statisticians, and physicists.

Careers in the Social Sciences and Services usually require a high-school diploma with good standing in mathematics, biology, and physics. Some trade and vocational programs in food service technologies require completion of Grade 10 only. Training is at the trade and vocational level, at community colleges, and at universities. Occupations include economists, geographers, cartographers, community planners, lawyers, police officers and detectives, guards, psychologists, bakers, dry cleaners, chefs, cooks, child-care workers, and social workers.

Information on specific careers is included throughout the encyclopedia; for example, with the entries on Advertising, Banking, Chemistry, Forestry, Nursing, Police, Teaching, and Zoology.

■ Cariboo Gold Rush

The Cariboo gold rush (1860-66) took place in the Cariboo region of British Columbia. It started when miners from the Fraser River rush of 1858 worked their way north, searching for the mother lode. The Cariboo rush opened up the B.C. interior and led to construction of the Cariboo Road. *See* **Gold Rushes; Overlanders.**

■ Cariboo Mountains

The Cariboo Mountains lie between the Fraser and North Thompson rivers in the central interior of British Columbia. The highest peak is Mount Sir Wilfrid Laurier (3520 m). These mountains were the site of the Cariboo gold rush in the 1860s. The area is noted for its canoe routes and ski facilities. *See* **Columbia Mountains.**

■ Cariboo Road

By 1860, miners were moving north from the Fraser River to richer goldfields in the Cariboo country. Governor James Douglas wanted the gold to travel out by the Fraser River, not through American territory. A road had to be built.

Governor Douglas gave the job of surveying the route to the Royal Engineers brought to British Columbia in 1859 by Colonel Richard Moody. In 1862 the engineers laid out a 650 km route from Yale — the highest point steamboats could reach on the Fraser — to the Cariboo. Much of the road had to be blasted from solid rock. The engineers themselves built the most dangerous parts in the Fraser Canyon. The rest was built by private contractors.

The Cariboo (or Great North) Road, completed in 1865, was a great success. Many other roads were built at the same time, and the ease of travel by wagon and stagecoach encouraged settlement of the interior of British Columbia. Part of the Trans-Canada Highway still follows its route.

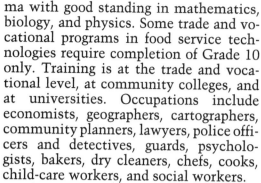

Caribou

The caribou (*Rangifer tarandus*) is a member of the deer family Cervidae. It is called "reindeer" in Europe and Asia. It is the only North American deer in which both sexes often bear antlers. In Canada five different subspecies are recognized: Peary, Grant's, barren ground, woodland, and reindeer.

Peary caribou, the smallest nearly white subspecies, occupies the arctic islands. Adult females may weigh less than 30 kg. Male woodland and barren ground caribou may weigh over 270 kg. The mainland subspecies are usually brown, with white markings on the throat, neck, belly, rump, and under the tail.

The barren ground caribou is migratory, frequenting the arctic tundra in summer and retreating south to the boreal forest in winter. They form herds of up to 50 000 or 100 000 animals prior to the spring migration, immediately after the fawns are born, and again before the autumn migration and breeding time. Between these times the animals disperse and form scattered herds of two to ten adults usually of the same sex. Most of the mating occurs in October and a single fawn is born. The fawn can stand within a half hour of birth and can run for a short distance only 90 minutes after birth.

The chief predators of caribou are man and the wolf. Grizzly bears, black bears, lynx, wolverines, and golden eagles may also prey on caribou. Caribou eat great quantities of lichen in the fall and winter. In summer they eat grasses, sedges, willow and blueberry branches, and even birch leaves and mushrooms. When lemmings are abundant, caribou have been seen to pursue and eat these "arctic mice."

Caribou are particularly well adapted to the harsh northern climate. Hair helps insulate its nose and toes. Its broad hooves serve as snow shovels and snowshoes. The long, hollow hairs of the coat hold an insulating layer of air and increase its buoyancy when swimming.

▷ SUGGESTED READING: Elizabeth Cleaver, *The Enchanted Caribou* (1985); Judy T. Ross, *Caribou* (1986).

Caribou Inuit, *see* Inuit

Carignan, Jean ("Ti-Jean")

Fiddler (*born in 1916 at Lévis, Que.; died in 1988 at Montreal, Que.*). Jean Carignan raised fiddling to a high art in Canada, winning the admiration of other fiddlers and a wide public. Taught at first by his fiddler father, "Ti-Jean" began playing at age four and was performing on the street corners of his village at five. At seven, he became enthralled by a recording of Joseph Allard. When his family moved to Montreal, he studied with Allard. He remained with Allard until he was 15, and learned the Celtic fiddle repertoire from recordings.

Carignan continued to perform in the streets during his first year in Montreal, but the police harassed him, so at 12 he became a shoemaker's apprentice. In his mid-teens he joined a Toronto band. In his early 20s he returned to Montreal and lived as a dance-band leader and sometimes as a factory worker. What made him remarkable — even apart from the brilliance of his playing — was his sense of responsibility towards the tradition of fiddling. He would have found it distasteful to change the 7000 jigs, reels, and other traditional dance tunes he took it upon himself to preserve.

At 40 he began driving a taxi so that he could make a living and reserve his fiddling for concerts and folk festivals. In 1973, 400 leading American and Canadian fiddlers travelled to Montreal to assist at the unveiling of a wood carving of Carignan by Georges Morisette. In 1975 the National Film Board of Canada produced the film *Jean Carignan, Violoneux* in tribute to him. Carignan retired in 1978 because of advancing deafness. His many recordings for London, Folkways, Philo, and Vanguard preserve his art for thousands of admirers.

Carle, Gilles

Filmmaker (*born in 1929 at Maniwaki, Que.*). Carle was one of the first Canadian filmmakers to achieve commercial and artistic success abroad. In the 1940s and 1950s, Carle was a graphic artist. He joined the National Film Board (NFB) in 1960, and made his first feature film, *La Vie heureuse de Léopold Z*, in 1965.

After the NFB rejected several projects, Carle became an independent filmmaker. He became successful with such films as *Le Viol d'une jeune fille douce* (1968), which combined sex and violence in a distinctly Québecois setting. He first gained international attention with *La Vraie Nature de Bernadette* (1972). In 1973 he began a series of films starring Carole Laure. The best known in Canada was *Maria Chapdelaine* (1983), adapted from Louis Hémon's classic story of a young woman in early 20th-century Quebec. The very successful *Les Plouffe* (1981) was a film based on Canada's first TV mini-series. In

Range of Caribou ●

Bull Caribou
photographed in the Yukon Territory (photo by Stephen J. Krasemann/DRK Photo).

1984 Carle made a sequel, *Le Crime d'Ovide Plouffe*.

Carle's fiction films are a clever blend of fantasy, romanticism, sex, and humour. Two recent dramatized histories, *Cinéma, cinéma* (1985), about the NFB, and *Vive Québec* (1987), about Quebec City, show the versatility of his talent.

■ Carleton, Guy (1st Baron Dorchester)

Colonial governor (*born in 1724 at Strabane, Ireland; died in 1808 at Maidenhead, England*). Sir Guy Carleton was the second governor of the Province of Quebec after the Conquest of 1760. He succeeded James Murray in 1768 and, like Murray, he was a British army officer.

Carleton was largely responsible for the Quebec Act of 1774, which preserved French laws and customs. The Act so angered English-speaking settlers in the Thirteen Colonies that it helped bring about the American Revolution. During the revolution, the Americans laid siege to Quebec City. The town survived the attack, but Carleton's military tactics were criticized. He resigned and left Canada in 1778.

Carleton had powerful friends in Britain, and in 1786 he was once more posted to Quebec. This time he was made governor-in-chief of the colonies of New Brunswick and Nova Scotia as well as Quebec. In addition, he was created Lord Dorchester. During this second period in office, the Province of Quebec was divided into Upper and Lower Canada (1791). Carleton believed that Britain's native people could be important allies in defending Canada. This view brought more criticism in Britain and Carleton resigned again. He returned to England in 1796.

▷ RELATED ARTICLE: **Province of Quebec.**

■ Carleton Place

Carleton Place, Ont., is a town on Canada's Mississippi River, 45 km southwest of Ottawa. It was founded in 1819 by William Morphy and his sons and was named for a square in Glasgow, Scotland. Two sawmills and a gristmill were the town's first major employers. One of the first woollen mills in Canada began here in 1830. The railway arrived in 1859. Today, electronics and computer industries are important to the economy. In 1986 the population was 6520. For information, contact the Town Clerk, 175 Bridge Street, Carleton Place, Ont., K7C 2V8.

■ Carleton University

Carleton University's campus, bordered by the Rideau River and the historic Rideau Canal, is just ten minutes from Parliament Hill and downtown Ottawa. A 5 km network of underground tunnels links the university's 27 buildings to provide cover in winter weather.

Carleton celebrates its 50th anniversary in 1992, but it has only been on its present campus since 1959. It was founded in 1942 as Carleton College and became a university in 1957.

Carleton offers nearly 50 undergraduate specializations leading to graduation in ten different degree programs. The primary language of instruction is English, but courses are also available in French in a number of disciplines. The university's 20 000 full-time and part-time students come from all across Canada and from about 90 foreign countries. Its programs in areas such as architecture, Canadian studies, and journalism attract students from across Canada. For more information, write to the Admissions Office, Carleton University, Ottawa, Ont., K1S 5B6.

■ Carling, Sir John

Brewer, politician (*born in 1828 at London Township, Upper Canada [Ontario]; died in 1911 at London, Ont.*). Carling joined his father's brewery in London when he was 21. He inherited the business in 1849 and remained president. He entered politics in 1857 as a Conservative. He was a member of the Ontario legislature and later of the House of Commons and finally of the Senate. He served as postmaster general 1882-85 and as minister of agriculture 1885-92.

■ Carmacks

Carmacks, Y.T., lies beside the Yukon River, 175 km north of Whitehorse. It is named for George Washington Carmack, one of the prospectors whose discovery along Bonanza Creek in 1896 touched off the Klondike gold rush. The village grew as a supply centre for boats on the Yukon River. The 1986 population of Carmacks was 280. It is now at the junction of the Klondike and Robert Campbell highways. For more information, contact the Clerk/Treasurer, Village of Carmacks, Y.T., Y0B 1C0.

■ Carman, Bliss

Poet and magazine editor (*born in 1861 at Fredericton, N.B.; died in 1929 at New Canaan, Connecticut, U.S.*). Though he was born and educated in Canada, and wrote most of his poems about the Canadian landscape, Carman spent most of his life in the United States. He went there in

Sir Guy Carleton was largely responsible for the Quebec Act, which helped to preserve French laws and customs (courtesy NAC/C-2833).

1890 to become editor of a New York religious weekly called the *Independent*. He also worked on several important magazines, such as the *Atlantic Monthly*.

Carman wrote hundreds of poems about nature and man's kinship with it. These were published in magazines, and gave pleasure to thousands of readers. One example is a poem called "Vestigia" in which Carman writes:

> I took a day to search for God,
> And found him not. But as I trod
> By rocky ledge, through woods
>   untamed,
> Just where one scarlet lily flamed,
> I saw his footprint in the sod.

His most famous book of poems is called *Low Tide on Grand Pré* (1893). In his lifetime, Carman was considered the best poet in Canada. He enjoyed the highest reputation in the United States and Great Britain ever held by a Canadian poet.

■ Carmichael, Franklin

Painter (*born in 1890 at Orillia, Ont.; died in 1945 at Toronto, Ont.*). Carmichael was a founding member of the Group of Seven (1920). He began as an apprentice with a Toronto commercial art company. He studied art in Europe and returned to paint the landscape of northern Ontario. His paintings often show a charm and gentleness along with strong composition.

■ Caroline

The *Caroline* was an American-owned steamer that assisted William Lyon Mackenzie after his unsuccessful rebellion in Upper Canada. Mackenzie and about 200 followers had retreated to Navy Island, on the Niagara River. There they were kept stocked with food and other supplies by the *Caroline*, which was based at Fort Schlosser on the American shore.

On the night of December 29, 1837, Commander Andrew Drew and a group of Canadian militia silently boarded the *Caroline*. After a brief fight in which one American was killed, they gained possession of the ship and forced the remaining crew ashore. They then set the *Caroline* alight and cut it from its moorings. The hull sank before reaching Niagara Falls, but some of the burning planks tumbled over the falls in a dramatic blaze of fire. The incident created a dispute between Canada and the U.S.

▷ RELATED ARTICLE: **Rebellions of 1837.**

■ Carr, Emily

Painter, writer (*born 1871 at Victoria, B.C.; died there 1945*). Carr, who lived and worked alone on Vancouver Island, is one of Canada's most famous artists. Although she decided to be an artist early in life, it was only when she was 57 years old that she began those paintings and writings for which she is remembered.

She studied art first in San Francisco and then in England, and visited France in 1910-11. As early as 1908 she decided to record the culture of the Northwest Coast native people, and travelled to remote villages to paint their totem poles and carved log houses. She was unable to support herself with her art, however. Discouraged, she began to run a boarding house in 1913. Although the boarding house was not sold until 1936, Carr returned seriously to painting in 1927 when her work was exhibited in a national show in Ottawa.

On her trip to the east, she met members of the Group of Seven, and Lawren Harris in particular encouraged and inspired her. She continued to paint Indian themes, but turned increasingly to nature. Her skies and forests are alive with energy, movement, and shimmering light. She also painted a splendid self-portrait. In these later years she travelled to New York and Chicago, and her work was widely exhibited and praised. She wrote several volumes of stories, many of which were based on her own life.

▷ RELATED ARTICLE: **Painting.**

Snow Clouds (1938), oil on canvas by Frank Carmichael (courtesy Franklin Carmichael/NGC).

Big Raven *(1931) by Emily Carr, oil on canvas, 86.7 x 113.8 cm. Carr's painting was deeply influenced by the art of the Northwest Coast Indians (courtesy Vancouver Art Gallery).*

▷ SUGGESTED READING: Ruth Gowers, *Emily Carr* (1987); Rosemary Neering, *Emily Carr* (1975); Kate Taylor, *Painters* (1989).

■ Carr, Shirley

Union leader (*born at Niagara Falls, Ont., date unknown*). Carr served in a local of the Canadian Union of Public Employees (CUPE). She became president of the Niagara local and moved to the provincial and then national levels. In 1986 she was elected president of the Canadian Labour Congress, the first woman to hold the position.

■ Carrier

The Carrier are an Athapaskan-speaking people who live in north-central British Columbia. Their name comes from the custom of the easternmost Carrier, which required widows to carry the bones of their dead husbands on their backs for about a year. Each group was associated with a hunting territory and fishing sites. The fur trade brought changes to their living patterns. Many settled near fur-trade posts, such as Fort St James. Today the Carrier live on reserves and work as seasonal labourers while continuing their hunting, trapping, and fishing. *See* **Native People: Subarctic.**

■ Carrier, Roch

Writer (*born in 1937 at Ste-Justine-de-Dorchester, Que.*). The author of poems, stories, novels, and plays, Carrier published his first book, a poetry collection, in 1956. But it was his novel, set in a Quebec village during World War II, *La Guerre, Yes Sir!* (1968), which launched his reputation. *La Guerre* was the first

Shirley Carr was the first woman to head Canada's largest union, CUPE.

novel in a trilogy. The other two books are *Floralie, Where Are You?* (1969) and *Is it the Sun, Philibert?* (1970). The trilogy is one of the most popular works in modern Quebec literature, and Carrier is one of the most widely read Quebec authors in English Canada.

In 1979 Carrier won a new audience of young readers when he published *Les Enfants du bonhomme dans la lune* (translated as *The Hockey Sweater and Other Stories*), a collection of delightful stories for children.

■ Carson, William

Physician, politician (*born in 1770 at Kirkcudbright, Scotland; died in 1843 at St John's, Nfld*). Carson was a surgeon, political reformer, social activist, politician, and a colourful writer who championed self-rule for Newfoundland.

He came to St John's in 1808 and became doctor to the local soldiers. Within a few years he began taking care of the needs of the town. He began a long campaign to improve medical and social conditions in Newfoundland and to gain local government for the colony. In 1832, in response to the efforts of Carson and others, Britain granted Newfoundland representative government. Carson ran for a seat as a Liberal in the House of Assembly. He was defeated but was elected in a by-election in 1833. He became Speaker in 1837.

In the Assembly, Carson continued to press for and get improvements in agriculture, education, transportation, and social conditions. In 1842 the governor appointed Carson to the Executive Council of Newfoundland.

■ Carter, Sir Frederick

Premier of Newfoundland (*born in 1819 at St John's, Nfld; died there in 1900*). Carter was a lawyer who was first elected to Newfoundland's House of Assembly as a Conservative in 1855. In 1861 the Conservatives formed the government and Carter was appointed Speaker. In 1864 he and Ambrose Shea represented Newfoundland as observers at the Quebec Conference on Confederation. Carter became premier in 1865. He supported the idea that Newfoundland should join Canada, but when he fought an election on the issue in 1869, he lost.

Carter remained in opposition until 1874, when he was again returned as premier. Joining Canada was no longer an issue. He left politics in 1878 and was appointed to the Supreme Court of Newfoundland, becoming chief justice in 1880.

■ Carter, Wilfred

Singer, songwriter (*born in 1904 at Port Hilford, N.S.*). Carter began to sing as a boy. He was influenced at an early age by a touring Swiss yodeller. He moved to Alberta in the 1920s and became a cowboy and part-time entertainer. He recorded hit tunes in Montreal in the 1930s and became popular on CBC radio and in the United States. His stage name in the U.S. was "Montana Slim." After he was seriously injured in a car crash in 1940, he could not perform for nine years. In the 1950s his travelling show was one of the most popular attractions in Canada.

■ Cartier, Sir George-Étienne

Politician (*born in 1814 at St-Antoine, Lower Canada [Quebec]; died in 1873 at London, England*). Cartier was one of the most important Fathers of Confederation and a longtime friend and ally of Sir John A. Macdonald. He grew up in the Richelieu Valley, graduated from the Sulpician's college in Montreal, and trained as a lawyer. As a young man, he was also a poet and Patriote. He wrote a song to his country ("O Canada, mon pays, mes amours"), and he fought against the British at St-Denis during the Rebellion of 1837. With the collapse of the rebellion, Cartier escaped to the United States, but was able to return home in 1838.

In 1848 Cartier was elected to the Province of Canada's Legislative Assembly. A member of the Parti Bleu, he joined

Sir George-Étienne Cartier was the key person in persuading French Canadians to accept Confederation (courtesy NAC/C-8007).

Macdonald in the government of 1857, and he became premier in the Cartier-Macdonald government of 1858-62.

Cartier was the key figure in persuading French Canadians to accept Confederation. Between 1864 and 1867 he devoted himself to this cause. After Confederation, he was a senior member of Macdonald's Cabinet, handling such important matters as British Columbia's entry into Confederation.

In 1872 Cartier's long-standing loyalty to the Sulpicians got him into a quarrel with the Bishop of Montreal, and he lost his Montreal seat in the elections. He took a Manitoba seat instead. By this time, Cartier was already ill with kidney disease. He went to England for treatment, but there was no cure, though he was optimistic to the last.

By nature, Cartier was energetic and confident. His Saturday night parties in Ottawa were legendary, with Cartier sitting on the dining-room table, singing paddling songs in his unlovely voice, pretending the table was a canoe and he was paddling it.

▷ RELATED ARTICLES: **Confederation; Parti Bleu; Province of Canada.**

■ Cartier, Jacques

Explorer (*born in 1491 at Saint-Malo, France; died there in 1557*). On April 20, 1534, French explorer Jacques Cartier set out from Saint-Malo with 61 men and two ships. He was commissioned by King François I of France to look for gold and a passage that would lead to Asia.

The ships reached Newfoundland on May 10 and entered the Strait of Belle-Isle on the 27th. He sailed along the west coast of Newfoundland; then, turning westward, he came across Prince Edward Island. He later reached the continental coast, followed it northward and entered Chaleur Bay, where he traded with the Micmac. Farther north, in the Baie de Gaspé, he met some Iroquois from the St Lawrence Valley who had come to fish in the bay. Cartier persuaded their chief, Donnacona, to allow two of his sons to return with him to France. He arrived back in Saint-Malo on September 5.

Second Voyage In the following year, Cartier returned to the Gulf of St Lawrence with 110 men and three ships, the *Grande Hermine*, the *Petite Hermine*, and the *Émérillon*. Donnacona's sons guided them to the St Lawrence River on August 13. Cartier sailed up this waterway as far as the village of Stadacona (now Quebec City), where Donnacona

lived. In early October, Cartier visited the Iroquois village of Hochelaga (Montreal), which was fortified. There he learned that rapids blocked navigation of the river to the west.

In late autumn, Cartier settled in with his men in a fort built near Stadacona. The time spent in winter quarters was a terrible ordeal. Most of the Frenchmen were afflicted with scurvy. Twenty-five died from the disease. The others survived because of a remedy learned from one of Donnacona's sons: a kind of tea made from the ground bark of white cedar. When he left the area in May 1536, Cartier seized Donnacona and nine other Iroquois, including four children, and carried them off to France.

Third Voyage Donnacona dazzled the French with tales of a Kingdom of Saguenay "where there are immense quantities of gold, rubies, and other rich things." Such talk set the French monarch dreaming, and he decided to found a colony in the New World. Again Cartier set out, this time under the command of La Rocque de Roberval, a nobleman.

Cartier was ready before Roberval and set out in May 1541 with five ships bearing sailors, soldiers, immigrants, livestock, and provisions. They reached Stadacona on August 23, but without the Iroquois he had taken to France, who had died earlier. Cartier established himself in Charlesbourg-Royal, at the mouth of the Rivière du Cap-Rouge, where he believed he had found diamonds and gold. During the winter the Iroquois became

Cedar Medicine

Most of the French were stricken with scurvy during their first winter in Canada. Many died before the Iroquois helped.

Cartier wrote, "They brought back from the forest nine or ten branches and showed us how to grind the bark and boil it in water, then drink the potion every other day and apply the residue as a poultice to swollen and infected legs."

Grande Hermine, *a replica of one of Cartier's ships (photo by K.P. O'Leary).*

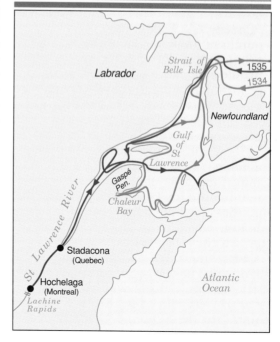

Explorations of Jacques Cartier 1534, 1535

more hostile. Cartier had broken his word by visiting their rivals at Hochelaga.

In June 1542, Cartier decided to set sail for France with all his men. In Newfoundland he met Roberval, who ordered him to turn back. However, anxious to show the king the gold and diamonds that he had discovered, Cartier slipped away and headed for France, where these so-called riches proved to be nothing but quartz and iron pyrites.

For King François, Cartier's expeditions had been a failure, but for the scholars of the age they were a major success. The accounts of his voyages made known the mighty St Lawrence River and its tributaries.

Cartier retired from the sea and spent the rest of his life quietly at Saint-Malo.

▷ RELATED ARTICLES: **Exploration; Kingdom of the Saguenay.**

▷ SUGGESTED READING: Daniel Conner, *Jacques Cartier and the People of the Eastern Woodlands* (1986).

■ **Cartography,** *see* **Maps and Mapping**

■ **Cartoons**

Cartoons are drawings that appear in newspapers, magazines, and books, and in animated form on film and television. There are two main kinds of cartoons: humorous or adventure cartoons (or comics) and serious cartoons that comment on the political and social events of the day.

By the end of the 19th century, cartoons were a popular feature in newspapers and magazines. Canada had a talented group of cartoonists, including J.W. Bengough, who launched his own satirical magazine, *Grip*, in 1873, and Henri Julien of the Montreal *Star*. Within a few years, however, newspapers, except for *La Presse* and *La Patrie* in Montreal, began to purchase their cartoons from features syndicates in the United States. Most Canadian cartoonists moved south in search of work, including Harold Foster, the creator of the adventure comic strip.

Comic books first became popular in the United States and Canada in the 1930s. It was a Canadian-born artist, Joe Shuster, who drew the first story about Superman, the most famous hero in comic-book history. In 1941 the supply of comics was cut off from the United States, and for the remainder of World War II there was a flourishing comic industry in Canada. While many adventure stories were based on American models, others featured such Canadian heroes as "Dixon of the Mounted" and "Nelvana of the Northern Lights." The favourite char-

acter of all was Leo Bachle's "Johnny Canuck," who single-handedly fought against Hitler and his generals. When the ban was lifted at the end of the war, Canadian publishers laid off their cartoon staff and simply printed American comics.

Around 1950, newspapers and magazines began once again to employ their own cartoonists. James Simpkin's "Jasper," a bear who lived in Jasper National Park but who shared many characteristics with a "typical" Canadian, appeared in *Maclean's* magazine (1948-69 and 1971-75). In 1950 Robert LaPalme joined *Le Devoir*, and his striking drawings of Ottawa and Quebec politicians were particularly hard-hitting; for example, he portrayed Premier Duplessis as a sleazy salesman trying to sell Quebec to the United States. Also in 1950, Len Norris joined the Vancouver *Sun*, and in 1958 Duncan Macpherson began work at the Toronto *Star*. Among younger political cartoonists, Terry Mosher ("Aislin") at the Montreal *Gazette*, Roy Peterson at the Vancouver *Sun*, and Jean-Pierre Girerd at *La Presse* all have their own individual style of drawing and a particular type of humour. They use caricature to exaggerate a person's physical features (such as Prime Minister Mulroney's large chin), and they use satire to ridicule the

Active Comics cover, February 1942 (courtesy NAC).

Johnny Canuck was a comic-book character who single-handedly fought against Adolf Hitler and the Nazis (courtesy NAC/C-99610).

Lynn Johnston

Lynn Johnston (*born in 1947*), who lives in Thunder Bay, Ont., is Canada's most widely syndicated cartoonist. Her strip "For Better or For Worse," based on the everyday activities of her own family, appears in more than 450 newspapers in 19 countries.

Duncan Macpherson

Duncan Macpherson (*born in 1924*) is Canada's best-known political cartoonist. He joined the Toronto *Star* in 1958 and made his mark for his biting and witty cartoons of Canada's prime ministers. He insisted on his right to be an independent commentator rather than a staff artist drawing illustrations for the editorial page. In the 1960s he experimented with cartooning for television. He did not have much success. The National Archives in Ottawa owns a large collection of his work (*untitled cartoon courtesy NAC/C-11273*).

powerful and privileged groups in society. They cover all aspects of contemporary life: Canadian and international politics, sports and entertainment, nuclear war, and unemployment. In their own way, they record a history of their times.

In recent years, three humorous Canadian cartoonists have enjoyed great international success. Jim Unger's "Herman" is known for his black humour. Ben Wicks's "The Outcasts" combines political comment with wit.

Lynn Johnston's "For Better or For Worse" is read daily by 50 million fans around the world. In addition, collections of cartoons published as books by cartoonists are extremely popular.

Although there was a small revival of Canadian comic books in the 1960s and 1970s, this branch of cartooning is still completely dominated by foreign imports. In Quebec, children's comic books such as *Capitaine Bonhomme* and *Bobino et Bobinette* have had some success. In English Canada, Dave Sim's "Cerebus the Aardvark" and Richard Comely's "Captain Canuck" are among the most interesting.

▷ SUGGESTED READINGS: *Portfoolio: The Year in Canadian Caricature* (1985, 1986, 1987, 1988, 1989); Peter Desbarats and T. Mosher, *The Hecklers* (1979); Maurice Horn, editor, *The World Encyclopedia of Comics*, 2 volumes (1976); D. Theaker, *An Introduction to Canadian Comic Books* (1986).

■ Cartwright, Sir Richard John

Politician (*born in 1835 at Kingston, Upper Canada [Ontario]; died there in 1912*). The Cartwrights were an old Loyalist family, and Richard had a successful business career before moving into politics in 1863. He started out as a Conservative, first in the Province of Canada and then, after Confederation, in the federal government. He broke with the Conservatives in 1869, when John A. Macdonald appointed Francis Hincks as finance minister. Cartwright had hoped that he would receive the appointment.

By 1873, Cartwright was in the councils of the Liberal Party and was the Liberals' financial expert. A strong believer in free trade, he claimed that tariffs were only justified by a government's need for revenue. A protective tariff, he said, was a tax on 95% of the population for the benefit of 5%. He served as finance minister in Alexander Mackenzie's Liberal government of 1873-78 and was a leading critic of Macdonald and the Conservative Party ever afterwards. Cartwright was so bitterly opposed to the Conservatives that the satirical magazine *Grip* pictured him as a knight on horseback, carrying a shield marked "Blue Ruin."

When Wilfrid Laurier came to power in 1896, Cartwright was appointed minister of trade and commerce, and so he remained until 1911. But he never had the power under Laurier that he had enjoyed with Mackenzie.

■ Casgrain, Thérèse

Reformer and leader of the Quebec suffrage movement (*born Thérèse Forget in 1896 at Montreal, Que.; died there in 1981*). For almost 20 years, Thérèse Casgrain fought to get Quebec women the right to vote in provincial elections. They did not gain this right until 1940, long after the other provinces had given women the vote.

After the vote was won, Madame Casgrain remained active in politics. As a longtime Liberal and wife of Liberal politician Pierre Casgrain, she came under heavy criticism in 1946 when she left the Liberals and joined the socialist Co-operative Commonwealth Federation (CCF). From 1951 to 1957 she was leader of the Quebec CCF, the first Canadian woman to be leader of a political party.

Both within the CCF and outside it, she worked to improve the lives of all people, not only women and not only Canadians. She campaigned for world peace, taking a strong stand against nuclear weapons. In 1960 she was a founding member of the League for Human Rights. In 1970 she was appointed to the Senate.

Thérèse Casgrain fought for 20 years to get women the vote in Quebec (courtesy NAC/C-68509).

Thérèse Casgrain's autobiography, *A Woman in a Man's World*, was published in 1972.

▷ RELATED ARTICLE: **Woman Suffrage.**

■ Casson, Alfred Joseph

Painter (*born in 1898 at Toronto, Ont.*). A. J. Casson was apprenticed to Franklin Carmichael, with whom he went sketching and camping. He joined the Group of Seven in 1926. He began painting small towns in Ontario, which remained his preferred subject. His painting is admired for its simplicity.

■ Castlegar

Castlegar, B.C., lies midway between Calgary and Vancouver on the west bank of the Columbia River, about 35 km north of the United States border. The area was first occupied by Interior Salish Indians.

The community began in the 1890s with the arrival of Irish and Scottish settlers. In 1908 it became a focus of Doukhobor settlement.

Castlegar's name comes from the Gaelic word for rock, "gar," combined with "castle" after the shape of a nearby rock formation. Always an important transportation centre, Castlegar's economy now relies on mining, the forest industry, and servicing the surrounding area. In 1986 the population was 6385. For further information, contact the City Clerk, 460 Columbia Avenue, Castlegar, B.C., V1N 1G7.

■ Castors

Castors were members of a faction in the Conservative Party in Quebec that emerged in 1882. They were strong nationalists who believed in a society dominated by the Catholic Church. They bitterly opposed some of their own party's policies. The name, French for "beavers," was a pen-name used by one of the group. Their influence had waned by the end of the century.

■ Cat

The name "cat" refers to members of the family of mammals called Felidae. The term is most often used for the domestic cat, but it also refers to large animals such as the lion. All cats, from the house cat to the tiger, are carnivorous (flesh eating). They have round heads, walk on their toes, and, except for the cheetah, have retractable claws. Cats move with fluid grace and occasional bursts of power. They have good night vision. They do not like water although they can swim. Most cats hunt alone, although the lion hunts in a group, called the "pride."

Domestic Cat Its origin is unknown, but it is one of the world's favourite pets. Most are mixed breeds, with long tails, straight ears, and short hair.

Pet cats are very popular in Canada. There are over 4 million, meaning that there is almost one for every two homes.

Lynx (courtesy Macmillan Illustrated Animal Encyclopedia).

Cougar, or mountain lion, is one of the three kinds of wild cat native to Canada (courtesy Macmillan Illustrated Animal Encyclopedia).

Wild Cats Three wild cats are native to Canada: the cougar (mountain lion), the lynx, and the bobcat.

▷ RELATED ARTICLES: **Bobcat, Cougar, Lynx.**

▷ SUGGESTED READING: Sheila Burnford, *The Incredible Journey* (1961); Laima Dingwall, *The Kid's Cat Book* (1984).

Catfish

There are seven freshwater species of catfish in Canada, which belong to the Ictaluridae family of fishes. The bodies of these fish do not have scales. They have barbels around the mouth which look like a cat's whiskers — hence their name, catfish. These barbels are covered with taste buds which enable them to find food. Catfish are very active at night. They eat aquatic insects, molluscs, crustaceans, other fish, and vegetation. They are scavengers and will eat chewing gum, soap, and cigarette butts.

Catfish are very attentive parents. After the eggs have been laid, the male and female of some species agitate them, which is necessary for them to hatch. After hatching, the young remain in a group for several weeks, under their parents' supervision. Once they are old enough to look after themselves, each fish goes its own way. In the United States, some species of this group are raised for food, but there is little interest in them as food in Canada.

There are three species of wolffish: Northern, Atlantic, and Spotted. They are all saltwater fish and are commonly called catfish.

Catherwood, Ethel

High jumper (*born in 1908 in North Dakota, U.S.; died in 1987 at Grass Valley, California, U.S.*). Catherwood was raised in Saskatoon and burst into the limelight in 1926 when, within a two-week period, she equalled the Canadian women's high-jumping record and then broke the world record. These jumps were at local meets in Saskatchewan, but soon Catherwood

Ethel Catherwood won a gold medal in the women's running high jump in the 1928 Olympic Games. She is the only Canadian woman to win an individual gold medal at the Olympics (courtesy Canada's Sports Hall of Fame).

was competing nationally. She was sponsored by the mining millionaire Teddy Oke, who gave her a job in Toronto and saw to her coaching.

She was in peak form for the 1928 Olympic Games in Amsterdam. There she sailed over the bar to win the gold medal for Canada in the women's running high jump. "The Saskatoon Lily" (as she was known) then gave up competitive jumping and withdrew from the public eye almost as quickly as she had emerged. In 1929 she moved to the United States, where she married. She is still the only Canadian woman ever to have won an individual gold medal in Olympics track and field.

Catholicism

Catholicism is the largest branch of Christianity worldwide, with over 900 million followers. About 50% of Canadians are baptised Catholics, though not all actively practise their religion. Catholics look to the leadership of the pope and the Church of Rome.

In the Catholic Church's belief, God the creator is father of all, and God the son (Jesus Christ) has a universal kingdom, which is the church. The Catholic Church recognizes seven religious acts, called sacraments: baptism, confirmation, communion, confession, ordination, marriage, and unction (performed on the seriously ill or dying). Catholics worship only God, but they also show deep reverence for those close to God, especially Mary, the mother of Jesus. They also respect holy places and objects, such as the cross.

The Catholic Church is divided into two major groups: the Roman Catholic and the Eastern Rite Catholic.

ROMAN CATHOLIC CHURCH

The Roman Catholic Church is governed by bishops, priests, and deacons, who are all under the authority of the pope, who is the bishop of Rome. All the clergy must be male.

History of the Church in Canada The Roman Catholic Church dates back to the 17th century in Canada. Samuel de Champlain encouraged the church in France to send clergy to the colony. The early priests, especially the Jesuits, were devoted to converting native people to Christianity. The Jesuits founded a mission among the Huron and raised money to build a college in Quebec. The church supported the colony and played an important role in politics. The Jesuits suf-

Notre Dame Church, *Montreal (photo by Malak, Ottawa).*

fered a setback in 1649 when their Huron mission was destroyed by the Iroquois and several priests were killed.

François de Laval, the first bishop of Quebec, arrived in 1659. He helped to organize the colony into parishes, which served the people of the countryside as well as those in the towns. The church was responsible for education and for care of the sick and needy.

After the Conquest of 1760, the Catholic Church had to deal with new British — and Protestant — rulers. This was difficult, because Catholics and Protestants were often mortal enemies in Europe. However, the terms of surrender guaranteed Catholics freedom of worship. The Quebec Act of 1774 further guaranteed Catholic rights and allowed Catholics to run for public office.
In the 19th century, Scottish and Irish Catholics came to Canada in large numbers, establishing Catholicism in English-speaking regions.

In Quebec, the clergy gained increasing influence in society after 1840. The church took care of the poor, the sick, and the orphaned. It controlled education, sent missionaries to western Canada and throughout the world, and continued to

influence politics. Meanwhile, it remained conservative in its views and was uneasy with change. Most Canadian Catholics actively practised their religion, regularly attending Mass (the main service of worship).

In the 1950s, change began to sweep through the Catholic Church. In Quebec, in particular, traditional religious values were questioned. Some groups within the church itself proposed modern solutions. During the Quiet Revolution of the 1960s, the state took over welfare, health, and education. At the same time, many Roman Catholics stopped practising the

Mary Crowned in Heaven, *on the dome of St Mary's Church in Yorkton, Sask. (photo by John deVisser).*

Ukrainian Catholic church in Hafford, Sask. (courtesy SSC Photocentre/photo by Gene Hattori).

faith, and fewer young men joined the priesthood.

Vatican II Catholicism worldwide underwent a whirlwind of change in the 1960s. From 1962 to 1965 church leaders met in Rome. The meetings, called Vatican II, brought forth many reforms to help the church adjust to the modern world. Forms of worship changed. For instance, priests now conduct Mass facing the people, and Mass is performed in the everyday language of the people instead of in Latin. The church has also leaned towards greater co-operation with other Christians.

In 1984, Pope John Paul II became the first pope to set foot in Canada. He was unable to visit Fort Simpson, N.W.T., because of fog, but he promised to go there on a later visit, and did so in 1987.

EASTERN RITE CATHOLIC CHURCHES

The Eastern Rite Catholic churches originated in eastern Europe. They grew apart from the church in Rome in disputes over leadership. Over the centuries the churches re-established the connection to Rome, but each kept many local traditions.

The largest Eastern Rite group in Canada was brought by Ukrainian immigrants in the 1890s and early 1900s. Canadian Ukrainian Catholics are organized under the Archbishop of Winnipeg and Metropolitan of All Canada. Priests are educated at the Seminary of the Holy Spirit in Ottawa and at the University of Ottawa.

Other Eastern Rite groups include Slovaks, Armenians, Melkites, and Maronites.

▷ RELATED ARTICLES: **Jesuits; Missionaries; Pilgrimage; Saints.**

■ Cattail

Cattails are perennial plants of the genus *Typha*, cattail family (Typhaceae). The name "typha" comes from the Greek *typhos*, meaning swamp or pond. The common cattail (*T. latifolia*) is found throughout the world. The narrow-leaved

Cattails *grow in damp places where they provide food and shelter to birds and mammals (artwork by Claire Tremblay).*

cattail (*T. angustifolia*) is native to Canada, and more rarely found. The two species grow in damp places where they form large colonies, thanks to the roots which gradually extend through the soil, giving rise to new above-ground stalks. These vertical stalks have very long and narrow leaves.

Each vertical stalk is crowned with a floral spike, consisting of two types of flowers: female ones at the base, male at the tip. The mature female spike is brown. It used to be dipped in a fuel and made into a torch for local festivals.

The fruit, covered in woolly hairs, was once used to stuff mattresses. Native people wove carpets and baskets with the leaves. The roots yield a sweet and nourishing flour. The white heart, at the base of the plant, is eaten like an artichoke heart.

The male spikes may be eaten green, like ears of corn. Cattails have an important role in the ecology. They hold muddy soils in place and build them up. They also offer food and shelter to various species of birds and mammals.

■ Caucus

A caucus is a meeting of all the elected members of one political party at either the federal or provincial level. A federal caucus may also contain senators. Caucus meetings are held regularly and they serve four purposes. One, they help the party leader and other important party members to explain party policy to their followers. Two, they allow all elected members of a party to state their opinions and ask questions. Three, they make it possible for party leaders to learn about the ideas and concerns of their followers and thus keep their parties united. Four, they provide an opportunity to plan party strategy, especially for parties in opposition who intend to fight a particular government proposal.

Caucus meetings are held in private and all discussions are supposed to be confidential. Only the party leader or another official spokesperson is supposed to comment on them publicly. Despite this, from time to time reports leak out and the media are always looking for information. Occasionally, a caucus can turn against its leader and a "caucus revolt" can occur. If a party member repeatedly refuses to accept caucus decisions, he or she can be expelled from the caucus (or can resign), and thus becomes an "independent."

▷ RELATED ARTICLES: **Government; Parliament.**

Cave

A cave is a natural cavity beneath the surface of the earth. Most caves are formed when water dissolves soluble rock, mainly limestone, underground. This process begins when water from the surface trickles down into the ground through tiny cracks. Over thousands of years, the water dissolves the limestone, forming caverns and passageways. The more acidic the water, the faster the rock will dissolve. Many caves have underground lakes, rivers, and waterfalls. Some caves are only a few metres deep; others are vast. The longest known cave is the Mammoth Cave-Flint Ridge System, in Kentucky, U.S.; it is over 500 km long. Some caves are as deep as 1.6 km.

Caves may also be formed by lava from an active volcano. As the lava flows, its surface hardens. The lava beneath this surface continues to flow and eventually drains out, leaving a cave. Other caves are formed by sea waves.

The longest known cave in Canada is Castleguard Cave in Banff National Park. It has 20 km of passages and extends far beneath the Columbia Icefield. Canada's deepest cave is Arctomys Cave, near Mount Robson, in the Rocky Mountains; it is 522 m deep.

Despite their danger, dampness, and darkness, caves are fascinating for their strange beauty. Perhaps the most spectacular features are the cones formed of calcite from dripping water: the icicle-like *stalactites* hanging from the ceiling, and the cone-like *stalagmites* forming on the floor. Few animals live in the darkest, innermost part of caves. Some are blind and have colourless skin, such as the small cave shrimp. Some caves are home to millions of bats.

Those who study caves are called *speleologists*, and those who explore them for fun are called *spelunkers*, or "cavers."

Cavers deep in the Castleguard Cave — the longest in Canada (photo by Derek Ford).

Ice Cave, in a glacier, Kluane National Park, Yukon (photo by J.A. Kraulis).

Cavendish

Cavendish, P.E.I., is situated on the north shore of the island, 38 km from Charlottetown. It was founded by Scottish immigrants in 1790 as a farming community. Today, it serves thousands of summer tourists, who flock to the beaches of nearby P.E.I. National Park. Lucy Maud Montgomery wrote *Anne of Green Gables* here and is buried in Cavendish cemetery. In 1986 the population was 94. For information, contact the Cavendish Area Tourist Association, P.O. Box 10, Cavendish, P.E.I., C0A 1N0.

Cedar

Cedars are conifers of the genus *Thuja*, belonging to the cypress family (Cupressaceae). They are also called *arbor vitae* ("tree of life"). They got this name from a traditional native drink made of the bark and leaves of the eastern white cedar (*T. occidentalis*); it cures scurvy and thus saved the lives of Jacques Cartier's men during their first Canadian winter in 1535. Two of the six cedar species are found in Canada: the white cedar around the Great Lakes and St Lawrence River, and the western red cedar (*T. plicata*), found on the Pacific coast and on the western slope of the Rocky Mountains. The western red cedar is a big tree that can reach 60 m in height and 3 m diameter (the eastern white cedar reaches 20 m at most).

The modified leaves (bracts) of the

Cedar *The Eastern White Cedar grows around the Great Lakes area of Canada. Because cedar wood is resistant to rot, it is used for posts, boats, shingles, etc. (artwork by Claire Tremblay).*

cedar are soft, unlike those of the juniper, which look very similar but are prickly. Cedars like neutral or alkaline soils. They are also found in acidic soils, provided these soils are also very wet (in bogs and swamps, for example). Since the wood is rot-resistant, it is used to make posts, boats, greenhouses, doors, frames, and shingles. The western red cedar played a very important role in the lives of the native people of British Columbia, who used it to build houses, huge canoes capable of carrying 50 people, and their famous totem poles.

■ CEGEP (Collège d'enseignement général et professionnel)

CEGEPs exist only in Quebec. Students who wish to continue their education in Quebec after high school must do so at a CEGEP. If they want to go to university, they take a two-year pre-university program at a CEGEP. Unlike community colleges in English Canada, the CEGEPs are pre-university. Credits cannot be transferred from a CEGEP to a university.

If students wish to qualify for a skilled trade, they take a three-year CEGEP program leading to a diploma. The first CEGEP opened in 1967 and there are now over 40 of them in Quebec, with about 140 000 students. They are intended to make post-secondary education more widely available for all students, regardless of location or background. They are also intended to meet the needs of the Quebec economy and to provide well-trained students for the universities.

■ Censorship

Censorship is the control over what can be printed, published, broadcast, or shown in a movie theatre. It may also apply to public speeches and to what may be shown in an art gallery. Censorship is frequently challenged because it denies basic democratic rights, such as freedom of the press and freedom of expression. Its defenders claim that it is necessary to maintain order and standards of morality. They claim that some materials are harmful, particularly to young people. Censorship has been used from very early times. For example, in ancient Athens, authorities condemned the philosopher Socrates for corrupting the morals of the young.

Censorship can be carried out in many ways. It can be carried out by intimidation and harassment. In the 1830s, a group of people did not like what William Lyon Mackenzie was writing about them in his newspaper. They broke into his office and threw his printing press into Toronto Harbour. Censorship of films is carried out by boards in the provinces, which declare what film may be shown. They also decide which films can be shown to which age group by classifying them. Censorship may be enforced by police action. It may be enforced by licensing, for example, the right to distribute handbills or flyers. It can be exercised by advertisers and decisions of the newspapers themselves. An owner of a publication may strongly influence what the editors print.

Obscenity In many countries, especially dictatorships, the main object of censorship is political comment. In Canada, the main object is sexual content. Under the Criminal Code of Canada, it is an offence to mail "obscene, indecent, immoral, or scurrilous" matter.

Obscenity is defined as that which is offensive to accepted standards. "Accepted" roughly means acceptable to an average person in the community. Whether the work has literary, artistic, political, or scientific value also plays a part. The Canadian Criminal Code reads: "For the purposes of this Act, any publication a dominant characteristic of which is the undue exploitation of sex, or of sex and any one or more of the following subjects: namely, crime, horror, cruelty, and violence, shall be deemed to be obscene." The courts decided what is "undue."

Wartime The strictest censorship in Canada has occurred in time of war. Government censors searched letters and newspapers for information that might aid the enemy. They also looked for political comments that they believed might somehow undermine the war effort.

Census

The word "census" comes from the Latin word *censere*, meaning "to assess." The first recorded census took place over 4000 years ago in China. The Chinese emperors used their surveys to set taxes and register young men for military service.

History When Jean Talon came to New France in 1666, he supervised the first census in Canada. He collected much of the information himself, visiting door to door. His census counted 3215 persons in New France. Thirty-five more censuses were conducted under French rule, as well as several in Acadia. Some of these censuses included crops, livestock, buildings, churches, mills, and even swords and guns.

A general census of Canada was taken in 1848. In 1851 a new Act required that a census be taken in 1852, 1861, and every ten years thereafter. In 1881 all census takers were required to take an Oath of Secrecy — an oath still required today. By the 1950s a mid-decade census was added to make information available more frequently. The census of 1986 was the fourth such mid-decade census.

Census Questions vary over time. Some questions have occurred on every census since 1941, for example, Is the dwelling you live in owned or rented? A question about wartime service was only asked in 1951, 1961, and 1971. A question about disability was asked for the first time in 1986.

In 1986, two different questionnaires were used. The short questionnaire was used in four-fifths of all households. It contained nine questions:
1. Name
2. Relationship to person 1
3. Date of birth
4. Sex
5. Marital status
6. Mother tongue
7. Aboriginal status
8. Person responsible for household payments
9. Dwelling owned or rented.

The longer questionnaires added 23 more questions, including place of birth, ethnic origin, years of schooling, place of work, and income.

Several questions, such as religion, date of first marriage, and number of bathrooms were asked in 1981 but not in 1986.

Taking a Census The process of taking a census of over 25 million people over a country as huge as Canada is complicated and expensive. First Statistics Canada consults governments, businesses, researchers, and others to see what questions should be included. Because a census aims to count every person within a certain area, it must be done with the aid of detailed maps. In Canada, over 40 000 maps were required for the census of 1986. The questionnaires were prepared and dropped off at each household before census day. They were completed and mailed back or picked up. The data were entered on computer, sorted, and published.

Accuracy A census can be inaccurate for several reasons. A census taker may miss a household. People may misunderstand the questions or refuse to answer. There may be errors when the data are entered on computer. Nevertheless, census information is the most detailed information available about a nation. It not only reveals patterns of growth or decline, but adds to our knowledge of economic and social conditions, variations among regions, and trends into the future.

▷ RELATED ARTICLES: **Demography; Population.**

▷ SUGGESTED READING: Statistics Canada, *Census Handbook* (1986).

Centennial Year

Centennial Year, 1967, was Canada's 100th anniversary of Confederation. Celebrations began at midnight on December 31, 1966, on Parliament Hill in Ottawa, when Prime Minister Lester Pearson lit the Centennial Flame. The flame is still alight today.

Every community in Canada was encouraged to mark the anniversary by doing something special. Many new buildings were constructed, including art galleries, libraries, theatres, and sports complexes.

The Centennial Train and Caravans crossed the country. These miniature museums of Canadian history and culture were visited by more than 10 million people. In the Voyageur Pageant, 12 canoes traced the old fur-trading route from Alberta to Montreal, where Expo 67 (a world fair) was being held. Expo was Canada's most spectacular Centennial event.

Festival Canada sponsored plays, musicals, operas, and ballets. The biggest

Census Facts, 1986
- 30% of Canada's population now lives in its 3 biggest cities: Toronto, Montreal, and Vancouver
- 1 in 4 elderly persons live alone

Census Question 6 (1986) Mother Tongue

6. What is the language you **first learned** in childhood and **still** understand?
☐ English
☐ French
☐ Italian
☐ German
☐ Ukrainian
☐ Other (*specify*)

sporting event was the Pan-American Games in Winnipeg. Residents of major cities saw the Centennial Tattoo, a celebration of 300 years of military history. There were also bathtub races, parades, and period costume parties. The year's biggest firework display took place in Ottawa on July 1.

Canada's birthday presents included a large engraved crystal ring from the United States, and 10 000 books and a Henry Moore sculpture from Great Britain.

■ Centipede

Contrary to what one might think, centipedes are not insects. They belong to a class of their own, called Chilopoda. Centipede means "100 feet." They are elongated creatures with at least 15 pairs of legs (and up to 179), one pair on each segment of the body. The rear segments may have more pairs. In comparison, millipedes (class Diplopoda) generally have two pairs per segment. Centipedes have flattened bodies, and their antennae are a little longer than their legs. Their colour varies from yellow to deep brown. Few are more than 3 cm long, but some Canadian species reach 8 cm.

There are about 70 species of centipede in Canada, including a dozen introduced from Europe. They have a pair of poisonous claws under the head, used to paralyse the little insects they hunt beneath stones and the bark of dead trees. Active by night, they prefer cool, moist areas, and quickly flee from light. In Canada, only one species can inflict painful bites (which, however, are not dangerous).

■ Ceramics

Ceramics come in two main types: earthenware (pottery) and porcelain. Both are made from clay mixtures. The clay is shaped into a pot, jar, plate, or some other object. A turntable ("wheel") is often used so that the piece is not lopsided. To set the object's shape, it is cooked at very high heat ("fired") in an oven ("kiln"). It is often coated ("glazed") with a waterproofing mixture. After glazing, it is fired a second time, at lower heat.

Earthenware is easily made from local clay. It was produced in Canada for hundreds of years by the native peoples. European settlers made their first Canadian pottery in the mid-1600s.

Pottery makes good containers because it is cheap, easy to make, sturdy, and attractive. However, the early clay mixtures and kiln temperatures were not scientifically controlled. As a result, much of the pottery was ruined.

Stoneware is a kind of earthenware made from very sandy clay. The first Canadian stoneware was made in the 1840s. Because stoneware is strong and naturally waterproof, it was popular for food preparation and storage — especially pickling and salting.

Early pottery had a distinct regional "look." Quebec earthenware was usually brown. Maritime earthenware was dark red. Upper Canada pottery had the most variety because it was made by so many different immigrant groups. Potteries flourished in this region because it was difficult to transport European ceramics.

After the British Conquest (1760), British earthenware was used widely in Canada, from Quebec farmhouses to governors' residences. Later, British bone china, a form of porcelain, became popular as the desire for fine quality replaced the need for sturdiness.

Several things contributed to the decline of Canadian ceramic production in the 1880s. Tableware was dominated by British and American products. Cheap glass containers were available for home canning, and more food preservation was being done in factories. By 1910, most potteries had closed.

Since the 1950s, the craft of ceramics has again become popular — both for traditional tableware and for experimental sculpture.

Governor General's Dinner Service (courtesy Government House/photo by Ray Kolly).

■ Chaleur Bay

Chaleur Bay (or Baie des Chaleurs) is situated between Quebec's Gaspé Peninsula and northern New Brunswick. It is the largest bay in the Gulf of St Lawrence. The Restigouche River drains into the western end. The bay is rich in nutrients,

Centipedes are not insects. They have a pair of poisonous claws under the head, which they use to paralyse the insects they hunt (artwork by Jan Sovak).

and supports important salmon, scallop, and clam fisheries. Jacques Cartier explored the bay in 1534 and traded with the native people there, who were probably Micmac. He named it *chaleur* (French for "warm" or "hot") for its mild climate. It is now a popular vacation spot.

■ Chalk River

Chalk River, Ont., is a village close to the Ottawa River, 210 km northwest of Ottawa. It was originally a stopping point on the Canadian Pacific Railway. In 1944, it became the site of the first nuclear reactor built outside the United States. There is now a complex of five reactors at the Chalk River Nuclear Laboratories. Residents now work at the nuclear plant, at the federal forestry reserve station, or at the Canadian Forces base at Petawawa. In 1986 the population was 923. For information, contact the Village Clerk, 15 Main Street, P.O. Box 59, Chalk River, Ont., K0J 1J0.

■ Champagne, Claude

Composer, educator (*born in 1891 at Montreal, Que.; died there in 1965*). Champagne was the most influential Quebec composer and music educator in the first half of the 20th century. His Irish mother taught him hymns. Local musicians gave him a sound, practical education in Montreal's own traditions. Alfred Laliberté admired Champagne's youthful compositions and arranged a scholarship for him to study at the Paris Conservatoire. After eight years there, Champagne returned to Montreal, a sophisticated musician in the French manner. In the 1930s he worked to reorganize Quebec's music education systems.

Champagne taught at McGill University and trained music teachers for the Catholic School Commission. His advice and help to young composers became his most important legacy. Violet Archer, Serge Garant, Roger Matton, Pierre Mercure, François Morel, Clermont Pepin, Gilles Tremblay, and Robert Turner are only a few of the best-known Canadian composers who learned from Claude Champagne.

Champagne composed elegantly in all forms. His most often-performed short work is the vigorous *Danse villageoise*. His best-known major work is the *Symphonie gaspésienne*.

■ Champlain, Samuel de

Explorer, mapmaker, founder of New France (*born around 1567 at Brouage, France; died in 1635 at Quebec*). Champlain's father was a sea captain and young Samuel was raised in a seaport on the west coast of France. He was a soldier in the king's service before he sailed to Spain, the West Indies, and Mexico in 1598. Champlain wrote and illustrated a book about his voyage, which was read and enjoyed by the king. In 1603 he joined a trading expedition to the St Lawrence River. It was the first of ten Atlantic crossings that he was destined to make to the "Great River of Canada."

Acadian Adventures The following year, 1604, Champlain sailed to the Bay of Fundy region. He was under the command of Pierre Du Gua de Monts, who had been granted a trading monopoly in the region. They spent their first winter on Sainte-Croix Island, five kilometres from the mouth of the St Croix River (in present-day Maine). It was an ill-chosen spot. Thirty-five of the 79 men died of scurvy. The post was moved across the bay to Port-Royal, where the men spent the next two winters (1605 and 1606). During these three years, Champlain explored the coasts of present-day New Brunswick and New England, making charts and recording his observations. In 1607 de Monts abandoned Port-Royal and Champlain returned to France.

The Founding of Quebec In 1608 de Monts placed Champlain in charge of an expedition to the St Lawrence River. Champlain's men erected a *habitation* at Quebec. He resumed the alliance he had made with the local Montagnais and Algonquin peoples in 1603. It was a pact of trade and mutual defence. To cement the arrangement, Champlain agreed to aid his new allies in their wars with the Iroquois.

Champlain's Native Allies and Enemies In 1609 Champlain took part in a battle near Lake Champlain. He killed two Iroquois chiefs and injured a third

Champlain's Astrolabe (courtesy The New York Historical Society).

with a single blast of his musket. The Iroquois, who had not seen such firepower before, fled in terror.

In 1615 Champlain travelled by canoe to Georgian Bay to strengthen the French alliance with the Huron. He joined another war party, travelling via Lakes Simcoe and Ontario to an Iroquois stronghold near present-day Syracuse, New York. The Iroquois were better prepared this time. Champlain was wounded and returned reluctantly to Huronia for the winter.

The Struggling Colony Champlain's task seemed hopeless at times. He faced mutiny by his own men, quarrels among the French traders, and problems with his native allies. By 1626, the entire population of New France numbered only about 60 souls. In 1629 he was betrayed by some of his own men, who led a group of English privateers up the river to Quebec. Champlain surrendered and was taken prisoner. He was taken to England, where he was released.

When Champlain returned to Quebec in 1633, the *habitation* was in ruins. He died only two years later, on Christmas Day. It is not known where he is buried.

Accomplishments Champlain's establishment of Quebec in 1608 was the true beginning of New France, and thus of European settlement in Canada. He tirelessly promoted the colony through his books, maps, and drawings. Today, his works are valuable records of native life. His vision of a French civilization in North America was later realized in New France and, ultimately, in the Province of Quebec.

▷ Related Articles: **New France; Order of Good Cheer; Port-Royal; Quebec.**

▷ Suggested Reading: J.C.W. Armstrong, *Champlain* (1988); Christopher Moore, *Samuel de Champlain* (1986).

■ Champlain Sea

The Champlain Sea formed in the St Lawrence Valley about 12 800 years ago. As the ice from the glaciers melted, sea levels rose, and the water surged into the valley. It lasted about 2000 years.

■ Channel-Port aux Basques

Channel-Port aux Basques, Nfld, on the southwest corner of the island, is the first community many visitors to the province see. It is the terminus for a ferry crossing to Nova Scotia and is the beginning of the Trans-Canada Highway across Newfoundland. Originally, the town was a collection of small fishing villages. Later, it became a railway centre with the build-

ing of the Newfoundland Railway in the 1890s. It is also a local business and government centre. In 1986 the population was 5901. For information, contact the Town Clerk, P.O. Box 70, Channel-Port aux Basques, Nfld, A0M 1C0.

■ Chant, Clarence Augustus

Professor of astrophysics (*born in 1865 at Hagerman's Corners, Canada West [Ontario]; died in 1956 at Richmond Hill, Ont.*). Chant has been called "the father of Canadian astronomy" because he trained so many of Canada's astronomers. He organized the department of astronomy at the University of Toronto, where he taught from 1891 to 1935. He built up the Royal Astronomical Society of Canada into one of the world's most successful organizations of its kind.

Chant took part in five expeditions to observe eclipses of the Sun, including the important expedition he led to Australia in 1922. In 1935, largely through his efforts, the magnificent David Dunlap Observatory was opened near Toronto. Its 1.88 metre optical telescope is still the largest in Canada. Chant devoted his life to promoting astronomy and wrote numerous articles and books on the subject, including his popular *Our Wonderful Universe* (1928). In 1987 Minor Planet No. 3314 was named after him.

■ Chant, Donald Alfred

Environmentalist (*born in 1928 at Toronto, Ont.*). Professor of zoology at the University of Toronto since 1967, Donald Chant has long been a spokesman on environmental issues. He has alerted the public to the dangers of pollution and pesticides, among other matters. Since his student years at the University of British Columbia, he has been involved in research on pest control by non-chemical methods (for instance, by controlling insect pests with predators that feed on them). He has also been active in environmental organizations, and in 1980 he became first chairman and president of the Ontario Waste Management Corporation. This organization looks for ways of treating harmful waste materials that are produced by industries during the manufacturing process. Chant's writings include *Pollution Probe* (1970) and *This Good Good Earth* (1971).

■ Chapais, Sir Thomas

Historian (*born in 1858 at St-Denis-de-Kamouraska, Canada East [Quebec]; died there in 1946*). Chapais trained as a lawyer, turned to journalism, and worked

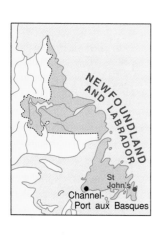

as a newspaper editor for several years. In 1892 he began a long career in public life when he was appointed to Quebec's Legislative Council. He was a member of three provincial cabinets, and in 1919 he was appointed to the federal Senate.

Chapais is best known as a historian. He wrote several works, including an eight-volume history of Canada, 1760 to 1867, and a study of Jean Talon, Intendant of New France. His histories earned him a knighthood in 1935.

■ Chapman, John Herbert

Space scientist (born in 1921 at London, Ont.; died in 1979 at Vancouver, B.C.). Chapman was the father of Canada's space program. Both as a scientist and administrator, he was the driving force that first put Canadian satellites in space and made Canada a leader in the Space Age.

Chapman was a senior scientist in Ottawa when the Soviets launched their satellite, *Sputnik I*, in 1957. He was soon deeply involved in a Canadian program to design and build satellites. He had his first great success in 1962 with the launching of Canadian-made *Alouette I*. Further satellites followed.

In 1967 Chapman headed a government task force on space policies which recommended using satellites to improve communications within Canada. This led to the formation of the organization known as Telesat Canada. From 1968 on, Chapman worked in the Department of Communications, and he was made deputy minister in 1974. At the time of his death, he was working on a project that would provide Canadians in remote areas with

John Chapman was the founder of Canada's space program (courtesy Department of Communications).

direct-to-home television by satellite.

▷ RELATED ARTICLE: **Satellite.**

■ Char

Char are fish belonging to the family Salmonidae. There are five species in Canada. All have a small fin in front of the tail, which is called *adipose* because it consists entirely of fatty tissue. Char can be distinguished from trout and salmon by the pale or variously coloured spots on their dark backs. They love cold, well-oxygenated water, and can be found in both fresh and salt water. All, however, reproduce in fresh water. Those who live in the sea must go upstream in fresh water to spawn. Char can be found throughout Canada: Arctic char (*Salvelinus alpinus*) in the north; Dolly Varden (*Salvelinus malma*) and Bull trout (*Salvelinus confluentus*), in the west; Brook or speckled trout (*Salvelinus fontinalis*) in the east; and finally the Lake trout (*Salvelinus namaycush*), the largest of the group, everywhere in the country. The succulent flesh and fighting spirit of all these species are prized by sport fishermen. Char have been the object of intensive pisciculture (fish raising) activity. They are used to restock water for sportfishing. The Splake, or wendigo, is created by crossing a Lake trout with a Brook trout. It is found primarily in the Great Lakes.

Char belong to the salmon family. The Arctic char, shown here, are found in the North. All char are prized by sport fishermen (artwork by Karen Klitz).

■ Charlebois, Robert

Singer (born in 1945 at Montreal, Que.). Charlebois took Quebec by storm in the 1960s with his multi-media shows and controversial hard rock music. He was the first Quebec rock singer to sing in *joual*, Quebec slang. This helped audiences identify with him and his songs. In 1969 he was awarded Le Trophée Felix Leclerc for his classic song "Lindberg." Charlebois slowly moved away from his hard-rock roots in the early 1970s to a more popular and sometimes humorous approach.

Charlebois studied at the National Theatre School in Montreal (1962-65) and also dabbled in the world of films in the 1970s. His numerous acting roles included the 1976 hit film *Un génie, deux associés, une cloche* by Sergio Leone. Musically, Charlebois continues to produce records that sell well in Quebec.

■ Charlottetown

Charlottetown is the capital and only city of Prince Edward Island. It is situated in the centre of the province, on the south shore. The city overlooks a fine natural harbour formed by the meeting of three rivers. Since it was founded in 1768, it has been a government centre, a busy port, and a market centre for the surrounding countryside.

Beginnings Charlottetown dates back to 1720 when a group of 300 French colonists built a small fortified post named Port La Joie across the harbour from the present city. When the British took control of the island in 1758, they deported most of the French settlers. At Port La Joie, they built defences and renamed the site Fort Amherst. Today, the fort is a national historic park.

After a few years the British decided to lay out a new townsite across the harbour from the fort. They called it Charlottetown, after Queen Charlotte, the wife of their king, George III. When the island became a separate colony the next year, in 1769, the new town was named the capital. It was located just across Northumberland Strait from Nova Scotia, and the three rivers made it easy for travellers to venture across the island.

A Growing Capital The area around Charlottetown was rich farmland, and the town grew slowly as a market centre. In the 1800s, several small factories ap-

Confederation Centre, Charlottetown, P.E.I. houses the Charlottetown Festival every year (photo by Malak, Ottawa).

peared, but the most important business was shipbuilding and sea-going trade out of the harbour.

In 1864 political delegates from the Maritime colonies and the Province of Canada met at Charlottetown to discuss union. The conference led to Confederation in 1867, although Prince Edward Island did not join Canada until 1873. By that time, the busy port was the eleventh-largest city in Canada.

By 1900, the age of the wooden sailing ship was over. However, Charlottetown's economy did not suffer. People found jobs in the harbour and in the factories. The city continued to serve the needs of the surrounding farmers, and since the 1930s tourism has been important.

Today, Charlottetown is a modern city which has preserved much of its old charm. The harbour front is a restored "Old Charlotte Town," with numerous shops. There are several historic churches, such as St Dunstan's Basilica. The city has two imposing historic sites: Province House, where the delegates met in 1864, and City Hall, built in 1888. The Confederation Centre of the Arts is a fine art gallery and from spring to fall houses the Charlottetown Festival. The festival is a showcase of musical theatre that includes the popular *Anne of Green Gables*.

The city still houses the provincial legislature and is home to the University of Prince Edward Island. Charlottetown today is the 48th-largest urban area in Canada, with a population of 53 868 (1986c). Because it is the capital and the largest city in Prince Edward Island, and because of its role as "the Cradle of Confederation," it has an importance which outweighs its small size. For information, contact the City Administrator, P.O. Box 98, Charlottetown, P.E.I., C1A 7K2.

Fathers of Confederation photographed at the Charlottetown Conference in September 1864. Sir John A. Macdonald (sitting) and Georges Etienne Cartier (holding the hat) are in the foreground (courtesy NAC/PA-90161).

Charlottetown Conference

The Charlottetown Conference was held in Province House, Charlottetown, P.E.I., between September 1 and 9, 1864. It was the first of the three conferences at which the plan for Confederation was set in motion. At first, the purpose of the meeting was to discuss a union of the Maritime colonies. The Maritimers were startled when the Canadians asked to attend.

Discussions of a Maritime union were quickly dropped as the Canadians proposed a scheme for a union of all the colonies. Twenty-three delegates from the Province of Canada, New Brunswick, Nova Scotia, and Prince Edward Island attended. The conference ended with an agreement to meet again in October at Quebec City. *See* photograph on previous page.

▷ Related Articles: **Confederation; Quebec Conference.**

Chasse Galerie

Chasse Galerie is the name of a French-Canadian legend. In most variations of the legend, lumbermen and voyageurs make a deal with the devil. They want a flying canoe to carry them home for a quick visit to their sweethearts, usually on New Year's Eve. In return, they promise not to say a holy word during the ride or the canoe will crash and the devil will take their souls. Usually, the flying canoe has several close encounters with church steeples and other forbidden objects. But in the end the men outwit the devil.

Château Clique

Château Clique was the nickname for the small group of men who held most of the power in Lower Canada until the 1830s. They were friends and acquaintances of the governor. They received appointments from him to the Legislative and Executive councils and to other important positions, such as judges.

Most of the Château Clique were English-speaking businessmen. They tended to favour policies that helped their own business interests rather than being concerned about the problems of the French-speaking majority. The nickname came from the governor's residence, the Château Saint-Louis at Quebec.

▷ Related Articles: **Family Compact; Lower Canada.**

Chateauguay, Battle of,

The Battle of Chateauguay, October 26, 1813, took place during the War of 1812. An American army of 4000 men was advancing on Montreal. A much smaller British force, led by Charles de Salaberry, encountered the Americans at the Chateauguay River in Lower Canada. Most of the Canadians were French-speaking Voltigeurs. The defenders blew horns in the woods to fool the Americans into thinking that they were far more numerous. The Americans were discouraged by this show of resistance and retreated after only two hours of fighting. The battle had an important effect on morale in Canada. It was the first battle in which the British forces were mainly made up of Canadians. It also showed convincingly that the French Canadians would remain loyal to the British.

▷ Related Articles: **Charles de Salaberry; Voltigeurs; War of 1812.**

Chatham

Chatham, N.B., lies near the mouth of the Miramichi River on the east coast of the province. It was founded about 1800 and for many years was dominated by Joseph Cunard of the famous shipping family. The forest industry has always been the mainstay of the local economy. In 1986 Chatham's population was 6219. For information, contact the Town Clerk, P.O. Box 309, Chatham, N.B., E1N 3A7.

Chatham

Chatham, Ont., lies on the Thames River, within easy reach of Lake St Clair. The site was chosen as a naval base by Governor Simcoe in 1793 and construction began the following year. It grew into an important shipbuilding, industrial, and agricultural centre in the 1800s.

Before the American Civil War, Chatham was the northern terminus for the "Underground Railroad" which served as a means of assisting slaves to escape from the United States. Descendants of these people still belong to the local population. Chatham continued to grow over the years and today has a number of food-processing companies, and automobile and plastics industries. In 1986 the population was 42 211. For further information, contact the City Clerk, 315 King Street W., P.O. Box 640, Chatham, Ont., N7M 5K8.

Chaudière River

The Chaudière River (or Rivière Chaudière in French) empties into the St Lawrence River opposite Quebec City. It is 193 km long. In 1775 American troops used the river on their way to attack Quebec. Its fertile floodplain, called Les Beaucerons, is used for farming.

■ Chautauqua

Chautauqua was a travelling variety show that was popular across Canada in the 1920s. The shows lasted several days. The program consisted of musical shows, lectures, plays, magicians, and puppets. The shows took place in huge brown tents which were carried along with the performers from town to town.

The tradition began at Chautauqua Lake, New York, and spread to Ontario in the late 19th century. Others appeared in the Maritimes in the 1920s. The largest show was brought to Alberta from the United States by John M. Erickson in 1917. It operated across Canada until 1935.

■ Chemical Engineering, *see* Engineering

■ Chemical Industry

Chemical industries turn materials found in nature, such as oil, natural gas, salt, and sulphide ores, into chemicals, such as ethylene, ammonia, chlorine, and sulphur dioxide.

Almost every manufacturing plant or mill in Canada uses one or more chemicals. To make paper white, for instance, pulp and paper mills use large quantities of chlorine or hydrogen peroxide. Plastic plants string ethylene into giant molecules of polyethylene, the material from which garbage bags are made.

Hundreds of thousands of chemicals are produced and used in Canada, and hundreds of new chemicals are introduced each year.

Directly or indirectly, the chemical industry produces hundreds of familiar things — adhesives, aspirin and other drugs; chloride, cosmetics, detergent, dyes, fertilizers, herbicides; man-made material such as nylon, polyvinyl, and polyester; paint, pesticides, polish, soap, tires, and wax, to name but a few of them.

Products The chemical industry produces three main kinds of products: petrochemicals (also known as organic chemicals); inorganic chemicals; and fine (or specialty) chemicals. It produces very large quantities of the first two kinds of chemicals, and relatively small quantities of the third kind.

The petrochemical industry produces complex organic chemicals such as ethylene from oil and natural gas. In turn, other manufacturing industries turn these chemicals into a host of familiar products, from antifreeze to nylon zippers. About 6% of the oil and gas consumed in Canada is turned into petrochemicals.

Most inorganic chemicals come from minerals found in the Earth, such as salt and potash. From salt (a compound of sodium and chlorine), electric currents can extract chlorine, a widely used industrial chemical. It is needed to bleach paper, for instance, and to purify the water in swimming pools. Canada is a major producer of fertilizer from potash. Canadian companies produce more than 50 inorganic chemicals. These are used by virtually all manufacturing industries.

Fine and specialty chemicals are made from a variety of raw materials, including oil and gas, animal fats, and vegetable oils. They are used in making cosmetics, foods, paints, detergents, polishes, adhesives, and more. Examples of fine chemicals made in Canada include rosin, which comes from pine trees and makes writing paper water resistant, and medicinal chemicals such as vitamins, hormones, and antibiotics.

THE MODERN INDUSTRY

The chemical industry is complex and diverse. It consists of both large and small companies, some Canadian, some foreign owned. A handful of large multinational companies, such as Dow Chemical Canada Incorporated, and Union Carbide Canada Limited, each produce a wide variety of products.

In its more than 1300 chemical plants, most of which are in Ontario, Quebec, or Alberta, the industry uses a small range of raw materials in a wide variety of ways. In 1986, the Canadian chemical industry sold more than $18.6 billion worth of chemicals, many to other countries, mainly to the United States.

Measuring size by sales, the chemical industry is one of the largest manufacturing industries in Canada, comparable in size to petroleum refining, pulp and paper, motor vehicles, and iron and steel. In 1986, some 87 600 people worked directly producing chemicals.

▷ RELATED ARTICLES: **Chemistry; Drug Industry; Fertilizer; Petrochemical Industry.**

■ Chemistry

Chemical changes occur naturally on Earth and make life possible. An example of a simple chemical change is the combination of iron and oxygen, which forms rust. Others occur as we burn gas or digest food. Chemistry is concerned with the structure and properties of matter and with the change of one form of matter into another. Matter is anything that has size and weight. Chemists measure how matter behaves under different conditions in order to understand natural processes. This is the basis of the production of many of the things that are essential to daily living; for example, food, drugs, clothing, and electricity.

The chemical industries use raw materials such as salt, oil, coal, and crops to make almost all the things we consume, including food, paper, paints, detergents, fertilizers, plastics, and cosmetics.

There are some 11 000 chemists in Canada employed in education, industry, and government. This includes chemical engineers and chemical technologists. Working at McGill University in Montreal at the beginning of this century, Ernest Rutherford discovered the nuclear structure of atoms. For this he won the Nobel Prize for Chemistry in 1908.

BASIC IDEAS OF CHEMISTRY

Atoms are the building blocks of the universe. Scientists have found that all matter consists of only 92 different kinds of atoms. These are the natural chemical elements. Everything we know, living or non-living, including ourselves, the planets, comets, and stars are made from them. Each element has been given a name and a one- or two-letter symbol, for example, O for oxygen and He for helium. The 92 elements fit into the Periodic Table. Elements 93 to 109 were artificially created by chemists and do not occur in nature.

Electrons bind atoms together to form *molecules*. Some molecules are made up of atoms of a single element. For example, oxygen is made up of two oxygen atoms. Its formula is therefore O_2, where the number 2 states the number of atoms.

When two or more different atoms combine, they form a *chemical compound*. Water is made up of two hydrogen atoms and one oxygen atom. Its formula is therefore H_2O. There are about seven million known chemical compounds.

Compounds form or break down through *chemical reactions*. Chemists write equations to describe these reactions. For example, $C + O_2 \rightarrow CO_2$ is the equation showing how carbon and oxygen molecules react to form carbon dioxide. This occurs when substances with carbon, such as coal, burn.

BRANCHES OF CHEMISTRY

The main branches of chemistry are organic, inorganic, physical, analytical, and biochemical.

Organic Chemistry is the study of those chemicals that contain carbon. Carbon has a strong tendency to share electrons with other atoms and to form large molecules. These molecules make up most of life. Carbon compounds are also the source of over one million man-made items, such as plastics, paints, detergents, drugs, and perfumes. Chemists have even learned how to imitate life, making new carbon compounds. The petrochemical, pulp and paper, and other industries are based on organic chemistry.

Biochemistry is the study of reactions brought about by tiny amounts of powerful *enzymes*. Enzymes are catalysts; that is, they bring about or speed up chemical reactions. Baking, brewing, and food processing are based on biochemical reactions, as are the growth and decay of all living things.

Biochemistry is the basis of medical science. A major Canadian contribution to biochemistry was the discovery of insulin, which controls the disease diabetes, by Frederick Banting and his co-workers in the early 1920s.

Inorganic Chemistry is the study of substances that do not contain carbon. This includes the study of the other 91 elements and their properties, such as magnetism, density, and boiling point. Inorganic chemists are concerned with the chemical changes in compounds and with the discovery of new compounds.

Geology and mining are based on inorganic chemistry. The development of Canada's mineral resources, such as nickel, potash, lead, and uranium, depends on inorganic chemistry.

Physical Chemistry is the measurement and calculation of the physical properties of atoms and molecules. They use the results of these studies to study such things as the energy involved in chemical reactions. Physical chemists use physics and mathematics to make models or maps of the intricate details of chemical reactions. In industry, physical chemists have developed ways of bleaching paper pulp, of recovering bitumen from oil sands, and other industrial applications.

Canada has made major contributions to physical chemistry. Gerhard Herzberg won a Nobel Prize for his work on the structure of molecules. A Nobel Prize was also won by John Polanyi for his discoveries about chemical reactions. Sidney Altman, a Canadian-born professor in the U.S. has also won the Nobel Prize for Chemistry in 1989.

Analytical Chemistry is the identifica-

Chemical Terms

- **matter,** anything that has size and weight
- **atoms,** the building blocks of all matter
- **element,** made up of one kind of atom
- **molecule,** combination of atoms held together by electrons
- **chemical compound,** combination of 2 or more different atoms
- **chemical reaction,** breakdown or forming of compounds

Careers in Chemistry

Chemists find employment in a variety of places, from teaching institutions to corporations and government laboratories. The minimum requirement for employment is an undergraduate degree, although those having more education are preferred. Teaching at the university level and some research positions generally require a PhD. Four-year undergraduate programs are offered at universities in every province. About 900 students graduate each year, the majority of them male.

Advanced study is available in every province but Prince Edward Island. About 150 students receive master's degrees each year, and about the same number earn PhDs. There are about 11 000 chemists in Canada.

tion and measurement of chemical elements and compounds in matter. For example, analytical chemists track down poisons such as mercury in lakes, in fish, and in people who eat the fish.

Analytical techniques may soon be able to detect single atoms and molecules. Many elements can now be measured in concentrations less than one part per billion. Computers are essential for this work.

▷ RELATED ARTICLES: **Frederick Banting; Biochemistry; Chemical Industry; Gerhard Herzberg; Harold Johns; Raymond Lemieux; Otto Maass; Petrochemical Industry; John Polanyi; Ernest Rutherford.**

■ Cheng, Angela

Pianist (*born in 1959 in Hong Kong*). When she was eight, Angela Cheng moved with her family to Canada, settling in Edmonton. She studied piano at the University of Alberta, at the Juilliard School in New York, and at Indiana University. She won first prize in the 1978 Canadian Music Competition, third prize in the 1986 Arthur Rubinstein International Piano Master Competition in Israel, first prize in the 1987 CBC Young Performers' Competition, and the $15 000 grand prize in the 1988 Montreal International Music Competition. She was the only North American to reach the finals in the Montreal competition and the first Canadian to win it. By the late 1980s, Cheng had appeared as soloist with all the major Canadian orchestras and with the Israel Philharmonic.

■ Chess

Chess is probably the oldest and most popular board game in the world. It was first played in Persia or India about 1300 years ago. Its name comes from the Persian word *shah*, which means "king." The rules are easy to learn and the game can be played at an early age. However, advanced chess is a very complex and challenging game.

About one in five adult Canadians play chess. Most games are played at home or in clubs. But chess is also a serious game of competition.

There are today over 13 000 players in Canada who have been nationally "rated" because of their results in competition. At the highest levels, Canada has nine men and seven women who have the title International Master. Three Canadian men are ranked at the even higher level of International Grandmaster: Abe Yanofsky, Duncan Suttles, and Kevin Spraggett. Yanofsky was a child prodigy. In 1939, at

Alex Fishbein of the U.S. and Alexandre Lesiège of Canada (right) at the New York Open Chess Tournament, March 1989 (photo by Jerome Bibuld).

the age of 14, he won a medal for Canada at the Chess Olympics in Buenos Aires. In 1989, Alexandre Lesiège of Quebec, age 13, defeated a Soviet Grandmaster at the World Open.

Canadians take part in a national championship, which is restricted to top-rated Canadian players. There is also a championship open to the best players in the world. Canada competes in the world team championships, called the Olympiad. Canadians do not take chess competition as seriously as many other countries. In the Soviet Union, for example, chess champions are as popular as hockey stars or rock musicians are in Canada. However, Canada has done well at the Olympiads. Some of Canada's best results have been 12th in 1964, 11th in 1970, 8th in 1976, tied for 7th in 1978 and tied for 8th in 1980.

■ Chester

Chester, N.S., lies on Mahone Bay, 72 km southwest of Halifax. The village is part of a larger district which has a population of 10 579 (1986c). The village itself contains 1170 people. Chester was colonized by New Englanders around 1761 and grew into an important shipbuilding, logging, and fishing centre. Today its sheltered bay, natural beauty, and collection of heritage buildings make it a popular summer resort. For information, contact the Village Clerk, P.O. Box 633, Chester, N.S., B0J 1J0.

■ Chesterfield Inlet

Chesterfield Inlet is a narrow finger of water stretching 160 km inland from the northwest coast of Hudson Bay. It was first sighted by Thomas Button in 1612-13 and is named for the Earl of Chesterfield. There is a small community at the mouth of the inlet, also called Chesterfield Inlet.

Chess Prodigies

Canada has not had many chess prodigies. Abe Yanofsky was one. He won a medal for Canada in 1939 at age 14.

Today, Alex Lesiège of Quebec, at age 13, is among Canada's best 50 players of any age. In 1989 he defeated a Soviet grandmaster in a tournament.

Breeding Range of:
**Black-capped
Chickadee** ●

■ Chestnut

The American chestnut (*Castanea dentata*) belongs to the beech family (Fagaceae). The generic name *Castanea* means chestnut, while the specific name *dentata* refers to the toothed (notched) outline of the leaf. The American chestnut is not widespread in Canada. Only a few are found north of Lake Erie, but its history is worth repeating. It once thrived in deciduous forests in southeastern Ontario and the northeastern United States. Its wood was used in carpentry, and its nuts were eaten. But a disease, the chestnut blight, caused by a fungus, was introduced into North America about 1900 on some plants imported from Asia; it caused the chestnut virtually to disappear. A few trees have survived into our time, thanks to suckers that developed on the roots; but these trees have grown to barely 10 m in height. They rarely manage to survive into maturity and produce chestnuts. Another species, the European sweet chestnut (*Castanea sativa*), is often planted as an ornamental. Finally, the horse chestnut (*Aesculus hippocastanum*) is sometimes confused with the American chestnut.

Chestnut trees are not common in Canada. They were almost wiped out by a fungus brought to Canada from Asia around 1900 (artwork by Claire Tremblay).

■ Chickadee

Chickadees are tiny, vocal members of the Paridae (titmouse) family of birds. There are over 40 species worldwide, of which six occur in Canada. They have a short, conical bill. Most chickadees have striking black and white head markings, with a black bib and white cheeks. They get their common name from their pleas-

Black-capped Chickadee is the most common chickadee. Chickadees are active even in the depth of winter (Macmillan Illustrated Animal Encyclopedia).

ant song: *chick-a-dee-dee-dee*!

Chickadees move about in small groups, except at nesting time, busily inspecting branches. They often hang upside down to pick insects and insect eggs from the underside of leaves and twigs. They are often found in company with kinglets, nuthatches, and woodpeckers. The Black-capped Chickadee (*Parus atricapillus*) is one of the most widespread. It lives in mixed forests and gardens. The Boreal Chickadee (*Parus hudsonicus*) prefers coniferous forests. The Mountain and Chestnut-backed Chickadee (*P. gambeli* and *P. rufescens*) and the Siberian Tit and Tufted Titmouse (*P. cinctus* and *P. bicolor*) are less widespread. Chickadees do not migrate. They nest in tree cavities and raise a large brood of young (from 5 to 12) each year.

Chickadees feed primarily on insects, some of them pests. They also eat seeds and some berries. They love animal fat and can easily be attracted by suspending a bit of suet from a branch or by sunflower seeds in a bird feeder. Their constant activity, even in the depth of winter, earns them their reputation for good humour and gaiety.

■ Chicoutimi

Chicoutimi, Que., lies on the Saguenay River, 200 km north of Quebec City. It is the regional capital of the Saguenay-Lac-St-Jean region. Located on a popular Indian canoe route, it was a fur-trade centre from the 1600s. Its name is from a Montagnais word meaning "the end of the deep waters." Peter McLeod Jr founded the town in 1842, building sawmills on nearby rivers. A large pulp and paper mill

operated from 1898 to 1929, when it closed. During World War II, many of the inhabitants found work at the new aluminum plant at nearby Arvida. Today, Chicoutimi is a major business, government, and religious centre. The city preserves its past through an active historical society. The remains of the old pulp factory have been preserved. Chicoutimi's population in 1986 was 61 083. For information, contact the Greffier, 201, rue Racine est, C.P. 129, Chicoutimi, Que., G7H 5B8.

Hydroelectric Plant built by Alcan in the Saguenay-Lac-St-Jean region of Quebec (courtesy Alcan Aluminum Ltd).

EMPLOYMENT BY INDUSTRY - 1988

Chicoutimi-Jonquière

Industry	%
Primary	0.9
Manufacturing	21.0 / 17.4
Trade	17.4 / 18.1
Construction	5.5
Finance, Insurance, and Real Estate	7.6
Transportation, Communication, and Other Utilities	7.1
Services	36.7 / 35.0
Public Administration	6.9

Legend:
- Primary
- Manufacturing
- Construction
- Transportation, Communication, and Other Utilities
- Trade
- Finance, Insurance, and Real Estate
- Services
- Public Administration
- Average of top 23 cities

Source: Statistics Canada

■ Chignecto Bay

Chignecto Bay is one of two narrow extensions at the head of the Bay of Fundy. The Petitcodiac River flows into the northwestern fork of the bay, while Sackville, N.B. is located at the head of the northeastern fork. The area was first settled by Acadians. Fundy National Park is located on its northern coast.

■ Chilcotin

The Chilcotin are an Athapaskan-speaking people who live along the Chilcotin River in west-central British Columbia. They were traditionally organized in bands, and hunted elk and caribou. Now deer and moose are the main game. They gathered in summer to fish salmon along the rivers, and traditionally moved to campsites near lakes in winter, where they could ice fish. In the 1860s the Chilcotin tried to resist the encroachment of their land, killing several labourers building a pack train trail in 1864. Five Chilcotin were executed for the killings. Today, the Chilcotin struggle to maintain their traditional way of life in spite of the spread of non-Indian settlement. *See* **Native People: Subarctic**.

■ Child Abuse

Child abuse is any kind of physical or emotional harm to children. It may result from violent or cruel acts by adults, usually the child's parents, or it may result from neglect.

Attention was drawn to the abuse of children in the 1960s when Dr Henry Kempe coined the term "battered child syndrome." People began to realize that child abuse is a leading cause of serious injury and death. It has also been recognized that sexual abuse and emotional maltreatment of children are as widespread as beatings.

Sexual Abuse is a widespread and destructive crime. It often remains unreported, perhaps because those who know it is happening do not want to meddle in what they may consider a private affair. Victims of the abuse fear what will happen to them and to their family if they tell.

Children of both sexes and all ages may be abused by members of their family. However, the most common form of sexual abuse is between father and daughter. The daughter may be as young as six to ten years when the abuse starts. It often continues over several years and may include more than one member of the family. Evidence shows that the victims' mother often knows what is happening, yet ignores it.

The results of child sex abuse are devastating to the victims. It may cause fear, anxiety, depression, anger, low self-esteem, sexually inappropriate behaviour, and even suicide. The most damaging abuses are experiences involving father figures, genital contact, and force.

Abuse and the Law Recent changes in

the law reflect a view in society that sexual abuse of children is a serious problem. Cases of abuse can result in criminal charges being laid. Evidence of children is now allowed in court. Each province has agencies which protect a child if there is a risk of abuse or neglect.

In all provinces, the public is required, by law, to report any suspicions of abuse or neglect. In the long run, however, eduction and support for families in distress will prove more effective than treating the results of abuse.

▷ SUGGESTED READING: Charlotte Vale Allen, *Daddy's Girl* (1980); Paul Kropp, *Not Only Me* (1987).

■ Child Labour

Child labour refers to the regular, full-time employment of boys and girls under 16 years of age. Today this is rare, since most children attend school. However, in Canada's pioneer days, and until the recent past, child labour was an accepted practice.

On the farms of New France, and later in the colonies of British North America, children played a useful part in the family economy. From an early age they helped and learned from their parents by doing chores. In the towns, youngsters became apprentices and learned a skill, such as printing or blacksmithing, while working for a master craftsman.

The coming of industry and the growth of cities after about 1850 had a dramatic impact on child labour. At the time, no laws required children to go to school. Many parents needed their children to work to help support the family. Children as young as 10 years old entered the work force in factories, mines, and mills.

Working conditions were sometimes frightful. Children sometimes worked 10 hours per day, six days a week, for a weekly wage of $1.50. Conditions in the mines and factories were often unhealthy and unsafe. Many children suffered serious injuries or illnesses. Many children died on the job, or lost limbs or their sight. There was no compensation for these children or their families.

As the worst abuses of child labour became known, some people argued that school was a better place for children. In the 1870s, provinces began to pass laws requiring young children to attend school regularly. At about the same time, other laws regulated child labour in factories and mines. However, these laws were slow to take effect and were not in effect in every province. It was not until well after World War I that most children under 14 were in school instead of on the job.

■ Children's Literature, *see* Literature for Children

■ Chilkoot Pass

The Chilkoot Pass is located on the British Columbia-Alaska border at an elevation of 1067 m. It is the main pass between the St Elias and Coast Mountains. It was used by the Tlingit Indians as a trade route. For tens of thousands of gold seekers during the great rush of 1897-98, it was the gateway to the Klondike goldfields. The North-West Mounted Police built a post there to keep the peace and collect customs duties. The pass was abandoned after a railway was opened over nearby White Pass in 1900. Today, the pass is part of a hiking trail, built in the 1960s, tracing the route of the Klondike gold rush.

■ Chilkoot Trail

The Chilkoot Trail extends 51 km from Dyea, on the Alaska Panhandle, across the Coast Mountains to Bennett, B.C. The original trail was used in 1897-98 during the Klondike gold rush. During the 1960s, the route was restored as a hiking trail. The terrain is rugged and the weather can be severe.

■ Chilliwack

Chilliwack, B.C., is on the south side of the Fraser River, 100 km east of Vancouver. It is chiefly an agricultural centre. The area's dairy farms supply much of the milk consumed in B.C. The region also produces grain crops, corn, berries, beef, poultry, and hogs. A number of lumber, wood products, and agriculture equipment industries are located in Chilliwack. Canadian Forces Base Chilliwack at nearby Vedder Crossing has 1500 military personnel and over 800 civilian employees. Cultus Lake and Harrison Lake, popular recreation areas, also lie nearby. Chilliwack became a city in 1908. The name is an Indian word meaning "valley of many streams" or "going back upstream." In 1986 the population of Chilliwack was 41 337. For information, contact the District Municipal Clerk, 8550 Young Rd S., Chilliwack, B.C., V2P 4P1.

■ Chilliwack

Chilliwack is a rock band that was formed in 1969 from the remains of the Collectors, one of the West Coast's best bands. Its lead singer and songwriter was Bill Henderson (*born in 1944 at Vancouver, B.C.*). Its lead guitarist was Brian

Treatment of Child Workers

In 1889 a government inquiry held interviews with child workers. Edward Gilfoy was a 15-year old who worked in a mill in Halifax:

Question: How long have you worked in the mill?
EG: Four years.
Q: Have you ever seen boys or girls getting whipped?
EG: Yes.
Q: What for?
EG: For playing.

Children in the Tobacco Factories

The 1889 report included this description:
"The testimony of children employed in cigar and tobacco factories was of a very painful nature. Boys and girls, not more than ten years of age, were found in these places in considerable numbers.... The evils were [made worse] by the fact that tobacco had stunted the growth of the witnesses and poisoned their blood."

"Too Loud" MacLeod (*born in 1952 at Halifax, N.S.*). Success came in 1977 with their sixth album, *Dreams, Dreams, Dreams*, which went platinum in Canada. Their ninth album, *Wanna Be a Star* (1981), was pushed to platinum sales in Canada by the singles "My Girl" and "Gone, Gone, Gone." The group split up after their last LP, *Opus X*, in 1982. Bill Henderson still performs, writes, and produces in Vancouver. His daughter Saffron is a singer. Brian MacLeod went on to form the Headpins.

Chimaera, like sharks, have a skeleton of cartilage, not bone. They live in very deep, cold water and are rarely captured (artwork by Karen Klitz).

■ Chimaera

There are three species of these fish on the Atlantic seaboard of Canada and another on the Pacific. They belong to the family Chimaeridae. Fish of cold sea waters, they are related to the shark and therefore have a skeleton of cartilage rather than bone. They have an unusual appearance: an elongated shape, a protruding and sometimes lance-like snout, a long, pointed tail, and pectoral fins that look like bird wings. Their large teeth are easily visible. They have no scales. Some of these fish measure 2 m. As with sharks, reproduction takes place internally. The male has special organs called claspers near his pelvic fins that allow him to deposit sperm in the female's body. After mating, the female lays the eggs, which are covered in a rigid casing. The young develop within these casings and are independent from birth. Fish of these species are rarely captured; they live in very deep water.

The Dr Sun Yat-sen Chinese Garden Ancient architecture, rare rock, pavilions, winding corridors, and ponds create a tranquil atmosphere. The garden is located in Vancouver's Chinatown (courtesy Dr Sun Yat-sen Garden).

■ Chinese

There are over 400 000 Canadians with some Chinese origin. Most large Canadian cities have a Chinatown, a district where the shops and restaurants are Chinese. Even the street signs are written in Chinese script. In these parts of town, one can find many aspects of Chinese culture.

The Chinese culture has very ancient roots. Centuries before the West was civilized, the Chinese had a highly advanced civilization. They were the first in the world to invent such things as printing and gunpowder. They were the first to build canals and locks. The Great Wall of China is among the wonders of the world. The Chinese were very skilled artists, poets, and philosophers. Despite this, Canadians of British origin treated them as inferiors during their early years in the country. There was a strong prejudice against Orientals, as the Chinese and Japanese were called.

THE PIONEERS

The first Chinese to set foot in Canada probably arrived in the late 18th century. They were associated with the fur trade across the Pacific Ocean. The first Chinese to stay arrived more than half a century later. They were men who had taken part in the California gold rush. They came north with other miners in 1858, during the Fraser River gold rush in British Columbia. In the 1860s they moved on to the Cariboo Mountains when gold was found there. Some joined in the search for gold or prospected for jade. Others provided services for the miners, and sold them fresh vegetables and other goods.

After the gold rushes, about 1500 Chinese stayed on in British Columbia. Some found jobs on Vancouver Island, as family servants in Victoria or as coal miners' helpers at Nanaimo. Others worked in the new salmon-canning factories. All were men who had come from poor families in China and were prepared to work hard for little pay. As a result, many more were brought direct from China when labourers were needed to build the Canadian Pacific Railway. More than 14 000 Chinese labourers worked on the railway in the early 1880s. Many died building the railway. They were given the most dangerous jobs, such as blasting a route through solid rock or building the line through the Fraser Canyon.

When the railway was completed in November 1885, politicians tried to force the Chinese to leave Canada. Some did return to China. Of those who remained, nearly all lived in British Columbia. There the prejudice against them was very strong. It became especially bitter in the early 1900s, when employers used Chinese and Japanese workers as strike breakers. They hired them at very low wages to replace coal miners who were on strike for better pay. In 1907 an English-Canadian mob destroyed many of the shops and homes of the Chinese and Japanese.

Meanwhile, the federal government made it more and more difficult for any Chinese to enter Canada. In January 1886 the government imposed a "head tax" of $50 which each Chinese immigrant had to pay. The tax was increased to $100 in 1900 and to $500 in 1904. This was far more than most Chinese could afford. Then, in 1923, the Chinese Immigration Act was passed (also known as the Chinese Exclusion Act). This Act had so many restrictions that only eight Chinese managed to enter Canada during the next 20 years.

THE MODERN ERA

The riots of the early 1900s caused many Chinese to leave British Columbia and settle elsewhere in Canada. By the 1940s they were spread across the country. But they still suffered from discrimination. In some provinces, Chinese were not allowed to vote. Chinese were kept out of the better paid professions. Most worked in service industries, running small shops or restaurants or laundries.

At the same time, a new generation of Chinese was growing up. Educated at public schools among other Canadians, they were more Canadian than Chinese in outlook and customs. Many of them were Christians. Missionaries had converted many Chinese from the traditional worship of their ancestors both in China and in Canada.

Gradually, the prejudice against Chinese faded. During World War II (1939-45), China was an important ally of Canada and Britain. Chinese Canadians benefited from this relationship. In 1947 they were finally accepted as citizens with the same rights as other Canadians, including the right to vote. Meanwhile, new immigration laws gradually made it easier for Chinese to enter Canada.

Since the 1960s, many thousands of Chinese have immigrated to Canada. Most have come from Hong Kong. Well-educated middle-class people who already speak English, they have fitted easi-

Chinatown Gate in Victoria, B.C. (photo by Malak, Ottawa).

ly into the Canadian community. Others, many of whom were French-speaking, arrived from Southeast Asia as "Boat People" in the late 1970s and early 1980s. They, too, quickly became part of the Canadian community, settling mainly in the larger cities.

Today, most Chinese do not live in Chinatowns. They live in suburbs or apartment blocks among fellow Canadians who are not of Chinese origin. Many do not eat Chinese food or know much about Chinese customs. Yet they are aware that they have a very rich cultural background and they are eager to know more about their Chinese heritage. There has been a renewed interest in Chinese art and literature, and in customs such as the celebration of the Chinese New Year. Such festivals are shared with other Canadians. All Canadians, whatever their origin, can enjoy visiting a big city's Chinatown.

▷ RELATED ARTICLES: **Ethnic Group; Immigration; Indochinese; Prejudice and Discrimination.**

▷ SUGGESTED READING: Vancy Kasper, *Street of Three Directions* (1988); Richard T. Wright, *In a Strange Land: A Pictorial Record of the Chinese in Canada 1778-1823* (1988); Paul Yee, *Saltwater City: An Illustrated History of the Chinese in Vancouver* (1988).

■ Chinook

Chinook is a warm, dry, and gusty westerly wind that in Canada blows in a broad belt along the eastern slopes of the Rockies. It occurs mainly in southern Alberta, but chinook-type winds sometimes reach

Chinook Wind blows from west (left) to east. As the air moves over the Rocky Mountains it releases moisture, picks up heat and sweeps onto the prairie. The Chinook brings a dramatic rise in temperature in southern Alberta (artwork by Steven Fick).

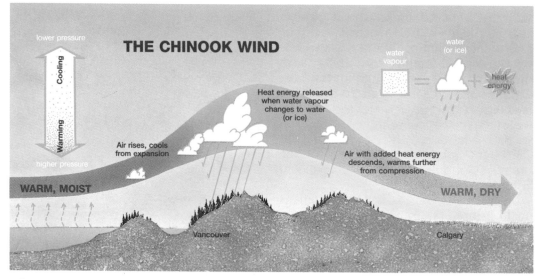

THE CHINOOK WIND

lower pressure

Cooling

Warming

higher pressure

Air rises, cools from expansion

Heat energy released when water vapour changes to water (or ice)

water vapour

water (or ice)

heat energy

Air with added heat energy descends, warms further from compression

WARM, MOIST

WARM, DRY

Vancouver

Calgary

Edmonton or southern Saskatchewan. Chinooks can raise temperatures more than 20°C in one hour, turning winter into spring-like conditions. Calgary receives an average of 30 to 35 chinook days each winter. Chinook is a native word meaning "snow eater," which describes how quickly the wind melts the snow.

A chinook originates as warm, moist air from the Pacific Ocean that is carried east by the prevailing westerly wind. This air loses its moisture as it climbs the western side of the Rockies, releasing heat energy in the process. When the air descends on the eastern slopes of the mountains, it warms up and becomes even drier. The air is now warmer and drier than it was at a comparable level on the windward side of the mountains.

This type of wind occurs in other places on Earth where there are similar geographical features as in western Canada: mountains at right angles to the prevail-

ing winds which carry warm, moist air from an ocean. Examples are California's Santa Ana and Europe's alpine *foehn*.

The chinook winds of southern Alberta melt snowcover and enable livestock to find forage. They encouraged the development of the ranching industry in the late 19th century. In some winters the chinooks do not occur, and hardships may be felt in the industry. The winds are often accompanied by a cloud formation, called a "chinook arch." An arch forms where milder, drier air has eaten away the cloud cover in the west.

Such winds seem to cause abnormal behaviour. Some people report feeling aggressive or listless just before chinook-type winds blow. Rates of accidents, crimes, and suicides increase.

▷ SUGGESTED READING: Robert E. Gard, *Johnny Chinook: Tall Tales From the Canadian West* (1945).

Chinook Arch in the sky of southern Alberta. The arch is created as clear air pushes the cloud cover westward (photo by Elliot & Nicole Bernshaw).

■ Chipewyan

The Chipewyan occupy the western Subarctic from Churchill, on Hudson Bay, to northeast Alberta and Great Slave Lake. They are an Athapaskan-speaking people. The name is a Cree word, referring to the pointed skin garments which the Chipewyan wore.

The ancestors of the Chipewyan may have occupied their territories for several thousand years. Their lifestyle was based on following and hunting the barren-ground caribou. They also relied on fish and small game. They lived in temporary shelters made from caribou skins. While they used bark canoes for some summer travel, they travelled extensively on foot, with the aid of snowshoes in winter, when they pulled their belongings on wooden toboggans. They dressed in garments made of caribou skins, decorated with porcupine quills, seeds, and red ochre or vermilion.

Chipewyans met English traders during the late 1600s and began to exchange furs and food for manufactured goods regularly during the 1700s. In their search for sources of furs, they expanded their ranges, trading with Indians to the northwest and settling in northeast Alberta. They became linked with European traders, who married Chipewyan women. Some of the offspring of these marriages became one source of the developing Canadian Metis. By the end of the 19th century, many Chipewyans lived in winter log cabin settlements and wore cloth clothing.

The Chipewyans signed several treaties from 1899 to 1921, in which they gave up title to their lands in exchange for reserves of land and other benefits. In 1988, the Chipewyans who live in the Northwest Territories signed a new land-claims agreement with the government as part of the Dene Nation.

The Chipewyans of today live on reserves, in towns, and in cities. In 1986, they numbered about 8400 people. They are still closely linked to their earlier ways of life, based on the resources of the "bush," while also relying on wage labour, professions, and even farming. *See* **Native People: Subarctic.**

Chipmunks find shelter in nests or holes in trees, and it spends the winter hibernating in a burrow (artwork by Jan Sovak).

The Chipmunk is easily identified by the white and black stripes on its head, back, and flanks (artwork by Claire Tremblay).

■ Chipmunk

Chipmunks are members of the squirrel family, Sciuridae. Five species of the genus *Tamias* are found in Canada: the eastern (*T. striatus*), the least (*T. minimus*), the yellow-pine (*T. amoenus*), the red-tailed (*T. ruficaudus*), and Townsend's (*T. townsendii*).

The chipmunk closely resembles the squirrel but it can be told apart by its shorter, less fluffy tail and by black and white stripes which run from its head to its rump. Chipmunks also have two large pouches inside their cheeks which they use for carrying food.

The least chipmunk is the most widely distributed in Canada with a range which extends from western Quebec to the central Yukon. It occupies habitats from arid sagebrush desert and semi-desert through brushy grasslands and coniferous forests into the alpine tundra of the mountains.

The other species are nearly always found in or beside forests. The burrow and its surrounding area make up the home territory, which is defended against other chipmunks. Winter dens are nearly always below ground. There, lengthy periods of hibernation are alternated with brief periods of arousal, feeding, and elimination of wastes. Summer dens may be in tree cavities or a nest built in the branches.

Chipmunks feed on seeds, grains, grasses, and berries, plus fungi, roots, and bulbs. Some invertebrates and a few bird eggs may be eaten. A great amount of food may be stored in shallow pits or within the burrow. Often uneaten tree seeds may sprout, thus aiding reforestation. Chipmunks are active during the day and retreat to their nests at night.

The weasel is the most important predator. Others include snakes, hawks, and occasionally an owl. Domestic cats kill chipmunks near urban areas.

▷ RELATED ARTICLE: **Squirrel.**

▷ SUGGESTED READING: S.E. Woods, Jr, *The Squirrels of Canada* (1980).

Range of Least Chipmunk ⬤

Range of:
Yellow Pine Chipmunk ⬤
Eastern Chipmunk ⬤

Range of:
Townsend's Chipmunk ⬤
Red-tailed Chipmunk ⬤

Chiriaeff, Ludmilla

Ballet dancer, choreographer, and director (*born in 1924 at Riga, Latvia*). Chiriaeff founded Les Grands Ballets Canadiens, one of Canada's major ballet companies. She trained in Berlin with excellent teachers and directed her own ballet company in Switzerland before she decided to immigrate to Canada in 1952. She immediately found work choreographing short ballets for the newly formed CBC French television in Montreal. She founded Les Ballets Chiriaeff, a performing group which appeared on television over 300 times between 1952 and 1958.

The company gave its first live performance in 1954, and in 1958 changed its name to Les Grands Ballets Canadiens. People laughed at the name, because the new company was not grand at all. But Chiriaeff was full of hope for the future. She remained as artistic director until 1974, and always selected dances that would show the small company to its best advantage and please the audience as well. In recent years she has taught at l'École supérieure de danse du Québec, the school which is associated with the company.

▷ RELATED ARTICLE: **Les Grands Ballets Canadiens.**

Chiropractor

Chiropractors treat ill and injured people by manually adjusting parts of the body, especially the spine.

History Chiropractic was invented in the late 19th century by Daniel David Palmer. When he was 20, Palmer left Port Perry, Ont., where he was born, and moved to the United States. He had contempt for doctors with their science, drugs, and surgery. In 1895, Palmer was 50 years old and living in Iowa. In that year he claimed that he cured a janitor of deafness by pushing back into position a bump on the man's neck, a misaligned part of the man's spine.

To Palmer, this success suggested that health depends on the flow of "energy" through nerves. If a section of the spine slips out of place, even just a little, it can push on a nerve, interrupting the normal flow of "energy." The result may be poor health. The cure is to push the section of the spine back into place, thus restoring normal function of the nerves and, consequently, good health.

Palmer gave the name "chiropractic," from the Greek words for "hands" and "practice," to the treatment based on this theory. His colourful son, Bartlett J.

Palmer, became a multimillionaire teaching chiropractic.

Medical doctors rejected the theory on which chiropractic was based, saying it was unscientific and unproven. Despite this, chiropractors managed to practise their skills.

Chiropractic Today Since about 1960, chiropractors have been increasingly accepted by patients and governments.

Without being able to explain scientifically how their technique works, chiropractors may help some people with a limited number of ailments, especially with headaches, migraines, or neck and back pain. They use only their hands. They give quick, forceful pushes of the spine, called adjustments, or light and prolonged pressures, called manipulations.

Chiropractic is now a well-established health-care profession in most industrialized countries. There are approximately 3300 chiropractors in Canada. Government health-care plans cover the cost of chiropractic treatment in all parts of Canada except Newfoundland and the Northwest Territories. About three-quarters of all Canadian chiropractors studied at the Canadian Memorial Chiropractic College, established in Toronto in 1945.

▷ RELATED ARTICLES: **Health; Health Care; Medicine.**

▷ SUGGESTED READING: Louis Sportelli, *Introduction to Chiropractic: A Natural Method of Health Care*, (8th ed, 1986).

Chisholm, George Brock

Psychiatrist (*born in 1896 at Oakville, Ont.; died in 1971 at Victoria, B.C.*). Brock Chisholm was one of the chief organizers of the World Health Organization and was its first director general (1948-53). Raised in Oakville, Ont., he served in the army during World War I, winning the Military Cross and bar. He then trained as a psychiatrist, for his wartime experiences had made him very curious about why people behave the way they do. He practised as a psychiatrist in Oakville and then Toronto before joining the regular army again in World War II.

During World War II, Chisholm applied his studies of human behaviour to the army. He worked out a system of tests so that soldiers could be given the tasks for which they were most suited. He was promoted in 1942 and appointed director general of the Canadian Army's medical services. Chisholm was the first psychiatrist to hold the position. He joined the Department of Health and Welfare to-

---

Chiropractic Careers
Chiropractors require at least two years of undergraduate training.

They are then admitted to the four-year Doctor of Chiropractic program.

In Canada this program is offered only at the Canadian Memorial Chiropractic College in Toronto. There are about 3300 chiropractors in Canada. About 200 graduate each year.

Brock Chisholm on Santa Claus

"Telling lies to a child does permanent damage to his mind. A child who believes in Santa Claus, who really and literally believes, because his daddy told him so, that Santa comes down all the chimneys in the world on the same night has had his thinking ability permanently impaired, if not destroyed."

Quoted in *Maclean's* Jan. 15, 1946

G. Brock Chisholm, 1944. Chisholm worked tirelessly fighting disease throughout the world (courtesy NAC/PA-115641).

wards the end of the war, and it was in this role that he became an organizer of the World Health Organization.

Chisholm was an outspoken person who was never afraid of saying what he thought, and this often brought him into the public eye. He caused an uproar in the 1940s by criticizing Santa Claus. He said that children should be told that Santa was a pleasant "make believe," not a real person. On another occasion he said, "We have messed up every aspect of living. No other animal in creation has made such a mess of it." He attempted to rectify the "mess" through his work for the World Health Organization. He wore himself out coping with outbreaks of disease in different parts of the world and trying to raise the standards of health in the poorest countries. There are many throughout the world who are grateful for his efforts.

Chokecherry

The chokecherry (*Prunus virginiana*) belongs to the rose family (Rosaceae). This shrub or small tree grows almost everywhere in North America, especially bordering fields or alongside enclosures. This cherry can be told from others by its clusters of flowers or berries (depending on the season). The colour of the ripe fruit varies from light to red to almost black, and sometimes yellow.

These cherries look wonderfully appetizing and would be delicious if only they were a touch sweeter and did not leave the mouth so puckered. Some birds eat the fruit, which they swallow whole and

then, having come to rest a little farther on (on a fence or a tree bordering a meadow, for example), they regurgitate it again, and thereby sow the seeds. Even though the chokecherry leaf is poisonous for humans and cattle, it provides food for tent caterpillars (so named for their "mosquito netting" of silk, a very effective way to protect themselves from birds that eat caterpillars). The native people knew the medicinal property of the bark. It is now used to improve the taste of cold syrups and in the past was used to flavour toothpaste. It also makes excellent jellies, syrups, and wine.

Cholera, see Epidemic

Chrétien, Jean

Lawyer and politician (*born in 1934 at Shawinigan, Que.*). After graduating from Laval University in Quebec City, Chrétien practised law for several years. He was first elected to the House of Commons as a Liberal in 1963. He rose quickly and held different positions in the Cabinets of both Prime Ministers Pearson and Trudeau. Chrétien was the first French Canadian to serve as finance minister.

A strong, emotional speaker, Chrétien was one of the most popular politicians in the country. He projected a sincerity that allowed ordinary Canadians to believe he understood their concerns. This quality is reflected in the English title of his best-selling autobiography, *Straight from the Heart* (1985).

In 1980 Chrétien led the fight against Quebec independence during the referendum debate in that province. As justice minister, he played an important role in preparing the Constitution Act, 1982, and the Charter of Rights and Freedoms.

Chrétien ran second to John Turner in

Jean Chrétien failed to gain the Liberal leadership in 1984 but prepared to fight for it again in 1989 (courtesy The Globe and Mail/L8832C7-9A).

the contest for leadership of the Liberal Party in 1984. Discouraged at not winning the leadership, he retired from Parliament two years later, returning to his law practice. In 1989 Turner resigned and Chrétien entered the race again for the leadership of the party. The convention was scheduled for June 1990.

■ Christianity

Christianity is the largest of all religions. It is estimated that well over one billion people call themselves Christian. The major divisions of Christianity are Roman Catholicism, Protestantism, and Eastern Orthodox. There are several independent churches of Eastern Christianity and many small sects throughout the world that also refer to themselves as Christian.

Life of Jesus Christianity was founded in Judea, now Israel, about 2000 years ago by Jesus of Nazareth. The Christian belief is based on Jesus being born the Son of God, also called the Messiah or Christ. The main sources of information about Jesus are the four Gospels of the Bible: Matthew, Mark, Luke, and John. Stories of his early days tell of his birth in Bethlehem, the flight to Egypt with his parents, and his preaching in the temple of Jerusalem. Nothing more is known until he began his public preaching and was baptized by John the Baptist. This was also when Jesus began to gather his twelve Apostles, or disciples. Further accounts tell of his healing the sick, raising the dead, and of his sermons to an increasing number of followers.

He entered Jerusalem during the final week of his life at age 33 and, after eating a last supper with the Apostles, was arrested and brought to trial before both a Jewish tribunal and the Roman governor, Pontius Pilate. Jesus was crucified on a hill called Calvary, and after his death his body was put in a tomb. Three days later, according to the Gospels, the tomb was found empty because Jesus had risen from the dead. His ascension into heaven 40 days after his resurrection is also reported in the Bible, in the Acts of the Apostles.

Spread Christianity, based on the belief that Jesus Christ was the resurrected Son of God, spread rapidly, despite 300 years of severe persecution. By the 4th century, it had become the official religion of the Roman Empire. Since the 16th century, Christianity has spread throughout the world because of intensive missionary efforts of both the Roman Catholic and Protestant churches.

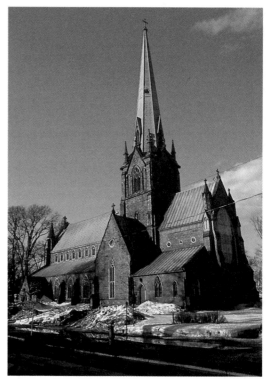

Christ Church Cathedral, *Fredericton, N.B., is one of the finest Christian churches in Canada (courtesy Environment Canada, Parks).*

Division The formal separation of the Eastern Orthodox Church and the Roman Catholic Church occurred in 1054 because of differences in belief and political considerations. The issues which still divide them are the role of the pope and the interpretation of the Trinity. One of the central beliefs in Christianity is the Trinity, the three aspects of divine power: God the Father, God the Son (Jesus), and God the Holy Ghost (the love of both Father and Son acting through people in this world).

Protestantism traces its roots back to the Reformation of the 16th century, which was a religious revolution against many practices of the church of Rome. Its greatest leaders were Martin Luther and John Calvin.

Rites A central rite of Christian worship is the Eucharist, which comes from a Greek word for "thanksgiving." It is also called the Lord's Supper, Holy Communion, and the Mass. The Eucharist is intended as a symbol of the unity of the Church and as a means of increasing that unity. All Christians would agree that the eating of the bread and the drinking of the wine at Holy Communion are a memorial recalling what Jesus Christ was, said, and did. Every Christian denomination sees this celebration as an integral symbol of the death of Christ on the cross. Most

Christian traditions teach that Jesus is present in the Eucharist, but they disagree on how this comes about.

Christians also maintain that Jesus Christ will return. This is called the Second Coming and will mark the end of the world. At that time the Last Judgement will occur, and all people alive and dead will be judged on their fitness to enter heaven. Early Christians believed that the event would happen soon and described in great detail how it would take place. Current tradition opposes speculation as to the exact time or manner of this final judgement.

The Christian calendar has several special days. Sunday is considered a day of rest and religious observance. Christmas, the time of Christ's birth, and Easter, the time of his resurrection, are the two most important festivals. The sacraments (visible signs ordained by Christ to indicate inward grace) are, for most Protestants, baptism and Holy Communion. Roman Catholic and Orthodox churches also include confirmation, penance, extreme unction (anointing with oil at the time of death), ordination, and marriage.

The major divisions of Christianity are well represented in Canada with 11.2 million Roman Catholics, 9.9 million Protestants and 362,000 Eastern Orthodox Christians.

■ Chuckwagon Races, *see* Calgary Stampede

■ Churchill

Churchill, Man., lies at the mouth of the Churchill River on the southwest coast of Hudson Bay. The Hudson's Bay Company built its first post near the mouth of the river in 1689. It was unsuccessful and was later replaced by Prince of Wales's Fort, which was an important trading centre for years.

With the completion of the Hudson Bay Railway in 1929, and a port facility in 1931, the town of Churchill developed. During World War II it prospered as a military base. However, it has never fulfilled hopes that it would become a major port. There is no road into Churchill. The only way to reach it is by train or by air. Churchill now attracts visitors for bird watching and for viewing beluga whales and polar bears. The town is on a polar bear migration route and occasionally these animals wander into town. In 1986 the population of the town was 1217. For information, contact the Resident Administrator, P.O. Box 459, Churchill, Man., R0B 0E0.

■ Churchill Falls

Churchill Falls, in southern Labrador, is 75 m high, making it higher than Niagara Falls. The Montagnais-Naskapi Indians believed that whoever looked at the awesome falls would be lured into its waters and perish. The first European to see the falls was John McLean of the Hudson's Bay Company in 1839.

The falls are the site of what was once the largest engineering project ever built in North America. The project took seven years to complete (1966-74), employed 30 000 people, and cost over $900 million. Eighty-eight dykes were built to collect water in a huge reservoir, named for Newfoundland Premier Joseph Smallwood. A massive underground powerhouse was the largest in the world to that time. Since power from the project passes through Quebec, it could only go ahead after an agreement between the governments of Newfoundland and Quebec. As a result, Quebec receives power from Churchill Falls quite cheaply and sells it at a profit to U.S. customers. Newfoundland is unhappy with the agreement and the dispute has dragged on for many years.

Churchill Falls, Labrador, is one of Canada's highest waterfalls (75 m) and the source of one of the world's largest electric power developments (photo by J.A. Kraulis).

■ Churchill River

The Churchill River, Labrador, rises in the rugged Labrador Plateau and flows east through mountainous terrain to Lake Melville, Hamilton Inlet, and the Atlantic Ocean. At 856 km, it is the longest river in the province of Newfoundland. It has great hydroelectric potential, aside from the Churchill Falls project, which is already producing. Originally called the Hamilton River, it was renamed in 1965 for British statesman Sir Winston Churchill. The renaming causes confusion because Canada already had a Churchill River (in Western Canada).

■ Churchill River

The Churchill River, 1609 km long, winds across the lowlands of northern Saskatchewan and Manitoba and empties into Hudson Bay at Churchill, Man. Its route is marked by many rapids and falls and a series of interconnected lakes. The river was used by Cree and Chipewyan Indians, and in the fur-trade era was an important link to the Athabasca country. It is named for John Churchill, an early governor of the Hudson's Bay Company. There is one hydroelectric station on the Saskatchewan part of the river. Most of the flow in Manitoba is diverted down the Burntwood River and into the Nelson River for power generation.

■ Chuvalo, George

Boxer (*born in 1937 at Toronto, Ont.*). Chuvalo became Canadian amateur heavyweight champion in 1955. He turned pro in 1956 and became professional champion in 1958 and lost and regained the title twice before 1968. He then held it for eleven years. Chuvalo fought the best boxers of his day, including Muhammad Ali. He was never knocked down. His lifetime record was 79 victories (70 by knockout), 15 defeats, and two draws.

■ Circuses

Circuses were a popular entertainment in Canada in the 19th century. Most came from the United States. The first circus performed in Canada in 1797. The Ricketts troupe from Philadelphia played for several months in Montreal and Quebec City. By the 1820s there were several dozen "mud shows" on tour. Managers would erect their tent, or backdrop, at a crossroads near an inn. The shows consisted of a few clowns tumbling and juggling, rope walkers, and perhaps a trick rider.

As roads improved, circuses became bigger. A mid-sized troupe would need 35 wagons and 60 horses for transportation. It might include a group of non-performing animals, such as monkeys or even an elephant.

In the early 20th century, the combined Ringling Bros. and Barnum & Bailey Circus needed 100 railway cars to carry their "Greatest Show on Earth." The circus parade of exotic animals, performing horses, clowns, and acrobats became a major event down the main street of the towns it visited. The shows were held in large canvas tents called "tops." People flocked to pay 50¢ admission (children 25¢) to the "big top," at a time when an average housemaid earned 20¢ a day.

Later circuses added spectacles and freak sideshows to their list of attractions. Performers in glittering costumes acted out familiar stories from history, the Bible, or fairytales. Troupes of giants, dwarfs, bearded women, two-headed calves, and five-legged lambs were paraded before the curious crowds. Andrew McAskill, "the Cape Breton giant," toured with a travelling show in the mid-19th century. Colourful festive billboards and posters advertised the circuses wherever they went.

By the time of World War I, the circus age was over. Large travelling shows had become too expensive to keep. Audiences were drawn to a new entertainment — the movies. Nevertheless, a few shows remained. Today, the Shriners' Circus from the U.S. and the Moscow State Circus tour Canada occasionally and perform in closed arenas. In the 1970s there was a revival of small domestic circuses. Five Canadian shows, including Puck's Travelling Circus, performed from town to town.

Le Cirque du Soleil, the Sun Circus, was founded in Montreal in 1984. It is based on traditions developed in Europe and China rather than in the U.S.

▷ SUGGESTED READING: Peter K. Alfaenger, *le Cirque* (1981); Hazel Elves, *Its All Done With Mirrors: A Story of Canadian Carnival Life* (1977); Alan C. Jenkins and Mark Peppe, *Circuses Through the Ages* (1972).

■ Cirque du Soleil, *see* Circuses

Cirque du Soleil performing The Trunk, *1988 (courtesy Cirque du Soleil/photo by Al Seib).*

Citizenship

All Canadian citizens are equally entitled to the rights, privileges, and responsibilities laid out in the laws of Canada. These rights include the rights to vote and run for office, and the rights to enter, remain in, and leave Canada. Only Canadian citizens can carry Canadian passports. All persons born in Canada are, with a few exceptions, Canadian citizens at birth. (One exception is the children of diplomats.) Children born abroad to Canadian citizens are also automatically citizens.

The process of becoming a Canadian citizen is laid out in the 1977 Citizenship Act. In the most common situation, a person comes to live in Canada with the status of a permanent resident. Adults who are admitted to Canada for permanent residence may qualify for citizenship after three or more years in Canada. Applications are heard by a citizenship judge. If the person qualifies, he or she will be sworn in as a Canadian citizen. If the person does not qualify, the judge's decision may be appealed. Citizenship may be taken away if it was gained under false pretences.

The Secretary of State is the federal government department responsible for citizenship. Its minister may waive some requirements for citizenship in the case of refugees, for example, or to reward those who have rendered exceptional services to Canada.

City

A city is a community larger than a village or town. Most cities in Canada have a population of at least 25 000. The point at which a town becomes a city varies from province to province. When it reaches sufficient size, a town applies to the provincial government to be elevated to city status. If successful, the town is given a charter and becomes a city.

A very high percentage of Canada's population live in *urban* areas (as cities, towns, and villages are called). In 1986 this percentage was over 76%, one of the highest in the world. Canada has 28 cities with populations over 100 000. Almost one in three Canadians live in Canada's three largest cities: Toronto, Montreal, and Vancouver.

Some large cities, called *metropolitan areas*, are actually collections of several urban areas. For example, Metropolitan Toronto includes five cities (the city of Toronto itself, North York, Scarborough, York, and Etobicoke) and other areas. Thus, the name Toronto applies both to a

Growth in Canada's Cities, 1976-86

Rank (1986)	Metropolitan Area	Population[1] (1976)	Population (1986)	Percentage Increase (1976-86)
1	Toronto	2 919 154	3 427 168	17.4
2	Montreal	2 833 378	2 921 357	3.1
3	Vancouver	1 166 340	1 380 729	18.4
4	Ottawa-Hull	717 398	819 263	14.2
5	Edmonton	615 574	785 465	27.6
6	Calgary	490 232	671 326	36.9
7	Winnipeg	583 922	625 304	7.1
8	Quebec	548 536	603 267	10.0
9	Hamilton	529 375	557 029	5.2
10	St Catharines-Niagara	340 412	343 258	.8
11	London	312 344	342 302	9.6
12	Kitchener	272 098	311 195	14.4
13	Halifax	267 991	295 990	10.4
14	Victoria	224 130	255 547	14.0
15	Windsor	252 244	253 988	.7

Average Percentage Change	12.7

[1] Based on 1986 area

city and to a metropolitan area. The population of the city of Toronto alone is about 612 000. Metropolitan Toronto has a population of about 3.4 million. The answer to the question, "What is Canada's largest city?" depends on whether the word "city" includes metropolitan areas. If it does not, Montreal is Canada's largest city. If it does (and it usually does), Metropolitan Toronto is Canada's largest city. Metro Toronto is also the seventh-largest city in North America. Montreal is the second-largest French-speaking city in the world.

Cities offer people a large variety of opportunities for work, services, and recreation. Cities are also centres of culture. The words "city" and "civilization" come from the same Latin word, *civis*. Most museums, art galleries, symphony orchestras, and theatres are found in cities and towns. Cities are also centres of higher education and government.

The original decision to build a town is usually based on geography. Most of Canada's cities are located near water transportation. Halifax, St John's, Vancouver, and Victoria, for example, are ocean ports. Toronto, Hamilton, Thunder Bay, and Sault Ste Marie are lake ports. Many Canadian cities are located on rivers, including Winnipeg, Montreal, Quebec, Saskatoon, and Edmonton.

When a town grows, it competes with other towns. For various reasons, over time some towns emerge as the largest cities in their respective regions. In many countries, a single city dominates all others. Paris, France, and London, England, are examples. Because Canada is so large, no one city can serve the whole country. Each of Canada's cities controls a region, though the influence of Toronto, Montreal, and Vancouver spread beyond their immediate zones. The successful cities are those which have gained the greatest advantage from geography, transportation, politics, or business.

Cities have always spread their influence through their economic and political power. Today, they are very powerful centres of communication as well. Cities such as Vancouver distribute their newspapers, television shows, and radio programs to the surrounding area.

HISTORY OF CANADIAN CITIES

Most of the villages of the native people were located on convenient water routes. Some of these sites were later chosen by the Europeans. For example, the cities of Montreal and Quebec are on the sites of the native villages of Hochelaga and Stadacona.

Colonial Towns Towns played a very important part in the European settlement of Canada. The earliest French and English colonists built their towns on the Atlantic coast or on rivers like the St Lawrence on which ocean-going ships could travel. These towns had to be close to the ocean, which was the lifeline to their mother countries.

The second consideration in choosing a site for a town was defence. Canada's oldest city, Quebec, was founded in 1608 near a high bluff overlooking the St Lawrence River. In combining strong defence and excellent transportation, Quebec became the most important town in New France. Most early towns were fortified by stone walls or wooden palisades. France built a huge fortress at Louisbourg, on Cape Breton Island, to defend the Gulf of St Lawrence. Britain responded by building the town of Halifax on the Atlantic coast in 1749. Several early Canadian towns suffered attacks in time of war, including St John's, Quebec, Montreal, and York (Toronto). When Quebec fell to the British in 1759, it marked the end of the French Empire in North America.

Colonial towns were centres for trade as well as defence. Quebec and Montreal were centres for the fur trade. Louisbourg, Halifax, and St John's, Nfld, were bases for the fishing fleets. The colonial towns traded directly with England and France, providing them with raw products such as furs and timber. They had little trade with each other. The main economic activities, the fur trade and timber trade, supported few people in the towns. For these reasons, the colonial towns remained small. Quebec was the largest town in early Canada. Its population was never much more than 8000 people during the days of New France.

Industrial Cities Colonial towns grew into cities when they became centres of industry. Montreal, for example, remained small for many years, even though it was the centre of trade in Canada. It grew into a large city in the mid-19th century when factories began to provide jobs for many workers.

By 1851, Canada's nine largest cities were (in order) Montreal, Quebec, Toronto, Saint John, N.B., Halifax, Hamilton, Kingston, Ottawa, and London. Over the next 30 years, several manufacturing towns in Ontario grew to almost 10 000 people. This second level of cities included Guelph, St Catharines, Brantford, and Belleville. By the 1880s, however, Montreal and Toronto began to outdistance all others.

Each city's growth or decline depends greatly on the prosperity of its surrounding area, which supplies food and products for sale and trade. It also provides a market for the city's goods. Toronto's location, for example, enables it to control the trade of the prosperous region of southwestern Ontario. It also enjoys convenient access to markets in the United States. The ability of each town to carry on commerce with nearby areas was greatly increased by the revolution in transportation that was brought about by the development of steam engines. Steamships began to appear in the 1820s and 1830s, railways in the 1840s and 1850s.

The railway played an extremely important role in the growth of cities in Canada. It provided arteries through which trade could flow year-round. Between 1881 and 1921, the railway brought a flood of settlement to the West. Most of the early settlers were farmers. Towns soon sprang up at regular points along the line. They serviced the railway, collected the wheat, and distributed goods to the surrounding areas. The decision to route the railway through Winnipeg was made in 1881 and it sparked the wildest boom in Canadian history. As the "Gateway to the West," Winnipeg grew at a phenomenal rate. It became a centre of finance, trade, and industry.

Equally dramatic was the growth of Vancouver, Calgary, and Edmonton from 1900 to 1913. Calgary grew 1000% from

1901 to 1911. Edmonton's population increased from 4100 in 1901 to 53 800 in 1916. Vancouver barely existed before the railway. It prospered both as a port and as the terminus of the Canadian Pacific Railway (CPR). By the 1920s it surpassed Winnipeg as Canada's third-largest city.

Western expansion also benefited cities in central Canada. It increased trade and enlarged the market for manufactured goods. Eastern factories produced farm machinery, rails, spikes, and railway cars. Merchants supplied farmers with goods and with services such as banking. As the headquarters of the CPR, Montreal benefited most from the expansion of the railways. Toronto secured its position as Ontario's prime city through its role as the hub of several railways.

Policies of the federal government on tariffs and railways strengthened the growth of manufacturing in the cities of Ontario and Quebec. At the same time, they weakened the position of the cities on the Atlantic coast. Quebec, Halifax, and Saint John were farther away from the booming activities of the western prairie. Their golden age of trade, which was based on the sailing ship, ended with the appearance of the steamship.

THE MODERN CITY

Most of the characteristics of the modern city had emerged by 1900. While earlier towns had a few functions, such as defence and trade, modern cities have many more functions and many more people. As cities grew, these different functions tended to become separated. Some areas were set aside for business, others for recreation, industry, homes, etc. These neighbourhoods were broken down further. For example, wealthier residents lived in certain neighbourhoods; poorer people in others. By the 1920s, the familiar pattern of tall office buildings downtown and sprawling suburbs on the fringe had appeared.

Electric streetcars played a very important role in the development of Canadian cities. Before streetcars, workers had to live near the factories, which were usually located downtown. Wealthy people moved into neighbourhoods farther out. By 1910, most cities had streetcars, which allowed working people to commute to work, and another ring of neighbourhoods was built. These neighbourhoods were laid out in grid patterns, along the streetcar lines. This pattern continued in the 1930s and 1940s.

Most Canadian cities had a significant growth spurt after World War II as a result of heavy immigration from Europe. This time the expansion was heavily influenced by the automobile. Both residents and factories moved to outer areas, called *suburbs*. Many of these suburbs were beyond the streetcar lines and could only be reached by car or bus. New expressways permitted people to travel to and from work more easily.

One of the earliest suburbs was Don Mills, on the outskirts of Toronto. Each of its four neighbourhoods centered on a school. The curved streets not only discouraged traffic, but were also interesting aesthetically, because they followed the terrain. Single-family dwellings, apartment buildings, offices, and factories were separated from one another. Don Mills was considered so successful that its pattern was repeated over and over throughout Canada.

Downtown The city centre has always held its most important buildings: city hall, large churches, offices, department stores, stadiums, etc. Recent decades have seen huge growth in the downtown areas of Canadian cities. As land has become more valuable, office buildings have risen higher. This has led to the building of large office towers and a great increase in the number of people who have to be moved to and from work each day.

The downtown office buildings also put stress on transportation. Every Canadian city except Toronto had given up its streetcars by the late 1950s. They were believed to be old fashioned. However, it soon became clear that cars and buses could not cope with all the people. The automobile, which had offered such freedom, began to devour huge areas of land in expressways and parking lots. It greatly increased air pollution. In response, first Toronto and then Montreal built subway systems. In recent years, Edmonton, Calgary, and Vancouver have built modern street rail lines, called Light Rapid Transit (LRT).

Urban Renewal In the late 1950s, urban renewal schemes were attempted across Canada to try to improve the conditions in the city cores. This renewal usually involved the tearing down of homes and businesses, and the building of new housing. These plans were resisted by working-class families who were displaced by the changes. The controversy over urban renewal continued into the late 1960s. The development industry responded to the vastly increased housing needs by building large apartment buildings, usually where handsome 19th-century houses had been demolished. Neighbourhood groups were formed in reaction to the destruction. In every major city, these groups battled with the developers and their supporters at city hall. By the mid-1970s, the apartment boom had come to an end.

Since then, renewal attempts have generally been more modest, such as improved street lighting, parks, decorative sidewalks, and community centres. Cities have begun to develop policies to strengthen downtown communities, rather than obliterate them. Attempts are being made to salvage what is left of the interesting buildings of the past. Areas such as Montreal's Old Town, Halifax's Heritage Properties, and Vancouver's Gastown have been preserved as tourist attractions.

City Life Since the 1950s, the number of people who are neither of French nor English origin has grown rapidly in Canadian cities. Most cities take pride in the celebrations of these cultures and attempt to encourage co-operation among them. These celebrations, together with arts events and sports, help to develop a sense of community. In this regard, Canada is recognized around the world for its orderly, clean, and safe cities. Cities still face problems, but Canada has shown that it has the resources and the willingness to make city life rewarding.

GOVERNMENT

All Canadian cities and towns elect a mayor (or sometimes a reeve). Mayors do not control the city government, like a premier or a prime minister. They preside over a council, which is also elected. They can have considerable influence if they have a strong personality, but in fact they have no more power than the council members.

City governments are organized by department, such as parks, public works, and social services. These departments are given directions by the council and mayor. Cities employ numerous workers: police, fire fighters, transit workers, and others.

About 37% of the money needed to run cities comes from taxes on property. Another 46% comes from grants from the provinces. The rest comes from other sources. About 40% of this money is spent on education, another 10% on transportation, and about 8% on police and fire fighting.

▷ RELATED ARTICLES: **Government; Industrial Revolution; Mayor; Railway; Urban Reform; Western Settlement.**

■ **Civil Defence,** *see* **Defence**

■ **Civil Engineering,** *see* **Engineering**

■ **Civil Law**

Civil law is the part of the law that resolves disputes between individuals or between organizations. It is separate from criminal law, which deals with crimes.

In all provinces, except Quebec, the rules of civil law are contained in court decisions (common law) and in legislation (statutes). In Quebec, the civil law is codified and contained for the most part in the Civil Code, which has well over 2000 articles.

The procedure used for the resolution of disputes in civil law is *adversarial*, that is, opposing parties argue against each other in court. In a typical case, an individual who believes he or she has suffered a wrong will consult a lawyer. This individual, called the *plaintiff*, may then bring an action against another individual called the *defendant*. The lawyer representing the plaintiff will attend the court and obtain a *writ* or other *summons* to be delivered to the defendant. The defendant will then be obliged to appear in court and answer the claim made by the plaintiff. In its initial phase, called discovery, the procedure is designed to compel the parties to reveal all the information relevant to the issues in dispute.

If the parties cannot agree on a settlement, they proceed to trial. Because of the large number of cases, the trial may not take place for months, or even years. Most civil trials take place before a judge but some can take place before a judge and a jury. In Quebec, however, no civil case goes to a jury. At the trial, each party presents evidence, usually in the form of documents, and calls witnesses. The judge renders a judgement for or against the plaintiff. After judgement, the losing party may choose to appeal to a higher court. The Court of Appeal may confirm or reverse the judgement, or in special cases order a new trial. If a defendant fails to comply with the judgement, his or her property may be seized and sold in payment of the debt confirmed in the judgement. In exceptional cases, where a party disobeys an express order of the court, this party may be sent to jail.

■ **Clam**

Clam is the common name given to the

class Bivalvia ("bi" meaning two and "valve" meaning shell) of the phylum Mollusca. They include the familiar oysters, scallops, clams, and mussels. They are aquatic animals found all over the world in fresh, salt, or brackish water and range in size from less than 1 mm to over 1 m in length.

Canada's largest bivalve is the Pacific geoduck which reaches 20 cm. Their soft bodies are protected from harm by a pair of hard shells which are generally hinged by a tough elastic ligament. The shells are opened and closed by adductor muscles. The firm white morsel of the scallop that you eat is actually its adductor muscle. Bivalves have no head. Their gills strain the microscopic food particles that they eat, from the water. Bivalves are not very mobile. The fastest is the scallop. By clapping its shells, it expels water from between them, creating propulsion. This makes them appear to swim in fast spurts. Others have a strong foot which is used for burrowing or hopping. Some bivalves do not move at all. Mussels tie themselves to the substrate by means of a bundle of threads called the byssus. Others like the oyster, cement themselves to rocks or other shells. Bivalves are an important link in the food chain for other molluscs, fish, birds, and mammals. They also strain harmful bacteria from polluted water.

■ Clancy, Francis Michael

Hockey player (*born in 1903 at Ottawa, Ont.; died in 1986 at Toronto, Ont.*). "King" Clancy was immensely popular as the leader of the Senators hockey team in his home town of Ottawa. In 1930 he was sold to the Toronto Maple Leafs for $35 000 and two players, a huge sum in those days. He was a small man but his speed and gritty play led the Leafs to their first great success. He was later well known for his witty and lively commentary on the game of hockey.

■ Clark, Brenda

Illustrator (*born in 1955 at Toronto, Ont.*). After graduating from Sheridan College, Clark became a freelance illustrator. Her first assignments were illustrations for anthologies and other school texts. She has also produced work for *Chickadee* magazine.

The first storybook that she illustrated was *The Yellow Flag* (1980), by Susanne McSweeney. Since then, she has illustrated a number of notable books, including Allen Morgan's *Sadie and The Snowman*

(1985), Paulette Bourgeois's *Franklin in the Dark* (1986), and Ted Staunton's *Puddleman* (1988). Clark's illustrations are closer to photographs than cartoons, but the round faces, and missing details and textures make them obviously paintings. Most of her compositions are simple, but she is developing effective variations. In Paulette Bourgeois's *Big Sarah's Little Boots* (1987), for example, she eliminates some backgrounds to focus attention on Sarah's feelings.

Big Sarah's Little Boots, *illustrated by Brenda Clark, 1987 (© 1987 Brenda Clark/courtesy Kids Can Press Ltd).*

■ Clark, Catherine Anthony

Writer (*born in 1892 at London, England; died in 1977 at Victoria, B.C.*). Clark came to Canada in 1914. She was the first writer to make significant use of Canadian materials in fantasy. She based the mountain settings for her six fantasies and her one historical novel on British Columbia's West Kootenay region, where she once had a ranch.

Clark's fantasies follow a pattern set in *The Golden Pine Cone* (1950). A boy and girl journey to a magical world where they undertake quests that restore moral order. They succeed because of courage, compassion, and generosity. Their adventure helps them to get along when they return home.

Two elements are distinctive in her fantasies. First, native Indian mythology and characters are important. Second, they contain many invented characters, such as the comical Rock Puck in *The Diamond Feather* (1962), who resemble the talking animals of folktales.

The Sun Horse (1951) won the Canadian Association of Children's Librarians Book of the Year medal.

Frank "King" Clancy was a star with the Ottawa Senators when he was traded to Toronto (courtesy Hockey Hall of Fame/artwork by Irma Coucill).

Charles Joseph Clark
16TH PRIME MINISTER OF CANADA

Born: June 5, 1939 at High River, Alta
Occupation: Journalist
Political Party: Conservative
First Elected: 1972
Chosen Leader: 1976
Period as Prime Minister: June 4, 1979, to
    March 2, 1980
(PHOTO BY JOHN DEVISSER)

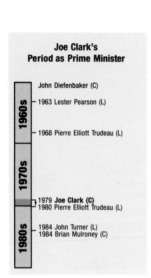

**Joe Clark's
Period as Prime Minister**

John Diefenbaker (C)

1960s
1963 Lester Pearson (L)

1968 Pierre Elliott Trudeau (L)

1970s

1979 Joe Clark (C)
1980 Pierre Elliott Trudeau (L)

1980s
1984 John Turner (L)
1984 Brian Mulroney (C)

■ Clark, Charles Joseph

Clark received a BA and MA at the University of Alberta. He worked as an organizer for the Conservative Party and was national student president of the party. He was first elected MP for Rocky Mountain, Alberta, in 1972, and has represented Yellowhead since 1979.

Clark vaulted into national attention in 1976 when he emerged as the surprise winner of the convention to choose a new leader of the Conservative Party. He had not been favoured to win but the convention was divided over the two leading candidates, Brian Mulroney and Claude Wagner. In May 1979 the Conservatives and Clark defeated the government of Pierre Trudeau and Clark became Canada's 16th prime minister. He was the youngest person to become prime minister (aged 40) and the first native-born westerner.

Prime Minister Clark had only gained a minority government, that is, the Conservatives had more seats than the Liberals, but not enough to govern without the support of the other parties, especially the NDP. He decided to press ahead with his program, which included the selling off of the government owned oil company, Petro-Canada, and cutbacks in government spending. The NDP combined with the Liberals to defeat the Conservatives in the House of Commons. Clark called an election and was defeated by a rejuvenated Pierre Trudeau in February 1980. Hence, Clark's time as prime minister was only nine months.

Defeat Clark was leader of the opposition from 1980 to 1983, during which time he fought Trudeau's plans for a new constitution until agreement was reached with the provinces. Although Clark and his party led the polls, many in his party believed that he could not win another election. He chose to settle the question of his leadership at a convention in June 1983, but lost to Brian Mulroney on the fourth ballot.

Minister Clark remained a respected member of the party, and when Mulroney became prime minister, he named Clark secretary of state for external affairs, a position he still holds (1990).

■ Clark, Joan

Writer (*born in 1934 at Liverpool, N.S.*). Clark is a graduate of Acadia University and she taught school before becoming a writer. She frequently uses parallel stories and symbols to explore her characters' search for identity. In her first book, *Girl of the Rockies* (1968), a bear cub's growth parallels that of the girl who kept it as a pet. In *The Hand of Robin Squires* (1977), the parallels are between a kidnapped English boy and a rebellious Micmac.

Symbols are a major element in two novels. In *Wild Man of the Woods* (1985),

Joan Clark often uses parallel stories and symbols to explore her characters' search for identity (courtesy Penguin Books).

a native mask that Stephen Gibson wears to scare bullies symbolizes his darker self. He is symbolically reborn after the mask is knocked off. *The Moons of Madeleine* (1987) explores female identity through the heroine's symbolic quest for First Woman in a parallel moon world.

Clark has also written two symbolic picture books, *Thomasina and the Trout Tree* (1971) and *The Leopard and the Lily* (1984).

■ Clark, Karl Adolf

Chemist (*born in 1888 at Georgetown, Ont.; died in 1966 at Victoria, B.C.*). Soon after leaving university, Clark was hired by the Research Council of Alberta to find a practical use for the tar-like form of oil called bitumen. In northeastern Alberta, as well as in other parts of Canada, there are huge tracts of bitumen-soaked sand, called oil sands. Starting in the 1920s, Clark pioneered a process which uses hot water to separate the bitumen from the sand.

In 1967, the year after Clark died, Great Canadian Oil Sands (now Suncor Ltd) opened an oil-sands mining plant at Fort McMurray, Alta. This plant, the first commercial oil-sands plant in the world, used Clark's hot-water recovery process. His process is also used at the Syncrude plant, which was built later at Fort McMurray. More than one-tenth of all the oil produced in Canada is extracted from oil sands by means of the hot-water process.

▷ RELATED ARTICLES: **Bitumen; Oil; Oil Sands; Petroleum.**

▷ SUGGESTED READING: Mary Clark Sheppard, *Oil Sands Scientist: The Letters of Karl A. Clark* (1989).

■ Clark, Paraskeva

Painter (*born Paraskeva Plistik in 1898 at St Petersburg [Leningrad], Russia; died in 1986 at Toronto, Ont.*). She learned abstract art in studios in Russia. She met Philip Clark in Paris, married him, and moved to Toronto in 1931. Her *Self-Portrait* (1933) shows an almost mask-like face that was influenced by the cubist painters, such as Picasso. She continued to paint portraits, still lifes, and flower studies with an individual flair.

■ Clarke, Charles Kirk

Psychiatrist (*born in 1857 at Elora, Canada West [Ont.]; died in 1924 at Toronto, Ont.*). The Clarke Institute of Psychiatry in Toronto is named after Charles Clarke, who laid the foundation of psychiatry as a medical science in Canada. Clarke built on the work of Joseph Workman and

Self-Portrait, *(1933) by Paraskeva Clark (courtesy NGC/183).*

Richard Bucke, two major pioneers in treating the mentally ill. Despite their efforts, most Canadians still thought that mental problems were untreatable. But Clarke maintained that "an insane person is one suffering from bodily disease just as much as the patient with typhoid fever." He therefore emphasized therapy, and he tried to get the name of the institutions changed from "lunatic asylum" to "hospital."

As a young man, Clarke had been Workman's assistant at the Provincial Lunatic Asylum in Toronto. He later worked at institutions in Hamilton and Kingston before returning to Toronto to be superintendent of the asylum in 1905. He gained such respect for his work that in 1911 he was appointed superintendent of Toronto General Hospital. He retained the position until 1918, while also serving as the University of Toronto's professor of psychiatry and dean of medicine.

▷ RELATED ARTICLES: **Richard Bucke; Joseph Workman.**

■ Clarkson, Adrienne Louise

Journalist, broadcaster (*born in 1939 in Hong Kong*). Clarkson is one of the best-known personalities on Canadian television. She arrived in Canada in 1942 with her parents and studied at both the University of Toronto and the Sorbonne in Paris. In 1965 she joined the CBC and was a popular host for several programs, in-

cluding "Take Thirty" and "the fifth estate." She travelled the world interviewing famous people, and was respected for the way she tackled controversial subjects with dignity and charm. In 1982 Clarkson was appointed Ontario's agent general in France, where she represented the province's trade and cultural interests. In 1987 she returned to Canada as president of the prestigious publishing house McClelland and Stewart, but in 1988 she went back to television as host of her own cultural program, "Adrienne Clarkson's Summer Festival." She has also published two novels, *A Lover More Condoling* and *Hunger Trace* with McClelland and Stewart.

■ Class

Social class is understood in two ways. One is based upon differences in wealth, status, job, education, residence, and similar factors. It leads to people being described as upper, middle, and lower class, sometimes with more specific terms such as upper-middle and lower-middle class. Obviously, these terms are not absolutely precise and it is not always easy to say to which exact class someone belongs.

The second definition of social class is found most often in Socialism. It distinguishes between people who own the "means of production" (for example, land, resources, factories, machines, etc.) and those who own only their "labour power" (for example, skill, strength, experience, etc.) The first group is the "bourgeoisie," or middle class. The second is the "proletariat," or working class.

Again, the terms are not always easy to apply. Where, for example, do lawyers, teachers, or actors belong? Where do managers, who have a lot of power but do not own things, belong?

In the socialist analysis, the middle class has most of the power, both in economics and in politics. For example, although business people and professionals make up only 10% of the Canadian population, they account for 75% of all those active in politics. Similarly, the poorest 20% of Canadians receive only 6.5% of total national income, while the richest 20% get 38.4%. Socialists believe that the working class must win more power.

Most Canadians see themselves as middle class and are unwilling to think in terms of social class. This has led the New Democratic Party to appeal not to "the working class" but to "ordinary Canadians."

▷ RELATED ARTICLES: **New Democratic Party; Socialism; Working-Class History.**

■ Clear Grits

The Clear Grits were a group of politicians in Canada West who broke away from the Reform Party around 1850. Seen as radicals, they looked to the United States, instead of to Britain, for their political ideas. For example, they thought that Canada should be a republic, like the United States. They wanted public officials such as judges to be elected rather than appointed. They believed that all signs of special privilege and aristocracy in Canada would then be destroyed and that everyone would be equal. They also wanted free trade and representation by population.

The Reform government of Robert Baldwin and Louis LaFontaine, which believed that Canada should continue British traditions, did not adopt the reforms these radicals wanted. The radicals therefore organized themselves into a separate movement in 1849 to work for change.

It is not certain how the Clear Grits got their name. The word "grit," which they were also called, means determination. Members of the movement sometimes said that they were "grit clear to the backbone." They meant that they were determined not to stop working until they got the reforms they wanted.

During the 1850s they came under the influence of George Brown, the Toronto newspaperman and politician. Brown managed to soften some of their extreme ideas. Gradually they began to work with other groups that had similar ideas. Finally, during the 1860s, they were absorbed into the new Liberal Party, led by Brown. In English Canada, the favourite nickname for the Liberal Party has always been "Grits."

▷ RELATED ARTICLES: **Political History; Reformers; Rep by Pop.**

■ Clearwater River

Clearwater River, 384 km long, flows west out of northwestern Saskatchewan into Alberta, where it joins the Athabasca River. It and the Fund du Lac River are the only westward-flowing rivers between Winnipeg and the Rockies. During the fur-trade era it was an important link between the Athabasca region and the south.

■ Cleaver, Elizabeth

Writer, illustrator (*born in 1939 at Montreal; died there in 1985*). Cleaver, who studied art in Montreal, won numerous awards for her 13 books.

Cleaver's subjects come from her love of fairy tales, myths, and legends. She illustrated four of William Toye's retelling of native legends: *How Summer Came to Canada* (1969); *The Mountain Goats of Temlaham* (1969); *The Loon's Necklace* (1977), winner of two major awards; and *The Fire Stealer* (1979). Shadow puppets illustrate her text of an Inuit myth, *The Enchanted Caribou* (1985). Her retelling of the Hungarian legend, *The Miraculous Hind* (1973), and *Petrouchka* (1980), inspired by a ballet, won further awards.

Cleaver's childhood love of cutout books influenced her technique of collage. She combined pictures printed from linoleum blocks with shapes cut and torn from paper. She also used a variety of materials, from leaves to lace, to create a three-dimensional effect.

Cleaver's collages make striking use of

Petrouchka, illustrated by Elizabeth Cleaver, 1980. Cleaver's subjects came from her love of fairy tales (courtesy Macmillan of Canada).

colour. In *The Mountain Goats of Temlaham*, for example, strips of bright colours suggest a mythic setting. Colours also convey mood, becoming darker when the evil men are punished and brighter when peace is restored.

▷ SUGGESTED READING: Cyrus MacMillan, *Canadian Wonder Tales* (1974).

■ Clergy Reserves

The clergy reserves were lands belonging to the Church of England (the Anglican Church) in Upper and Lower Canada. By the Constitutional Act of 1791, one-seventh of each township was set aside to support "Protestant clergy." The aim was to provide the Church of England with an income. By leasing its lands, it could pay its clergy and cover other expenses. The government believed that members of the Anglican Church were more loyal to Britain than members of other religions. It hoped that by giving the Anglicans this kind of advantage, they would make the church stronger and better able to win the support and loyalty of new settlers. A church that receives this kind of help from a government is called an "established church."

The government's plan did not work. Instead of increasing the loyalty of new settlers, the clergy reserves caused much resentment. In fact, Anglicans were soon a minority, even in Upper Canada. Most of the new settlers who poured into the colony were not Anglicans. They were Methodists, Baptists, and Presbyterians, and they did not share in the proceeds from the clergy reserves. Neither did the Roman Catholics. Another complaint was that the reserves were scattered across each township, rather than being concentrated in one area. This made settlement difficult.

From the 1820s on, there were increasing complaints about the clergy reserves.

The Mountain Goats of Temlaham, *illustration by Elizabeth Cleaver, 1969. Cleaver accurately depicts the art styles of the native people of the West Coast and, in presenting the swirling waters, communicates the fear the tiny goat feels when mistreated by the children (© Oxford University Press).*

Cold Front *as a broken line of showers and thunderstorms (© A&J Verkaik/Skyart).*

Warm Front *showing several layers of cirrus clouds in advance of the front (© A&J Verkaik/Skyart).*

Thunderstorm, *showing a single thundershower with a heavy rain core. Thunderstorms usually erupt at the end of a hot summer day (© A&J Verkaik/Skyart).*

Snow Squalls *showing a bank of heavy cloud embedded with cells of snow. Most people in the world never see snow, but in the Canadian climate, it is part of our everyday life in winter (© A&J Verkaik/Skyart).*

Soil Erosion *caused by an intense thunderstorm squall lifting the soil off the fields. Air moves because it is heated by sunlight, rises, then cools and descends. This churning of the atmosphere results in wind — the flow of air from place to place (© A&J Verkaik/Skyart).*

In 1840 a bill was passed distributing profits from the lands among all the leading religious groups. In 1854 the lands were finally removed from church ownership.

■ Climate

Climate is the temperature and moisture conditions of the layer of air near the surface of the Earth over a long period of time. The term "weather" refers to these conditions as they occur from day to day.

Because Canada is such a large country, it has many different climates. These differences result from the unequal distribution of the energy of the Sun. The heat received by a particular area depends on the angle at which the Sun's rays strike the Earth. This angle varies with the time of day, the latitude of the area, and the season of the year. The length of the day is also important. For example, in December, southern Canada receives eight hours of daylight, while the northern tip receives none.

Heat that reaches the Earth is absorbed by land and water, and is released again into the atmosphere. Canada is a northern country, and for much of the year, more heat is lost than gained. As a result, large areas of the North experience long, cold winters and short, cool summers.

Land areas absorb heat rapidly, and they also cool off rapidly. Water areas warm up slowly and cool off slowly. Hence, there is almost always a difference in temperature between land and nearby bodies of water. As a result, large land areas can have very large variations in moisture and rain. This is called a *continental* climate. Areas that are under the influence of nearby oceans are known as *marine* climates. Marine climates have less variation in temperature and rain.

The movements of large air masses have a major effect on climate. In Canada, most of these air masses move from west to east, as the winds are predominantly *westerly* (blowing from the west). Canada's climate is generally dominated by cool polar air masses. Southern Canada is often a combat zone between this cool polar air and warm, moist air from the south. The result is often the storms that are so typical of Canadian weather. These storms, powered by the westerly winds, track from west to east. When a storm hits western Canada, it is probable that it will soon reach the east.

The land surface has an important effect on the climate of Canada. The Pacific mountain ranges block the warm, moist air blowing in from the west. As the air

Winter Wind Storm, *Pincher Creek, Alberta (photo by Thomas Kitchin).*

reaches the mountains, it rises, cools, and releases its moisture on the western slopes. The regions to the east of the mountains are therefore drier than areas to the west.

The Atlantic and Pacific oceans have a powerful influence on the west and east coasts of Canada. The Pacific Ocean is relatively warm and helps to bring milder winters to British Columbia. On the Atlantic, in contrast, the cold Labrador Current has a cooling effect. The Great Lakes bring more rain and snow, and milder winters, to the climate of southern Ontario. Hudson Bay, on the other hand, freezes over in winter and brings a much cooler climate to the land nearby.

MEASURING CLIMATE

The most common measurements for climate are temperature and moisture. These are useful, but more complex measurements are needed to decide what crops can be grown in certain areas.

Temperature is the degree of warmth or coldness. In winter, when northern Canada receives very little solar radiation, temperature differences from north to south are great. In summer, northern days are longer and the difference between north and south is less.

Moisture is the water that falls to Earth as rain, snow, hail, or in other forms. Moisture is measured in millimetres. Since warm air can hold more moisture than cold air, southern Canada has more precipitation than the North.

Growing Season The length of the growing season is the number of days between the spring date and the autumn date when the mean of 5.5°C occurs.

Frost-Free Days are the average number of days between the last killing frost in the spring and the first killing frost in the autumn. This measurement is more useful than "growing season" for the farmer who grows tender plants such as

tomatoes and beans.

Heating Degree Days (HDDs) measures the coldness of a place. HDDs sum up the temperatures below 18°C, the point at which furnaces are likely to be turned on. Southern Ontario has 4000 HDD; the High Arctic has 12 000. HDDs are also used to help match the right crop to the climate.

Potential Evapotranspiration (PE) is a way of measuring both heat and moisture. Moisture is of great importance to agriculture, but the simple measure of total precipitation is inadequate. It fails to take into consideration all the ways in which water may be stored in the ground, or may run off or evaporate. Much of the water that falls in Canada evaporates again into the atmosphere. Much of it also runs off into rivers and lakes. PE is the amount of water that would evaporate or transpire from vegetation in a certain area. The High Arctic islands, with a PE of 200, receives very little heat. The warmer areas of Canada measure over 600. This measure also shows that southern Alberta and the interior valleys of B.C. have the greatest water deficiencies. Moisture surpluses are highest on the West Coast.

CLIMATE REGIONS

Canada can be divided into regions according to any of the above measurements. There are six main regions:

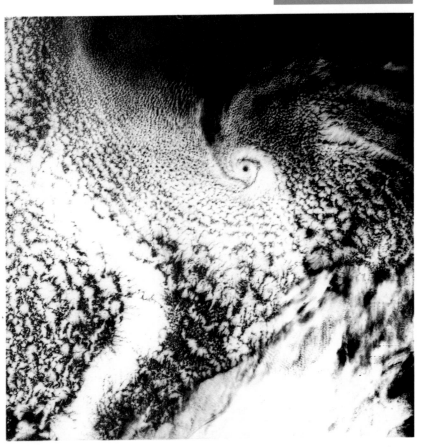

Storm Pattern *over the Davis Strait in northern Canada. The spiral pattern is typical of severe storms. Canada's climate is dominated by cool polar air masses (courtesy Canada Centre for Remote Sensing).*

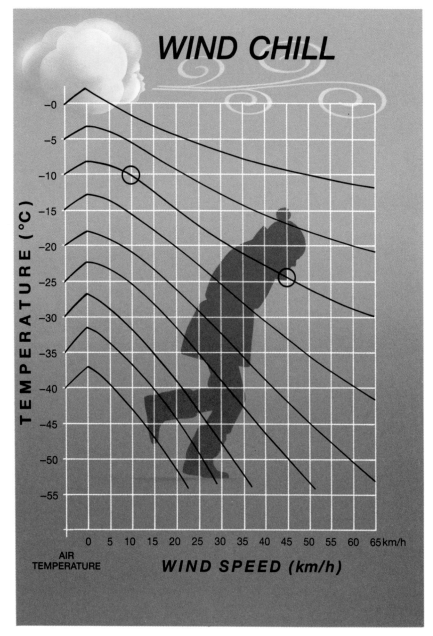

WIND CHILL

TEMPERATURE (°C)

-0
-5
-10
-15
-20
-25
-30
-35
-40
-45
-50
-55

0 5 10 15 20 25 30 35 40 45 50 55 60 65 km/h

AIR
TEMPERATURE

WIND SPEED (km/h)

Wind Chill is the combined effect of temperature and wind. The graph shows that if the temperature is -10°C and wind speed is 10 km/h, there is little added effect. But if the temperature is -10°C and the wind is 45 km/h, the air temperature is the equivalent to -25°C (artwork by Michael Lee).

Arctic Region The Arctic has been called a cold desert. It is well known that the region is cold. No monthly mean is above 10°C. It is less well known that the region is very dry, especially the western Arctic.

East Coast Precipitation is uniform through the year, and only in July is there less water than is needed

Great Lakes Precipitation is fairly uniform, but the PE is greater than on the East Coast.

Prairie Annual precipitation is inadequate in many areas. Precipitation in the winter is not enough to restore moisture in the soil.

West Coast Mean monthly temperatures are usually above 3°C, and water is needed in every month at Victoria.

Mountain Region Varies according to altitude and wind direction. Some very dry, others covered with permanent ice.

CLIMATE CHANGE

Changes in climate take place slowly, over many years. Yet even minor changes can have major, even catastrophic, effects on life.

Climates change for a number of reasons. Not all are understood. The climate of North America is much warmer today than it was 12 000 years ago. At that time, glaciers covered most of Canada. As the Earth warmed, the ice melted, exposing the land.

Climate changes can be caused by variations in the amount of energy given off by the Sun. Volcanic eruptions can change the climate by spreading dust in the atmosphere and blocking the sunlight. Humans may be altering the climate by burning fossil fuels and cutting down forests, thus increasing the amount of carbon dioxide in the atmosphere. Carbon dioxide allows the Sun's warmth to enter the atmosphere but prevents it from leaving, causing the Earth to heat up as a result of the "Greenhouse Effect."

CLIMATE AND MAN

There is hardly an aspect of life that is not affected by climate in some way. Climate determines life's essentials: heat, moisture, and light. It affects the way we dress, how and what we eat, how we feel, what we pay to heat our homes. It is essential to the production of trees and the management of water resources. It restricts agriculture, forestry, and other economic activities, and therefore has a great effect on where we live. Changes in climate, through drought, flood, or other natural causes, can be catastrophic.

Climate affects humans most closely in farming. Crops that are grown in Canada include wheat on the Prairies, potatoes in the Maritimes, and special crops where local climate conditions allow, such as fruit trees in the Okanagan Valley of B.C. and grapes in southern Ontario. Agriculture can be successful only when the climate is suitable for the type of crop a farmer wishes to grow. For every plant there is an ideal condition. The peach tree, for example, cannot withstand winter temperatures below -29°C. Therefore the only parts of Ontario where peaches can be grown are the warmer southern areas, such as the Niagara Peninsula.

All agricultural areas in Canada suffer from drought, frost, wind, heavy precipitation, hail, and flooding.

Precipitation is the source of all fresh water. Canada contains more usable fresh water than any other nation. However, the demand on these resources is great.

Canada consumes more energy per person than any other nation. This thirst for energy is largely a result of Canada's extreme climate. About one-third of our energy goes to heat or cool our homes and offices.

Climate also has an effect on transportation. Snow removal costs in Canada each year can be over $1 billion. Snow causes delays in traffic and heavy increases in fuel consumption. Fog and ice are perils to all forms of transportation.

Climate plays an important role as well in human health. Climate-related problems include colds, hypothermia, hay fever, asthma, frostbite, and headaches.

Climate plays a major role in our recreation. Ski areas, for example, depend on snowfall. A lack of snow between Christmas and New Year's Day can spell disaster for resort operators.

Climate also affects our comfort and safety. Winter is the most stressful time of year.

▷ SUGGESTED READING: Lydia Dotto, *Thinking the Unthinkable* (1988).

■ Climo, Lindee

Painter, author (*born in 1948 in Massachusetts, U.S.*). Climo grew up loving to work with animals and to paint. In 1974 she moved to Prince Edward Island, where she did both. Her paintings have been exhibited across Canada.

Her two books celebrate the simple life on old-fashioned farms. *Chester's Barn* (1982) describes a day on the farm. The pictures are filled with the activities of the animals, and rich brown colours create a sense of warmth and security. *Clyde* (1986) is about a farm horse who feels unwanted when the farmer buys a new trac-

---

Clyde, *illustrated by Lindee Climo, 1986 (© 1986 Lindee Climo/Tundra Books).*

tor. He foolishly imagines that he can become something else, but finally discovers that the farmer really needs and loves him. The illustrations reveal how foolish Clyde's daydreams are.

■ Clockmaker, or The Sayings and Doings of Sam Slick of Slickville, The (1836)

These short, humorous, satirical sketches by Thomas C. Haliburton feature Sam Slick, a clever clockmaker from the United States who sold his wares in rural Nova Scotia. He was able to sell clocks at a large profit because he used what he called "soft sawder," or flattery, on his customers. They found themselves buying a luxury item they did not need and could not afford.

Slick often commented on the people he met, pointing out their weaknesses, especially their laziness.

The short sketches were first published in the *Novascotian* newspaper and were later printed in book form. The sketches were very popular in Canada, England, and the U.S. The first series of the book rivalled Charles Dickens in popularity. Many later writers of humour were influenced by Haliburton's sharp satire, his humorous exaggeration, and his clever characterization.

■ Cloud

A cloud is a visible mass of water droplets or ice crystals floating in the air. When you "see" your breath outdoors on a cold day, you are seeing a cloud form. Molecules of water and particles of "dust" are always present in the atmosphere. Often these dust particles are coated with a film of water, giving rise to particles we call haze. Water molecules in the air constantly bombard these haze particles, and molecules from the haze are constantly leaving to enter the air. As the air cools, the rate at which water molecules leave the haze particles slows down, but the rate of bombardment remains the same. Thus, the haze drops grow and a cloud forms. This process is called condensation. Water vapour condenses when you breathe out into cold air, or when warm, moist air rises and cools as a result of expansion. In both cases, tiny droplets of water form, droplets so tiny (less than one-hundredth of a millimetre in diameter) that they float in the air like smoke — a cloud.

Clouds have short lives, from a few minutes to several hours. Either they evaporate — their usual fate — or they drop their water as precipitation in the

---

Sayings of Sam Slick

"Of all the seventeen senses, I like common sense as well as any of 'em, arter all."

"If a bear comes after you, Sam, you must be up and doin' or it's a gone goose with you."

Cirrus Clouds are wispy white clouds formed of tiny ice crystals at high altitudes. Those in this photo are stretched out into what are called "mares' tails." Cirrus clouds are often the first to appear in a clear blue sky (© A&J Verkaik/Skyart).

Altocumulus Clouds are fleecy cloud formations which usually appear in a rippled pattern. They may form when cool air moves in and pushes warm air masses upward (© A&J Verkaik/Skyart).

Cumulus Clouds have a flat base and rounded tops, built up like mountains. They grow upwards because of the upward movement of air. Cumulus clouds are warm-weather clouds (© A&J Verkaik/Skyart).

Altocumulus Clouds (top) with cumulus clouds in the distance (© A&J Verkaik/Skyart).

Severe Storm A classic storm structure shows a high, sharp top on the clouds, like an anvil. On the flanks are growing towers. Such cumulonimbus clouds form in late afternoon on a hot day, when currents of warm air rise to the greatest altitude (© A&J Verkaik/Skyart).

form of rain, hail, or snow. It takes about a million cloud droplets to form one raindrop.

The cloudiest parts of Canada are the East and West Coast where, on average, 80% or more of winter skies are covered by clouds. The Prairie Provinces and the Arctic are relatively cloud-free.

Fog A fog is a cloud that forms at ground level and is so dense that you cannot see more than 1000 m through it. (If you can see farther, it is called a mist, not a fog.) Because it so reduces visibility, fog is a peril on roads, in the air, and at sea.

Most fog in Canada occurs along the Pacific, the Arctic, and especially the Atlantic coasts. In summer, the coasts of Nova Scotia and Newfoundland are often blanketed in fog. This fog forms when warm, moist air is chilled by the very cold waters of the Labrador Current. St John's, Nfld, reports fog an average of more than one in every three days. The seas off Newfoundland, in fact, are among the foggiest in the world.

In inland areas of Canada, fog can form early in the morning, particularly after cloudless nights in autumn, when the air has been radiating its heat upwards and thus becoming cool. Such fogs persist until they are evaporated by the heat of the Sun.

Often the droplets in a fog remain liquid at temperatures below the freezing point of water. Such droplets are said to be supercooled. They may then freeze into beautiful patterns on trees, wires, and other objects. However, supercooled fog can also lead to dangerous ice build-ups on aircraft and electrical transmission lines.

In the North, the air can be so bitterly cold that water vapour is deposited as tiny crystals of ice rather than as liquid, thus forming a sparkling ice fog. This tends to happen when temperatures are colder than -30°C.

▷ RELATED ARTICLES: **Climate; Precipitation; Thunderstorm; Tornado; Weather.**

■ Clover

The true clover is the name given to plants of the genus *Trifolium*, of the pea family (Leguminosae). Most people are familiar with the species brought over from Europe to be grown as forage. There are 12 native species; all but one are found on the west coast of B.C. An important cattle food, protein-rich clover is preferably eaten dried. Clovers have trifoil leaves and clusters of round, compact flowers, which may be purple, white, pink, red, or yel-

Clover is an important cattle food. White clover (bottom) and alsike clover (upper left) are grown for honey production. Red clover (upper right) is used to calm coughs (artwork by Claire Tremblay).

low, depending on the species. The roots bear swellings, or nodules, containing bacteria that are able to fix nitrogen from the air and transform it into nitrates, which the plant then absorbs.

The white clover (*Trifolium repens*) and the alsike clover (*T. hybridum*) are grown for honey production. Clover flowers, with their rich, perfumed smell and pleasant taste, are put in soups, used as a substitute for tea, or mixed with onion juice and hot honey to soothe a cold. A tea drink made from red clover (*T. pratense*) calms coughs, relieves diarrhea, and cleanses the system of toxins. A "four-leaf clover" is a symbol of good luck, wealth, and fertility.

Club Moss

Club moss, commonly known as "ground pine" or "trailing evergreen," belongs to genus *Lycopodium* of the club moss family (Lycopodiaceae). These low evergreen plants grow on forest floors. Unlike the club mosses, which lived hundreds of millions of years ago and grew to tree height, today's versions are rarely more than 25 cm tall.

A club moss plant often consists of a long trailing stalk, either underground or clinging to the soil, from which rise vertical secondary stalks. These branches are covered in small, single-veined leaves like those found on mosses (hence the name). Club mosses reproduce through spores that form in special organs, the sporangia, which are found on the upper face of certain leaves. In most Canadian species, the leaves form a cone, called a sporophyll, in which the sporangia are housed. The sporophylls are usually clustered in long spikes found in the tips of the upright branches. Some club mosses can also reproduce from small buds that detach themselves from the plant and give birth to new plants. In the past, club mosses were sold commercially as Christmas decorations. The spores had a variety of uses: as a coating for pills, as a drying powder for baby care, or even, because of their flammability, to imitate lightning in theatres and in fireworks.

Clutesi, George Charles

Nootka artist and author (*born in 1905 at Port Alberni, B.C.; died in 1988 at Victoria, B.C.*). George Clutesi was the author of *Son of Raven, Son of Deer: Fables of the Tse-shaht People* (1967) and *Potlatch* (1969), both of which he illustrated himself. He was one of the first native people to write about native legends and customs, bringing them to a non-native audience. Previously, native cultures had most often been described by anthropologists or folklorists, rather than by native people themselves.

Clutesi was a fisherman and pile driver for 21 years, but in the 1940s he broke his back. While he was recovering, he began to record and teach the stories, songs, and art of his people. He became an accomplished artist as well as a writer, and in 1967 he painted a large mural for the "Indians of Canada" pavilion at Expo 67, the world fair held in Montreal.

▷ SUGGESTED READING: George Clutesi, *Potlatch* (1969).

CN Tower

The CN Tower in Toronto is the world's tallest free-standing structure. The concrete tower is 450 m high and is topped by a 100 m steel mast, giving it a total height of 553 m. It was completed in 1976 and cost $52 million. The tower has two main functions: communications and observation. It transmits both broadcast and microwave signals, and it is also a popular tourist centre. Each year, thousands of visitors ride in glassed-in elevators to a revolving restaurant and wide observation decks, which are 342 m above the ground. The tower overlooks Lake Ontario and soars above the SkyDome stadium.

CN Tower *is the tallest free-standing structure in the world. From this angle, it soars above the SkyDome (courtesy Aerocamera Services Inc., Orangeville, Ont.).*

■ Cnidaria

This phylum consists of corals, hydrozoa, jellyfish, and anemones. Cnidaria are the most primitive form of life, after sponges. Cnidaria have long been classified as zoophytes, which in Greek means animal-plant. The individuals live alone or in colonies, and may have either of two different types of body structure. One is the polyp type, with a tube-shaped body that is usually surrounded by a crown of tentacles. This type must be attached to some surface and includes corals and anemones.

The other type is a flowing, swimming kind, the jellyfish type, with a gelatinous, umbrella-shaped body. Several species take both forms during the course of their development.

The body of either type is made up of two layers of cells, with a mouth either on the top (polyp types) or on the bottom (jellyfish types). The inner layer of cells is the stomach lining, while the outer layer is the protective covering. The outer layer has little stinging cells called cnidoblasts, which they use for defence and to capture their food. The cnidoblasts are particularly abundant on their tentacles. Cnidaria are all aquatic, and almost all are sea creatures. They are usually small, but some jellyfish have a diameter of 2 m and have tentacles 10 m long. The hydrozoa and some anemones can reproduce through budding: that is, young ones grow out of an adult, a little like a twig out of a branch, and detach themselves once fully formed. Some Cnidaria are luminescent and give off a feeble bluish light in the dark.

▷ RELATED ARTICLES: **Anemone; Coral; Jellyfish.**

■ Coady, Moses

Priest and teacher (*born in 1882 at North East Margaree, N.S.; died in 1959 at Antigonish, N.S.*). A community organizer as well as a priest, Coady was the founder of the Antigonish Movement.

Coady was a teacher at St Francis Xavier University in Antigonish, Nova Scotia. In 1930 he launched a program of adult education. The Antigonish Movement, as it was called, helped people in the Maritimes to work for their own economic betterment. It organized dozens of co-operatives that allowed people to obtain consumer goods, housing, and medical care at a cost they could afford.

During the bleak years of the Great Depression, Coady also fought for the right of Maritime workers to form unions. His writings were translated into several languages. By the time of his death, his ideas of community self-help had been taken up in many poorer countries.

In 1959 the Coady International Institute opened. At St Francis Xavier University, its task has been to train organizers from around the world.

▷ RELATED ARTICLES: **Antigonish Movement; Co-operative Movement.**

▷ SUGGESTED READING: Malcolm A. MacLellan, *Coady Remembered* (1985).

■ Coaker, Sir William

Union leader (*born in 1871 at St John's, Nfld; died in 1938 at Boston, Mass.*). Coaker believed that the fishermen could only improve their conditions if their union played a strong role in politics. He began organizing the Fishermen's Protective Union (FPU) in 1908 and it had 20 000 members by 1914. The FPU did well in the election of 1913 and Coaker joined the Cabinet of Premier Squires in 1919. However, he failed to solve the long-standing problems of the Newfoundland fishing industry.

■ Coal

Coal is a black or dark brown mineral. It is mostly made up of carbon and can burn. It is by far the most abundant fossil fuel and is an important source of energy.

Formation Coal lies in veins beneath the surface of the Earth, sandwiched between layers of rock. It formed from 360 to 280 million years ago. The climate was warmer and wetter then and supported vast areas of dense vegetation. When the plants died, they were slowly buried, crushed, and heated beneath the Earth's surface. Over millions of years, the plants turned to coal.

Uses Today, coal is used mainly to generate heat and electricity. In 1988, 18% of Canada's electricity was generated from coal. The coal is used to produce steam, which is used to turn the generators that produce electricity. Heat from coal is also used to produce metals, such as steel. Coal itself is used to make chemicals and plastics.

Distribution Canada has 4% of the coal in the world, enough to last over 100 years at the present rate that it is being used. Most of Canada's coal is mined in Alberta, B.C., Nova Scotia, and Saskatchewan.

HISTORY OF COAL MINING

Coal was first mined in Canada in 1639 at Grand Lake, in present-day New Brunswick. In the 1720s, French soldiers based at Louisbourg on Cape Breton Island kept warm by burning coal that was mined nearby.

During the 19th century, coal gradually replaced wood as the most important source of energy. Coal burns hotter than wood and is easier to transport. It powered the steam engines that brought about the Industrial Revolution.

Canada's coal-mining industry first developed on Cape Breton Island. By the time of Confederation, coal mines on Cape Breton supplied most of Canada's coal.

The first coal mine in western Canada opened in 1836 near Fort McNeil, on Vancouver Island. Larger mines around Nanaimo, B.C., opened in the 1850s. These mines supplied fuel for coastal steamboats. When the railway crossed the prairies in the 1880s, coal mines opened along the way to fuel the locomotives. Western Canada passed Nova Scotia in production by 1912. By mid-century, coal supplied one-half the energy used in Canada.

The coal era ended abruptly when large reserves of oil and gas were discovered in the 1940s and 1950s. Oil and gas replaced coal in heating homes, in industry, and in transportation. Coal dropped from 50% to only 10% of Canada's energy supply. Many coal-mining communities closed down.

COAL MINING TODAY

In the mid-1960s new markets developed for Canadian coal in Japan, Korea, Brazil, and elsewhere. New towns came to life, such as Tumbler Ridge in northwestern B.C., to supply the new markets. In 1987, $1.7 billion in coal was exported from Canada to over 15 countries.

In Alberta, Saskatchewan, New Brunswick, and Nova Scotia, coal is shipped short distances to electric-generating stations. However, most coal must be carried long distances to sea ports and to industrial markets in Ontario.

Coal in mined using two different methods: surface (or strip) and underground.

Surface Mines Over 90% of Canada's coal comes from surface mines, most of them in western Canada. First, mechanical shovels strip away the clay and rock that lie above the coal seams. Then draglines (the world's largest land machines), track shovels, and other machines remove the coal. Trucks haul it away.

Once the coal is removed, the earth and topsoil are replaced and the grass and trees are replanted.

Underground Mines Less than 10% of all the coal mined in Canada comes from underground mines. There is only one underground mine located in the mountains of the West. The most extensive underground coal mines in Canada are those on Cape Breton Island. They have been worked for over 200 years; together with the associated iron and steel works, they are the region's most important industry. Some of the tunnels extend beneath the Atlantic Ocean, more than 8 km beyond the shoreline. A chain conveyer carries the coal back towards the mine entrance.

HAZARDS OF COAL

Coal mining is sometimes a dangerous occupation. Cave-ins are more frequent in underground coal mines than in other kinds of mines, because the rocks from which the coal is dug are soft and weak. Methane, an explosive gas, is often present in underground coal mines, and coal dust itself can explode. When inhaled, the dust causes lung disease.

Mining disasters have killed many coal miners. Between 1881 and 1969, a total of 424 miners died in the coal mines of

---

Types of Coal

● **Anthracite:** the most valuable, highest heating value, the cleanest burning; mixed with bituminous coal to make coke for the iron and steel industry, and the chemical industry.

Found in B.C. and the Yukon.

● **Bituminous:** second-most valuable; used in steelmaking, as thermal coal in electric-power generation.

Found in Alberta, Newfoundland, Nova Scotia, New Brunswick, and B.C.

● **Sub-bituminous:** is used for heat and for steam, as well as coal liquifaction and coal gasification. Found in Alberta, B.C., Yukon, and N.W.T.

● **Lignite:** the lowest grade; used as for sub-bituminous coal.

Found in all but the Atlantic Provinces and Quebec.

● **Peat:** early stage in formation of coal; high water content makes it an unsuitable energy source but can be dried and burned; covers almost 12% of Canada.

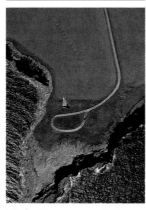

Light Beacon on Cape Tryon, northeast coast of P.E.I. Navigation aids are needed along the lengths of Canada's coastline that are used for shipping (photo by J.A. Kraulis).

Springhill, N.S., alone. The worst coal-mine disaster in Canada occurred on June 19, 1914, at Hillcrest, Alta. Dust explosions burned away all the oxygen in the long, deep tunnels of the mine, and 189 men died.

Coal can create serious environmental damage, not only when it is mined but also when it is being shipped, and especially when it is burned. To reduce the hazards of shipping coal, it is cleaned to remove the dust and to reduce the amount of methane present. When coal is loaded into a train car it is sprayed with water to clean it.

The burning of coal creates many pollutants, including sulphur dioxide (the main ingredient of acid rain). Coal from western Canada contains much less sulphur than the coal that Ontario Hydro imports from elsewhere for generating electricity. Substituting Canadian coal for American coal would thus reduce acid rain — but it would also increase Ontario Hydro's operating costs. Other solutions are emission control devices, such as scrubbers, in the smoke stacks. Scrubbers remove sulphur dioxide before it reaches the atmosphere.

Burning coal also increases the amount of carbon dioxide in the atmosphere, thus contributing to the "Greenhouse Effect."

▷ RELATED ARTICLES: **Cape Breton Island; Cape Breton Strikes; Climate; Disasters; Fossil Fuels.**

■ Coast

Canada's mainland coasts front on three oceans, the North Pacific, the Arctic, and the North Atlantic. Including the coasts of Newfoundland, Cape Breton, and Prince Edward Island, Canada's coastline

Gaspé Coast shows the effect of tides and waves, which, in time, erode the hardest rocks (photo by Thomas Kitchin).

measures 71 262 km. There are, in addition, over 172 000 km of coastline along Canada's islands.

A coast is an unstable meeting of land and water. The most important forces of change are tides and waves. The energy in waves can, in time, erode the strongest rocks, forming steep cliffs. Wind and waves erode the soft limestone cliffs, forming sand, which builds up into beaches. The beaches may be small pockets or long stretches of sand.

Ice has had a major role in shaping many of the details of Canada's coasts. The glaciers of the last Ice Age, for instance, carved the deep, steep-walled gorges, called *fjords*, along the rugged coasts of British Columbia and of Baffin and Ellesmere islands.

The east coast of Canada is long and irregular, with many islands, bays, and peninsulas. Jagged coastlines like this are produced by flooding. Part of Canada's mountainous eastern rim was submerged when the glaciers of the last Ice Age melted. Huge amounts of water were released from the ice sheets, causing the sea level to rise. The rise was very rapid at first, and it continues slowly today.

▷ RELATED ARTICLES: **Glaciation; Natural Regions; Oceans.**

■ Coast Mountains

The Coast Mountains are a chain of mountains, 1600 km long, running along the Pacific coast from the Fraser River near Vancouver, B.C., north into the Yukon. Often they rise abruptly from the water's edge. In parts, annual rainfall is the heaviest in North America, producing dense, coniferous forests. Mount Waddington (4019 m) is the highest peak in the chain.

■ Cobalt

Cobalt, Ont., is a mining town near Lake Timiskaming on the Quebec border in northern Ontario. In 1903, J.H. McKinley and Ernest Darragh were scouting for timber for railway ties when they spotted something glittering in the lake. It turned out to be silver. Shortly after, Fred LaRose found a piece of silver as big as his hand. Almost overnight, a town sprang alive with thousands of miners hunting for silver. By 1910, Cobalt's mines were producing the fourth-largest amount of silver in the world. Production peaked in 1911 but then declined. By the 1940s, Cobalt had fallen on hard times. There was a sudden demand for the cobalt metal (used in fighting cancer) for which the town was originally named. Some silver mines reopened in the 1960s, but the town has never recovered its glory days, when its population was over 10 000. In 1986 the population of Cobalt was 1640. The Cobalt Mining Museum has the world's largest display of raw silver.

Cobalt

Cobalt is a silvery white metal, which closely resembles iron and nickel. Small amounts of cobalt are recovered from copper and nickel ores in Canada. The town of Cobalt, in northern Ontario, takes its name from the metal. It was the world's leading producer of cobalt from 1905 to 1927.

Cobalt gives a blue colour to glass and ceramics and has been known for some 4000 years. However, its remarkable chemical and physical properties were only discovered in this century. It is used for magnets, as an alloy, and in the treatment of cancer.

In 1987 Canada produced over $46 million worth of cobalt. Most was exported.

Cobourg

Cobourg, Ont., lies on the shore of Lake Ontario, 112 km east of Toronto. Founded by Loyalists in 1798, it grew as a lake port and as a business centre for the farming region to the north. Originally called Amherst, it was renamed Cobourg in 1819. By the 1830s, Cobourg was one of the most important centres in Upper Canada. To symbolize the confidence of the growing town, the leaders decided to build a grand town hall. However, when the Cobourg railway failed, the town was almost ruined. By the 1870s, Cobourg was a favourite vacation spot for wealthy Americans, who built several beautiful mansions. Today, the economy relies on a variety of industries. Victoria Hall, the ornate town hall, is a national historic site. In 1986 the population was 13 197. For information, contact the Town Clerk Administrator, 55 King Street W., Cobourg, Ont., K9A 2M2.

Cochrane

Cochrane, Alta, is a town in the foothills, 35 km west of Calgary. It is on the Canadian Pacific Railway main line and near the Trans-Canada Highway. Senator Matthew Henry Cochrane established his Cochrane Ranche here in 1881. One of the first large-scale ranching ventures in western Canada, it is now a historic site. The town is still a ranching and farming centre, but it also takes advantage of nearby timber and natural gas. Many residents commute to work in nearby Calgary. In 1986 the population was 4190. For information, contact the Town Manager, P.O. Box 10, Cochrane, Alta, T0L 0W0.

Cochrane

Cochrane, Ont., is in northern Ontario, 375 km northwest of North Bay. Founded in 1908 as a railway townsite, it grew slowly as a local business centre. It serves as the departure point for the Polar Bear Express, the popular excursion train to Moosonee. Francis Cochrane was an Ontario cabinet minister. In 1986 the population was 4662. For information, contact the Town Clerk/Treasurer, 171 4th Avenue, P.O. Box 490, Cochrane, Ont., P0L 1C0.

Cochrane, Tom

Tom Cochrane (*born in 1953 at Lynn Lake, Man.*) is the leader and songwriter of the group Red Rider. The group also includes Ken Greer, guitar; John Webster, keyboard; Ken "Spider" Sinnaeve, bass; Randall Coryell, drums; and Peter Mueller, guitar. The son of a bush pilot, Tom Cochrane has earned a reputation as a rock-and-roll poet since his first album, *Hang On To Your Resistance*, in 1974. Red Rider's first four albums went platinum in Canada. In 1986 the group changed the name to Tom Cochrane and Red Rider. From that point on, they became international stars. Their hit single, "Lunatic Fringe," is one of the most requested songs on radio in the U.S. They won the Juno in 1987 as Group of the Year. Their 1988 album, *Victory Day*, was considered by many their best ever. Cochrane won the 1988 Juno for Composer of the Year.

Cockburn, Bruce

Singer, songwriter (*born in 1945 at Ottawa, Ont.*). He began playing guitar in Ottawa rock bands and went on to become a folksinger. He released his first LP in 1970 and began to use his music to draw attention to the plight of the native people, the environment, the people of Central America, and other major concerns, such as the threat of nuclear war. He has written songs in both English and French, including "If I Had a Rocket Launcher," "Stolen Land," and "If a Tree Falls." He is known internationally for his poetic style. He has won 10 Juno Awards.

Cockroach

Cockroach is the name usually given to insects of the order Dictyoptera – *Diktuon* meaning "net," or "web" and *pteron*

Characteristics of Cobalt

Formula: Co
Appearance: a silvery/white metal
Properties: hard, magnetic; a melting point of 1495°C
Atomic Weight: 58.93
Uses: permanent magnets and high-temperature superalloys.

Cobalt-60, a radioisotope, is used in treatment of cancer; cobalt oxide gives a bluish colour to ceramics and glass.

Bruce Cockburn has used his music to draw attention to the plight of native people, the environment, and other causes (courtesy True North Records).

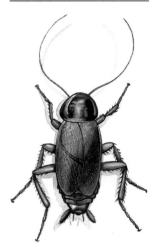

Cockroaches eat food, clothing, and books and leave behind foul-smelling excrement (artwork by Jan Sovak).

meaning "wing" — because of the network of veins on their wings. Cockroaches have flattened, oval bodies, with long antennae, and six long legs well adapted to walking and running. Their front wings are thick, the rear ones membranous. Some species have no wings. This group is widespread in the tropics.

In Canada, there are 17 species, only a few of which are native. The others arrived from Europe or the tropics in imported goods. Because they will eat food, clothing, and books, and leave behind foul-smelling excrement, cockroaches are universally hated by householders. The native species live in the woods, under rocks and dead trees, and are very rarely found in buildings. Active at night, cockroaches prefer dark, damp environments. They have an incomplete metamorphosis: the larva looks like the adult but is smaller, and its wings are less well developed. It moults several times before it becomes an adult.

■ Cod

In Canada, we have about 24 species of the family Gadidae. With the exception of the freshwater burbot, they are generally found in oceans. They live in cold water, usually close to the bottom. The most important species in Canada is the Atlantic cod (*Gadus morhua*). It can be recognized by its heavy body, large head, three dorsal fins, two anal fins, and squared-off tail. Like several species of this family, the Atlantic cod has a single whisker on its lower jaw. It can weigh up to 90 kg, but most specimens weigh between 3 and 4 kg. The young feed on small crustaceans. The adults are carnivores, eating, for example, capelin and herring. Atlantic cod are very fertile. A single female can produce 12 million eggs. Atlantic cod is one of the world's leading food fishes. It has been fished for centuries off the North Atlantic coast by vessels from many countries. Nevertheless, overfishing has caused stocks to drop drastically.

▷ RELATED ARTICLE: **Fishing Industry.**

■ Cogswell, Fred

Poet and editor (*born in 1917 at East Centreville, N.B.*). Cogswell taught in the English department of the University of New Brunswick in Fredericton from 1952 into the 1980s. As editor of *The Fiddlehead* magazine (1952-67) and founder of a series of poetry books, he gave a voice to many of the region's young writers. He also translated Quebec poetry and published 13 volumes of his own verse.

Leonard Cohen is one of Canada's best-known poets and popular singers (photo by Alexander W. Thomas).

■ Cohen, Leonard

Writer, singer (*born in 1934 at Montreal, Que.*). Cohen grew up in Montreal, and the city's atmosphere is a strong influence on his writings. He attended university at McGill and Columbia but has been a full-time writer most of his life.

Cohen achieved fame with his first two books of poetry: *Let us Compare Mythologies* (1956) and *The Spice-Box of Earth* (1961). The latter book gave him a reputation as a romantic love poet. However, Cohen's imagination is dark and despairing. As a Jew, Cohen has been acutely aware of the horror of the Holocaust, when millions of Jews were killed. This vision reached its peak in the novel *Beautiful Losers* (1966), which is at once religious, obscene, and comic. It is the most radical and perhaps most beautiful experimental novel ever published in Canada.

Cohen is best known around the world as a singer. His songs combine the same black humour and mixed images of sex, death, religion, and beauty as his poems and novels. He sings in a gruff monotone which emphasizes the meaning of the words. Among his most famous songs are "Suzanne," "The Window," and "Famous Blue Raincoat."

Cohen's work has been widely translated. He is especially popular in France and Germany.

▷ SUGGESTED READING: Stephen Scobie, *Leonard Cohen* (1978).

■ Cohen, Matt

Novelist, short-story writer (*born in 1942 in Kingston, Ont.*). Cohen's writings are noted for their vivid characters, their explorations of relationships, and their intensity. He has written poetry (*In Search of Leonardo*, 1986), collections of short stories (*Café Le Dog*, 1983), novellas

(*Johnny Crackle Sings*, 1971), a children's book (*The Leaves of Louise*, 1978), and novels (*Living on Water*, 1988). His writing is influenced by his southeastern Ontario background, as in the Salem Quartet, four novels set in the imaginary town of Salem, near Kingston, Ont. Other influences on his writing are his travels and knowledge of history, as in *The Spanish Doctor* (1984), and his Jewish heritage, as in *Nadine* (1986).

■ Cohen, Morris (Moishe) Abraham

Adventurer (*born in 1889 at London, England; died in 1970 at Salford, England*). Many stories have been told about the man known as Two-Gun Cohen. An unruly youth, his family sent him to Saskatchewan to learn farming. But Cohen learned how to handle guns and cards as well as horses. In 1912 he moved to Edmonton, where he grew rich through gambling and speculating in real estate. He was a warm-hearted man, prepared to champion causes for those in need. He was viewed as a hero by Chinese Canadians after he knocked out a burglar who was robbing a Chinese restaurant.

Cohen became a spokesman for Chinese Canadians, representing their interests at all levels of government and trying to stem the anti-Asian prejudice that was common in Canada at that time. Some years earlier, he had met the Chinese leader Dr Sun Yat-sen, who was visiting North America. In 1922, Dr Sun invited Cohen to China to serve as one of his bodyguards. Although Sun died in 1925, Cohen stayed on in China for more than 20 years. He was imprisoned by the Japanese during World War II and was later sent home to Canada. After the war, he was still welcome in Communist China and also in Taiwan, and he tried without success to bring the two Chinas together.

▷ SUGGESTED READING: Charles Drage, *The Life and Times of General Two-Gun Cohen* (1954).

■ Coins

Coins are pieces of metal used as money. They were used in Asia and Europe for centuries before Europeans brought them to Canada. When we talk about coins, we use the terms "obverse" and "reverse," also known as "heads" and "tails." The obverse side is stamped with an impression of the monarch's head (or the head of a national leader if a country has no monarch). The reverse has the value, date, and design of the coin.

Early Colonial Years Canada suffered from a severe shortage of coins until the

Lower Canada Coin, *1837, obverse (left) and reverse (right).*

New Brunswick Half-penny, *1854, obverse (left) and reverse (right).*

Nova Scotia One-Penny Token, *1856, obverse (left) and reverse (right).*

Upper Canada Coin, *1833, obverse (left) and reverse (right).*

Decimal Coin of Queen Victoria, *1882, obverse (left) and reverse (right).*

Decimal Coin of George VI, *5 cents, 1937, obverse (left) and reverse (right).*

Decimal Coin *to mark the occasion of the Montreal Olympics ($10), reverse only*

Decimal Coin *of Elizabeth II ($100), reverse only*

Province of Canada *coin, showing the Bank of Montreal building*

(courtesy Currency Museum, Bank of Canada, all photos by James Zagon).

mid-19th century. In New France, copper coins of small denominations were used, but they had to be imported from France. There were never enough of them. The first coins made especially for use in the French colonies were made of silver and stamped with the words "Gloriam Regni." New France also received copper coins after 1717, but they were not used widely.

After the British took over New France in 1763, the official coinage became British sterling (pounds, shillings, and pennies). For the first 50 years of British rule, the Canadian colonies received only occasional shipments of badly worn British copper coins. As a result, colonists accepted any money available — British sterling, Spanish, U.S., and Portuguese dollars, and even flattened buttons.

Tokens The lack of a reliable standard currency to pay wages and to buy everyday necessities led governments, banks, and merchants to issue copper "tokens." They were like coins, because they represented a certain value; but they were not true coins, because they were made without the authority of the British government. Even when these tokens were counterfeited, they were still accepted because of the lack of anything better.

The first token was issued in 1794 by the Copper Company of Upper Canada. In 1815 Sir Isaac Coffin issued coins for use on the Îles de la Madeleine, which were granted to him as a seigneury. They had such inspiring mottos as "Success to the Fishery." The "habitant" series used a Quebec farmer for its design. The British government declared the coins illegal.

Colonial Issues The various colonies issued their own coins, as well as using coins from Britain and from other parts of North America. In 1813 Prince Edward Island created a "holey dollar"; the centre was removed and used as a coin of smaller value. One of the most beautiful coinages was issued in Nova Scotia in 1856. The reverse side had a very fine engraving of a mayflower plant from a design by a Halifax botanist. Newfoundland was the only British colony to have a gold coin, worth $2. British Columbia made $10 and $20 gold coins in 1862, but they were never issued. These gold coins are the rarest Canadian coins. Only about ten of each are known to exist. When the colonies joined Confederation, they stopped issuing their own coins.

Canadian Issues A Canadian decimal (dollars and cents) system had been introduced in 1858, and in 1870 the first coins

of the new Dominion of Canada were issued. They were silver 5¢, 10¢, 25¢, and 50¢ pieces. For all, the reverse design was a crown and maple leaves, and this design did not change very much until 1937. A bronze cent was issued in 1876, and a silver dollar in 1935. The standard Canadian coin values have not changed.

The coins themselves, however, have changed in size, design, and inscription, and in the metals used. In 1920 the 1¢ piece was reduced to its current size. In 1922 the silver 5¢ piece became a bigger coin made of nickel, and after many changes it is now made of a copper-nickel alloy. In 1968, nickel replaced silver in 10¢, 25¢, 50¢, and $1 coins.

Minting From 1858 to 1907, most Canadian coins were made at the Royal Mint in London, England. In 1908 the Royal Mint opened a branch in Ottawa. This came under Canadian control in 1931 and was renamed the Royal Canadian Mint. It strikes coins for foreign countries as well as for Canada, and in 1974 it opened a branch in Winnipeg.

1937 Issue A completely new coinage was introduced in 1937. For the first time, each coin had its own reverse design created by Canadian artists, one of whom was Emanuel Hahn. The designs were chosen because of their importance to Canada's heritage: two maple leaves (1¢), a beaver (5¢), the schooner *Bluenose* (10¢), a caribou (25¢), the Canadian coat of arms (50¢), and a voyageur ($1). Except for the dollar, these designs are still on our coins today.

The design on the dollar was frequently changed to honour special events. In 1987 a new dollar coin was introduced, called the "loonie" because of its design of a swimming loon. It is made of tombac, a copper-zinc alloy.

1967 Issue To celebrate Canada's Centennial, a special coinage was issued in 1967. The designs were created by artist Alexander Colville. They were a dove in flight (1¢), a running hare (5¢), a mackerel (10¢), a bobcat (25¢), a howling wolf (50¢), and a Canada goose in flight ($1).

Commemorative Coins Since 1954, special coins for collectors have been issued in standard metals, as well as in gold (1967) and silver (1971). They are sold in sealed packages, individually or in sets.

Canada's most complete currency museum is located in the Bank of Canada, Ottawa.

▷ RELATED ARTICLE: **Money.**

▷ SUGGESTED READING: Bank of Canada, *The Star of Canada's Currency* (1981).

Colborne, Sir John

Colonial governor and army officer (*born in 1778 at Lyndhurst, England; died in 1863 at Torquay, England*). Sir John Colborne was lieutenant-governor of Upper Canada from 1828 to 1836. He was then appointed commander-in-chief of the armed forces in both Upper and Lower Canada, and in 1838-39 he was governor general of the two Canadas.

During Colborne's eight years in charge of Upper Canada, he organized a system of immigration to bring settlers from the British Isles. Through this scheme, he more than doubled the population of Upper Canada and improved communications by getting roads and bridges built in the countryside. In 1829 he founded Upper Canada College as a school where future leaders could be educated.

Colborne was a strong supporter of British traditions, including the Church of England (Anglican Church). This was not popular with many of the people of Upper Canada, and his policies added to the discontent which led to the Rebellion of 1837. As chief of the armed forces during the rebellion, Colborne put down opposition with great severity. In December 1837, he personally led the assault on St-Eustache in Lower Canada, where many Patriotes were burned to death in a church.

After returning to Britain in 1839, Colborne was made a lord.

Cold Lake

Cold Lake, Alta., is a town on the shore of Cold Lake, 290 km northeast of Edmonton. Its history began with the Chipewyan Indians who hunted and trapped nearby. The Hudson's Bay Company built a post there, and settlers came in 1905 to cut timber and farm. Canadian Forces Base Cold Lake was established here in 1952. This boosted the local economy and Cold Lake became a town in 1955. The military base is a self-contained community, with its own shopping mall, schools, churches, etc. The base is Canada's largest. Jobs are provided by farming, tourism, and heavy oil developments. Cold Lake is surrounded by vast reserves of heavy oil. The lake is one of Alberta's largest. It has kilometres of sandy beaches and is well known for its excellent fishing. A native legend told of Kinosoo, a monster fish that lived in the lake and could snap a canoe in two. In 1986 the population was 3195. For information, contact the Town Administrator, P.O. Box 98, Cold Lake, Alta, T0A 0V0.

▷ SUGGESTED READING: Laura Skarsen, editor, *Treasured Scales of the Kinosoo* (1980).

Coldwell, Major James William

Teacher and politician, leader of the federal CCF (*born in 1888 at Seaton, England; died in 1974 at Ottawa, Ont.*). Trained as a teacher, Coldwell came to Canada from England in 1910. He was active in teachers' organizations, and began his political career as a Regina alderman. In 1932, in the midst of the Great Depression, he became leader of the Saskatchewan Farmer-Labour Party. This group later merged with the Co-operative Commonwealth Federation (CCF).

Coldwell ran unsuccessfully in the Saskatchewan election of 1934; he then moved to federal politics as a member of the CCF. He was elected in 1935 and remained a member of Parliament until 1958.

Coldwell became leader of the CCF in 1942. He was a member of the Canadian delegation to the founding of the United Nations after World War II. During his leadership, the CCF enjoyed a peak of support in the mid-1940s, then went into a slow decline through the 1950s. He led the party in five general elections, retiring in 1960 just as the CCF was preparing to reorganize itself as the New Democratic Party.

Coleman, Kathleen

Newspaper columnist (*born Kathleen Blake in 1864 near Galway, Ireland; died in 1915 at Hamilton, Ont.*). "Kit of the Mail" was the first woman journalist to be in charge of her own section of a Canadian newspaper. In the 1890s and early 1900s, she ran a seven-column page in the Toronto *Mail*. Called "Woman's Kingdom," it came out once a week and was so outspoken that it attracted a wide following, including Prime Minister Wilfrid Laurier. She tackled anything that interested her: political commentary and theatre criticism, as well as fashion notes and recipes. In one of her most popular features she gave advice to the lovelorn.

Coleman was cynical about love, for her parents had married her off at 16 to an elderly Irishman. Widowed at 20, she migrated to Canada in 1884 and worked as a secretary until she married her boss, Edward Watkins. When Watkins died in 1889, she turned to journalism to support their two children. She worked for the *Mail* until 1911. Meanwhile, she married a third husband, Theobald Coleman. Kit became the first woman in the world to be a war correspondent. This was in 1898

M.J. Coldwell speaking into a CKCK microphone from Regina on the night the CCF was elected to the government of Saskatchewan (courtesy Saskatchewan Archives Board/photo by Michael West).

Kit's Advice to the Lovelorn
"Kit of the Mail" was one of the first journalists to give advice to readers who wrote in. Her outspoken comments attracted many readers. Here is an example:

"Maria: Asks me to tell her 'what it signifies when a gentleman gets a lady's handkerchief and keeps it.' It probably means, Maria, that he has a head-cold."

Kathleen (Kit) Coleman had a number of "firsts" for a woman in journalism (from Canadian Women, Past and Present, c1903)

when she went to Cuba to report on the Spanish-American War. After 1911 she sold "Kit's Column" to dozens of newspapers across the country.

▷ RELATED ARTICLE: **Journalism.**

▷ SUGGESTED READING: Ted Ferguson, *Kit Coleman: Queen of Hearts* (1979).

■ Colicos, John

Actor (*born in 1928 at Toronto, Ont.*). Colicos has excelled as an actor in film, television, and on the stage in both classical and contemporary roles. He began his career in Montreal, Que., but made his mark in Shakespearian plays at the Old Vic in London, England, and in Shakespeare festivals at Stratford, Connecticut, and at Stratford, Ont. He made an impressive Winston Churchill in the stage play *Soldiers*, and a believable Lord Beaverbrook in a CBC television drama about the famous Canadian businessman. He has also appeared in such popular television shows as "General Hospital" and "Star Trek." He played Thomas Cromwell in the film *Anne of the Thousand Days* (1969) and also acted in *The Changeling* (1979) and *The Postman Always Rings Twice* (1981).

■ Collège Classique

Before the Quiet Revolution of the 1960s, most high-school education in Quebec was provided by classical colleges, or *collèges classiques*. They were run by the Catholic Church and were fee-paying schools, though there were some scholarships and bursaries. Their name came from the fact that they concentrated heavily on classical subjects, such as Latin, Greek, religion, and philosophy. Students also studied math and modern languages. The *collèges* were much criticized in the 1960s for taking too few students and for neglecting science and technical subjects. In the 1960s they were replaced by the kind of high-school system found in other provinces.

■ Collège des Jésuites

The Collège des Jésuites was Canada's first boys' school. It was founded in 1635 in the tiny settlement of Quebec and was run by Jesuit priests. By the 1660s the college was teaching a broad range of subjects that included grammar, theology, some science, and classical subjects such as Latin, Greek, and philosophy.

■ Collège dominicain de philosophie et de théologie

The Collège dominicain de philosophie et de théologie is located in Ottawa and Montreal. It offers university degrees through the departments of pastoral studies, philosophy, and theology. Instruction is in French. The college was founded in 1909 by the Order of Friars Preachers in Canada. In 1967 it received university status. There are 180 full-time students. For further information, write the Registrar's Office, Collège dominicain de philosophie et de théologie, 96 Empress, Ottawa, Ont., K1R 7G3.

■ Collingwood

Collingwood, Ont., is a town on the southern shore of Georgian Bay, about 100 km north of Toronto. It was originally settled by the Huron. It was settled by Europeans in 1835 and named for a British naval hero. It has an excellent harbour, and until 1986 it was a major shipbuilding centre. In 1855 the railway arrived, and Collingwood became a trans-shipment point for goods headed west. It became a town in 1858.

Collingwood is a major industrial town. The largest employer is LOF Glass. Other products include automobile wheels, whisky, furniture, rubber, carpet, mining equipment, and fabrics. Collingwood is world famous as a pottery capital, based on glazed clay from nearby Blue Mountain. In winter, it is Ontario's most popular ski resort. In 1986 the population was 12 172.

■ Collip, James Bertram

Biochemist, a discoverer of insulin (*born in 1892 at Belleville, Ont.; died in 1965 at London, Ont.*). Collip was the biochemist

James B. Collip worked with Banting and Best on the discovery of insulin (courtesy NAC/C-37756).

working with Frederick Banting and Charles Best on Professor J.J.R. Macleod's research team at the University of Toronto from 1921 to 1922. He was the one to produce the first insulin suitable for use on human beings. Until then, millions of people had died of diabetes. Now the disease could be treated, even though insulin was only a treatment and not a cure for diabetes.

Collip was chosen as a member of Macleod's team while on a travelling research fellowship in Toronto. Still a young man, he had a lifetime of medical research ahead of him. He was professor of biochemistry at the University of Alberta (1922-28) and at McGill (1928-47), before becoming dean of medicine at the University of Western Ontario (1947-61). Collip became a world leader in hormone research. He found a way of extracting hormones from the parathyroid glands to provide relief to people suffering from spasms. Another project was his study of hormones associated with fertility and reproduction. Despite his reputation, Collip was modest about his achievements, more interested in the research work itself than in the fame it brought him.

▷ RELATED ARTICLES: **Sir Frederick Banting; Insulin.**

▷ SUGGESTED READING: Michael Bliss, *The Discovery of Insulin* (1982).

▪ Collura, Mary-Ellen Lang

Writer (*born in 1949 at Vancouver, B.C.*). Collura grew up in Vancouver and has worked at a variety of occupations, from printing-press operator to horseback-riding instructor. She lives on a small farm and teaches high school in Campbell River, B.C. Her two novels, *Winners* (1984) and *Sunny* (1988), are both horse stories that deal with the troubled lives of young people and their eventual success. In *Winners*, a young native boy who has grown up in a variety of foster homes finds his real family and his sense of himself through taming a wild horse. In *Sunny*, a girl and her mentally handicapped brother weather a family breakup through their shared love of an injured race horse. Collura writes powerfully of the tensions in a young adult's life and lyrically of the natural world.

▪ Colombo, John Robert

Poet and compiler of anthologies (*born in 1936 at Kitchener, Ont.*). Colombo has been called Canada's "master gatherer." He has a passion for searching out details about Canada. He has compiled more than 77 books, many of which are collections of Canadian facts, quotations, jokes, legends, mysteries, ghost stories, and so on. He has also made his name as a poet and broadcaster.

Educated at the University of Toronto, Colombo began his career as an editor in Toronto. He first gained national attention with *Colombo's Canadian Quotations* (1974) and *Colombo's Canadian References* (1976). Since then, his books have ranged from *The Poets of Canada* (1978) and other literary collections to quiz books such as *999 Questions About Canada* (1989).

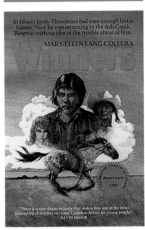

Winners, *a novel by Mary-Ellen Collura (1984). The anger and frustration of the main character, the two people who influence him, and his feeling of freedom riding across the prairies are all presented on the cover of* Winners *(Illustration by Oni; © Western Producer Prairie Books).*

John Robert Colombo is Canada's "master gatherer" of facts and details about Canada (photo by Camilleri).

Colonial Office

The British government established the Colonial Office in 1825 to handle the affairs of its colonies. The Colonial Office wielded much power. It decided what kind of government a colony would have. It appointed the governor, gave him his instructions, and supervised his work. It examined colonial laws to make sure they did not contradict laws already passed in Britain. Occasionally it gave money to a colony to help pay for an expensive project. Sometimes it helped recruit settlers. When a colony got a new constitution, the Colonial Office was responsible for getting the approval of the British Parliament.

Even after Confederation, when Canada became a Dominion, the Canadian government continued to deal with Britain through the Colonial Office. In 1907 the Colonial Office established a special division to deal with the Dominions. In 1925 this responsibility shifted out of the Colonial Office to a new Dominions Office.

Colonization Companies

Colonization companies were formed at various times in Canada's history to bring immigrants to Canada and settle them on the land. Usually, a company received

Snowcoaches on the Columbia Icefield, Jasper National Park (photo by Scott Rowed/Take Stock Inc.).

land cheaply from the government. In return, it advertised abroad for settlers, organized their travel to Canada, and provided services and perhaps some equipment to help them through the first years of settlement. The earliest companies date back to the 17th century in New France. During the 19th century, two prominent colonization companies were the Canada Company (in Upper Canada) and the British American Land Company (in Lower Canada).

Columbia Icefield

The Columbia Icefield, on the British Columbia-Alberta border, is the largest mass of ice in the Rocky Mountains. It lies at the geographic apex of North America, the point from which all land falls away. It is a remnant of the great ice sheet that once covered most of Canada. Its meltwaters feed six major river systems flowing into three oceans. It is about 230 km² in area and up to 365 m deep.

Columbia Mountains

The Columbia Mountains include four mountain ranges which form parallel lines running north-south in southeastern British Columbia. The four mountain ranges are the Purcell, Selkirk, Monashee, and Cariboo.

Columbia River

The Columbia River rises in Columbia Lake in southeastern British Columbia. It flows north around the Cariboo Mountains before turning south to cross the United States border, about 800 km from its source. It then flows across Washington State to the Pacific Ocean. It is 2000 km long in total. The long, powerful river has the third-largest drainage basin in North America. It was named by American trader Robert Gray after his ship. Gray visited the river's mouth in 1792, but it was 1811 before fur trader David

Columbia River, B.C. (courtesy B.C. Hydro).

Thompson explored the length of the river. The Hudson's Bay Company built Fort Vancouver at the mouth in 1824-25, and the river was an important supply route to the interior. The Columbia was recognized as the border between American and British territory until the actual border was set at the 49th parallel in 1846. Three major dams were built on the Canadian section of the river as part of a massive hydroelectric development. A fourth dam was completed in 1983. Before the dams, the river was one of the world's largest spawning grounds for salmon.

Columbia River Treaty

The Columbia River Treaty is an international agreement designed to regulate development on the Columbia River basin in both British Columbia and Washington State.

Canada and the United States signed the treaty on January 17, 1961. However, British Columbia argued with the Canadian government over the terms of the treaty. The result was that it did not become effective until September 16, 1964. Under the terms of the Columbia River Treaty, Canada built two dams on the Columbia River and one of the Kootenay River. These dams control the flow of water in the river. This enables more power to be produced downstream in Washington. It also affords a degree of flood protection there. The U.S. paid $273.3 million for the electric power generated by the project. It also paid $69.3 million for the flood protection.

One-half of the additional power produced by the development was to belong to Canada. However, instead of taking the power and using it in B.C., the provincial government decided to sell it, for a period of 30 years, to American customers. In 1994 that agreement will end.

Columbine

Of the genus *Aquilegia* and the buttercup family (Ranunculaceae), columbines are perennial plants that grow from 10 to 120 cm. The name comes from the Latin word for "claws of an eagle." Six of the 70 species found worldwide grow in Canada. The wild columbine (*A. canadensis*) is one of our most beautiful wildflowers. It grows east from Saskatchewan. Its jagged leaves are slim and bright green. Its horn-shaped flowers have five petals each, with bright yellow centres and vivid red exteriors, which end in long, curve-tipped spurs. The columbine is found in the woods and in mountainous and rocky places. It flowers in early summer. The garden columbine (*A. vulgaris*), originally from Europe, has inspired generations of gardeners to create many spectacular hybrids with large flowers (7-8 cm long) and varied colours. These curious flowers are pollinated by hummingbirds and various insects, who must pierce the tip of the spur in order to reach the nectar. All parts of the plant are poisonous when swallowed. Several native Indian groups used the columbine as a remedy for stomach problems and rubbed it against the scalp to get rid of fleas.

Colville, Alexander

Painter (*born in 1920 at Toronto, Ont.*). Colville's family moved to Nova Scotia when he was nine. He studied painting at Mount Allison University and joined the army as a war artist when he graduated.

After the war, he returned to Canada and taught at Mount Allison until 1963, when he was able to quit teaching and concentrate on his painting. His paintings are always based on careful measurements, using thousands of tiny brush strokes to show subjects from his immediate environment: his family (*Family and Rainstorm*), the landscape around his home (*French Cross*), and his animals (*Hound in Field*). The titles sound like familiar themes, but the artist's precise details and cool colours make the paintings seem distant and private, even mysterious. His work is sometimes also disturbing: two people appear together but seem to have no connection (*January*); a horse gallops full speed towards an oncoming train (*Horse and Train*).

French Cross, *1988, by Alex Colville, shows the cool and mysterious quality typical of the artist's work (courtesy Alex Colville 1990/VIS*ART Copyright Inc.).*

Colville works on one painting or silk-screen print at a time and completes only three or four a year. His work is very popular in North America and in Europe, and he is one of Canada's most successful painters. He designed the Centennial coins in 1967, and the Governor General's Medal in 1978. He was made a Companion of the Order of Canada in 1982.

■ Come by Chance
Come by Chance, Nfld, overlooks the head of Placentia Bay at the narrow neck of the Avalon Peninsula. It has always been sparsely populated. The population was 44 in 1921, 42 in 1945, and only 266 in 1986. The settlement leaped to prominence in the 1970s with the construction of a huge oil refinery. The refinery began producing in 1973, but closed only three years later. It opened again in 1987 and now produces 80 000 barrels of oil a day. It is operated by Newfoundland Processing Ltd and employs about 200 people. For information, contact the Town Clerk, P.O. Box 89, Come by Chance, Nfld, A0B 1N0.

■ Comet
A comet is an object in space. When a comet is far from the Sun, it is a small, solid object. It is composed partly of frozen water and other matter. When the comet comes near to the Sun, however, the substances evaporate and glow with an eerie light. A comet usually has a head and two tails. The head consists of a small body (like a dirty snowball). One tail consists of gases being blown away from the Sun. The second tail, composed of dust, is also directed away from the Sun but tends to be curved. One tail is often behind the other, leaving only one visible from Earth. In recorded history, about 750 comets have been observed. Of these several have been observed more than once.

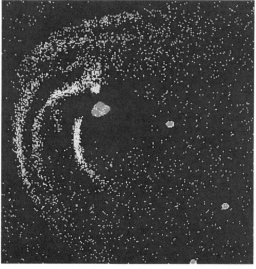

Image of Halley's Comet obtained by Canadian astronomer C.J. Pritchet in March 1986 with the Canada-France-Hawaii telescope. Jets of material are ejected from spots on the comet's nucleus. The jets are made into spirals by the clockwise rotation of the nucleus and are being swept towards the left by radiation and particle pressure issuing from the Sun (image by C.J. Pritchet and S. Van den Bergh).

All of these comets likely belong to our solar system and are orbiting the Sun.

Comets are named after their discoverers. For example, Comet Van den Bergh was discovered in 1974 by Canadian astronomer Sidney Van den Bergh. Another Canadian astronomer, Rolf Meier, has had four comets named for him.

The most famous comet is Comet Halley. In the 17th century, English astronomer Edmond Halley showed that his comet approached Earth every 76 years. It was last seen in 1985-86 and will return in 2061. Canadian astronomers C.J. Pritchet and Sidney Van den Bergh obtained a remarkable image of the comet from the Canada-Hawaii telescope.

■ Comics, *see* Cartoons

■ Commonwealth
The Commonwealth is a loose association, or grouping, of 49 countries, rich and poor alike, which were once part of the British Empire. Canada, Great Britain, and India are major members, as are Australia and New Zealand.

The Commonwealth is a voluntary association. Members are free to leave the Commonwealth at any time. They can also be part of any other grouping of countries. The Commonwealth is not an alliance like NATO; members make no promises to defend one another or to consider an attack on one as an attack on all. Commonwealth countries promise nothing to one another, except to try to co-operate and to talk over mutual problems.

The Commonwealth includes more than a billion people, one-quarter of the world's population, from territories in the six continents and five oceans. Sixty percent of the Commonwealth's population are under the age of 25.

History The Commonwealth was formed when the territories of the British Empire, which were controlled by Great Britain, became self-governing. The original members of the Commonwealth — Great Britain, Canada, Australia, New Zealand, South Africa, and Ireland — were countries whose governments were mainly controlled by whites.

At a conference held in Ottawa in 1932, Commonwealth countries agreed to give a lower duty or tariff to each other's trade. This was called the imperial preference. It is no longer in effect, but for many years it was responsible for much trade among Commonwealth members.

In the late 1940s India, Pakistan, and Ceylon (Sri Lanka) became independent and chose to join the Commonwealth.

Commonwealth

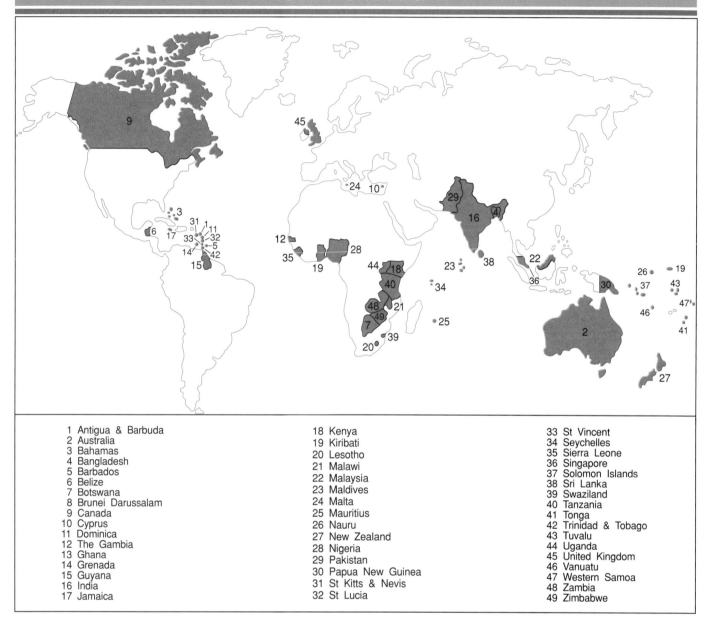

1 Antigua & Barbuda	18 Kenya	33 St Vincent
2 Australia	19 Kiribati	34 Seychelles
3 Bahamas	20 Lesotho	35 Sierra Leone
4 Bangladesh	21 Malawi	36 Singapore
5 Barbados	22 Malaysia	37 Solomon Islands
6 Belize	23 Maldives	38 Sri Lanka
7 Botswana	24 Malta	39 Swaziland
8 Brunei Darussalam	25 Mauritius	40 Tanzania
9 Canada	26 Nauru	41 Tonga
10 Cyprus	27 New Zealand	42 Trinidad & Tobago
11 Dominica	28 Nigeria	43 Tuvalu
12 The Gambia	29 Pakistan	44 Uganda
13 Ghana	30 Papua New Guinea	45 United Kingdom
14 Grenada	31 St Kitts & Nevis	46 Vanuatu
15 Guyana	32 St Lucia	47 Western Samoa
16 India		48 Zambia
17 Jamaica		49 Zimbabwe

The Commonwealth was becoming multiracial.

Beginning with Ghana in 1957, almost all the British colonies in Africa became Commonwealth members after they achieved independence, as did several British colonies in the Caribbean, Asia, and the Mediterranean Ocean. The Commonwealth was now truly an association of many races and cultures, and it took great pride in that fact.

Some Commonwealth countries, such as Canada, have kept the British monarch (the King or Queen of England) as the head of state of their own country. Other countries, such as India, have a republican form of government, with a president as their head of state.

South Africa left the association in 1961 after its policies towards its African population received heavy criticism at a Commonwealth conference that year. The Commonwealth has been trying ever since to bring an end to *apartheid*, the system that discriminates against Blacks and keeps them in an inferior position to Whites in South Africa. The Black countries of the Commonwealth, however, want stronger action than some other member countries are willing to agree to. White countries, particularly Great Britain, have economic interests in South Africa and they do not want these harmed.

Commonwealth Declaration of Principles, 1971 A 1971 meeting of the govern-

ment leaders of member countries agreed that the Commonwealth stands for the following:
- support of the United Nations
- equal rights for all citizens, regardless of race, colour, religion, or political belief
- representative institutions and guarantees of personal freedom under the law
- opposition to racial prejudice
- efforts to overcome poverty, ignorance, and disease
- the freest possible flow of trade between countries
- consultation, discussion, and co-operation among Commonwealth members
- the rejection of the use of force in international relations.

These are aims only. Not all Commonwealth countries follow them. Each has its own strong interests which are more important than the Commonwealth tie.

Organization Queen Elizabeth of Great Britain is the head of the Commonwealth. All the Commonwealth, therefore, accepts the Queen as the symbol of the co-operation they are trying to achieve. She has no power, although some Commonwealth leaders seek her advice from time to time.

The association is run by civil servants in London, England, who come from all over the Commonwealth. This group is called the Secretariat, and its chief is the Secretary General. The first Secretary General of the Commonwealth, from 1965 to 1975, was a Canadian, Arnold Smith. The Secretariat advises on technical matters, distributes information, helps organize programs of Commonwealth co-operation, and arranges meetings and discussions between members. English is the working language of the Secretariat.

The Commonwealth heads of government meet every two years to discuss problems and ways to co-operate. Meetings are kept as small and relaxed as possible. Two examples of the results of these gatherings are the 1971 Declaration of Principles (above) and the 1977 Gleneagles Agreement against sporting contacts between South Africans and citizens of Commonwealth countries.

Other Commonwealth politicians, such as ministers of finance, education, and agriculture, also have regular meetings.

Commonwealth Activities The richer Commonwealth countries give economic help (also known as development assistance) to poorer members. This began with the Colombo Plan of 1950, when Canada, Australia, Ceylon (now Sri Lanka), Great Britain, India, New Zealand, and Pakistan agreed to work together in fighting against the poverty of South and Southeast Asia. Under the plan, Canada makes agreements to give developing nations such as India financial aid.

The Colombo Plan still exists, but it is not nearly as important as it once was. The main development assistance tool is now the Commonwealth Program for Technical Co-operation. Canada is the biggest contributor to this fund ($18.5 million, 1988-89). The fund arranges for highly specialized experts to be sent to Commonwealth countries.

The Commonwealth Youth Program, established in 1973, helps young people get education and training.

Commonwealth Scholarships are awards given for study in a university of another country. Commonwealth Scholarships, for example, allow Canadians to study at Oxford and Cambridge universities in England.

The Commonwealth Foundation gives money to encourage exchanges between organizations and societies in Commonwealth countries.

In addition to the official work of the Commonwealth and its many agencies, there are about 300 other Commonwealth "non-governmental" groups. For example, there are Commonwealth associations for architects and journalists. The association that puts on the Commonwealth Games every four years is another example.

Canada's Part in the Commonwealth Canada has always been a leader in the Commonwealth. We were the first British territory to become a country on our own, in 1867. We led the movement in the 1920s and 1930s towards a Commonwealth of equal nations, where each country could make its own decisions and consult with the other members as much or as little as it wanted. In the late 1940s we helped to keep India in the Commonwealth, which was important if the institution was going to be representative of the world's peoples. Canadian criticism of South Africa in the early 1960s had a lot to do with that country's decision to leave the association. Prime Minister Pierre E. Trudeau helped keep the Commonwealth together through some difficult times in the 1970s and 1980s.

The Commonwealth is not nearly as important as it once was, either to the Canadian government or people. Only 4% of Canada's trade in the late 1980s was with Commonwealth countries (it was about 20% in the 1960s).

Still, we remain leaders, contributing experts, money, and ideas to the Commonwealth. Almost 35% of Canada's total development assistance budget is given to Commonwealth countries.

▷ RELATED ARTICLE: **External Relations.**

■ Commonwealth Games

The Commonwealth Games are held every four years among the countries of the Commonwealth. They were originally called the British Empire Games. The first games were held in 1930 at Hamilton, Ont. They have since been held in Vancouver, B.C., in 1954, and Edmonton, Alta, in 1978. At the Edmonton games, in which 1500 athletes from 46 countries competed, Canada had its best showing, winning 45 gold medals (England was second with 27). In recent years, many countries have refused to participate in the games for political reasons. Some countries, which object to the policies of other countries to South Africa, have boycotted the games. Nigeria boycotted the Edmonton Games in 1978, while 32 countries boycotted the games in Edinburgh, Scotland, in 1986. *See* **Commonwealth.**

■ Communications

Communications are an attempt to overcome distance between human beings. This may be done by transportation, which moves the people themselves. It may be done through exchanges of information; for example, by letters in the post.

Over the past 100 years, the means of sending and receiving information have been revolutionized by technology. The telegraph, telephone, computer, and facsimile transmission (FAX) machine have made information exchanges almost instantaneous.

On another level, radio, television, newspapers, and magazines have spun a communications web across the world. This kind of communication, called mass communication, sends messages to very large audiences.

From its beginnings, Canada has presented an enormous challenge in communications. The tiny outposts of New France had no way of sending or receiving news across the Atlantic except by mail, carried over the ocean by sailing ships. Meanwhile, in North America itself, the colony's merchants set up a trading network based on the canoe and river routes learned from the native people.

By the time of Confederation, in 1867, the steam engine had greatly speeded up transportation. Railways and steamships increased the speed at which people and information could travel. The telegraph used electric batteries and magnets to send messages in a code of dots and dashes (called Morse Code for its inventor). The telegraph could send fairly complicated messages and was used almost at once by newspapers. In 1866 a telegraph cable was laid across the Atlantic Ocean (from Valencia, Ireland, to Heart's Content, Nfld). This cable made it possible to send a message from Europe to America in a few minutes.

Ten years later, Alexander Graham Bell, a Scottish immigrant to Canada, invented the telephone (1876). Like the telegraph, it was a vast improvement over earlier methods of communication, such as horse, ship, and rail. It permitted communication by wire over long distances almost immediately.

A Canadian also played an important role in the next stage: sending messages without wire (or "wireless"). In 1895, an Italian inventor, Guglielmo Marconi, sent signals through space by what he called a *wireless telegraph*. (We call it "radio"). In 1901 he received messages sent across the Atlantic to St John's, Nfld. At first, Marconi's device only sent Morse code signals; but in 1900, Canadian scientist Reginald Fessenden attached a mouthpiece to a wireless and transmitted voice by radio. Fessenden made the world's first public broadcast in 1906.

Canada's first radio licence was issued in 1919 to station XWA in Montreal. Radio created a brand-new challenge. Within a few years, Canadian listeners were being bombarded by American stations. Many Canadian stations were receiving interference. In 1929 a government commission recommended that Canada should have a publicly owned radio corporation. An organization was set up in 1932 to control and carry on broadcasting in Canada. By 1936, about one million Canadian households had radios.

Radio emphasized the problem faced by Canada in being next to the most powerful communications nation in the world — the United States. Its solution, still in practice today, was to mix access to American programs with encouragement of a Canadian presence. As well, Canada has a mixture of public and private ownership of broadcasting.

Microwave Station, Manning Park, B.C. *Microwave networks made it possible to send TV signals over long distances (photo by Thomas Kitchin).*

The most powerful communications technology today is television. It was developed in the 1930s and 1940s. A TV network was set up in Canada in the 1950s. Microwave networks made it possible to send TV signals over long distances. In the 1960s and 1970s, the cable-television industry grew more rapidly in Canada than any other nation.

The modern communication system can now carry many different types of messages, including telegraph, voice, television images, video, and computer data.

Communist Party members on March, B.C. District, May 1930s (courtesy Vancouver Public Library/ #8786).

Modern communications are extremely important to the Canadian economy. They make it possible to increase efficiency. They also provide Canada with sales of equipment and services to other countries.

However, mass communications are a mixed blessing for Canada. The spread of cable TV has expanded the choice of American programs in Canadian homes. It has also contributed greatly to the "Americanization" of Canada and has reduced opportunities for Canadians to have access to their own media.

It is perhaps not a coincidence that the best-known communications commentator in the world, Marshall McLuhan, was a Canadian. McLuhan drew attention to the fact that the media themselves reshape our very way of thinking. "Media events" are created so that they will make "good television." Politicians can avoid issues in a campaign if they can control how they are presented on television.

Communications open new opportunities and create new problems. The way that it is controlled and used will play a great part in Canada's future.

▷ RELATED ARTICLES: **Alexander Graham Bell; Reginald Fessenden; Frederick Gisborne; Inventors and Inventions; Marshall McLuhan.** *See also* the articles on the various types of communication.

▷ SUGGESTED READING: Bobbie Kalman, *How We Communicate* (1987); Dan Mackie and Paul Hayes, *Communications* (1987).

■ Communism

The central idea in communism is that all things should be owned in common rather than privately. In this view, private ownership leads to greed, selfishness, and inequality. A few people become rich and powerful while the majority become poor and powerless. Communists disagree how much, if any, private property should be allowed. Strict communists believe that all private property should be abolished. Others are prepared to allow personal possessions, such as books and clothes. In this more flexible view, private property is acceptable if it does not lead to some people controlling others.

There are many kinds of communism, and in various forms it can be found throughout history. Some early Christians held similar views about private ownership, as did Canada's native people. Hutterite colonies practise a type of communism.

Today, the word "communism" is most commonly applied to the ideas of Karl Marx and to the Soviet Union. In this sense, communism has come to mean not only the abolition of private property, but also dictatorship, a one-party state, centralized planning, and a lack of freedom. In fact, the word is often used in Canada as a political insult.

As a political movement, communism was most active in Canada in the 1930s. The Communist Party of Canada was founded in 1921. In 1932 Tim Buck and seven other leaders were convicted of being members of an illegal organization. The party was outlawed from 1940 to 1943. Party members were active in many strikes and demonstrations. Today, Canada's Communist Party is very small, but it regularly contests elections. Party representatives have been elected to city councils and school boards.

▷ RELATED ARTICLE: **Timothy Buck.**

Community College

Community colleges provide education for people who have graduated from high school but do not intend to go directly to university. Many community colleges specialize in technical and vocational education. Some also offer academic programs that lead on to university. In 1987, there were over 319 000 students in community colleges across Canada.

The first Canadian colleges were built in the 1960s and were part of the general educational expansion of the period. They were the result of two ideas: 1) everyone has a right to education after high school; and 2) more and more jobs need more training and education than can be provided at school. Community colleges vary widely from province to province, but they are all under provincial government control, with their teachers being government employees. They largely decide what they will teach, but government decides whether or not their programs will be funded. They do not possess the freedom enjoyed by universities.

The term "community college" was meant to indicate that colleges responded to and were controlled by the local community, but this is true only in a few cases. They have their own national organization: The Association of Canadian Community Colleges.

▷ RELATED ARTICLE: **CEGEP.**

Comox

Comox, B.C., lies in the shadow of the Beaufort Mountains on the east coast of Vancouver Island, 223 km north of Victoria. The Salish Indians first inhabited the area and the name Comox comes from their word for abundance. The first European settlers were brought in by a naval vessel in 1862. The Comox Air Base was constructed in 1942 and is still in operation. The military base is situated at the edge of town and is well known for its search-and-rescue operations on the Pacific Coast. The region has recently become a rich agricultural area. Nearby Forbidden Plateau and Mount Washington are two of B.C.'s most popular winter sports areas. In 1986 Comox's population was 6873. For information, contact the Town Clerk, 1809 Beaufort Ave., Comox, B.C., V9N 4B8.

Compagnie des Cent-Associés

Compagnie des Cent-Associés (the Company of One Hundred Associates) was a fur-trade company chartered in France in 1627. The French government gave it monopoly control of New France. In return, the company was supposed to bring in colonists and develop the colony. However, in 1645 it sublet its monopoly to the Communauté des Habitants. In 1663 it went out of business when the French king took over direct control of New France.

Company of Young Canadians

The Company of Young Canadians (CYC) was a voluntary agency created by the federal government in 1966. The young recruits were trained in "social animation" techniques and worked for a small salary. They were sent out into the community to help different groups organize themselves in an effort to improve their lives. Many of the projects were creative and successful, but others failed. Some of the volunteers were accused of being radical troublemakers because of their Marxist or separatist views. In 1969 the government imposed controls on the CYC, which caused further friction between the councillors and the recruits, and in 1976 the organization was abolished.

Computer-Assisted Learning

There are three main forms of computer-assisted learning (CAL). One is the use of computers to make the routine work of teaching easier, for instance by keeping records, by identifying students' difficulties, by testing, and by marking tests and worksheets. A common example is the use of computerized report cards. The second form of CAL is the use and study of computers themselves, as in computer science courses. The ability to use a computer is seen as increasingly important, since more and more jobs involve some

Careers in Computing
Careers in the computer field occur in a broad range of areas.

In *operations*, people work directly with the computer (for example, computer operator, and data control clerk).

Programmers design instructions for a computer so that it can do a certain task.

In *systems*, people find the best computer, program, or system to do a certain task.

In *data communications*, people work with the networks used to communicate information between computers.

In *data base administration*, people are responsible for a data base or data bases.

People in the *technical* area work in computer equipment installation or repair. Other careers include word-processor operators, sales, and management.

Computer science may be learned at trade or vocational schools, community colleges, and universities. Trade school programs usually last one year, those at community colleges two years. Over 4500 students graduate from such programs each year.

Another 3500 graduate from university undergraduate programs, which last four years.

Applicants should have a high-school diploma with courses in English (or French) and mathematics. Credits in business and computer science are desirable.

About 60 000 people work in some aspect of computing science; the field will no doubt continue to grow.

School Children *at the computer, Yellowknife, N.W.T. (photo by Malak, Ottawa).*

use of computers. The third form is the use of computers for teaching and learning a wide range of subjects, so that the computer becomes a resource, like a textbook or an atlas. Microcomputers are being used more and more in schools.

The Uses of CAL The five most common uses of CAL are for drill and review, for acquiring new information, for practising skills, for solving problems, and for creativity.

● Drill and review are used to help students remember what they have already learned (for example, formulas in science or definitions in social studies).

● Acquiring new information through CAL can be done by using a computer much like a textbook, or by allowing for student creativity (for example, in creating and analysing shapes in geometry).

● Practising skills involves activities such as solving problems in mathematics or using maps in geography.

● Problem solving usually involves interaction between students and the computer. For example, in a computer geography program, students play the part of a farmer, making decisions on such matters as planting crops and buying equipment, while the computer presents new information about weather, prices, etc.

● Creativity involves using CAL to encourage students to do something new (eg., to compose a tune in music).

The "Pros" and "Cons" of CAL Supporters of CAL claim it has several advantages. Students can learn at their own speed instead of being locked into the whole class. CAL can be fun. Computers never get angry and thus do not frighten students. Computers can help some students who cannot be reached by regular teachers.

Critics of CAL argue that it makes learning too isolated because students work on their own with the computer,

rather than with each other. Critics also point out that often the student has to fit in with the computer program, whereas a teacher can be much more flexible. Another criticism is that CAL makes learning too inhuman and mechanical.

In fact, everything depends on how CAL is used. It is generally agreed that CAL will not replace teachers but that it is a tool that teachers should use as needed. A major problem is that good CAL programs are very complicated to produce. One hour of CAL time generally requires 100 to 300 hours of development, involving many specialists. Because of this, there are many poor, cheaply made programs. Because of the cost, it has been difficult to get good Canadian programs. However, some provincial governments and universities are now correcting this. One of the skills that teachers now need is the ability to select good CAL programs and to decide when to use them.

■ Computers

Computers are machines that process information according to instructions which they are able to remember, modify, and carry out.

Computers are small, reliable, versatile, powerful, and inexpensive tools. Given detailed instructions, they can do complex calculations, store vast amounts of information, run video games, guide missiles, regulate human hearts, record television programs while you sleep, and do a great deal more. Computers continue to become smaller, "smarter," faster, and cheaper.

There are now computers in factories, offices, schools, and homes, in every corner of every industrialized society, including Canada. In 1965 there were about 1000 computers in Canada, all large machines owned by large companies or government. In the late 1980s there were at least 25 000 large computers in Canada, and more than 2 million small personal computers. As well, there are countless tiny special-purpose computers, called *microprocessors*, controlling wristwatches, car engines, and many other machines.

HOW COMPUTERS WORK

Most modern computers are what are known as digital electronic computers. They reduce all information — pictures, numbers, sounds, words — to long strings of the numbers one and zero. The numbers are called *bits*, and a string of eight bits is called a *byte*. To represent the number one, a circuit is switched on, and a pulse of electricity flows through it. To represent the number zero, a circuit is switched off, and no electricity flows through it. There are a great many such electrical circuits inside a computer.

In handling information, all computers do four main things:
• accept information, such as the set of instructions known as a *program*, or data such as numbers or words. Such input usually comes on a floppy disk, or is typed in on a keyboard.
• store information. Computers memorize or recall information with blazing speed — at rates of a few million words per second.
• process information, for instance, add or compare numbers.
• output information. For instance, they can display numbers on a screen, similar to that of a television, or print words on a printer.

The physical parts of a computer — keyboards, screens, circuits, and so on — are called *hardware*. The programs that tell a computer what to do are known as *software*.

HISTORY

Abacus Since ancient times, people have used tools to ease the work of computing — of adding, subtracting, and so on. The earliest of these tools was the abacus. It consists of beads strung on columns. To keep track of calculations, you can move beads from place to place. The abacus is still in use in China, though China also uses highly advanced computers.

The First Electronic Computers In electronic computers, electrical currents are switched on to keep track of calculations, much as beads are switched in the abacus. The first electronic computer was built in the United States during World War II. It was designed to calculate the paths followed by shells fired from big guns.

Scientists at the University of Toronto built a model of an electronic computer in 1948. In 1951, U of T purchased a computer called FERUT. It was a huge machine, filling a whole room, and had many flashing red, green, and blue lights.

Within seconds, FERUT could do calculations that before would have kept a team of mathematicians busy with calculators for many days. This computer and others like it were used to help design nuclear power plants, to calculate water levels in the St Lawrence Seaway, and more.

In the 1950s several Canadian universities began offering courses in computer science. Businesses based on the computer began to emerge. Most offered services. Some provided ways for distant computers to send data over telephone lines. Others designed software, such as the computer programs that, in 1962, began controlling traffic lights through the Toronto area — the world's first computer-controlled traffic system.

Chips In the 1960s scientists invented the *chip*. Chips are flat squares, smaller than a fingernail, made of materials such as silicon. Many electrical circuits can be packed on a single chip. These circuits use the miniature electrical switching device known as the transistor.

The cost of making chips, and thus of computers, has been going down, while the complexity of the circuits packed onto a single chip has been increasing.

The pattern of circuits on the first chips was about as complex as the street plan of a small town. Such miniature circuitry was complex enough to make the first hand-held calculators. Today, in the early 1990s, the pattern of the circuits that can be packed on a chip is about as complex as that of a detailed map of a city as big as a continent.

The brain of a computer, which in the 1950s was as big as a room, became in the 1960s as big as a refrigerator. In the 1970s such a brain could be squeezed onto a single chip.

Chips have created a remarkable reduction in the size and cost of computers. They have created a new branch of tech-

Human Heart *shown from the side in a computer graphic. Colours outline heart chambers and blood vessels (courtesy First Light).*

Computer Art *Computers can be used to produce drawings and paintings. The creativity, however, is limited to the program and to the operator (courtesy First Light).*

Computers *are valuable tools in teaching pilots to fly. They can simulate complex situations that a pilot might face. This photo shows a computer simulation of a CF-18 military fighter (photo by Brian Milne/First Light).*

Computer Graphics *are used to help architects design buildings (courtesy First Light).*

nology called microelectronics. They have created revolutionary changes in how people work, play, communicate, and think of the world.

USES OF COMPUTERS

It is becoming difficult to find activities in which computers are not used.

Government agencies were among the first users of computers. Computers are used to store great quantities of information about Canadians, such as the taxes they pay and the crimes they commit.

In business, computers were first used to calculate workers' pay cheques, and to keep track of goods and bills. Many offices use computers for *word processing*. Running a word-processing program, a computer can, among other things, remember words typed in, and it can correct spelling errors. (This encyclopedia was entered, revised, and typeset by computer. Computers also kept track of every entry and sorted them alphabetically.)

Computers are being linked with telephones to speed the flow of information over great distances. Computers tell travel agents what seats are available on flights. They make it possible to withdraw money from your home bank, even

Piping Design *generated on a computer to help design a complex plumbing system (courtesy First Light).*

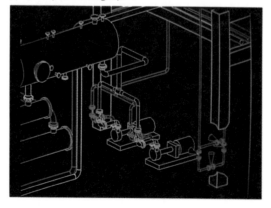

when you are away from home.

Computers keep medical records at most hospitals. By quickly searching such records, they help match donors of organs with people to whom the organs can be transplanted. They also give doctors three-dimensional pictures of parts of the body.

In schools, computers are used to help teach students.

They serve scientists, lawyers, business people, and journalists as stores of information.

Computers are used to control complex operations in, among other things, refineries, pipelines, and power plants. Many industries, especially the automotive industry, now use robots. Controlled by computers, robots can automatically do jobs, such as welding and painting. As well as helping to manufacture cars and other products, computers are also helping design them, by producing blueprints and making calculations.

Computers are also used to animate films, to make music, and to run toys.

Computers *in use at the Dofasco steel mill, Hamilton, Ont. (photo by Gregg Stott/Masterfile).*

COMPUTER-BASED BUSINESSES IN CANADA

In 1987 Canadians spent more than $10 billion on computer goods and services. Very little of this was spent on hardware made in Canada, but Canadian companies have been successful in developing software.

Most computer companies offer specialized services to business and industry. One of Canada's specialties is merging computers and communications. Northern Telecom Ltd of Mississauga, Ont., led the world in sending telephone messages coded in the digital language used by computers.

Northern Telecom is one of the very few Canadian companies which actually makes chips. Most computer-based companies in Canada buy chips from other countries. In the mid-1980s, in order to help Canadian firms develop the ability to make chips, some provincial governments set up organizations such as the Alberta Microelectronics Centre and the Ontario Centre for Microelectronics.

SOCIAL IMPACT

Privacy Many people are not aware that details of their lives are being recorded and exchanged between computers, such as those run by banks and the Canadian government. It is no longer as easy as it once was to remain private. Some people are concerned that information about them may be wrong, misused, or given too easily to other people.

Jobs Computerized machines, quicker and more accurate than most humans, are taking over work once done by humans. Machinists, assembly-line workers, factory workers, bank tellers, secretaries, and others may lose jobs to computers. On the other hand, computers increase efficiency in industry. Their proper use can help make Canada's economy more competitive.

Computers also create some new jobs. Most of these jobs, such as selling, repairing, and designing computers, require more specialized skills than the jobs being lost. As the number of computers in the workplace increases, jobs become more skilled.

Information Economy The computer is sometimes linked with means of communication, such as telephones and satellites. This combination is creating what some people call a new "information economy." One of the new features of the information economy is that much that was once done using paper is now done electronically. If you have a computer and a device called a *modem*, which allows your computer to communicate over the telephone lines, you can purchase goods from your home or office, send and receive messages, and get information from data banks.

In the 1940s, two-thirds of the jobs done by Canadian workers required strength or physical skill. Today, most people work in banks, insurance and real estate companies, theatres, book shops, schools, and other places where they handle not things but information.

The information industries are growing in size, employing more and more Canadians. Information, some say, is replacing natural resources as the most valuable resource in the Canadian economy. Computers have played the major role in that change.

▷ RELATED ARTICLES: **Robots; Technology.**

▷ SUGGESTED READING: Stewart Brand, editor, *Whole Earth Software Catalogue* (1985); A.K. (Keewatin) Dewdney's column, "Computer Recreations" in the magazine, *Scientific American*; Laura Greene, *Computer Pioneers* (1985); Marvin Minsky, *The Society of Mind* (1986); Theodore Roszak, *The Cult of Information: The Folklore of Computers and the True Art of Thinking* (1986); Kathlene R. Willing and Suzanne Girard, *The Junior Computer Dictionary* (1984).

■ Conacher, Lionel Pretoria

Athlete (*born in 1902 at Toronto, Ont.; died in 1954 at Ottawa, Ont.*). Called "The Big Train," Conacher was the greatest athlete Canada has produced. He excelled in football, lacrosse, baseball, boxing, wrestling, hockey, and track and field. He grew up in a tough area of Toronto, one of ten children. He was light-heavyweight boxing champion of Canada and later carried his fisticuffs into the hockey arena. He led the Toronto Argonauts to victory in the 1921 Grey Cup game, scoring 15 of his team's 23 points. He helped Toronto to the Lacrosse championship the following year. He played defence for Pittsburgh, New York, Chicago, and Montreal in the National Hockey League, making the first all-star team in 1934.

Conacher entered politics in 1937, serving in the Ontario legislature and then the House of Commons. He died during a charity softball game in Ottawa.

▷ SUGGESTED READING: Frank Cosentino, *Lionel Conacher* (1981).

Lionel Conacher excelled at football, hockey, boxing, and other sports. He was voted Canada's outstanding athlete of the century (courtesy Canada's Sports Hall of Fame).

■ Conception Bay

Conception Bay, 70 km long, on the north side of the Avalon Peninsula, was the site of the earliest settlements in Newfoundland. Its coastline varies from rugged cliffs and narrow fjords to sandy beaches and excellent harbours. The name commemorates the Feast of the Immaculate Conception.

■ Conception Bay South

Conception Bay South, Nfld, is a town that stretches 32 km along the southeast shore of Conception Bay on the Avalon Peninsula. The largest town in Newfoundland, it was created in 1971 by merging several small villages, most of which were founded before 1800. For most of their history, these villages depended on the small-boat inshore cod fishery and on some vegetable farming. The scenic area is now a popular summer resort. Many residents now commute to work in nearby St John's, although some mining and port facilities also provide employment. In 1986 the population was 15 531. For information, contact the Town Clerk, P.O. Box 280, Manuels, Nfld, A0A 2Y0.

■ Concert Halls, *see* Music

■ Concession

Concession is a block of land in rural Ontario. When the townships were first surveyed, they were subdivided into concessions and then into smaller blocks called *lots*. The size and layout of concessions within townships varied at different times and places. Roads were later built along the boundaries of the concessions. These concession roads are also sometimes known as concessions.

■ Concordia University

Concordia University is located on two campuses in Montreal. It offers more than 160 graduate and undergraduate programs in four faculties: arts and science, commerce and administration, engineering and computer science, and fine arts. The university has strong traditions in part-time education and many of its students work full-time during the day. Instruction is in English, but assignments and examinations, with some exceptions, may be submitted in French.

Concordia was founded in 1974 with the merger of Sir George Williams University and Loyola College. There are about 26 000 students. For further information, write the Admissions Centre, Concordia University, Montreal, Que., H3G 2S2.

■ Confederation

Confederation refers to the birth of Canada on July 1, 1867. The word is also used to describe the events that led to Confederation. The four original provinces were Nova Scotia, New Brunswick, Quebec, and Ontario.

The idea of uniting the British colonies of North America had been discussed for many years, but little interest was shown until a plan was drawn up in 1864 by several leaders in the Province of Canada. In September 1864, the Canadians presented

Reading the Proclamation, July 1, 1867, Market Square, Kingston, Ont. (courtesy Queen's University Archives).

their scheme to the leaders of the Maritime colonies in Charlottetown, P.E.I. The following month, there was another meeting at Quebec City to work out the details. Three years later, the new Dominion of Canada was proclaimed.

The birth of Canada was in many ways unique. It was not achieved by war or revolution. It was not a popular uprising of the people. Nor was it a call for independence from Great Britain. Each colony faced problems that it seemed unable to solve on its own. As Great Britain wished to draw away and as the United States grew more powerful, the solution more and more seemed to lie in a union that would be better able to deal with the economic and political challenges of a changing world.

BACKGROUND

Colonies of the British Empire Before 1867, North America had only one independent nation — the United States. Perched along its northern border were a number of colonies which were still largely dependent upon Britain and had little contact with one another.

On the Atlantic coast were the colonies of Newfoundland, Nova Scotia, Prince Edward Island, and New Brunswick. Each of these colonies had developed a way of life based on seafaring, fishing, shipbuilding, and the timber trade. Each looked outward to markets in Britain or the U.S., but they had very little contact with the inland colony of the Province of Canada.

To the north and west was a vast, mostly unsettled, land. The Hudson's Bay Company claimed much of this territory and called it Rupert's Land. It was populated by Indians, Metis, and a few thousand fur traders and settlers at Red River. Far to the west, on the Pacific coast, there had been a British colony since 1849 on Vancouver Island and since 1858 on the mainland.

Although the separate colonies along the Atlantic coast had much in common, the united Province of Canada contained two very different sections. The population of Canada West was primarily English-speaking and Protestant. Canada East was mostly French-speaking and Roman Catholic.

Troubles in the Canadas Britain had created the united province in 1841 in the hope that the English population would dominate and that the use of French would disappear. In this it failed, because the French-speaking sector not only survived but gained much skill in politics.

The union also failed to provide the colony with good government. Both Canada East and Canada West were given the same number of seats in the government. In the beginning, this favoured Canada West because it had the smaller population. Later, as the population of Canada West grew and outnumbered the East, the arrangement favoured Canada East. First one side, then the other, complained that the system was unfair. Disputes often became bitter. French Canadians feared for the survival of their way of life. English Canadians believed that the French Canadians were blocking their progress. Their battle cry, under their leader George Brown, was "rep by pop," meaning that the section with the greatest population should have the greatest representation (that is, the greatest number of seats in the Assembly).

By the late 1850s, the government of the Canadas had come almost to a standstill. Political parties tried to get support in both sections, but the party that was strong in one section was weak in the other. The Conservatives were strong in Canada East, where they were called *Bleus*, but they were weak in the West. The Reformers, often called "Grits" in the West and *Rouges* in the East, were strong in the West and weak in the East.

As a result, no party could hold power for very long. For example, one government fell when it tried to choose a site for a capital city. Finally, when Queen Victoria provided a compromise by choosing what became Ottawa, both sections were disappointed. Yet another government fell.

FORCES BEHIND CONFEDERATION

By the 1860s, most Canadian leaders agreed that their government was not working. Their determination to change was the spark that put Confederation in motion. But first the deadlock had to be broken among men who strongly disliked one another. Thus it was a great surprise when George Brown approached his old enemy John A. Macdonald to make a deal. Brown would join a *coalition*, as long as everyone would co-operate in looking for a better system. Macdonald agreed, and so did George-Étienne Cartier, the leader of the largest French-Canadian group.

The main idea of this "Great Coalition," as it was called, was that all the British North American colonies should unite. This idea had not been acted on before, but now there were a number of pressures that made it seem urgent.

Joseph Howe *was the great patriot of his province of Nova Scotia. He loudly denounced Confederation as the "botheration scheme." In 1867-68, he travelled to England to try to keep Nova Scotia out of Confederation (courtesy NAC/C-22002).*

Alexander Tilloch Galt *was a powerful businessman who first called for a union of the colonies in 1858. He was a member of the Great Coalition, attended both conferences, served in the Cabinet after Confederation, and was Canada's first representative in Britain. The story of his life has been called "the history of Canada in the 19th century" (courtesy NAC/PA-13008).*

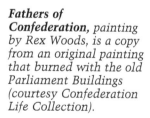

Delegates at the Charlottetown Conference,1864. This famous photo shows John A. Macdonald seated in the front row, centre. George-Etienne Cartier is standing to his right, holding his hat. Directly behind Cartier is Thomas D'Arcy McGee, who was later assassinated (courtesy NAC/C-733).

Fathers of Confederation, painting by Rex Woods, is a copy from an original painting that burned with the old Parliament Buildings (courtesy Confederation Life Collection).

Threat from the South One of the greatest concerns of the colonists was the terrible Civil War in the United States which had broken out in 1861. Many people remembered that the Americans had already bought or seized a great deal of land in North America. They had seized Texas from Mexico in 1845. The following year they obtained the huge Oregon territory from Britain. In 1812 and before, American troops had tried to invade Canada. Now the leaders in the northern states were angered by Britain's support of the South and the British North American colonists feared that the Americans would turn their anger on them. After an incident at sea in 1861, 15 000 British troops were rushed to defend Canada. They arrived in Halifax, but had a slow, cold, and painful trip to Quebec. This proved to Canadians how helpless they would be if the Americans attacked. To make matters worse, a group of Irish rebels, called Fenians, added to these fears by attacks at several places along Canada's borders.

Economic Pressures One advantage of being a colony was that the colonists always knew they could sell their products in Great Britain. By the 1840s, however, Britain began to buy its wheat, fish, and timber elsewhere. The colonists now looked more and more to the U.S. as a new market for their goods. In 1854 an agreement called the Reciprocity Treaty was signed with the U.S. It greatly increased trade between the colonies and the republic to the south. Reciprocity brought prosperity to the colonies, but in the early 1860s the U.S. threatened to end the agreement. Once again, the colonists felt weak and at the mercy of others.

Railways If economics and politics made a union seem necessary, it was the railway that made it possible. Large-scale railway building only came to Canada in the 1850s but it quickly changed the colonists' way of life. Where before there

had been only muddy forest roads and rivers that froze in winter, the iron rails now offered fast, year-round transportation. The railway could link the Canadas with the Maritimes and with the Northwest and even British Columbia.

ACHIEVING CONFEDERATION

Charlottetown Conference Confederation was helped along by some luck. Canadian leaders discovered that Maritime leaders planned to meet at Charlottetown, P.E.I., to discuss their own plans for a union. The Canadians asked if they could attend, and they were accepted.

Few people in Charlottetown noticed the arrival, on September 1, 1864, of Macdonald, Brown, Cartier, and the other Canadians as they entered the harbour aboard their ship, *Queen Victoria*. A circus was in town and promised to be far more interesting. On September 2 the Canadians explained their proposal: first, the colonies would unite under one central government. This would give power to the nation as a whole to deal with matters such as defence and trade with other countries. Second, each of the Canadas and the Maritime colonies would become a province with its *own* government to deal with local matters and to preserve the special character of each area. This system, with two levels of government, is called a *federation*. As part of the plan, the central government would build a railway to connect the colonies. It seemed to offer something for everybody. But was it enough?

The Maritimers agreed to put aside their own plans. All agreed to meet again, in Quebec City, and to try and work out the details.

Quebec Conference By October 10, 1864, 33 delegates had gathered in Quebec City from Nova Scotia, New Brunswick, Prince Edward Island, and the Province of Canada. Newfoundland sent two observers only, since it had no firm plans to join. Before the end of the first day, it was agreed that the "future prosperity of British North America would be promoted by a federal union under the Crown of Great Britain."

Working out the details of the union, however, was not so easy. There were long arguments over how many seats each province should have in the central government. George Brown insisted on "rep by pop," which would give his home province, Canada West, 82 seats. Canada East would get only 65 seats, and Prince Edward Island only five. This quickly ended enthusiasm among the Islanders. Nor was P.E.I. much interested in Canada's promise to build a railway to the Maritimes; it would be of little use to an island! Disputes also broke out about which powers would be kept by the central government and which would go to the provinces. Nevertheless, when the conference ended on October 27, an agreement had been worked out between New Brunswick, Nova Scotia, and the Canadas. The agreement included 72 points on which the delegates agreed and is known as the 72 Resolutions.

Most of the items were in John A. Macdonald's own handwriting. He was the one who ironed out many of the problems and who persuaded each colony that its separate nature would be protected. Although Macdonald was not the first to propose Confederation, he proved the ablest man to bring it about.

Opposition to Confederation The scheme had strong opponents. In Canada West, Reformers opposed union with the Maritimes and the cost of building a railway to Halifax, but Brown rallied their support. In Canada East, a leading French Canadian declared that Confederation would "oppress us ... and send us to the scaffold and into exile," and many agreed with him. But Cartier won over many French Canadians with his argument that Quebec's only real chance for survival in North America was as part of Canada. The resolutions passed, 91 votes *for* and 33 *against* (with the members from Canada East voting 27 *for* and 22 *against*).

Opposition was even stronger in the Maritimes. The influential newspaperman and politician Joseph Howe of Nova Scotia called Confederation the "botheration scheme." He attacked it in the newspapers and demanded an election. Charles Tupper, the leader of the government in Nova Scotia, supported Confederation but was afraid to put it to a vote. There was trouble in New Brunswick as well, where Leonard Tilley fought an election on the issue and lost.

Triumph While opposition mounted in New Brunswick and Nova Scotia, Confederation was eagerly supported in Great Britain. The British were finding the defence of the colonies very expensive. A new governor was sent to New Brunswick to help put Tilley back into power. Meanwhile, Fenian raids flared up along the borders of New Brunswick and the Canadas. In March 1865 the U.S. announced that it would end Reciprocity in 1866. Thus, the old fears were raised

Sir John A. Macdonald *proved the most able leader in bringing about Confederation. He was shrewd, knowledgeable, and tenacious. He was so involved in the discussions at Quebec that most of the resolutions were in his own handwriting. In 1866, Macdonald took the resolutions to England for approval. After his first exhausting day, he fell asleep and was awakened by a raging fire that had been set off by a burning candle. It must have seemed typical of all the problems in achieving Confederation. In recognition of his accomplishment Macdonald was the unanimous choice to become the first prime minister of the new nation (courtesy NAC/C-27638).*

Samuel Leonard Tilley *played a most important role in bringing New Brunswick into Confederation. The scheme's darkest hour came when he lost an election over the issue in 1865. However, he regained power the following year (courtesy NAC/PA-26346).*

again: danger along the border and loss of a trading partner.

Supporters breathed a sigh of relief when Tilley was swept back into power. New promises were made to Nova Scotia and Tupper finally gained the support of the Nova Scotia Assembly.

At a third conference, held in London, England, further details were worked out. In March 1867 the British Parliament passed the British North America Act. Macdonald wanted to call the new nation the "Kingdom of Canada," but the British feared that the word "kingdom" would offend the United States. The name Dominion was chosen instead. There was never any question that the new nation would be called Canada.

First of July, 1867 Booming cannons and parades celebrated Confederation in many parts of Canada, but black crepe was hung in windows elsewhere, as if for a funeral. The new prime minister, John A. Macdonald, knew that Confederation was only a beginning; much was left to be done. *See* **Responsible Government** (for an explanation of how the government of the colonies worked) and **Federalism** (for a description of the system today).

▷ RELATED ARTICLES: **George Brown; George-Étienne Cartier; Joseph Howe; John A. Macdonald.**

▷ SUGGESTED READING: Michael Bliss, *Confederation: A New Nationality* (1981); Stan Garrod, *Confederation* (1982).

■ Confederation of National Trade Unions

The CNTU is a union group in Quebec. It is second in size only to the Quebec Federation of Labour. In 1986 there were 1717 unions and 218 865 members in the CNTU. Most of the members are public servants and hospital workers.

The CNTU was founded in 1921. It was originally called the Canadian Catholic Confederation of Labour, because many of its member-unions were formed by Catholic priests. By 1960 the organization had lost its ties to the church and took its present name. The French name of the CNTU is Confédération des syndicats nationaux, or CSN.

When it is bargaining with the government for better pay and working conditions, the CNTU sometimes joins forces with teachers and other workers. This *Common Front* approach won important gains for members during the 1970s.

■ Conifers

Conifers were the first trees to appear on Earth, some 300 million years ago. They are an order (Coniferales) of non-flowering plants. As their name suggests, most conifers bear cones, composed of scales. The male cones, small and numerous, appear in early spring. They then produce a large amount of pollen that, wind-borne, enters between the scales on the female cones. These scales each carry two or more ovules that, after pollination, turn into winged seeds. Conifer leaves may be broad and scale-like (as in cedars and some juniper species) or narrow and needle-like (as in pine, fir, hemlock, spruce, yew, larch, and tamarack). With the exception of larches and tamaracks, conifers keep their leaves throughout winter; hence their name of *semper virens* (evergreen). Another characteristic of most conifers is that they produce resin.

The huge conifer forests that cover much of Canada are important for several reasons. First, they purify the air by absorbing carbon dioxide and producing the oxygen we need to breathe. Second, with their branches (which may droop far enough to touch the ground) conifers prevent soil erosion and provide shelter and food to a wide variety of wildlife. Finally, their wood plays an important part in Canada's economy, since it is used for construction and for wood pulp.

■ Connor, Ralph

Writer (*born in 1860 at Glengarry County, Canada West [Ont.]; died in 1937 at Winnipeg, Man.*). Using the pen name of Ralph Connor, Charles William Gordon became a successful author of international bestsellers. Ordained a Presbyterian minister in 1890, he did three years' missionary work at Banff, in the Rockies, before becoming a pastor in Winnipeg. He began writing to raise money for his Winnipeg parish.

Black Rock (1898) and *The Sky Pilot* (1899), the books that made him famous, are based on his experiences in Banff. They contain lots of action, interesting scenes of frontier life, and brave heroes who defend Christian principles.

Gordon based two popular books on childhood memories. The hero of *The Man from Glengarry* (1901) is pictured as the ideal Christian pioneer. *Glengarry School Days* (1902) sketches pioneer social life in and around the one-room school.

Among other accomplishments, Gordon was a chaplain in World War I, a labour mediator, and the moderator of the Presbyterian Church in Canada.

▷ Suggested Reading: John Lennox, *Ralph Connor and his Works* (1988); Keith Wilson, *Charles William Gordon* (1981).

■ Conquest

The Conquest is the term that is used to describe the events surrounding the military takeover of New France by Great Britain.

The French surrendered the fortress of Quebec to British forces on September 18, 1759. A year later Montreal fell. On September 8, 1760, both sides agreed to the terms of surrender. The British guaranteed not to deport or mistreat the people of New France. They allowed anyone to leave, taking their possessions with them. They guaranteed the French the right to take part in the fur trade and to worship in the Catholic religion. New France formally became a British colony by the Treaty of Paris, February 10, 1763.

The effect of the Conquest on the 70 000 French colonists has been debated by historians. The French maintained their language, religion, and customs. However, they lived under the threat that these rights could be taken away. The governor and officials were English. The economy was controlled by English and Scottish merchants. Nevertheless, under British rule, the French-Canadian populace were able to vote and elect members of the Assembly.

Some modern historians see the Conquest as a disaster for French Canadians, making them second-class subjects. Others claim that the majority of people were affected very little by the event. One thing is certain. The Conquest resulted in Canada containing two very different cultures: French and English.

■ Conscription

Conscription is a government policy which requires citizens to join the armed forces. There has never been conscription in Canada in peacetime, but it was used during the two world wars, causing bitter divisions between French and English Canadians.

WORLD WAR I

In 1917 the Conservative government of Robert Borden introduced conscription because it feared there were not enough volunteers to keep up the strength of the Canadian army fighting in Europe. The policy upset many French Canadians, who thought that a war in Europe was not their affair.

Other groups, such as farmers and some newcomers from Europe, also opposed conscription. So did Wilfrid Laurier and many of his supporters in the Liberal Party. Other Liberals, especially those from English Canada, joined with Borden to form a coalition government strong enough to force the measure through Parliament. Reaction across the country was bitter. Some farmers challenged conscription in the courts. There was an anti-conscription riot in Quebec City over Easter weekend in 1918. For many years the Conservative Party found it hard to get votes in Quebec.

WORLD WAR II

At the outbreak of World War II, politicians remembered the problems that conscription had caused in 1917-18. Both the Conservatives and the ruling Liberals promised there would be no conscription. However, after Germany conquered Holland, Belgium, and France in May-June 1940, Prime Minister King introduced the National Resources Mobilization Act. This law gave the government the authority to make young men serve in the forces, but they could only serve in Canada or to defend home territory. There was criticism of these "zombies" who did not have to fight overseas. Some English Canadians believed that the French Canadians in particular were not doing their part to fight the war.

As the war progressed, political pressure for all-out conscription mounted. In 1942 King called a plebiscite, asking voters to release him from his pledge not to use conscription for duty overseas. Quebec said "no," but the rest of Canada said "yes."

Knowing how conscription had divided Canadians in World War I, King still hesitated to act. By late 1944, King's minister of defence, J.L. Ralston, was telling him that Canadian soldiers were dying in Europe because of shortages of men. King fired Ralston, but his replacement, A.G.L. McNaughton, also failed to find more volunteers. All-out conscription was finally introduced at the end of 1944. However, since the war was almost over, few conscripts actually took part in the fighting.

▷ Related Articles: **World War I; World War II.**

■ Conservation

Conservation is the wise use of resources. The word is most often applied to natural resources, but it also refers to energy, works of art, heritage buildings, languages, and cultures.

Conservation often requires trade-offs between economic gain and the loss of re-

---

Time Line: Conquest

- **1759** Fall of Quebec
- **1760** Surrender of New France
- **1763** Treaty of Paris creates Old Province of Quebec (a British colony)
- **1774** Quebec Act enlarges the boundaries of Quebec, guarantees religious rights of French Canadians
- **1791** Constitutional Act creates Upper and Lower Canada (two separate British colonies)

sources. Without resources there is no economic gain and without a sound economy there is no money to fund conservation programs.

Renewable and non-renewable resources require different approaches. The conservation of renewable resources, such as forest and grasslands, requires using only as much as nature replaces. Conservation of non-renewable resources, such as minerals and fossil fuels, means avoiding waste, such as oil spills and overheated houses. It also means promoting the recycling of materials.

HISTORY OF THE CONSERVATION MOVEMENT

Until the end of the last century, Canada's vast resources seemed inexhaustible. However, signs began to appear that there were limits to how rapidly resources could be taken. The great pine forests of eastern Canada rapidly disappeared. Most of the great bison herds that once roamed the prairies were killed by hunters. The wilderness splendour of North America was quickly disappearing to the farmer's plough and the lumberman's axe.

Most of the first conservationists were naturalists, who fought to preserve natural areas and wildlife. They worked to establish bird sanctuaries and parks.

The conservation movement later turned its attention to the loss of natural resources. Powerful new tools sped up the rate at which forests, fish, and soil could be used. Chain saws, for example, felled trees far faster than hand saws. Large, well-equipped factory-trawlers scooped up greater numbers of fish than simple fishing boats with nets on the east coast of Canada.

Another factor that led to increased use of resources was the failure to consider the cost to society and the future. For example, the cost of oil is very low, in part because it does not include the cost of damage to the environment when oil spills occur, or the cost to future generations when supplies run out.

In the 1960s, a growing number of Canadians joined the conservation movement, because they were concerned about pollution and the destruction of the environment that supports all life. Today the conservation movement has joined with the environmental movement. Together they sometimes come into conflict with those who support measures to spur economic development.

CONSERVATION TODAY

The idea that conservation benefits the whole society is slowly gaining acceptance. There is a trend to see resources as borrowed from future generations, rather than inherited from the past. Thus, support has grown for the protection of wildlife and their habitats, and for careful environmental planning.

Canadians, on the average, used less energy to heat their homes in the 1980s than they did in the 1970s. With the assistance of government, they often insulated their homes more effectively. Their cars and furnaces are more efficient. The forest industry is increasingly aware of the need to replant trees and to limit their cutting.

Canada and many other countries now include the goal of development in their planning. They are trying to find a balance between economic development, which is needed to provide jobs, and conservation, which we all need if we are to survive. Nevertheless, there is a wide gap between such talk and the sacrifices needed to achieve the goal of a society that is concerned as much for the future as for the present profit.

Information on various aspects of conservation can be obtained by writing to the following organizations: The Canadian Nature Federation, 453 Sussex Drive, Ottawa, Ont., K1N 6Z4; Canadian Wildlife Federation, Suite 203, 1673 Carling Ave., Ottawa, Ont., K2A 3Z1; and Energy Probe Research Foundation, 225 Brunswick Ave., Toronto, Ont., M5S 2M6. You may also find useful information in *Owl*, a magazine published by the Young Naturalist Federation and in *Ranger Rick*, a magazine published by the Canadian Wildlife Federation.

▷ Suggested Reading: Monte Hummel, editor, *Endangered Spaces: The Future for Canada's Wilderness* (1989).

■ Conservatism

Conservatism is a term used in Canada to refer to a belief in tradition, respect for the law, and opposition to rapid change. The term is often confused with the American use of the word, which refers to a kind of political thought that stresses individualism and freedom from state interference.

People who call themselves conservatives hold a wide range of views. Conservatives may oppose government interference in certain economic matters, while supporting interference in moral issues, such as abortion. Usually, however, they support authority and prefer things as they are.

Conservatives are not limited to the Progressive Conservative Party. Some

The Old Flag, The Old Policy, The Old Leader *was the appeal to the old ways on which John A. Macdonald built the power of the Conservative Party (courtesy NAC/C-6536).*

support smaller parties, such as the Reform Party in the West, or the Social Credit Party in British Columbia. It is possible to speak of the "conservative wing" of the Liberal Party or even of the New Democratic Party.

■ Conservative Party, *see* Progressive Conservative Party

■ Constitution

A constitution is the rules that govern how an organization is supposed to work, whether it is a small club or the government of a country.

Components of the Canadian Constitution Most countries today have written constitutions, that is, one document that contains all the important rules. Examples are the United States and the Soviet Union. However, some countries have an "unwritten" constitution, in the sense that they have no one written document. The best-known example is Great Britain, whose constitution consists of many different Acts of Parliament. It also contains court decisions, and traditions and customs that stretch back over centuries. Before 1982, Canada was close to the British example. The British North America

(BNA) Act of 1867 declared that Canada had "a constitution similar in principle" to Great Britain. In the 1950s, Canada's Constitution was made up of six components: 1) the BNA Act and its amendments; 2) Acts of the Canadian Parliament; 3) Acts of the British Parliament; 4) court decisions; 5) customs and traditions; and 6) other. In 1982, the Constitution Act, 1982, was added to the Constitution. The BNA Act was renamed the Constitution Act, 1867.

The most important parts of Canada's written Constitution include the following:

● the *Quebec Act of 1774*, which guaranteed the use of the French language and civil law in Quebec;

● the *Constitutional Act of 1791*, which created elected assemblies in Quebec and Ontario;

● the *British North America Act of 1867*, which created the basis of the federal system and laid down the division of powers between federal and provincial governments. This Act was renamed the *Constitution Act, 1867* in 1982 ;

● decisions of the Supreme Court;

● the *Statute of Westminster of 1931*, which recognized Canada's full independence within the Commonwealth. It stated that no law made by the Parliament of the United Kingdom would extend to any Dominion, except at the request of that Dominion;

Queen Elizabeth II *signing the Constitution document as Prime Minister Trudeau and his aides Michael Pitfield (centre) and Michael Kirby (right) look on; Ottawa, Ont. (courtesy SSC Photocentre).*

- the Acts that created new provinces after Confederation, for example, the Manitoba Act (1870) and the Alberta and Saskatchewan Acts (1905);
- the *Canada Act, 1982*, which was the last Act passed by Great Britain that affected Canada. It states that "No Act of the Parliament of the United Kingdom ... shall extend to Canada as part of its law;"
- the *Constitution Act, 1982*, which made a number of changes to the British North America Act;
- the *Canadian Charter of Rights and Freedoms*, which entrenches certain rights in the Constitution.

In 1981 the Supreme Court ruled that the Constitution consists of unwritten constitutional "conventions," or customs, as well as written documents, such as laws and Acts of Parliament. Conventions have developed over the years, sometimes over centuries, and are widely accepted, although they are nowhere written down. The Cabinet, for example, is not mentioned in the Constitution. Similarly, the custom that says the government must have a majority in the House of Commons and must resign if it loses the confidence of the House, is not mentioned in the Constitution.

Bringing Home the Constitution For many years, Canada was an independent country, in spite of the fact that its constitution (the BNA Act) was an Act of the British Parliament. Efforts to "bring home" the Constitution failed because the federal and provincial governments could not agree on an "amending formula" by which the Canadian Parliament would be able to change the Constitution. Quebec, in particular, was concerned that the English-speaking majority of Canadians would use their votes to limit Quebec's rights concerning French language and culture.

The issue of bringing the Constitution to Canada (or "patriating" it) dominated Canadian politics between 1980 and 1982. In 1980, as part of a campaign to defeat Quebec separatism, Prime Minister Pierre Trudeau promised to reform the Canadian Constitution. During 1980 the federal and provincial governments entered into tough and difficult negotiations over the shape of a new constitution. When they could not agree, Prime Minister Trudeau announced that the federal government would act on its own and ask the British Parliament to hand the BNA Act back to Canada. The Conservatives, in opposition, bitterly opposed this plan, as did some provinces. Although Ontario and New Brunswick supported the federal government, the other eight provinces were opposed. Some of them asked the courts to decide whether the federal government could act on its own. Both sides presented their own plans to the public. In 1981 the federal government agreed to send the dispute to the Supreme Court.

Kitchen Compromise The Supreme Court ruled that the federal government had a legal right to act on its own. However, it also ruled that there was an unwritten convention that, when provincial government rights might be affected, the federal government had to work with the provinces. This decision led to further negotiations and to a final conference in November 1981. This conference lasted four days and seemed likely to end in deadlock. Then a private meeting among three ministers (Jean Chrétien of the federal government, Roy McMurtry of Ontario, and Roy Romanow of Saskatchewan) led to a compromise. This meeting took place in a kitchen and has become known as the Kitchen Meeting. The compromise was amended and accepted by the other provinces, except for Quebec, which was not consulted. Premier René Lévesque of Quebec protested bitterly against these secret negotiations, which he saw as a betrayal of Quebec, and he refused to sign the proposed constitution.

The formula is summarized in the following table:

Amending the Constitution

Changes	Agreement Required
• To the office of the Queen, Governor General, Lieutenant-Governor, the use of French or English, and the make-up of the Supreme Court of Canada	• Unanimous (the federal and all the provincial governments)
• To the boundaries between provinces, and to the use of English or French within a certain province	• The federal Parliament and the provinces to which the changes apply
• To the Senate and House of Commons	• The federal Parliament alone
• To the Constitution of a province	• That province alone
• General (meaning cases not covered by the above)	• The federal Parliament and 7 of the 10 provinces representing at least 50% of the population of all the provinces

The New Constitution The Constitution Act of 1982 is the document that brings together the discussions of 1980-82. Essentially, it does three things:

1) it brings together most of the earlier documents that make up the Constitution;

2) it includes the Charter of Rights and Freedoms, together with the "notwithstanding" clause that was part of the Kitchen Meeting compromise; and

3) it provides a formula by which the Constitution can be amended with the agreement of the federal Parliament and two-thirds of the provinces making up 50% of Canada's population. If an amendment involves changing the Supreme Court, the monarchy, or the amending formula itself, all ten provinces and the federal Parliament must agree. This complicated system is intended to protect the rights of the provinces while also allowing for the Constitution to be changed to meet new circumstances.

In 1987 Prime Minister Brian Mulroney and the provincial premiers drew up the Meech Lake Accord in order to bring Quebec into the Constitution.

▷ RELATED ARTICLES: **Canadian Charter of Rights and Freedoms; Government; House of Commons; Meech Lake Accord; Parliament.**

▷ SUGGESTED READINGS: Robert Sheppard and M. Valpy, *The National Deal: The Fight for a Canadian Constitution* (1982); George F.G. Stanley, *A Short History of the Canadian Constitution* (1969).

■ Constitution Act, 1867

The Constitution Act, 1867, is the modern name for the British North America Act, which was renamed in April 1982. The Act created the Dominion of Canada in 1867, making it a federal nation with two levels of government — federal and provincial. It distributed powers between the two levels of government and outlined how the system was to work. *See* the article on **Federalism**, which describes the form of government established by the Act.

▷ RELATED ARTICLES: **Confederation; Constitution Act 1982.**

■ Constitution Act 1982

The Constitution Act, 1982, is part of the Constitution of Canada. It made several changes to the British North America Act, including renaming it the Constitution Act, 1867.

The Constitution Act, 1982, contains the Canadian Charter of Rights and Freedoms.

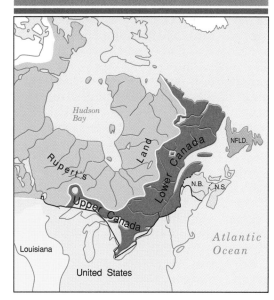

Constitutional Act 1791

■ Constitutional Act, 1791

The Constitutional Act came into effect on December 26, 1791. Its main terms were as follows:

● it divided the old Province of Quebec into two, *separate colonies*: Upper Canada and Lower Canada (*see* map, above);

● it gave each colony an *elected assembly* with the power to raise taxes;

● it gave each colony a *legislative council*, chosen by the governor;

● it guaranteed the ownership of land of the old *seigneurial system* in Lower Canada; and

● it created the *clergy reserves* in Upper Canada.

By limiting the power of assemblies, which were elected by the people, the Act set the stage for future conflict.

▷ RELATED ARTICLES: **Clergy Reserves; Lower Canada; Political History; Upper Canada.**

■ Continental Divide

The Continental Divide is the height of land which separates areas drained by rivers that flow to opposite sides of North America. In Canada there are two divides. One runs north-south along the top of the Rocky Mountains. Water in the rivers west of this line flows eventually into the Pacific Ocean, while rivers to the east flow either to the Arctic or Atlantic oceans. The second divide, running east-west across the continent, is low and less obvious. Starting in the Rockies, it crosses the southern plains and central Ontario and Quebec. Water in rivers to the north of this line flows into the Arctic Ocean or Hudson Bay.

▷ RELATED ARTICLES: **Geology, Mountains.**

Continental Drift

Until recently it was believed that the Earth's surface was stable, that the continents are now where they always were. It was not until the 1950s and 1960s that evidence was found by scientists, including Canadian John Tuzo Wilson, to prove otherwise. It is now believed that at one time all the world's continents were one single land mass, which is called Pangaea. Pangaea broke up and the continents have since been moving, much like closely packed icebergs on the Arctic Ocean. The Earth is also divided into many plates of which continents are part. These plates move a few centimetres each year. The reasons for this movement are not known, though some scientists believe that it is caused by forces beneath the Earth's crust. Where the plates clash, the result is earthquakes and volcanoes.

▷ RELATED ARTICLES: **Plate Tectonics; John Tuzo Wilson.**

Cook, James

British naval explorer (*born in 1728 near Marton, England; died in 1779 in Hawaii*). Cook was the greatest navigator of his day. He did more than any other explorer to add to our knowledge of the Pacific Ocean. He first appeared off Canada's shores as an officer in the British navy in 1758 during the siege of the French fortress of Louisbourg. He was a skilled surveyor. Early in 1759 he charted part of the Gaspé and the St Lawrence River. From 1763 to 1767 he mapped the treacherous coast of Newfoundland, including the harbour at St John's.

Pacific Voyages Cook is best known for his great voyages of discovery into the Pacific which twice took him around the world. On the first voyage (1768-71) he led a scientific expedition to the island of Tahiti and charted New Zealand and the east coast of Australia. He sailed home by way of Java and the Cape of Good Hope.

On his second voyage (1772-75), Cook sailed along the edge of the icy coast of the Antarctic. Despite the extreme risks, Cook sailed farther south than any other

navigator before him, and there was only one death among his crew.

Voyage to Nootka Sound Cook's next and last voyage (1776-79) brought him to the coast of North America in search of a Northwest Passage through the Arctic. On the way across the Pacific he discovered the Hawaiian Islands, then known as the Sandwich Islands. He arrived at Nootka Sound on the west coast of Vancouver Island on March 29, 1778, and remained there for four weeks, repairing his vessels and trading with the native people. He sailed north as far as Icy Cape on the Alaska coast, but was forced to turn back. He returned to Hawaii, where he was killed in a dispute with the Hawaiian people.

Cook's crewmen brought back word of the rich supplies of furs to be found on the coast of Vancouver Island, sparking an interest that led to a British claim of the coast of British Columbia.

▷ RELATED ARTICLES: **Exploration; Nootka Sound.**

▷ SUGGESTED READING: Daniel Conner, *James Cook and the Nuu-Chah-Nulth* (1986); Roger Hart, *The Voyages of Captain Cook* (1973).

Cook, William Harrison

Chemist (*born in 1903 at Alnwick, England*). Brought up on an Alberta homestead, Cook began his formal education at agricultural school when he was 17. By 1924 he was assisting Robert Newton in research on the drying of damp wheat. He joined the National Research Council (NRC) in 1932 and became its director of biology in 1941.

Having experimented with refrigerated greenhouses (which were designed to simulate farming conditions on the prairies), Cook's work during World War II included converting freighters into refrigerated food ships. After the war, he reorganized the NRC's food research laboratories. He also did original research on a seaweed used by the food industry. He was associated with the NRC until 1974.

Cook is the author of more than 150 scientific and technical papers. He has also written a memoir of his cowboy youth and a book about his years with the NRC.

Co-operative Commonwealth Federation (CCF)

The CCF was founded in 1932. It brought together a number of socialist, farm, and labour groups who wanted to reform society by changing the values on which it is based. They wanted a society in which everyone would co-operate for the common good, hence the name "co-operative com-

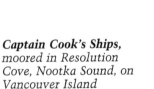

Captain James Cook was the foremost explorer of his day. He explored both Canada's east and west coasts (courtesy the National Maritime Museum, London).

Captain Cook's Ships, moored in Resolution Cove, Nootka Sound, on Vancouver Island (courtesy NAC/C-11201).

Tommy Douglas standing under a CCF billboard shortly after his election (courtesy Saskatchewan Archives Board/R-B2895).

monwealth." They were intensely critical of capitalism, which they believed encouraged inequality, selfishness, and greed. In 1933 in Regina, the CCF chose J.S. Woodsworth, a Winnipeg Labour member of Parliament, as its first leader. It also adopted the Regina Manifesto as its program. The manifesto called for public ownership of key industries. It put forward programs for social services such as pensions, medicare, family allowances, and unemployment insurance. It promised that the CCF would work tirelessly to eliminate capitalism by democratic means.

The CCF quickly won a handful of seats in Parliament, but its major political successes occurred at the provincial level. In 1943 it became the official opposition in Ontario, and in 1944 it formed the government of Saskatchewan with T.C. (Tommy) Douglas as premier.

Some of the CCF's opponents tried to discredit it by claiming that it wanted to establish a dictatorship, as in the Soviet Union. In fact, the CCF was firmly opposed to communism. In 1956 the Regina Manifesto was replaced with a much more moderate document in an attempt to gain more voters' support. Nevertheless, the party did poorly in the 1958 federal election. It elected only eight MPs.

After much discussion, the CCF and the Canadian Labour Congress joined to organize a new political party which could make democratic socialism more popular with Canadian voters. In 1961 the CCF became the New Democratic Party. Although the CCF had formed a government only in Saskatchewan, some of its ideas were taken up by other parties. The federal Liberals adopted CCF policies such as old-age pensions, unemployment insurance, family allowances, and medicare.

■ Co-operative Movement

The co-operative movement is a social and economic movement which emerged in the 19th century in response to the growth of industry. As organizations grew larger and larger, dominating more and more of everyday life, co-operatives appeared to many people to be a way of regaining control over their lives.

Co-operatives are businesses owned and managed by the people they serve. There are three basic types: consumer co-operatives such as retail stores; producer co-operatives such as wheat pools or fish canneries; and credit unions which provide savings, loans, and other "banking" services to their members. Co-ops exist in almost every area of the economy, from housing, insurance, funeral services, and transportation, to day care, filmmaking, and theatre.

All co-operatives are owned and controlled democratically by their members, and their savings or "profits" are returned to the members in their own communities and are not sent away to outside investors.

History The earliest co-ops appeared in Canada in the 1840s, but they met with limited success. It was among farmers that co-ops began to achieve their best results towards the end of the century. Eastern dairy farmers in particular united to produce and sell their cream, milk, and cheese through co-ops.

In western Canada, grain growers formed the first large-scale co-operatives. Led by E.A. Partridge, they founded the Grain Growers' Grain Company in 1906 to sell their wheat. They eventually formed co-ops to run grain elevators, stores, and farm-equipment factories.

The co-operative idea caught fire in other parts of the country as well. In Que-

Manitoba Wheat Pool tents at the Co-operative headquarters, Brandon, Manitoba Fair, 1928 (courtesy Western Canada Pictorial Index).

Characteristics of Copper

Formula: Cu
Appearance: a reddish metal that takes on a greenish colour in the moist air
Properties: tough, soft, excellent conductor of heat and electricity
Atomic Weight: 63.54
Uses: electrical wires and motors, cable, roofing, munitions, coinage, jewellery, copper chemicals, and airplane parts.

Alloyed with zinc to form brass, with tin and zinc to form bronze, and with zinc and nickel to form German silver. Alloys are used in pipes, car radiators, ships' propellors

bec, Alphonse Desjardins organized the first *caisse populaire* ("people's bank") in 1900; within ten years, there were a hundred of these co-op banks in the province.

The Maritimes had its own co-operative network, the Antigonish Movement, which was started in 1928. It sponsored stores, fish plants, sawmills, and other co-op projects in the region in the 1930s.

Since World War II, co-ops of different kinds have continued to flourish and play an important role in the Canadian economy. In 1989, Canadian co-operatives had 12 million members and total assets estimated at $70 billion. Information about co-operatives is available from the Canadian Co-operative Association, Suite 400, 275 Bank Street, Ottawa, Ont., K2P 2L6.
▷ RELATED ARTICLES: **Antigonish Movement, Alphonse Desjardins, E.A. Partridge.**

■ Coot

The American coot (*Fulica americana*) is an aquatic bird which belongs to the same family of birds (Rallidae) as rails and gallinules. Of the 10 species in the world, this is the only one in North America. A dark grey bird with a white bill, the coot is the size of a small duck, about 40 cm long. The membrane edges to its toes give it a semi-webbed foot, useful when it swims or runs on the surface of the water to take flight. Like the gallinule, the coot bobs its head while swimming. It feeds on seeds, insects, and snails. Preferring large, open stretches of water, the coot nests in freshwater marshes and on lakes and ponds. It winters either on fresh or brackish water, usually somewhere on the eastern or southern coasts of the United States. Its nest may float or be attached to living plants. For 23 or 24 days, the female or male incubates the 8 to 12 eggs. A few hours after hatching, the young are already swimming and can move across the

Coot nests in marshes, near lakes and ponds. It bobs its head while swimming (artwork by Claire Tremblay).

vegetation. Very noisy when in a group, coots are easily noticed.

■ Copper

Copper is a soft but tough, reddish metal with many useful properties. It is an excellent conductor of electricity and heat. About half of the copper used in Canada is in electrical wires. For instance, there is copper in telephones, radios, and televisions. There is also copper in the motors of refrigerators and vacuum cleaners. Copper is mixed with other metals to form an *alloy* which is used to make pipes, automobile radiators, ships' propellers, and many other things.

Copper was one of the first metals used by man. Copper from the Coppermine River area of the N.W.T. and from the shore of Lake Superior was used by the native people. Today, British Columbia and Ontario are Canada's main producers. Refined copper is produced in Montreal (the world's largest refinery), Timmins, Ont., and Sudbury, Ont. In 1987 Canadian mines produced 794 t of copper, worth about $1.9 billion. In 1986, Canada was fourth among the copper-producing countries of the world. It ranked after the USSR, the United States, and Chile.
▷ RELATED ARTICLE: **Mining.**

■ Copper Inuit, *see* Inuit

■ Coppermine

Coppermine, N.W.T., is a community on the mainland coast near the mouth of the Coppermine River in the central Arctic. In 1916 a trading post opened on the site, and gradually the local Inuit settled permanently. Residents rely on hunting, trapping, and craftwork. In 1986 the population was 888. For information, contact the hamlet, Coppermine, N.W.T., X0E 0E0.

■ Coppermine River

The Coppermine River, 845 km long, rises in the Barren Lands of the Northwest Territories and flows northwest into Coronation Gulf on the Arctic Ocean. In 1771 Samuel Hearne became the first European to reach the river. He named it for the copper found in the area.

■ Coquitlam

Coquitlam, B.C., is one of the growing residential suburbs of Vancouver. The name comes from a Salish Indian word meaning "small red salmon." In 1909-10, French Canadians arrived from Quebec to work in logging. They settled at Maillardville, which is still the largest French-speaking community in B.C. Coquitlam

Breeding Range of:
American Coot ●

is mainly residential, but several industries have located there. Its population in 1986 was 69 291. For information, contact the District Municipal Clerk, 1111 Brunette Ave., Coquitlam, B.C., V3K 1E9.

■ Coral

Corals are tiny marine animals that resemble upside-down jellyfish. They range from a few millimetres in diameter up to 25 cm. Young corals secrete a skeleton of calcium carbonate that anchors them to a surface.

Colonial corals grow on top of each other. Young corals attach themselves to the slowly accumulating mound of dead coral beneath them. The result can be massive reefs. Some coral reefs extend 1400 m into the sea. When they take circular form, they create an *atoll*. The Great Barrier Reef of Australia is composed of coral. It is about 1900 km long and is some 20 to 30 million years old. The reef-building corals are always associated with algae. For this reason, they can only live in waters that never drop below 18°C; and since the algae needs light to survive, they are not found more than 36 m deep.

The cold Canadian waters support no coral reefs; but there are numerous stony corals, none larger than 10 cm, in all Canadian oceans.

▷ RELATED ARTICLE: **Cnidaria.**

■ Cordillera

A Spanish word, cordillera, is the general term for groups of mountain ranges. One example runs parallel to the Pacific coast, from Alaska to Cape Horn, the southern tip of South America.

The North American portion is called the Western Cordillera. It was mainly formed by the colliding of plates. In the case of the Western Cordillera, the Pacific plate met the American plate and was pushed beneath it. As the Pacific plate was being forced down, it buckled the American plate near its edge and also forced it to uplift. The mountain ranges in eastern North America is sometimes called the Eastern Cordillera.

▷ RELATED ARTICLE: **Mountains.**

■ Cormack, William Eppes (or Epps)

Merchant, explorer (*born in 1796 at St John's, Nfld; died in 1868 at New Westminster, B.C.*). The first non-native to cross Newfoundland on foot, Cormack made important additions to knowledge about the geography of the island and its Beothuk Indians.

While earning his living as a merchant,

William Cormack was a keen explorer and student of nature. In 1822 he made a difficult trek across Newfoundland with a Micmac guide. Along the way he hoped to meet up with some of the Beothuk people, who were fast disappearing from the island.

On this expedition and on a second one in 1827, Cormack failed to make contact with the Beothuk. Later he looked after Shawnadithit, the last surviving Beothuk, and helped to preserve some memory of their culture. Around 1830 he left Newfoundland, settling finally in British Columbia.

▷ RELATED ARTICLE: **Beothuk.**

▷ SUGGESTED READING: Bernard D. Fardy, *William Epps Cormack: Newfoundland Pioneer* (1985).

■ Cormorant

Cormorants belong to the family of birds Phalacrocoracidae. There are four species in Canada: the Great Cormorant (*Phalacrocorax carbo*) on the Atlantic coast; the Pelagic Cormorant (*P. pelagicus*) on the Pacific coast; and the Double-crested Cormorant (*P. auritus*) from the Atlantic coast to Alberta. Brandt's Cormorant breeds on some of the small islands off the west coast of Vancouver Island. Cormorants are large waterfowl, black and shiny, measuring 66 to 91 cm. They have very hooked and tapering bills, pouches on their throats, small featherless patches near the eyes, long and rigid tails, and webbed feet.

Cormorants plunge into the water to catch fish. They often fly in a V formation like ducks. When at rest, they tend to spread and gently fan their wings so as to dry them.

Living in colonies on cliff and island ledges, cormorants build their nests with branches and marine grasses. They lay 3 to 4 eggs once a year. Both parents incubate the eggs for some 28 to 31 days. They

Breeding Range of **Double-crested Cormorant** ●

Breeding Range of:
Great Cormorant ●
Pelagic Cormorant ●

Cormorants plunge into the water to catch fish (artwork by John Crosby).

feed their young by regurgitating predigested fish, which the babies seek so avidly they sometimes push their bills down their parent's throat. The fledglings begin to fly two months after birth. The colour of the throat pouch differs in each species: yellow with a white border on the Great Cormorant; orange-yellow on the Double-crested Cormorant; dark red on the Pelagic Cormorant; dull blue on Brandt's Cormorant.

■ Corn Laws

The Corn Laws (1791-1846) were British laws which set customs duties on wheat and other cereals imported into Britain. By the 1820s these laws favoured British colonies, such as Upper and Lower Canada. These colonies were charged far less import duty than grain growers who were not part of the British Empire.

In 1846 Britain repealed the Corn Laws as part of a movement towards free trade. It was a blow to Canadian farmers, who lost their favourable trading terms, along with an assured British market for their wheat. They began to look to the United States as an alternative trading partner.

The repeal of the laws had an effect on politics in Canada. Since Britain was trading more freely with a range of countries, it no longer relied so much on trade with its colonies. As a result, it no longer felt the need to control colonial politics. Nor did it want the continued expense of doing so. Britain was therefore willing to let the British North American colonies take charge of their own affairs under a system of responsible government.

▷ Related Articles: **Free Trade; Responsible Government.**

■ Corner Brook

Corner Brook lies at the head of a long arm of the Bay of Islands on the west coast of Newfoundland. The fjordlike arm is a deep-water port, open to oceangoing vessels year-round. The second-largest city in Newfoundland, Corner Brook became a city in 1956 when it was combined with three other towns.

Settlers were first attracted to the area by fishing, farming, and lumbering. By 1864 Corner Brook had a sawmill. By 1925, the Newfoundland Power and Paper Company had opened a large pulp and paper mill, and a power plant at nearby Deer Lake. In 1938 the mill was purchased by a British company, Bowater-Lloyd, and Corner Brook became prosperous. When Bowater announced in 1984 that the company was leaving Corner Brook, the city's future was threatened. However, the mill was sold again and continues to operate. Several other industries, including fish-processing plants, provide employment. Sir Wilfred Grenfell College located here in 1975. Marble Mountain, about 18 km away, offers the best skiing in Atlantic Canada and is being developed as a year-round resort. In 1986 the population of Corner Brook was 22 719. For information, contact the City Clerk, City Hall, P.O. Box 1080, Corner Brook, Nfld, A2H 6E1.

■ Cornwall

Cornwall, Ont., is a city on the north bank of the St Lawrence River, about 40 km west of the Quebec border. Founded by Loyalists in 1780, it is one of English Canada's oldest settlements. These early settlers were joined in 1784 by Loyalist soldiers and in 1786 by a large number of Highland Scots. In 1797 the original name of New Johnstown was changed to Cornwall, in honour of the Duke of Cornwall, the eldest son of King George III.

Cornwall became a town in 1834 and began work on a canal to enable ships to pass the Long Sault Rapids. The canal was opened in 1842 and brought prosperity. Water power from the canal was used to run local woollen, saw, and flour mills. The completion of the Grand Trunk Railway between Montreal and Toronto in 1856 put Cornwall in a good position to attract more industry. A paper mill was established in 1883 and rapidly expanded; it is now a division of Domtar Ltd and is one of the city's biggest employers. Canadian Industries Ltd (CIL) operates a large chemical plant. Other plants manufacture furniture, recording discs, lacrosse sticks, etc.

Cornwall became a city in 1945. It is located on the St. Lawrence Seaway and is linked to New York State by an interna-

Cornwall, Ont., has benefited from its position on the St Lawrence Seaway (photo by John deVisser/Masterfile).

tional bridge. The nearby Robert H. Sanders power-generating station supplies power for eastern Ontario. In 1958 Cornwall residents observed "Inundation Day," as a seaway dam was blown up, flooding some of the longest-settled areas in Ontario. In 1986 the population was 46 425 and 28.19% claimed French as their mother tongue. For information, contact the City Clerk, 360 Pict Street, P.O. Box 877, Cornwall, Ont., K6H 5T9.

Cornwallis, Edward

Founder of Halifax (*born in 1713 at London, England; died in 1776 at Gibraltar*). Cornwallis served 17 years in the British army and in 1749 was appointed governor of Nova Scotia. He arrived that June with 2576 settlers, mostly from London, and began to build the town of Halifax.

Cornwallis's arrival marked a new British policy for Nova Scotia. Efforts were made to settle the infant colony and to strengthen it with army and navy posts, thus establishing a strong British presence in the region. By the time Cornwallis left in October 1752, he had set up the beginnings of a system of government and a system of law courts, and several new military posts. He was criticized by the authorities in Britain for spending too much money.

Never one to give in to criticism, Cornwallis had a stormy career in the years that followed. But he was the son of a lord and had powerful friends, so continued to get important appointments. His final posting was as governor of Gibraltar (1762-76).

▷ RELATED ARTICLE: **Halifax.**

Cornwallis Island

Cornwallis Island (6996 km²) forms the north side of Barrow Strait in the middle of the Arctic Archipelago. It was visited by William Parry in 1819 who named it for Sir William Cornwallis, a British admiral. In 1947 an airstrip was built at Resolute, which is now the major communications and transportation centre in the archipelago.

Coronach

Coronach, Sask., lies near the United States boundary in southern Saskatchewan. It was founded in 1926 with the arrival of a Canadian Pacific Railway line. Cattle and wheat are the economic mainstays of the town, but in the 1970s a power plant and a coal mine brought new prosperity. In 1986 Coronach's population was 1006. For information, contact the Town Administrator, P.O. Box 90, Coronach, Sask., S0H 0Z0.

Coronation Gulf

Coronation Gulf is a broad strait of water separating Victoria Island from the Arctic mainland. It forms part of the original Northwest Passage through the Arctic Archipelago. It was named by John Franklin in 1821 for the coronation of King George IV.

Corriveau, Marie-Josephte

Murderess (*born in 1733 at St-Vallier, New France; died in 1763 at Quebec*). There are many stories about "La Corriveau," the infamous daughter of Joseph Corriveau. Her ghost is said to haunt the roads of St-Vallier, Que., appearing to lone travellers at night.

In real life she was a habitant who outlived her first husband. In 1761 she married for a second time — to a farmer named Louis Dodier. Two years later, in January 1763, she killed Dodier by hitting him on the head with an axe one night as he slept. She was tried for murder and hanged.

As a grim warning to others, her dead body was then placed in a cage which was displayed on the roadside at Lauzon, near Quebec. All passers-by could see it. The ghost stories, myths, and legends began to circulate about a century later when the cage was found in Lauzon Cemetery. Among those who incorporated the grisly tale in their books was Philippe-Joseph Aubert de Gaspé, author of *Les Anciens Canadiens* (1863).

Corte-Real, Gaspar

Explorer (*born about 1450; died at sea in 1501*). Corte-Real was one of the explorers whose voyages early in the 16th century laid Portugal's claim to North America. In 1500, and again in 1501, he scouted the coast of Labrador and Newfoundland. On the second voyage he disappeared. A search party led by his brother Miguel, in 1502, also disappeared.

▷ RELATED ARTICLE: **Exploration.**

Corvée

Corvée was unpaid labour done by habitants in New France. It was required by the government so that roads, bridges, and other communal projects could be built. Some seigneurs made habitants work for them for free too, though this was illegal.

▷ RELATED ARTICLES: **New France; Seigneurial System.**

Cougar

The cougar or mountain lion (*Felis con-*

Cougar sniffing for another predator's scent (photo by Thomas Kitchin).

color) is a member of the cat family, Felidae. This cat is also locally called the puma or panther. The largest member of the cat family in Canada, an adult male can weigh 63-75 kg and reach up to 2.4 m in total length. This long-tailed cat is usually tawny, with white throat, breast, and abdomen, a black strip on each side of the muzzle, and a black tip on the tail. At one time the cougar was the most widespread mammal in the western hemisphere. It was found from the Atlantic to the Pacific Ocean and from the Yukon to the southern tip of South America. Vigorous hunting greatly reduced their range by 1900 and the cougar was absent from most of eastern North America. Cougars were killed for sport and because they killed livestock (but rarely people). Today, most of Canada's cougars live in Alberta and British Columbia, but they are reoccupying areas in Saskatchewan, Manitoba, Ontario, Quebec, and perhaps even Nova Scotia and New Brunswick. Researchers estimate there are about 600 to 700 in the Alberta wilderness.

The cougar is secretive and elusive. It is a solitary hunter and its chief prey is deer, but it will take beaver, hares, elk, young moose, and sometimes porcupines. Cougars usually ambush their prey, leap onto the victim's back and kill it by biting through the back of the neck, head, or by biting down on its throat while the cat maintains its grip with its sharp claws. Male cougars (called toms) may kill kittens or young adults. Females (called queens) attending kittens will attack and drive toms away. Cougars defend their territories and alert other cougars to the territorial boundaries by making scrapes in the snow or on the ground, and through urine marking.

The cougar has acute hearing and sees well at night. It is an excellent climber and usually seeks refuge from a threat by climbing a tree. It can make graceful leaps 7 m long and 6 m high. It is an excellent sprinter and although it can swim, like

Range of Cougar ●

most cats it avoids water. Today, man is the only significant predator of cougars.

Females have their first litter between the ages of 20 and 36 months of age. After breeding and a gestation period of three months, one to six kittens are born. Births may occur in any month, but most kittens are born between June and September. They accompany their mother for up to two years. Cougars may live 18 years.

■ Coulthard, Jean

Composer (*born in 1908 at Vancouver, B.C.*). Her teachers included Frederick Chubb in Vancouver and Ralph Vaughan Williams and Arthur Jacob in England. She also took the unusual step of submitting her work for criticism to other composers, such as America's Aaron Copland. She had begun teaching by 1934 and taught composition at the University of British Columbia from 1947 to 1973. She became a beacon for young composers seeking to develop their own styles. Coulthard's music remained personal and serene, and yet is by no means easy to explain. Her *String Quartet No. 2*, for example, is sad and mysterious. With Canadian music's gradual turning away from the systems and trends of the 1950s, Coulthard's music has become more and more widely performed.

Jean Coulthard's music is personal and serene (photo by Andreas Poulsson).

■ Council of Twelve

Council of Twelve was part of the government of Nova Scotia. It was established in 1719. It consisted of 12 councillors who were appointed by the British governor and served for life.

The councillors were generally military officers or wealthy merchants. Their main role was to advise the governor and help him decide policy. Many people objected to the council's promotion of Halifax and its elite. In 1837 the council was enlarged and split into two: an Executive Council of 12 members and a Legislative Council of 19 members.

■ Coureurs des bois

Coureurs des bois (French for "runners of the woods") were young men who left the villages of New France to go among the native people. They made trading agreements and collected furs. They learned the native languages and became skilled at wilderness travel and the native way of life. The government tried to prevent the men from leaving the colony, for it wanted to keep firm control over the fur trade. The church objected to the effect of native ways on the young men's Christian beliefs. Nevertheless, the lure of independence drew many men to the woods, even in violation of the law. By 1680 there were as many as 500 coureurs in the woods around Lake Superior. Perhaps the most famous coureur des bois was Pierre Radisson. In their eagerness to profit from furs, the coureurs expanded the trade and added to the knowledge of the North American interior.

▷ RELATED ARTICLES: **Fur Trade; New France; Pierre Radisson.**

■ Courtenay

Courtenay, B.C., is a city on the east coast of Vancouver Island, 219 km north of Victoria. It is named for naval officer George William Courtenay, who surveyed the area from 1846 to 1849. A Hudson's Bay Co. store was established in the 1850s, and the first settlers arrived in the 1860s. Today, it is a service centre for the surrounding logging, fishing, and farming region. Nestled against a backdrop of mountains, it has emerged as an attractive ski centre.

The city forms part of the regional district of Comox-Strathcona. In 1986 Courtenay's population was 9631. For information, contact the City Clerk, 750 Cliffe Avenue, Courtenay, B.C., V9N 2J7.

■ Courts of Law

The Court System The courts apply the laws of Canada. They resolve disputes between individuals, between individuals and the state, between organizations, and between governments. The courts apply and interpret all laws, whether passed by the federal Parliament, a provincial legislature, or a municipality.

Responsibility for establishing and operating the courts is divided.

The provinces set up and administer all courts in the provinces. The federal government appoints the judges of the superior and county or district courts. The lower, or "inferior," provincial courts are staffed by provincial appointees. The exceptions to this division are the federal courts, which are both administered and staffed by the federal government.

FEDERAL COURTS

The Supreme Court of Canada The Supreme Court is Canada's final court of appeal. It consists of nine judges, three of whom must come from Quebec. It hears selected appeals from provincial appeal courts. These appeals are ones which are of importance to the entire country. They frequently involve the constitutional validity of federal or provincial laws. Many of these appeals now concern laws that may violate the Canadian Charter of Rights and Freedoms.

The Federal Court of Canada is a specialized court which hears claims against or by the federal government.

It also deals with patent, copyright, and maritime cases.

PROVINCIAL COURTS

Courts of Appeal In each province there is a court, usually called the Court of Appeal, which hears appeals from lower courts in the province. Although certain cases may go on to the Supreme Court of Canada, the Court of Appeal's decision is normally final. It and the provincial supreme or superior courts are collectively called "superior courts."

Supreme and Superior Courts These courts have broad authority to hear all civil matters, as well as serious criminal matters such as murder, treason, and piracy. In every province, a jury, made up of 12 people, may be put together for such criminal cases.

County or District Courts are courts only found in Nova Scotia, Ontario, and British Columbia. They hear important civil and criminal cases that do not fall into the jurisdiction of a superior court.

Provincial or Magistrates Courts deal with lesser criminal and civil matters while **Family and Juvenile Courts** deal with cases involving the custody of children, support obligations, adoption, and offences by children.

Small Claims Courts are responsible

for cases involving sums of money limited to a specific minimum amount. For example, in certain provinces, the upper limit is $1000 to $4000.

▷ RELATED ARTICLES: **Supreme Court; Young Offenders.**

■ Cowansville

Cowansville, Que., is a town near the United States border on a branch of the Yamaska River. It is about 75 km southeast of Montreal. The first settler was Capt. Jacob Ruiter who came from New York in 1798. Ruiter built a mill and was followed by more settlers from the U.S. The town is now mostly French speaking. It was named Cowansville after Peter Cowan who opened the first post office in 1839. The town grew as a farming, milling, and transportation centre and now contains several industries. A federal penitentiary opened in 1966. The town's beautiful 19th-century architecture is an important tourist attraction. Its population in 1986 was 11 643. For information, contact the Greffier, 220, place Municipale, Cowansville, Que., J2K 1T4.

■ Coyote

The coyote (*Canis latrans*) is a member of the dog family, Canidae. It occurs in most parts of Canada, except in the Arctic tundra, thanks to the great reduction in wolves in areas occupied by man. The coyote looks like a medium-sized dog. The coat is tawny grey, the throat and belly off-white, and nearly all coyotes have a uniform grey area on the side of the nose

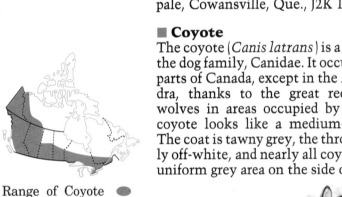

Range of Coyote ●

Coyotes hunt with a partner or in a pack. A pack may attack deer or domestic livestock (artwork by Jan Sovak).

Coyotes feed on mice, rabbits, deer, and other prey (photo by Stephen J. Krasemann/DRK Photo).

midway between the eyes and nose pad. Coyotes mate with dogs to produce coydogs. Often the best way to identify coydogs is from the nose colour, which is not the uniform grey of the coyote nose. The long guard hairs both on the body and tail of the coyote are tipped with black. A frightened coyote runs with its tail low or tucked between its legs in contrast to a wolf which carries its tail higher. Coyotes bark and howl. If other coyotes are in hearing distance, they will join to form a chorus.

The coyote is usually most active during twilight or at night. It feeds on small mammals, birds, amphibians, reptiles, and carrion. Even though it sometimes attacks cattle, the coyote helps farmers by eating large numbers of destructive rodents. (It also feeds on berries and fruit.) Coyotes hunt alone, with a partner, or in a pack. Packs may attack deer, dogs, and domestic livestock. Mating takes place between late January and late March. After three months, three to ten pups are born. Both parents attend the young. The pups usually disperse in the fall, but if resident coyotes evict them from neighbouring areas they may return to the parental territory and become part of a pack. They do not customarily mate until they have their own territory. Most females give birth near their first birthday; a few do not mate until they are nearly two.

■ Crab

The crab belongs to the order of crustaceans, Decapoda (meaning "ten-footed"), along with crayfish, shrimp, and lobster. The head bears two sets of antennae. The flattened body is divided into two parts, the cephalothorax on top and the abdomen below. It has five pairs of legs. The front ones end in pincers, which are used for grasping and tearing and for defence. The abdomen is very flattened and curves back upon the cephalothorax, with a distinctive shape for each sex. That of the female is U-shaped and large; that of the male is small and triangular. The female carries her eggs under her abdomen. When hatched, the young go through several moults before becoming adults. The crab's skeleton is in fact its external shell and is called an exoskeleton.

In order to grow, the crab moults. It grows a new shell under the old one, which it then sheds. The new shell remains soft for several hours, giving the crab time to puff itself up with water and stretch the shell. Once the shell has hardened, the crab loses the water and has room to grow. If a crab loses one of its legs, it can grow it back. In Canada, crabs live in deep estuaries and intertidal waters. The hermit crab, whose shell never hardens, protects itself by living in the empty shell of a mollusc. When this shell becomes too small, it moves to a larger one.

■ Cradle Board

Cradle board is a device for carrying babies that was used by native people in almost every region of Canada. A mother could carry the board on her back, prop it close to where she was working, or hang it from a tree in the fields. Eastern Woodland groups made flat boards, Plains people used stiffened rawhide, Subarctic groups sewed birchbark cradles, and Northwest Coast people wove cedar baskets. Sometimes a hoop at the top of the board protected the child's head from possible injury. Cradle boards were usually beautifully decorated, and reflected the close bond between parents and children.

Inuit women carried their babies in pouches inside their parkas to keep them warm.

■ Craft Unionism, see Unions

■ Crafts

Crafts or "handicrafts" involve making useful — and often beautiful — objects by hand from ordinary materials. Today, most things are manufactured in factories, using machines and high technology. Before the Industrial Revolution in the 19th century, household items and furniture, farming tools, wagons, jewellery, and every other object had to be made one at a time by craftspeople.

Crafts include blacksmithing, ceramics, weaving, leatherworking, metalworking, carpentry, knitting, and sewing. Crafted objects can include woodenware, glass bowls, silver plates, leather bags and harnesses, woven baskets, clay pipes and pots, patchwork quilts, and hooked rugs.

Before the 20th century, settlements were more isolated than our communities are today, and crafts developed regional styles. Because of modern transportation and communication, crafted objects are now much the same across Canada. Exceptions are Quebec's brightly coloured woven sashes (ceinture fléchée), Newfoundland's hooked rugs, and Nova Scotia's quilts.

We no longer rely on handcrafted items to carry on our daily lives. However, in recent years they have become popular again. There has been an increase in the number of people making crafts for a living. Canadians are rediscovering the joy of creating things with their own imagination and hands.

Some craftspeople do it just for their own pleasure. Some turn their crafts into businesses, as in olden times. Many people would rather pay more for a beautiful, handmade object than for one that looks like thousands of others made by machine. Traditionally, craftspeople handed down their skills to their children or to apprentices. Today, children and adults can learn crafts in many places, such as schools, art schools, and community colleges.

The Canadian Guild of Crafts is an association that promotes crafts in Canada. It organizes exhibitions and helps to maintain high standards. It has also encouraged native Indian and Inuit people to take up their traditional crafts again.

▷ SUGGESTED READING: Canadian Museum of Civilization, *Masters of the Crafts* (1989); Rosemary Neering and Stan Garrod, *In the Pioneer Home* (1978).

■ Craig, Sir James Henry

Governor general (*born in 1748 at Gibraltar; died in 1812 at London, England*). Craig was governor general of the Canadas from 1807 to 1811. He and his allies among the leading English merchants tried to eradicate French-Canadian nationalism in the colony. He interfered with elections, and he imprisoned, without trial, the leaders of the Parti Canadien in 1810.

■ Craig, John

Author (*born in 1921 at Peterborough, Ont.; died there in 1982*). Craig served in the Royal Canadian Navy during World War II. He then earned a BA from the University of Manitoba and an MA from the University of Toronto. While working as a marketing executive in the 1950s, he began to write books.

Careers in Crafts
Crafts may be studied at an art school or community college. Programs usually last from two to four years, and are offered in most provinces in Canada. Crafts can be studied at all of Canada's major art schools, namely, the Emily Carr College of Art and Design in Vancouver, Alberta College of Art in Calgary, Ontario College of Art in Toronto, and the Nova Scotia College of Art and Design in Halifax. Admission requirements vary, but usually include presentation of a portfolio of the applicant's past work.

Sir James Craig was governor general of the Canadas from 1807 to 1811 (courtesy NAC/C-24888).

Four of his books are about the difficulties teenage boys face as they grow up: understanding themselves and their roles, and learning to accept the differences of other individuals and cultures. In *The Long Return* (1959), Thad Cameron, a pioneer boy, learns to respect his Ojibwa captors and begins to discover his inner strengths on his long journey back home. *No Word for Good-bye* (1969) is about the troubled friendship between Ken Warren and an Ojibwa boy he meets during summer vacation. The title hero of *Zach* (1972) travels across the United States and Canada searching for traces of his native Indian ancestors, meeting many people who become close friends. *The Wormburners* (1975) is about an inner-city track team that overcomes jealousies and wins the cross-country championship.

■ Craigellachie

Craigellachie, B.C., is just west of Revelstoke in the mountainous interior, at the west entrance to Eagle Pass. It is famous as the spot where, on November 7, 1885, Donald Smith drove the "last spike" to complete the building of the Canadian Pacific Railway across Canada.

▷ RELATED ARTICLE: **Canadian Pacific Railway.**

■ Cranberry

Cranberries belong to the genus *Vaccinium* of the heath family (Ericaceae). They owe their name to their flower, which looks like the head of a crane. The small bog cranberry (*V. oxycoccus*) and the American, or large cranberry (*V. macrocarpon*) grow in bogs. Their trailing branches, long and delicate, mix with the moss. They produce red fruit that grows larger than their tiny leaves, and the fruit becomes even more juicy after a few good frosts. Too sour and acidic to be eaten raw, they are transformed into the jelly traditionally associated with Christmas and Thanksgiving turkeys, or into cranberry juice. Grocery store supplies largely come from commercially grown American cranberries. The cuttings are planted on the damp sand of old bogs that have been cleaned and dyked. When it is time for the harvest, the plantation is flooded. The fruit, which comes loose from its branches, floats to the surface of the water and is then collected. The bog is left flooded all winter to protect the plants against frost. Two other plants bear the name cranberry: the mountain cranberry (*V. vitis-idaea*) which grows on dry rocks in cold regions, and the highbush cranberry (*Viburnum opulus*) a shrub of the honeysuckle family (Caprifoliaceae).

■ Cranbrook

Cranbrook is a city lying in the Rocky Mountain Trench, in the southeast corner of British Columbia. It was within the territory of the Kootenay Indians. Colonel James Baker, who settled in the area in 1885, named his land Cranbrook Farm after his English birthplace, and the name stuck. Baker persuaded the Canadian Pacific Railway to locate on his homestead when the rail line was built through the Crowsnest Pass in 1898. The railway has been important to the city's forest and mining industries. Forestry, mining, manufacturing, tourism, and transportation make up the local economy. Cranbrook's mild climate and nearby mountains attract tourists. East Kootenay Community College opened in 1975. Today, Cranbrook is the main commercial centre in the East Kootenay region. In 1986 the population was 15 893. For information, contact the City Clerk, 40 10th Avenue S., Cranbrook, B.C., V1C 2M8.

■ Crane

Cranes form their own separate bird family, Gruidae. They are large migrating birds that can reach 1.4 m in length. They have long legs and necks, and a straight bill that is even longer than the head. Cranes look like herons, but unlike herons their rumps appear more tufted and they stretch their necks while flying. They gather marsh plants in shallow water to make their nests. For 30 to 35 days the parents care for their two eggs. There are 14 species in the world, with only two in Canada: the Whooping Crane (*Grus americana*) and the Sandhill Crane, (*G. canadensis*).

The Whooping Crane, Canada's tallest bird, is pure white, except for its black-tipped wings and red face. Almost extinct, it can be found only in Wood Buffalo National Park, where it nests, and in the salty marshes of the Aransas National Wildlife Refuge, in Texas, where it winters. It can be seen between these two places during migration. The nesting population is estimated at about 100 individuals. The Sandhill Crane, found more widely across the country, is grey with dull red on the top of its head and a little black on its wings. It nests throughout Canada west of Quebec and winters from the southern United States to central Mexico.

▷ RELATED ARTICLE: **Whooping Crane.**

Whooping Crane nesting grounds on a small island in Wood Buffalo National Park (photo by E. Kuyt).

Breeding Range of Whooping Crane

Breeding Range of Sandhill Crane

Crawford, Isabella Valancy

Novelist and poet (*born in 1850 at Dublin, Ireland; died in 1887 at Toronto, Ont.*). In 1869, Crawford settled with her family in Peterborough, Ont., where she began to write and sell poems and stories. After her father's death in 1875, she supported her family with her writing, moving to Toronto to further her career, where she wrote novels and popular verse. *Malcolm's Katie, and Other Poems* (1884), a book of poems, was the only book published in her lifetime. It sold 50 copies. Crawford's poems are admired for their feeling for the unique Canadian landscape. Works published after her death include *Selected Stories of Isabella Valancy Crawford* (1975) and *Fairy Tales of Isabella Valancy Crawford* (1977), both edited by Penny Petrone.

▷ SUGGESTED READING: D. Farmiloe, *Isabella Valancy Crawford: Life and Legends* (1983).

Crawley, Frank Radford

Film producer (*born in 1911 at Ottawa, Ont.; died in 1987 at Toronto, Ont.*). He was known by his nickname "Budge." Crawley Films, the company he ran with his wife Judith Crawley, is one of the few long-term success stories in Canada's film industry. Crawley, with his energy and enthusiasm, was one of its best-loved figures. He produced hundreds of films in his 40-year career, and many were award winners. *Île d'Orléans* (1938), made by the Crawleys on their honeymoon, won an award for best amateur film. *The Loon's Necklace* (1948) was named Film of the Year at the first Canadian Film Awards. *The Man Who Skied Down Everest* (1975) won an Academy Award.

During World War II, Crawley Films worked with the National Film Board to produce training films. In the 1950s, Crawley produced films for television and established an animation division. He produced two animated series for American television, "The Tales of the Wizard of Oz" (1962) and "Return to Oz" (1963). Crawley's feature films include *The Luck of Ginger Coffey* (1964) and *The Rowdyman* (1972), starring Gordon Pinsent. A generation of Canadian filmmakers learned their skills with Crawley Films.

Crawley, Judith

Filmmaker (*born in 1914 at Ottawa, Ont.; died there in 1986*). As wife and partner of Frank Crawley, she was an important contributor to film in Canada. They made their first film, *Île d'Orléans* (1938), on their honeymoon. Most of the films Judith Crawley made were educational documentaries. She directed the "Ages and Stages" series (1949-57) on child care. After 1961, she concentrated on producing and writing. In 1976 the husband-and-wife team won an Academy Award for *The Man Who Skied Down Everest* (1975). Crawley was president of the Canadian Film Institute, 1979-82.

Crayfish

The crayfish is a freshwater crustacean which resembles a small lobster. It shuns light and prefers shadowy locations. By day it hides in holes or under rocks; by night it hunts for food. It is brownish green in colour, but heat destroys these pigments and gives it a red pigmentation instead. That is why the crayfish, like the lobster, turns red when cooked. Crayfish are omnivorous; they will eat animal and vegetable material, living or dead, fresh, or rotten. Towards the end of summer, like other crustaceans, they moult. They are capable of breaking off their own legs, usually when in the grasp of a predator. The break occurs near the body and quickly closes over so as to avoid excessive loss of blood. During later moults, the lost limb grows back. Crayfish are found on every continent except Africa. A total of 300 crayfish species exist. Eleven are found in Canada, two west of the Rockies; the others in the East.

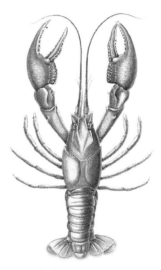

Crayfish is a crustacean. Unlike the lobster, which it resembles, the crayfish lives in freshwater (artwork by Kendal Morris).

Credit

Credit allows people to buy things now and pay for them later. For example, many people borrow money when they buy a house. They use credit, in this case a mortgage loan, to buy the house now and then pay the loan back over a number of years. The word credit is derived from the Latin word *creditum*, which means "put trust in." A history of a person's past loans and repayments is called a *credit rating*, and special firms called *credit bureaus* sell this information to banks and other institutions to help them decide whether to approve a loan.

A very common use of credit occurs when purchases are made using credit cards. Banks pay the seller and then send a bill to the purchaser once a month. In effect, banks are lending the customer the money to make the purchase.

The amount of credit used by individuals, firms, or governments is their *debt*. The cost of credit is the interest rate paid on the debt. At the end of 1988, Canadian households had total debts amounting to about $220 billion. Total business debt was about $340 billion, and the federal government debt was about $340 billion.

■ Créditistes

The Créditistes were a political party active in Quebec in the 1960s and 1970s. They supported the adoption of Social Credit policies. They burst into politics with their fiery leader Réal Caouette in 1962, winning 26 seats in Quebec during the federal election. The party briefly allied with the Social Credit Party and held the balance of power in the House of Commons until 1963. In 1970 the party entered Quebec provincial politics, winning 12 seats. Both the federal and provincial parties were weakened by internal splits. The provincial party was wiped out in 1973. The federal party declined steadily, disappearing in 1980.

The Créditistes represented Quebec's rural population. They supported the expansion of the French language and opposed the independence movement in Quebec.

▷ RELATED ARTICLE: **Réal Caouette.; Political Parties; Social Credit.**

■ Cree

The Cree are an Algonquian-speaking people. The name was an Ojibwa word and was adopted by the French. The Cree have other, local names for themselves. Cree live over a greater area than any other native group, from Alberta to Quebec. There are three brood groups: East Main Cree (James Bay), West Main Cree (around Hudson Bay), and Western Woods Cree (forests west of Hudson Bay). The latter are often called Plains Cree. Their population in 1988 was nearly 147 000.

The Cree may have lived on their lands for thousands of years. During the 1600s they met British traders on Hudson Bay. A large group acquired horses and began to live on the plains. They adapted quickly to the plains way of life, following the bison. By the 1880s, this life had ended with the destruction of the bison herds, and the Cree moved onto reserves.

Cree lived in the forests by hunting, fishing, and trapping. They travelled by canoe in summer and by snowshoe in winter. They lived in small bands most of the year and gathered into larger groups in summer for socializing and ceremonies.

From the 1870s to 1921, the federal government negotiated a series of treaties with the Cree, who gave up title to their land in exchange for reserves and other benefits.

Today, many Cree live in towns or cities for much of the year, going into the bush to hunt and trap for part of the time. Cree in Quebec negotiated special pay-

Cree Pipe Stem Bearer by artist Paul Kane (courtesy of the Royal Ontario Museum).

Interior of Cree Indian Tent, 1820 (courtesy Glenbow Museum).

Cree Indians in blanket costume (courtesy PAA/B766).

ments and rights with the Quebec and federal governments in 1975, during the building of the James Bay power development. *See* **Native People: Subarctic.**

▷ SUGGESTED READING: Eleanor Brass, *I Walk in Two Worlds* (1987); *Medicine Boy and Other Cree Tales* (1978); Joseph F. Dion, *My Tribe, The Crees* (1979); Ken Hodgins, *The Art of the Nehiyawak: Exploring the Art and Crafts of the Woods Cree* (1988).

■ Creeper

The Brown Creeper (*Certhia americana*) is the only species of the bird family Certhiidae in North America. A small bird, its camouflage of brown and white streaked plumage allows it to conceal itself against a tree trunk. It uses its slender, curved, and very pointed bill to dislodge insects from the tree bark. Like a woodpecker, it braces itself against the trunk with its long straight tail. The creeper has an unusual way of hunting for food. It starts at the base of the tree and, in little jerky hops, spirals its way to the top. Then it flies to the base of another tree

and starts over. The creeper is a solitary bird, though sometimes it will join groups of chickadees in winter. It does not usually migrate, though some creepers living at the northern edge of their territory will move farther south for the winter. Its nest is hidden under a bit of loose bark on a tree trunk. The number of eggs can vary from four to eight.

■ Creighton, Donald Grant

Historian (*born in 1902 at Toronto, Ont.; died in 1979 at Brooklin, Ont.*). Creighton joined the history department of the University of Toronto in 1927 and remained there for his entire career. In 1937 he published his first book, *The Commercial Empire of the St Lawrence*. In it he argued that the St Lawrence River formed the basis for the future development of Canada as a nation, creating a strong east-west tie. The book made his reputation as English Canada's leading historian.

Creighton was a graceful writer who thought that writing history should be a literary art. His two-volume biography of John A. Macdonald won two Governor General's Awards (1952, 1955). He wrote several other books, including a one-volume history, *Dominion of the North*, and numerous articles. In 1967 he was named a Companion of the Order of Canada.

Creighton was a strong Canadian nationalist. He opposed American influences on Canada, and like his hero, John A. Macdonald, believed in a strong central government.

▷ SUGGESTED READING: Carl Berger, *The Writing of Canadian History*, Chapter 9, "Donald Creighton and the Artistry of History" (2nd ed. 1986).

■ Creighton, Helen

Folklorist (*born in 1899 at Dartmouth, N.S.; died in 1989 at Halifax, N.S.*). Creighton began collecting folk stories and folksongs in the late 1920s, when hardly anyone was interested in the culture of ordinary people. She often travelled around Nova Scotia on foot, pushing a melodeon in a wheelbarrow and writing down the songs she heard. Later she worked for the National Museum in Ottawa for 20 years. Altogether she collected more than 4000 songs in English, French, Micmac, and other languages. One of them was the famous ballad, "Farewell to Nova Scotia." She published 16 books of folklore and songs, including a children's book, *With a Heigh-Heigh-Ho* (1986).

▷ RELATED ARTICLES: **Folk Music; Folklore.**

▷ SUGGESTED READING: Helen Creighton, *A Life in Folklore* (1975).

■ Crerar, Henry Duncan Graham

Army officer (*born in 1888 at Hamilton, Ont.; died in 1965 at Ottawa, Ont.*). General Crerar was one of Canada's top military commanders in World War II. He was commissioned a lieutenant in the artillery in 1910. During World War I he fought in the Battle of Ypres, surviving the German gas attack of April 1915. He was commandant of the Royal Military College at Kingston, Ont., when World War II broke out in 1939.

In 1940 Crerar was appointed chief of the general staff, based in Ottawa. From 1942 on he commanded Canadian forces in Europe. He led 1st Canadian Corps during the tough fighting in Italy in 1943. He succeeded General McNaughton as commander of First Canadian Army on March 20, 1944, leading it in the invasion of France that year. He then commanded the army during the campaign in northwestern Europe. He retired from the military in 1946.

General H.D.G. Crerar commanded the Canadian army in Italy and France (courtesy NAC/PA-166584).

■ Crerar, Thomas Alexander

Farm leader and politician (*born in 1876 at Molesworth, Ont.; died in 1975 at Victoria, B.C.*). Crerar was the first leader of the Progressive Party (1920-22). He was raised in Manitoba, where he taught school and farmed, before becoming pres-

Breeding Range of
Brown Creeper ●

Donald Grant Creighton *was one of Canada's foremost historians, known particularly for his skilful writing (courtesy NAC/PA-123984).*

General Crerar's Rules of Conduct

"Whatever you do, do it with all your might. Do to others as you would have them do to you. Lead always, drive rarely, but when you must, drive hard."

Thomas Alexander Crerar, around 1945. He led the Progressive Party to a stunning success in 1921. Crerar could not unite the party and quit in 1922 (courtesy PAM/N11570).

ident of the Grain Growers' Grain Company, a farmer-owned co-operative in Winnipeg. He was active in farm politics, won election to the House of Commons in 1917, and joined Prime Minister Borden's Cabinet as minister of agriculture.

Crerar quit Borden's government in a dispute over tariff policy. In 1920, when farmers formed the Progressive Party, he became its leader. The next year the party had a stunning success, winning 65 seats in a federal election. Yet Crerar could not unite the Progressives under his leadership, and he quit in 1922.

Crerar returned to politics as a Liberal. He served in the Cabinet of Prime Minister Mackenzie King in 1929, and again between 1935 and 1945. He finished his career as a member of the Senate from 1945 to 1966.

Creston

Creston, B.C., is in the mountainous Kootenay area of southeast British Columbia. It lies at the edge of a large floodplain near where the Kootenay River empties into Kootenay Lake. Settlers followed the Kootenay River north across the U.S. border in the 1860s, lured by gold and silver in the nearby mountains. Much of the surrounding valley is reclaimed marshland, and it produces grain, alfalfa, fruit, and vegetables. Forestry, tourism, mining, and brewing also provide employment. The federal government created the floodplain using dykes to produce a fertile agricultural area. The nearby Creston Valley Wildlife Management Area conserves wetlands which are vital to waterfowl. It is open to the public from May to October. In 1986 the population of Creston was 4098. For information, contact the Town Clerk, 904 Vancouver Street, Creston, B.C., V0B 1G0.

Cricket

Cricket is a game played with a ball and bat between two teams of eleven players per side. The game is one of the most popular in Great Britain, Australia, New Zealand, India, Pakistan, and parts of the West Indies. Like baseball, the two teams take turns at bat and in the field.

The game was brought to Canada about 150 years ago by the British army. It has most frequently been played in private schools, such as Upper Canada College in Toronto. The game declined in popularity in the 1920s, especially with the growth of baseball. Cricket has recently regained some popularity in most regions of Canada.

Cricket at Trinity College, Port Hope (photo by John deVisser).

Cricket

Crickets are well-known insects of the order Grylloptera. They have elongated bodies which may be brown, black, or green and have chewing mouthparts. They are frequently flightless; if wings are present, there are two pairs lying flat on top of the abdomen. The first pair are small and thick, covering the second, which fold up like a fan when the cricket is resting. Crickets have a pair of jumping legs at the back of the body but, even so, are poor jumpers. The male produces the familiar sound heard especially in late summer and early autumn. This sound, caused by rubbing the forewings together, is used to attract the female and claim territory. Both sexes have a pair of ears on each of the front legs. The female usually has a long needle-like appendage, called the ovipositor, at the tip of the abdomen. She digs it into moist soil and lays one egg at a time. Twenty to 300 eggs are laid. The cricket overwinters as an egg. In spring the little nymph, very like the adult, emerges from the ground. The nymph goes through several moults before becoming an adult (by about August). Active mainly at night, crickets eat the

Crickets make their familiar sound when the male (shown here) rubs the forewings together (artwork by Claire Tremblay).

leaves of plants, seed pods, and vegetables. Cave and house crickets often move into building basements as cold weather approaches. There are about 95 species in Canada.

■ Crime

Crime is an act that is prohibited by law. Many acts, or failures to act, may be viewed as wrong or immoral, but they are not crimes unless they are prohibited by law.

The decision as to what makes a crime varies from culture to culture. Some kinds of sexual activity, for example, are considered crimes in some societies but are acceptable behaviour in others.

In most early societies, crime — even murder — could be settled by compensation. This was the case in early England where all crimes could be settled by compensation, except crimes against the body of the king. Over time, all criminal acts came to be seen as breaches of the king's peace. This is why, even today, a crime is charged as having been committed against the Crown.

In Canada, most offences are set out in the Criminal Code. Other provincial and federal laws can also create offences. There are about 40 000 offences for which Canadians can be prosecuted. Generally, ignorance of these offences is not a defence.

There were nearly 3 million offences reported to the police in 1988. However, it is very difficult to state exact figures for particular crimes. In 1987 about one in four Canadians reported that they were the victim of at least one crime. Over one-half were personal crimes, such as robbery and assault. About one-third were crimes such as break and enter, theft of household property, and motor vehicle theft. Property offences and impaired driving or dangerous driving offences are the most common crimes dealt with in the courts.

Control of Crime In 1988 there were over 53 000 police and 26 000 correctional personnel (for example, prison guards) in Canada. The cost of these services was over $1.4 billion. Society also pays for crime prevention through extra street lights, security, and other measures.

The main way that society tries to prevent crime is through punishment. However, there is no clear evidence that punishment does deter crime. Measures such as work, education, and treatment have also been tried, without much success.

Crime is now seen largely as a social

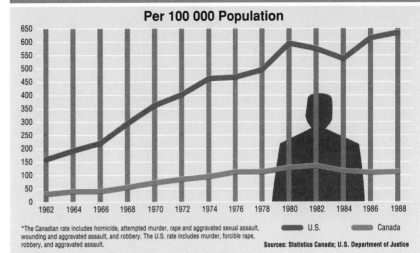

SERIOUS CRIME RATES* IN CANADA AND THE U.S. - 1962-1988

Per 100 000 Population

*The Canadian rate includes homicide, attempted murder, rape and aggravated sexual assault, wounding and aggravated assault, and robbery. The U.S. rate includes murder, forcible rape, robbery, and aggravated assault.

■ U.S.   ■ Canada

Sources: Statistics Canada; U.S. Department of Justice

and political problem. Those who hold this view feel that crime can be lessened by reducing poverty, as well as by improving education and opportunities for jobs. Recently emphasis is being placed on helping the victims of crime, based on the idea that it is the victim, as well as the state, that is hurt by crime.

▷ RELATED ARTICLES: **Capital Punishment; Police; Prison.**

■ Criminal Code

The Constitution of Canada provides the federal Parliament with the authority to pass laws dealing with crime. The Criminal Code contains most of the serious criminal offences. However, some criminal offences (for example, those concerning drugs) are contained in other statutes.

The Criminal Code defines the kind of conduct that is considered a crime. It also sets out the kind of punishment that may be imposed when a person is convicted of an offence. Almost 40% of the Code deals with the procedures to be followed in prosecuting a crime.

The Code groups offences under different categories, such as offences against the person, offences against property, sexual offences, etc.

The Code was originally passed in 1892. It has never been fully revised, but amendments are made almost every year. The Code has had to change as society changes. For example, new offences have recently been created dealing with computer crimes, the misuse of credit cards, and impaired driving. Nevertheless, the Code has been severely criticized for failing to reflect the attitudes of Canadians today. Many sections have been struck down because they are not consistent with the Canadian Charter of Rights and

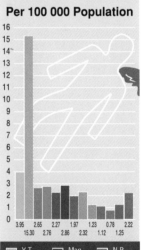

HOMICIDE RATE IN CANADA-1988

Per 100 000 Population

3.95 2.65 2.27 1.97 1.23 0.78 2.22
15.30 2.76 2.86 2.32 1.12 1.25

□ Y.T.   □ Man.   □ N.B.
□ N.W.T.   □ Ont.   □ P.E.I.
□ B.C.   □ Que.   □ N.S.
□ Alta   □ Nfld   □ Canada
□ Sask.   Source: Statistics Canada

Freedoms. At present, the federal government is studying the Criminal Code with a view to making it more up-to-date and simpler.

Criminal Law

Criminal law is concerned with protecting the public and maintaining the values of society. These values include the preservation of morality (for example, obscenity laws), protection of the person (for example, crimes of violence such as murder), protection of property (for example, theft), protection of the public peace (for example, causing a disturbance), and protection of the state (as in treason).

There can be no crime or punishment if there is no fixed law. There are many legal wrongs that are not crimes. These fall in the field of civil law. Civil actions are brought to court by one person against another or by one organization against another. In contrast, a crime is a wrong against the community as a whole, rather than against an individual victim.

A crime may be divided into two elements. One element is the act itself. Another equally important element is the "guilty mind." The prosecution must prove that it was in the mind of the accused to commit a crime. In fact, many criminal trials are contested on the question of whether a person intended to commit a crime, rather than on whether he or she actually committed the deed.

Under criminal law, others beside the person who commits the crime can be held responsible. Those who help can also be convicted. In addition, the attempt to commit an offence is a crime.

Presumed Innocent One of the most important principles of criminal law is that a person is presumed to be innocent. The court must *prove* that the accused is guilty beyond a reasonable doubt.

Defences The law allows several defences in which those who commit acts will be found not guilty. Some examples of these defences are self-defence, duress, necessity, and entrapment. There are other defences, for example, provocation and intoxication, in which the accused may be found not guilty of the original charge, but guilty of a lesser and included offence.

A person may be found not guilty by reason of insanity. This verdict is different from a finding of not guilty. The accused is not allowed to leave the courtroom but is detained in a secure mental hospital for treatment. A special board decides when it is safe to release the person.

Finally, it should be pointed out that a child under the age of 12 cannot be convicted of a criminal offence.

PROCEDURES

The process of trying a crime is set in motion when a *charge* is laid — usually by a police officer. A charge states that there is good reason to believe that a person (the *accused*) has committed a crime.

In the case of a serious crime a preliminary hearing sometimes precedes a trial. The purpose of the hearing is to determine whether there is sufficient evidence to justify a trial.

All offences may be classified as *indictable* (a serious crime) or *summary* (less serious). A conviction for a summary crime carries a maximum punishment of $2000 or six months in jail.

In both types of crime, the accused is called upon to plead guilty or not guilty. If the plea is not guilty, the case will go to trial. If the plea is guilty, the judge will pronounce a sentence.

In Canada, the legal system is *adversarial*. This means that the proceeding is a dispute between the Crown (known as the plaintiff in all Canadian criminal cases) and the accused (known as the defendant). Both parties must gather and present evidence. However, the Crown must prove that the accused is guilty. The accused is not required to give evidence. The court must acquit the accused if the Crown does not prove its case. This system favours the accused in order to protect individual rights.

▷ Related Articles: **Civil Law; Courts; Juvenile Justice; Judiciary; Law; Police.**

Criminals in History

From the earliest days to the present, criminals have posed problems for Canadian society. Pirates, such as Peter Easton (early 1600s), Henry Mainwaring (1587-1653), and Maria Lindsay and Eric Cobham (early 1700s), prowled our Atlantic coast. La Corriveau (1733-63) shocked Quebec when she murdered her husband. For many years the pirate and smuggler Bill Johnston (1782-1870) terrorized the Thousand Islands of the St Lawrence River. On February 4, 1880, near Lucan, Ont., a long feud came to a bloody climax when a vigilante mob murdered five members of the Donnelly family. On the Prairies the crimes of American whisky traders led to the formation of the North-West Mounted Police in 1873. The West had native Indian outlaws too; notably Almighty Voice (1874-97) and Charcoal (1856-97). In the 1870s the McLean Gang, three of them teenagers, robbed and murdered in the district of Kamloops, B.C. During the winter of 1931-32 the Mad Trapper of Rat River led police on a wild Arctic chase before being killed in a gunfight. In 1946 Evelyn Dick became the centre of one of Canada's most grisly murder cases when her husband's mutilated torso was found in Hamilton, Ont.

Some Canadian criminals left colourful stories in our history and folklore, and have inspired writers and filmmakers. A few have even become legendary figures, romanticized so that they appear as heroic Robin Hoods. Most of them, however, led violent and tragic lives, and wound up in prison or on the gallows. The following are some of Canada's most outstanding criminal stories.

Reginald Birchall, murderer *(born in 1866 at Accrington, England; died in 1890 at Woodstock, Ont.).* Birchall was an English gentleman, educated at Oxford. After squandering his money, he turned to crime. He conned two young men, Douglas Pelly and Frederick C. Benwell, into paying him £500 each for the purchase of a farm near Woodstock. They travelled to Canada, where they were to be partners on the farm. Birchall's plan was to kill them and keep the money. On February 17, 1890, he shot Benwell to death in a swamp. Later he tried unsuccessfully to kill Pelly. Birchall was arrested for murder by John W. Murray, Canada's famous "Great Detective." Because of his upper-class background, Birchall's case was widely reported in Canada, the U.S., and Europe. He was hanged in Woodstock.

Edwin Alonso Boyd, bank robber *(born in 1914 at Toronto).* The son of a policeman, Boyd spent his youth as a hobo and served with the Canadian Army in World War II. After the war he became dissatisfied with his employment as a labourer and turned to robbery. He began as a lone bandit. He was captured in 1951, but escaped with a number of other robbers who joined to form the "Boyd Gang." The gang robbed several banks, most of them in the Toronto area. Boyd was recaptured, but escaped from jail again. In 1952 two of Boyd's men killed a Toronto police detective and were subsequently hanged. Boyd had no part in the homicide. He was sentenced to life imprisonment for his robberies and jail breaks. He was eventually paroled and retired to private life under a new identity.

Thomas Neill Cream, doctor, murderer *(born in 1850 at Glasgow, Scotland; died in 1892 at London, England).* Cream was one of Canada's most unusual murderers. He studied medicine at McGill University, but was a thief, arsonist, and blackmailer. He did most of his killing with poison. His known victims include the American husband of one of his mistresses, and at least five women in London, England. He is also suspected of killing his Canadian wife and a Canadian mistress. He served time in prison in the U.S. for one of his murders and was finally sentenced to death in England. On the gallows he was reported to say "I'm Jack..." Though he could have been responsible for some unsolved murders in London, he was in prison in 1888 when the Jack the Ripper murders occurred.

Alvin Karpis, gangster *(born Albin Karpowicz in 1908 at Montreal, Que.; died in 1979 at Torremolinos, Spain).* Karpis was known to his criminal pals as "Old Creepy." He learned thievery as a boy and grew up to be a professional bank robber and kidnapper. During the Depression years of the 1930s, he was a gunman for the infamous Barker Gang. Karpis and the Barkers terrorized the American Midwest until the Federal Bureau of Investigation broke up the gang. Once the Barkers were gone, police declared Karpis "public enemy number one" — the most wanted fugitive in the country. He was captured in New Orleans in 1936. He served a record 26 years in Alcatraz Penitentiary. In 1969 he was paroled and deported to his native Canada. His autobiography, *Public Enemy Number One,* was published in 1971.

Norman Ryan, bandit *(born in 1895 at Toronto, Ont.; died in 1936 at Sarnia, Ont.).* "Red" Ryan's long criminal career earned him the nickname "The Canadian Jesse James." He began as a small-time thief in his teens and became one of the most notorious gangsters of his day. He robbed banks in Ontario, Quebec, and the U.S., and in 1923 made a spectacular escape from Kingston Penitentiary. He was recaptured and sentenced to life in prison. He was involved in the killing of a man, but Ryan did not do the killing. After serving a long prison term, he persuaded many authorities, including the prime minister of Canada, that he had reformed. With much public sympathy, Ryan was paroled in July 1935. He was presented as living proof that the correctional system worked, and became a spokesman for prison reform. However, Ryan was secretly engaging in criminal activities. Ten months after his release he was killed while robbing a liquor store.

Bill Miner, outlaw (*born in 1847 at Bowling Green, Kentucky, U.S.; died in 1913 at Covington, Georgia, U.S.*). Bill Miner was one of the most infamous stagecoach robbers of the Old West. His polite manners gained him the nickname "The Gentleman Bandit." He is believed to have been the first outlaw to use the term, "Hands up!" Miner served a long prison term in California and then moved to B.C. in 1904. He posed as a rancher while continuing his criminal career. He robbed the Canadian Pacific Railway in 1904 and in 1906. He was captured and imprisoned in New Westminster Penitentiary. In 1907 Miner escaped and fled to the U.S., where he continued to rob banks and trains. He died in a prison in Georgia. An award-winning Canadian film, *The Grey Fox*, tells the story of his adventures in Canada.

Donald Morrison, outlaw (*born in 1858 near Megantic, Canada East [Quebec]; died in 1894 at Montreal, Que.*). Known as "The Megantic Outlaw," Morrison was the son of Scottish settlers who farmed near Lake Megantic in what is now Quebec. He spent several years working as a cowboy in western Canada and the U.S. When his family's farm was lost to businessman Malcolm McAulay, Morrison felt he had been swindled and swore revenge. McAulay hired a gunman, Jack Warren, to arrest Morrison. Instead, Morrison killed Warren in a gunfight. For several months Morrison evaded capture, aided by farmers who considered him a hero. They felt McAulay was the real villain. Morrison was caught April 21, 1889, and sentenced to 18 years in prison. He died after serving five years. He has become a legendary figure in eastern Quebec and has been called "The Canadian Rob Roy" after the Scottish hero.

Patrick James Whelan, tailor, convicted assassin (*born about 1840 in Ireland; died in 1869 at Ottawa, Ont.*). On April 7, 1868, Thomas D'Arcy McGee, a Father of Confederation, was shot to death in Ottawa. Within hours police arrested Whelan. They suspected him of being a member of the Fenians, a terrorist organization dedicated to the liberation of Ireland from British rule. There was no solid evidence that Whelan was a Fenian. The testimony which placed him at the murder scene was not reliable. In a controversial trial, Whelan was convicted and sentenced to death. He pleaded his innocence throughout his trial and on the scaffold, where he was publicly hanged.

▷ RELATED ARTICLES: **Almighty Voice; Marie-Josephte Corriveau; Donnelly Family; Albert Johnson; John Wilson Murray; Pirates.**

▷ SUGGESTED READING: Ed Butts and H. Howard, *Bandits and Privateers* (1987); M. Lamb and B. Pearson, *The Boyd Gang* (1976); T.P. Slattery, *They Got To Find Mee Guilty Yet* (1972).

David Cronenberg *is one of Canada's greatest film directors. His movies include* The Fly *and* Dead Ringers *(courtesy NAC/MISA/The Mantle Clinic II, Ltd).*

■ Cronenberg, David

Filmmaker (*born in 1943 at Toronto, Ont.*). Cronenberg studied English literature at the University of Toronto in the 1960s, and while there made several experimental films. He has since become one of Canada's most brilliant and successful filmmakers.

Shivers (1976), which Cronenberg wrote and directed, launched his reputation as "The King of Horror." It was followed by *Rabid* (1977), *The Brood* (1979), *Scanners* (1980), and *Videodrome* (1983). *The Dead Zone* (1983), and *The Fly* (1986) brought international fame.

Dead Ringers (1988), a psychological thriller, is very different from his earlier films. It was bizarre and unsettling in its exploration of the different natures, and yet dependencies, of twin doctors.

■ Cross of Valour

Cross of Valour is the highest civilian Canadian medal for bravery. It is awarded for acts of outstanding courage in situations of extreme danger. The few people who have won the medal have all risked death for the sake of others. Some have died as a result of their actions.

The Cross of Valour was first awarded in 1972. At the same time, two other ranks of bravery award were also introduced: the Star of Courage and the Medal of Bravery. Any person or group can recommend someone for a bravery medal by writing to Government House, Ottawa.

The following are recipients of the award:

Lewis John Stringer (1930-69) and *Vaino Olavi Partanen* (1928-69) were the first to be awarded the Cross of Valour. The ship HMCS *Kootenay* was in the English Channel, homeward bound for Canada, on the morning of October 23, 1969, when an explosion in the engine room started a roaring fire. Many dashed for safety but Chief Warrant Officer Partanen stayed behind, grabbed the phone and alerted the officer of the watch. By taking those extra few moments to warn others, he sealed his own fate. Seconds later he was dead, engulfed by the flames.

Meanwhile, smoke and flames swept through the ship. Sergeant Stringer saved many lives by remaining calm and directing the trapped men to safety. Only when the last man was safely out did Stringer leave his post. Weak from the smoke in his lungs, he collapsed in the galley. Although he was rescued from there, he did not survive.

Mary Dohey (1933-). Dohey, an airline stewardess, was caught in an airplane hijacking on November 12, 1971. A masked man carrying a sawn-off shotgun took over Flight 812 from Calgary. Holding the gun at Dohey's head, he demanded a ransom of $1.5 million. He made Dohey hold two wires of a dynamite bomb. For eight terrifying hours Dohey remained calm. She persuaded the hijacker to release the passengers and most of the crew. But when he said she could leave the plane too, she refused. It was this extra act of courage — willingly risking her life for the sake of others — that earned her the Cross of Valour. Fortunately, the pilot was able to subdue the hijacker.

Kenneth Bishop (1945-). On March 30, 1974, about 15 km from Vegreville, Alta, George McAdie lay helpless in the road. A few minutes earlier, the fuel tanker he was driving collided with an oncoming truck. Dazed and bleeding, he lay on the shoulder of the road while fuel from the ruptured tanker flowed around and over him.

As soon as Ken Bishop reached the

Cross of Valour, *Canada's highest civilian medal for bravery (courtesy Rideau Hall).*

scene, he moved in to help. Just then the fuel caught fire, exploding, and hurling Bishop to the side of the road. Bishop plunged back into the sea of fire and pulled the injured man from the blaze. Both were severely burned, but both survived. Bishop was awarded the Cross of Valour for "the finest example of selfless courage."

Jean Swedberg (1926-74). Jean Swedberg was on duty at the front desk of the Valnicola Hotel in Merritt, B.C., when a fire broke out on September 4, 1974. She ran from room to room, pounding on doors, shouting warnings. While others were escaping, she raced upstairs to warn the guests, and there she died. Her prompt and courageous action saved at least 12 people.

Thomas Hynes (1958-77). On a cold December day in 1977, Tom Hynes plunged into frigid waters near his home village of Jacques Fontaine, Nfld, to help his eight-year old cousin Keith, who had fallen through the ice. Tom held Keith up until Keith could grasp hold of a long stick which some boys on the bank pushed to him. Keith survived, but Tom drowned before rescuers arrived. He was only 19 years old.

Gaston Langelier was one of several hostages taken during a prison break at Laval Penitentiary on July 11, 1978. In a struggle with the gunman, Langelier was shot twice in the face and once in the arm. In the course of the breakout, one guard and one inmate were killed. Four other inmates escaped, though all were later recaptured. Langelier recovered from his wounds.

Amédéo Garrammone (1955-) was a private stationed at Canadian Forces Base Halifax in 1978. On the evening of November 4, he saw Private Bradley Quinn being beaten and stabbed by three men. Garrammone ran to help him. The man with the knife then turned on Garrammone and stabbed him in the chest. The tip of the knife penetrated Garrammone's heart. The attackers fled. Quinn died shortly after, but Garrammone survived after open-heart surgery.

Lester Fudge (1927-), ***Harold Miller*** (1958-), and ***Martin Sceviour*** (1941-) were three Newfoundland fishermen who saved the crew of a Danish trawler on the night of November 19, 1978.

There was a violent storm that night, with winds of 100 km/h and temperatures of -25°C. The three men were ashore at Nain, Labrador, when a distress call came from the Danish trawler *Remoy*. It was stranded on a sand reef about 13 km out from Nain. Lashed by the wild seas, it had iced over and lost its power and light. A trawler that went to its aid could not get close enough to rescue the crew, for fear of running aground. Fudge, Miller, and Sceviour volunteered to man a small motorboat that would take the crew from the *Remoy* to the other trawler. Since the motorboat was too small to take more than seven at a time, they had to make two trips through the treacherous seas, bailing out water all the way to avoid being swamped.

Anna Lang (1940-). She "displayed selfless courage to a very high degree," says the official citation describing Lang's worthiness for Canada's highest medal of bravery.

On September 9, 1980 Lang and her friend Lana Walsh were driving home with Walsh's four-year-old son Jaye. Lang stopped at a red light by the bridge over the Hammond River, 30 km northeast of Saint John, N.B. A gasoline truck close behind ploughed into her car, and both plunged into the river. The driver of the truck jumped free, but the two women and the child landed in the river. They escaped from the car through an open window, but the river was on fire with burning gasoline. Jaye's mother held his head up to keep him from drowning, but had to duck him each time his hair caught fire.

Anna Lang reached the shore first, but she plunged back into the blazing river. She grabbed hold of Jaye, pulling him and his mother towards the bank. All recovered from their injuries, though Anna Lang was in the hospital the longest. She suffered concussion, and two cracked vertebrae, as well as serious burns.

Robert Teather (1947-). An RCMP diver with the Surrey Detachment in British Columbia, Corporal Bob Teather was called out at four o'clock on September 26, 1981 to rescue two fishermen whose boat had been run down by a freighter and lay upside down.

The two fishermen were trapped in the engine room of the capsized boat, where there was still a small pocket of air above water level. Teather found the men in the darkness and the oily water. One man could not swim. He panicked and struggled, and by the time Teather got him to the surface, both men were half drowned. Nevertheless, Teather went straight back to rescue the other man.

René Marc Jalbert (1921-) won the Cross of Valour for his cool-headed courage when a man armed with two submachine guns shot his way into the National Assembly building in Quebec City, killing three people and wounding 13 others. This was on the morning of May 8, 1984. The gunman, Denis Lortie, intended to kill Premier René Lévesque, but Lévesque was not there. Lortie sprayed the chamber with bullets each time he saw anyone move. Jalbert was sergeant-at-arms of the Assembly. He entered the Assembly Chamber and said firmly to Lortie, "Stop firing. I'm coming to talk to you." Then, unarmed, he walked boldly into view. Lortie held his fire. Over the next four hours, Jalbert persuaded Lortie to surrender to police.

Jalbert's ice-cold courage drew great admiration across the country. In 1985 he was appointed to the position of gentleman usher of the black rod at the Senate of Canada in Ottawa.

David Gordon Cheverie (1956-) has won both the Cross of Valour and the Star of Courage. As a constable with the Charlottetown Police Department, he won the Star of Courage for rescuing a man from a house fire in March 1986. The Cross of Valour was also awarded for extreme bravery during a fire. On May 16, 1987, Cheverie and his patrol partner saw flames through the living-room window of a house. Entering the fiercely burning building, Cheverie found a little girl unconscious on the floor. He carried her out and then ran straight back into the house to search for her sisters. He found them upstairs and carried one under each arm, racing through a tunnel of flames to get to the front door. The house exploded into a fireball seconds after all were safely out of the building.

▷ SUGGESTED READING: John Melady, *Cross of Valour* (1985); Carlotta Hacker, *Bravery* (1989).

■ Crow

This family of birds (Corvidae) includes the largest perchers: jays, magpies, ravens, crows, and nutcrackers. Most have a strong, tapering bill, which is usually almost as long as the head. Their nostrils are covered with stiff feathers which resemble bristles. Some species hop along the ground (jays), while others walk (crows). Except for some jays, they are loud, noisy birds. Crows are valuable to man as scavengers and destroyers of insects. On the other hand, they often eat fruit and grain, especially corn.

Crows are thought to be the most intelligent birds. The American Crow can learn to count to three or four and can also imitate human speech. It has excellent memories and it can learn from experience. Jays are also mimics who can whistle and chuckle and imitate other birds. They can also solve problems. For example, they catch ants, place them in their feathers, and scratch. The acid secreted by the ant eases the skin irritation caused by lice and fungus.

The American Crow (*Corvus brachyrhynchos*) breeds across southern Canada, from interior B.C. to Newfoundland. It is a resourceful bird that prefers open places while looking for food but chooses wooded areas for nesting. It has profited from the spread of farming, and in winter it frequents garbage dumps. The adults are black, with violet or greenish gloss. It is known for its familiar cry — *caw*. The Northwestern Crow (*Corvus caurinus*) is somewhat smaller. It is found only on the coast and islands of British Columbia. They are beachcombers but may also be found in nearby farming areas.

The Common Raven (*Corvus corax*) is much larger than the American Crow. The adult male's wingspan may reach 437 cm (compared to 321 cm in the crow). It also has a heavier bill and long, pointed feathers on its throat. It is all black, with a purplish gloss. The Common Raven is easily confused with the Common Crow. It can be told apart by its habit of taking

two or three hops before it become airborne, while the crow jumps directly into flight. Its croak (*kwawk*) is very different from the crow's *caw*. The Common Raven is found in all parts of Canada (including the Arctic) except for the southern prairie regions of the West.

The Black-billed Magpie (*Pica pica*) is a large black-and-white bird with a very long tail. It is easily identified by its flashing white patches on the wing tips when it flies, and by its *yak-yak-yak* call. It breeds only in western Canada, from the southern Yukon to western Manitoba.

Jays are more brightly coloured than other crows and are usually smaller. Several species have a crested head and a long

Crow Family includes the Common Crow (top), Black-billed Magpie (middle), and Blue Jay (bottom). Crows are believed to be the most intelligent birds (courtesy Macmillan Illustrated Animal Encyclopedia).

Breeding Range of:
Northwestern Crow ●
Common Crow ○

tail. Three live permanently in Canada: the Blue Jay (*Cyanocitta cristata*) in central and eastern Canada; Steller's Jay (*C. stelleri*) in the West, and the Gray Jay (*Perisoreus canadensis*) almost everywhere except the arctic and prairie West. Jays accommodate to people easily, often coming into camping grounds and helping themselves to the campers' food. Clark's Nutcracker (*Nucifraga columblana*) is found in the evergreen forest and mountains of southern British Columbia and Alberta.

▷ RELATED ARTICLES: **Birds; Jay; Magpie.**

■ Crowfoot

Blackfoot chief (*born about 1830 near the Belly River [Alta]; died in 1890 at Blackfoot Crossing [Alta]*). Crowfoot was widely respected for his wisdom and statesmanship during a period of great change for the native people of the plains. During his lifetime the bison, long the staple of his people, became scarce. His homeland was occupied by agricultural settlers whose culture was much different from that of his people.

Crowfoot was a leading chief of the Blackfoot Confederacy. He was a member of the Blood tribe by birth and of the Blackfoot tribe by adoption. He first attracted notice as a teenager. His bravery during an attack on a Crow camp earned him the name Isapo-muxika ("Crow Indian's Big Foot," or Crowfoot). His outstanding courage drew increasing admiration. His most heroic deed was in 1866 when, single-handedly with only a lance as a weapon, he attacked and killed a grizzly bear that had just mauled a Blackfoot youngster.

As Crowfoot grew older, he became an influential peacemaker. During the 1860s, he established friendly relations with traders and missionaries. He formed a long-lasting friendship with the missionary Albert Lacombe. Early in the 1870s he made peace with the Cree, who were traditional enemies of the Blackfoot, and adopted a young Cree, Poundmaker, as a son. In 1874, when the North-West Mounted Police arrived in the West, Crowfoot made them welcome. He willingly co-operated with their senior officer, James Macleod, in establishing law and order on the western prairies.

Crowfoot was a key figure during negotiations for Treaty No. 7 (1877). His decision to sign the treaty caused other chiefs to follow his lead. Similarly, his decision to keep the Blackfoot neutral during the North-West Rebellion (1885) influenced

Crowfoot, chief of the Blackfoot, 1887 (courtesy Glenbow Archives/NA-29-1).

other natives to stay out of the fighting too. By then he no longer trusted the government, but he had the foresight to realize that the Blackfoot could not win such a fight. Like Chief Red Crow of the Blood tribe, he acted with great skill and diplomacy during very difficult times as he strove for the best interests of his people.

▷ RELATED ARTICLES: **Native People: Plains; North-West Rebellion.**

▷ SUGGESTED READING: Hugh Dempsey, *Crowfoot* (1972); Carlotta Hacker, *Crowfoot* (1977).

■ Crown, *see* Parliament

■ Crown Corporation

A crown corporation is a business which is owned either by the government of Canada or the government of one of the provinces. Some crown corporations do business solely with other government departments. Others provide goods and services to the public. Crown corporations perform many functions, including transporting mail, running lotteries, providing electric power, producing and broadcasting television programs, operating railways, producing Canadian money, and operating gas stations. Although a crown corporation is owned by a government, it is supposed to operate as an independent business and to be free from constant government interference.

Crown corporations are usually managed by independent boards. However, Cabinet ministers responsible for the corporations exert some influence on them.

Canadian governments have created crown corporations for many reasons. Often the government decided that privately owned businesses (those owned by individuals) either would not or should not be involved in providing important services to the public. Sometimes the government argued that the creation of a crown corporation to compete with privately owned businesses, which were often foreign owned, would provide Canadians with more control over their economy and resources. In some cases, the government has created a crown corporation by taking over a privately owned business which is in danger of closing.

Many Canadians believe that the government should reduce its involvement in business activities. They believe that the government should "privatize" many crown corporations by selling them to private owners. The government of Prime Minister Brian Mulroney and the governments of several provinces have announced plans to sell some crown corporations. By 1989 the most notable example of the activity was the sale of Air Canada.

Ten of the largest crown corporations are Canada Post, PetroCanada, Canadian National Railway, CBC, Atomic Energy of Canada, Ontario Hydro, Caisse de dépôt et placement du Québec, Alberta Government Telephones, and BC Hydro.

■ Crown Land

Crown land is land that is owned by the federal or provincial governments. About 89% of Canada is crown land (41% federal, 48% provincial). Most of the federal crown land is in the Yukon and Northwest Territories. Rights to the resources of these lands may be leased to private enterprises such as mining companies. As well, some of the land is allocated for national and provincial parks, Indian reserves, and military bases.

■ Crow's Nest Pass Agreement

The Crow's Nest Pass Agreement was signed in 1897 between the Canadian Pacific Railway Company (CPR) and the Government of Canada. Valuable minerals had been discovered in southern British Columbia, and the CPR wanted to have exclusive rights to develop them. The government wanted cheap transportation rates for farmers' belongings and for grain in order to attract farmers to the prairies.

In the agreement, the CPR received a

Crowsnest Pass, Turtle Mountain. The Frank Slide is on the left (photo by Cleve Wershler).

government subsidy of $3.3 million to build a rail line from Lethbridge through the Crowsnest Pass to Nelson in southern B.C. In return, the CPR agreed to transport grain and flour from the prairies to eastern markets at a cheap rate, and to ship "settlers' effects" from the east to the prairies, also at cheap rates. These reduced rates were of great importance during the settlement of the West.

Prairie farmers came to rely on the "Crow rate." Any changes or threat to the agreement caused great dissatisfaction in the West. However, in a long process that culminated in the Western Grain Transportation Act in 1983, grain-shipping costs were allowed to be increased gradually, provided that they never exceed 10% of the world price for grain.

■ Crowsnest Pass

The Crowsnest Pass (elevation 1357 m) is the most southerly of the important railway passes crossing the Rocky Mountains. It is situated on the British Columbia-Alberta border, 70 km north of the United States border. The surrounding area is known for coal production.

▷ SUGGESTING READING: Frank W. Anderson and Elsie G. Turnbull, *Tragedies of the Crowsnest Pass* (1984).

■ Crustacean

Crustaceans are invertebrates (having no backbone) of the animal phylum called Arthropods (which also includes insects, spiders and centipedes). They include shrimp, barnacles, crayfish, crabs, lobsters, and other similar species — some 40 000 in all.

The main characteristic of crustaceans is their two pairs of antennae. All other arthropods have at the most one pair.

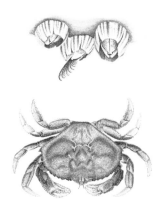

Crustaceans include barnacles (above) and crabs (below). All crustaceans are invertebrates; that is, they have no backbone (artwork by Kendal Morris).

Breeding Range of
Black-billed Cuckoo ●

Breeding Range of
**Yellow-billed
Cuckoo** ●

Old Houses, Montreal,
*painted around 1908 by
Maurice Cullen. Many of
his paintings, such as
this, were night or dusk
scenes (courtesy The
Montreal Museum of
Fine Arts).*

The crustacean body is generally divided into three parts: head, thorax, and abdomen. Each part is made up of segments, which serve for locomotion, breathing, reproduction, defence, and handling food. Some species carry their eggs in these appendages on their abdomens. Like all invertebrates, they have a shell (called the "exoskeleton") rather than having an internal skeleton. To grow, they must moult; that is, they must lose their old shell when it becomes too small and develop a larger one.

Crustaceans are extremely varied, as can be seen by comparing a crab and a barnacle. Most crustaceans have separate sexes, but some, like barnacles, are both sexes in one; others, like some shrimp, change sex as they age. In some crustaceans, the blood, because of the presence of copper, is bluish in colour. Crustaceans are important products in the fishing industry. They also provide food for fish and whales.

▷ RELATED ARTICLES: **Barnacle; Crab; Crayfish; Lobster; Shrimp.**

Crysler's Farm, Battle of

The Battle of Crysler's Farm on November 11, 1813, was a British victory during the War of 1812. An 800-strong force, consisting of British regular soldiers, Canadian militiamen, and native soldiers, defeated the rearguard of a 7000-strong American army. The battle took place on the farm of John Crysler, a militia captain, on the banks of the St Lawrence River near present-day Morrisburg, Ont. It was an important battle since it marked the end of American attempts to take Montreal and isolate Upper Canada. After the battle, the Americans withdrew across the St Lawrence.

▷ RELATED ARTICLE: **War of 1812.**

Cuckoo

The cuckoo family (Cuculidae) includes more than 125 species worldwide. Only two are found in Canada: the Black-billed Cuckoo (*Coccyzus erythropthalmus*) and the Yellow-billed Cuckoo (*C. americanus*). The two are almost identical, except that the Black-Billed Cuckoo has a reddish ring about the eye, no rusty tint under the wings, and a pure black beak. Cuckoos have slender, elongated bodies, long, tiered tails, and slightly downcurved bills. They live in open woodlands in bushes or thickets.

Unlike European species of cuckoo, which lay their eggs in the nests of other species, Canadian ones build their own fragile nests of twigs. The female lays two to four bluish green eggs. Cuckoos are very useful birds, eating large quantities of insects, caterpillars in particular. Once numerous, cuckoos have become rare. They winter in South America.

Cullen, Maurice Galbraith

Painter (*born in 1866 at St John's, Nfld; died in 1934 at Chambly, Que.*). Cullen moved to Montreal in 1870. He began his art training as a student of Louis-Philippe Hébert, a sculptor. Like other artists of his time, he then moved to Paris to study. Arriving in 1889, he decided to become a painter. He learned the current style of Impressionism and applied it to the Montreal cityscape on his return in 1895. His colours were darker than the Impressionists, and many of his scenes, such as *Old Houses, Montreal* (*circa* 1908), were of night or dusk. His special gift was an ability to capture light and mood.

Culleton, Beatrice

Writer (*born in 1949 at Winnipeg, Man.*). Culleton grew up in several foster homes. After the suicide of one of her sisters, she decided to write a novel based on her own and her family's tragic experiences.

In Search of April Raintree (1983; revised in 1984 under the title of *April Raintree*) describes the heroine's life from a baby to a young woman. Alcohol, prejudice, suicide, violence, and a broken marriage make April's life very unhappy. However, she struggles courageously to succeed. *Spirit of the White Bison* (1985) is narrated by the spirit of a buffalo who tells of the senseless destruction of the great bison herds during the 19th century. Culleton's books reflect her pride in her native ancestry, her anger at how her people have suffered, and a belief that better times will come for them.

■ Culture

The word *culture* is used in many ways. It suggests something which is developed or refined. One anthropologist described culture as cooked, compared to nature, which is raw. In one widely held view, culture is the music of Beethoven or the writing of Shakespeare. For an anthropologist, culture contains much more than classical music or the paintings in museums. In this view, rock and roll is just as much a part of culture as Beethoven.

Culture is Learned To an anthropologist, culture is all learned or acquired ideas, beliefs, and knowledge that are shared by several individuals. Thus, culture includes many different things, from pots and pans to ideas about God. It includes customs, sports, gestures (such as the handshake), art, laws, and language.

All aspects of culture are learned. They are not inherited. No child is born with culture. A child raised away from society would have no language, religion, or technical knowledge. Culture is what separates humans from animals. Human behaviour is overwhelmingly determined by culture.

Culture is Shared Culture is shared among people in a group and spreads from group to group. It is passed on from generation to generation.

Some traits are observed by all people in a given culture, for example, language and laws. There are also attributes shared by all known cultures. All humans have developed tools to cope with their environment. They have a language, a body of knowledge, a system of beliefs, and a social structure. All cultures have prohibitions against killing or stealing. All have rules of politeness and hospitality. Every human group has funerals for its dead.

Cultural Groups The term *culture* is often used to describe particular groups. Anthropologists speak of the culture of the Northwest Coast native people, for example. It is difficult, however, to apply the term to a nation, such as Canada. Canada is a complex mixture of cultures, beginning with two major communities, French and English. Within these two communities there are a series of subcultures. These have their own characteristics, although they remain parts of the larger French and English cultures.

Confusion with Other Terms The terms nation, country, society, and race are often confused with the idea of culture used by anthropologists. A *nation*, or country, is a political entity. A nation may contain a single culture, or more likely, it will include many. Culture is also confused with *society*. Culture is a complex of learned ideas, while society is a group of individuals who live and interact with each other other.

Race refers to groups of people who possess certain distinct characteristics, which are inherited. Race has nothing to do with culture.

Beliefs are accepted without proof. They are a part of every culture because humans are always seeking explanations for their lives and the universe. Science adds to our knowledge, but it also raises more questions with each new answer.

Values refer to the goals that people consider important in life. They are important in determining the behaviour of individuals. In all human societies, people judge behaviour as either "good" or "bad."

CULTURE CHANGE

Culture generally resists change. Most of those who share a culture want to preserve it as it is. Nevertheless, culture does change. Change and resistance to change are often in conflict within a culture. Change may affect one aspect of a culture and leave others untouched. In Canada, most people accept changes in technology. At the same time, Canadians resist changes in other areas, such as in our political system or family arrangements.

Much culture change occurs as a result of invention. The invention of the automobile, for example, changed the way we move, where we live and work, and how we build our cities. In a little over 100 years, the telephone, radio, radar, television, atomic bomb, transistor, airplane, and computer have changed almost every culture on Earth.

Dominance of Cultures The spread of ideas from more powerful cultures to the less powerful is called *acculturation*. This process may end in one culture totally disappearing as a distinct entity. This is called *assimilation*. When a group comes to Canada from a different culture, there is pressure to conform to Canadian beliefs, customs, etc., in order to be able to live at ease in the society. In time, many immigrants become assimilated.

Influences from outside are not the only causes of culture change. A culture may change even though it is cut off from others. It may respond to changes in the

---

Symbols

Symbols make human communication, and therefore culture, possible.

Humans are the only beings who communicate by symbols. A symbol is an object, sound, colour, odour, to which humans have attached a meaning. There is no necessary relationship between the symbol and the thing. These symbols, such as words, are invented, as are the rules for their use.

Cultural Knowledge

Every culture has a body of knowledge which has been gained by testing understandings about the world. The Inuit, for example, have a thorough knowledge of the habits of the animals they live amongst.

People who live by the sea understand the nature of tides, currents, and winds.

Canadian Culture

Is there a Canadian culture? Many people think so, but they have difficulty in describing it.

It is easier to describe Canada as a group of cultures.

The native people alone have many different cultures.

The two "founding peoples," French and English, are separate cultures.

These two groups also contain subcultures. For example, the English contain English, Scots, Irish, and Welsh.

The many ethnic groups who have come to Canada since the 19th century also form a separate group. Most of these people adopt English as their working language. Many still speak their former language.

The challenge of Canada as a nation is to recognize these differences, while drawing them together.

Sir Samuel Cunard was one of the first Nova Scotians to build a business empire (artwork by Irma Coucill).

physical environment or to conflicts within itself.

CULTURE CONFLICT

People resist change partly because culture helps them to cope, to understand the world, and to feel that their lives have meaning. When people have confidence in their culture it often leads to the view that other cultures are inferior. The very act of saying that you are part of one group excludes you from others.

When different cultural groups are forced to live together, as they have been in Canada, the result is often uncertainty, prejudice, and discrimination.

The necessity to defend our group leads us to fear others. Fear of change and fear of uncertainty leads us to fear differences. In fact while we may even come to value differences, a group must also have some unity and faith in its principles.

▷ RELATED ARTICLES: **Ethnic Groups; Immigration; Prejudice and Discrimination.**

■ Cumberland

Settlement began at Cumberland, B.C., on the east coast of Vancouver Island, after coal was discovered in the 1880s. The population grew steadily as coal production increased, and it stood at 3000 when Cumberland was made a city in 1897.

Workers came from far and wide to work the mines. By 1911 the population had grown to over 10 000, including about 3000 Chinese and 1000 Japanese. As coal mining activity decreased in the area, Cumberland's population fell dramatically. The mines closed in 1953, and in 1958 Cumberland's status fell from city to village. Its population in 1986 was 1853.

Cumberland's history as a coal-mining town was sometimes stormy. There was a large labour strike from 1912 to 1914. Explosions in the mines in 1901, 1903, 1922, and 1923 killed 130 men. For information, contact the Village Clerk, P.O. Box 340, Cumberland, B.C., V0R 1S0.

■ Cumberland House

For its first hundred years, the Hudson's Bay Company (HBC) expected the native peoples to bring furs to them at Hudson Bay, but when competitors from Montreal took away the trade, the Company had to move inland. In 1774 Samuel Hearne chose a site on the main trade route from York Factory to the Saskatchewan River, and Cumberland House became the first of the HBC's inland trading posts. The site was moved in 1789. In 1793 the North West Company built its own Cumberland House close by.

The HBC still has a trading post at Cumberland House, which is the oldest continuously occupied European settlement in Saskatchewan.

▷ RELATED ARTICLE: **Hudson's Bay Company.**

■ Cumberland Sound

Cumberland Sound (300 km long) is a major inlet on the east coast of Baffin Island. Its steep sides, indented with deep fjords, rise to glacier-covered uplands. The area was first occupied by Dorset people, ancestors of the modern Inuit. After 1840, British and American whalers made annual visits. Pangnirtung is the main settlement.

■ Cummings, Burton

Singer, songwriter (*born in 1947 at Winnipeg, Man.*). Cummings was the lead singer for the Canadian rock group Guess Who from 1968 to 1975. He began a solo career in 1975 and had a string of hit singles, including "Stand Tall" and "I'm Scared." Cummings is known for his rich voice and emotional lyrics. He has won numerous awards and critical acclaim for his singing and songwriting.

■ Cunard, Sir Samuel

Businessman and shipowner (*born in 1787 at Halifax, N.S.; died in 1865 at London, England*). Founder of the Cunard Line of steamships, Samuel Cunard was the son of a Halifax carpenter and timber merchant. After serving in the War of 1812, he played an increasing role in his father's business, building its few sailing ships into a large fleet, which traded in a range of products. By the 1830s he had become very wealthy.

In 1839 Cunard and a group of British partners won a contract to run a mail service by steamship across the Atlantic. They had four side-wheelers built for the mail service and began operations in 1840, when their *Britannia* crossed from Liverpool to Halifax in 12 1/2 days. With fast and reliable steamships gradually replacing sailing ships, Cunard's company grew steadily.

Cunard was one of the first Nova Scotians to build a successful business empire. His company grew to be one of the great 20th-century passenger lines, launching such famous ships as the *Queen Mary* and *Queen Elizabeth*.

▷ SUGGESTED READING: John M. Bassett, *Samuel Cunard* (1976); T.W.E. Roche, *Samuel Cunard and the North Atlantic* (1971).

■ Cupids

Cupids, Nfld, lies on the southwest shore

of Conception Bay on the Avalon Peninsula. It was one of the first English settlements in America and the site of the first attempt to colonize Newfoundland. It began in 1610 when John Guy and 39 settlers planted a colony in a beautiful harbour then known as Cuper's Cove. He was harassed by pirates, who carried off some of his men. Visiting fishermen, who looked on Newfoundland as their own, refused to recognize Guy's authority. The colony soon collapsed, but Cupids remained a popular fishing harbour. The fishing industry still provides the main source of employment in the community, which had a population of 789 in 1986. Archaeologists have unearthed remains of buildings that may date back to the Guy settlement. For information, contact the City Clerk, City Hall, P.O. Box 99, Cupids, Nfld, A0A 2B0.

■ Curling

Curling is a sport in which two teams slide stones over an ice surface towards a target. The object is to place a stone closest to the centre of the target circle. Curling first developed in Scotland, and Scottish soldiers brought the sport to Canada. The first sports club in Canada was the Royal Montreal Curling Club, founded in 1807. The early clubs in Canada used local materials for "stones," such as iron or maple wood.

Canada was an ideal place for curling to flourish, because of its long winters and abundant ice. In fact, curling was often too cold to play outdoors. Curlers quickly took their sport indoors. Indoor rinks built for curling were often used in the early days of ice hockey. By the early 20th century, almost every town in western Canada had an indoor rink. Winnipeg became the curling centre of Canada, with more clubs than Toronto and Montreal combined.

Early Canadian curlers were considered "barbarians" by the Scots, but they soon gained respect. The first Canadian team toured Scotland in 1908. It won 23 of its 26 matches. Unlike many other sports, curling quickly became a sport for both men and women.

The curling championship, called the Brier, began in 1927 and is held every year. Teams from each of the provinces compete and the winner represents Canada at the world championships, which grew out of competition between Canada and Scotland. It first took place in Montreal in 1968. Air Canada presented the Silver Broom trophy for the event, which

was won by Canada's Ron Northcott. Canada won the first five championships, but curling grew in other countries, such as Sweden, Switzerland, Germany, and the United States. Canada did not win from 1973 to 1979. However, Canadian teams have won most of the championships of the 1980s. Curling was a demonstration sport at the 1988 Calgary Olympics, where Canada won a gold medal in the women's event and a bronze medal in the men's event. The Scottish bagpipes heard at many matches, or "bonspiels," are reminders of the sport's Scottish origin.

■ Currant

Red currants (genus *Ribes*) belong to the gooseberry subfamily of the family of plants called Saxyfragaceae. Currants and gooseberries are fruit bushes. Their leaves are quite similar in appearance. They are usually divided into five lobes, with veins running from the base to the tip of each lobe. Currants, unlike gooseberries, have no thorns. They flower early in spring and produce clusters of red or black berries. Among the 14 wild species, one red- and one black-berried variety stand out for their special perfume: that of a skunk! (It is given off by the leaves when bruised or the fruit when cooked.)

Whatever their individual differences, all the currants are rich in pectin and possess a slightly sour taste. They make delicious jellies and preserves. Wild currants, unfortunately, harbour a microscopic fungus which attacks the white pine, killing the tree in a few years. Cultivated black currants have a distinctive fragrance: they are used to make a jelly of intense flavour and a special liqueur. Their leaves are mixed with tea to make a tisane with that special aroma.

■ Currency, *see* Coins; Money

■ Curriculum

The word curriculum comes from the Latin word, *currere*, which means "to run." Thus, a curriculum is like a racecourse; it has a beginning and an end, and it has to be covered in a certain time. The word now means a program of studies, made up of courses and subjects to be taken by students. Sometimes it refers to a whole program, as in the high-school curriculum or the university curriculum. Sometimes it refers to a specific course, as in the Grade 4 music curriculum or the Grade 10 geography curriculum.

All the provinces and territories have

an officially approved curriculum. It specifies what subjects have to be learned in each grade.

This curriculum is usually accompanied by officially approved textbooks and sometimes by end-of-year exams. Teachers are legally obliged to follow the curriculum and are inspected by principals or superintendents. Thus, the curriculum is the officially approved view of what students are supposed to learn.

In practice, the curriculum is usually drawn up by a committee of teachers appointed by the Minister of Education of a province or territory. Often these curriculum committees include a few members who are not teachers, such as school trustees or representatives of community groups.

The curriculum is written out as an official document. It usually consists of a statement of goals and objectives. It contains descriptions of the subject matter and a list of teaching resources.

In the 1960s and 1970s, curriculum controls were loosened and teachers were given a great deal of freedom to decide what to teach. In the 1980s, most provinces and territories tightened up their control of curricula in order to ensure that students learned certain skills and subjects. This was a response to arguments that Canada needed highly skilled workers in order to compete economically with other countries.

▷ RELATED ARTICLE: **Education.**

Sir Arthur Currie
insisted that Canadian troops fight together so they could take pride in fighting together as Canadians (by permission of the British Library).

■ Currie, Sir Arthur William

Army officer (*born in 1875 at Strathroy, Ont.; died in 1933 at Montreal, Que.*). Currie was one of the most outstanding generals in World War I. He was the first Canadian appointed to command the Canadian Corps. Previously, the corps had been commanded by officers from the British army.

Currie started his career as a schoolteacher and businessman in British Columbia. He was also a keen member of the militia and had reached the rank of lieutenant-colonel when war broke out in 1914. A first-rate military leader, he rose quickly in rank during the war. In June 1917 he succeeded Sir Julian Byng as commander of the Canadian Corps. That same year he was knighted and promoted to lieutenant-general. Currie determinedly kept the Canadian divisions together as one corps, rather than having them mixed in with various British units, as the British generals wanted. As a result, Canadian troops were able to take pride in fighting together as Canadians, and in winning as Canadians. Inspired by Currie's leadership, they waged an especially successful campaign during the last 100 days of the war (between August and November, 1918).

Currie served as inspector general of the militia forces in Canada from 1919 to 1920. From 1920 until his death he was principal and vice-chancellor of McGill University. At McGill, he applied the same organization and enthusiasm that had brought him such success as a general.

▷ RELATED ARTICLE: **Byng of Vimy.**

▷ SUGGESTED READING: Daniel G. Dancocks, *Sir Arthur Currie: A Biography* (1985).

■ Cuso

CUSO is a non-profit Canadian organization which sends people and money to help the poor of less developed countries help themselves. The organization was formerly known as Canadian University Service Overseas, but is now known simply as CUSO. The name change reflects a change in the make-up of the volunteers, who are increasingly skilled tradespeople as opposed to university graduates. Started in 1961, CUSO finds volunteer Canadians of many ages to go overseas (usually for two years) to Africa, Asia, Latin America, and the Caribbean as educators, managers, and health workers, and as teachers of such skills as farming, fishing, and running a business. CUSO also gives grants of money to Third World community groups to aid in the setting up of small businesses, such as medical clinics, and other projects. CUSO is a completely private organization, with headquarters in Ottawa and with offices in major Canadian cities and local committees across the country.

Information can be obtained by writing to the Communications Department, CUSO, 135 Rideau Street, Ottawa, Ont., K1N 9K7.

▷ RELATED ARTICLE: **Foreign Aid.**

■ Cut Knife Hill, Battle of

This battle took place west of Battleford, in what is now Saskatchewan, on May 2, 1885, during the North-West Rebellion. It was a victory for the Cree and Stoney in Chief Poundmaker's camp, who routed over 300 government soldiers commanded by Colonel William Otter.

Otter's aim was to punish Poundmaker's band for ransacking Battleford early in April. But the native people learned of Otter's approach and attacked first. After six hours of fighting, they forced the government troops to retreat. Poundmaker himself took no part in the fighting, and he prevented his men from pursuing the fleeing troops. This saved many lives. Only eight of Otter's force died in the battle; native losses were five or six.

▷ RELATED ARTICLES: **North-West Rebellion; William Otter; Poundmaker.**

■ Cuttlefish

Cuttlefish are part of the Cephalopod class of Mollusca. There are more than 100 species worldwide. In Canada, we have five species of the closely related genus *Rossia*.

Unlike other molluscs, cephalopods have no external shells. They have an internal shaft known as the "cuttlebone." The head is only visible from the back, where one can see the two eyes. Connected to the head of the cuttlefish are ten tentacles. Eight of the tentacles are short and bear suction cups on the internal surfaces. The other two are long and slender, with cups only at their enlarged tips. It is these two tentacles that are used to capture food. The mouth is surrounded by the tentacles and has two powerful jaws made of a horny material. The rest of the body is enclosed by the mantle.

The cuttlefish lives in coastal waters. It can change its colour to blend into its surroundings and so pass unnoticed. To swim, the cuttlefish forcefully expels water from an opening near its head, a propelling motion that allows it to swim rapidly. These bursts of speed help it evade its enemies and catch its prey. Moreover, when under attack, the cuttlefish can create a "smokescreen" — it has an internal sac full of a dark liquid which, once expelled, roughly takes on the shape of a cuttlefish and so serves as a decoy. The real cuttlefish then turns pale and escapes. Sepia ink, long an artist's medium, is derived from this liquid.

▷ RELATED ARTICLE: **Mollusc.**

■ Cycling, *see* Bicycling

■ Cypress

The cypress (*Chamaecyparis*), more accurately called false cypress, are conifers of the cypress family (Cupressaceae). Only one species is native to Canada, the Alaska cypress, or yellow cypress (*C. nootkatensis*), which is found in the coastal forests of British Columbia. The tree is of medium height (15 to 40 m), with scaly leaves like those of the cedar, but more prickly. The rather small cones, consisting of only four or six scales, hang in pairs, alternating at right angles. The Alaska cypress reaches its greatest growth in moist, temperate forests with deep soils. They can live over 1000 years. Chemical substances in the tree protect it from certain microscopic fungi; this explains its extraordinarily long life. The tree's wood, a lovely yellow shade and very decay-resistant, is much in demand for boats, greenhouses, cabinetry, and sculpture. The tree is also planted close to buildings as an ornamental. The native people frayed its inner bark to use as a bandage and for washing their infants. They also mixed it with down and wool and spun it into coverlets and clothing.

Cypress Trees can live up to 1000 years. The Alaska cypress is found on the coast of B.C. Cypress wood is very resistant to decay and is used for boats and cabinets (artwork by Claire Tremblay).